New Perspectives on
Microsoft®
Windows® 95

ADVANCED

The New Perspectives Series

The New Perspectives Series consists of texts and technology that teach computer concepts and the programs listed below. Both Windows 3.1 and Windows 95 versions of these programs are available. You can order these New Perspectives texts in many different lengths, software releases, bound combinations, and CourseKits™. Contact your CTI sales representative or customer service representative for the most up-to-date details.

The New Perspectives Series

Computer Concepts

dBASE

Internet Using Netscape Navigator

Lotus 1-2-3

Microsoft Access

Microsoft Excel

Microsoft Office Professional

Microsoft PowerPoint

Microsoft Windows 3.1

Microsoft Windows 95

Microsoft Word

Microsoft Works

Novell Perfect Office

Paradox

Presentations

Quattro Pro

WordPerfect

New Perspectives on
Microsoft®
Windows® 95

ADVANCED

Harry L. Phillips
Santa Rosa Junior College

A DIVISION OF COURSE TECHNOLOGY
ONE MAIN STREET, CAMBRIDGE, MA 02142

an International Thomson Publishing company I(T)P

Albany • Bonn • Boston • Cincinnati • London • Madrid • Melbourne • Mexico City
New York • Paris • San Francisco • Singapore • Tokyo • Toronto • Washington

New Perspectives on Microsoft Windows 95 — Advanced is published by CTI.

Managing Editor	Mac Mendelsohn
Series Consulting Editor	Susan Solomon
Product Manager	Joan Carey
Production Editor	Catherine D. Griffin
Text and Cover Designer	Ella Hanna
Cover Illustrator	Nancy Nash
Technical Writer	Crane Technical Writing

© 1996 by CTI.
A Division of International Thomson Publishing, Inc. – I(T)P

For more information contact:

Course Technology
One Main Street
Cambridge, MA 02142

International Thomson Publishing Europe
Berkshire House 168-173
High Holborn
London WCIV 7AA
England

Thomas Nelson Australia
102 Dodds Street
South Melbourne, 3205
Victoria, Australia

Nelson Canada
1120 Birchmount Road
Scarborough, Ontario
Canada M1K 5G4

International Thomson Editores
Campos Eliseos 385, Piso 7
Col. Polanco
11560 Mexico D.F. Mexico

International Thomson Publishing GmbH
Königswinterer Strasse 418
53227 Bonn
Germany

International Thomson Publishing Asia
211 Henderson Road
#05-10 Henderson Building
Singapore 0315

International Thomson Publishing Japan
Hirakawacho Kyowa Building, 3F
2-2-1 Hirakawacho
Chiyoda-ku, Tokyo 102
Japan

ISBN 0-7600-3572-5

Printed in the United States of America

10 9 8 7 6 5 4 3 2

From the New Perspectives Series Team

At Course Technology, Inc., we have one foot in education and the other in technology. We believe that technology is transforming the way people teach and learn, and we are excited about providing instructors and students with materials that use technology to teach about technology.

Our development process is unparalleled in the higher education publishing industry. Every product we create goes through an exacting process of design, development, review, and testing.

Reviewers give us direction and insight that shape our manuscripts and bring them up to the latest standards. Every manuscript is quality tested. Students whose backgrounds match the intended audience work through every keystroke, carefully checking for clarity and pointing out errors in logic and sequence. Together with our own technical reviewers, these testers help us ensure that everything that carries our name is error-free and easy to use.

We show both *how* and *why* technology is critical to solving problems in college and in whatever field you choose to teach or pursue. Our time-tested, step-by-step instructions provide unparalleled clarity. Examples and applications are chosen and crafted to motivate students.

As the New Perspectives Series team at Course Technology, our goal is to produce the most timely, accurate, creative, and technologically-sound product in the entire college publishing industry. We strive for consistent high quality. This takes a lot of communication, coordination, and hard work. But we love what we do. We are determined to be the best. Write us and let us know what you think. You can also e-mail us at info@course.com.

The New Perspectives Series Team

Joseph J. Adamski	Kathy Finnegan	Dan Oja
Judy Adamski	Robin Geller	June Parsons
Roy Ageloff	Chris Greacen	Sandra Poindexter
David Auer	Roger Hayen	Mark Reimold
Rachel Bunin	Charles Hommel	Ann Shaffer
Joan Carey	Chris Kelly	Susan Solomon
Patrick Carey	Terry Ann Kremer	John Zeanchock
Barbara Clemens	Melissa Lima	Beverly Zimmerman
Kim Crowley	Mac Mendelsohn	Scott Zimmerman
Jessica Evans		

Preface The New Perspectives Series

What is the New Perspectives Series?

Course Technology's **New Perspectives Series** combines text and technology products that teach computer concepts and microcomputer applications. Users consistently praise this series for its innovative pedagogy, creativity, supportive and engaging style, accuracy, and use of interactive technology. The first New Perspectives text was published in January of 1993. Since then, the series has grown to more than thirty titles and has become the best-selling series on computer concepts and microcomputer applications. Others have imitated the New Perspectives features, design, and technologies, but none have replicated its quality and its ability to consistently anticipate and meet the needs of instructors and students.

How is the New Perspectives Series different from other microcomputer applications series?

The **New Perspectives Series** distinguishes itself from other series in at least four substantial ways: sound instructional design, consistent quality, innovative technology, and proven pedagogy. The texts in this series consist of two or more tutorials, which are based on sound instructional design. Each tutorial is motivated by a realistic case that is meaningful to students. Rather than learn a laundry list of features, students learn the features in the context of solving a problem. This process motivates all concepts and skills by demonstrating to students *why* they would want to know them.

Instructors and students have come to rely on the the high quality of the **New Perspectives Series** and to consistently praise its accuracy. This accuracy is a result of Course Technology's unique multi-step quality assurance process that incorporates student testing at three stages of development, using hardware and software configurations appropriate to the product. All solutions, test questions, and other CourseTools (see below) are tested using similar procedures. Instructors who adopt this series report that students can work through the tutorials independently, with a minimum of intervention or "damage control" by instructors or staff. This consistent quality has meant that if instructors are pleased with one product from the series, they can rely on the same quality with any other New Perspectives product.

The **New Perspectives Series** distinguishes itself with its innovative technology. This series innovated truly *interactive* learning applications—CTIWinnApps, Interactive Labs, and CTI Windows 95 Applications. These applications have set the standard for interactive learning.

How do I know that the New Perspectives Series will work?

Some instructors who use this series report a significant difference between how much their students learn and retain with this series as compared to other series. With other series, instructors often find that students can work through the book and do well on homework and tests, but still not demonstrate competency when asked to perform particular tasks outside the context of the text's sample case or project. With the **New Perspectives Series**, however, instructors report that students have a complete, integrative learning experience that stays with them. They credit this high retention and competency to the fact that this series incorporates critical thinking and problem solving with computer skills mastery.

How does the book I'm holding fit into the New Perspectives Series?

New Perspectives microcomputer applications books are available in the following categories—

Brief books are about 100 pages long and are intended to teach only the essentials of the particular microcomputer application.

Introductory books are about 300 pages long and consist of 6 or 7 tutorials. An Introductory book is designed for a short course on a particular application or for a one-term course to be used in combination with other Introductory books.

Comprehensive books consist of all of the tutorials in the Introductory book, plus 3 or 4 more tutorials on more advanced topics. They also include the Brief Windows tutorials, 3 or 4 Additional Cases, and a Reference Section.

Intermediate books take the 3 or 4 tutorials at the end of 3 or 4 Comprehensive books and combine them. Additional Cases and Reference Sections are also included.

Advanced books begin by covering topics similar to those in the Comprehensive books, but cover them in more depth. Advanced books then go on to present the most high-level coverage in the series. Additional Cases and Reference Sections are also included.

Four-in-One books and **Five-in-One** books combine a Brief book on Windows with 3 or 4 Introductory books. For example, *New Perspectives on Microsoft Office* is a Five-in-One book—it combines Brief Windows with Introductory Word, Excel, Access, and PowerPoint.

Finally, as the name suggests, **Concepts and Applications** books combine the *New Perspectives on Computer Concepts* book with various Brief and Introductory microcomputer applications books.

Custom Books Course Technology offers you two ways to customize a text to fit your course exactly: **CourseKits**, 2 or more texts packaged together in a box, and **Custom Editions**, your choice of New Perspectives books bound together. Both options offer significant price discounts.

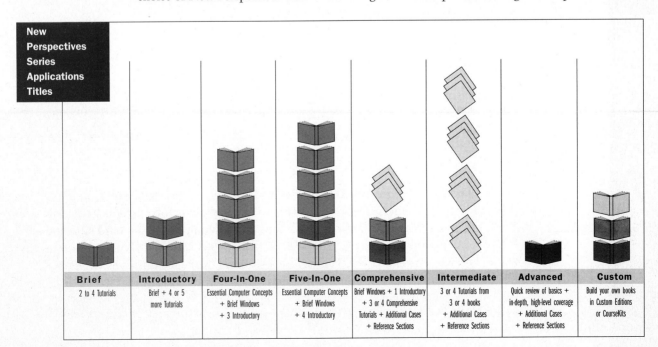

New Perspectives Series Applications Titles

Brief	Introductory	Four-In-One	Five-In-One	Comprehensive	Intermediate	Advanced	Custom
2 to 4 Tutorials	Brief + 4 or 5 more Tutorials	Essential Computer Concepts + Brief Windows + 3 Introductory	Essential Computer Concepts + Brief Windows + 4 Introductory	Brief Windows + 1 Introductory + 3 or 4 Comprehensive Tutorials + Additional Cases + Reference Sections	3 or 4 Tutorials from 3 or 4 books + Additional Cases + Reference Sections	Quick review of basics + in-depth, high-level coverage + Additional Cases + Reference Sections	Build your own books in Custom Editions or CourseKits

What is unique about the Advanced New Perspectives books?

The Advanced New Perspectives books are designed to fit a need not addressed by other books in that they cover concepts and skills required of advanced students. Research indicates that students in upper-division courses need a higher level of coverage. In the past, professors have had to use trade books to attain this level of coverage, but these books did not provide the pedagogical foundations for advanced learning. For example, trade books typically do not have end of chapter questions and exercises by which students can test and measure their understanding of the material. The Advanced New Perspectives books combine the high level coverage with reinforcing pedagogical features.

In what kind of course could I use this book?

This book can be used in any course in which you want students to learn all the most important topics of Microsoft Windows 95. In this book, students explore the Windows 95 operating system, beginning with the desktop, property sheets, the Recycle Bin, and online Help. They learn to customize the desktop, work with drives, folders, and files, and use Find and Windows Explorer. Students also are introduced to more advanced topics, such as troubleshooting Windows 95, working with a Startup Disk, using DOS with Windows 95, implementing a backup strategy, and optimizing disks with Scan Disk and Disk Defragmenter. They also learn to work with applications, use object linking and embedding, and use the connectivity features of Windows 95 with networks, including the Internet and the World Wide Web. This book assumes students have taken an introductory operating system course, but does not require any previous knowledge of Windows 95.

What features are contained in Advanced Windows 95 editions of the New Perspectives series?

Large Page Size   If you've used a *New Perspectives* text before, you'll immediately notice that the book you're holding is larger than the Windows 3.1 series books. We've responded to user requests for a larger page, which allows for larger screen shots and associated callouts. Look on page ADVWIN 67 for an example of how we've made the screen shots easy to read.

Design   We have designed this book to help students easily differentiate between what they are to *do* and what they are to *read*. The steps are easily identified by their shaded background and numbered steps. Furthermore, this design presents steps and screen shots in a large, easy to read format. Some good examples of our design are on pages ADVWIN 150 and ADVWIN 350.

"Read this Before You Begin" Page   This page is consistent with Course Technology's unequaled commitment to helping instructors introduce technology into the classroom. Technical considerations and assumptions about hardware and software are listed in one place to help instructors save time and eliminate unnecessary aggravation. The "Read This Before You Begin" page for this book is on page ADVWIN 2.

Tutorial Case Each tutorial begins with a problem presented in a running case that is meaningful to students. The problem turns the task of learning how to use an application into a problem-solving process. The problems increase in complexity with each tutorial. The running case touches on multicultural, international, and ethical issues—so important to today's business curriculum.

Step-by-Step Methodology This unique Course Technology methodology keeps students on track. They click or press keys always within the context of solving the problem posed in the tutorial case. The text constantly guides students, letting them know where they are in the course of solving the problem. In addition, the numerous screen shots include callouts that direct students' attention to what they should look at on the screen. On almost every page in this book, you can find an example of how steps, screen shots, and callouts work together.

TROUBLE?

TROUBLE? Paragraphs TROUBLE? paragraphs anticipate the mistakes that students are likely to make and help them recover from these mistakes. By putting these paragraphs in the book, rather than in the Instructor's Manual, we facilitate independent learning and free the instructor to focus on substantive conceptual issues rather than on common procedural errors. Two representative examples of TROUBLE? are on pages ADVWIN 16 and ADVWIN 28.

REFERENCE window

Reference Windows Reference Windows appear throughout the text. They are short, succinct summaries of the most important tasks covered in the tutorials. Reference Windows are specially designed and written so students can use them for their reference value when doing the Tutorial Assignments and Case Problems and after completing the course. Page ADVWIN 13 contains the Reference Window for Starting an Accessory.

HELP DESK

Help Desks The Help Desk feature encourages students to use online Help to explore additional methods for completing a task. The more exposure the students have to the online Help system, the more comfortable they will be getting help for tasks that are new to them. Each Help Desk includes instructions for starting Help and accessing the correct Help tab. It provides the keyword they should enter, and then names the topic that contains the information. Although the Help Desks do not replace the step-by-step tutorial, students can explore the Help Desk topics while they are working through the tutorial, or they can come back to them later during review. Page ADVWIN 14 contains a Help Desk for locating information on new features of Windows 95.

Task Reference The Task Reference is a summary of how to perform common tasks using the most efficient method, as well as helpful shortcuts. It appears as a table at the end of the book. In this book, the Task Reference is on pages ADVWIN 459–464.

Tutorial Assignments and Case Problems Each tutorial concludes with a Tutorial Assignment, which provides students with additional hands-on practice of the skills they learned in the tutorial. The Tutorial Assignment is followed by four Case Problems that are comparable to the tutorial case, require critical thinking skills, and that carry the student's skills one step further.

Additional Cases The Additional Cases synthesize the skills and concepts they've learned over the course of the book. Each case challenges students to handle a comprehensive operating system problem that draws on a variety of connected skills and topics. The Additional Cases can be completed by each student individually, or by a group of students working together.

What CourseTools are available with this text?

Instructor's Manual The Instructor's Manual is written by the author and is quality assurance tested. It contains answers and solutions to all of the Tutorial Assignments, Case Problems, and Additional Cases. This is available in hard copy and electronic form.

Acknowledgments

This textbook exemplifies the effective teamwork that forms the core of Course Technology's commitment to its authors and the instructors and students who use this book. Thanks are owed to many people for their involvement at all stages in the development and production of this textbook.

My appreciation goes to our reviewers, whose comments and suggestions helped shape this book: Patrick Carey, University of Wisconsin–Madison; and Bill Petersen, Mount Hood Community College.

I would also like to thank all the members of the New Perspectives team who helped in the development and production of this book. Special thanks go to Joan Carey, who not only successfully managed this project but also contributed her invaluable insight to the direction and content of this book.

Additional thanks go to the unequaled quality assurance and technology support from Jim Valente and the QA testers, Chris Hall and Ujin Wong; to the excellent production work of Cathie Griffin, and the staff at Gex; to the thorough copyediting done by Jane Pedicini and proofreading done by Joyce Churchill; and to the editorial direction and support of Mac Mendelsohn.

Harry L. Phillips

Table of **Contents**

New Perspectives on

Microsoft® Windows® 95

ADVANCED

TUTORIALS

Read This **Before You Begin**

STUDENT DISKS

To complete the tutorials, Tutorial Assignments, and Case Problems, you need four Student Disks. Your instructor will either provide you with Student Disks to copy or ask you to make your own.

If you are supposed to make your own Student Disks, you will need four blank, formatted disks. You will need to copy a set of folders from a file server or standalone computer onto your disks. Your instructor will tell you which computer, drive letter, and folders contain the folders you need. The following table shows you which folders go on each of your disks:

Disk	Write this on the disk label	Put these folders on the disk
1	Student Disk 1: Tutorial 3	Training folder plus all 44 files in the root directory
2	Student Disk 2: Tutorial 4	Overhead Transparencies, Templates, Training
3	Student Disk 3: Tutorials 7 & 8	MEI_INC
4	Student Disk 4: Tutorials 9 & 10	VAI

When you begin each tutorial, be sure you are using the correct Student Disk. See the inside front or inside back cover of this book for more information on Student Disks, or ask your instructor or technical support person for assistance.

Some of the Case problems will ask you to make a copy of your Student Disk so that you can use the copy to complete the case problem.

USING YOUR OWN COMPUTER

If you are going to work through this book using your own computer, you need:

■ **Computer System** Microsoft Windows 95 must be installed on your computer. This book assumes a typical installation of Microsoft Windows 95.

■ **Student Disks** Ask your instructor or technical support person for details on how to get the Student Disks. You will not be able to complete the tutorials or exercises in this book using your own computer until you have Student Disks.

To complete the tutorials in this book, your students must use a set of Student Files. These files are stored on the Student Files Disks that are included with the Instructor's Manual. Follow the instructions on the disk labels and the Readme.doc file to copy them to your server or standalone computer. You can view the Readme.doc file using WordPad or Write.

Once the files are copied, you can make Student Disks for the students yourself, or tell students where to find the files so they can make their own Student Disks. Make sure the files get correctly copied by following the instructions in the Student Disks section above.

CTI DATA FILES

You are granted a license to copy the Student Files to any computer or computer network used by students who have purchased this book. The files are included with the Instructor's Manual and may also be obtained electronically over the Internet. See the inside front or inside back cover of this book for more details.

TUTORIAL 1

The Windows 95 Operating System

Evaluating Windows 95 at Resource Management

OBJECTIVES

In this tutorial you will:

- Distinguish the basic functions of an operating system

- Identify new operating system components in Windows 95

- Explore the Windows 95 desktop

- Change the properties of the taskbar

- Work with date, time, and time zone settings

- View information on system and device properties and performance

- Learn about the difference between a 32-bit and 16-bit operating system

- Explore properties of the Recycle Bin

- Use online Help to search for information

CASE

Resource Management

Resource Management is a rapidly growing company that helps communities around the globe set up recycling programs. The company relies on computers for practically every facet of its operation. Sally Browne, a microcomputer specialist at Resource Management, has been preparing to upgrade the company computers to Windows 95. Sally has asked you to load Windows 95 on your computer and then evaluate it. She would like you to study, in particular, how Windows 95 interacts with a computer's hardware and software, how to optimally configure and customize computers for yourself and other employees, how employees can monitor their system's performance, and how the company as a whole can increase its productivity with Windows 95. Furthermore, she wants you to evaluate the Windows online Help prior to showing other staff members how to use it so you can answer their questions.

Using the Tutorials Effectively

These tutorials will help you learn about Windows 95. The tutorials are designed to be used at a computer. Each tutorial is divided into two sections. You should be able to complete each section in about 45 minutes, but take as much time as you need. It's also a good idea to take a break between each section.

Before you begin, read the following questions and answers. They are designed to help you use the tutorials effectively.

Where do I start?

Each tutorial begins with a case, which sets the scene for the tutorial and gives you background information to help you understand what you will be doing in the tutorial. Ideally, you should read the case before you start the tutorial.

How do I know what to do on the computer?

Each section contains steps that you will perform on the computer to learn how to use Windows 95. Read the text that introduces each series of steps. The steps you need to do at a computer are numbered and are set against a shaded background. Read each step carefully and completely before you try it.

How do I know if I did the step correctly?

As you work, compare your computer screen with the corresponding figure in the tutorial. Don't worry if your screen display is somewhat different from the figure. The important parts of the screen display are labeled in each figure. Check to make sure these parts are on your screen.

What if I make a mistake?

Don't worry about making mistakes—they are part of the learning process. Paragraphs labeled TROUBLE? identify common problems and explain how to get back on track. Follow the steps in a TROUBLE? paragraph *only* if you are having the problem described. If you run into other problems:

- Carefully consider the current state of your system, the position of the pointer, and any messages on the screen.

- Complete the sentence, "Now I want to..." Be specific because you are identifying your goal.

- Develop a plan for accomplishing your goal, and put your plan into action.

How do I use the Reference Windows?

Reference Windows summarize the procedures for many operations you learn in the tutorial steps. Do not complete the actions in the Reference Windows when you are working through the tutorial. Instead, refer to the Reference Windows while you are working on the assignments at the end of the tutorial. For reference information on short, simple tasks, consult the Task Reference at the end of the book.

How can I test my understanding of the material I learned in the tutorial?

After you have completed the entire tutorial, you should complete the Tutorial Assignment. The Tutorial Assignment is carefully structured so you can review what you have learned and then apply your knowledge to new situations.

What if I can't remember how to do something?

You should refer to the Task Reference at the end of the textbook; it summarizes how to accomplish common tasks.

How do I use Help Desks?

Help Desks tell you where you can find additional information in online Help about the current topic. Each Help Desk explains how to access online Help and what topic to search for.

Now that you've seen how to use the tutorials effectively you are ready to begin.

What Is an Operating System?

Sally gives you a copy of Windows 95, which you install and start. Installation goes smoothly and you're ready to begin. You touch base with Sally and the two of you decide that it would help employees understand the company's reasons for upgrading to Windows 95 if you gave a brown-bag lunch seminar on how Windows 95 is a step forward in operating system technology. An **operating system** is a software product that manages the basic processes within a computer, coordinates the interaction of hardware and software, and provides support for the use of other software. Operating systems also display a **user interface**, the combination of elements on the screen that let you interact with the computer. Although operating systems vary in the scope of tasks that they manage, all operating systems handle the following tasks:

- Booting a computer
- Configuring and customizing a computer
- Managing hardware, including disk drives and disks
- Displaying a user interface
- Interpreting user commands and requests
- Providing services to software applications
- Allocating and managing memory
- Managing folders and files
- Resolving system errors and problems
- Providing online Help
- Optimizing system performance
- Providing troubleshooting tools

Following the explosion of mass-marketed computer technology in the 80's that made microcomputers, or PCs, indispensable in many offices, schools, and homes, the most commonly used operating system until the early 90's was **DOS**, an abbreviation for "disk operating system." DOS is actually a generic name for three related operating systems: PC-DOS, MS-DOS, and IBM-DOS. Over the years, Microsoft and IBM worked cooperatively to develop different versions of PC-DOS or IBM-DOS for IBM microcomputers, while Microsoft developed MS-DOS for compatibles. IBM now develops its own versions of IBM-DOS for IBM microcomputers. Although there are subtle differences between PC-DOS, MS-DOS, and IBM-DOS, all manage the hardware and software resources within a computer in similar ways, provide access to similar types of features, and include similar utilities for enhancing the performance of a system.

The DOS operating system and other operating systems like it (UNIX and VAX/VMS, for example) use a **command line interface** where you communicate with the computer by typing commands, one line after another, after an operating system prompt, as shown in Figure 1-1. An important feature of command line interface operating systems is that they operate in **text mode**, where the computer monitor displays only text, numbers, symbols, and a small set of graphics characters using white characters on a black background.

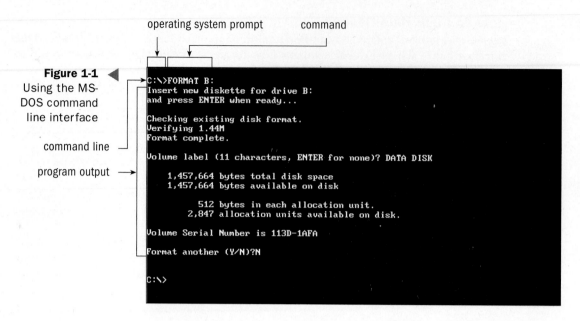

Figure 1-1
Using the MS-DOS command line interface

command line

program output

In 1985, Microsoft introduced the Windows operating environment. An **operating environment** is a software product that performs the same functions as an operating system, except for booting a system and handling the storage and retrieval of data in files on a disk. Although Windows 3.1, the most commonly used version of this operating environment, uses DOS in the background to handle basic file functions, its interface is completely different. Instead of displaying a command line interface in text mode, Windows 3.1 uses a **graphical user interface** (known as a **GUI**), which you interact with not by typing commands but by choosing options from task-related lists and boxes that appear on the screen. GUIs operate in graphics mode rather than text mode. In **graphics mode**, a monitor can display text in a variety of fonts and formats, shapes, and drawings, and displays greater **resolution**, or screen detail, using a wide variety of colors. GUIs, like the Windows 3.1 graphical user interface shown in Figure 1-2, generally provide a more visual and supportive working environment than command line interfaces like DOS, making it easier for you to interact with the operating system and the computer's hardware and software resources.

Figure 1-2
The Windows 3.1 graphical user interface

Program Manager application window

desktop

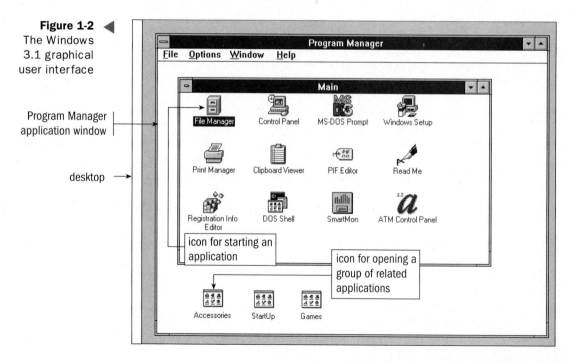

The Windows graphical user interface uses **windows,** or defined rectangular areas of the screen, to organize your view of applications and documents; **icons** or graphical images, to represent hardware and software resources (such as drives and applications); **menus** that list options for performing different types of command operations; **dialog boxes** that open when you choose commands, letting you clarify what you want to do; and a **mouse** for selecting objects and options from menus, windows, and dialog boxes.

In 1995, Microsoft released Windows 95, a new operating system. When you install Windows 95 onto a computer that uses DOS, Windows 95 replaces DOS as the operating system. In addition to performing the same core functions as DOS and other operating systems, Windows 95 includes these important additional features, which you'll work with over the course of this book:

- A new system architecture

- An object-oriented interface

- Robustness

- Plug and Play

- Multimedia support

- Support for online services

- Network support

- Support for portable computers

Since Windows 95 represents a major change in the way in which employees at Resource Management will use their computers, Sally asks you to emphasize in your seminar not only the significant new features in Windows 95 that will improve computer performance and increase productivity, but also how easy it will be to learn and use.

The most important feature of Windows 95 is its new **system architecture,** a term which refers to the internal design and coding of an operating system. The improved system architecture of Windows 95 takes advantage of the 80386, 80486, Pentium, and even newer microprocessors. This system architecture not only incorporates a new operating system technology, but also provides support for operating modes of earlier microprocessors, such as the 8088, 8086, and 80286 microprocessors. It supports the use of DOS applications developed for all microprocessors from the original 8088 to the newest type of microprocessor. The ability to handle hardware and software designed for earlier systems is called **backward compatibility.** Many companies, including Resource Management, consider this a crucial quality of Windows 95, since it still allows them to use their current software applications. This architecture also sets standards for the development and use of new hardware and software technologies.

One of the things you'd really like to emphasize at your seminar is an important shift in the way you work with documents. The enhanced graphical user interface lets you change from an application-oriented interface to a document-oriented interface. In an **application-oriented interface,** you first open the software application you want to use, then you locate and open the document you want to use. In a **document-oriented interface,** you locate and open the document you want to use, and then the operating system opens the application you originally used to produce that document. This document-oriented approach permits you to work with your computer in a more logical way: by locating, for example, a spreadsheet or word processed document, rather than the application that created it. Moreover, if you work with several similar types of applications, such as two word processing applications or two spreadsheet applications, you do not have to remember which application you used to produce a document; the operating system does it for you.

To further increase the effectiveness and reliability of Windows 95, the system architecture includes new design features that increase the stability, or **robustness**, of the operating system and that protect important system resources. These features ensure that a single malfunctioning application does not crash other running applications or the entire computer, and, in some cases, these features permit you to save information that you might otherwise lose.

Employees at Resource Management will be glad to hear that Windows 95 also makes it much easier to install new hardware on their computers. The Windows 95 **Plug and Play** (or PNP for Plug 'N Play) feature automatically configures hardware components in your computer when you install Windows 95. Later, if you add new hardware components to your system, Plug and Play automatically configures those hardware components as well. Previously, it was not uncommon for users to encounter what seemed like irresolvable configuration problems when they added new hardware to their computer. Plug and Play consists of a set of specifications that free you from manually configuring hardware devices, such as a mouse, CD-ROM drive, or modem. Plus, Plug and Play eliminates or identifies conflicts among installed hardware devices. Although Plug and Play is primarily designed for future hardware that supports these new specifications, this feature does recognize and configure hardware currently in use on computers today. The Plug and Play technology simplifies the installation of multimedia components, such as CD-ROM drives and sound cards, and provides smoother and faster operation of CD-ROM applications and games. Moreover, it supports new, emerging multimedia technologies.

Another broad area of support provided by Windows 95 is **connectivity support**. Resource Management has offices all over the world, and the ability to share data among offices is becoming more and more vital to the company's international operations. The new system architecture of Windows 95, as well as new built-in communication features, supports the use of communications software and hardware, access to online services, networking, and the use of portable computers. The Microsoft Network, which you can access from Windows 95, provides a variety of online services. These services include electronic mail for sending and receiving messages, bulletin boards for posting messages, chat rooms for online discussions, and file libraries with software and clip art.

Windows 95 provides enhanced support for connecting to networks and network operating software, including Novell NetWare. It can interact with network application software and hardware (such as printers), access documents and information on networks, and manage the operation of a network.

For mobile users who depend increasingly on portable computers, as Sally does when she travels to branch offices, Windows 95 provides tools for connecting to networks so that she can access shared resources, such as software, printers, e-mail, and files. Furthermore, Windows 95 includes other features for portable computers, such as power management, automatic updating of files, fax services, document viewers, and deferred printing.

The graphical user interface in Windows 95 simplifies the user's interaction with the operating system, and provides a standardized operating environment for the development of new software. The diverse range of features in Windows not only expands the role of an operating system, but also emphasizes the importance of integrating applications and features to optimize the performance of a computer, more effectively manage its resources, and increase its productivity.

Launching Windows 95

To **launch**, or start, Windows 95, you turn on your computer's power. Like its predecessor, MS-DOS, Windows 95 handles the booting of a computer. During the booting process, it checks the computer for installed hardware components and compares its findings with information it stores in a configuration database called the **Registry**. After it configures your computer, Windows 95 might first display a Welcome dialog box, as shown in Figure 1-3. The Welcome dialog box displays a tip that briefly describes the use of a Windows 95 feature. From the Welcome dialog box, you can also start a Windows Tour, discover what's new in Windows 95, register Windows 95 online, obtain a product catalog, or view other tips. If you do not see the Welcome dialog box, don't worry; it simply means that this feature has been turned off.

Figure 1-3 ◀
Welcome dialog
box

tip of the day

click to deselect
this option

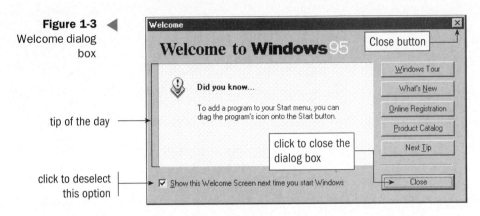

If your computer is connected to a network, Windows 95 automatically detects the network and displays an Enter Network Password dialog box, as shown in Figure 1-4, so that you can enter a password and connect your computer to that network. If you decide that you do not want to use the network immediately, you can always connect to the network later with Network Neighborhood.

Figure 1-4 ◀
Enter Network
Password
dialog box

user name
shown here

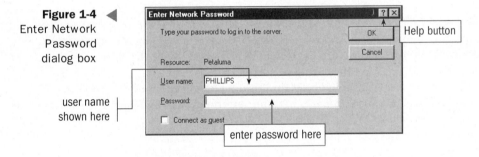

To launch Windows 95:

1. If your computer is turned off, turn on the power switch.

2. Click the **Show this Welcome screen next time you start Windows** check box if you don't want this dialog box to appear.

3. Click the Welcome dialog box's **Close** button ⊠ or the equivalent **Close** button in the lower-right corner.

4. Enter a password if prompted, then click the **OK** button.

   After Windows 95 boots your computer, it displays its graphical user interface. See Figure 1-5. Your desktop might differ from the one shown in the figure. For example, you might see icons for installed applications.

Figure 1-5 ◀
The Windows
95 graphical
user interface

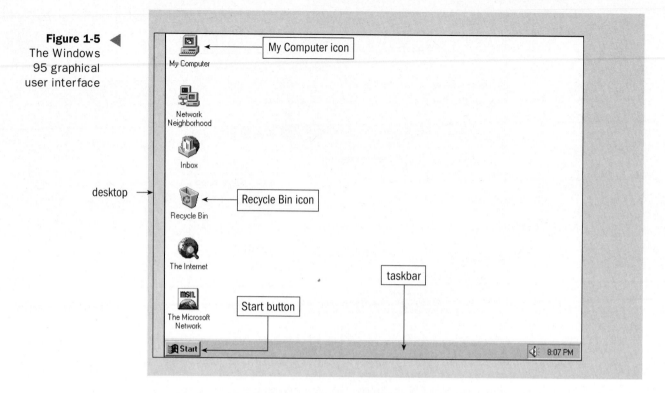

Navigating the Desktop

One of the things you'd like to do in your seminar is run through a quick session with your audience to show how easy it is to use Windows 95. After you start Windows 95, the graphical user interface displays the **desktop**, the large area you see on the screen that includes a set of graphical objects or icons for interacting with the operating system, as shown in Figure 1-5.

The box below is an example of a Help Desk, a reference tool in this book that directs you to an online Help topic containing more information. You'll learn the specifics of using online Help later in this tutorial.

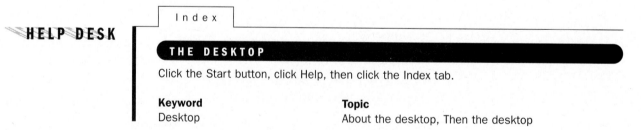

HELP DESK

Index

THE DESKTOP

Click the Start button, click Help, then click the Index tab.

Keyword	Topic
Desktop	About the desktop, Then the desktop

Beneath the desktop at the bottom of the screen is a horizontal bar called the **taskbar**, which displays a Start button for starting programs or opening documents, as well as buttons for currently open software applications and documents.

Clicking the Start button opens the Start menu, from which you can start software applications installed on your computer, locate recently used documents, change system settings, locate a file or folder, access online Help, run a program, or shut down your system.

You decide to show your audience how to find and then start one of the Windows 95 accessories, Paint, which replaces Paintbrush in Windows 3.1 and lets you create and work with graphic images.

To start Paint:

1. Click the **Start** button. The Start menu opens, as shown in Figure 1-6. Your Start menu might contain additional options.

Figure 1-6 ◀
Start menu

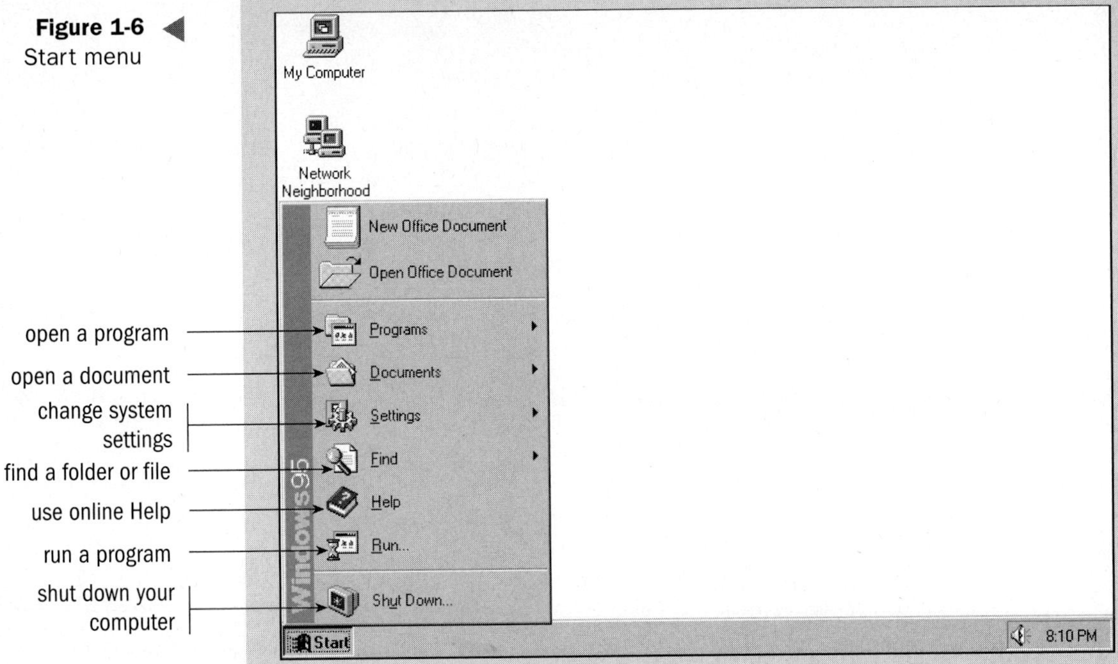

open a program ────▶ Programs
open a document ────▶ Documents
change system ──── Settings
settings
find a folder or file ──── Find
use online Help ──── Help
run a program ──── Run...
shut down your ──── Shut Down...
computer

The default Start menu contains seven items: Programs, which lists the programs on your computer; Documents, which lists recently opened documents; Settings, which gives you easy access to options for configuring your PC; Find, which helps you locate folders and files; Help, which starts online Help; Run, which you can use to start a program, open a folder, or open a file and its application; and Shut Down, which gives you options for shutting down or restarting your computer. If Office 95 is installed on your computer, as is the case for the computer used to produce Figure 1-6, then your Start menu will also contain New Office Document for creating a new document with one of the Office 95 applications, and Open Office Document for opening an existing document and the Office 95 application that produced that document. To navigate the Start menu, you point to an item followed by an arrow to open a new menu with more options, or you click an item without an arrow to select a document or program.

2. Point to **Programs** on the Start menu. The Programs menu opens, as shown in Figure 1-7.

Figure 1-7 ◀
Opening the
Programs menu

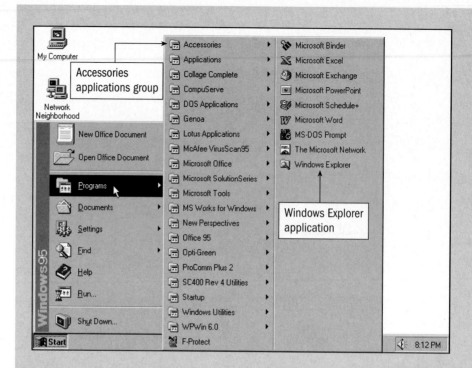

The Programs menu lists folders that contain a group of related applications (such as the Accessories folder), or individual applications (such as Windows Explorer). Notice that in Windows 95, you can accomplish many things just by pointing and clicking. Users of Windows 3.1 might notice that Windows 95 minimizes the need to double-click (click twice in quick succession), which requires dexterity and is difficult for the very young, the very old, and for those with limited use of their hands.

3. Point to **Accessories** on the Programs menu and, when the Accessories menu opens, click **Paint**, then click the **Maximize** button ☐ to maximize the Paint window to the full screen. The Paint accessory opens, and a Paint button appears on the taskbar. See Figure 1-8. Every program that you run in Windows 95 has a corresponding button that appears on the taskbar; this feature makes it easy to switch quickly among applications.

Figure 1-8 ◀
Paint
application
window

menu bar

toolbox

color box

status bar

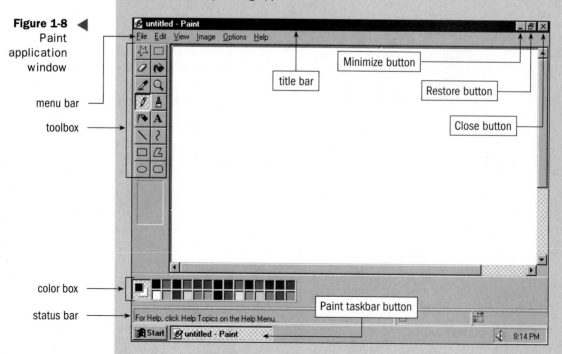

TROUBLE? If you can't find Paint on the Accessories menu, it's possible that your site did not install the Paint accessory. Try opening a different accessory.

If you need to reduce the open window to a button on the taskbar, you just click the Minimize button for that window.

4. Click the **Minimize** button 🔳 to reduce the Paint window to a button on the taskbar. Windows 95 returns you to the desktop. The Paint accessory is still running in the background.

5. Click the **Paint** button on the taskbar to reopen the Paint window.

6. Click the **Close** button ❎ to close Paint.

REFERENCE
window

STARTING AN ACCESSORY

- Click the Start button.
- Point to Programs on the Start menu.
- Point to Accessories on the Programs menu.
- Click the accessory name, or point to an Accessories group, then click an accessory name.

The buttons that appear on the taskbar can correspond to programs that are running or to other open windows. To switch from window to window, you simply click the button on the taskbar, as you just did to reopen Paint. The Windows 3.1 Alt and Tab key combination still works to move you from window to window.

HELP DESK

Index

SWITCHING WINDOWS

Click the Start button, click Help, then click the Index tab.

Keyword
Task switching

Topic
The Basics

Examining Objects and Their Properties

Sally's department has come up with a strategy for establishing Windows 95 as the standard operating system at Resource Management, and she wants you to explore the desktop on your computer to learn how to find information about your computer's configuration.

Finding information about your computer has never been easier. You can think of your computer as an interconnected collection of hardware and software. Each hardware device and each software application is an **object** in the sense that it is an entity that your computer will use to complete a specific task. A modem is an object. Your spreadsheet package is an object. Your hard drive is an object. Moreover, the parts of many hardware and software objects are also considered objects. In your spreadsheet package, for example, a cell range is an object, a column is an object, a chart is an object, and a label is an object. There are two things you can say about every object: it has actions associated with it and it has properties. **Actions** are operations you can do with or to the object. For example, you can perform a variety of actions on a hard drive: you can explore its contents, rename it, and store other objects on it. **Properties**, on the other hand, are characteristics of an object that you can view and sometimes change. Your hard drive, for example, has properties: its size, the company that manufactured it, how much of it is used up, and how much of it is free space. Your word processing program also has properties: its name, version number, its location on your hard drive, how much space it takes on your hard drive, when it was last used, and who holds its copyright. The desktop itself has properties: its color, whether it's using a screen saver, its resolution, and the font it uses to display text.

HELP DESK

Index

PROPERTIES

Click the Start button, click Help, then click the Index tab.

Keyword
New features

Topic
The new look and feel of Windows, then Properties

Windows 95 is called an **object-oriented operating system** because it manages all the actions and properties associated with an object and gives you immediate access to these actions and characteristics. All you need to do is right-click the object or the icon that represents the object. To right-click, you point to the object, then press the right mouse button once and release it. After you right-click, a **shortcut menu** opens, which gives you access to the actions and properties of the object. Because every object has a shortcut menu associated with it, you can use the same method of performing actions and examining properties, whether the object is a CD-ROM drive or a piece of clip art pasted into a document. The rest of this chapter focuses on exploring the properties of some of the most important objects on the desktop, starting with the taskbar.

HELP DESK

Index

SHORTCUT MENUS

Click the Start button, click Help, then click the Index tab.

Keyword
New features

Topic
The new look and feel of Windows, then Shortcut menus

Opening Property Sheets

Windows 95 makes it easy for you to explore the properties of an object because it pulls together all the properties of an object into a **property sheet**, a dialog box that opens when you right-click the object and then click the Properties command. From the property sheets, you can examine object properties and change them to customize your system.

Sally suggests you first find out what property settings Windows 95 defines for the taskbar so that you can determine whether you and other staff members might benefit from changing any of those property settings.

To display the property sheet for the taskbar:

1. Point to an unused area of the taskbar, then right-click. Windows 95 displays a shortcut menu. See Figure 1-9.

Figure 1-9 ◀
Taskbar
shortcut menu

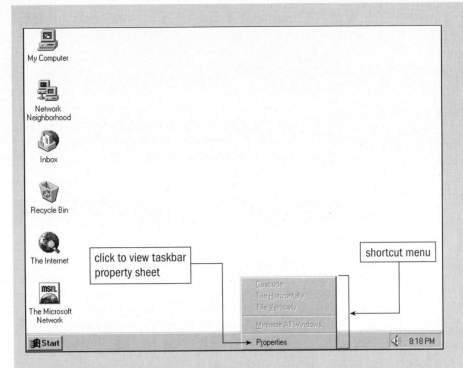

click to view taskbar
property sheet

shortcut menu

TROUBLE? If you are left-handed and have already changed the button configuration for your mouse from right-handed to left-handed so that you can select an
object or option by clicking the right mouse button, then you must click the left
mouse button to open the shortcut menu.

2. Click **Properties** on the shortcut menu. Windows 95 displays a Taskbar
   Properties dialog box. See Figure 1-10.

Figure 1-10 ◀
Taskbar
Properties
dialog box

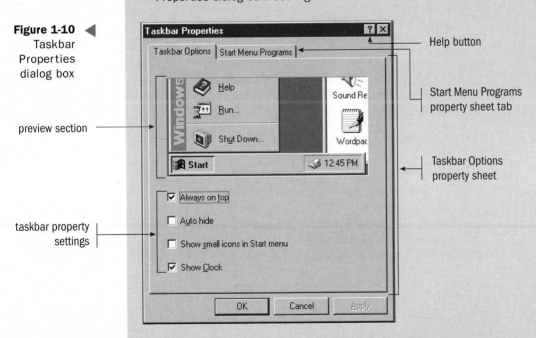

Help button

Start Menu Programs
property sheet tab

preview section

Taskbar Options
property sheet

taskbar property
settings

The Taskbar Properties dialog box is a **tabbed dialog box**, a dialog box with tabs
along the top that you can click to access different groups of property settings.
The first tab, Taskbar Options, appears on top and displays four options for customizing the taskbar: Always on top, Auto hide, Show small icons in Start menu,
and Show Clock. The second tab, Start Menu Programs, allows you to customize
the programs on the Start and Documents menus.

3. Click the **Start Menu Programs** tab to look at options for customizing the Start menu. As you can see, tabbed dialog boxes group information very efficiently and are an important new feature of Windows 95.

4. Click the **Taskbar Options** tab to return to the first tab.

Above the four property setting options is a preview section that displays an image of part of the desktop with the taskbar and part of an open window. As you change a property setting, the image in this preview section changes so that you can see the effect of that setting.

Recording Property Settings

Before you examine and change information on property settings, it is important that you keep a record of which settings were active and which were inactive. If you work in a shared environment, such as a college's computer lab network, you will need to restore any settings you change. You can, of course, simply write the property settings down in a notebook, but if you have quick access to a printer, you might find that it's quicker to get a hard copy of the property sheet. The Taskbar Properties dialog box should still be open on your screen, with the Taskbar Options tab displayed.

To make a hard copy of the Taskbar Options property settings:

1. Press and hold down the **Alt** key and press the **Print Screen** key. Although nothing appears to happen, a copy of the active window was just placed on the Clipboard. Pressing two keys at the same time is called a **key combination**. The Alt + Print Screen key combination prints a copy of the active window to the Clipboard. If you had just pressed the Print Screen key without the Alt key, Windows 95 would have copied the entire screen to the Clipboard, not just the open window. Now that you have a copy of the Taskbar Properties dialog box in the Clipboard, you can paste the image into Paint and print it from there.

TROUBLE? If you can't find the Print Screen key on your keyboard, you might have a key labeled "Prt Scr." If you are unsure about which key to use, or if you discover the key does not work as you expect, then ask your instructor or technical support person for assistance.

2. Click the **Start** button, point to **Programs**, point to **Accessories**, click **Paint**, then, if necessary, click the **Maximize** button ☐.

TROUBLE? If you can't find the Paint accessory on the Accessories menu, it's possible that your site didn't install Paint. Check the Accessories menu again and, if the WordPad accessory is installed, you can use it instead of the Paint accessory. If you cannot find either accessory, ask your instructor or technical support person for a suggestion on which application to use. If you are using your own computer, you can use the Windows 95 Setup disk to find and install the Paint and WordPad accessories.

3. Click **Edit** on the Paint menu bar, then click **Paste**.

TROUBLE? If a message box appears asking to enlarge the bitmap, click Yes. The contents of the Clipboard appear in the Paint window, as shown in Figure 1-11.

Figure 1-11
Pasting the
contents of the
Clipboard

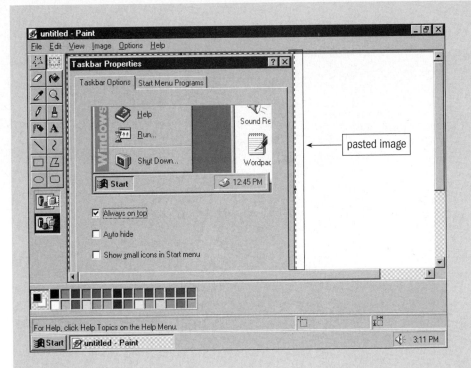

4. Make sure your printer is on and operational.

5. Click **File**, click **Print**, then click the **OK** button in the Print dialog box after you check the Print settings. You now have a hard copy of the Taskbar Properties dialog box, which you can use to reset any settings you change. Get into the habit of taking this precaution for every dialog box you change.

6. Click **File** then click **Exit**.

7. When a Paint dialog box appears asking if you want to save your file, click the **No** button. Windows 95 again returns you to the desktop, and the Paint button disappears from the taskbar.

REFERENCE
window

PRINT A COPY OF A PROPERTY SETTINGS SHEET

- Right-click the object, then click Properties on its shortcut menu.
- Press Alt + Print Screen.
- Click the Start button, point to Programs, point to Accessories, then click Paint.
- Click Edit then click Paste.
- Click File, click Print, then click OK.
- Click File, click Exit, then click No.

Getting Help on Property Settings

As you examine property settings in property sheets, you can use one of several Help features to understand property settings and options. If you click the [?] button and then click a property setting or option, Windows 95 opens a **pop-up window**, a small window containing a brief explanation of that setting or option. You can also right-click a property setting or dialog box option to open another shortcut menu with one option, "What's This?", and then select that option to display the same type of help.

Try using both these Help features to get more information on the taskbar property sheet options.

To view Help on property settings:

1. Click the **?** button ⬚, then point to the **Always on top** check box.

   After you select the ? button, notice that the mouse pointer shape includes a question mark ⬚. This mouse pointer shape is called Help Select.

2. Click the **Always on top** check box. A pop-up window opens, explaining that this option ensures that the taskbar is always visible, even if you open an application and view that application's window. See Figure 1-12.

Figure 1-12 ◄
Displaying Help
in a pop-up
window

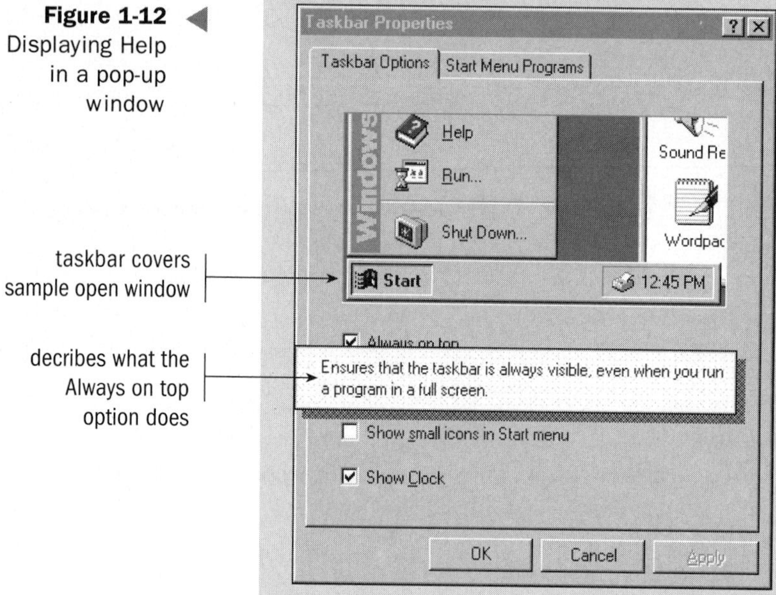

taskbar covers
sample open window →

decribes what the
Always on top
option does

If this option is checked, the taskbar in the preview section at the top of the dialog box covers the sample open window. If this option is not checked, then the sample open window covers part of the taskbar.

3. Click the **pop-up window**. The pop-up window closes. If you click Always on top a second time, rather than click the area in the dialog box, you will change this property setting.

4. If necessary, click the **Always on top** check box to place the check mark in the check box, then examine the appearance of the taskbar in the preview section.

5. Click the **Always on top** check box to remove the check mark from the check box, then examine the preview section again. Notice how the appearance of the taskbar changes in the preview section after you change this property setting.

6. Using your records, restore the original setting for the **Always on top** check box.

Next, you want to examine some of the other taskbar properties. Since you do not know what Auto hide means, you decide to use the Help feature on a shortcut menu.

To find out the purpose of Auto hide:

1. Right-click the **Auto hide** check box. A shortcut menu opens with one option, "What's This?" See Figure 1-13.

Figure 1-13 ◄
Using a Help
shortcut menu

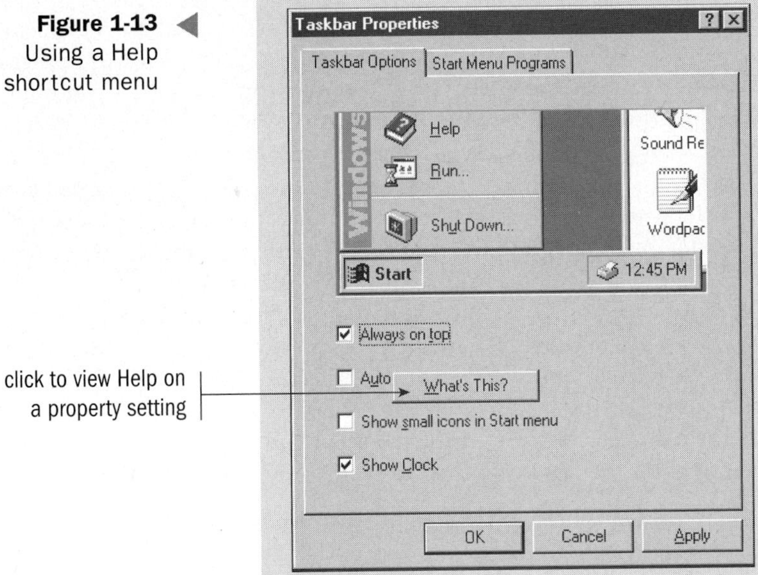

click to view Help on
a property setting

2. Click **What's This?** A pop-up window opens, and informs you that this property setting reduces the size of the taskbar to a thin line at the bottom of the screen after you use the Start menu or the taskbar. You can redisplay the taskbar by pointing to the thin line. The advantage of using this option is that the taskbar uses less of the space available for an application window. Furthermore, if you select the Always on top and Auto hide options, the taskbar is available even when you run a program and maximize the application window.

3. Click the **pop-up window** to close this Help window.

4. If necessary, click the **Auto hide** check box to remove the check mark in the check box, then examine the appearance of the taskbar in the preview section.

5. Click the **Auto hide** check box to place a check mark in this check box, and then examine the preview section again. If this option is checked, the taskbar changes to a thin bar and you cannot see the Start button. If this option is not checked, then the taskbar appears in its normal height and you can see the Start button.

6. Use the Help button or shortcut menu to view information about the use of each of the next two property settings. The Show small icons in Start menu option, if active, displays a smaller Startup menu. The Show Clock setting, if active, displays a digital clock on the right side of the taskbar.

7. Select each of the two last options and examine how the settings change the taskbar in the preview section, then restore the original settings. Refer to the hard copy of this dialog box, which you made when you began, to be sure the settings are the same.

8. Restore the Auto hide check box option to its original setting.

9. Leave this property sheet open as you continue with the next section.

As you've seen, pop-up windows can give you quick answers to questions about Windows 95 features you see in the property sheets. You'll learn later how to access the full Windows 95 online Help system.

Changing Taskbar Property Settings

If you change the property settings for the taskbar, you customize or change the appearance of the taskbar without affecting the configuration of your computer. However, if you change other property sheet settings for other objects within your computer, you might not only change the configuration of your computer, but also adversely affect the performance of Windows 95. In some cases, Windows 95 displays warnings that you should not change certain property sheet settings unless you are an advanced user. An **advanced user** is one who knows and understands the effects of different system settings, understands how a change in one setting might affect other settings on a computer, and knows how to restore settings on a system if a change in a setting adversely affects system performance. Before you change an important property setting, keep a hard copy of the original setting and the change that you made, as well as how to locate the property sheet for this setting. Later, if you experience problems, you can locate and check the property setting you changed and, if necessary, restore the property for that object to its original setting.

After evaluating the property settings for customizing the taskbar, you decide that it is safe to change these settings so that you can directly evaluate how they affect the use of your computer.

To change taskbar properties:

1. If necessary, click the **Always on top** and **Show Clock** check boxes to select these options, and then click the **Auto hide** and **Show small icons in Start menu** check boxes to deselect these options.

   Your selections should match those shown in Figure 1-14.

Figure 1-14 ◀
Choosing taskbar property settings

turn these settings on

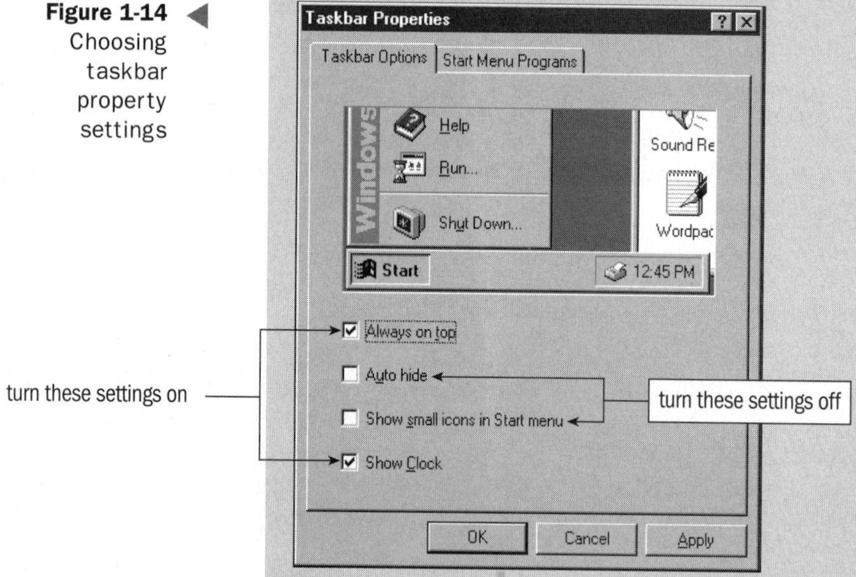

2. Click the **OK** button. The Taskbar Properties dialog box closes, and you see the Windows 95 desktop with a digital clock on the right side of the taskbar.

Working with Date and Time Settings

Windows 95 tracks both the date and time, including the time zone, and makes it very easy for you to change and view these settings. Sally has often had to field requests from Resource Management employees who don't know how to change their time settings when daylight savings time starts and when it ends, so she wants to be sure employees understand how easy it is to change these settings on their own.

HELP DESK

Index

CHANGING A COMPUTER'S DATE

Click the Start button, click Help, then click the Index tab.

Keyword
Date/Time

Topic
Changing your computer's date

One of the objects on the taskbar is the clock, which you displayed in the previous section. To adjust time settings, you use one of the actions on the taskbar shortcut menu.

To view the date and time settings:

1. Point to the **clock** and let the mouse pointer rest on the clock for a second.

   A pop-up window displays the current date along with the day of the week. See Figure 1-15.

Figure 1-15 ◀
Displaying the current date

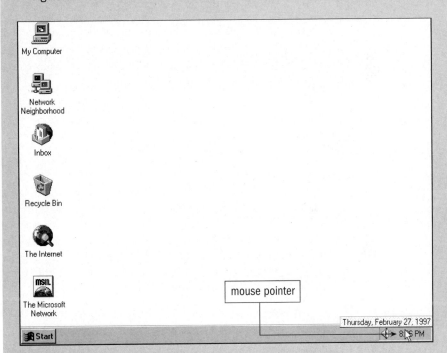

mouse pointer

My Computer

Network Neighborhood

Inbox

Recycle Bin

The Internet

The Microsoft Network

Thursday, February 27, 1997

Start   8:15 PM

2. Right-click the **clock**. The taskbar shortcut menu opens, but this time with an additional command on the top of the menu, Adjust Date/Time. Notice that the Adjust Date/Time command is highlighted. Many shortcut menus have one highlighted command. When you double-click the object instead of right-clicking it, the highlighted action is performed. Try closing the shortcut menu and then using the double-click method to adjust date and time settings.

3. Click a blank area of the desktop to close the shortcut menu, then double-click the **clock**. Windows 95 opens the Date/Time Properties dialog box, which has two property sheets. See Figure 1-16.

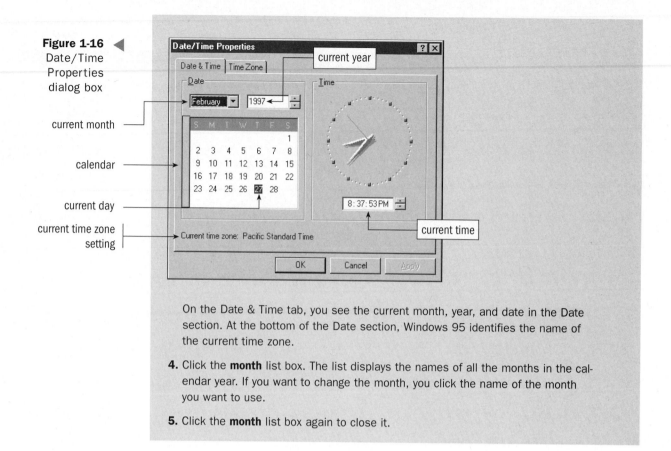

Figure 1-16
Date/Time
Properties
dialog box

current month

calendar

current day

current time zone
setting

On the Date & Time tab, you see the current month, year, and date in the Date section. At the bottom of the Date section, Windows 95 identifies the name of the current time zone.

4. Click the **month** list box. The list displays the names of all the months in the calendar year. If you want to change the month, you click the name of the month you want to use.

5. Click the **month** list box again to close it.

If you need to change the calendar year, you click the up or down spin arrow to the right of the year box until you locate the year you want to use. If you want to change the day shown in the calendar, you click the day you want to use.

In the Time section, Windows 95 displays an analog clock with a second hand. If you want to change the time on your computer, you point to the hour, minutes, seconds, or AM or PM designation in the box below the clock, click that component of the time, then you use the up or down spin arrows to change the settings.

HELP DESK

Index

CHANGING A COMPUTER'S TIME

Click the Start button, click Help, then click the Index tab.

Keyword
Date/Time

Topic
Changing your computer's time

On the Time Zone tab, you can view the current time zone setting and, if necessary, change that setting.

HELP DESK

Index

CHANGING TIME ZONE SETTINGS

Click the Start button, click Help, then click the Index tab.

Keyword
Date/Time

Topic
Changing your computer's time zone

To examine the time zone setting:

1. Click the **Time Zone** tab. Windows 95 displays a Mercatur map of the world. See Figure 1-17.

Figure 1-17 ◄
Time Zone
property sheet

current time zone
setting

Mercatur map of
the world

option for adjusting
clock for daylight
saving time

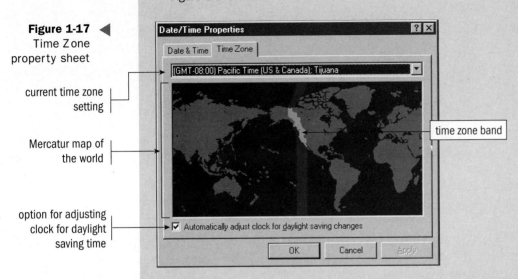

time zone band

The time zone band indicates the time zone that Windows 95 is currently using. Above the world map, the time zone box shows information on the current time zone in use. Each time zone uses Greenwich, England, as a standard reference point. In this figure, the time zone is 8 hours (08:00) west of Greenwich Mean Time (GMT). The minus sign (−) before 08:00 indicates that Pacific Time is west of Greenwich, England, and that the time on the west coast of the United States is eight hours earlier than that in Greenwich, England. If you see a plus sign (+) before the time, the location is east of Greenwich, England, and the time is later in that location than it is in Greenwich, England. In the figure, the time zone runs through the United States and Canada, as well as Tijuana, Mexico. Below the world map is a check box for daylight savings time. If you activate this option, Windows 95 will automatically change the time on your computer to account for daylight savings time.

2. Click the **Automatically adjust clock for daylight saving changes** check box if it is not selected.

If you need to change the time zone on your computer, you can use the time zone list to select another time zone.

To change the time zone:

1. Click the **time zone** list arrow.

From the list, you can also identify a time zone if you know the continent, region, state, or city. Next, you want to select one of the other time zones.

2. Click **Eastern Time (US & Canada)** or a time zone that is different than the one for your location. The Mercatur map moves, and the time zone selection changes. See Figure 1-18.

Figure 1-18 ◀
Selecting a
new time zone

new time zone setting ────

drag to select another ────
time zone

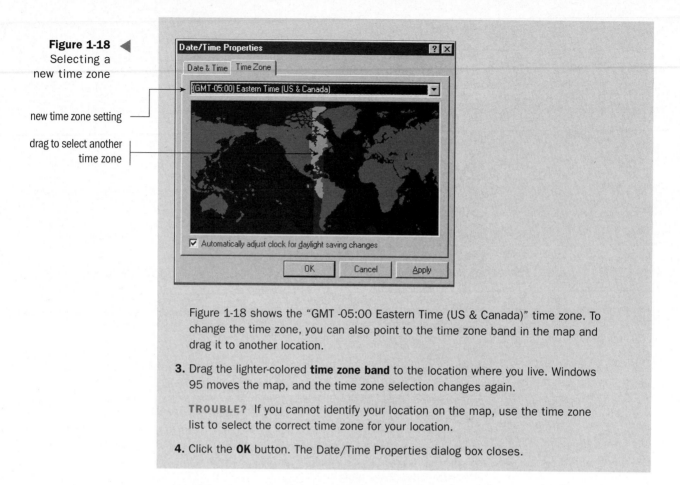

Figure 1-18 shows the "GMT -05:00 Eastern Time (US & Canada)" time zone. To change the time zone, you can also point to the time zone band in the map and drag it to another location.

3. Drag the lighter-colored **time zone band** to the location where you live. Windows 95 moves the map, and the time zone selection changes again.

TROUBLE? If you cannot identify your location on the map, use the time zone list to select the correct time zone for your location.

4. Click the **OK** button. The Date/Time Properties dialog box closes.

Since Resource Management has branch offices directing recycling efforts around the globe, employees often need to call those in other time zones. You are sure that this feature will be welcomed by Resource Management staff.

If you want to take a break and resume the tutorial at a later time, you can do so now. If you are on a network, close any open applications and dialog boxes, and leave Windows 95 running. If you are using your own computer, you can click Start on the taskbar, click Shut Down, click Shut down the computer, and then click Yes. When you resume the tutorial, launch Windows 95 again, then continue with the tutorial.

● ● ●

Viewing System Properties

So far you have worked with properties of two Windows objects: the taskbar and the clock. You can use the same method to view the properties of a much more important object: your computer. Windows 95 assigns a special icon to your computer: the My Computer icon. You can use the property sheet associated with the My Computer icon to examine the resources and properties of your computer, configure your computer, and, in the process, understand how the Windows 95 operating system functions. As you examine system properties, you can change settings and reconfigure your computer. However, before you make any changes, use the Print Screen method described earlier to make hard copies of property sheets in their original form, then record any additional information you might need later, such as the location and name of the property sheet and how to get to that property sheet. By knowing this information, you can restore an original setting if you discover that the change you made affects adversely the performance of your computer. Also, *please pay attention to warnings that Windows 95 might provide on the effects of changes that you intend to make.*

HELP DESK

Index

MY COMPUTER

Click the Start button, click Help, then click the Index tab.

Keyword	**Topic**
New features	The new look and feel of Windows, then My Computer

If you start by exploring property sheets and examining settings for the Windows 95 operating system and for the hardware and software resources that Windows 95 manages, you can develop an important overview of the organization and relationship of interconnected components. Then, you are in a better position to make changes that might affect a variety of resources within your computer.

HELP DESK

Index

UNDERSTANDING SYSTEM PROPERTIES

Click the Start button, click Help, then click the Index tab.

Keyword	**Topic**
System properties	More ways to customize Windows, then System properties

Now that you understand how to work with property sheets and the importance of documenting system settings before you change them, you are ready to examine the resources of the computer you are using and improve your understanding of Windows 95.

To view your system's resources:

1. Right-click the **My Computer** icon on the desktop.

2. Click **Properties** on the shortcut menu. Windows 95 displays a System Properties dialog box with four tabs. See Figure 1-19.

Figure 1-19 ◀
System
Properties
dialog box

General property
sheet

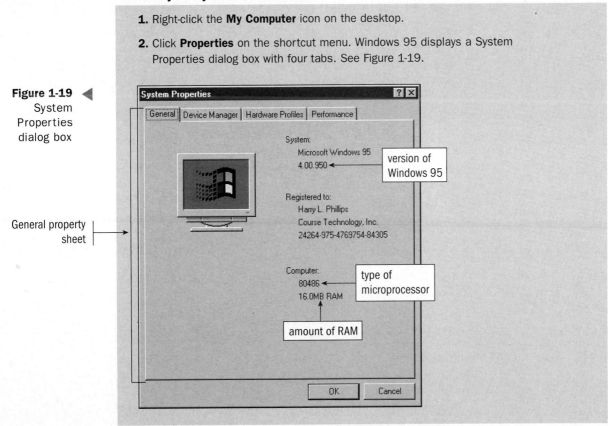

On the General tab, Windows 95 displays three types of information about your system. First, it identifies which version of Windows 95 your computer is using. This information is important to know. If your computer has a problem and you decide to call Microsoft's technical support line, a technician might first ask you for the version number of Windows 95 before attempting to troubleshoot the problem. That information might be a key to solving the problem. The General tab also identifies the registered user of this version of Windows 95, as well as the type of microprocessor and the amount of memory, or RAM, in the computer. In this figure, the computer contains an 80486 microprocessor and 16.0MB (megabytes) of RAM.

Viewing Device Properties

The General tab of the System Properties dialog box gives you very general information about your computer. The other tabs give you more specific information about, for example, your **hardware devices**, or the physical components of your computer, which include your disk drives, your CD-ROM drive (if you have one), your keyboard, your modem (if you have one), and all the other devices that contribute to the functioning of your computer. Windows 95 not only automatically identifies hardware components within a computer, but it also automatically configures those components using its Plug and Play specifications.

The Device Manager tab lists the hardware components within a computer. You can select a hardware device from this list and examine its properties in more detail.

So that you can more fully understand the makeup of your computer and the interaction of the hardware components, Sally recommends that you examine information on some of the hardware components in your computer.

To view information on hardware devices:

1. Click the **Device Manager** tab. Windows 95 opens the Device Manager property sheet and displays a list of all the hardware components that it found when first installed on your computer. Windows 95 updates the list of devices when you add new hardware to your computer. You can view the information in one of two ways, by type of device or by type of connection.

2. If the View devices by type radio button is not already selected, click the **View devices by type** radio button. This option lists devices, or components, by hardware category. See Figure 1-20.

Figure 1-20
Device Manager property sheet

choose to view devices by type

categories of hardware devices (your list might be different)

Ports selection box

click to view hardware properties

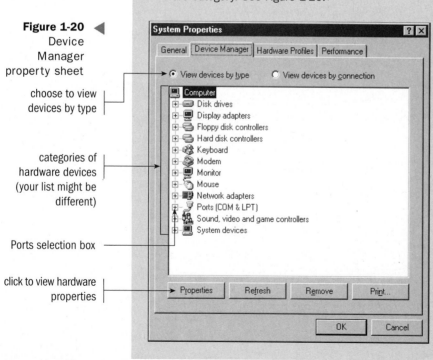

On the computer used for this figure, the list shows that this computer contains disk drives, display adapters, floppy disk controllers, hard disk controllers, a keyboard, a modem, a monitor, mouse, network adapters, ports, sound, video, and game controllers, and system devices. As it turns out, the computer used for this figure has no network adapters, but Windows 95 still claims there are these types of hardware devices in the computer. Your list will probably be different, but more than likely it will include some of the same hardware categories for standard devices. Some of the categories have just one item (for example, there is probably just one keyboard) while others might have more than one (computers today often have more than one disk drive).

If you want to see what hardware is available within each category, you click the plus sign that appears to the left of each hardware category, as shown on Figure 1-20. For example, clicking the Ports selection box with the plus sign shows what ports you have available on your computer (a **port** links your computer to a peripheral device like a modem or a printer).

To examine information on the ports category:

1. Click the **selection box** with the plus sign next to Ports (COM & LPT). Windows 95 now lists the ports within your computer. Although the types and number of ports vary with different computers, you will more than likely see at least two listings, one for a Communications Port (COM1) and one for a (parallel) Printer Port (LPT1). If you see an "X" through a device icon, then that hardware component has been disabled for some reason. If you see a circled exclamation point over the device icon, then there is a problem with the configuration of that hardware component. By using the Properties button, you can view more detailed information on a device, including information about hardware problems.

2. Click **Printer Port (LPT1)**, then click the **Properties** button. The Printer Port (LPT1) Properties dialog box opens. See Figure 1-21.

Figure 1-21 ◀
Printer Port
(LPT1)
Properties
dialog box

indicates whether
device is working
properly

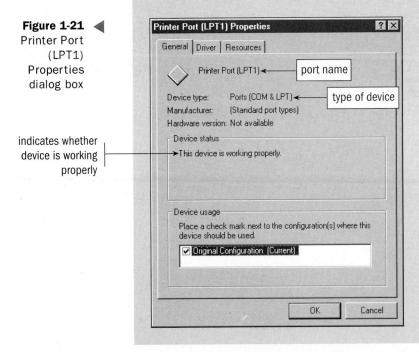

The device property sheets usually have three tabs: General, Driver, and Resources. In Figure 1-21, the General tab displays general information about the device, such as its type and manufacturer. In the Device Status section on the General tab, Windows 95 reports whether the device is operating properly. If you are experiencing problems with a device, or suspect that there is a problem or conflict between two different devices within your computer, this is the property sheet you would examine first.

3. Click the **Driver** tab. The Driver tab lists the name of the device driver or drivers that Windows uses for this hardware component. See Figure 1-22.

Figure 1-22 ◀
Driver property
sheet

name and location of
device driver

manufacturer of this
device driver

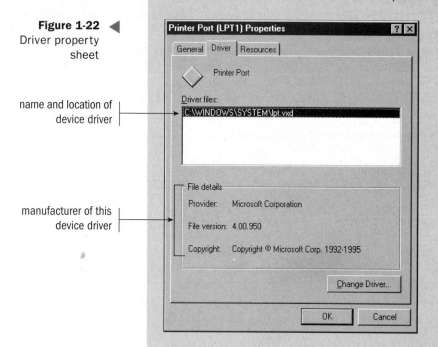

TROUBLE? If you are working on a network, you might not see a Driver tab.

A **device driver** is a file that contains program code that enables the operating system to communicate with and control the operation of a hardware or software component. When you need to troubleshoot problems with your hardware devices, this is where you look to identify the driver, usually the source of the problem.

4. Click the **Resources** tab.

On the Resources tab, Windows 95 displays the resources that a device uses. See Figure 1-23.

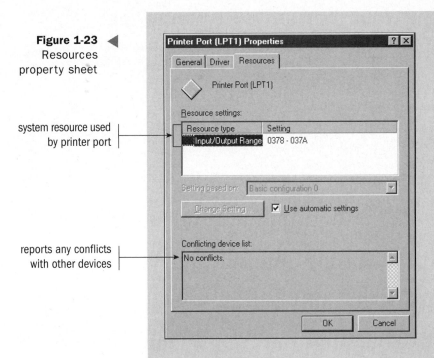

Figure 1-23
Resources
property sheet

system resource used
by printer port

reports any conflicts
with other devices

This property sheet can also help you troubleshoot problems with devices because it alerts you to any conflicting devices. In Figure 1-23, the resources used by this device do not conflict, or interfere, with resources used by other devices within the computer. If a conflict existed, Windows 95 would report information on the type of conflict. For example, two devices might attempt to use the same Input/Output range or some other system resource.

5. Click the **Cancel** button to close the Printer Port (LPT1) Properties dialog box. The Properties dialog box for this hardware device closes, and you see the System Properties dialog box. Clicking the Cancel button prevents you from making changes to properties that you don't intend to make.

The Device Manager tab of the System Properties dialog box should still be active. If you display devices by connection, Windows 95 shows which devices are connected to which hardware components. If you select the Refresh button, Windows 95 updates the device list, but you might have to wait several minutes for it to complete this process. If you need to remove a device, use the Remove button. If you want to print a summary with information on your computer's devices, you can use the Print button.

Sally suggests that the two of you take some time tomorrow to document all the settings on your computer system.

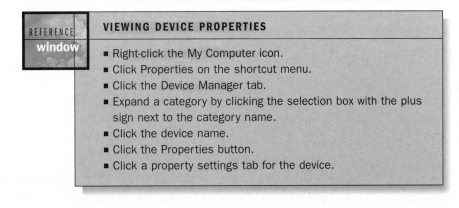

REFERENCE
window

VIEWING DEVICE PROPERTIES

- Right-click the My Computer icon.
- Click Properties on the shortcut menu.
- Click the Device Manager tab.
- Expand a category by clicking the selection box with the plus sign next to the category name.
- Click the device name.
- Click the Properties button.
- Click a property settings tab for the device.

Evaluating Your System's Performance

The Performance tab in the System Properties dialog box includes summary information on some of the important factors that affect your system's speed and overall performance. This information might help you anticipate potential problems.

To view performance specifications:

1. Click the **Performance** tab. Windows 95 displays a Performance property sheet with information on six system properties. See Figure 1-24.

Figure 1-24 ◀
Performance
property sheet

performance settings ⟶

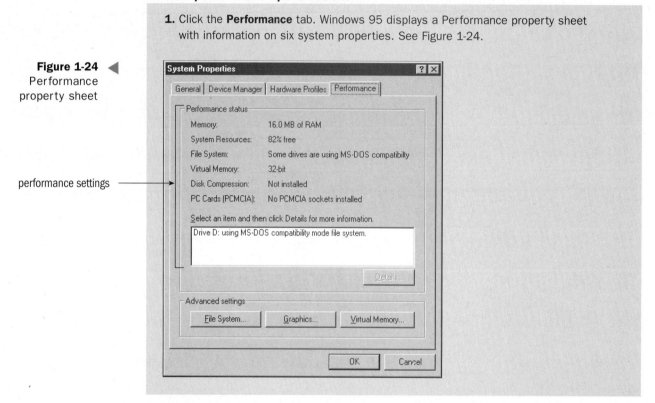

All six of these items help you characterize your system's performance, but there are two important things you can learn from these properties about your system. First, you can evaluate how your computer accesses memory, and second, how it accesses files. Windows 3.1 users will see some important improvements in these two areas in Windows 95.

How Windows 95 Accesses Memory

The first item on the Performance tab is Memory. This information verifies what you already learned about available memory by examining the General tab. The second item, System Resources, informs you that a certain percentage of the systems resources are free. The fourth item, Virtual Memory, tells you how your system uses the hard drive when it needs extra memory. **Virtual memory** refers to space on a hard disk that an operating system can use as extra memory to supplement the memory available in RAM. If the amount of memory within a computer is limited, or if the available RAM is almost completely used up, Windows 95 can temporarily swap unused parts of the program code for open applications and parts of open document files to storage space on a hard disk in order to free up memory for other uses. In essence, the operating system performs a complex juggling task to manage multiple applications, documents, tasks, windows, and dialog boxes on a computer with limited memory.

Your system can retrieve information from RAM, that is, the predominant type of memory within your computer provided through the use of memory chips on the motherboard, much more quickly than it can retrieve information from virtual memory stored on your system's hard drive. The less your system has to rely on virtual memory, the faster it will run, and the more RAM you have, the less you have to rely on virtual memory. As a general rule, Windows 95 should have no less than 8 MB of RAM for "good" performance. However, increasing the memory to 16 MB of RAM will result in a significant increase in speed when you run many applications or when you run resource-intensive applications. Use the Windows 95 pop-up windows to get a better understanding of these issues.

To learn more about the Performance tab memory settings:

1. Right-click **System Resources**, then click **What's This?** In the pop-up window, Windows 95 explains that, if this number becomes too low, your computer might function more slowly. As you open more applications, files, windows, dialog boxes, and other objects, system resources will decrease and the overall performance of your computer will also decrease. You can free up resources by closing unused files, applications, windows, and dialog boxes.

2. Click the **pop-up window** to close it.

3. Right-click the **setting** for Virtual Memory, then click **What's This?** Read the information, then close the pop-up window. You'll learn more about the 32-bit option in the next section.

   TROUBLE? If you accidentally right-click the Virtual Memory button rather than the setting, you will see a different pop-up window. Be sure to right-click the setting and not the button.

If Sally or you need to check the performance of a co-worker's computer, you know exactly where to locate the information you need. Then, you can determine what you next need to do to correct a problem or improve the performance of a computer.

How Windows 95 Accesses Files

An important aspect of your system's performance is how efficiently it retrieves files from your hard disk. There are two property settings on the Performance tab that help you evaluate how your computer accesses files: File System and Disk Compression. Take a look at the settings for how your computer accesses files.

To evaluate how your computer accesses files:

1. Right-click the **setting** to the right of File System, then click **What's This?** This setting indicates what type of filing system Windows 95 is currently using. A **filing system** refers to specific techniques used by an operating system to access data stored on disk. Windows 95 will choose one of two options: a 32-bit filing system (the default), or an MS-DOS filing system. Help also notes that Windows 95 performs optimally when it uses its own 32-bit filing system.

   TROUBLE? If you accidentally right-click the File System button rather than the setting, you will see a different pop-up window. Be sure to right-click the setting and not the button.

2. Close the **pop-up window**.

3. Right-click the **setting** for Disk Compression, click **What's This?**, examine the information in the pop-up window, then close it. This setting indicates what type of disk compression you are using on your computer, if any, and whether it is either 32-bit software or software compatible with MS-DOS. Disk compression utilities, such as Stacker and Microsoft's Doublespace and DriveSpace, are examples of software products that substantially increase the storage capacity of hard disks and even disks. In some cases, storage capacities are doubled, or more than doubled.

4. Click the **Cancel** button to close the System Properties dialog box.

The 32-bit setting for File System (and for Virtual Memory) is a very important one for Windows 95 because it is this capability that most significantly improves the performance of your computer over previous versions of Windows. The other option for both the File System and Virtual Memory settings (as you saw when you opened the pop-up windows) is MS-DOS compatibility mode (also called real mode), which slows down the performance of your system. How does a 32-bit filing system differ from the MS-DOS filing system? How do these two different approaches handle virtual memory? To answer these questions, you must delve deeper into the differences between the capabilities of various types of microprocessors and the operating systems designed for these chips.

What Is a 32-Bit Operating System?

One of the most important features of Windows 95 is that it is a 32-bit operating system. A **32-bit operating system** contains program code that enables it to use the full capabilities of the 80386 and later microprocessors. DOS, on the other hand, is a **16-bit operating system** that contains program code originally designed to enable it to function on the early types of microprocessors. The "32-bit" and "16-bit" designations refer to specific features of the microprocessors that these operating systems exploit.

The early microprocessors used on microcomputers—the 8088 (used in IBM PCs and XTs), the 8086 used in XT compatibles, and the 80286 used in IBM PC/ATs and 286s—were **16-bit chips**, or chips that could internally process 16 bits of data at once. The 80386 and 80486 are **32-bit chips**, or chips that can internally process 32 bits of data at once. Although the 32-bit chips operate internally twice as fast as the 16-bit chips, the overall performance of the microprocessors in these systems also depends on how much data each microprocessor can transmit to or receive from devices. The actual number of bits that a microprocessor transmits and receives might differ from the number of bits that it can process internally. For example, the 8088 transmits and receives 8 bits at a time. The 8086, 80286, and 80386SX (the low-end 80386) transmit and receive 16 bits at a time. The 80386DX (the full-featured 80386), 80486SX, and 80486DX all transmit and receive 32 bits at a time.

Another important difference is the amount of memory that each type of microprocessor can address. To use the memory within a computer, the microprocessor must be able to form a unique address for each memory location. The address identifies the location of one byte, or one character, of data. The 8088 and 8086 microprocessors use a 20-bit addressing scheme that allows them to address a total of 1MB of memory. In other words, they form addresses using 20 bits. Since each bit can either be a 0 (zero) or 1, the microprocessor can form 2^{20} addresses, or 1,048,576 addresses. Since each byte of memory is assigned an address, you can access 1,048,576 bytes, or 1MB, of memory. The 80286 uses a 24-bit addressing scheme that allows it to form 2^{24} addresses and access 16MB of memory. The 80386 and 80486 employ a 32-bit addressing scheme that allows them to form 2^{32} addresses and thereby access 4096MB, or 4G (gigabytes), of memory.

As a result of these differences in how microprocessors process data and in how they address memory, the operating systems used with these microprocessors are either 16-bit or 32-bit operating systems. DOS is a 16-bit operating system that can only address 640K of memory, even on computers that contain 80386 and 80486 microprocessors. Windows 95 is a 32-bit operating system that can address the full 4G of memory accessible to 80386 and subsequent microprocessors.

DOS applications are called **16-bit applications** because DOS employs a 16-bit memory addressing scheme for these applications, and that scheme allows these applications to operate within the 640K of memory that DOS manages. Applications written specifically for Windows 95 are called **32-bit applications** because Windows 95 employs a 32-bit memory addressing scheme for these applications. To maintain backward compatibility with DOS applications, Windows 95 can address memory using both approaches. Microsoft Corporation now refers to DOS applications as **Win16-based applications**, and the newer Windows 95 applications, such as Office 95, as **Win32-based applications**.

Another important distinction between the two operating systems is that DOS operates in real mode while Windows 95 operates in protected mode. **Real mode** is an operating mode used by 8088 and 8086 microcomputers in which the microprocessor itself can only address 1MB of memory. **Protected mode** is an operating mode that allows 80286, 80386, 80486 and subsequent microprocessors to address more than 1MB of memory and to provide memory protection features. 80386 and subsequent microprocessors can also operate in Virtual 8086 mode. **Virtual 8086 mode** is an operating mode that allows the 80386 (or subsequent) microprocessor to perform as multiple 8086 microprocessors. In virtual 8086 mode, the microprocessor creates **virtual machines**, each of which acts like an 8086 microprocessor and each of which is capable of running an operating system and an application. Each virtual machine is a computing environment that functions as if it were a complete computer. **Virtual mode,** on the other hand, refers to the ability of an operating system to use storage space on a hard disk as extra memory.

Windows 95 contains both 32-bit and 16-bit program code, so that it can function with applications developed for Windows 95 and with DOS applications. Windows 95 uses 32-bit program code for its filing system, device drivers, memory management, scheduling, and process management while DOS uses 16-bit program code for these same system resources. The Windows 95 32-bit program code provides faster response times, more efficiently uses system resources, and improves overall system performance.

Your exploration of property sheets has yielded much valuable information about your computer, which you report to Sally. Sally is pleasantly surprised to hear how much easier it is to get an instant overview of a computer with Windows 95. She is confident that this will speed up diagnostic efforts on computers that are having problems.

Examining Properties of the Recycle Bin

Sally asks if you've discovered any other interesting things about Windows 95 as you've explored the desktop. You tell her about a feature that you're sure will save Resource Management employees from much frustration: the Recycle Bin. Resource Management is upgrading to Windows 95 from Windows 3.1. Under Windows 3.1, if you deleted a file, there was no easy way to recover it. You could use DOS and third party utilities to help recover deleted files, but not everyone at Resource Management had these utilities or knew how to use them. The Windows 95 Recycle Bin makes it much easier to recover deleted files.

No matter how much storage capacity your hard disk drive has, you need to periodically remove unneeded folders, data files, and software from your computer so that you can reclaim valuable storage space for use by other software applications and data files. Newer types of software applications require increasingly larger amounts of storage space to install the program and auxiliary files provided with the product. As you build more complex, compound documents that contain text, tables, charts, clip art, and linked objects, your file sizes will increase dramatically.

When you perform your next system cleaning, you can archive important document files by copying them from your hard disk to floppy disks or some other type of permanent storage device in the event you need them again in the future. If you discover duplicate copies of files, such as clip art files, you can archive them or delete them from your system. Periodically, you might also want to reorganize the folder, or subdirectory structure of your hard disk so that you can more efficiently organize files. If you store important sets of document files on floppy disks and work from those disks on different computers at different business or work sites, you might need to decide periodically which files you no longer need and remove them from a disk.

When you are ready to remove unneeded files, software, folders, or other objects from your computer, you can drag them to the Recycle Bin, which stores them as long as it can (how long depends on how you configure the Recycle Bin). Until you empty the Recycle Bin, you can recover items stored there, either to their original location or to a new location. By default, Windows sets aside 10% of your hard disk as storage space for files and folders that you place in the Recycle Bin. If you have a 500MB hard disk drive, then Windows 95 uses up to 50MB for the contents of the Recycle Bin. If hard disk space storage is a premium for you, as it is for most people, you could more efficiently use your hard disk by limiting the size of the Recycle Bin. Furthermore, you might simply not need to set aside that large amount of storage space for the Recycle Bin.

The setting you choose might also depend on the types of applications and documents you use. If you create relatively small documents with word processing and spreadsheet applications, then you can use a low setting for the size of the Recycle Bin and still be able to recover a document file that you or someone else deliberately or inadvertently deleted. However, if you create large documents with word processing or spreadsheet applications, or if you work with large database, video, and graphic files, then you should allow more space in the Recycle Bin for those files.

Sally wonders how much space the Recycle Bin on her computer is taking up right now, because space is really at a premium on her hard disk. She has already filled 80% of her hard disk with utilities and software applications as well as files containing procedures, training materials, and other types of information. She has used approximately 400MB of her 500MB hard drive. She'd like to conserve as much space as possible, so she decides to reduce the size of the Recycle Bin. The two of you sit down at her computer, and you show her what you've learned.

To examine properties of the Recycle Bin:

1. Right-click the **Recycle Bin** icon on the desktop.

2. Click **Properties** on the shortcut menu. The Recycle Bin Properties dialog box opens, with options for changing settings of the Recycle Bin. See Figure 1-25.

Figure 1-25
Recycle Bin
Properties
dialog box

global property
settings

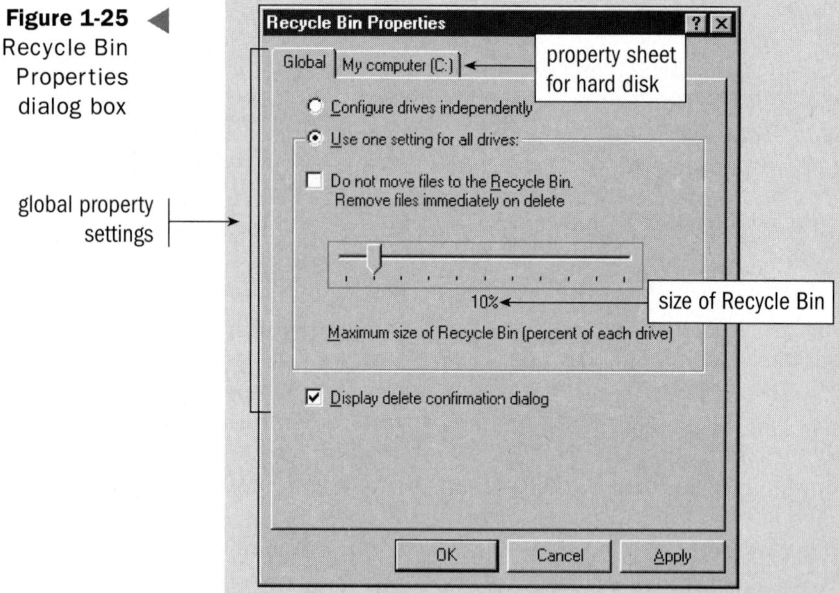

In addition to the Global tab, which displays system-wide settings, there is a tab for each of your hard disk drives. Each hard disk drive tab identifies the volume name, or label, assigned to the drive, if any, as well as the drive name itself. The computer in Figure 1-25 has only one hard drive—drive C.

The top radio buttons on the Global property sheet give you the option of configuring each hard disk drive separately or of using one setting for all drives. If you configure each drive separately, you can specify how much storage space is allocated for the Recycle Bin on each drive. You also have the option of immediately deleting files rather than storing them in the Recycle Bin until you empty it. If the Display delete confirmation dialog check box is checked, Windows 95 will ask you to confirm a file or folder deletion. This feature prevents you from inadvertently deleting important files or folders.

You can use the slider control to set the maximum size of the Recycle Bin as a percentage of each drive or, if the Configure drives independently radio button is selected, then you can switch to the tab that contains the Recycle Bin property settings for a specific drive and adjust the slider control for that drive alone. For example, if your slider control shows that Windows 95 is currently using 10% of your hard disk for the Recycle Bin, you can change that setting to 1%. If your hard disk has 500MB of storage space, this change would reduce the size of the Recycle Bin from 50MB to 5MB. The 45MB that you gain from changing this setting means that you will not run the risk of storing an additional 45MB of deleted files and folders in the Recycle Bin, which could take up valuable disk space. You must weigh the importance of having the disk space against the importance of having the safeguards provided by the Recycle Bin, and decide how much of your hard disk to allot to Recycle Bin space.

Since disk space is a valuable resource on your computer, you decide to change the setting for the size of the Recycle Bin from its current setting to 1% on drive C.

To change the size of the Recycle Bin:

1. Make sure the Configure drives independently check box is selected, then click the tab for your drive C.

2. Drag the **slider control bar** from its current setting to 1%, then release the mouse button. As you drag the slider control, the percent shown on the property sheet changes.

3. If you want to make this change to your hard disk drive, click the **OK** button.

If you fill up the Recycle Bin without emptying it, Windows deletes the oldest files to make room for new files.

Sally is curious about how you would retrieve a file from the Recycle Bin if you did delete it by mistake. The two of you decide to use online Help to find out.

Using Online Help

The Windows 95 online Help is a valuable resource for quickly locating information on specific features and tasks. You can even use online Help to access property sheets so that you can configure your computer. You access online Help from the Start Menu. Once you open online Help, you can view information on specific topics from the table of contents, or you can search for information by topic or by keyword.

Locating How To Help

Sally suggests you start with the How To Help topics to locate information on using the Recycle Bin.

To find Help on recovering files from the Recycle Bin:

1. Click the **Start** button.

2. Click **Help** then click the **Contents** tab.

On the Contents tab, the four top-level books introduce you to Windows 95, describe how to locate "how to" information, explain new tips and tricks, and access Windows 95 online troubleshooters to resolve system problems. See Figure 1-26.

Figure 1-26
Help Topics
dialog box

Contents tab

quick tour

books with related
topics

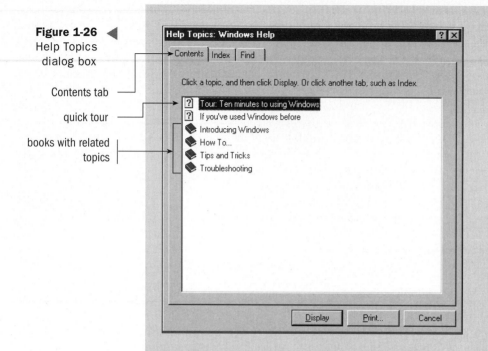

3. Click the **How To** book, then click the **Open** button. The book opens and shows topics within the How To book. See Figure 1-27.

Figure 1-27
Opening the
How To book

books for learning
how to perform tasks

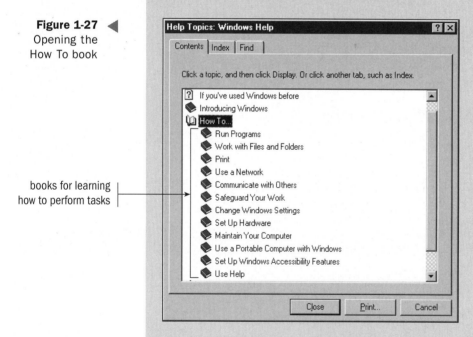

4. Click the **Work with Files and Folders** book, then click the **Open** button. More specific how-to topics for working with files and folders appear.

5. Click **Retrieving deleted files or shortcuts**, then click the **Display** button. A Windows Help dialog box opens and instructs you to start by double-clicking the Recycle Bin icon. See Figure 1-28.

Figure 1-28 ◀
Windows Help
dialog box

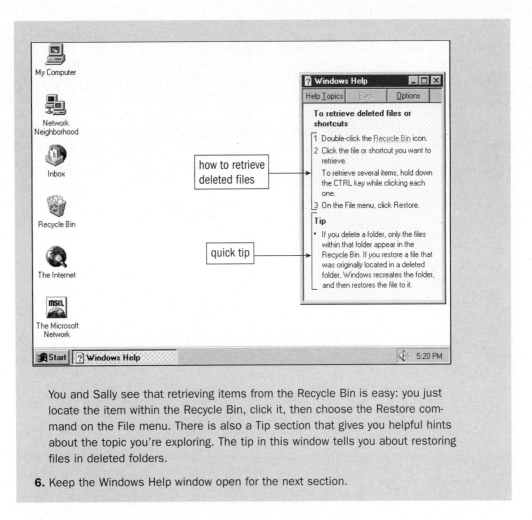

You and Sally see that retrieving items from the Recycle Bin is easy: you just locate the item within the Recycle Bin, click it, then choose the Restore command on the File menu. There is also a Tip section that gives you helpful hints about the topic you're exploring. The tip in this window tells you about restoring files in deleted folders.

6. Keep the Windows Help window open for the next section.

Sally and you realize that the online Help could be used as a valuable tool in some upcoming training sessions on the use of Windows 95.

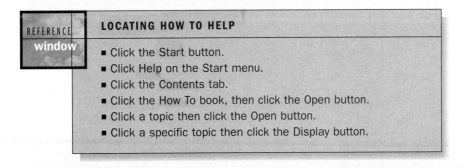

REFERENCE **window**

LOCATING HOW TO HELP

- Click the Start button.
- Click Help on the Start menu.
- Click the Contents tab.
- Click the How To book, then click the Open button.
- Click a topic then click the Open button.
- Click a specific topic then click the Display button.

Searching for Information in the Help Index

The main Help window has two other tabs that give you access to information: Index and Find. By using the Index tab, you can go directly to a specific topic and locate information on how to perform an operation. Unlike the Contents tab, which provides general information on various procedures and features, the Index tab allows you to quickly pinpoint information on a specific topic.

Recently, you adjusted the setting for the Recycle Bin. Now you and Sally want to find out how much storage space remains on your hard disk.

To examine disk usage:

1. In the Windows Help window, click the **Help Topics** button to return to the main Help window, and then click the **Index** tab. In the Step 1 text box on the Index tab, you enter the topic for which you want to locate information by typing in the first few characters of the topic. See Figure 1-29.

Figure 1-29 ◀
Help Index tab

enter a search topic ————

select an index entry ————

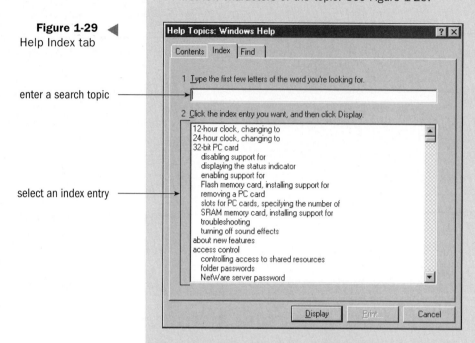

TROUBLE? If you closed the Windows Help window earlier, click the Start button, click Help to display the Help Topics dialog box, then click the Index tab.

2. In the Step 1 text box on the Index tab, type **hard disk space**. Windows 95 adjusts the view in the Step 2 index entry box on the Index tab to show topics that fall under the index entry "hard disk space." See Figure 1-30.

Figure 1-30 ◀
Searching for
Help on hard
disk space

search topic ————

matching index entry
found

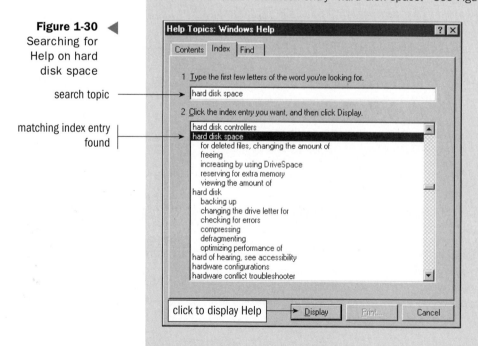

Below that index entry, you can see a more specific index entry, "viewing the amount of."

3. Click **viewing the amount of** under the hard disk space topic in the index entry list, then click the **Display** button. In the Windows Help window that opens, Windows 95 explains how to determine how much space is available on a disk. As you work, you can choose to keep this window on top so that you can see the steps for this operation.

4. Click the **Options** button, point to **Keep Help on Top**, then click **On Top** from the cascading menu. Now, you can follow the steps shown in the Windows Help window. First, you have to double-click the My Computer icon, and then click the disk drive you want to check.

5. Double-click the **My Computer** icon, then maximize the window. The My Computer window opens. See Figure 1-31. The contents and arrangement of your My Computer window may differ from that shown in the figure.

Figure 1-31 ◀
My Computer window

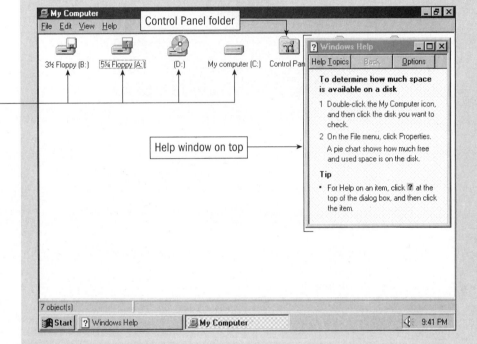

TROUBLE? Once you open My Computer, you might not be able to see the entire window with Help on Top. You can readjust the size of either the My Computer or the Windows Help window. Just point to a size or corner border, drag one or more sides of a window until the window outline is close to what you want, then release the mouse button. If you cannot see a window border, click the Restore button 🔲 to return the window to its original size.

Next, you select drive C.

6. Click the **drive C** disk icon. As shown in the Windows Help window, you next select the File menu, then the Properties option on the File menu.

7. Click **File** then click **Properties**. In the Properties dialog box for drive C, Windows 95 shows the label, or volume name, assigned to the drive, if any. See Figure 1-32. Next to Type, Windows 95 identifies whether the drive is a local hard disk drive or a network drive. On the computer in this figure, 475MB of the 503MB hard disk is already in use and only 27.8MB is available. The pie chart for drive C illustrates the percentage of space used and the percentage of space still available.

Figure 1-32 ◄
Properties
dialog box for a
hard disk

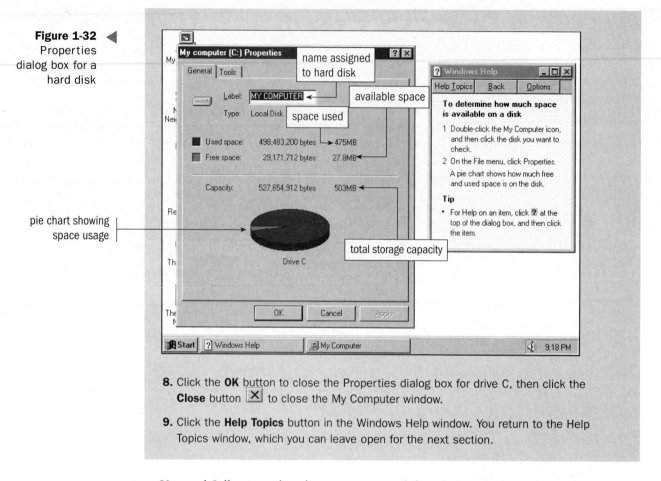

pie chart showing
space usage

Figure 1-32 ◄
Properties
dialog box for a
hard disk

8. Click the **OK** button to close the Properties dialog box for drive C, then click the **Close** button ⊠ to close the My Computer window.

9. Click the **Help Topics** button in the Windows Help window. You return to the Help Topics window, which you can leave open for the next section.

You and Sally agree that the company can definitely benefit from the ability to locate important information about a computer when you need to assist users in troubleshooting problems.

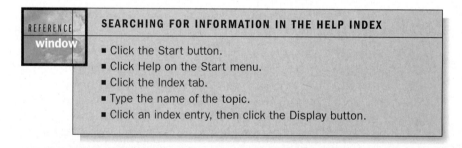

REFERENCE
window

SEARCHING FOR INFORMATION IN THE HELP INDEX

- Click the Start button.
- Click Help on the Start menu.
- Click the Index tab.
- Type the name of the topic.
- Click an index entry, then click the Display button.

Searching Online Help with Keywords

When you use the Index tab, you specify a category, such as printer, to locate a set of topics related to the use of printers. By using the Find tab, you can search for specific words and phrases within information on a help topic, rather than a specific topic. For example, if you search for information on "sans," "serif," or "sans serif" using the Index tab, you will not find any Help information. However, if you use the Find tab, you will locate information on "Finding similar fonts." If you are looking for information on a specific hardware device, for example, using the Index tab is faster. However, if you want to expand your search to include more words and phrases, using the Find tab is more effective.

After you and Sally have worked together for several hours on this computer, you decide to display information on the percentage of system resources that Windows 95 is currently using, but you do not remember which property sheet contains this information. You decide to use the Find tab in online Help to assist you in this process.

To locate information on displaying system resources:

1. Click the **Find** tab. The first step is to type a word that identifies what you want to do. See Figure 1-33.

Figure 1-33
Help Find tab

enter a search topic

select a matching word

select a topic

number of topics found

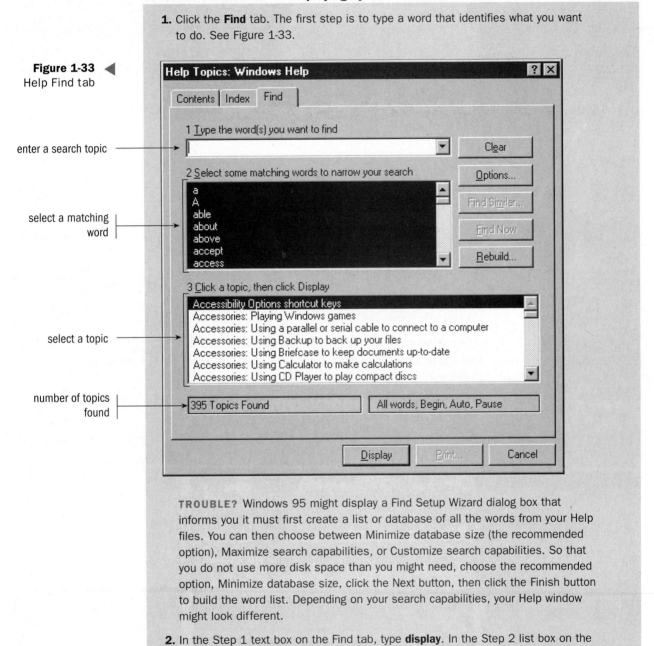

TROUBLE? Windows 95 might display a Find Setup Wizard dialog box that informs you it must first create a list or database of all the words from your Help files. You can then choose between Minimize database size (the recommended option), Maximize search capabilities, or Customize search capabilities. So that you do not use more disk space than you might need, choose the recommended option, Minimize database size, click the Next button, then click the Finish button to build the word list. Depending on your search capabilities, your Help window might look different.

2. In the Step 1 text box on the Find tab, type **display**. In the Step 2 list box on the Find tab, Windows lists matching words in the word list box. See Figure 1-34.

Figure 1-34
Searching for
Help on
"display"

search topic

matching words

selected topics

number of topics
found

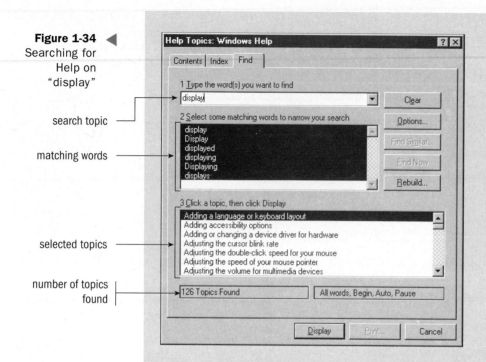

In the Step 3 topic list box on the Find tab, Windows 95 displays an alphabetical list of topics associated with the word you entered. On the computer in this figure, Windows Help found 126 topics. You want to narrow the search even further.

3. In the word list under Step 2, click **Displaying** (*do not click "displaying" with the lowercase "d"*). On the computer in this figure, Windows Help narrowed the list under Step 3 to six topics. See Figure 1-35.

Figure 1-35
Fine-tuning a
search

select this matching
word

selected topics

number of topics
found

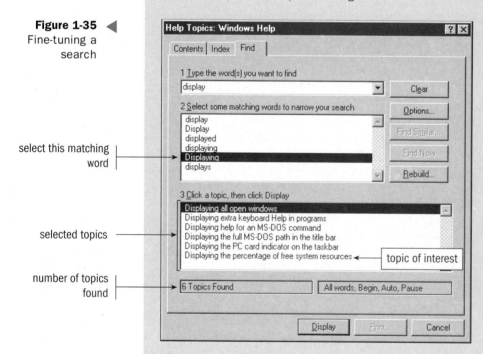

topic of interest

The topic you want is the last one.

4. In the topic list under Step 3, click **Displaying the percentage of free system resources**, then click the **Display** button. In the Windows Help window, Windows 95 instructs you in Step 1 to click the button to display the Performance information.

5. Click the button for the one and only step in the Windows Help window.

This system property sheet shows you the available system resources. Chances are the percentage will be different from what it was earlier. See Figure 1-36.

Figure 1-36 ◄
Checking the
available
system
resources

amount of available
system resources

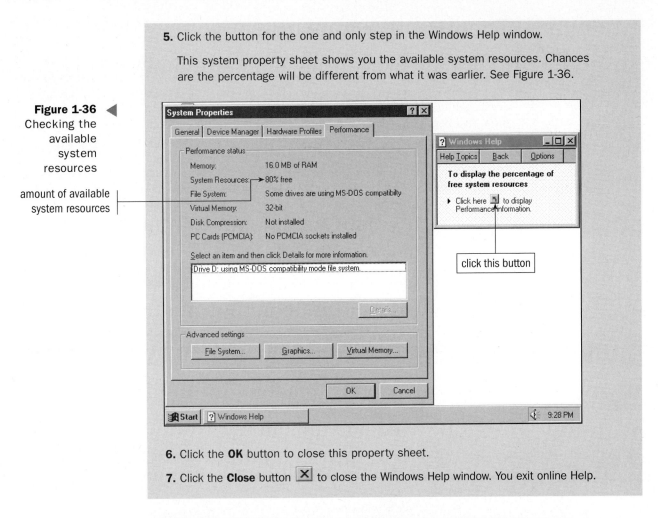

click this button

6. Click the **OK** button to close this property sheet.

7. Click the **Close** button ☒ to close the Windows Help window. You exit online Help.

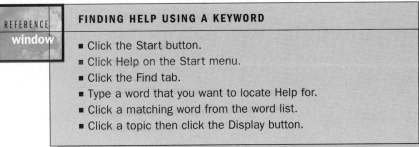

REFERENCE
window

FINDING HELP USING A KEYWORD

- Click the Start button.
- Click Help on the Start menu.
- Click the Find tab.
- Type a word that you want to locate Help for.
- Click a matching word from the word list.
- Click a topic then click the Display button.

● ● ●

You have plenty of subject matter for your brown-bag seminar. You've seen that Windows 95 provides not only an impressive graphical user interface with icons for all the objects within your computer, but it also includes easy-to-access online Help to explain and to guide you through the use of new features. Plus, property sheets permit you to quickly customize your Windows desktop. During your seminar, you can accent these features so that the staff can get up to speed quickly.

Tutorial Assignment

As Sally and you install Windows 95 on new computers for employees at Resource Management, she wants the two of you to check the settings in Device Manager for each of the disk drives, keyboard, monitor, and mouse, and ensure that there are no device conflicts that might cause potential problems for employees. She asks you to start with Beth Gilbert's new computer on which you just installed Windows 95. As you leave your office, she asks you to print a system summary for that new computer.

1. Launch Windows 95.
2. Right-click the My Computer icon, then click Properties on the shortcut menu.
3. When the System Properties dialog box opens, click the Device Manager tab.
4. If necessary, click the View devices by type radio button.
5. Click the selection box with the plus sign to the left of Disk drives to display a list of drives.
6. Click the hardware option for the hard disk drive, then click the Properties button.
7. On the General tab, check the Device status section and verify that this hardware device is working properly.
8. Click the Settings tab, verify the drive letter assigned to this disk drive, then click the Cancel button to close the dialog box without making any changes.
9. Click the hardware option for your floppy disk drive or, if you have two floppy disk drives, choose the first one, then click the Properties button.
10. On the General tab, check the Device status section and verify that this hardware device is working properly.
11. Click the Settings tab, verify the drive letter assigned to this disk drive, then click the Cancel button to close the dialog box without making any changes.
12. Click the selection box with the plus sign to the left of the Keyboard category to display the keyboard model, click the keyboard model name, then click the Properties button.
13. On the General tab, check the Device status section and verify that this hardware device is working properly.
14. Click the Resources tab, check the Conflicting device list section and verify that there are no conflicts with other devices, then click the Cancel button to close the dialog box without making any changes.
15. Click the selection box with the plus sign to the left of the Monitor category to display the monitor model, click the monitor model name, then click the Properties button.
16. On the General tab, check the Device status section and verify that this hardware device is working properly, then click the Cancel button to close the dialog box without making any changes.
17. Click the selection box with the plus sign to the left of the Mouse category to display the mouse model, click the mouse model name, then click the Properties button.
18. On the General tab, check the Device status section and verify that this hardware device is working properly, then click the Cancel button to close the dialog box without making any changes.
19. Click the Print button on the Device Manager tab.
20. When the Print dialog box opens, click the System summary radio button in the Report type section, then make sure there is no check mark in the Print to file check box.
21. Make sure your printer is on and operational, then click the OK button.
22. On the Device Manager tab, click the Cancel button to close the System Properties dialog box without making any changes to configuration settings.

Case Problems

1. Evaluating Newly Installed Computers at Southbay Title Company Southbay Title Company researches information on titles for new homeowners and their lending institutions. To increase her employees' productivity, the president, Sharon Wainright, recently hired a consultant to install Windows 95 on their five new computers. Before staff members start using their computers and making changes to settings, she asks you to document information on the hardware devices of each computer. She recommends you start by compiling a list for one computer, then you can use that table to verify that the other computers are using the exact same settings.

1. Launch Windows then open the System Properties dialog box.
2. Select the Device Manager tab, then choose the option to display devices by type.
3. Use the Alt + Print Screen key combination to place a copy of the Device Manager tab on the Clipboard, then open Paint and print a copy of this property sheet.
4. Using the table in Figure 1-37 as a guideline, document the properties of standard and optional hardware components for your or another computer system. If a hardware device is not available, enter N/A for the Type, Brand, or Manufacturer, Driver(s), and Resource(s) columns.
5. After you compile the information for this table, select the Disk drives category and open the Print dialog box. For Report type, specify that you want a report by Selected class or device, then print the report.

Figure 1-37 ◄

Hardware Component	Type, Brand, or Manufacturer	Driver(s)	Resource(s)
Hard Disk Drive			
First Floppy Disk Drive			
Second Floppy Disk Drive			
Monitor			
Mouse			
Keyboard			
CD-ROM Drive			
Modem			
Tape Drive			

2. Contingency Planning at McKinlay Flooring & Interiors, Inc. Timothy McKinlay operates a small home improvement business that sells floor and wall products. At a recent meeting of the local Chamber of Commerce, one business member described how she recently lost several days of business when she experienced problems with one of her computers. Timothy realized that it might be a good idea to take an inventory of settings on his computer system so that, if he experienced any difficulties, he would have a record of the original settings. He asks you to set aside some of your time to document the properties of adapters and controllers in the computer system that the business uses to track customer accounts and its business income and expenses.

1. Launch Windows then open the System Properties dialog box.

2. Select the Device Manager tab, then choose the option to display devices by type.

3. Use the Alt + Print Screen key combination to place a copy of the Device Manager tab on the Clipboard, then open Paint and print a copy of this property sheet.

4. Using the table in Figure 1-38 as a guideline, document the properties of standard and optional adapters and controllers for your or another computer system. If your computer does not have one of the adapters or controllers shown in the table, enter N/A for the Type, Brand, or Manufacturer, Driver(s), Resource(s), Conflicts, and Working Properly? columns.

5. After you compile the information for this table, select the Hard Disk Controller category and open the Print dialog box. For Report type, specify that you want a report by Selected class or device, then print the report.

Figure 1-38 ◄

Device Type	Type, Brand, or Manufacturer	Driver(s)	Resource(s)	Conflicts	Working Properly?
Display Adapter					
Hard Disk Controller					
Floppy Disk Controller					
Sound Controller					
Gameport Controller					

3. Upgrading Computers at Maestri & Lyman Desktop Publishers, Inc. Maestri & Lyman Desktop Publishers, Inc. have grown rapidly over the last three years, and now handle a variety of large business accounts in southern California. The owners, Carolyn Maestri and Mark Lyman, have decided that it is time to upgrade some of their computers by adding modems and tape drives to those computers. Since this process will involve reassigning ports, they want you to prepare a list of port settings for the computer that you use. If hardware conflicts develop, then the dealer from which they purchased the computers will have the necessary information to trace and resolve the source of the problem.

1. Launch Windows then open the System Properties dialog box.

2. Select the Device Manager tab, then choose the option to display devices by type.

3. Use the Alt + Print Screen key combination to place a copy of the Device Manager tab on the Clipboard, then open Paint and print a copy of this property sheet.

4. Using the table in Figure 1-39 as a guideline, document the properties for the following ports for your or another computer system. If your computer does not have a certain port shown in the table, enter N/A for the Type, Brand, or Manufacturer, Driver(s), Resource(s), Conflicts, and Working Properly? columns.

5. After you compile the information for this table, select the Ports (COM & LPT) category and open the Print dialog box. For Report type, specify that you want a report by Selected class or device, then print the report.

Figure 1-39 ◄

Port	Type, Brand, or Manufacturer	Driver(s)	Resource(s)	Conflicts	Working Properly?
LPT1					
LPT2					
LPT3					
COM1					
COM2					
COM3					
COM4					

4. Troubleshooting Hardware Conflicts on a Bayview Travel Service's Computer Bayview Travel Service relies heavily on its computers to track information on travel packages and to make reservations for its clients. Like many other businesses that want to expand their services, Bayview Travel recently added a modem to one of its computers so that employees could connect to online services and access information on vacation tours and resorts. Now, the mouse and the modem on that computer do not work. The manager, Earl Sykes, has asked you to troubleshoot the problem. Based on your experience, you assume that the likely source of the problem is that those two hardware devices are attempting to use the same port. After checking the computer, you find that one device is connected to the first serial communications port, COM1, while the other is connected to the second serial communications port, COM2.

1. Prepare a brief outline that lists the strategy you would follow to locate the source of the problem. For each step in this outline, list any resources, including online Help, that Windows 95 can provide you as you attempt to determine the cause of the problem.
2. After you prepare the outline, print a copy of the settings for the ports installed on your computer system.

Customizing Windows 95

Creating Desktops for a Diverse Work Force

CASE

Thorsen Pharmaceuticals Corporation

Thorsen Pharmaceuticals Corporation is an international firm that produces and sells new pharmaceuticals around the world. Over the last 25 years, Thorsen Pharmaceuticals developed new medications in its research labs in Great Britain, France, and Sweden. Like many other pharmaceutical companies, its management realizes that many new strains of bacteria have developed resistance to the use of traditional types of antibiotics, such as penicillin. In response to the need for new antibiotics, Thorsen Pharmaceuticals recently opened a new research facility in the United States that uses gene-splicing technology to accelerate the process for finding new classes of antibiotics. To increase the productivity of its staff, Thorsen Pharmaceuticals has purchased 125 desktop Pentiums for its administrative, office, scientific, and technical support staff at this new division. The manufacturer from which they purchased the Pentiums has already installed Windows 95 on the hard disks of these computers with the default desktop settings in Windows 95. Over the next several weeks, Jaime Navarro, a microcomputer systems specialist at this new research facility, will help staff members customize their desktops. Also, since employees in this division must communicate on a regular basis with other divisions outside the United States, Jaime must show employees how to use international language settings on their computers.

Thorsen Pharmaceuticals has discovered that its policy of hiring individuals from diverse backgrounds has enabled the company to expand its operations beyond its traditional markets and to draw on the talents of a diverse pool of people. As Jaime helps employees customize their desktops, he wants to provide them with options that will help them perform their jobs efficiently and effectively.

Changing Desktop Properties to Increase Productivity

As Jaime has discovered from past experience, employees are more productive if the software they use lets them customize their working environment. Personal, cultural, and ethnic differences often affect the choices that employees make when they customize their desktops.

Since Jaime and you work together on various projects, he suggests that the two of you customize your own desktops before you start showing others how to customize their desktops. Then, you can discuss the pros and cons of using different types of desktop settings. Before you start, Jaime tells you that you can customize the Windows 95 desktop using many of the same types of options that are available in the Windows 3.1 operating environment. You can select a background pattern or wallpaper, select or define a color scheme for the desktop and each of the components of a window, choose a screen saver, implement energy savings features, change the screen resolution, and select fonts. Jaime suggests that the two of you first change the background patterns for your desktops.

If you have installed Microsoft Plus! for Windows 95, which has more features than the standard version of Windows 95, then you will have to complete the following steps before you can work with background patterns. These steps turn off the Desktop Themes feature so that you can work with background patterns. If you are using the standard version of Windows 95, instead of Microsoft Plus! for Windows 95, do not complete the following steps; instead, start with the steps labeled "To view desktop property settings."

If you use Microsoft Plus! for Windows 95:

1. Click the **Start** button, point to **Settings**, then click **Control Panel**.

2. Double-click the **Desktop Themes** icon, then click the **Theme list arrow**.

3. In the Theme list box, locate and click **Windows Default**.

4. Close the Desktop Themes dialog box.

5. Close the Control Panel.

The desktop property settings are located on the property sheets in the Display Properties dialog box.

To view desktop property settings:

1. Point to a unused area of the desktop, then right-click.

   Windows 95 displays a desktop shortcut menu. See Figure 2-1.

Figure 2-1
The desktop
shortcut menu

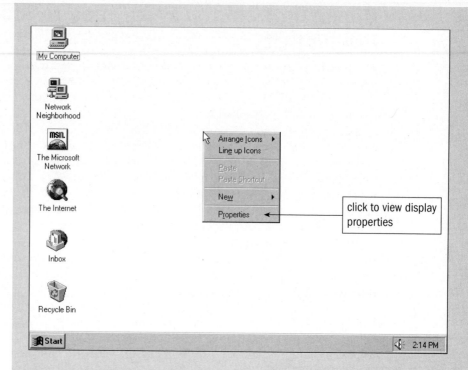

2. Click **Properties** on the shortcut menu.

Windows 95 opens the Display Properties dialog box, which contains tabs for four sets of property settings: Background, Screen Saver, Appearance, and Settings. See Figure 2-2.

Figure 2-2
Display
Properties
dialog box

Background tab

select a background
pattern from
this list box

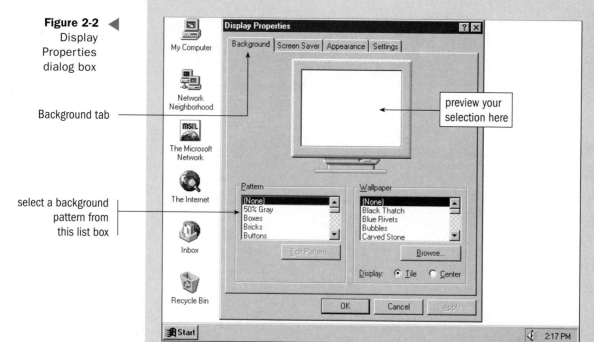

TROUBLE? The computer you are working on might have already been customized by another user or by a technical support person. Don't worry if your desktop properties look different from the ones in the figures.

TROUBLE? If you are using Microsoft Plus! for Windows 95, you will see five property sheets. The extra property sheet is labeled Theme and allows you to design desktop themes.

3. If necessary, click the **Background** tab.

The Background tab contains two settings that determine the appearance of your desktop: Pattern and Wallpaper. By using the Pattern setting, you can display a predefined pattern, such as a box, in a specific color. The Wallpaper setting offers a set of more complex, three-dimensional designs, such as bubbles or a honeycomb, that replace the current color and pattern. You can also click the Browse button to select a bitmap file as your desktop background, like a company logo, a beautiful mountain scene, a familiar face, and so on.

HELP DESK

Index

CREATING YOUR OWN BACKGROUND

Click the Start button, click Help, then click the Index tab.

Keyword	Topic
Bitmaps, displaying in the background	Overview: Using pictures, patterns, and colors

When you choose a different pattern or wallpaper, Windows 95 displays a preview of how the desktop background will appear with this new setting on the image of the monitor.

Jaime suggests that the two of you first examine the pattern and wallpaper options so that you can discuss how other employees might benefit from what you find.

To examine background patterns:

1. Before you make any changes, make a note of the Pattern, Wallpaper, and Display settings for your system so that you can restore the settings later.

2. Click the **title bar** of the Display Properties dialog box, then drag it to the right side of the desktop so that you can see your desktop icons and part of the desktop.

3. If necessary, scroll to the top of the Pattern list box, click **(None)**, then examine the appearance of the desktop in the preview section.

4. Press [↓] and examine the next pattern in the preview section.

The 50% Gray pattern appears in the preview area in the image of the monitor. This pattern darkens the background by adding gray to the current background color.

TROUBLE? If you do not have the 50% Gray pattern on your computer, select the next pattern. If nothing happens when you select a pattern, you might have already selected a Wallpaper. Wallpaper settings take precedence over patterns. Click (None) in the Wallpaper list (scroll to the top if necessary), then repeat Steps 3 and 4. If you still have trouble, ask your instructor for assistance.

5. Press [↓] to select each of the other patterns, and examine the patterns as they appear in the preview section.

If you installed Windows 95 as an upgrade to Windows 3.1, then you will see new patterns available in Windows 95, such as the Circuits and the Scales patterns, as well as patterns such as Scottie that were available in Windows 3.1. Jaime suggests that you might like the Rounder pattern for your desktop.

6. Scroll to Rounder in the Pattern list box, click **Rounder**, then click the **Apply** button.

By applying this pattern to the desktop, rather than previewing it, you have a better feeling for the three-dimensional perspective of this pattern. The desktop icons appear to float on an invisible layer above the desktop background pattern. See Figure 2-3. You realize that the improvements to the Windows 95 graphical user interface are reflected in small touches such as the one you are currently viewing.

TROUBLE? If you do not find the Rounder pattern, then choose another pattern and apply that pattern to the desktop.

Figure 2-3 ◀
The Rounder
background
pattern

Rounder pattern
applied to desktop

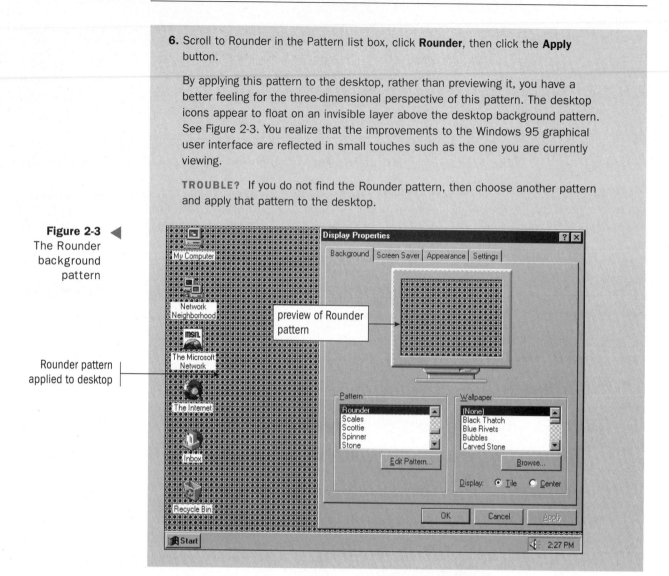

Editing a Pattern

On the Background tab of the Display Properties dialog box, you notice a button for editing patterns. You mention to Jaime that employees can not only choose a pattern, but can also modify the pattern to create new patterns that might be more interesting to them. He suggests that you select one of the other patterns that appeals to you, and modify it.

To edit an existing pattern:

1. Scroll to the Boxes pattern, click **Boxes**, then click the **Apply** button.

Windows 95 changes the background pattern to match the new pattern you have chosen.

TROUBLE? If you do not have the Boxes pattern, pick another pattern to edit.

2. Click the **Edit Pattern** button.

In the Pattern Editor dialog box, you see the name of the pattern in the Name list box, an enlarged view of the pattern in the Pattern section, and a view of the pattern as it would appear on the desktop in the Sample section. See Figure 2-4.

Figure 2-4
Pattern Editor
dialog box

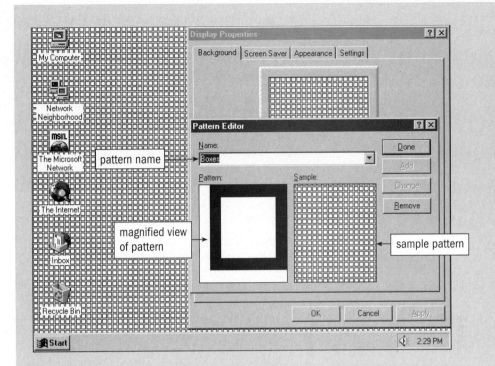

The square you see in the Pattern section is just one of the small squares in the Sample section. The enlarged pattern itself is composed of blocks. To edit a pattern, you point to part of the pattern in the Pattern section and click. Each time you click, you reverse the color of a block. You decide to start by adding a dark square in the middle of the pattern.

3. Click the **center** of the black square.

A black square appears in the center of the larger black square, and the pattern in the Sample section changes.

4. Click the **blocks** above, to the right, below, and to the left of the first block you selected, then click the **blocks** in each of the diagonal corners.

You create a more elaborate pattern, as shown in Figure 2-5.

Figure 2-5
Using the
Pattern Editor

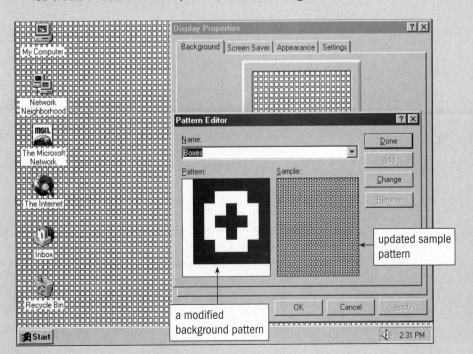

To keep the original pattern and this new pattern, you must assign a name to the new pattern.

5. If the pattern name Boxes in the Name list box is not already highlighted, double-click **Boxes**, then type **Filled Boxes**.

6. Click the **Add** button then click the **Done** button.

This adds the new name to the list of patterns and closes the Pattern Editor dialog box. You now see the new name in the Pattern list box, and the new pattern in the preview section.

TROUBLE? If a pattern named "Filled Boxes" already exists, repeat Steps 3 and 4 but this time use a different name.

7. Click the **Apply** button.

The new pattern appears on your desktop. Although your background color might be different, your new pattern will be similar to that shown in Figure 2-6.

Figure 2-6 ◀
Applying a new
desktop
background
pattern

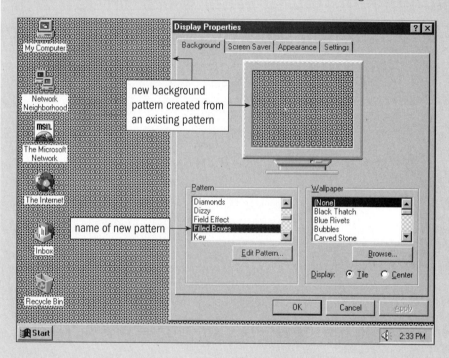

new background
pattern created from
an existing pattern

name of new pattern

REFERENCE
window

CHANGING THE DESKTOP BACKGROUND

- Right-click an unused area of the desktop.
- Click Properties on the shortcut menu.
- Click the Background tab.
- In the Pattern list box, choose a pattern then click Apply to view the new pattern on the desktop.
- If you want to change the pattern, click the Edit Pattern button, use the mouse to modify the pattern in the Pattern section, enter a name for the new pattern in the Name box, click the Add button, then click the Done button.
- Click the Apply button to view the new pattern on the desktop.
- Close the Desktop Properties dialog box.

Selecting Wallpaper

While you created a background pattern, Jaime examined the wallpaper options. Jaime then notes that most employees will probably prefer to choose a wallpaper over a background pattern. Some of the wallpapers contain beautiful designs and three-dimensional perspectives that dramatically enhance the appearance of the desktop and provide a more stimulating work environment. So that you have a better feeling for the effect created by a wallpaper pattern, Jaime suggests that you choose the Red Blocks wallpaper.

To select a wallpaper pattern:

1. Scroll the Wallpaper list box so that you can see the Red Blocks option, click **Red Blocks**, then for the Display options, click the **Tile** radio button, if it is not already selected.

   TROUBLE? If Red Blocks does not appear, you might not have installed the complete set of Windows 95 wallpapers. You can install the complete set only if you have the original installation disks or CD.

   The Tile option repeats whatever wallpaper pattern you choose, while the Center option only shows the wallpaper pattern in the center of the screen. If you choose Center, an open window might hide the one and only copy of the wallpaper pattern displayed on the desktop.

   Although Windows 95 updates the preview of this wallpaper option, you can appreciate the full effect by closing the Display Properties dialog box.

2. Click the **OK** button.

   In Figure 2-7, Windows 95 displays the Red Blocks wallpaper.

Figure 2-7 ◀
The Red Blocks
wallpaper

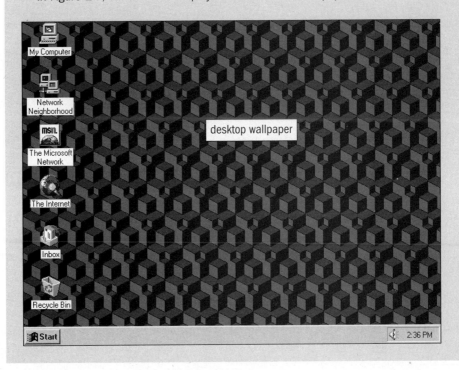

REFERENCE
window

CHANGING THE WALLPAPER

- Right-click an unused area of the desktop.
- Click Properties on the shortcut menu.
- Click the Background tab.
- In the Wallpaper list box, choose a display option, choose a wallpaper pattern, then click the Apply button to view the new pattern on the desktop.
- Close the Desktop Properties dialog box.

Changing Color Schemes

Joyce Renaldi, the director of Human Resources at Thorsen Pharmaceuticals, asks you and Jaime to help her choose and customize a color scheme that incorporates the colors from the company's logo on her desktop and that provides enough contrast for her to discern different elements of the desktop. The company's logo uses blue and teal colors for the company's initials on a dark red background.

Using the Appearance tab in the Display Properties dialog box, you can change the appearance of many different Windows 95 screen elements at the same time by selecting a scheme. A **scheme** is a combination of settings that include different colors, sizes, and formats. Windows comes with a set of default schemes that were created by artists and designers for an aesthetic appearance. You can select the name of an existing scheme from the Appearance tab, or you can create and name your own scheme. You can also select an individual screen component and change its appearance.

Jaime suggests to Joyce that it would be a good idea to first choose a color scheme from one of the schemes included with Windows 95, then adjust individual components as the need arises. Before you start, Jaime suggests that you record the current settings.

To view and select color schemes:

1. Right-click the **desktop**, then click **Properties** on the shortcut menu, and when the Display Properties dialog box opens, drag it to the right side of the screen.

2. On the Background tab, change the Pattern to **(None)**, then change the Wallpaper to **(None)**.

3. Click the **Appearance** tab.

   In the preview section at the top of the Appearance tab, Windows 95 shows how screen elements look using the current color scheme. See Figure 2-8.

Figure 2-8 ◀
Appearance
property sheet

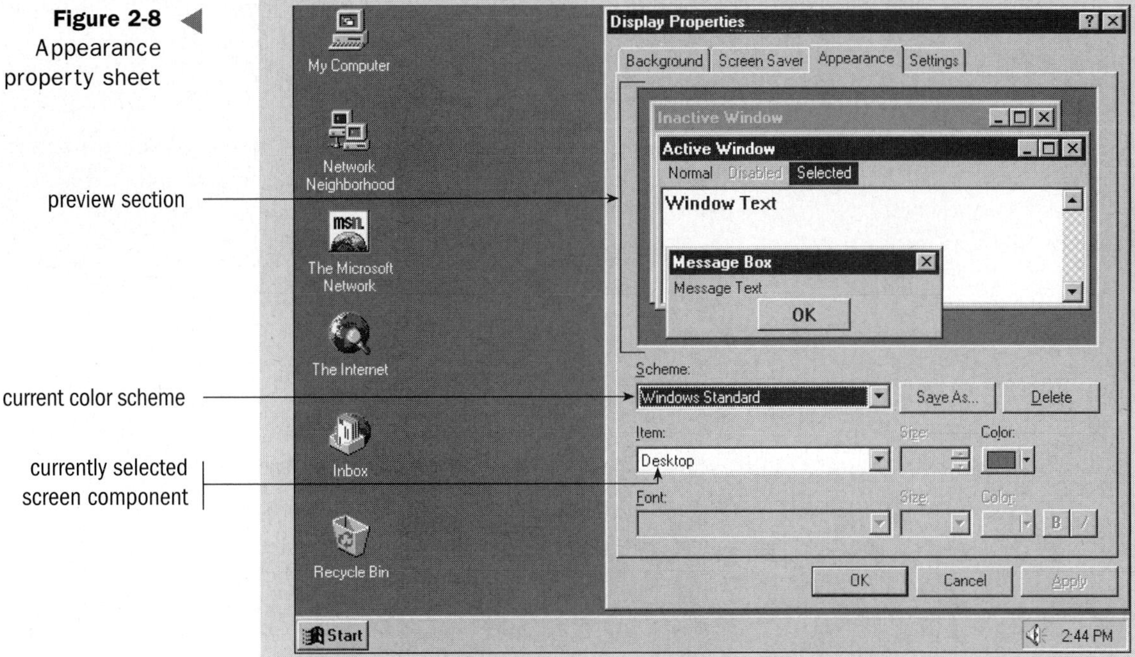

preview section ——————

current color scheme ——————

currently selected
screen component

Below the preview section, you can select a scheme from the Scheme list box or you can select an individual screen component from the Item list box and make changes to its color scheme. So that you can compare different options with the standard scheme used in Windows 95, you decide to start with that scheme for the desktop.

TROUBLE? Figure 2-8 shows a customized screen called "Windows Standard." Your scheme might be different.

4. Before you make any changes, make a note of the name of the current color scheme in the Scheme list box.

TROUBLE? If you do not see a name for the current color scheme, click the Save As button, type "My Original Color Scheme" in the Save Scheme dialog box, then click the OK button.

5. If the Windows Standard scheme is not displayed in the Scheme list box, click the **Scheme list arrow**, scroll until you can see the Windows Standard scheme, then click **Windows Standard**.

In the preview section, the title bars of the active window and message boxes, as well as selected menu names, appear dark blue. The desktop itself appears as teal. Since the company's logo uses a dark red background, you want to choose dark red for the desktop.

6. Click the **Color list arrow**.

A color palette appears, with 20 colors. The color palette includes a color very close to the dark red used in the company's logo.

7. Click **dark red** (the dark red color on the second row and in the second column).

In the preview section, you now see a dark red background. Now you want to view this color scheme on the desktop. Since you are no longer using all the elements of the Windows Standard color scheme, the Scheme text box no longer has the name for that scheme.

8. Click the **OK** button.

The desktop color is now dark red.

Earlier, you noticed that Windows 95 displays an Inactive Window's title bar in a dark gray. So that this title bar stands out more clearly on the screen, you decide to change its color to teal, one of the other colors used on the company's logo.

To change the Inactive Window's title bar:

1. Right-click an unused area of the desktop, then click **Properties** on the shortcut menu, and when the Display Properties dialog box opens, click the **Appearance** tab.

2. If necessary, drag the Display Properties dialog box to the right side of the screen.

3. Click the **Inactive Window** title bar in the preview section.

   The name of the selected screen component, Inactive Title Bar, appears in the Item list box. Options such as size and font now become active.

4. Click the **Color list arrow** to the right of the Item list box and, from the color palette, click the **teal color** located on the third row and in the fourth column.

   The Inactive Window title bar changes from a dark gray to a teal color. Jaime notes that you can further improve the contrast by using the Size spin box arrows for the selected item to increase or decrease its size or height.

5. Note the current settings for the size of the selected item in the Item list box, the name of the font, the font size, and the font color.

6. To the right of the option Inactive Title Bar in the Item list box, click the **Size up arrow** until it displays **26**.

   In the preview section, the height of the Inactive Title Bar and other title bars increases, as well as the size of the Minimize, Maximize, and Close buttons on these bars.

7. Click the **Size down arrow** until the size is restored to its original setting.

   Now you want to try a different font. A **font** is a set of characters that have a specific **typeface**, or character style, a specific **point size**, or character height, and attributes like bold or italic.

8. Click the **Font list arrow**, scroll to Times New Roman, then click **Times New Roman**.

   TROUBLE? If you do not see the Times New Roman font, it is not installed on your computer. Select another font for the remaining steps.

   Now you want to change the point size of the font. Point sizes are measured in $\frac{1}{72}$nds of an inch. A 72-point font is one inch tall, a 36-point font is one-half inch tall, and the commonly used 12-point font is one-sixth of an inch tall.

9. To the right of the Font list box, click the **Size list arrow**, then click **12**.

   TROUBLE? Since the available point sizes depend on the font you use, 12 might not appear in the Size list box. If you do not have this point size, select another font size close to 12.

   Notice that the character height of text displayed in all title bars shown in the preview section is larger, and that the value for the size of the selected item also increases. See Figure 2-9.

Figure 2-9 ◀
Designing a
new scheme

size of screen
component

screen component

color of screen
component

font for screen
component

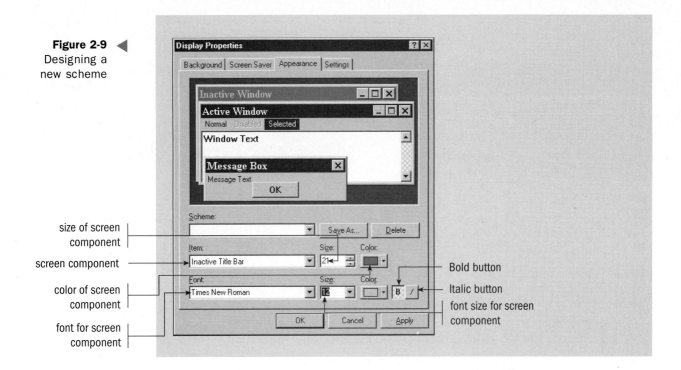

Bold button

Italic button

font size for screen
component

Jaime tells you that you can also improve the contrast of an image on the screen by changing the attributes of the text in the title bars with the Bold or Italic buttons shown in Figure 2-9. The Bold button is already selected for the Inactive Title Bar screen component. You decide to experiment with the Bold and Italic buttons.

To test the bold and italic features:

1. Click the **Bold** button, the button with the letter "B" located to the right of the font Color button.

Boldfacing is removed from the text in the preview section.

2. Click the **Bold** button again.

The text in the preview section now appears in boldface.

3. Click the **Italic** button located to the right of the Bold button.

The text in the preview section is now italicized.

4. Click the **Italic** button.

The italic attribute is removed from the text in the preview section.

Before you restore your original settings, you want to save this color scheme so that you and Joyce can later retrieve the color scheme and modify other screen components.

To save your new color scheme:

1. Click the **Save As** button.

Windows 95 displays a Save Scheme dialog box. See Figure 2-10.

Figure 2-10 ◄
Saving a new
color scheme

enter new color
scheme here

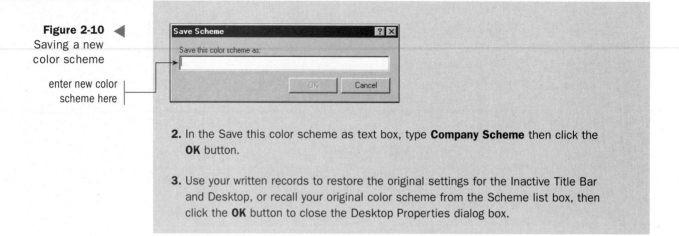

2. In the Save this color scheme as text box, type **Company Scheme** then click the **OK** button.

3. Use your written records to restore the original settings for the Inactive Title Bar and Desktop, or recall your original color scheme from the Scheme list box, then click the **OK** button to close the Desktop Properties dialog box.

You've seen how to change individual screen components: you simply select a screen component from the Item list or, if the screen component is shown in the preview section, you can click it to select it. Then, depending on the screen component you select, you might be able to change the color, element size, font, and font size, and you might also be able to enable (or disable) boldface and italics.

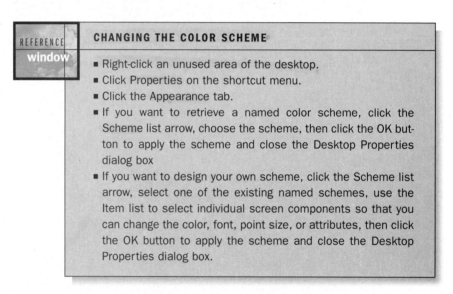

REFERENCE
window

CHANGING THE COLOR SCHEME

- Right-click an unused area of the desktop.
- Click Properties on the shortcut menu.
- Click the Appearance tab.
- If you want to retrieve a named color scheme, click the Scheme list arrow, choose the scheme, then click the OK button to apply the scheme and close the Desktop Properties dialog box
- If you want to design your own scheme, click the Scheme list arrow, select one of the existing named schemes, use the Item list to select individual screen components so that you can change the color, font, point size, or attributes, then click the OK button to apply the scheme and close the Desktop Properties dialog box.

Customizing a Screen Saver

As you make changes to the appearance of Joyce Renaldi's desktop, she notices the tab labeled Screen Saver, and asks Jaime about the purpose and use of a screen saver. Jaime explains that a **screen saver** is a program that either blanks the screen or displays moving images on the screen when you do not use a computer system for a certain amount of time. Although computer systems with VGA monitors do not need screen savers, many people find them interesting and useful for concealing sensitive or confidential information when they step away from their computer system. If you have an older monitor, a screen saver is even more useful because it prevents an image of the current display from being burned into the screen.

Then, Jaime explains that it is possible to create a screen saver that displays the company's name if the computer is not used for a certain period of time. He suggests that Joyce and you choose the Scrolling Marquee option and then modify it to display the company's name.

To select a screen saver:

1. Right-click the **desktop**, then click **Properties** on the shortcut menu.

2. Click the **Screen Saver** tab.

3. Click the **Screen Saver list arrow**.

A list of available screen savers appears. See Figure 2-11. The names of your screen savers might differ from those shown in the figure.

Figure 2-11 ◀
Selecting a
screen saver

Screen Saver tab ———

list of screen savers ———

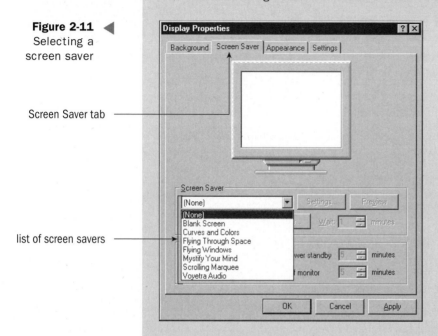

4. Click **Scrolling Marquee**.

The Scrolling Marquee option appears in the Screen Saver list box. You can use this screen saver to display text of your own choosing on the screen. When you select this option and enter text, the text moves across the screen. If you have already created a scrolling marquee, then you will see it in the preview section.

TROUBLE? If you do not see Scrolling Marquee listed as a screen saver, then you might have a screen saver named just Marquee. Click that screen saver. If you do not have an option for Scrolling Marquee or Marquee, then you can skip to the next section or you can select another screen saver and customize it. If you do select another screen saver, the options for customizing it with the Settings buttons will be different than the steps that follow for a scrolling marquee, so you will have to generalize these steps. For example, if you choose another screen saver, you can still use the Settings button to customize it; however, the options will be different, but you can still save those options and use the Preview button to see how the screen saver you customized will work.

5. Click the **Settings** button.

The Options for Scrolling Marquee dialog box opens. See Figure 2-12. You can enter the text for the scrolling marquee, format the text, indicate where to display it on the monitor, adjust its speed, and select a background color.

Figure 2-12 ◀
Designing a
scrolling
marquee

select position for
marquee

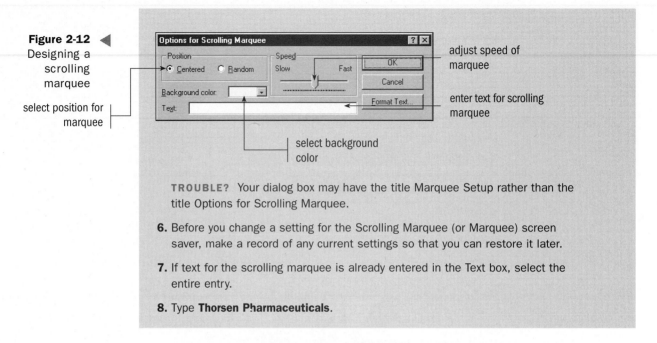

adjust speed of
marquee

enter text for scrolling
marquee

select background
color

TROUBLE? Your dialog box may have the title Marquee Setup rather than the title Options for Scrolling Marquee.

6. Before you change a setting for the Scrolling Marquee (or Marquee) screen saver, make a record of any current settings so that you can restore it later.

7. If text for the scrolling marquee is already entered in the Text box, select the entire entry.

8. Type **Thorsen Pharmaceuticals**.

Next, you want to select a font, font style, size, and color that closely matches that of the company logo. You also want to pick a background color, select a position for displaying the scrolling marquee, and finally test your choices.

To customize the scrolling marquee:

1. Click the **Format Text** button.

   The Format Text dialog box opens. See Figure 2-13.

Figure 2-13 ◀
Formatting the
marquee text

select a font style
here

select a font here

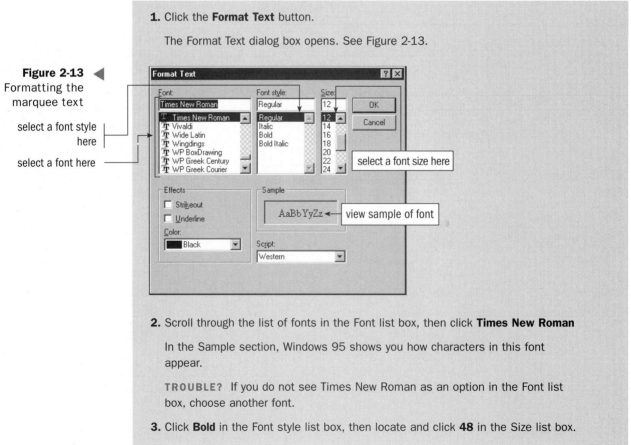

select a font size here

view sample of font

2. Scroll through the list of fonts in the Font list box, then click **Times New Roman**

   In the Sample section, Windows 95 shows you how characters in this font appear.

   TROUBLE? If you do not see Times New Roman as an option in the Font list box, choose another font.

3. Click **Bold** in the Font style list box, then locate and click **48** in the Size list box.

TROUBLE? If the Bold style is not available for the font you select, choose the Italic style or do not choose a style. If a size of 48 is not available for the font you select, select a size slightly smaller than 48.

Next, Joyce wants to display the company name in a dark red color against a light green or teal background.

4. Click the **Color** list arrow, and from the list of colors locate and click **Maroon**, then click the **OK** button.

5. Click the **Background** list arrow, scroll halfway through the list of colors, then click **light green**.

6. Click the **Random** radio button in the Position section, then click the **OK** button.

In the preview section, you see a sample of what the scrolling marquee will look like.

7. Click the **Preview** button then *do not move* the mouse.

TROUBLE? If you move the mouse, you return to the Display Properties dialog box. Click the Preview button again and do not move the mouse.

Now, you see a full-screen view of your screen saver. See Figure 2-14.

Figure 2-14 ◀
Previewing a
scrolling
marquee

marquee

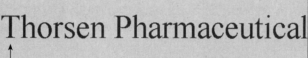

Thorsen Pharmaceutical

8. Move or click the mouse to return to the Display Properties dialog box.

Now that Joyce has selected the enhancements she wants to use for the screen saver, she wants to set the time for 5 minutes.

9. Click the **Wait up** arrow until it displays 5 (for 5 minutes).

10. If you are working in a computer lab, use your records to restore the settings for the Scrolling Marquee (or Marquee) screen saver, then click the **OK** button to close the Desktop Properties dialog box.

Joyce is impressed with how easy it is to select and then customize desktop settings. Now that she knows how to access the Desktop Properties dialog box, she can try other desktop settings and find what works best for her.

SELECTING A SCREEN SAVER

- Right-click the desktop then click Properties on the shortcut menu.
- Click the Screen Saver tab.
- Select a screen saver from the Screen Saver list box.
- Customize the screen saver with the Settings button.
- Test the screen saver using the Preview button.
- Set the Wait time to the number of minutes you want Windows 95 to wait before it displays the screen saver.
- Click the OK button.

Implementing Energy Saving Features

Recently, Thorsen Pharmaceuticals, at the urging of environmentally-conscious employees, launched a drive to conserve energy. Adrian Lemus, the Data Systems Manager at Thorsen Pharmaceuticals, suggested that employees use the energy saving features in Windows 95 to reduce power consumption when their computers remain idle for any length of time.

Many newer computer systems offer energy saving features that put components such as the monitor, mouse, or keyboard "to sleep" when they have been idle for a predetermined period of time so that they consume less energy. Even the microprocessor can idle down. For a moderately heavy computer user, the savings in utility costs can reach $50 or more a year. If you have an Energy Star computer, then that computer includes software that will cycle down each of these components, one at a time, whenever the computer system remains idle for a specific period of time. That power management, or energy saving, software must be loaded after you turn on your computer system, and you must use it with the operating system for which it was designed.

Since the monitor in a computer system typically consumes far more power than other components, Windows 95 includes two energy saving features for monitors that are Energy Star compliant. Manufacturers of Energy Star compliant monitors use a set of specifications, known as VESA Display Power Management Signaling (DPMS) specifications, that enable software to place the monitor in standby mode or turn it off when the monitor is inactive for a certain period of time. The Low-power standby option switches your monitor to standby mode if your computer is idle for the number of minutes shown in the Minutes box, and thereby conserves power. The Shut off monitor option turns off your monitor after a certain period of time and conserves even more power.

Jaime asks you to turn off your screen saver and then test the energy saving feature so that you can determine what settings will work best for you.

 Be sure your monitor is Energy Star compliant before you start these steps; otherwise, your computer might crash.

To test the energy saving features:

1. Right-click the **desktop**, click **Properties** on the shortcut menu, then click the **Screen Saver** tab.

2. Click the **Screen Saver list arrow**, then locate and click **(None)** from the top of the Screen Saver list.

   If you later reselect the Scrolling Marquee option from the Screen Saver list box, you will find that Windows 95 retains all your settings.

3. If the Low-power standby option is not selected, click the **Low-power standby** check box, then click the corresponding **Minutes down arrow** until it displays **1**.

TROUBLE? If the Low-power standby and the Shut off monitor options are grayed or if no settings are visible, then your computer might not be properly configured or it might not support these energy saving features. If you know that your computer supports power management features, click the Settings tab in the Display Properties dialog box, then click the Change Display Type button. In the Change Display Type dialog box, click the Monitor is Energy Star compliant check box. If the Adapter Type and Monitor Type settings in the Change Display Type dialog box are not correct, you will need to select the appropriate Change button and select the proper adapter type or monitor type from a Select Device dialog box. However, before you make changes to the configuration of your computer system, make sure you know what the proper settings should be. When you are done, click the Screen Saver tab again.

4. If necessary, click the **Shut off monitor** check box to select this option, then click the corresponding **Minutes up arrow** or **down arrow** until it displays **2**.

   Your settings should match those shown in Figure 2-15.

Figure 2-15 ◀
Implementing energy saving features

Low-power standby option

Shut off monitor option

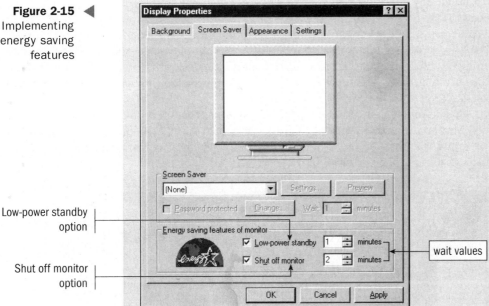

wait values

5. Click the **OK** button.

6. *Do not touch any key on the keyboard or move the mouse for one minute*, and watch your monitor's status light indicator.

   Windows 95 switches your monitor to standby and blanks the screen. Your monitor's status light might change from a steady green indicator to a steady amber indicator.

7. Move the mouse or press a key.

   The image on the monitor appears, and your monitor's status light might change from a steady amber indicator to a steady green indicator.

8. *Do not touch any key on the keyboard or move the mouse for two minutes*, and watch your monitor's status light indicator.

   Windows 95 first switches to standby mode after one minute, then another minute later it shuts off your monitor. Your monitor's status light might change from a steady green indicator to a steady amber indicator, then to a blinking amber indicator.

9. Move the mouse or press a key.

The image on the monitor appears. Your monitor's status light might change from a blinking amber indicator to a steady green indicator.

TROUBLE? If your monitor does not automatically turn on, then check the monitor's hardware manual for power up instructions. You might need to turn the monitor's power switch off, wait a few seconds, then turn it back on.

10. If you intend to use these energy saving features, adjust the wait values for Low-power standby and Shut off monitor options to values you want to use; otherwise, deselect the options, then click the **OK** button to close the Display Properties dialog box.

Jaime suggests to Joyce that she might want to use a screen saver in combination with these two energy saving features. She could, for example, set the wait value for the screen saver to 5 minutes, the Low-power standby to 10 minutes, and the Shut off monitor to 15 minutes. The wait values for the Low-power standby mode and the Shut off monitor mode must be the same, or greater than, the wait value for the screen saver. The wait value for the Shut off monitor mode must be the same, or greater than, the wait value for the Low-power standby mode. Windows 95 will not let you set the Shut off monitor setting at a value less than the Low-power standby setting or the Wait value for the Screen Saver setting, and it will not let you set the Low-power standby setting at a value less than the Wait value for the Screen Saver setting.

After testing the energy saving features on your computer, Joyce decides to use Jaime's recommendations and set the values for the screen saver, Low-power standby, and Shut off monitor so that they are five minutes apart. If she is away from her desk for more than 5 to 15 minutes, one or more of these settings will kick in.

REFERENCE window	IMPLEMENTING ENERGY SAVING FEATURES
	■ Right-click the desktop then click Properties, on the shortcut menu.
	■ Click the Screen Saver tab.
	■ Click the Low-power standby check box, then adjust its wait value.
	■ Click the Shut off monitor check box, then adjust its wait value.
	■ Click the OK button to close the Display Properties dialog box.

Adjusting Screen Resolutions

One of the characteristics of your monitor display is the sharpness of the image that appears on your screen, or its resolution. When your computer operates in graphics mode, each image is composed of thousands of individual dots called **pixels** (for picture elements). The number of pixels across the width of the screen and down the length of the screen determines the resolution. Your computer's monitor is attached via the monitor cable to a **display adapter**, a device inside your computer that controls the image you see on the screen. This device is also called a **video card** or **video adapter**. At a resolution of 640 by 480, the display adapter produces 640 pixels across the width of the screen and 480 pixels down the screen. Many display adapters can operate in different display modes other than 640 by 480, such as 800×600, and 1024×768. The more pixels the adapter displays across the width of the screen and down its length, the greater the resolution, the sharper the image, and the smaller the characters appear.

In addition to controlling resolution, the display adapter determines the number of colors you can see. Today's monitors offer an increasingly precise representation of color. Standard VGA adapters, for example, are 4-bit video display adapters that display 2^4 or 16 colors. The "4-bit" refers to the number of bits used by the video adapter to define individual colors. With four bits, there are a maximum of 16 possible combinations of 0 (zero) and 1. As you may recall, the 0 (zero) and 1 are the only two digits available in the binary numbering system. By combining these 0's and 1's, you can produce codes that uniquely define a color. Adapters capable of using 8-bit video can display 2^8 or 256 colors. 16-bit video display adapters can display 2^{16} or 65,536 colors, a feature referred to as **High Color**. 24-bit video display adapters can display 2^{24} or 16,777,216 colors, a feature referred to as **True Color**. The resolution you choose also determines the number of colors that you can view.

One important new feature of Windows 95 is that you can change the screen resolution "on the fly" (that is, without having to reboot) if you have a video adapter that supports multiple display modes and colors. If, however, you change your Color palette setting, you do have to reboot so that the new settings take effect.

Under Windows 3.1, if you changed the screen resolution, you had to reboot the computer. Now, you can change the screen resolution dynamically without rebooting.

Since researchers at Thorsen Pharmaceuticals want to connect their desktop computers to sophisticated and extremely sensitive scientific equipment to record the results of scientific experiments, Jaime and you will need to reconfigure those computers so that they use the highest possible screen resolution and maximum number of colors.

To change the screen resolution:

1. Right-click the **desktop** then click **Properties** on the shortcut menu.

2. In the Display Properties dialog box, click the **Settings tab**.

   The Settings tab contains options for adjusting the resolution and the number of colors displayed in the color palette. See Figure 2-16. The computer system used for this figure has a video adapter card that currently displays 256 colors and uses a screen resolution of 640 x 480 pixels (a standard VGA resolution). At certain resolutions, you can also change the font size.

Figure 2-16 ◀
Settings
property sheet

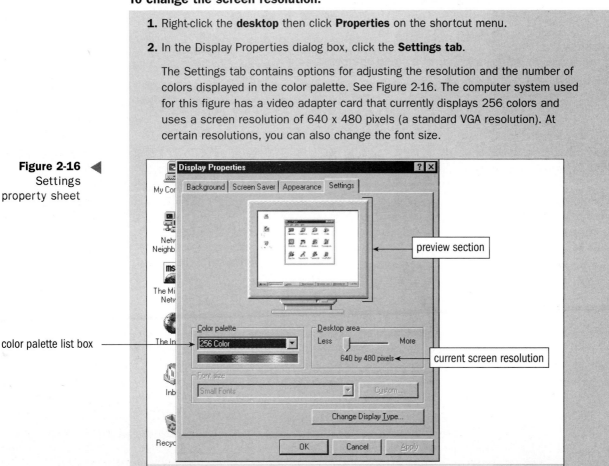

3. Click the **Color palette list arrow**.

Windows 95 lists the color options available for your display adapter and monitor.

If you are working in a computer lab, do not change the following setting because it requires that you restart the computer.

4. Click the **Color palette list arrow** again to close the list box *without* selecting a different one. (Selecting one causes your computer to reboot, which might disrupt lab computers.)

5. In the Desktop section of the Settings tab, drag the **slide bar** right to the next available resolution.

For example, if you are currently using a resolution of 640 x 480, a standard VGA resolution, drag the slider bar to select 800 x 600 pixels or another resolution. After you make this change, check the image in the preview section (the picture of the monitor). If the image is distorted or if the image does not display properly, then you do not want to change to this resolution.

TROUBLE? Depending on the type of video display adapter and monitor in your computer system, you may or may not be able to change your screen resolution.

6. Click the **OK** button.

In the Display Properties message box, Windows 95 informs you that it will now resize the desktop. See Figure 2-17. It also warns you that if Windows does not display properly, wait 15 seconds, and it will automatically restore your original settings.

Figure 2-17 ◄
Adjusting the
resolution

what will happen ——

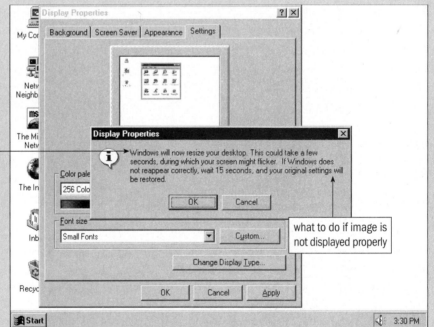

7. Click the **OK** button.

Windows 95 resizes the desktop and displays a Monitor Settings dialog box so that you can choose whether or not to keep the new setting. See Figure 2-18. On the computer used in this figure, the screen resolution increased to 1024 x 768, and the size of text and screen components decreased. At this point, it is important to carefully examine the screen and determine whether there are any potential problems, such as distortion of the image or loss of part of the image.

Figure 2-18
Monitor
Settings dialog
box

desktop displayed at
a resolution of 1024
x 768 (yours might
differ)

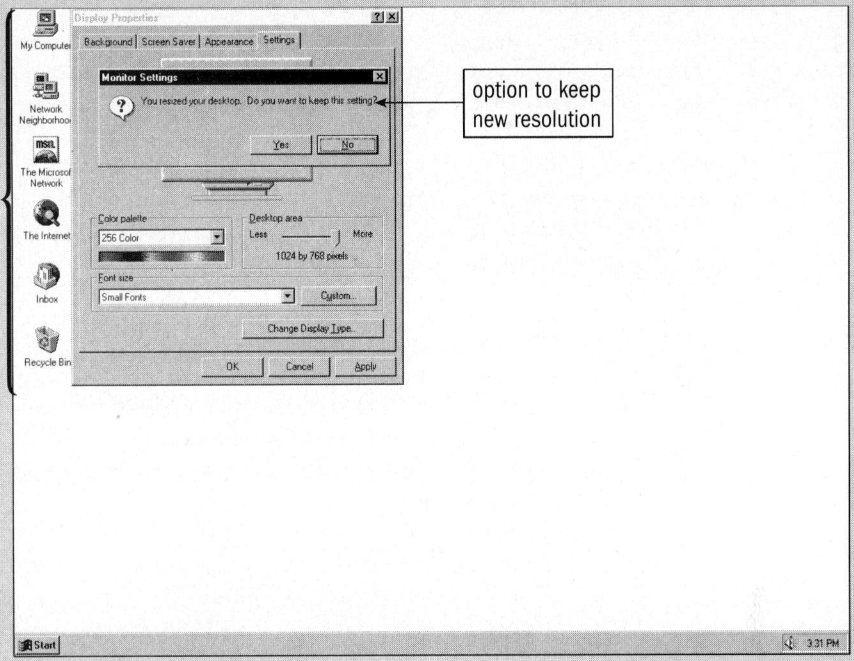

option to keep
new resolution

8. *Do not* click the Yes or No buttons; instead, wait 15 seconds.

Windows 95 restores the original resolution, and informs you of this fact in the Display Properties dialog box. See Figure 2-19.

Figure 2-19
Restoring a
desktop's
original size

original desktop
resolution restored

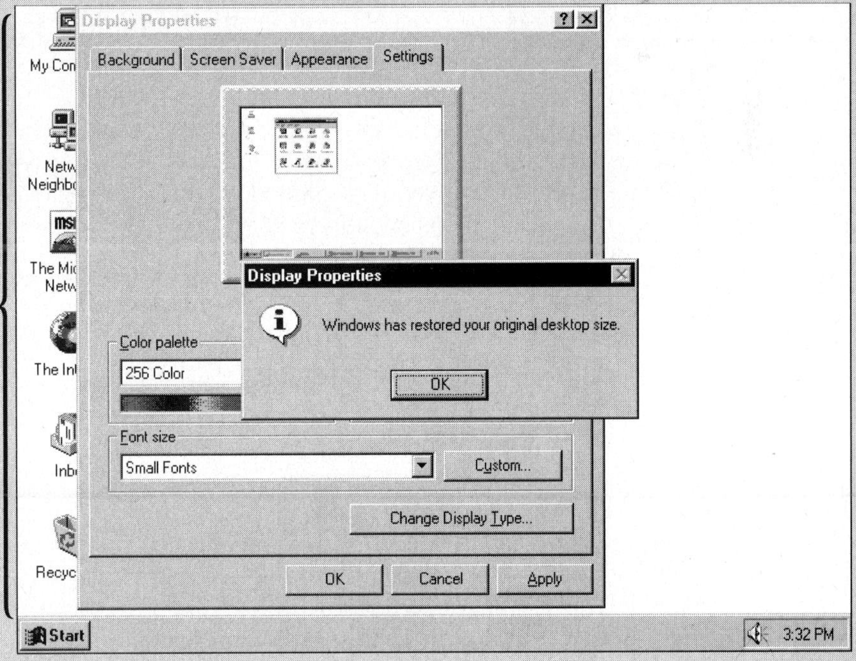

9. Click the **OK** button.

Windows 95 restores the original settings on the Settings tab.

10. Click the **OK** button to close the Display Properties dialog box.

It is important to note that increasing the screen resolution and the number of colors that you can see places additional demands on the resources of your computer system, including processing power and memory. As your microprocessor manages more and more pixels *and* colors, the performance of your system slows down. If you need to operate your system at greater screen resolutions and display more colors, you can add a **video accelerator adapter**, a device that assists the microprocessor with the task of drawing and displaying images. Alternately, you can add a graphics coprocessor to your computer system to speed up the process of creating and displaying images. You can also add additional memory, called VRAM or Video RAM, to your display adapter to store multicolored, high-resolution images.

REFERENCE window	**CHANGING THE SCREEN RESOLUTION**
	■ Right-click the desktop, click Properties on the shortcut menu, then click the Settings tab.
	■ Drag the Desktop area slider bar to select another screen resolution.
	■ Click the OK button.
	■ Read the information and warning in the Display Properties dialog box, then click the OK button.
	■ After Windows 95 resizes the screen and displays the Monitor Settings dialog box, examine the screen resolution and properties.
	■ If you want to use the new resolution, click the OK button; otherwise, wait 15 seconds for Windows 95 to restore your original settings.
	■ Close the Display Properties dialog box.

If you want to take a break and resume the tutorial at a later time, you can do so now. If you are on a network, close any open applications and dialog boxes, and leave Windows 95 running. If you are using your own computer, you can click Start on the Taskbar, click Shut Down, click Shut down the computer, then click Yes. When you resume the tutorial, launch Windows 95 again, and then continue with the tutorial.

● ● ●

Working with Regional Settings in a Global Marketplace

The employees at the United States division of Thorsen Pharmaceuticals work in close cooperation with the other divisions in Great Britain, France, and Sweden. Each day office, research, and technical staff communicate with their counterparts in other divisions. Office personnel transmit information on the financial, legal, and business operations of Thorsen Pharmaceuticals to other divisions and to the main headquarters in Great Britain. Researchers share the results of their findings, so that the research efforts of one lab directly benefit the efforts of other Thorsen Pharmaceuticals laboratories. Technical staff share their wealth of knowledge on the operation of complex scientific equipment, as well as the computer systems that Thorsen Pharmaceuticals increasingly relies on to manage its business, with staff in other divisions.

Financial, legal, business, scientific, and technical documents and files are prepared and transmitted daily from one office to another. Since each division of Thorsen Pharmaceuticals resides in a different country with a different language, and since languages differ in how they sort numbers, currency, dates, and times, employees draw on the tools and resources at their disposal to prepare these documents and files.

Alan Lee, the new assistant financial analyst, is ready to prepare a financial summary for Thorsen Pharmaceuticals' headquarters in Great Britain. He has asked Jaime to help him change the regional settings on his computer system so that he can use settings appropriate to Great Britain.

Jaime asks you to accompany him so that you can learn how to change these settings. As you walk to Alan Lee's office, he emphasizes the importance of using caution when you make changes to regional settings, because they affect all the other applications that you use. For example, if you select regional settings for a country like Great Britain that uses a different currency symbol, then currency figures in financial documents are displayed with that symbol rather than the dollar sign symbol used in this country whenever you format values for currency. As you prepare a financial document, you will still have to use your spreadsheet application to perform the proper conversion from one currency amount to another, because Windows 95 will change, for example, $100 to £100 without applying a conversion rate.

After arriving at Alan Lee's office, Jaime introduces you to Alan, then the three of you sit down at Alan's computer so that Jaime can show you how to change regional settings. You will use the **Control Panel**, a centralized collection of settings controls that contains a variety of tools for configuring and customizing your computer system, including tools for installing hardware and software.

To view regional settings for Great Britain:

1. Click the **Start** button, point to **Settings**, click **Control Panel**, then maximize the Control Panel window.

The Control Panel opens. See Figure 2-20.

Figure 2-20
Control Panel window

menu bar

accessibility options icon

number of objects

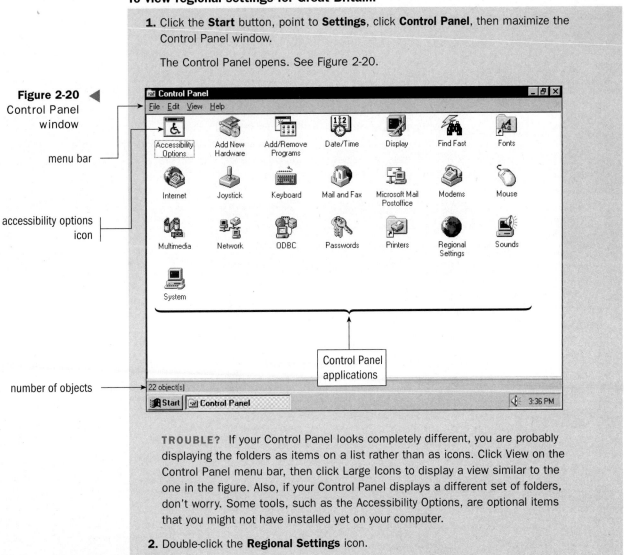

Control Panel applications

TROUBLE? If your Control Panel looks completely different, you are probably displaying the folders as items on a list rather than as icons. Click View on the Control Panel menu bar, then click Large Icons to display a view similar to the one in the figure. Also, if your Control Panel displays a different set of folders, don't worry. Some tools, such as the Accessibility Options, are optional items that you might not have installed yet on your computer.

2. Double-click the **Regional Settings** icon.

The Regional Settings tab in the Regional Settings Properties dialog box shows the regional setting that Windows 95 is currently using on your computer system. See Figure 2-21. If you live in the United States, Windows will more than likely be using the English (United States) regional setting.

Figure 2-21 ◄
Regional
Settings
Properties
dialog box

regional setting in use
on this computer

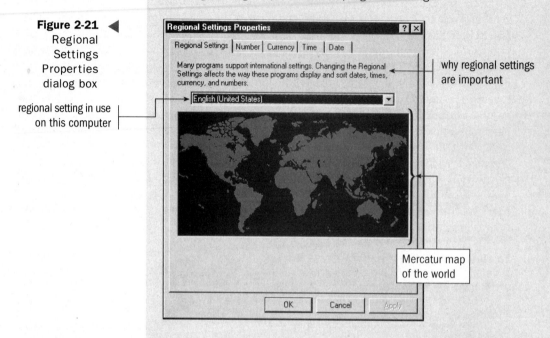

why regional settings
are important

Mercatur map
of the world

3. Click the **Regional Settings list arrow**, then scroll so that you can see all the regional settings for the English language.

Note that there are regional settings for Australia, Great Britain, Canada, the Caribbean, Ireland, Jamaica, New Zealand, South Africa, and, of course, the United States. See Figure 2-22. Although English is the primary language spoken in all of these countries, settings for date, time, currency, and numbers vary.

Figure 2-22 ◄
Regional
Settings list
box

regional settings for
English-speaking
countries

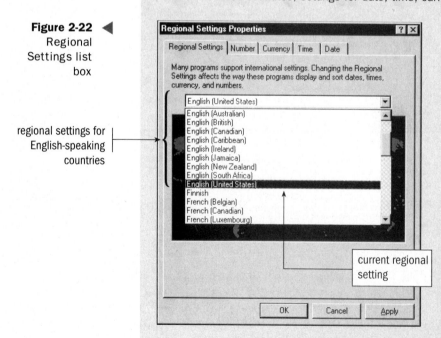

current regional
setting

If you are working in a computer lab, do not change the following setting, because it requires that you restart the computer. Instead, skip to the summary at the end of this section.

4. Click **English (British)**.

5. Click the **Currency** tab.

Windows 95 displays a Change Regional Settings message box, asking you if you want to restart your system so that these settings can take effect. See Figure 2-23.

Figure 2-23 ◀
Change
Regional
Settings
warning box

regional setting

option to restart
computer

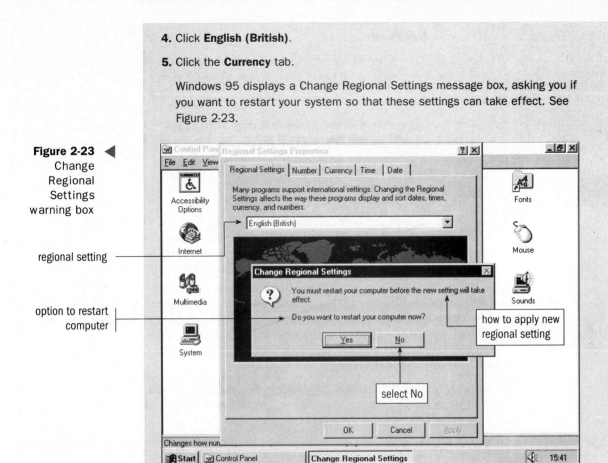

how to apply new
regional setting

select No

6. Click the **No** button.

Windows 95 switches to the Currency tab and shows the Currency settings for this region. See Figure 2-24. Although the currency format settings are similar to the United States, the British use the British pound as their currency symbol instead of the dollar sign.

Figure 2-24 ◀
Currency
property sheet
for Great
Britain

examples of currency
figures

British currency
symbol

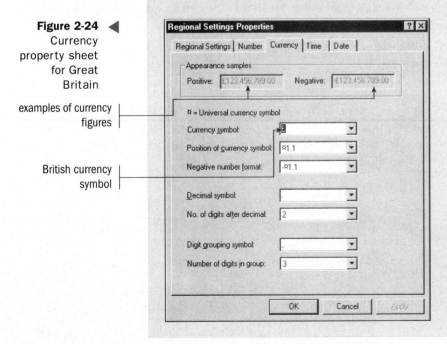

7. Click the **Number** tab.

Although the number format settings are similar to the United States, the British use the metric system instead of the U.S. measurement system.

8. Click the **Date** tab.

The Short date style is different than that used in the United States. As shown in the Short date sample box, in Great Britain, the day number appears before the month number. In the United States, the month and day numbers are reversed: the month number appears before the day number.

9. Click the **Time** tab.

The time style is also different. As shown in the Time sample box, Great Britain uses a military style format with seconds, and does not use either the AM or PM suffix.

Now, Alan can prepare his document, and choose a currency format for values that uses the British currency symbol rather than the dollar sign. After he saves and prints his document, he wants you to help him restore his original settings.

To restore your original settings:

1. Click the **Regional Settings** tab, click the **Regional Settings list arrow**, then locate and select the regional settings originally used on your computer system, probably English (United States).

2. Click the **OK** button.

Windows 95 displays a Change Regional Settings dialog box, asking you if you want to restart your system so that these settings can take effect. Since you did not restart your computer when you selected the regional settings for Great Britain, you can select No here to switch back to the English (United States) regional settings without rebooting your computer.

3. Click the **No** button.

The Change Regional Settings dialog box closes. The next time you start your system, Windows 95 will use your original settings.

4. Click the **Cancel** button to close the Regional Settings Properties dialog box without making any changes.

Windows 95 support for international language settings will encourage software manufacturers to provide support within their individual applications for implementing these new settings and will meet the needs of an increasing number of businesses, such as Thorsen Pharmaceuticals, that rely on global markets.

REFERENCE window	**CHANGING A REGIONAL SETTING**

- Click the Start button, point to Settings, then click Control Panel.
- Double-click the Regional settings icon in the Control Panel.
- On the Regional Settings tab of the Regional Settings Properties dialog box, click the Regional Settings list arrow, then locate and click the Regional Setting you want to use.
- When Windows 95 displays a Change Regional Settings dialog box, asking you if you want to restart your computer with these new systems, click Yes if you want to switch to these new settings, otherwise, click No.
- Close the Regional Settings Properties dialog box.

Selecting Keyboard Layouts

If you configure your computer to work with another language system, you must select a keyboard setting that provides support for that language system and that allows you access to that language's character set. For example, if you need to enter currency amounts using the British pound sterling (£) instead of the dollar sign ($), you need a keyboard layout that provides that character. You might also need another keyboard that contains the symbols for that language system's characters on the keys. Although it is now possible to use a word processing application command to insert a special character, like the British pound sterling, it is easier to use a keyboard that provides that symbol, especially if you use that and other symbols repeatedly within a document.

To protect Thorsen Pharmaceuticals' research discoveries, patent and legal experts from each of Thorsen Pharmaceuticals' divisions are currently meeting at its division in the United States to prepare a document that contains guidelines for researchers to follow prior to publishing research findings in scientific journals. The staff in the United States division must prepare copies of this document for Thorsen Pharmaceuticals' divisions in Great Britain, France, and Sweden. Not only must the staff choose the appropriate regional setting, but they must also use the proper keyboard layout so that they can prepare copies of the translated document. The three staff members responsible for preparing these documents have asked Jaime to show them how to adjust the regional settings and keyboard layouts on their computer systems.

If you are working in a computer lab, do not change the following setting, because it requires that you restart the computer. Instead, skip to the summary at the end of this section.

To change keyboard layout settings:

1. If necessary, click the **Start** button, point to **Settings**, then click **Control Panel**.

2. Double-click the **Keyboard** icon in the Control Panel.

   The Keyboard Properties dialog box opens. See Figure 2-25. From this dialog box, you can use the Speed tab to adjust the response time of the keyboard, the Language tab to select a keyboard layout, and the General tab to view the keyboard type.

Figure 2-25 ◀
Keyboard
Properties
dialog box

click to view keyboard
type

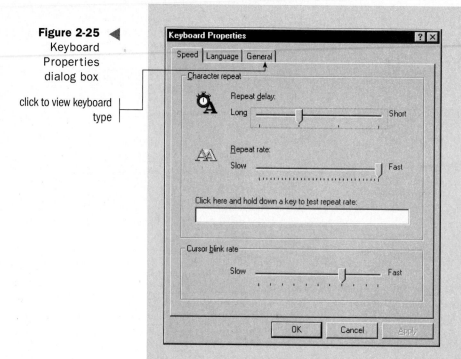

3. Click the **General** tab.

In the Keyboard type box, you see the setting that Windows 95 identified for the type of keyboard in your computer system. If you replace your current keyboard with a new model, then you can use the Change button to install the proper software for that keyboard.

4. Click the **Language** tab.

In the Language list box, Windows 95 shows the current languages and keyboard layouts selected for use on your computer system. See Figure 2-26. Your list of keyboard settings might differ from that shown in the figure if you have already installed other keyboard layouts.

Figure 2-26 ◀
Language
property sheet

currently installed
language and layout

choose to add
another keyboard
layout

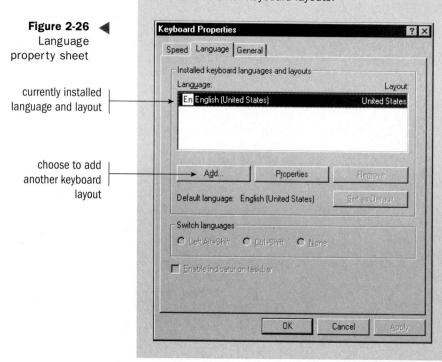

On the computer system in this figure, the current language setting is that of the English language in the United States. On the right side of this dialog box, you see the name of the corresponding keyboard layout. Windows 95 loads instructions for using this language and keyboard layout into memory every time the computer system starts. If you are using more than one language and keyboard layout setting, then you can click the Enable indicator on taskbar check box on the Language property sheet so that Windows 95 displays a language indicator on the taskbar. To quickly switch to another language or keyboard layout, you can click this indicator to display a menu with a list of all languages and keyboard layouts. You also have the option of designating a keyboard shortcut for quickly switching between keyboard layouts.

While he installs the keyboard layout for Sweden on one computer, Jaime asks you to assist him by installing the keyboard layout for France on another computer. First, the two of you want to enable the option for displaying the language indicator on the taskbar.

To enable the language indicator option:

1. Click the **Add** button.

An Add Language dialog box opens.

2. Click the **Language list arrow**.

3. Locate and click **French (Standard)**.

The option you selected appears in the Language list box on the Add Language dialog box.

TROUBLE? If you have already installed the French (Standard) language and keyboard layout, choose another language and keyboard layout that you might want to use on your system.

4. Click the **OK** button.

The option you selected now appears in the Language list. See Figure 2-27.

Figure 2-27 ◀
Installing a new
language and
keyboard layout

newly installed
language

option to display
language indication

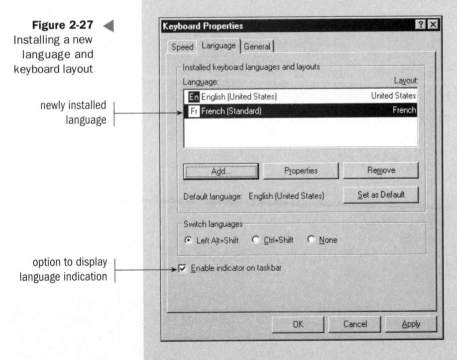

5. If the Enable indicator on taskbar check box is not already selected, click the **Enable indicator on taskbar** check box.

6. If you intend to install this setting from your Windows 95 CD-ROM installation disk, insert that disk in your CD-ROM drive, then click the **OK** button.

TROUBLE? If you do not have the Windows 95 CD-ROM installation disk, click the Cancel button, acknowledge the error messages that appear, then skip Step 7.

7. If Windows 95 prompts you for an installation disk, insert it into the appropriate disk drive, then, if necessary, click the **OK** button.

TROUBLE? If you do not have the Windows 95 installation disk, click the Cancel button, then acknowledge the error messages that appear.

Windows 95 completes the installation and displays the Control Panel.

Now you want to test the use of the language indicator on the taskbar before employees start to use the computer.

To switch to another keyboard layout:

1. Close the Control Panel.

If you enabled the Enable indicator on taskbar setting, then you should see an indicator on the right side of the taskbar to the left of the digital clock. The language indicator has a two-character code, such as En for English, that identifies the language and keyboard layout setting used on your computer system.

2. Click the **language indicator** on the Taskbar.

Windows displays a menu that lists the installed language and keyboard layouts on your computer system. See Figure 2-28.

Figure 2-28 ◀
Displaying a
menu of
installed
languages

TROUBLE? If you have not installed two or more language and keyboard layouts on your computer system, you will not be able to complete this section. Continue to the next section. Don't worry if your list of language and keyboard layouts is different than that shown in the figure.

3. Click **French (Standard)** or the new keyboard layout you installed.

The language indicator now shows Fr for the French (Standard) language and keyboard layout.

TROUBLE? If the language indicator does not change from En to Fr, the keyboard layout might not be properly installed.

4. Click the **language indicator** on the taskbar.

5. Click **English (United States)** or the language and keyboard layout you regularly use on your computer system.

Another staff member who works in the same office inadvertently added a language and keyboard layout that he does not need. Jaime asks you to remove that language layout.

To remove a language and keyboard layout:

1. Click the **Start** button, point to **Settings**, then click **Control Panel**.

2. Double-click the **Keyboard** icon in the Control Panel.

3. Click the **Language** tab in the Keyboard Properties dialog box.

4. In the Language list box, locate and click **French (Standard)** or the name of the language and keyboard layout setting that you previously added to the computer you are using.

5. Click the **Remove** button.

    Windows 95 removes the setting from the Language list box.

6. Click the **OK** button to close the Keyboard Properties dialog box.

7. If Windows 95 displays an error message, click the **Yes** button to continue.

8. Close the Control Panel.

Next, you need to restart your computer system so that Windows 95 uses the proper language and keyboard layout for the next section and for other programs that you might use.

 If you are working in a computer lab, do not complete the next two steps because it requires that you restart the computer.

To restart your computer:

1. Click the **Start** button then click **Shut Down**.

2. Click **Restart the computer** then click the **Yes** button.

As Jaime shows employees how to select background patterns, wallpaper, color schemes, screen savers, and the proper screen resolutions, his co-workers discover how easy it is to customize a desktop with Windows 95 with the wide variety of options that are available. Furthermore, by implementing energy savings features on everyone's computer, staff members realize their goals of a more energy efficient workplace. For those employees who must work with different regional settings and language and keyboard layouts, their job is easier than ever with the support provided in Windows 95 for using country specific settings.

SELECTING A KEYBOARD LAYOUT

- Click the Start button.
- Point to Settings then click Control Panel.
- Double-click the Keyboard icon in the Control Panel.
- Click the Language tab then select a keyboard layout.
- Close the Keyboard Properties dialog box, then close the Control Panel.

Using Accessibility Options for Employees with Disabilities

Each year the President of the United States recognizes companies that contribute to the well being and success of their employees in a special awards ceremony held at the White House. Thorsen Pharmaceuticals recently received the highest commendation for its outstanding programs for hiring and promoting the efforts of individuals with disabilities. The employees at Thorsen Pharmaceuticals are proud of their company's efforts and recognition for creating a diverse work force and for drawing on the talents of many different types of people. Its success in the global marketplace is a direct result of its diverse work force.

With the Accessibility Options feature available in the Windows 95 operating system, Jaime and other staff members who provide computer support for staff in Thorsen Pharmaceutical's divisions around the world can provide a more effective working environment for employees with disabilities.

The Accessibility Options in Windows 95 operate with both Windows and DOS-based applications. Although the Accessibility Options are not automatically installed when you first set up Windows 95 on your system, you can easily install them later.

HELP DESK

Index

CUSTOMIZING FOR DISABILITIES

Click the Start button, click Help, then click the Index tab.

Keyword
Accessibility

Topic
Overview: customizing for disabilities

Alison Weichel, an employee in one of the research labs, asks Jaime and you to assist her in installing the Accessibility Options. Since she has limited use of her hands, she finds it difficult to use a keyboard and mouse. Jaime tells her that he can help her explore the Keyboard and Mouse accessibility features so that she can select options that help her in her job. First, however, Jaime asks you to install the Accessibility Options on her computer system.

If you are working in a computer lab, do not change the following setting, because it requires that you restart the computer. Instead, continue with the next section.

To install the Accessibility Options.

1. Click the **Start** button, point to **Settings**, then click **Control Panel**.

If you see an Accessibility Options icon, then the accessibility features are already installed on your computer system. You can then skip to the next section.

2. If you do not see the Accessibility Options icon and you want to install the Accessibility features on your computer, double-click the **Add/Remove Programs** icon in the Control Panel.

The Add/Remove Programs Properties dialog box opens. The second tab, Windows Setup, allows you to install or remove a Windows 95 component.

3. Click the **Windows Setup** tab.

On the Windows Setup tab, you see a list of Windows 95 components. See Figure 2-29.

Figure 2-29 ◀
Add/Remove
Programs
Properties
dialog box

Accessibility Options
component

description of
component

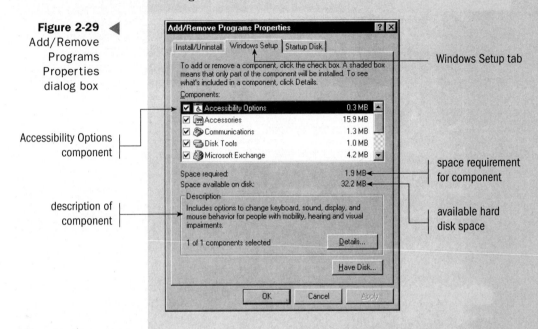

Windows Setup tab

space requirement
for component

available hard
disk space

A check mark in the box next to an option indicates it is already installed. If the check box has a check mark and is also shaded, only part of that component is installed. Your options might differ from those shown in the figure.

4. In the Component list box, click **Accessibility Options**.

In the Description section, Windows 95 explains that this component includes options for changing the keyboard, sound, display, and mouse for the hearing and sight impaired. It also shows how much disk space that component will require on a hard drive.

5. If the Accessibility Options are already installed, click the **Cancel** button to close the Add/Remove Programs Properties dialog box, then skip to the next section.

6. If you want to install the Accessibility Options, click the **OK** button.

Windows 95 displays an Insert Disk dialog box, prompting you for a CD-ROM installation disk.

TROUBLE? If you do not have the Windows 95 installation disk(s), you will not be able to complete this part of the tutorial. Click the Cancel button to close the Add/Remove Programs Properties dialog box. You might want to read the explanatory paragraphs in this part of the tutorial so that you are aware of the types of Accessibility features that are available. You might need to recommend them to someone else, or use some of the features yourself later.

7. Insert the CD-ROM installation disk into your CD-ROM drive, or insert the installation disk into your disk drive, then click the **OK** button.

As it installs this software component, Windows 95 displays a Copying Files dialog box. Then, it displays a System Settings Change dialog box that informs you that you must restart Windows 95 before the settings will take effect.

8. Click the **OK** button.

Windows 95 restarts your computer system.

Simplifying Keyboard Operations for an Employee with Limited Mobility

After installing the Accessibility Options on Alison's computer, Jaime asks you to show Alison how to select and use the Keyboard and Mouse accessibility options.

If you are working in a computer lab, and if you find that the Accessibility Options are not installed on your network, then you will not be able to complete the remainder of the tutorial.

To examine Keyboard accessibility options:

1. Click the **Start** button, point to **Settings**, then click **Control Panel** to open the Control Panel.

2. Double-click the **Accessibility Options** icon.

The Accessibility Properties dialog box opens. See Figure 2-30. The Keyboard and Mouse tabs provide alternate methods for working with the standard keyboard and for using keys to control mouse pointer movement. The Keyboard tab allows you to use StickyKeys, FilterKeys, and ToggleKeys.

Figure 2-30 ◄
Accessibility
Properties
dialog box

Keyboard tab

Sticky Keys feature

Filter Keys feature

Toggle Keys feature

extra Help feature

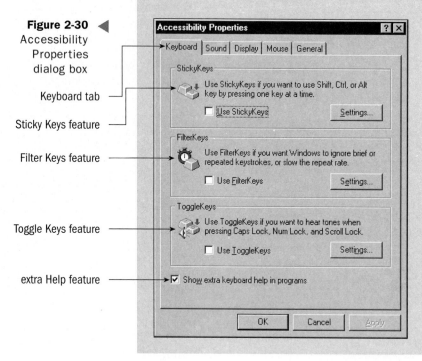

The StickyKeys, FilterKeys, and ToggleKeys features can all help make Alison's computer easier to handle. Many applications provide for the use of **shortcut keys,** or key combinations, that allow you to quickly perform an operation or select a command. These shortcut key combinations use a **modifier key,** such as the Control, Alt, or Shift key, with another key. For example, in Windows applications, you press and hold down the Control key and then press the S key to save your document. This key combination is usually indicated by Ctrl + S. Pressing two keys simultaneously can be difficult for many computer users, even individuals who do not have limited use of their hands. If you activate the StickyKeys feature, you can press the Control, Alt, or Shift key, then release the key before you select another key. The application or Windows 95 then treats the two keys as if they had been pressed simultaneously. This feature is especially useful for individuals who cannot press two keys at the same time.

The FilterKeys feature prevents an application from responding to a key that was touched momentarily or that was accidentally brushed against for a split second. A key must be held for a certain period of time before Windows 95 or the application recognizes the key. Someone with limited hand mobility might easily touch a key while attempting to select another key.

The ToggleKeys feature instructs Windows 95 to emit a high sound when you toggle the Caps Lock, Scroll Lock, or Num Lock keys. A **toggle** key alternates between two different uses each time you press the key. If you toggle off any one of these three keys, Windows 95 emits a low sound.

If an application supports the use of extra Help for the keyboard, you can enable Windows 95 support for that feature on the Keyboard tab by checking the Show extra keyboard help in programs check box.

Now that you have installed the Accessibility Options, you are ready to show Alison how to use these Keyboard accessibility features.

To view StickyKey settings:

1. Click the StickyKeys **Settings** button.

In the Keyboard shortcut section, the Use shortcut check box, if checked, allows you to press the Shift key five times to turn this feature on or off. See Figure 2-31. In the Options section, you can choose an option that locks the modifier key if you press it twice. The modifier key stays active until you press it a third time. You can also turn the StickyKeys feature off if you press a modifier key and another key at the same time. In the Notification section, you can instruct Windows 95 to emit a sound when you press a modifier key and to display a status indicator on the taskbar when the StickyKey feature is active. Alison asks you to enable this feature so that she can test it.

Figure 2-31 ◀
Settings for
StickyKeys
dialog box

StickyKeys options ────────▶

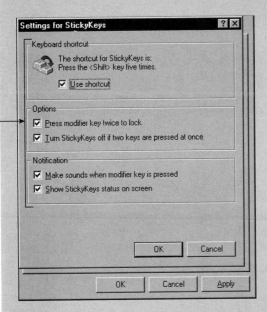

2. If necessary, click the **Use shortcut** check box in the Keyboard shortcut section to select this option.

3. Click the **OK** button to close the two dialog boxes.

The Accessibility Properties dialog box closes.

To test the StickyKeys feature, you suggest to Alison that she use a shortcut key for one of the Edit menu options in the Control Panel.

To test the StickyKeys feature:

1. Click **Edit** on the Control Panel menu bar.

   On the Edit menu, you can select all the icons in the Control Panel by selecting the Select All option or by pressing its shortcut key combination, Ctrl + A.

2. Click **Edit** a second time to close the Edit menu.

3. Press **Ctrl + A**.

   Windows 95 selects all the icons in the Control Panel.

4. Press **A**.

   Windows 95 removes the selection.

5. Double-click the **Accessibility Options** icon, click the **Use StickyKeys** check box to select this option, then click the **OK** button.

6. Press **Ctrl**.

   If you have a sound card, Windows 95 might emit a tone, indicating that you have selected a modifier key.

7. Press **A**.

   Windows 95 selects all the icons in the Control Panel.

8. Press **A** a second time.

   Windows 95 removes the selection.

9. If you are in a computer lab or if you want to turn off this feature, double-click the **Accessibility Options** icon, click the **Use StickyKeys** check box to deselect this option, then click the **OK** button.

These features are not only useful for individuals with disabilities. First-time computer users, as well as experienced computer users, can benefit from these features. For example, first-time computer users invariably find it difficult to press two shortcut keys simultaneously. If they enable the StickyKeys feature, they can use shortcut keys without pressing both keys simultaneously. Later, they can turn this feature off as their keyboard skills improve.

REFERENCE
window

CHOOSING KEYBOARD ACCESSIBILITY OPTIONS

- Click the Start button, point to Settings, then click Control Panel.
- Double-click the Accessibility Options icon.
- On the Accessibility Properties dialog box, select the Keyboard tab.
- Select the type of Keyboard accessibility feature that you want to use, then use the Settings button to customize that accessibility feature.
- Click the OK button to close the Settings dialog box, then click the OK button to close the Accessibility Properties dialog box.

Changing Mouse Properties for an Employee with Limited Mobility

Jaime explains to Alison that the Mouse application in the Control Panel folder and the Mouse tab on the Accessibility Options Properties dialog box provide options for customizing the use of the mouse. Jaime suggests that you and Alison examine the Mouse application first.

To view general mouse settings:

1. If necessary, click the **Start** button, point to **Settings**, then click **Control Panel**.

2. Double-click the **Mouse** icon in the Control Panel.

   The Mouse Properties dialog box opens. See Figure 2-32.

Figure 2-32 ◀
Mouse
Properties
dialog box

choose a button
configuration

adjust double-click
speed

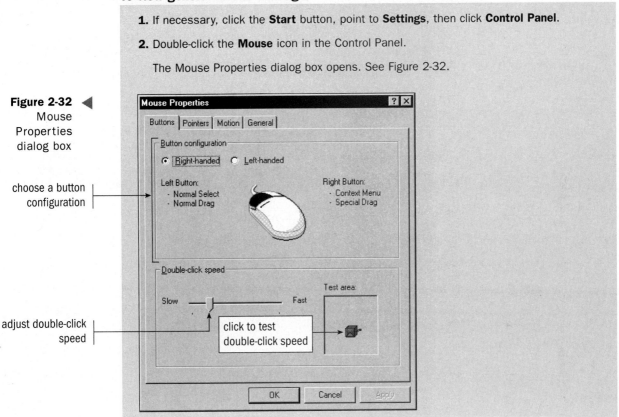

On the Buttons tab, you can change the Button configuration and the Double-click speed. For each Button configuration, the property sheet shows what the left and right mouse buttons do. If you are left-handed, you can use the options in the Button configuration section to swap the use of the left and right mouse buttons.

For the Double-click speed option, you can adjust the response recognition time of Windows 95 to your double-clicking. A slower speed allows you to double-click more slowly; a faster speed requires that you double-click more quickly for Windows 95 to recognize the double-click. You can use the Test area to test changes you make to the double-click speed. If you double-click in the Test area and Windows 95 recognizes the double-click, a jack-in-the-box will pop out of the box. If you double-click again, Windows 95 closes the box. If you double-click and you do not see the jack-in-the-box, or the box does not close, the double-click speed setting is too high. Adjust it downward and try again.

Before you and Alison examine the other mouse property sheets, she wants to reduce the double-click speed for the mouse.

To adjust the double-click speed:

1. If you are left-handed and want to swap the left and right mouse buttons, click the **Left-handed** radio button in the Button configuration area.

2. In the Double-click speed section, drag the **slider bar** so that it is approximately one-quarter the distance between Slow and Fast.

TROUBLE? If you chose the Left-handed option in the previous step and tried to drag the slider bar with the right mouse button, either nothing will happen or a shortcut menu might appear. You must click the OK button and close the Mouse Properties dialog box before the left-handed option becomes active. If you do close the Mouse Properties dialog box, open it before you start the next step.

3. Point to the box with the rotating crank in the Test area, then slowly double-click the **box**.

The jack-in-the-box pops out of the box, as shown in Figure 2-33.

Figure 2-33 ◄
Testing the
double-click
speed setting

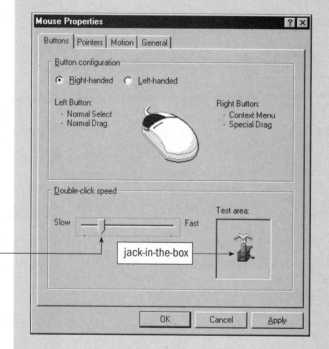

double-click speed
setting

jack-in-the-box

TROUBLE? If the jack-in-the-box did not pop out of the box, then you might have double-clicked too slowly. Double-click again at a slightly faster pace.

4. Double-click the **jack-in-the-box** in the Test area to close the box.

Alison tells you that this double-click speed is just right. Next, the two of you want to examine the Pointers property sheet.

5. Click the **Pointers** tab, then scroll through the pointers box.

In the Pointers list box, Windows 95 lists the default pointer shapes that it uses. If you want to use another pointer shape, you can click the Browse button, locate a folder with files that contain cursor shapes, and then select a replacement for the currently selected Windows 95 pointer.

6. Click the **Motion** tab.

On this sheet, you can adjust the speed at which the pointer moves across the screen, and you can use mouse pointer trails. See Figure 2-34. If you select the Show pointer trail option, images of previous positions of the mouse pointer on the screen appear to create a trail that extends to the current position of the mouse pointer. This feature makes the mouse pointer easier to see on an LCD screen, something to consider with vision-impaired users. You can also adjust the trail length. Alison does not need pointer trails on her computer, but she wants the mouse to move more slowly so that she can more easily select objects.

Figure 2-34
Controlling
mouse pointer
motion

Motion tab

adjust pointer speed

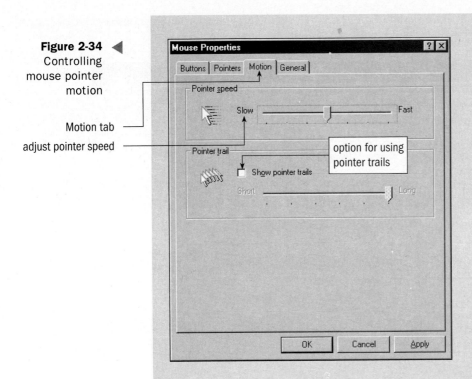

7. In the Pointer speed section, drag the **slider bar** left to the next setting on the slider bar, then click the **Apply** button.

8. Click the **General** tab.

   On the last tab, you see the name for your mouse model. If you change the mouse on your computer, you might need to use the Change button to set up the new mouse.

9. Click the **OK** button to accept the changes or the **Cancel** button to cancel.

   The Mouse Properties dialog box closes. The changes Alison made to her mouse settings are now activated.

REFERENCE
window

CHANGING MOUSE PROPERTIES

- Click the Start button, point to Settings, then double-click Control Panel.
- Double-click the Mouse icon.
- On the Buttons tab, choose the Button configuration you want and adjust the double-click speed.
- On the Pointer tab, select the mouse pointers settings that you want to use.
- On the Motion tab, adjust the mouse pointer speed and enable or disable pointer trails.
- Click the OK button to close the Mouse Properties dialog box.

Next, Alison wants to find out about the MouseKeys accessibility option.

The MouseKeys accessibility option allows you to control pointer movement with the numeric keypad. If you activate the MouseKeys feature, you can use the directional keys on the numeric keypad to move the mouse pointer and to perform mouse operations, such as click, double-click, and drag. See Figure 2-35.

Figure 2-35 ◄
Using the
Numeric
Keypad for
Mouse
Operations

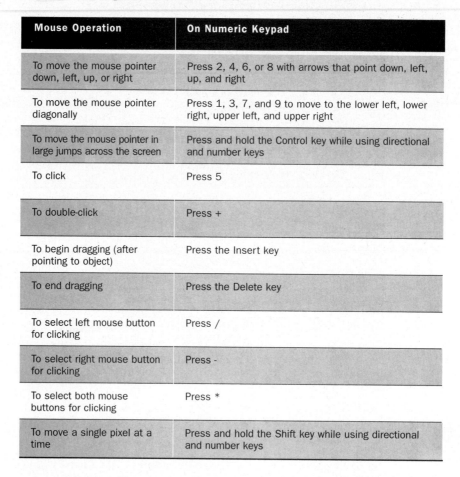

Mouse Operation	On Numeric Keypad
To move the mouse pointer down, left, up, or right	Press 2, 4, 6, or 8 with arrows that point down, left, up, and right
To move the mouse pointer diagonally	Press 1, 3, 7, and 9 to move to the lower left, lower right, upper left, and upper right
To move the mouse pointer in large jumps across the screen	Press and hold the Control key while using directional and number keys
To click	Press 5
To double-click	Press +
To begin dragging (after pointing to object)	Press the Insert key
To end dragging	Press the Delete key
To select left mouse button for clicking	Press /
To select right mouse button for clicking	Press -
To select both mouse buttons for clicking	Press *
To move a single pixel at a time	Press and hold the Shift key while using directional and number keys

To view the Mouse tab options:

1. If necessary, click the **Start** button, point to **Settings**, then click **Control Panel**.

2. Double-click the **Accessibility Options** icon.

3. Click the **Mouse** tab.

Although Alison thinks the adjustments to mouse settings that she made on the Mouse Properties property sheet might be all she needs, she wants to view the options for MouseKeys.

4. Click the **Settings** button.

In the Settings for MouseKeys dialog box, you can choose to use a shortcut for turning MouseKeys on and off, you can adjust pointer speed and pointer acceleration with a slider bar, you can use the Control and Shift keys to speed up or slow down the mouse pointer, you can use MouseKeys with Num Lock on or off, and you can display a MouseKeys status indicator on the taskbar. See Figure 2-36. Alison decides not to use any of these features just yet, but she is glad that they exist if she finds that she needs them later.

Figure 2-36 ◀
Settings for
MouseKeys
dialog box

MouseKeys options ————

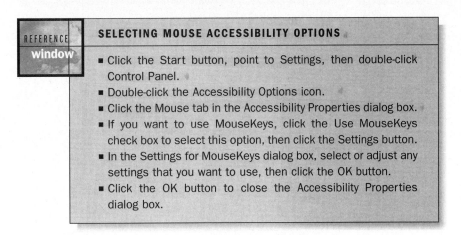

5. Click the **OK** button to close the Settings for MouseKeys dialog box.

6. Click the **OK** button to close the Accessibility Properties dialog box.

REFERENCE
window

SELECTING MOUSE ACCESSIBILITY OPTIONS

- Click the Start button, point to Settings, then double-click Control Panel.
- Double-click the Accessibility Options icon.
- Click the Mouse tab in the Accessibility Properties dialog box.
- If you want to use MouseKeys, click the Use MouseKeys check box to select this option, then click the Settings button.
- In the Settings for MouseKeys dialog box, select or adjust any settings that you want to use, then click the OK button.
- Click the OK button to close the Accessibility Properties dialog box.

Setting Display Accessibility Features for an Employee with Limited Vision

Douglas Montoya, a research scientist at Thorsen Pharmaceuticals, relies heavily on his eyeglasses to discern the detail that he sees on his computer's monitor. He asks Jaime if there is any way that he can improve the contrast on his computer. He comments that many of the newer applications use dark shades of gray which make it more difficult for him to spot and interpret information. Jaime asks you to show Douglas how the Display accessibility features in Windows 95 might help him.

You start Windows 95 and note that the Display accessibility features allow you to increase the size of text on the monitor and to use a high-contrast color scheme, both of which might benefit Douglas.

To view Display accessibility features:

1. If necessary, click the **Start** button, point to **Settings**, click **Control Panel**, then click the Maximize button 🔲.

2. Double-click the **Accessibility Options** icon.

3. Click the **Display** tab.

   On the Display tab, Windows 95 suggests that you use the High Contrast option if you want it to use colors and fonts that are designed for easy reading.

4. If necessary, click the **Use High Contrast** check box to select this option.

5. Click the **Settings** button.

   On the Settings for High Contrast dialog box, Windows 95 displays the shortcut key for switching between High Contrast and your original color scheme. See Figure 2-37. It also allows you to select a High Contrast color scheme.

Figure 2-37 ◀
Settings for
High Contrast
dialog box

choose a high
contrast color scheme ─────

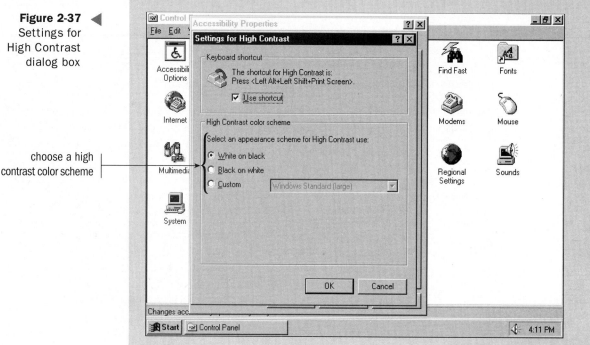

6. If Black on white is not already selected in the High Contrast color scheme section, click the **Black on white** radio button to select this option, then click the **OK** button.

7. In the Accessibility Properties dialog box, click the **OK** button.

   Windows 95 switches the screen display to high contrast. See Figure 2-38. Notice that text is displayed in black on a white background, and the text is also displayed in a larger size. Screen elements, such as the title bar, are shown in high-contrast colors. If you open an application, such as Microsoft Word or Excel, Windows 95 will override the application's settings for displaying its application window and use the same high contrast color scheme.

Figure 2-38
Displaying a
high contrast
screen display
with black on
white

larger title bar,
buttons, and
menu bar

larger taskbar

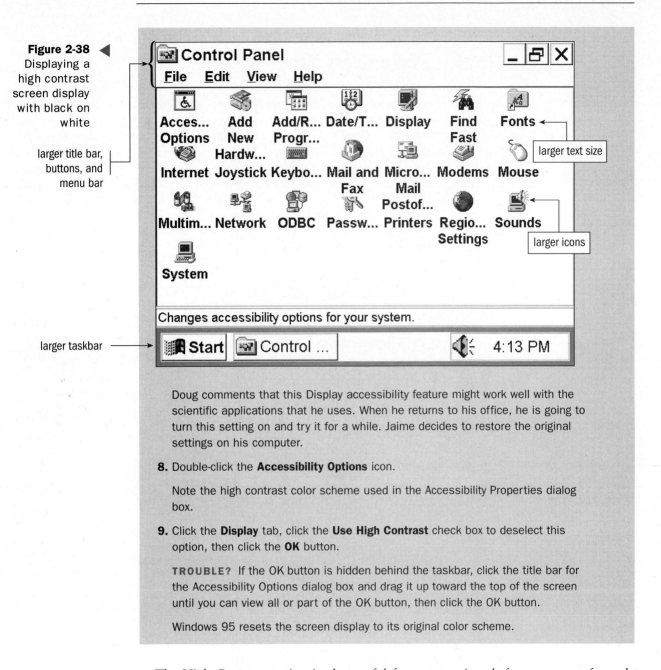

Doug comments that this Display accessibility feature might work well with the scientific applications that he uses. When he returns to his office, he is going to turn this setting on and try it for a while. Jaime decides to restore the original settings on his computer.

8. Double-click the **Accessibility Options** icon.

Note the high contrast color scheme used in the Accessibility Properties dialog box.

9. Click the **Display** tab, click the **Use High Contrast** check box to deselect this option, then click the **OK** button.

TROUBLE? If the OK button is hidden behind the taskbar, click the title bar for the Accessibility Options dialog box and drag it up toward the top of the screen until you can view all or part of the OK button, then click the OK button.

Windows 95 resets the screen display to its original color scheme.

The High Contrast option is also useful for presentations before a group of people when you are using an LCD display panel and an overhead projection and need to increase the contrast of the displayed image.

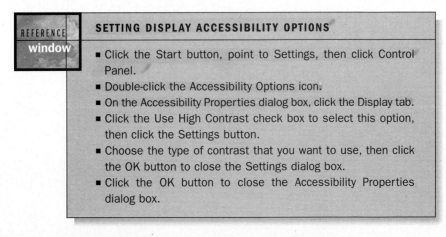

REFERENCE
window

SETTING DISPLAY ACCESSIBILITY OPTIONS

- Click the Start button, point to Settings, then click Control Panel.
- Double-click the Accessibility Options icon.
- On the Accessibility Properties dialog box, click the Display tab.
- Click the Use High Contrast check box to select this option, then click the Settings button.
- Choose the type of contrast that you want to use, then click the OK button to close the Settings dialog box.
- Click the OK button to close the Accessibility Properties dialog box.

Using Sound Accessibility Features for Hearing-Impaired Employees

Rafaela Hidalgo, the CEO of the United States division of Thorsen Pharmaceuticals, is deaf and relies on sign language and an interpreter to communicate with her hearing and deaf employees. Like every other employee, she has a desktop computer that she uses to prepare speeches, her annual report, and daily memos and letters. In a recent conversation with Jaime, she learned that Windows 95 includes two Sound accessibility features that provide visual clues when an application emits a sound. She asks Jaime to drop by her office when he has a free moment, and show her how to access and use these features. Jaime, who learned sign language from one of his deaf parents, suggests that he stop by first thing tomorrow morning, and invites you to go along.

To view the Sound accessibility features:

1. If necessary, click the **Start** button, point to **Settings**, then click **Control Panel**.

2. Double-click the **Accessibility Options** icon.

3. Click the **Sound** tab.

   Jaime signs to Rafaela that she can activate SoundSentry, ShowSounds, or both Sound accessibility features from the Sound tab. See Figure 2-39. SoundSentry, if activated, instructs Windows to flash an area of the screen when the computer emits a sound. ShowSounds instructs applications to display visual information, such as captions or other types of textual information, for sounds and speech they emit. Jaime also notes that future software applications will take advantage of these new Sound accessibility features in Windows 95.

Figure 2-39
Viewing Sound accessibility options

SoundSentry option

ShowSounds option

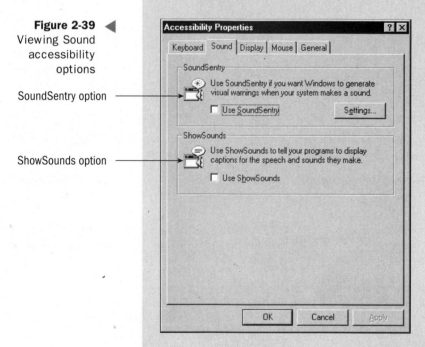

4. In the SoundSentry section, click the **Settings** button.

   In the Settings for SoundSentry dialog box, Jaime notes that Rafaela can use this option to identify which part of the screen should flash for windowed, full screen text, or full screen graphics programs.

5. Click the **Warning for full windowed programs list arrow**.

For this category of programs, Jaime points out to Rafaela that she can instruct Windows 95, for example, to flash the active window or the desktop when the computer emits a sound.

6. Click the **Warning for full windowed programs** list arrow to close the list box.

7. Click the **OK** button to close this dialog box, then click the **OK** button to close the Accessibility Properties dialog box.

8. Close the Control Panel.

CHOOSING SOUND ACCESSIBILITY OPTIONS

- Click the Start button, point to Settings, then click Control Panel.
- Double-click the Accessibility Options icon.
- On the Accessibility Properties dialog box, select the Sound tab.
- Select the type of Sound accessibility feature that you want to use, then, if available, use the Settings button to customize that accessibility feature.
- Click the OK button to close the Settings dialog box, then click the OK button to close the Accessibility Properties dialog box.

● ● ●

Rafaela thanks Jaime for showing her these accessibility features and notes that she will try them in the near future with the applications that she currently uses. Rafaela also takes this opportunity to thank Jaime for the support that he provides the diverse work force at Thorsen Pharmaceuticals. She notes that several employees have recently complimented him on his professional approach to his job, and that his efforts make her job more rewarding.

Tutorial Assignment

Thorsen Pharmaceuticals has decided to open another research facility in Mexico. The scientists at that facility will study the flora of the rain forests of South America in an effort to discover new drugs that Thorsen Pharmaceuticals can develop and market. Jaime has been asked to customize the first set of computers that the company will ship to its new research facility. To meet a short deadline, Jaime enlists your assistance. Jaime has already prepared a list of directions for customizing the computers, so that all the computers have the same settings. He asks you to customize half the computers as follows:

1. Launch Windows 95.
2. Right-click the desktop then click Properties on the shortcut menu.
3. When the Display Properties dialog box opens, choose the Forest Wallpaper pattern on the Background tab, select the Tile Display option, then apply the wallpaper to the desktop. *Note:* If your computer does not have the Forest Wallpaper pattern, choose another pattern.

4. Select the Screen Saver tab, select the Curves and Colors screen saver, then select the Settings button. On the Options for Curves and Colors dialog box, use the slider bar to set the Speed and Shape to Fast, set the number of Lines and Curves to 10, use the slider bar in the Density and colors section to select Dense. Select the Multiple random colors option, then close this dialog box. Then use the Preview button to test the screen saver. Set the Wait value for the screen saver to 5 minutes. *Note:* If your computer does not have this screen saver, choose another screen saver and explore the options for customizing the screen saver, then test it.

5. If your computer supports energy savings features, enable the Low-power standby and Shut off monitor options in the Energy savings feature of monitor section on the Screen Saver tab, set the wait values to 1 minute, test these options, then set the wait values to 15 minutes.

6. Select the Appearance tab. From the Scheme list box, choose the Teal (VGA) color scheme, if available, or choose another color scheme that you prefer, then change the Desktop color to dark blue. Select the Menu screen element in the active window, then change its color to royal blue (a bright blue). Select the Save As button and assign your name to this color scheme, apply the new scheme to the desktop, then close the Display Properties dialog box.

7. Open the Control Panel.

8. Open the Regional Settings Properties application.

9. On the Regional Settings tab of the Regional Settings Properties dialog box, locate and select Spanish (Mexican) in the Regional Settings list box.

10. Select the Currency tab, and when Windows 95 asks you if you want to restart your computer, click the No button.

11. Note the Currency symbol for this regional setting, then select the Number tab and find out what measurement system this regional setting uses.

12. Select the Date and Time tabs, and note date and time formats used for this regional setting.

13. Select the Regional Settings tab again, locate, select English (United States) in the Regional settings list box, then close the Regional Settings Properties dialog box. When Windows 95 asks if you want to restart your computer, click the No button.

14. Open the Accessibility Options from the Control Panel, then select the Mouse tab in the Accessibility Properties dialog box.

15. Select the Use MouseKeys option, then close the Accessibility Options dialog box.

16. Close the Control Panel.

17. Using Figure 2-35 provided in this tutorial as a guideline, test the options for moving the mouse pointer with the arrow keys on the numeric keypad and with the Ctrl and Shift keys combined with the arrow keys on the numeric keypad. This approach to controlling mouse operations allows you to prepare precision drawings in a program such as Paint.

18. Open the Control Panel, open Accessibility Options, select the Mouse tab, and disable the Use MouseKeys option. Close the Accessibility Properties dialog box, then close the Control Panel.

19. Open the Display Properties dialog box and restore your computer's original color scheme, screen saver, and wallpaper or background. Then, close the Display Properties dialog box.

Case Problems

1. Designing a New Color Scheme for Computers at Northbay Landscaping Northbay Landscaping sells and rents landscaping equipment and supplies for homeowners and business. Eric Baum, the owner, has asked you to design a new desktop color scheme for the computers used by his full-time employees in the administrative support office. Eric also asks you to keep a brief record of the changes you make so that you can prepare a short report that new employees can use to customize their desktops. As you complete these steps, choose colors that complement each other. If you find that you cannot change a screen component in the version of Windows 95 that you are using, then note that it is not available.

1. Open the Display Properties dialog box, then select the Appearance tab.
2. From the Scheme list box, select the Windows Standard scheme.
3. From the preview section or the Item list box, select the Active Title Bar, change its color, increase its size, and change its font.
4. Select the Active Window Border from the preview section or the Item list box, change its color and increase its size.
5. Select the Inactive Title Bar screen element, and change its color and select the Bold attribute.
6. Select the Menu screen element, change the size of the menu bar, choose a new color, change the font and font size and font color, and select the Bold attribute.
7. Select the Scrollbar screen element, and decrease the size of the scroll bar.
8. Select the Window element, and change the color of the window.
9. Select the Save As button, then assign a new name to this color scheme.
10. Close the Display Properties dialog box, examine your desktop, and decide whether you need to make any further changes.
11. Prepare a short list that details the specific changes you made to each screen element.
12. Optional: If you have access to a color printer, press the Print Screen key to copy an image of the desktop to the Clipboard, open Paint, and choose Edit, then Paste to paste a copy of the desktop into Paint. Use the Save As command on the File menu to save a copy of the image in a file on disk. Use the Print command on the File menu to print a copy of the image.
13. Change the color scheme back to the Windows standard scheme or the original color scheme used on your computer.

2. Choosing Screen Resolutions for Computers at Desktop Publishing Unlimited Desktop Publishing Unlimited is a rapidly-growing desktop publishing business in New Orleans, which employs 11 graphics artists. Marsha Hartman, the owner and senior graphics artist in the firm, wants to purchase new computer systems for herself and her staff. As she and other graphics artists have discovered, screen resolution is one of the major considerations when purchasing a new computer system. She asks you to prepare a summary of the available screen resolutions, colors, and font sizes for your computer. Then, she will use this information when she shops for the new computer systems for her firm.

 If you are working in a computer lab, do not change the following setting because it requires that you restart the computer.

As you complete the following steps, keep a record of the screen resolution, Color Palette setting, and any screen distortions in the preview section so that you can prepare a table of your results.

1. Open the Display Properties dialog box and select the Settings tab.
2. Examine the setting in the Color palette list box. What color setting is used on your computer? How many colors does this setting allow Windows 95 access to?
3. Examine the setting in the Desktop area section. What screen resolution does your computer use?
4. If the slider bar is not set to the lowest possible screen resolution, move the slider bar to the left side of the bar. What is the lowest possible screen resolution on your computer? Does the color setting change when you reduce the screen resolution? Do you see any screen distortion in the preview section?
5. Move the slider bar to the right to the next available screen resolution. What is that resolution? Does the color setting change? Do you see any screen distortion in the preview section?
6. Move the slider bar to each of the next available screen resolutions, check for distortion in the preview section, and check for a change in the color setting.
7. Prepare a table that summarizes your findings. Note which screen resolutions are available, the Color palette setting for each screen resolution, and whether any distortion occurs in the preview section.

3. Using Regional Settings at Salerno & Associates   Salerno & Associates is an international law firm that specializes in corporate law. Employees at each of its offices in the United States, Europe, and Latin America prepare multilingual documents that require access to different regional settings. So that staff at each of its offices are familiar with the settings used in other regions, you have been asked by your supervisor, Jonathan Stratton, to prepare a table detailing the most common regional settings for the United States, Switzerland, and Mexico.

1. Open the Control Panel, open Regional Settings, and, if necessary, select the Regional Settings tab.
2. If necessary, select English (United States), then record information on the regional settings shown in Figure 2-40. If Windows 95 asks if you want to restart your computer system when you change a regional setting, click the No button.

Figure 2-40 ◀

	English (United States)	French (Swiss)	Spanish (Mexican)
Currency Symbol			
Alternate Currency Symbol			
Measurement System			
Alternate Measurement System			
Short Date Style Sample			
Time Style Sample			
AM Symbol			
PM Symbol			

3. Select the Regional Settings tab, then select French (Swiss) from the Regional settings list box. Record information on the regional settings used by French-speaking nationals in Switzerland in your copy of Figure 2-40.
4. Select the Regional Settings tab, then select Spanish (Mexican) from the Regional settings list box. Record information on the regional settings used in Mexico in your copy of Figure 2-40.

4. Using Keyboard Accessibility Options in an Enabling Services Training Program at Tri-City Community College Tri-City Community College in Pennsylvania specializes in a wide assortment of Enabling Services training programs for individuals with disabilities. In its upcoming employee contract training workshop on Accessibility Options in Windows 95, Lorraine Jeffries wants to demonstrate the use of Keyboard accessibility features. She asks you to assist her in the preparation of a handout for the employees who will participate in this workshop.

1. Open the Control Panel then open Accessibility Options.
2. Select the Keyboard tab.
3. Activate the option for FilterKeys, then select the Settings button.
4. In the Filter options section, click the radio option button labeled Ignore quick keystrokes and slow down the repeat rate. Click in the box labeled Click and type here to test FilterKey setting. Test how Windows 95 responds to the press of a key.
5. Close the Settings for FilterKeys dialog box, then close the Accessibility Properties dialog box.
6. Test the FilterKey option in the Control Panel folder by selecting the Close option on the File menu. Press the Alt key to access the menu bar, then type "C" for Close on the File menu. Note any visual or audible clues provided by Windows 95 as you use the FilterKey option.
7. Open the Control Panel, open Accessibility Options, then select the Keyboard tab.
8. Turn off the FilterKeys feature.
9. Activate the option for ToggleKeys, then select the Settings button.

10. Examine the information in the Settings for ToggleKeys dialog box. Use the ? button to display help information on the ToggleKeys feature.

11. Close the Settings for ToggleKeys dialog box, then close the Accessibility Properties dialog box.

12. Perform the ToggleKeys test that you designed, then record the results. Note any visual or audible clues provided by Windows 95 as you use ToggleKeys.

13. Open the Control Panel, open Accessibility Options, then turn off the ToggleKeys feature.

14. Prepare a short summary of the types of tests that you performed with the FilterKeys and ToggleKeys accessibility features, and briefly describe your results.

15. Optional: Prepare a one-page handout on the StickyKeys, FilterKeys, and ToggleKeys features that you might be able to use as handout during an actual training session.

Working with Drives, Folders, and Files

Organizing Templates on a Staff Resource Disk

OBJECTIVES

In this tutorial you will:

- Format, copy, and view the contents of a floppy disk

- Change display options for viewing folders and files

- View drive properties

- Create a shortcut

- Open and create folders

- Rename and delete files

- Use Quick View

- Move and copy files to folders

CASE

Delta Oil Company

Delta Oil is a small company with headquarters located in New Orleans, Louisiana. Delta Oil not only sells oil but also develops and sells a variety of petroleum based products, including motor oils. Like many other small companies, Delta Oil has relied on the use of a minicomputer to handle its data processing requirements. A year ago, the president of Delta Oil decided to purchase desktop computers for each employee to free up resources on the company's minicomputer. Employees can still access information stored on the minicomputer to produce management reports and other types of documents, but now most of the processing occurs on their desktop computers rather than the minicomputer.

Michelle Cressler, a staff resource specialist in the Data Systems Department, assisted employees with the transition from working on a minicomputer to using a desktop computer. So that employees could work more efficiently and effectively, Michelle designed templates for different types of documents. A **template** is a file that contains the structure, formatting, and standardized text and data required for a specific type of document, including presentation materials for use in on-site and off-site company training programs. Templates help give company documents a consistent look. Michelle plans to share the template files with everyone in the company, and she wants to organize and distribute them as efficiently as possible. She asks you to prepare a distribution disk for the staff so that they can have easy access to the templates, and quickly locate the ones they need.

Managing Drives, Folders, and Files

Whether you work on a desktop computer or on a computer connected to a network, one of the most important tasks you face is the management of drives, folders, and files. A **drive** is a name assigned by the operating system to all or part of the storage space on a physical disk (like a hard disk, a floppy disk or CD-ROM disk) or a virtual disk (like a RAM drive that you designate as a temporary storage location). A disk in a drive contains **folders**, or organized collections of objects such as files or perhaps other folders. A **file** consists of a collection of data, such as a program or document, stored in a folder on a drive. Figure 3-1 shows the relationship between drives, folders, and files.

Figure 3-1
The relationship of drives, folders, and files

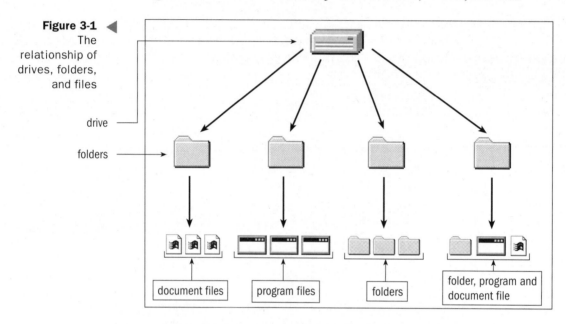

The operating system assigns drive names to drives within a computer system. You (or your installation software) assign folder names and filenames to folders and files so that you can identify the contents of these objects. The features built into an operating system for naming, organizing, and storing folders and files constitutes its filing system.

HELP DESK

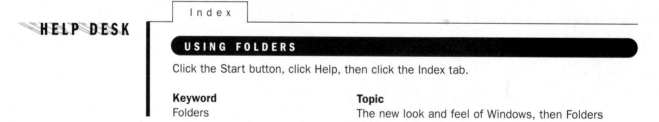

Index

USING FOLDERS

Click the Start button, click Help, then click the Index tab.

Keyword	**Topic**
Folders	The new look and feel of Windows, then Folders

As you work with the operating system and the applications on your computer, you access different drives so that you can work with the folders and files stored in these different locations. You select different folders and files to view information contained in those objects and, as needed, to move, copy, rename, and delete folders and files. You must develop effective strategies for organizing the many different types of files that you create and work with on a daily basis so that you can locate those files quickly and easily. If you work primarily on a hard disk drive, these tasks can be complicated by the increasingly greater storage capacities of hard disk drives and the increasingly larger sizes of software products. When you install an operating system or an application, hundreds of files are copied to folders on your hard disk. Since most users today must juggle a greater variety of applications and files stored on multiple drives, folder and file management becomes of paramount importance. Windows 95 offers a powerful array of techniques to help you manage, organize, navigate, and view the drives, folders, and files on your computer.

Formatting a Disk

Many Delta employees practice "telecommuting" from home offices one or more days a week using modern telecommunication products that keep them in touch with the office. They load data on floppy disks for easy transport from work to home and back. Michelle likes to keep a fresh supply of blank, formatted disks on hand for those who need them in a hurry, and she allows employees to drop off disks containing unneeded data to her department for reformatting. She then clears disks of sensitive data so they can be reused. Formatting a disk is one of the most important operations that you perform on a computer system, because the formatting process prepares the disk so that it can store data, creates the necessary structures for tracking information on folders and files that you eventually place on the disk, and verifies the integrity of the disk's surfaces. Once a disk is formatted, an operating system can store files on the disk, and retrieve those files later when you need them. The company or dealer that sold you your system formatted your hard disk, so this is one operation that you might never need to perform (though some hard disk problems are solved with reformatting as a last resort). These days, most disks that you purchase are preformatted so that you can immediately use them. However, if you purchase unformatted disks, you must format them first before the operating system can store files on the disk. Also, if you find that you no longer need the files stored on a disk, you can reformat the disk and erase whatever is stored on it so you can reuse that disk.

HELP DESK

Index

FORMATTING DISKS

Click the Start button, click Help, then click the Index tab.

Keyword	**Topic**
Formatting	Disks

During the formatting process, a formatting program subdivides the disk into storage compartments. First, the program creates concentric recording bands, called **tracks**, around the inner circumference of the disk. Then, the formatting program subdivides each track into equal parts, called **sectors**. Figure 3-2 shows a formatted 3½-inch disk with 80 concentric tracks, each of which is divided into 18 sectors. On disks and many hard disk drives, a sector contains 512 bytes. A **byte** is the storage space required on a disk for one character.

Figure 3-2 ◀
Tracks and sectors on a formatted 3 ½-inch diskette

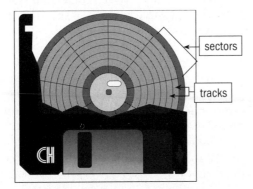

sectors

tracks

Figure 3-3 lists the similarities and differences of formatted 5¼-inch and 3½-inch double-density and high-density disks.

Figure 3-3 ◀
Disk
Specifications

Name	Size	Density	Number of Sides Formatted	Number of Tracks	Number of Sectors/ Track	Number of Bytes/ Sector	Storage Space (Bytes)	Sectors per Allocation Unit	Maximum Number of Files	Number of Pages*
360K	5¼ inch	Double	2	40	9	512	368,640	2	112	105
1.2MB	5¼ inch	High	2	80	15	512	1,228,800	1	224	350
720K	3½ inch	Double	2	80	9	512	737,280	2	112	210
1.44MB	3½ inch	High	2	80	18	512	1,474,560	1	224	420

*Assuming a single-spaced page that contains approximately 3,500 characters (or bytes)

Once the formatting program defines the tracks and sectors on a floppy disk, it creates a boot record in the first sector on the first track of the disk. The **boot record** (sometimes called the **boot sector**) is a table that contains information about the version of the operating system used to format the disk, as well as information on the physical characteristics of the disk. This information includes the number of bytes per sector, the number of sectors per allocation unit, the maximum number of files per disk, the total number of sectors, and the number of sectors per track. An **allocation unit**, or **cluster**, consists of one or more sectors of storage space, and represents the minimum amount of space that an operating system allocates when saving the contents of a file to disk. For example, on a double-density disk, an allocation unit or cluster consists of two sectors. On a high-density disk, an allocation unit or cluster consists of one sector. On a hard disk drive, the number of sectors in an allocation unit or cluster varies, but might consist of four, eight, or more sectors. That means that a small file, such as a short memo which is no larger than a sector in size, requires two sectors of storage space on a double--density disk, one sector of storage space on a high-density disk, and four, eight, or more sectors of storage space on a hard disk because space is allocated not on a sector-by-sector basis, but rather on a cluster-by-cluster basis. Any space allocated to a file, but not used to actually store the contents of the file, is wasted space.

The formatting utility also creates a table that keeps track of which allocation units (or clusters) are available or unused, used to store the contents of files, defective and unusable, and reserved for use by the operating system, as shown in Figure 3-4. This figure shows a partial view of how an operating system tracks cluster usage for a single file that uses clusters 102-104 and 106-107. Each cluster contains the number of the next cluster for a file. The last cluster of a file contains an **end-of-file** marker. In MS-DOS, this table is called a File Allocation Table, and it forms the basis of the filing system used by MS-DOS to keep track of the location of files stored on disk. Because the File Allocation Table is so important to the operating system's ability to locate files, the formatting utility places two copies of this table onto a disk. One copy is called FAT1, the other is called FAT2. Each time the operating system saves a new or modified file to disk, it updates both tables. If the area of the disk where FAT1 is stored fails, then the operating system uses FAT2 to locate the clusters that belong to a file.

Figure 3-4 ◀
Partial view of
cluster use in
the File
Allocation Table

cluster numbers
calculated by
operating system

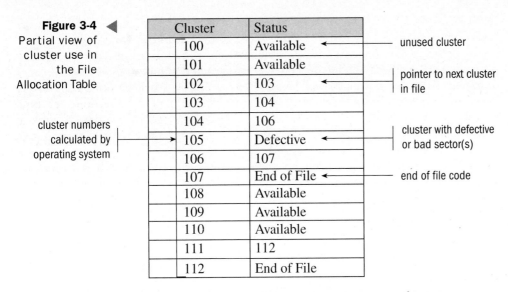

Cluster	Status
100	Available ◀──── unused cluster
101	Available
102	103 ◀──── pointer to next cluster in file
103	104
104	106
105	Defective ◀──── cluster with defective or bad sector(s)
106	107
107	End of File ◀──── end of file code
108	Available
109	Available
110	Available
111	112
112	End of File

To maintain backward compatibility with MS-DOS and Windows 3.1 applications, Windows 95 uses the MS-DOS File Allocation Table as a foundation for its own filing system, but expands the capabilities of that filing system with the use of a virtual device driver. Recall that a device driver is a program that enables an operating system to communicate with and control a hardware or software component (or device) within a computer. Under MS-DOS, a device driver manages the use of a system resource for a single application. A **virtual device driver** manages a hardware or software resource so that more than one application can use that resource at the same time. Virtual device drivers therefore allow an operating system to support multitasking. A virtual device driver, also referred to as a **VxD**, is a special type of device driver that Windows 95 uses when it operates in protected mode and uses the full capabilities of 80386 and later microprocessors to address more memory and provide memory protection features. The Windows 95 filing system is called the **VFAT filesystem**, for Virtual File Allocation Table. VFAT provides faster disk access and supports the use of long filenames (up to 255 characters for each filename).

Finally, when formatting a disk during the formatting process, the formatting program creates a root directory file to keep track of the folders and files stored in the root directory of the disk. This root directory file is another table that contains the names of folders and files, as well as information on their sizes, dates and times of creation or modification, and any special **attributes**, or characteristics, assigned to the folder or file by the operating system. Attributes include the Read-Only, Hidden, System, Archive, and Directory attributes. Files with Read-Only attributes can be read, but not modified or deleted; those with the Hidden attribute are not displayed in file listings; those with the System attribute are operating system files; those with the Archive attribute are newly-created or newly-modified files; and those with the Directory attribute are folders. The directory file also contains the number of the starting cluster for each folder and file on a disk. By using the directory file and File Allocation Tables, the operating system can locate all the clusters used by a folder or file. Figure 3-5 shows a partial view of the root directory of a floppy disk that contains a folder named RESUMES and the files named RESUME1.DOC, RESUME2.DOC, and RESUME3.DOC—folders and files that you might see on your computer.

Figure 3-5 ◀
Root directory
file

a folder (or directory)

document files

File name	File Extension	File Attributes	File Time	File Date	Starting Cluster	File Size
RESUMES		D	10:31:49	04/23/97	576	0
RESUME1	DOC	A	10:45:21	04/23/97	1011	3502
RESUME2	DOC	A	14:23:33	05/12/97	1297	6793
RESUME3	DOC	A	09:11:59	06/03/97	1486	4281

With Windows 95, you can format a disk from the My Computer window by using the Format command on a drive icon's shortcut menu or the File menu. For a floppy disk, the process takes a minute or two, and Windows 95 can format a disk in your floppy disk drive while working with applications elsewhere on your computer.

Jonathan Belansky, a financial analyst at Delta Oil, asks Michelle for a copy of her most recent set of templates so that he can prepare some financial projections and forecasts for an upcoming manager's meeting. Since Jonathan works three days a week at home, Michelle asks you to format a diskette and then copy the templates from one of her original diskettes.

Even if you use preformatted disks, reformat a disk so that you know how to perform this operation in Windows 95. Make sure the disk you are about to format does not contain important data.

To format a disk:

1. Make sure you see the Windows 95 desktop, then place a blank high-density or double-density disk in drive A that is not write-protected.

2. Double-click the **My Computer** icon. Windows 95 opens the My Computer window. See Figure 3-6. In the My Computer window, you see icons representing the drives within your computer and folders that provide you with access to specific applications that control your computer and its peripherals. Although the contents of your My Computer window might differ from that shown in the figure, you should see at least two folders, one labeled Control Panel and one labeled Printers. Once you open the My Computer window, you can then choose the drive that you want to format.

Figure 3-6 ◀
My Computer
window

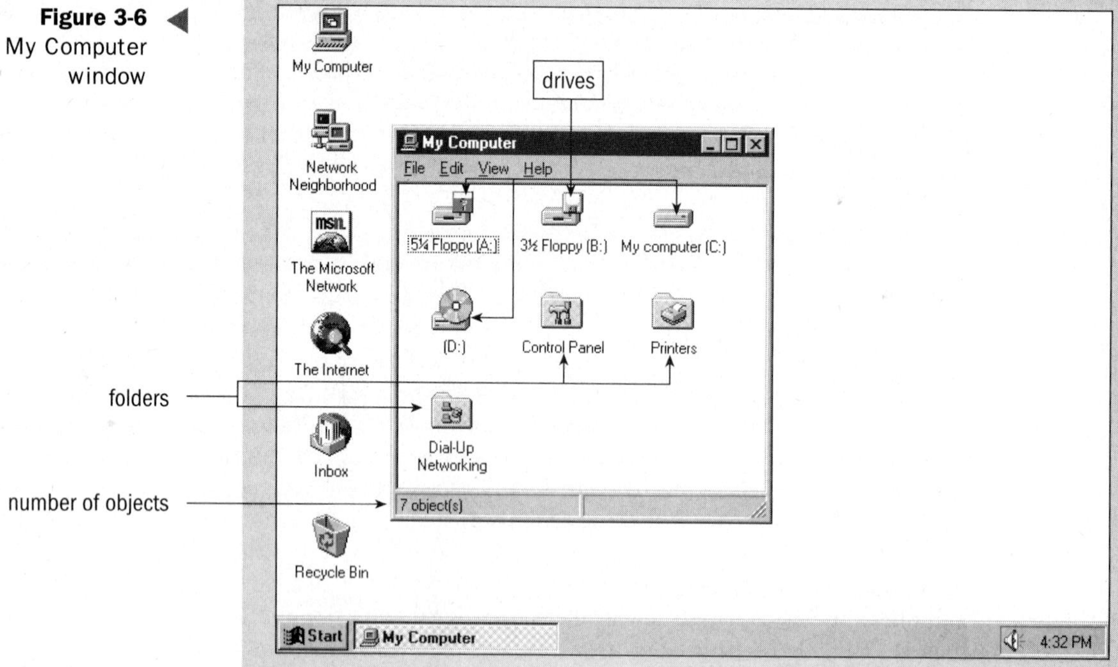

3. Right-click the **disk drive** icon for drive A or B, then click **Format** on the shortcut menu. Windows 95 opens a Format dialog box for the type of disk drive you chose. See Figure 3-7. The computer in this figure and throughout the tutorial has drive B as the 3½" high-density drive. In the Capacity list box, you choose the appropriate formatting capacity for the type of disk you intend to use.

TROUBLE? If you double-click instead of right-clicking, a window opens that displays the disk's contents. You must close this window before you can format the disk.

Figure 3-7 ◀
Format dialog
box

choose a format
capacity

choose the type of
format

enter a disk label

select to view a
summary

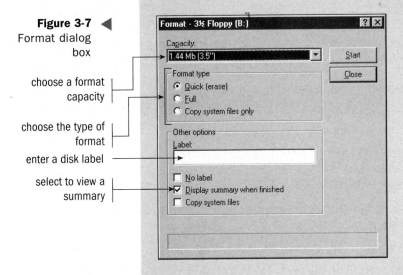

4. Click the **Capacity list arrow**. A list of available format capacities for your disk drive appears.

5. In the Capacity list box, click the **format capacity** you want to use.

TROUBLE? If you do not know the format capacity of the diskette that you want to format, use these guidelines to determine the format capacity. High-density diskettes are often labeled HD (for high density) or DS/HD (for double sided/high density), while double-density diskettes are often labeled DD (for double density) or DS/DD (for double sided/double density). High-density 3½-inch disks have a storage capacity of 1.44MB, while double density 3½-inch disks have a storage capacity of 720K. High-density 5¼-inch disks have a storage capacity of 1.2MB, while double-density 5¼-inch disks have a storage capacity of 360K. Manufacturers often list the storage capacity of the disk, such as 720K (for double density) and 1.44MB (for high density), on the diskette. In some cases, double-density 3½-inch disks are labeled 1MB instead of 720K, while high-density disks might be labeled 2MB. Also, double-density 3½-inch disks have one square hole for the write-protect tab, while high-density 3½-inch disks have two square holes, one directly opposite the other on the sides of the diskette. If you are still not able to determine the format capacity of a disk, ask your instructor or technical support person.

In the Format type section, you can specify a Quick or Full format. The Quick format reformats a disk that has already been formatted once. It erases the contents of the File Allocation Table and the root directory file, thereby removing any reference to what was originally stored on the disk. However, it does not physically erase the files on the disk. Also, it does not perform a surface scan. During a **surface scan**, the formatting program records dummy data onto each sector of the disk and reads it back. If it is unable to record data in a sector or read data from a sector, it records in the File Allocation Table that the cluster with that sector is defective. Then, the operating system will not attempt to store any data in the defective or bad cluster. By skipping the surface scan, which takes time, and by erasing the contents of the File Allocation Table and root directory file, the formatting utility can quickly reformat a disk.

The Full format steps through the complete process for formatting a new or previously used disk. This option divides the disk into tracks and sectors, creates a boot sector, creates two File Allocation Tables, creates a root directory file, and examines the surface of the disk for defects. If you are formatting a brand new (unformatted) disk, you must use the Full format option. If you are reformatting a disk that you know does not have defective sectors, then you can use the Quick format to save time.

Since you do not want to run the risk of giving Jonathan a disk that might contain defective sectors, you decide to do a Full format.

To continue the formatting process:

1. In the Format type section, click the **Full** radio button. Next, you want to assign the company name to the disk.

2. In the Other options section, click the **Label** text box, then type your last name. Labels, or **volume names**, for disks are limited to 11 characters, and cannot contain periods. You can use spaces as part of a label.

3. If the Display summary when finished check box in the Other options section is not already selected, click the **Display summary when finished** check box.

4. Click the **Start** button. A progress indicator bar appears at the bottom of the Format dialog box that provides you with a visual idea of where you stand in the formatting process. After Windows 95 formats the disk, it indicates that it is creating a file system for the disk. Then, the Format Results dialog box opens, as shown in Figure 3-8, and Windows 95 identifies the total amount of disk space on the diskette in bytes, the number of bytes used by system files, the number of bytes of bad sectors, and the total available space on the disk. Your summary information might differ from that shown in the figure. The summary also shows you the size of each allocation unit, the total number of allocation units on the disk, and the disk's serial number. From the size of the allocation unit, you can determine how many sectors are contained in an allocation unit, or cluster. For example, on the high-density disk used in the figure, each allocation unit is 512 bytes, or one sector, in size.

Figure 3-8 ◀
Format Results
dialog box

total disk space ——

no bad sectors ——

size of an allocation
unit

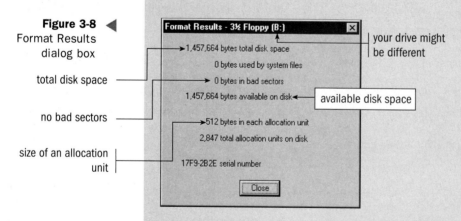

5. Determine the number of sectors in each allocation unit on the disk that you just formatted.

6. Click the **Close** button [X] to close the Format Results dialog box.

7. Click the **Close** button [X] to close the Format dialog box.

8. Remove the disk from the disk drive, place a label on the disk, then write your name on the disk.

9. Click the **Close** button ☒ on the My Computer window.

REFERENCE window

FORMATTING A DISK

- Double-click the My Computer icon.
- Right-click the disk drive icon containing the disk you want to format, then click Format on the shortcut menu.
- In the Capacity list box, select the correct format capacity.
- In the Format type section, select the Format type option.
- In the Other options section, select any other formatting options.
- Click the Start button.
- Close the Format Results dialog box, then close the Format dialog box.

Before you copy Michelle's template files to Jonathan Belansky's newly formatted floppy disk, you want to examine its contents and verify that it contains the files he will need.

Viewing the Templates Disk

To view the contents of a floppy disk, you open the My Computer window and then open another window for the floppy disk. Once you open a window, you should select any display settings that you want to use for that window, so that you can more easily understand and work with the contents of a window and its objects.

HELP DESK

Index

SEEING WHAT'S ON YOUR COMPUTER

Click the Start button, click Help, then click the Index tab.

Keyword	Topic
My Computer	Overview: Seeing what's on your computer

Michelle asks you to open the My Computer window, specify the display settings you want to use, then open a window to view the contents of the templates disk. Then, you can verify that the disk contains all the files that Jonathan needs. Check the "Read This Before You Begin" page to verify that you are using the correct disk for this tutorial before proceeding.

To select the display settings for viewing folders and files:

1. Insert your Student Disk in a floppy disk drive.

2. Double-click the **My Computer** icon.

Before you open a new window for the floppy disk drive, Michelle suggests that you set your options for viewing each new window you open.

3. Click **View** then click **Options**. On the Folder property sheet in the Options dialog box, you have two options for browsing files. See Figure 3-9. If you choose the first browsing option, Windows 95 creates a new window each time you open a folder. The previously opened window remains open. If you choose the second browsing option, Windows 95 updates the current window to show you the contents of the next folder you open. You only have one open window and, when you close that window, you return to the desktop. The second browsing option is the more useful of the two browsing options because you do not need to close every window that you open. However, if you want to be able to return to the previous window to select another folder, or if you need to switch between windows as you work (perhaps to drag files from one window to another), then choose the first browsing option.

Figure 3-9 ◀
Options dialog
box

Folder property sheet ────

choose to view a
single window

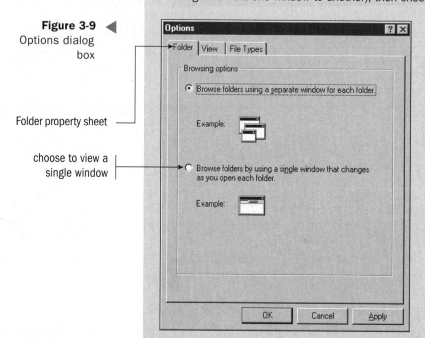

4. Click the **Browse folders by using a single window that changes as you open each folder** radio button.

While you are in the Options dialog box, Michelle recommends that you select the option for viewing file extensions, so that you know the full filename of each file.

5. Click the **View** tab. The last option on this tab that allows you to display or hide file extensions for registered files. See Figure 3-10. A **registered file** is a file associated with a specific application. When you register a file, you tell Windows 95 that files with the same file extension are ones that it should open with a specific application. For example, files with the file extension .DOC might be registered with Microsoft Word for Windows.

Figure 3-10 ◀
View property
sheet

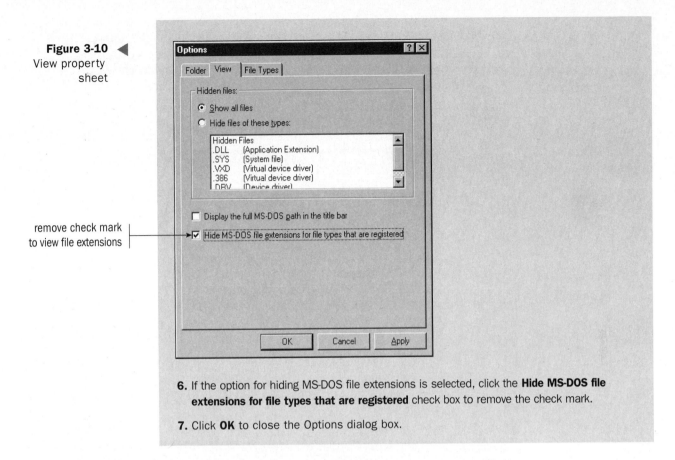

remove check mark
to view file extensions

6. If the option for hiding MS-DOS file extensions is selected, click the **Hide MS-DOS file extensions for file types that are registered** check box to remove the check mark.

7. Click **OK** to close the Options dialog box.

Now that you have specified all the settings you need for viewing files, you are ready to open a window for the floppy disk drive to view its contents.

To view the contents of the floppy disk drive:

1. Double-click the **floppy disk drive** icon. Notice that the window showing the contents of the floppy disk drive replaces the My Computer window. See Figure 3-11.

Figure 3-11 ◀
Floppy disk
drive window

folder icon

file icon

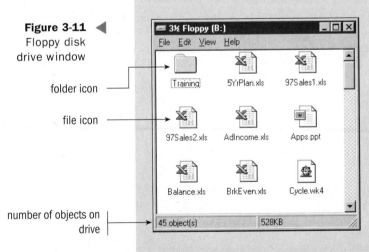

number of objects on
drive

2. Maximize the floppy disk drive window. In this window, you see a partial view of the contents of the disk. Since there are different ways to arrange the contents of a drive window, Michelle suggests that you choose the settings for automatically arranging icons in a window, and for displaying a toolbar in the drive window so that you can more easily change views. Your view might be different.

3. If you do not see a toolbar below the menu bar, click **View**, then click **Toolbar**. A toolbar appears at the top of the window. The last four buttons on the right side of the toolbar allow you to adjust the way in which Windows 95 displays folders and files.

4. Point to the **Large Icons** button on the toolbar. Windows 95 displays a ToolTip that identifies this button as the Large Icons button. See Figure 3-12.

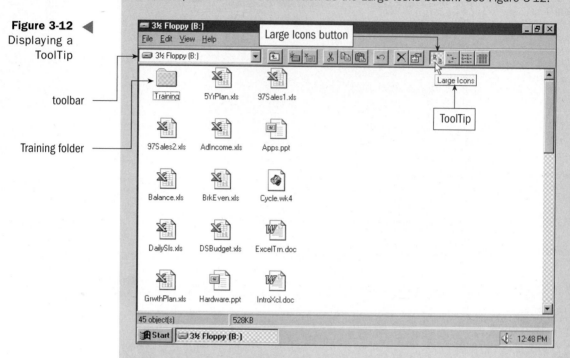

Figure 3-12
Displaying a
ToolTip

toolbar

Training folder

5. If you do not see large icons similar to those shown in Figure 3-12, click the **Large Icons** button . In the upper-left corner of the window, Windows 95 represents a folder by using an icon of a folder. See Figure 3-12. The Training folder contains a group of related files. The other icons are file icons. Windows 95 uses specific icons for files produced by different types of applications, such as Lotus 1-2-3 for Windows, dBASE for Windows, Microsoft Excel for Windows, and Microsoft Word for Windows. The status bar at the bottom of the window shows that there are 45 objects on the disk.

6. Click **View**, then point to **Arrange Icons**. Windows 95 displays the Arrange Icons menu, as shown in Figure 3-13.

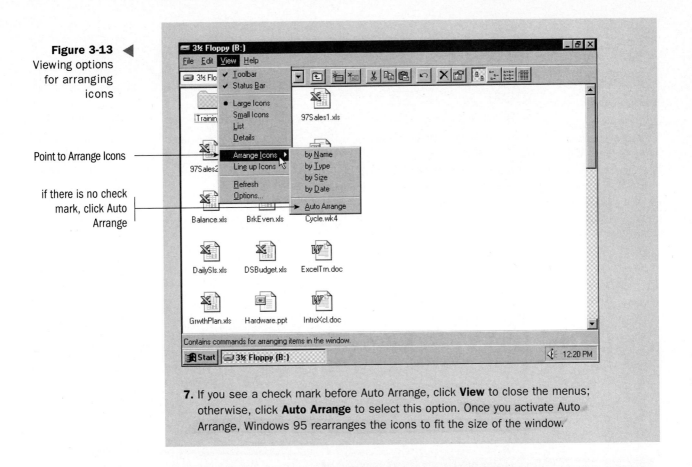

Figure 3-13 ◀
Viewing options
for arranging
icons

Point to Arrange Icons ────────

if there is no check
mark, click Auto
Arrange

7. If you see a check mark before Auto Arrange, click **View** to close the menus; otherwise, click **Auto Arrange** to select this option. Once you activate Auto Arrange, Windows 95 rearranges the icons to fit the size of the window.

Changing Your View of Files

Michelle mentions that other employees might prefer a view other than the large icons, especially if a disk contains a large number of files. Michelle suggest that you try each of the other available views and determine their advantages and disadvantages.

The current view of your Student Disk shows files using large icons. If a folder contains a large number of files, you can view the files using small icons so that you can see more files within the window. You can arrange the files in a list, and you can also view file details. Each view provides a different perspective and different types of information. You can quickly switch views by using buttons on a window's toolbar.

HELP DESK

Index

CHANGING YOUR VIEW OF FILES

Click the Start button, click Help, then click the Index tab.

Keyword
My Computer

Topic
Changing the appearance of items in a folder

Michelle notes that you can access the other three ways of viewing files just by clicking buttons on the toolbar.

To change views of files in a folder window:

1. Click the **Small Icons** button 🔳 on the toolbar. Now you can see all the folders and files in the current window without scrolling. See Figure 3-14.

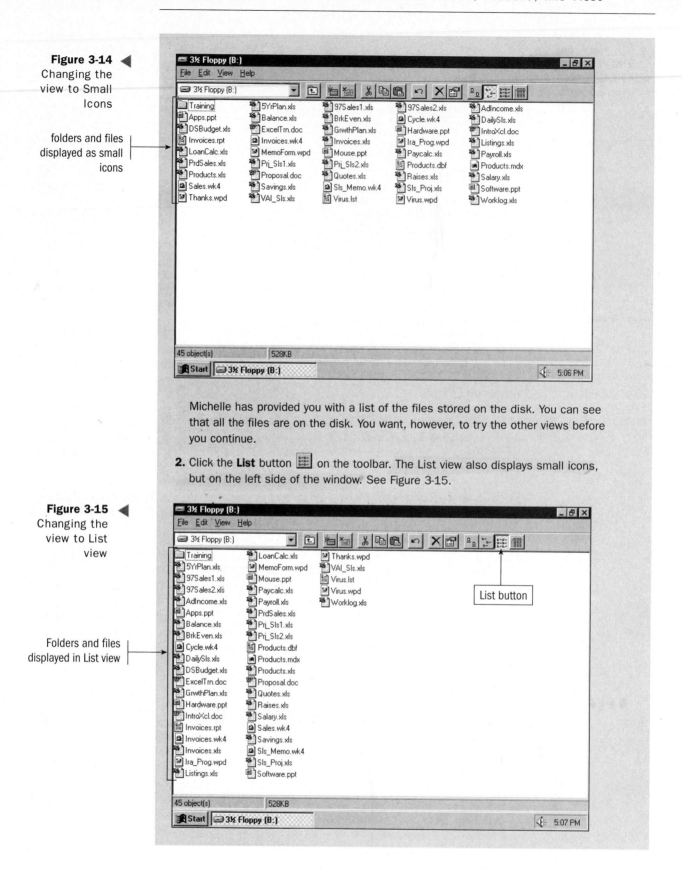

Figure 3-14
Changing the
view to Small
Icons

folders and files
displayed as small
icons

Michelle has provided you with a list of the files stored on the disk. You can see
that all the files are on the disk. You want, however, to try the other views before
you continue.

2. Click the **List** button on the toolbar. The List view also displays small icons,
but on the left side of the window. See Figure 3-15.

Figure 3-15
Changing the
view to List
view

Folders and files
displayed in List view

3. Click the **Details** button 🁢 on the toolbar. The Details view displays detailed information on the files in a window. See Figure 3-16. The files are listed in alphabetical order by filename. In addition to the full filename, you also see the file size, the file type, and the date and time of creation or last modification. The file type identifies either the application that produced the file, or just the extension of the file if Windows 95 does not know which application produced that file. So that you can view all the information in that column, you want to widen the Type column.

Figure 3-16 ◄
Change the view to Details view

folder and filenames listed in alphabetical order

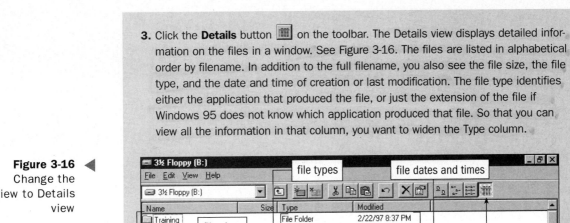

4. Point to the border between the Type and Modified columns until you see a double-head arrow ⬌, then double-click the **border**. The Type column widens to show all the information on the application that produced the document and the type of document. See Figure 3-17.

Figure 3-17 ◄
Widening the Type column

double-click on border to adjust column width

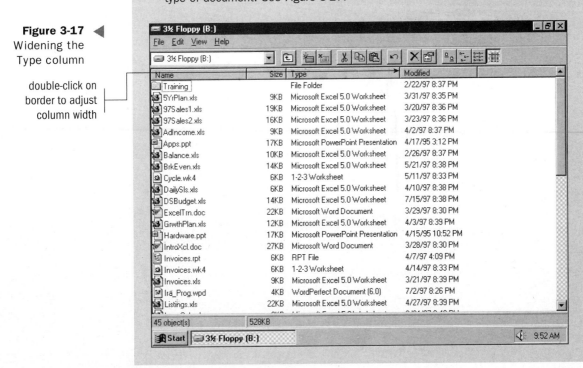

5. Click the **Up One Level** button to close the floppy disk drive window. Now you return to the My Computer window. See Figure 3-18. Notice that the List view of the My Computer window provides details on the contents of My Computer, including the size and free space on drive C.

Figure 3-18
Moving up one level in the folder structure

view of details in the My Computer window

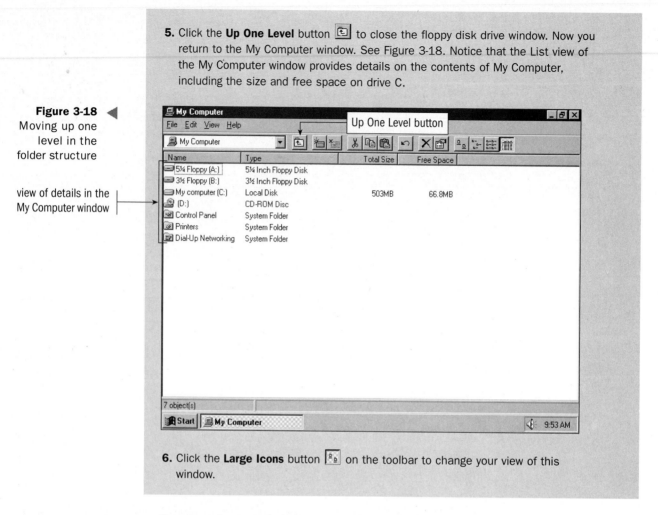

6. Click the **Large Icons** button on the toolbar to change your view of this window.

You have just verified that the copy of the templates disk that you have made for Jonathan contains the correct set of folders and files.

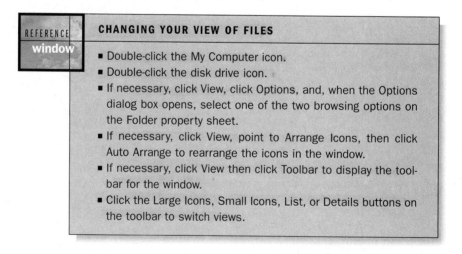

REFERENCE window

CHANGING YOUR VIEW OF FILES

- Double-click the My Computer icon.
- Double-click the disk drive icon.
- If necessary, click View, click Options, and, when the Options dialog box opens, select one of the two browsing options on the Folder property sheet.
- If necessary, click View, point to Arrange Icons, then click Auto Arrange to rearrange the icons in the window.
- If necessary, click View then click Toolbar to display the toolbar for the window.
- Click the Large Icons, Small Icons, List, or Details buttons on the toolbar to switch views.

The templates disk contains all the files Jonathan will need. You not only will give Jonathan the disk, but you will also explain how he can view the files on the disk.

Copying a Disk

As a precautionary measure, you decide to make a duplicate of Jonathan's floppy disk. If for some reason one disk fails, then Jonathan will have a second disk with the files that he needs.

You can make a copy of a disk from the My Computer window by selecting the Copy Disk option on the shortcut menu. When you copy a disk, the operating system makes a sector-by-sector copy of the original disk, called the **source disk**, and records the exact information to another disk, called the **destination disk**. The source and destination disks must be the same size and same storage capacity. If your computer only has one floppy disk drive, or if it has two floppy disk drives—one for 3½-inch and one for 5¼-inch disks, then you must use the same disk drive for the source and destination disks. The disk copy program first asks you for the source disk, then copies and stores the contents of the disk in RAM, then asks you for the destination disk, and finally copies the contents of the source disk from RAM to the destination disk.

The disk copy operation replaces any information already stored on the destination disk with the contents of the source disk. After the disk copy is complete, the source and destination disks are identical, except for their serial numbers. To protect your original disk during the disk copy operation, write protect it, as described in the next set of steps. If you do not write protect your original disk, and if you insert the disks in the wrong order, you end up with two blank disks (if the destination disk is a newly formatted diskette). After the disk copy operation, you can remove the write protection.

Now you are ready to make a copy of Jonathan's disk.

To copy a disk:

1. Remove your Student Disk from the floppy disk drive to write protect it.

2. If you are using a 3½-inch disk, hold the Student Disk so that the label on the disk faces away from you and the metal shutter is at the bottom. With your fingernail, press on the square tab in the write protect notch until it slides up and exposes an open, square hole in the disk.

   TROUBLE? If you are using a 5¼-inch disk, place a piece of tape over the square write-protect notch cut into the side of the disk.

3. Insert your Student Disk back into the appropriate floppy disk drive. This is the source disk.

4. If you have closed the My Computer window, double-click the **My Computer** icon.

5. Right-click the **disk drive** icon for the disk drive you want to use, then click **Copy Disk** from the shortcut menu. In the Copy Disk dialog box, Windows 95 highlights the name of the drive that you selected in the previous step. See Figure 3-19. If you only have one floppy disk drive, that drive name will be highlighted as the Copy from and the Copy to drive.

Figure 3-19 ◀
Copy Disk
dialog box

source drive ——————

destination drive ——————

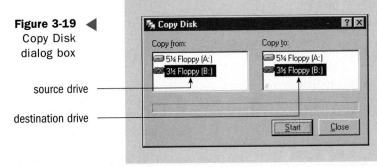

TROUBLE? If you see two drives in the Copy from and the Copy to boxes and if the drives are for different sized disks or for disks with different format capacities, then you must use the same disk drive as the Copy from and the Copy to drive. In this case, select the same drive in the Copy from and Copy to drives. If you have two drives that are the same size and the same format capacity, then you can copy from one drive to another.

6. Click the **Start** button. Windows 95 reads the contents of your source disk, and stores it in RAM. Then it displays a Copy Disk dialog box that prompts you to insert the destination disk. Make sure you insert a blank, formatted disk as the destination disk. Otherwise you might lose important information.

7. Remove your Student Disk from the disk drive, insert the disk that you are going to copy to (the destination disk), then click the **OK** button. Windows 95 reports that it is now writing to the destination disk, then it should report that the copy was successfully completed.

8. Click the **Close** button to close the Copy Disk dialog box.

9. Remove the copy of your Student Disk from the disk drive, and label the disk "Delta Oil Templates Copy." If you experience problems with the Student Disk that you use for this tutorial, then you have a copy that you can turn to. You will use this copy in the exercises at the end of the tutorial. You decide to remove the write protection from the disk you copied so that Jonathan can make changes to the template files if necessary.

10. If you are using a 3½-inch disk, hold the Student Disk so that the label on the disk faces away from you and the metal shutter is at the bottom. With your fingernail, press on the square tab in the write-protect notch until it slides down and covers the previously open, square hole in the diskette.

TROUBLE? If you are using a 5¼-inch disk, remove the piece of tape that you previously placed over the square write-protect notch cut into the side of the disk.

REFERENCE window	**COPYING A DISK**
	▪ Double-click the My Computer icon.
	▪ Right-click the disk drive icon, then click Copy Disk on the shortcut menu.
	▪ In the Copy Disk dialog box, select the Copy from and the Copy to drives.
	▪ Click the Start button.
	▪ When prompted, insert the source disk.
	▪ When prompted, insert the destination disk.
	▪ When the copy is complete, close the Copy Disk dialog box.

Jonathan thanks you for preparing the copies of the disk with the template files. Now, he can prepare the financial documents that he needs for tomorrow's meeting.

Viewing Drive Properties

Over the last few months, Michelle has added many new template files to her master disk. Before she continues to add more files to this disk, she asks you to check the amount of available storage space on the disk. You can easily do this by examining the properties of the disk.

Windows 95 keeps track of the properties of different types of disk drives within your computer system. You can view those properties and, in some cases, change one or more properties of a drive. You can also monitor the available space on any type of disk drive you have in your computer system. This feature is particularly important in the case of a hard disk drive. If you want to install a new operating system or software application or if you want to copy files from another computer to your computer, you need to check first to make sure you have enough space for the new software or new files.

To view drive properties:

1. Insert your Student Disk into a disk drive.

2. If you closed the My Computer window, double-click the **My Computer** icon, and, if necessary, maximize the window.

3. Right-click the **disk drive** icon for the drive that contains your Student Disk.

4. From the shortcut menu, click **Properties**. The Properties dialog box opens for the particular type of disk drive that you selected. See Figure 3-20.

Figure 3-20
A floppy drive properties dialog box

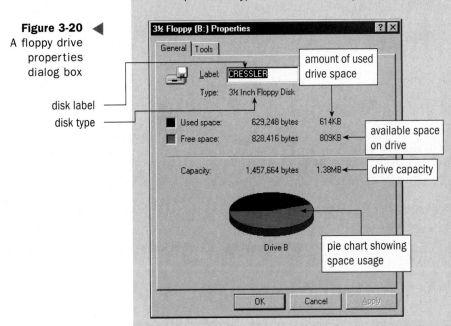

Your Properties dialog box might differ from that shown in the figure. If you are working on a network, then you might see a Sharing tab, which allows you to specify whether you want to share this resource with other users. On the General tab of the disk used for the figure, Windows 95 shows the type of disk and information on how much space is used and how much is free. On the disk in this figure, the files take up 614KB (or kilobytes) of storage space; 809KB of storage space remains free. The total storage space on this disk is 1.38MB (or 1,457,664 bytes). (*Note*: Windows 95 arrives at 1.38MB by dividing 1,457,664 bytes by 1,024 twice. There are 1,024 bytes in a kilobyte, and 1,024 kilobytes in a megabyte.) The pie chart shows the relative proportions of used and unused space on the disk. Most of the storage space on this disk is still available.

5. Click the **OK** button to close the drive Properties dialog box.

VIEWING DRIVE PROPERTIES

- Double-click the My Computer icon.
- Right-click the disk drive icon, then click Properties on the shortcut menu.
- View the information on the General property sheet.
- Click the OK button to close the Properties dialog box.

After examining the space usage on the diskette, you tell Michelle that the templates disk has plenty of room for new template files that she might want to add to the disk. Also, employees who work off a copy of this disk will have plenty of space to store final documents that they create from the templates.

If you want to take a break and resume the tutorial at a later time, you can do so now. If you are on a network, close any open applications and dialog boxes, and leave Windows 95 running. If you are using your own computer, you can click Start on the taskbar, click Shut Down, click Shut down the computer, and then click the Yes button. When you resume the tutorial, launch Windows 95 again, and then continue with the tutorial.

●   ●   ●

Creating a Shortcut

Michelle and you will frequently access your floppy disk drive as you prepare copies of the master templates disk for other employees. Michelle asks you to create a shortcut to that floppy disk drive, and place it on the desktop so that the two of you can switch to the drive in one step. A **shortcut** is a feature that allows you to quickly access an object within your computer system. You can create shortcuts to drives, applications, documents, files, and printers, and place the shortcuts on the desktop or in folders where you frequently work. The shortcut icon is similar to the icons for a specific object, but it has a small arrow in the lower-left corner of the icon. To use a shortcut, you double-click the shortcut icon.

HELP DESK

Index

USING SHORTCUTS

Click the Start button, click Help, then click the Index tab.

Keyword	Topic
Shortcuts	More ways to customize Windows, then Shortcuts on the desktop

Because shortcuts establish a direct link to a drive, folder, application, file, or printer, you do not have to open multiple windows, folders, and menus to locate an item. For example, if you create a shortcut to a floppy disk drive, you can immediately access that drive from the desktop by double-clicking the shortcut, as shown in Figure 3-21. You do not have to double-click the My Computer icon, then double-click the floppy disk drive icon to access that drive.

Figure 3-21
Using a
shortcut

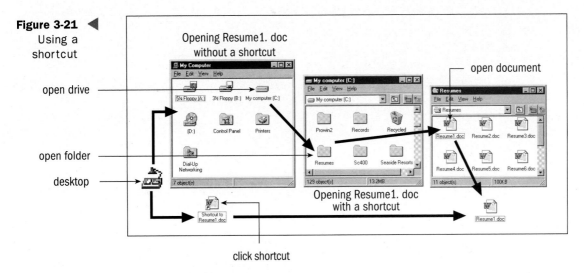

click shortcut

Shortcuts are useful in many situations; for example, you can place a shortcut to your word processing program, or even to a document that you access regularly, on the desktop or in any folder that you commonly use. When you double-click the shortcut, you open and access that object. Shortcuts are also useful in networked environments because you do not have to browse the network looking for a network resource.

After you create the floppy disk drive shortcut, you should check the shortcut to verify that there are no problems.

To create a shortcut to your disk drive:

1. Click the **Restore** button 🔲 on the My Computer window.

2. If necessary, drag the My Computer window to another location on the desktop so that you can see the section of the desktop where you want to place the shortcut.

3. Point to the **disk drive** icon in the My Computer window for which you want to make a shortcut, then right-click and drag the icon to the desktop, as shown in Figure 3-22.

   Windows 95 displays a shortcut menu with an option for creating a shortcut to the icon that you just dragged to the desktop.

Figure 3-22 ◀
Dragging a disk
drive icon onto
the desktop

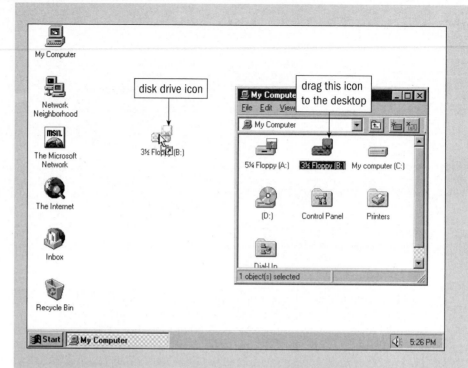

TROUBLE? If you right-click then drag with the left mouse button, Windows 95 displays a warning that you cannot move that object, but you can still create a shortcut to the object. If this occurs, click the Yes button and skip the next step.

4. Click **Create Shortcut(s) Here**. Windows 95 places a shortcut to your disk drive on the desktop. See Figure 3-23.

Figure 3-23 ◀
Shortcut to
floppy drive

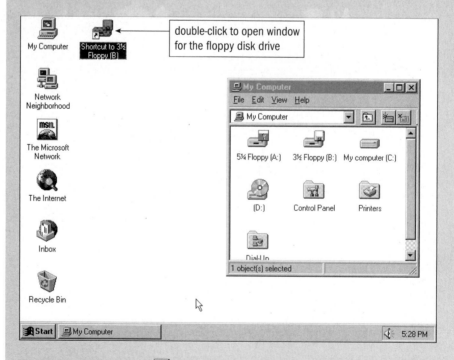

5. Click the **Close** button ☒ on the My Computer window. Now you want to try the shortcut to make sure it works.

6. Double-click the **Shortcut** to your floppy disk drive. Although you can accomplish the same operation using the My Computer window, the shortcut is faster.

7. Click the **Minimize** button ⬛ on your floppy disk drive shortcut window.

8. On the desktop, right-click the **Shortcut** to your disk drive, then click **Properties**. Windows 95 also assigns properties to shortcuts. See Figure 3-24. On the General tab, you see information on the type of object (a Shortcut), the object's location (Desktop), the object's size, its MS-DOS name, and the dates and times the shortcut was created, last modified, and last accessed. Windows 95 also summarizes the status of the object's attributes, or characteristics. The LNK file extension in the MS-DOS name is an abbreviation for "link," and emphasizes that a shortcut is a direct link to a specific object.

Figure 3-24 ◄
Shortcut
Properties
dialog box

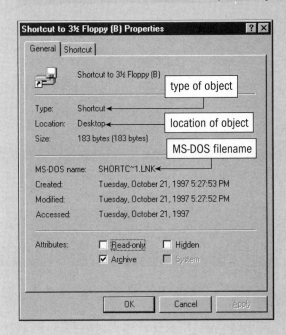

If you want more information about the link between the shortcut and the object, you can select the Shortcut tab.

To check the nature of the link:

1. Click the **Shortcut** tab. On the Shortcut property sheet, the Target type identifies the type of item that the shortcut points to. See Figure 3-25. In this case, the shortcut points to a file folder that displays the contents of the diskette in the drive. The Target location identifies the original location of the object that the shortcut points to. In this case, it is the root directory, or main file folder, for the diskette in drive A (or B). The Start in text box identifies the folder, if any, that contains other files a program might need. You have the option of assigning a **shortcut key**, or key combination, that lets you quickly choose a shortcut from the keyboard. In the Run list box, you can choose the size of the window for the object once you select the shortcut. You can open the object in a Normal window (or standard screen view), a maximized window (or full screen), or a minimized window as a button on the taskbar. The Find Target button takes you directly to the object from this property sheet. The Change Icon button allows you to select another icon for the shortcut. Now that you have verified the link for Michelle, you can close the property sheet for the shortcut.

Figure 3-25 ◀
Shortcut
property sheet

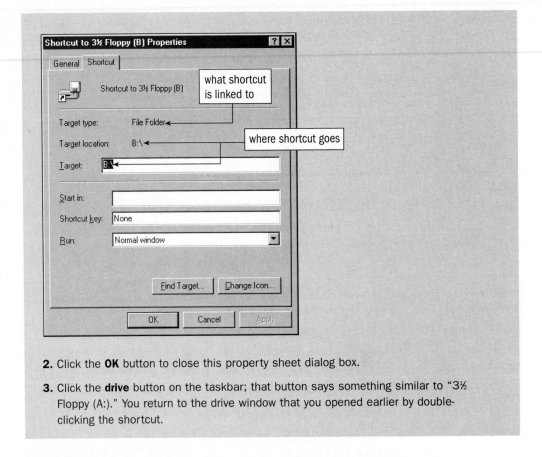

2. Click the **OK** button to close this property sheet dialog box.

3. Click the **drive** button on the taskbar; that button says something similar to "3½ Floppy (A:)." You return to the drive window that you opened earlier by double-clicking the shortcut.

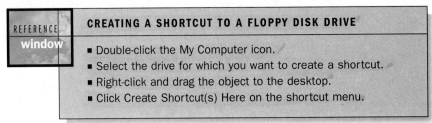

REFERENCE
window

CREATING A SHORTCUT TO A FLOPPY DISK DRIVE

■ Double-click the My Computer icon.
■ Select the drive for which you want to create a shortcut.
■ Right-click and drag the object to the desktop.
■ Click Create Shortcut(s) Here on the shortcut menu.

This shortcut makes it easier for both you and Michelle to access the contents of the master templates disk and to check copies that you make of the disk.

Planning a Folder Structure for the Templates Disk

Over the last several months, Michelle has discovered that employees waste a lot of time looking for files on disks. She suggests that the two of you develop a strategy that shows employees the importance of organizing their files into folders, so that they can quickly locate files and work more effectively. Michelle suggests that the best place to start is with your own set of files. Although the two of you are familiar with the files on the templates disk, you could take the time needed to organize them into folders. Employees who use the templates disk can discover from your folder structure how easy it is to organize files into folders. She suggests that the two of you start by developing a diagram of the folder structure that you want to implement on the templates disk.

Like drives, folders and files are objects that serve as important tools in the Windows 95 GUI. Just as you store paper copies of documents in paper folders, you store electronic copies of documents in electronic folders. Folders allow you to organize your documents into logical groups (for example, one folder for every class you're taking) so that you can easily locate a file by looking for it in a folder containing related files. Although folders are containers for files, you can store other types of objects, such as shortcuts, within a folder. You can also store folders within a folder, just as you would store several paper folders within a hanging folder in a filing cabinet.

The Windows 95 shortcut feature fundamentally changes the way in which you work with objects on your computer. By storing shortcuts to commonly used objects, such as folders, files, and devices, within different folders, you can use the shortcut to go directly to the object. You do not have to open and close folders, or step through menus, always following the same path, to locate and use a folder, file, or device.

After Michelle and you discuss the types of files stored on the templates disk, you decide to organize the files into three groups, as shown in Figure 3-26. Since the majority of files on the diskette are templates, you plan to organize these files into a Templates folder so that employees know where to go to find the type of template they need. When they view the contents of this folder with a specific application, that application will show them only the files produced by that application. You plan to organize the other two, smaller groups of files into a new Overhead Transparencies folder and the existing Training folder. By providing employees with the necessary tools for creating presentations, you also encourage and promote small group training. All of a sudden, Michelle and you realize that the mere process of organizing files on what has been known as the master templates disk has led you to the discovery that you actually have a staff resource disk instead. By expanding the use of this disk, you can use it as a tool to increase the variety of resources that you provide staff and also to promote staff development.

Figure 3-26 ◀
Planning a
folder structure

floppy disk drive

folders for organizing
files on a floppy disk

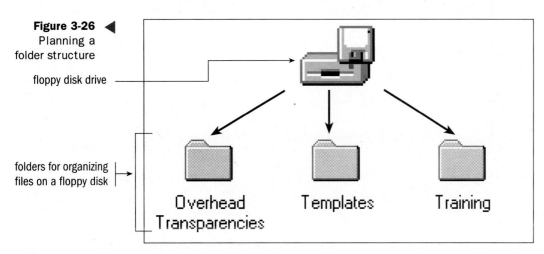

Opening a Folder

As a first step in reorganizing the templates disk, Michelle recommends that you first examine the files in the Training folder. To navigate the folder structure of a drive, you double-click the first folder you want to open. If you want to open another folder, you then double-click that folder. In this way, you navigate down the folder structure of the disk.

If you have set your window browsing option so that each window replaces the previous window, you can choose the Up One Level button 🔼 on the window toolbar to go back to the previous window and move up the folder structure of the disk. Alternatively, you can close the current window and go directly back to the desktop. If you have set your window browsing option so that a new window appears each time you open another folder, you can close the current window to go back to the previous window.

To examine the contents of the Training folder:

1. If you have already closed the floppy disk drive window and returned to the desktop, double-click the **Shortcut** to the floppy disk drive.

2. If necessary, maximize the floppy disk drive window.

3. If you do not see a toolbar in this window, click **View** then click **Toolbar**.

4. If you do not see large icons in the window, click the **Large Icons** button on the toolbar. If Large Icons is already selected, the Large Icons button will appear as if it is pressed.

5. Click **View**, point to **Arrange Icons**, then, if there is no check mark next to Auto Arrange, click **Auto Arrange**; otherwise, click **View** to close the menu.

6. Double-click the **Training** folder, then, if necessary, maximize the Training folder window. In the Training folder window, you can see the five files contained in this folder. See Figure 3-27.

Figure 3-27 ◄
Viewing the
contents of the
Training folder

files in the Training
folder

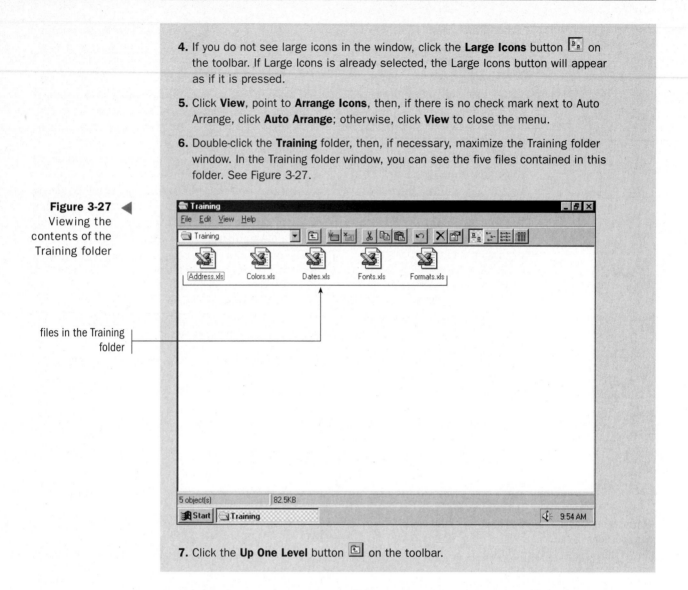

7. Click the **Up One Level** button on the toolbar.

Michelle uses these files to prepare outlines for training sessions. These files are already placed in the correct folder.

Renaming a File

Michelle wants you to change the name of one of the files so that it more accurately reflects the contents of the file. Originally, she had named it Proposal.doc because it contained a proposal for a training session on computer basics. Now, she wants to call the file Basics.doc.

HELP DESK

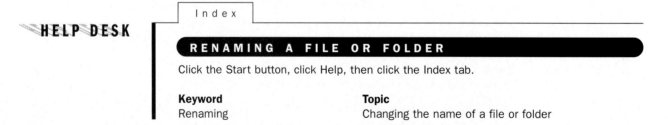

Index

RENAMING A FILE OR FOLDER

Click the Start button, click Help, then click the Index tab.

Keyword
Renaming

Topic
Changing the name of a file or folder

To rename a file:

1. Right-click the **Proposal.doc** icon, then click **Rename**. Windows 95 highlights the filename.

2. Type **Basics** then press the **Enter** key. In the Rename dialog box, Windows 95 warns you that, if you change the extension of this file, the file might become unusable, and asks you if you are sure you want to change it. What Windows 95 actually means is that, if you change the file extension and then later double-click the file's icon, it will not be able to find the original application that produced the file and might substitute another application, which might not be able to handle the file.

3. Click the **No** button. Windows 95 highlights the name again.

4. Click after the "s" in "Basics," type **.doc** (remember to type the period before "doc"), then press the **Enter** key. The new filename is now Basics.doc. See Figure 3-28.

Figure 3-28 ◀
Renaming a file

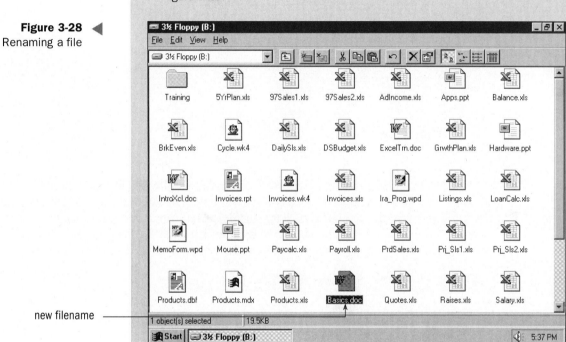

new filename ──────

Deleting a File

After you change the name of Proposal.doc to Basics.doc, Michelle asks you to delete the file named Virus.lst. She notes that there is already a copy of this file on the disk under another name, and there is no need to clutter the disk with duplicate copies of files.

To delete a file:

1. Click the **Small Icons** button [icon] on the toolbar.

2. Click the **Virus.lst** file to select it.

3. Press the **Delete** key. A Confirm File Delete dialog box appears, asking you to confirm this operation.

4. Click the **Yes** button. Windows 95 deletes the file. See Figure 3-29.

Figure 3-29 ◄
Deleting a file

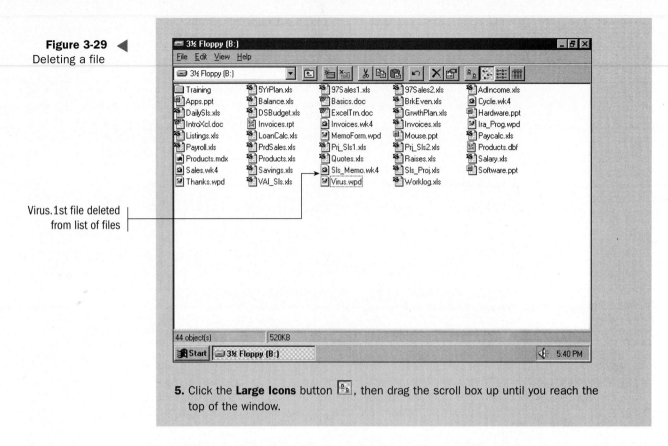

Virus.1st file deleted
from list of files

5. Click the **Large Icons** button , then drag the scroll box up until you reach the top of the window.

Michelle emphasizes that it is important to remind employees whenever possible that the two most important resources in a computer are the amount of available storage space on a hard disk and the amount of available memory. If all employees periodically set aside some time to remove extra or unneeded files from their hard disks and floppy disks, then they will not waste valuable storage space that they might need for software or other files.

Using Quick View to Examine a Presentation File

To help you reorganize the files into folders, Michelle suggests that you use the Windows 95 Quick View feature to assist you with the process of placing files in the correct folder.

Quick View lets you view the contents of a file without opening the application used to create the file. This feature is useful if you want to quickly view a file's contents to remind you what it contains. It is also useful if you are working on a computer, such as a portable computer, that does not have the application that produced a file and you want to examine that file's contents.

If you select a file, then right-click to display the shortcut menu for that file, and you will see the Quick View option on the shortcut menu. You can also select a file, select the File menu on the menu bar, and then select the Quick View option. If Quick View is not available for a particular type of file, then the shortcut menu and File menu will not display a Quick View option.

HELP DESK

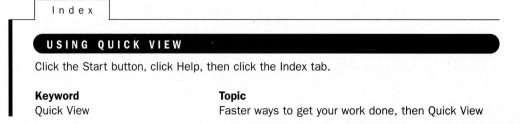

Index

USING QUICK VIEW

Click the Start button, click Help, then click the Index tab.

Keyword	Topic
Quick View	Faster ways to get your work done, then Quick View

Michelle suggests that you place the files produced with Microsoft PowerPoint in the Training folder, along with some of the Microsoft Word and Microsoft Excel files, since those files are primarily used for training. She mentions that the PowerPoint files have the file extension PPT. She suggests that you try the Quick View feature on one of the PowerPoint files so that you know how it works.

To use the Quick View feature, it must be installed on the computer system that you use. Quick View is one of the applications in the Windows 95 Accessories group. If it is not installed on your computer, then you will not be able to complete this section until you install it. If it is not available, skip to the next section.

To view the contents of a file:

1. Right-click the **Apps.ppt** icon, then click **Quick View** on the shortcut menu. Windows 95 displays an Apps.ppt - Quick View window. See Figure 3-30. This file contains a PowerPoint presentation used to produce an overhead transparency. Notice that you see the formatted document in its final form. If you click the Open File for Editing button, or select Open File for Editing on the File menu, then Windows 95 opens the document in the application that produced it. However, for this feature to work, you must have the application on your computer system.

Figure 3-30 ◀
A Quick View window

Quick View menu ——

Quick View toolbar ——

a view of a PowerPoint file

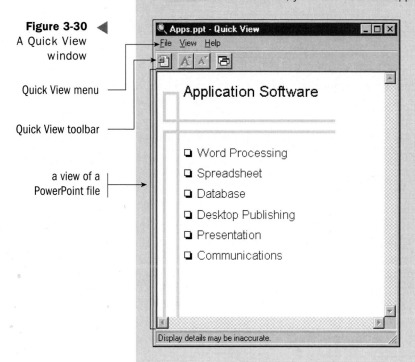

TROUBLE? If you do not see the Quick View option on the shortcut menu, then the Quick View application is not installed on your computer system, or it is not available for the type of file that you selected. Skip to the next section.

2. In the Apps.ppt - Quick View window, click **View**, then click **Page View**. You now see a full-page view of the document. See Figure 3-31. As you change views, other options on the View menu, such as Landscape, Rotate, and Font, might become available.

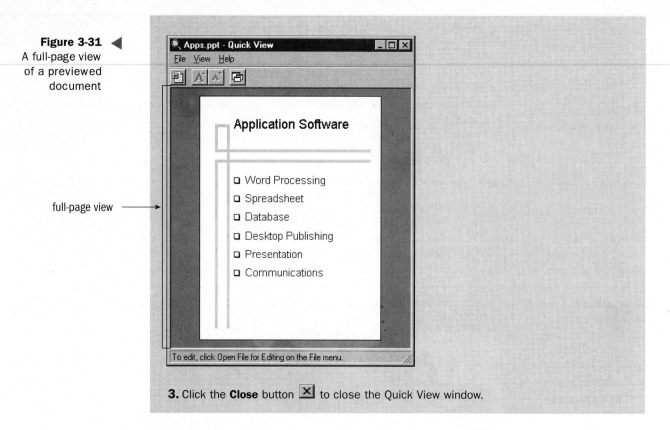

Figure 3-31
A full-page view
of a previewed
document

full-page view

3. Click the **Close** button ⊠ to close the Quick View window.

As you organize the files into folders for Michelle, you can use the Quick View feature to examine the contents of the file before you decide in which folder to place the file.

Creating a Folder

Now that you are familiar with how to open folders and view files, you are ready to organize the files into folders for easy access. You begin by creating the additional folders that Michelle and you chose for the files on the templates disk.

Before you create a folder, you should make sure you are positioned at the correct level of the folder structure of a drive so that the new folder is in the right place. If you want to add the folder to a drive, open the drive's folder, then create the new folder. The **drive folder** is the first folder created on a disk or drive by a formatting utility. When you open a drive folder, you are viewing the contents of that disk drive. If you want to add a new folder to an existing folder, open the drive folder, open an existing folder within the drive folder, then create the new folder.

Since the two additional folders you want to create for the templates diskette must be at the same level as the Training folder, you must be working in the drive folder.

To create a new folder:

1. Click the **Training folder** icon to select it.

2. Click **File**, point to **New**, then click **Folder**. Windows 95 creates the new folder, and adjusts your view so that you can see the new folder at the bottom of the drive window. See Figure 3-32. Windows 95 gives it the name New Folder, and highlights the name so that you can replace it with one of your own. Since this folder will store the template files, you want to name it Templates.

Figure 3-32 ◀
Creating a new
folder

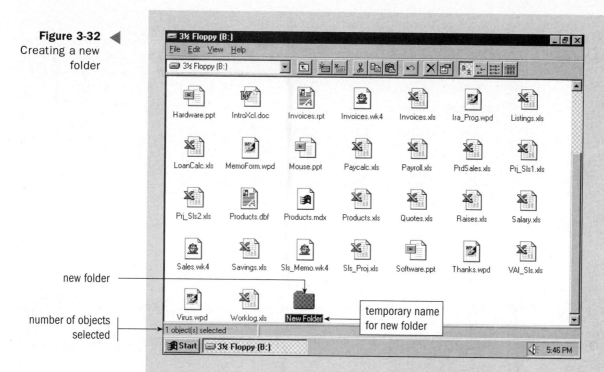

new folder

number of objects
selected

temporary name
for new folder

1 object(s) selected

TROUBLE? If you open the File menu and find two New commands, or if you
click a New command and Windows 95 opens, or attempts to open, PowerPoint,
then the Apps.ppt file icon is still selected, and Windows assumes you want to
open a new file similar to the one that is selected. Select the Training folder icon
before you select New on the File menu. Then Windows 95 knows you want to
create a folder.

3. Type **Templates** then press the **Enter** key. You have now named the folder. Note
that the filename contains nine characters, one more character than the MS-DOS
operating system permits. As noted earlier, Windows 95 allows you to create filenames with up to 255 characters. Now, you can create the third folder. This folder
will store overhead transparencies.

4. Click **File**, point to **New**, click **Folder**, and when the new folder appears, type
Transparencies then press the **Enter** key. After naming the new folder, you realize
you made a mistake. You wanted to name it Overhead Transparencies.

5. Right-click the **Transparencies** folder, then click **Rename**. Windows 95 highlights
the folder name.

6. Click at the beginning of the folder name, type **Overhead**, press the **Spacebar** to
insert a space between "Overhead" and "Transparencies;" then press the **Enter** key.

Note that you might not see the word "Transparencies" within the window, but it
is still part of the folder name.

To make it easier to work with the new folders, you want to place them next to
the Training folder.

7. Click **View**, point to **Arrange Icons**, then click **by Name**. Windows rearranges the
folders on the disk. See Figure 3-33.

Figure 3-33
Rearranging
folders and files
by filename

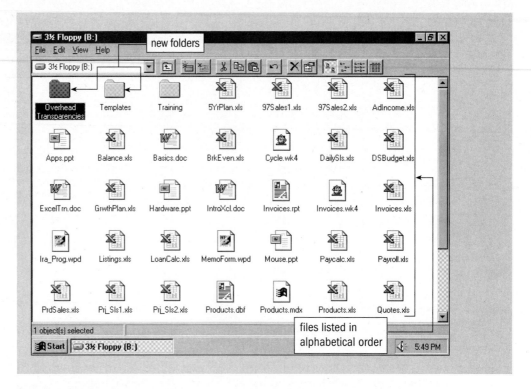

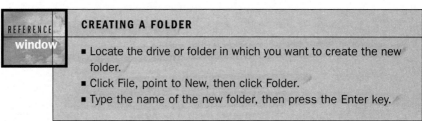

REFERENCE
window

CREATING A FOLDER

- Locate the drive or folder in which you want to create the new folder.
- Click File, point to New, then click Folder.
- Type the name of the new folder, then press the Enter key.

Now you have completed the second step in reorganizing the disk by creating the additional folders you need.

Moving Files

Michelle has revamped her list of files stored on the disk and indicated the folder in which to place each file. There are several ways to move files from one location to another, and which method you use depends on the circumstances. Dragging is often quickest for a single file when both the file and the destination folder are visible; a selection rectangle is useful for dragging a group of adjacent files. Cut and paste is useful when you want to move files that are scattered throughout a folder. You can manage files most efficiently by learning a few quick selection methods that help you highlight several or all files at once, either grouped or scattered. Try using these methods to rearrange the file structure on your staff resources disk.

Dragging a File to a Folder

The first file on Michelle's list is 5YrPlan.xls, which she wants you to move to the Overhead Transparencies folder. To move a file to a folder, you can drag the file and place it on top of the folder. Since the file 5YrPlan.xls is right next to the folders, you can quickly drag it to the folder where you want to store it.

To move a file:

1. Drag the **5YrPlan.xls** icon to the Overhead Transparencies folder, as shown in Figure 3-34. Windows briefly displays a Moving dialog box, and moves the file to the Overhead Transparencies folder. Since it occurred so quickly, you want to verify that it worked.

Figure 3-34
Dragging a file
to a folder

ghost of file icon on
top of folder icon

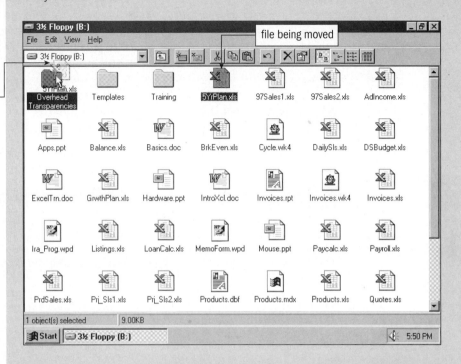

2. Double-click the **Overhead Transparencies** folder. In this folder window, you see the file that Windows 95 moved to this folder. See Figure 3-35.

Figure 3-35
Contents of
Overhead
Transparencies
folder

file dragged to
Overhead
Transparencies folder

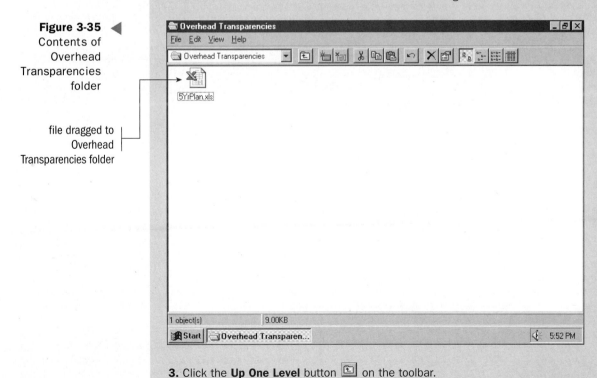

3. Click the **Up One Level** button on the toolbar.

Moving Groups of Files Using the Selection Outline

The next set of files on Michelle's lists are four Lotus 1-2-3 files, all of which must be moved to the Overhead Transparencies folder. You can select and move a group of files to a folder, rather than move each file one at a time. First, you arrange the files in an order that makes them easier to select as a group. If you choose the option to arrange files by Type, then Windows 95 arranges the files by the type of application that produced the file. Files with the same file extension are grouped together, and arranged in alphabetical order within the group. Next you select the files by drawing a selection rectangle around the files with the mouse. After you release the mouse, Windows 95 highlights the selected files. Once you select the files, you point to one of the selected files, then drag it to the folder. Once you highlight the folder, you release the mouse button and Windows 95 moves all the files.

HELP DESK

Index

USING DRAG AND DROP

Click the Start button, click Help, then click the Index tab.

Keyword
Drag and drop

Topic
Overview: Using drag and drop

Before you move the Lotus 1-2-3 files with the drag-and-drop method, you need to rearrange the files so that you can easily select them as a group.

To select and move a group of files:

1. Click **View**, point to **Arrange Icons**, then click **by Type**. Now, the file icons are arranged by file type; in other words, in alphabetical order by the applications that produced them. See Figure 3-36. The four Lotus 1-2-3 files are grouped together.

Figure 3-36 ◀
Arranging folders and files in order by file type

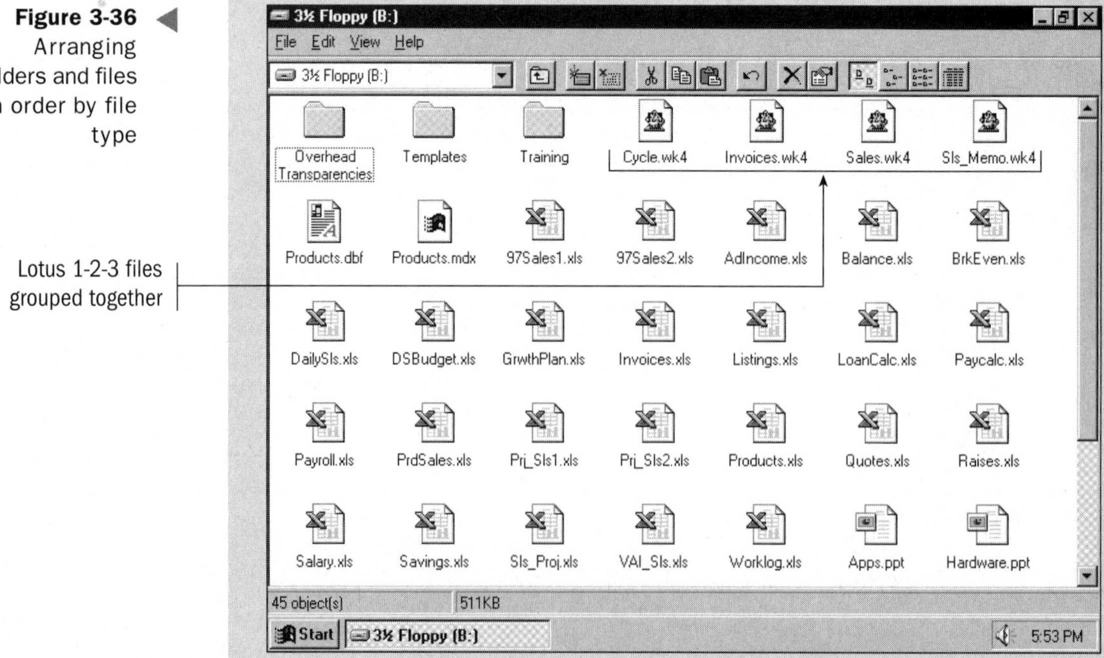

Lotus 1-2-3 files grouped together

2. Point to the white space to the left and above the Cycle.wk4 icon, drag to draw a selection rectangle around the next three Lotus 1-2-3 files (with the file extension wk4) on the first row, as shown in Figure 3-37, then release the mouse button. As you drag, Windows 95 displays a dotted rectangle around the group of files you are selecting, and highlights each selected file icon and name.

Figure 3-37 ◀
Selecting a group of files to move

number of objects selected

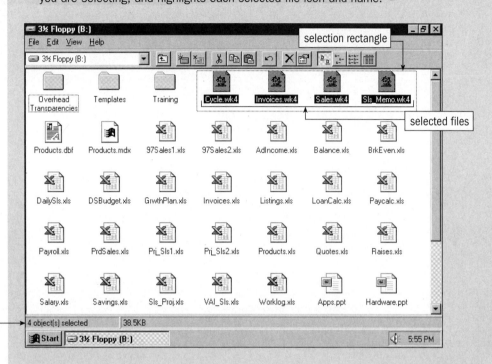

3. Point to **Cycle.wk4**, drag that icon to the Overhead Transparencies folder, as shown in Figure 3-38, and once the Overhead Transparencies folder is highlighted, release the mouse button. As you drag, you will see outlines of all the selected file icons. Windows 95 displays a Moving dialog box, lists the original location and name of each file that it is moving, and identifies the new location for each file.

Figure 3-38 ◀
Dragging a group of files to a folder

file icon dragged to folder

outlines of other selected files

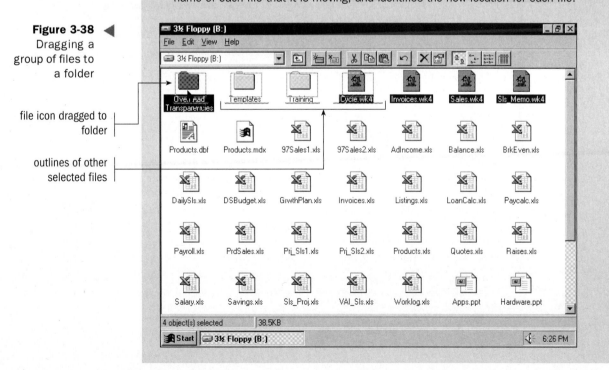

4. Double-click the **Overhead Transparencies** folder, then, if necessary, maximize the window. After the Overhead Templates folder opens, you see all the files that you just moved. See Figure 3-39.

Figure 3-39
Contents of
Overhead
Transparencies
folder

files dragged as a
group to folder

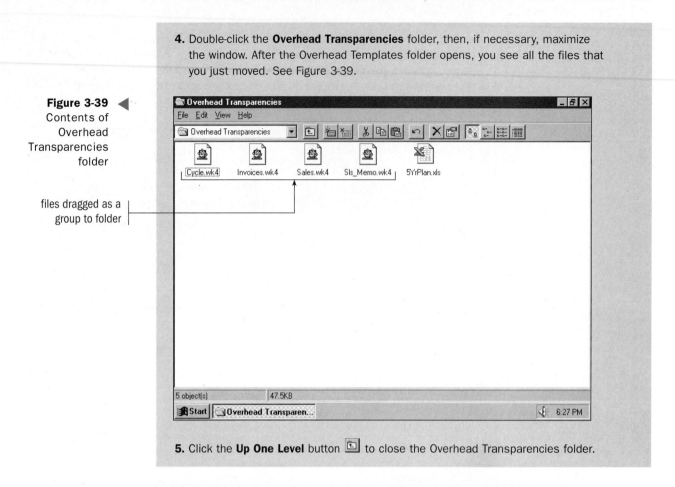

5. Click the **Up One Level** button to close the Overhead Transparencies folder.

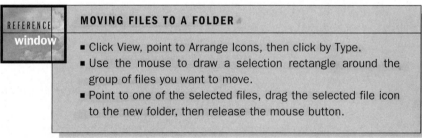

REFERENCE
window

MOVING FILES TO A FOLDER

- Click View, point to Arrange Icons, then click by Type.
- Use the mouse to draw a selection rectangle around the group of files you want to move.
- Point to one of the selected files, drag the selected file icon to the new folder, then release the mouse button.

Using Cut and Paste to Move Adjacent Files

After looking at Michelle's list, you notice that you next have to move the Microsoft Excel files to the Templates folder. However, this time there are many more files to move at once.

To make this process easier, you first change to List view so that you can see many more files at the same time. Then, you arrange the files by Type so that Microsoft Excel files with the file extension XLS are grouped together so you can select them by group. Although you could drag the files as a group to the folder where you want to store them, it is easier to cut and paste. To use this approach, you cut the files from their original location, open the folder where you want to store the files, then paste them into the new folder.

To move a group of files:

1. Click the **List** button ⊞ on the toolbar. The files and their icons are listed in columns across the width of the window.

   TROUBLE? If you do not see a toolbar in your drive or folder window, click View then Toolbar.

2. Click **View**, point to **Arrange Icons**, then click **by Type**. Now, the file icons are arranged by file type; in other words, in alphabetical order by the applications that produced them. Next, you want to select the Microsoft Excel files.

3. Click **97Sales1.xls**, then press and hold the **Shift** button and click **Worklog.xls**. Windows 95 selects all the files between 97Sales1.xls and Worklog.xls. See Figure 3-40.

Figure 3-40 ◄
Selecting a group of files in List view

click first file icon →

selected files →

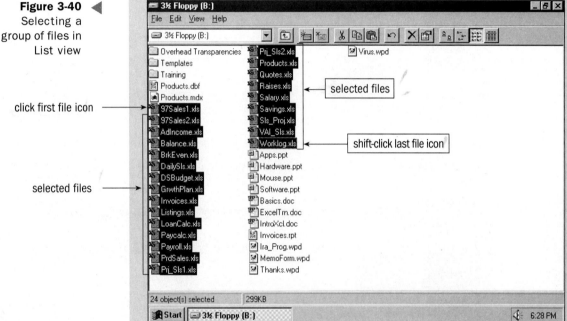

Pressing the Shift key and clicking the mouse is called the **shift-click** method. This technique is commonly used in many Windows applications to select adjacent objects or a block of text.

4. Click the **Cut** button ✂ on the toolbar. Windows 95 displays a ghost of the cut files. See Figure 3-41.

Figure 3-41 ◀
Using cut and
paste to move
files

ghosts of cut files ⟶

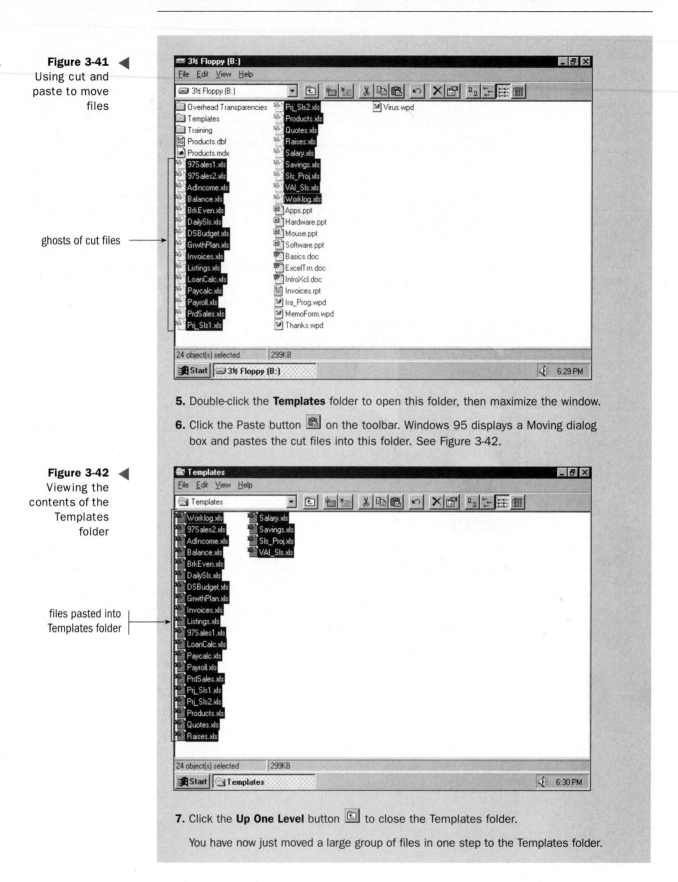

5. Double-click the **Templates** folder to open this folder, then maximize the window.

6. Click the Paste button 🖹 on the toolbar. Windows 95 displays a Moving dialog
box and pastes the cut files into this folder. See Figure 3-42.

Figure 3-42 ◀
Viewing the
contents of the
Templates
folder

files pasted into
Templates folder

7. Click the **Up One Level** button 🖻 to close the Templates folder.

You have now just moved a large group of files in one step to the Templates folder.

MOVING A GROUP OF FILES TO A FOLDER

- Select the type of view you want to use.
- Select the way in which you want to arrange the files by using Arrange Icons on the View menu.
- Click the name of the first file in the group, then press and hold the Shift key and click the name of the last file in the group.
- Click the Cut button on the toolbar.
- Double-click the folder you want to move the files to.
- Click the Paste button on the toolbar.

Moving Non-adjacent Files

You notice that the next set of files on Michelle's list have different file extensions, and therefore they cannot be arranged so that they are adjacent to each other. You ask Michelle if it's possible to select and move them at the same time. She points out that the easiest way to select these four files is to press and hold the Ctrl key while you click on the icon for each file.

To move a collection of files:

1. If necessary, click the **Large Icons** button on the toolbar.

2. Click the **Invoices.rpt** icon.

3. Press and hold the **Ctrl** key.

4. Click the **Thanks.wpd** icon, then click the **Virus.wpd** icon.

   TROUBLE? If you select the wrong icon, then click it a second time while holding the Ctrl key, and Windows 95 will remove it from the selection.

5. Release the Ctrl key. You have selected three files, as shown in Figure 3-43.

Figure 3-43
Selecting a
collection of
files

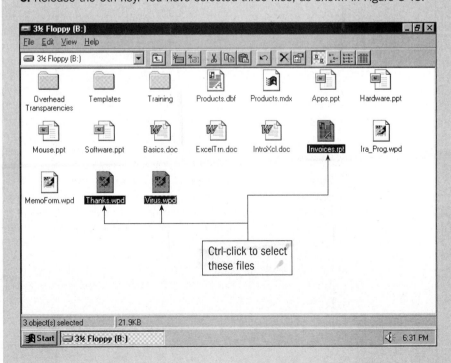

6. Click the **Cut** button on the toolbar. Windows 95 displays ghosts of the selected files.

7. Double-click the **Overhead Transparencies** folder.

8. Click the **Paste** button on the toolbar. Windows 95 pastes the four selected files into this folder.

9. Click the **Up One Level** button to close the Overhead Transparencies folder.

Next, you want to move another collection of files to the Templates folder using the same approach.

To move another collection of files to another folder:

1. Click the **Products.dbf** icon.

2. Press and hold the **Ctrl** key.

3. Click the **Products.mdx** icon, click the **Ira_Prog.wpd** icon, then click the **MemoForm.wpd** icon.

4. Release the **Ctrl** key.

5. Click the **Cut** button on the toolbar. Windows 95 displays ghosts for the file icons.

6. Double-click the **Templates** folder.

7. Click the **Paste** button on the toolbar. Windows 95 pastes the cut files into the Templates folder.

8. Click the **Up One Level** button to close the Templates folder.

Moving the Remaining Files Using Select All

To move the remaining files on Michelle's list to the Training folder, you can use the Select All option on the Edit menu to select the files, then use drag-and-drop or cut-and-paste to move the files. Now you are ready to move the last set of files as a group.

To select and move all files:

1. Click **Edit** then click **Select All**. All the folders and files in the current window are selected. You need to remove the folders from the selection by "unselecting" them.

2. Press and hold the **Ctrl** key and click the **Overhead Transparencies** folder, the **Templates** folder, and the **Training** folder. Now, only the files in this window are selected.

3. Drag one of the selected file icons to the Templates folder, then release the mouse. Windows 95 displays a Moving dialog box, and moves the remaining files. All of a sudden, you realize you made a mistake! You meant to move these files to the Training folder. You can use the Windows 95 Undo feature to reverse folder and file operations.

4. Click the **Undo** button (now Undo Move) on the toolbar. Windows 95 moves the files back to their original location, then deselects them. Now, you have to repeat the selection.

Instead of using the Undo button, you can use the Undo command on the Edit menu. This command, as well as the ToolTip for the Undo button, always describes the last operation you can undo. For example, if you moved files, the Edit command shows the Undo Move option.

5. Click **Edit** then click **Select All**.

6. Press and hold the **Ctrl** key, and click the **Overhead Transparencies** folder, the **Templates** folder, then the **Training** folder, then release the Ctrl key.

7. Drag one of the selected file icons to the Training folder.

8. Double-click the **Training** folder, then maximize the window. Windows 95 has moved the remaining files to this folder.

9. Click the **Up One Level** button 🖻 on the toolbar to go back to the drive folder. The current drive now has only three folders in its root directory. See Figure 3-44.

Figure 3-44 ◄
Folders on
floppy disk

you organized all the
files into these folders

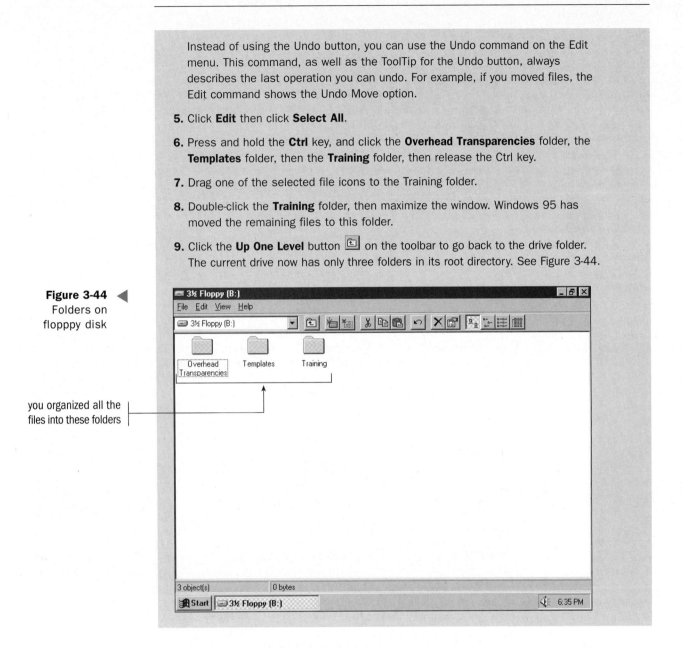

You have successfully reorganized all the files on the templates disk for Michelle! Now, other employees who rely on this diskette and its files can go directly to the folder that contains the set of files that they want to work with.

Copying a File from Folder to Folder

Earlier, you moved the file 5YrPlan.xls to the Overhead Transparencies folder so that Michelle and you could locate the file whenever you needed to make a transparency. Michelle wants to place a copy of this file in the Templates folder so that employees can easily locate this template and use it to build Five Year Growth Plans for Delta Oil.

If you need to copy a file from one folder to another folder, you can use copy-and-paste. After you select a file and then select the Copy option, Windows 95 places a duplicate of the original file on the Windows Clipboard so that you can paste it on a disk or in a folder where you need it. The copy that you paste in a new location is a completely separate file. It is not a shortcut, and it is not linked to the original file. You can work on the duplicate without affecting the original.

Now you are ready to make a copy of 5YrPlan.xls in the Overhead Transparencies folder, and place the new copy in the Templates folder.

To copy a file:

1. Double-click the **Overhead Transparencies** folder to open this folder.

2. Click the **5YrPlan.xls** icon.

3. Click the **Copy** button 🖹 on the toolbar. Windows 95 places a copy of the 5YrPlan.xls file on the Clipboard.

4. Click the **Up One Level** button 🖿 to return to the drive folder.

5. Double-click the **Templates** folder to open this folder.

6. Click the **Paste** button 🖹 on the toolbar. Windows 95 pastes a copy of the 5YrPlan.xls file in the Templates folder. See Figure 3-45.

Figure 3-45 ◄
Using copy-and-paste to copy a file to a folder

file copied from
Overhead
Transparencies folder

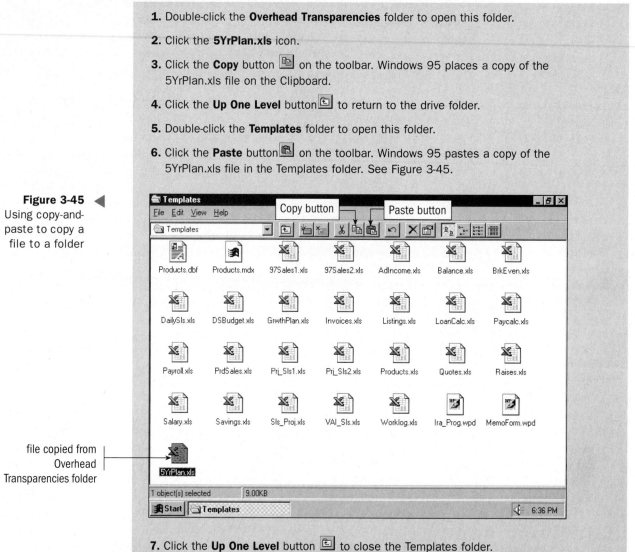

7. Click the **Up One Level** button 🖿 to close the Templates folder.

REFERENCE window	**COPYING A FILE FROM FOLDER TO FOLDER**
	▪ Select the file you want to copy, then click the Copy button.
	▪ If necessary, click the Up One Level button to return to the previous folder.
	▪ Double-click the folder that you want to copy the file to.
	▪ Click the Paste button.

The staff resource disk is now organized more efficiently. Staff wanting to find a file quickly will not have to scroll through a long set of files, but can move immediately to the folder they need and locate the file there.

Printing a Copy of the Resource Disk's Folder Structure

Before you start another task, you want to document the changes that you have made to the staff resource disk. If you reorganize the folder structure of a disk, especially a hard disk, it is a good idea to document the folder structure before and after you reorganize it on the disk. If you need to rebuild the folder structure or return to your original folder structure, then you have a record from which you can work. One way to document important changes is to print a copy of the folder structure using the Paint accessory included with Windows 95.

Michelle suggests that you store a copy of the folder structure shown in the My Computer window on the Clipboard, then open Paint and paste the contents of the Clipboard into Paint's drawing area. Then you can print your documentation.

To document the folder structure:

1. Press and hold down the **Alt** key and press the **Print Screen** key. Although nothing appears to happen, a copy of the active window was just placed on the Clipboard. Now that you have a copy of the My Computer window in the Clipboard, you can paste the image into Paint and print it.

   TROUBLE? If you can't find the Print Screen key on your keyboard, you might have a key labeled "Prt Scr." If you are unsure about which key to use, or if you discover the key does not work as you expect, then ask your instructor or technical support person for assistance.

2. Click **Start**, point to **Programs**, point to **Accessories**, then click **Paint**.

   TROUBLE? If you can't find Paint on the Accessories menu, it's possible that your site didn't install Paint. Check the Accessories menu again and, if the WordPad accessory is installed, you can use it instead of Paint. If you cannot find either accessory, ask your instructor or technical support person for a suggestion on which application to use. If you are using your own computer, you can use the Windows 95 Setup disk to find and install the Paint and WordPad accessories.

3. Click **Edit**, then click **Paste**.

   TROUBLE? If a message box appears asking to enlarge the bitmap, click the Yes button.

   The contents of the Clipboard appear in the Paint window, as shown in Figure 3-46.

Figure 3-46 ◀
Pasting an
image from the
Clipboard into
Paint

image of folders in
floppy disk drive
window

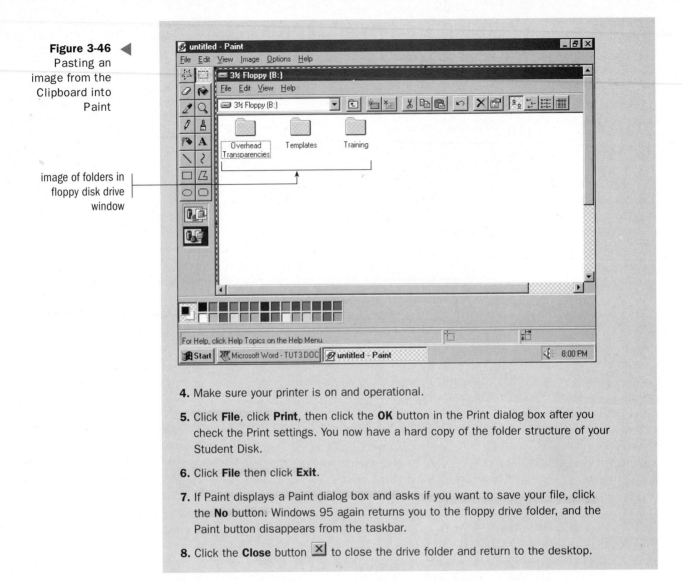

4. Make sure your printer is on and operational.

5. Click **File**, click **Print**, then click the **OK** button in the Print dialog box after you check the Print settings. You now have a hard copy of the folder structure of your Student Disk.

6. Click **File** then click **Exit**.

7. If Paint displays a Paint dialog box and asks if you want to save your file, click the **No** button. Windows 95 again returns you to the floppy drive folder, and the Paint button disappears from the taskbar.

8. Click the **Close** button ⊠ to close the drive folder and return to the desktop.

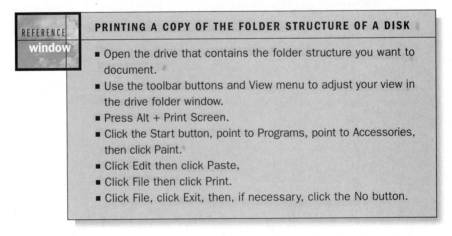

REFERENCE window

PRINTING A COPY OF THE FOLDER STRUCTURE OF A DISK

- Open the drive that contains the folder structure you want to document.
- Use the toolbar buttons and View menu to adjust your view in the drive folder window.
- Press Alt + Print Screen.
- Click the Start button, point to Programs, point to Accessories, then click Paint.
- Click Edit then click Paste.
- Click File then click Print.
- Click File, click Exit, then, if necessary, click the No button.

● ● ●

Michelle is pleased with the changes that you made to the original templates disk. Not only will it be more valuable to employees who depend on the disk, but she can now expand the use of the disk and offer new resources to the staff. She suggests that the two of you now refer to the disk as a staff resource disk to emphasize its new role.

Tutorial Assignment

Michelle receives a call from Brad Samuels, one of the staff members in the Human Resources Department at Delta Oil Company. Brad is preparing a PowerPoint presentation for an upcoming orientation session for new employees, and needs a copy of your templates disk. So that Brad can focus on just the files he needs for this new employee orientation, Michelle asks you to take a copy of the original templates disk and customize the disk for Brad. First, she wants you to create a new folder just for Brad's presentations files, and then to move the presentation files that Brad needs to that folder.

To complete this Tutorial Assignment, use the copy of the Student Disk that you made at the beginning of Tutorial 3 that you labeled "Delta Oil Templates Copy." *Do not use your Student Disk with the reorganized folder structure.*

1. Insert the copy of the Student Disk into a floppy disk drive.
2. Double-click the shortcut to your floppy disk drive.
3. If you do not see a toolbar, click View then click Toolbar.
4. Click File, point to New, then click Folder.
5. After Windows 95 creates a new folder icon, change the folder name. Type Presentations then press the Enter key.
6. Click View, point to Arrange Icons, then click by Type.
7. Click the List button on the toolbar.
8. Click the Apps.ppt file icon, then shift-click Software.ppt.
9. Click the Cut button on the toolbar.
10. Click the Large Icons button on the toolbar.
11. Double-click the Presentations folder icon.
12. Click the Paste button in the Presentations folder window.
13. Click Software.ppt, right-click Software.ppt, click Quick View, then click the Close button after you view the contents of this file.
14. Right-click Apps.ppt, click Rename on the shortcut menu, then type Applications.ppt as the new filename and press the Enter key.
15. Click the Up One Level button on the toolbar to close the Presentations folder window.
16. Click View, point to Arrange Icons, then click by Type.
17. Press Alt + Print Screen.
18. Click the Start button, point to Programs, point to Accessories, then click Paint.
19. After Paint opens, click Edit, then click Paste.
20. Make sure your printer is on and operational.
21. Click File then click Print.
22. Click File, click Exit, then click the No button.
23. Close the floppy drive window.

Case Problems

1. Creating a Folder for Reports at Peninsula Child Care Peninsula Child Care is a non-profit agency that provides child care services for parents who are reentering the job market. Federal, state, and county agencies, as well as corporations, fund their programs with special grants. To ensure that the center has sufficient funding to meet all its needs, James O'Connor prepares periodic financial reports, cashflow reports, invoice summaries, and financial projections for the staff and the Board of Directors. To simplify the task of locating the files that he needs, James has decided to create a folder just for reports.

To complete this Case Problem, use the copy of the Student Disk that you made at the beginning of Tutorial 3. *Do not use your Student Disk with the reorganized folder structure.*

1. Insert your copy of the Student Disk into a floppy disk drive.
2. Open a window for your floppy disk.

3. If necessary, display a toolbar for the drive window and change the view to Large Icons.

4. Verify that Windows 95 is using the browsing option that displays each folder in a new window.

5. Create a new folder named Reports.

6. Arrange the folders and files in order by file type.

7. Move the files named 5YrPlan.xls, Balance.xls, GrwthPln.xls, and Invoices.rpt to the Reports folder.

8. Open the Reports folder then press Alt + Print Screen.

9. Open Paint, paste the contents of the Clipboard into the drawing area, then print a copy of the Reports folder.

10. Exit Paint without saving the file.

11. Close the Reports folder and return to the desktop.

2. Creating a Folder for Financial Models at Financial Management, Inc. Financial Management, Inc. assists new business owners with the task of preparing and analyzing financial forecasts so that these individuals can build a strong foundation for their new businesses. Maria Hernandez, their senior financial analyst, has prepared a set of files that she uses to create the documents that her clients need. Maria wants to organize these files into one central folder so that she can locate the financial models she needs for different types of clients. She also wants a duplicate folder that contains the same set of files, so that she can experiment with ways to improve these models.

To complete this Case Problem, use the copy of the Student Disk that you made at the beginning of Tutorial 3. *Do not use your Student Disk with the reorganized folder structure.*

1. Insert your copy of the Student Disk into a floppy disk drive.

2. Open a window for your floppy disk.

3. If necessary, display a toolbar for the drive window and change the view to Large Icons.

4. Create two new folders, one named Models and the other named Experimental Models.

5. Arrange the folders and files in order by file type.

6. Copy the following collection of files to the Models folder: 97Sales1.xls, 97Sales2.xls, BrkEven.xls, Payroll.xls, Prj_Sls1.xls, Prj_Sls2.xls, and Sls_Prj.xls.

7. Click the Up One Level toolbar button.

8. Select the same files, then move these files to the folder named Experimental Models.

9. Arrange the folders and files in order by file type, and adjust your view so that you can see the folders on your diskette.

10. Press Alt + Print Screen.

11. Open Paint, paste the contents of the Clipboard into the drawing area, then print a copy of the view of the folders on your diskette.

12. Exit Paint without saving the file.

13. Close the floppy drive window.

3. Creating a Property Listings Folder for Midland Realty Company Midland Realty Company sells prime real estate in a rapidly growing region of California north of San Francisco. Marion Tompkins, the leading sales person on their staff, uses a laptop computer to provide clients with information on the spot. As she shows clients properties, she can use her laptop to estimate the monthly mortgage payment based on the amount of the down payment, the current interest rate, and the term of the loan. Periodically, she downloads updated listings of properties onto her laptop so that she can quickly select properties to show customers who are looking for properties within a certain price range. In addition to maintaining a duplicate copy of these important files on her hard disk, Marion also wants to store a copy of these files in a folder on a diskette so that you can work on her laptop and on her office computer. She also wants to create a shortcut to this folder.

To complete this Case Problem, use the duplicate copy of the Student Disk that you made at the beginning of Tutorial 3. *Do not use your Student Disk with the reorganized folder structure.*

1. Insert your copy of the Student Disk into a floppy disk drive.
2. Open a window for your floppy disk drive.
3. If necessary, display a toolbar and arrange the folders and files in order by file type.
4. Create a new folder named Property Listings.
5. Use drag-and-drop to move the following collection of files to the Property Listings folder: Listings.xls, LoanCalc.xls, and Savings.xls.
6. Restore the floppy drive window to its original size.
7. Right-click the Property Listings folder then drag a copy of the folder icon to the desktop, then choose the option to create a shortcut.
8. Close the window for your floppy disk drive, and return to the desktop.
9. Double-click the Shortcut to the Property Listings folder.
10. Press Alt + Print Screen.
11. Open Paint, paste the contents of the Clipboard into the drawing area, then print a copy of the files in this folder.
12. Exit Paint without saving the file.
13 Close the Property Listings folder, then delete the Property Listings folder from the desktop.

4. Creating a Paint Shortcut for Students at Middletown High School As the result of a generous donation from a local corporation, the staff at Middletown High School was able to open a new computer lab for high school students to use. Charles Prescott, a teacher in one of the design classes that uses this lab, wants to create a shortcut to the Paint accessory for his students.

1. Open the My Computer window, then open a window for drive C.
2. Locate, and open, the Windows folder on drive C.
3. Choose the viewing option that arranges folders and files in order by file type.
4. Locate the program named Pbrush.exe.
5. Drag the Pbrush.exe icon, which appears as an artist's palette, to the desktop and create a shortcut to this program.
6. Close the window on drive C, and return to the desktop.
7. Open the Properties dialog box for the Pbruh.exe shortcut icon, and click the Shortcut tab to select it.
8. Press Alt + Print Screen to copy the shortcut Properties dialog box to the Clipboard.
9. Close the Shorcut Properties dialog box.
10. Double-click the Shortcut to the Paint accessory.
11. Paste the contents of the Clipboard into the drawing area, then print a copy of the dialog box.
12. Exit Paint without saving the file.

Locating Files with Windows Explorer

Tracking Financial Documents at MultiGrain Cereals

In this tutorial you will:

- Navigate the Windows 95 filing system
- Use Find to locate folders and files
- Open Windows Explorer
- View the folder structure of a computer
- Search for files using wildcards
- Use date and advanced options to find files
- Use the Explorer to create, copy, and delete folders
- Move and copy files with Windows Explorer
- Create a shortcut to Windows Explorer

CASE

MultiGrain Cereals Co.

MultiGrain Cereals produces five popular types of cereals for the United States market—Pinyon Pine Delight, Hazelnut Crunch, Golden Currant Crisp, Sugar Maple Flakes, and Blueberry Almond Crunch. Over the last 10 years, its sales of these products have increased at an average rate of 12.5% per year. Since recent market research studies show that customers increasingly prefer a variety of choices in the products available to them, MultiGrain Cereals has decided to develop new varieties of cereals.

Jason Mulholland works as an assistant financial analyst in the company's finance department. Jason and his supervisor are busy preparing sales summaries, analyses, and projections to provide the management at MultiGrain Cereals with the information that it needs to expand its operations and introduce new products. To produce the documents needed by management, Jason must locate and pull together information from a variety of documents stored in different files on his computer system. Then, he will use several different applications, along with his own template files, to prepare the new financial analyses and projections.

Navigating My Computer

Jason's supervisor, Nadine Alexander, recently ordered Jason a Pentium computer that runs Windows 95, and the Data Systems Department has loaded the applications that Jason needs. Jason is eager to learn how Windows 95 handles the software he uses to get his work done.

When you install a software product on your computer, that product's installation program creates one or more folders on your hard drive that contains the software and its supporting files. Jason uses Microsoft Office Professional, which contains four or five separate applications. When it was installed on his system, it created a folder named MSOffice, which contained additional folders, called subfolders, for each of the applications in this office suite.

Likewise, when he installed Windows 95 on his computer, it created a folder named Windows, along with a variety of subfolders, such as Command, Desktop, Help, Start Menu, and System, to store related files together. Figure 4-1 illustrates the types of relationships that exist between these and other folders.

Figure 4-1 ◀

A partial view of the hierarchy of folders within the Windows folder

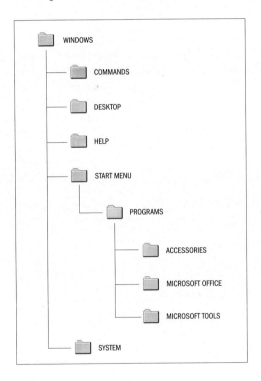

Although you can store your document files in application folders, you can also create folders to help organize your files on a computer. For example, you might organize your files by project, client, account, or document types so that you can easily and quickly locate a file.

Windows 95 uses an application's full path to locate and then to load the file that contains the program instructions for that application. Similarly, if you want to use a specific document file, Windows 95 uses that file's full path to locate and then open the file. The **full path** is the notation that identifies the drive and sequence of folders that lead to a folder or a file. Windows 95 refers to the full path as the **MS-DOS path** because this feature was introduced in and used by the MS-DOS operating system.

For example, if you want to start the popular spreadsheet application, Microsoft Excel, Windows 95 must be able to locate the Excel program file, which is named Excel.exe. The default installation stores this file in the Excel folder, which by default is stored in the MSOffice folder on your hard disk. The full path for this program file in a default installation on the drive C is:

C:\MSOffice\Excel\Excel.exe

The first piece of information in the full path is the name of the drive where the application is stored. The first backslash immediately after the drive name refers to the first folder created on drive C after formatting the disk. Within this folder is the MSOffice folder, which contains all the subfolders and files for the applications that come with this office suite. Since Microsoft Excel is one of these applications, you find an Excel subfolder within the MSOffice folder. Finally, within the Excel subfolder is the actual program file, Excel.exe. In a path, the folder name, subfolder name, and filename are separated from each other by a backslash symbol (\). The full path is important because it describes the *exact* location of an object on a computer system.

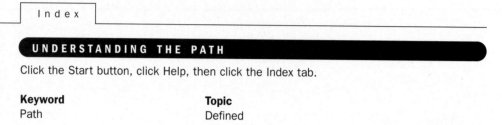

HELP DESK

Index

UNDERSTANDING THE PATH

Click the Start button, click Help, then click the Index tab.

Keyword	**Topic**
Path	Defined

In the Windows 95 graphical operating environment, the path actually starts with the Desktop, and then proceeds to My Computer before it reaches the drive, because there could be several drives available to a computer. Figure 4-2 shows the location of the Microsoft Excel application within the Windows 95 operating environment.

Figure 4-2
The path to the Microsoft Excel 5.0 for Windows application file

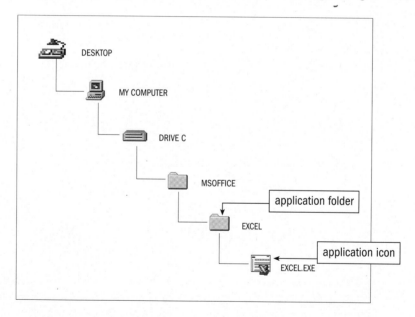

The Windows 95 operating system makes it easy for you to visualize following a path from the Desktop to a file. In this example, you access the program file Excel.exe by first opening My Computer on the desktop. Next, you open drive C. Then, you locate and open the MSOffice folder. Next, you locate and open the Excel subfolder. Finally, you locate the application icon for the file Excel.exe. You use the same approach to locate other types of files, including document files.

Jason uses Excel regularly to create financial spreadsheets. Before he starts locating and printing financial statements for management, he wants you to verify that the Arial font, the standard font he uses for most of his printed documents, has been loaded on his computer. He asks you to print a sample of the Arial font for him. So that you have a frame of reference as you navigate the folder structure, he suggests that you also display the full MS-DOS path name.

If you are working on a networked computer that does not have a drive C, then ask your instructor or technical support person for the name of the network drive that contains the Windows folder and the Fonts subfolder.

To navigate the folder structure using the MS-DOS path name:

1. Make sure you see the Windows 95 desktop.

2. Double-click the **My Computer** icon, then maximize the My Computer window. Before you continue to navigate the folder structure, check your view settings so they match the figures in this tutorial.

3. If you do not see a toolbar, click **View**, then click **Toolbar**.

4. Click **View** then click **Options**. The Options dialog box opens, and you see the browsing options on the Folder tab. See Figure 4-3.

Figure 4-3 ◀
Options dialog
box

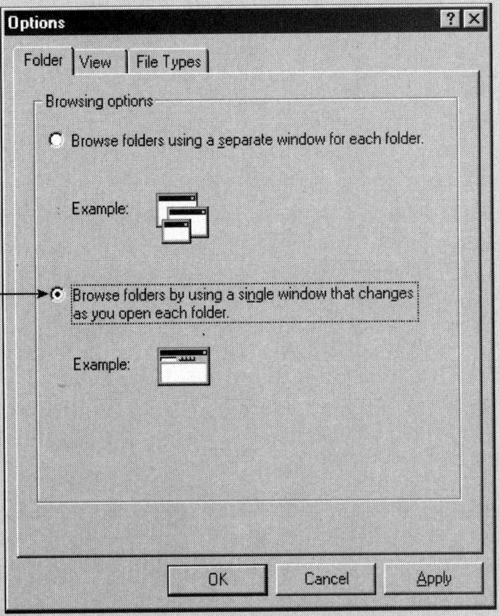

choose this option to
browse with a single
window

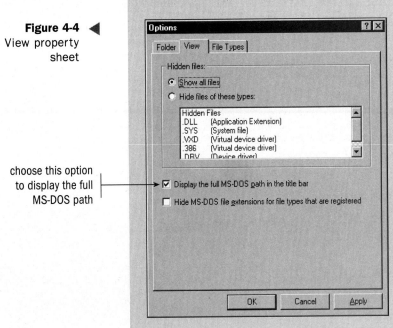

5. If it is not already selected, click the **Browse folders by using a single window that changes as you open each folder** radio button.

6. Click the **View** tab. On the View property sheet, you have an option for displaying the MS-DOS path. See Figure 4-4.

Figure 4-4 ◀
View property
sheet

choose this option
to display the full
MS-DOS path

7. If it is not already selected, click the **Display the full MS-DOS path in the title bar** check box.

8. If it is selected, click the **Hide MS-DOS file extensions for file types that are registered** check box to remove the check mark.

9. If necessary, in the Hidden files section, click the **Show all files** radio button to select this option, then click the **OK** button.

Now that you have specified the settings you need for each window, you can locate the Fonts folder.

To continue the navigation of the folder structure:

1. After you return to the My Computer window, double-click the **disk drive** icon for drive C. On the title bar of the drive window, you see the current path, C:\. This path tells you that you are in the first folder created on drive C after the disk was originally formatted. Like MS-DOS, Windows uses the \ (backslash symbol) to identify the first folder on a disk. You also see the subfolders on drive C.

   TROUBLE? If your computer does not have a drive C, then double-click the network drive that contains the Windows 95 program files. If you do not know the name of this drive, ask your instructor or technical support person.

2. If necessary, scroll down the drive window and locate the Windows folder.

3. Double-click the **Windows** folder.

4. If necessary, click the **Large Icons** button 🔲 on the toolbar. In the Windows folder, you see subfolders and files. See Figure 4-5. Your folder names might differ from those shown in the figure. Note that the MS-DOS path for the Windows folder is C:\WINDOWS. Also, as you open each window, Windows 95 places a button on the taskbar with the MS-DOS path.

Figure 4-5 ◀
Windows folder

MS-DOS path

drive

main folder on drive

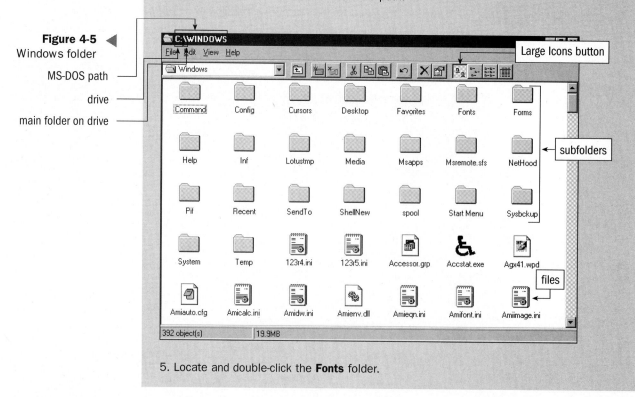

5. Locate and double-click the **Fonts** folder.

In the Fonts folder window, Windows 95 displays icons for the individual font files. See Figure 4-6. Your set of fonts might differ from those shown in the figure. If the Arial font is installed on your computer, you see a file icon labeled Arial. The MS-DOS path for the Fonts folder is C:\WINDOWS\FONTS.

Figure 4-6 ◄
Fonts folder

MS-DOS path

current folder

Arial font file

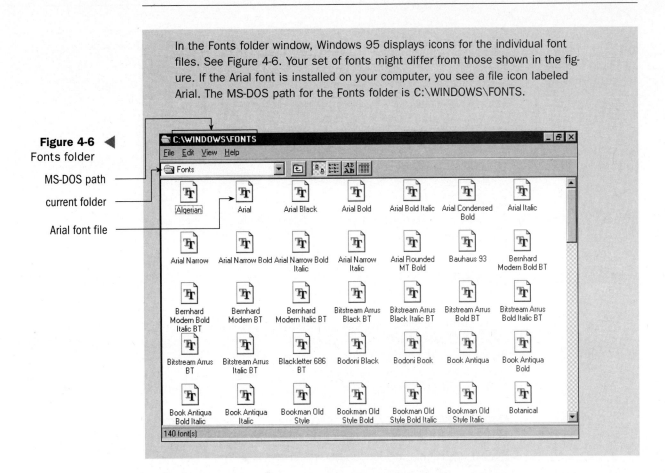

Next, you want to open the Arial font file and print a sample of the design style for this font.

To print a copy of the design style for the Arial font:

1. Double-click the **Arial** icon, then maximize the Arial (True Type) window. This window contains information about this font, shows the characters available in this typeface, and then illustrates samples of different point sizes. See Figure 4-7.

Figure 4-7 ◄
Arial (TrueType)
window

character set

examples of various
point sizes

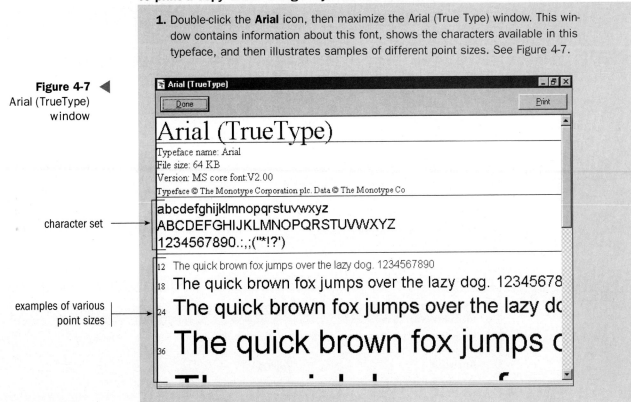

TROUBLE? If your computer does not have the Arial font file, then choose another font file.

2. Make sure your printer is on and operational.

3. Click the **Print** button, click the **OK** button in the Print dialog box.

4. Click the **Done** button to close this window. You return to the Fonts folder.

5. Click the **Up One Level** button 🔼 on the toolbar. You return to the Windows folder.

6. Click the **Up One Level** button 🔼 on the toolbar. You return to the highest-level folder on drive C.

7. Click the **Up One Level** button 🔼 on the toolbar to return to the My Computer folder.

8. Click the **Close** button ❎ to close the My Computer window. You return to the desktop.

As you close each window, you step up the folder structure and return to the parent folder. The **parent folder** is the folder above the current folder in the folder structure of a drive. For example, the parent folder for the Fonts subfolder is the Windows folder. If you want to close a set of open windows that originated from the same window and return directly to the desktop, you can press the Shift key and click the Close button at the same time.

REFERENCE window

DISPLAYING THE MS-DOS PATH

- Double-click the My Computer icon.
- Click View then click Options.
- Click the View tab in the Options dialog box.
- Click the Display the full MS-DOS path check box in the title bar to select this option.
- Close the Options dialog box.

Jason can use the same process to navigate the folder structure of his disk as he looks for important financial documents. As he looks for files that he needs, he can use the file viewing option that displays the path on the title bar of each folder's window so that he knows exactly where he is within the folder structure of a disk.

Navigating Folders with Windows Explorer

Jason has told you that Windows 95 includes a tool called **Windows Explorer**, which helps you navigate the folder structure of your computer. You and he decide to take a look.

Windows Explorer displays the contents of your computer, including drives, folders, subfolders, and files, in a diagrammatic representation of the hierarchy, or order and relationship, of your computer's resources. It also lets you move, cut, copy, and paste folders and files without having to open multiple windows.

HELP DESK

Index

USING WINDOWS EXPLORER

Click the Start button, click Help, then click the Index tab.

Keyword
Windows Explorer

Topics
The new look and feel of Windows, then
Windows Explorer

Jason and you use Windows Explorer to study the folder structure of Jason's new computer from top to bottom.

To open Windows Explorer:

1. From the desktop, click the **Start** button.

2. Point to **Programs** on the Start menu and, when the Programs menu appears, click **Windows Explorer**. The Windows Explorer title bar informs you that you are exploring the highest level folder on your hard disk drive.

3. If necessary, click the **Large Icons** button [icon]

4. Maximize the Exploring - C:\ window. In the All Folders window, you have an overview of the organization of your entire computer. See Figure 4-8. Although the details of your view might differ from those shown in this figure, you will find many of the same components. Your view of the information in the Contents window on the right depends on the view options and settings that you specify.

Figure 4-8 ◄
Exploring -
C:\window

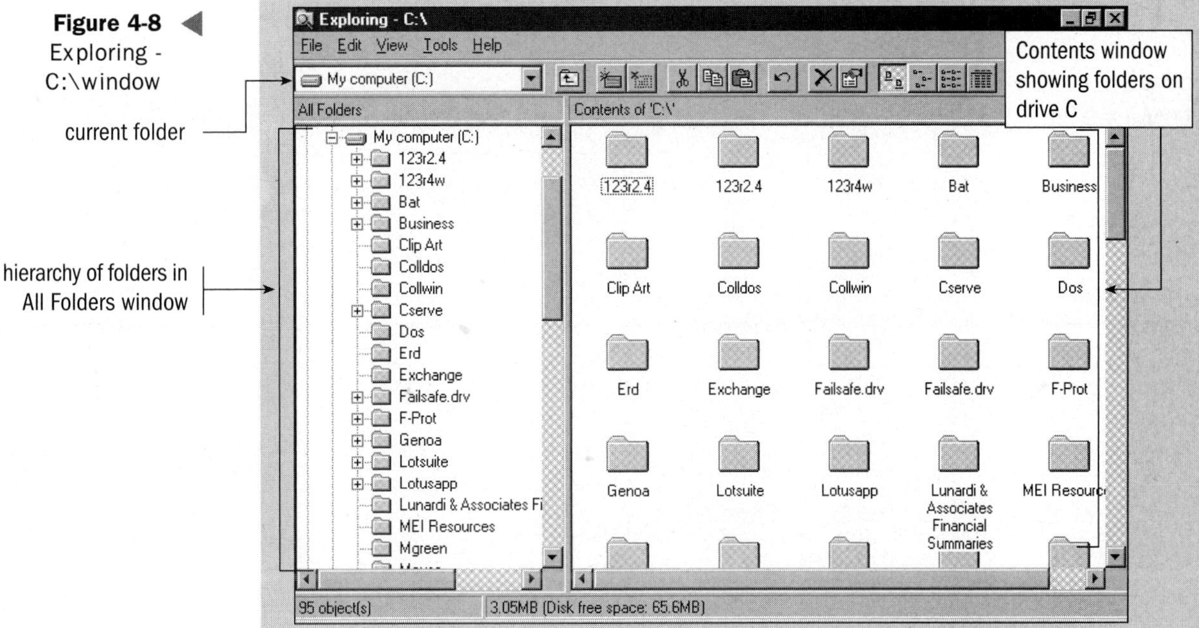

current folder

hierarchy of folders in
All Folders window

Windows Explorer has the same menu bar and toolbar as a drive or folder window that you access from My Computer. However, below the toolbar, there is an All Folders window that displays the hierarchy of resources on your computer. There is also a Contents window that displays information on the system resource, tool, drive, folder, or file that is currently selected in the All Folders window. You can change the view of folders and files in the Contents window by selecting the Large Icons, Small Icons, List, or Details button on the toolbar.

By default, Windows Explorer shows you a view of the contents of your hard disk drive C in the All Folders window. Under the icon and name of your hard disk drive C, you see the first level of folders below the folder for drive C. The plus sign (+) to the left of a folder means that there are subfolders below that folder.

HELP DESK

Index

BROWSING WITH WINDOWS EXPLORER

Click the Start button, click Help, then click the Index tab.

Keyword
Windows Explorer

Topics
Overview: Browsing,
then using Windows Explorer

Jason realizes that drive C is only one part of the folder structure of his computer. He asks you to adjust the view of the All Folders window so that you can see where drive C fits within that folder structure.

To examine the complete hierarchy of your computer:

1. Scroll to the top of the All Folders window. Under Windows 95, the hierarchy of resources within your computer begins with the Desktop. See Figure 4-9. Below the Desktop is My Computer. The first vertical dotted line on the left side of the All Folders window shows what objects are subordinate to the Desktop.

Figure 4-9 ◀
Hierarchy of
folders

My Computer

drives

folders

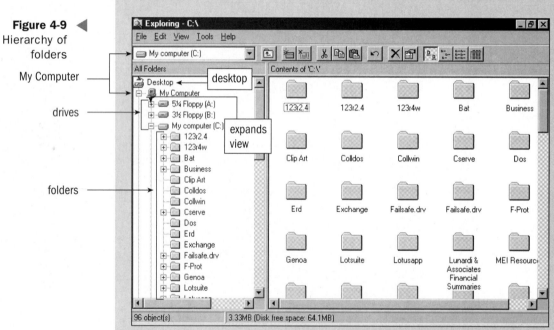

2. Scroll slowly to the bottom of the All Folders window and, as you do, notice the relationship of folders to each other. See Figure 4-10. Near the bottom of the window, Jason discovers that the Recycle Bin is another system resource or tool that is, like My Computer, below the Desktop.

Figure 4-10 ◀
Adjusting the
view of the
hierarchy of
folders

Go to a different
folder list arrow

folders

drive

system folders

system tools

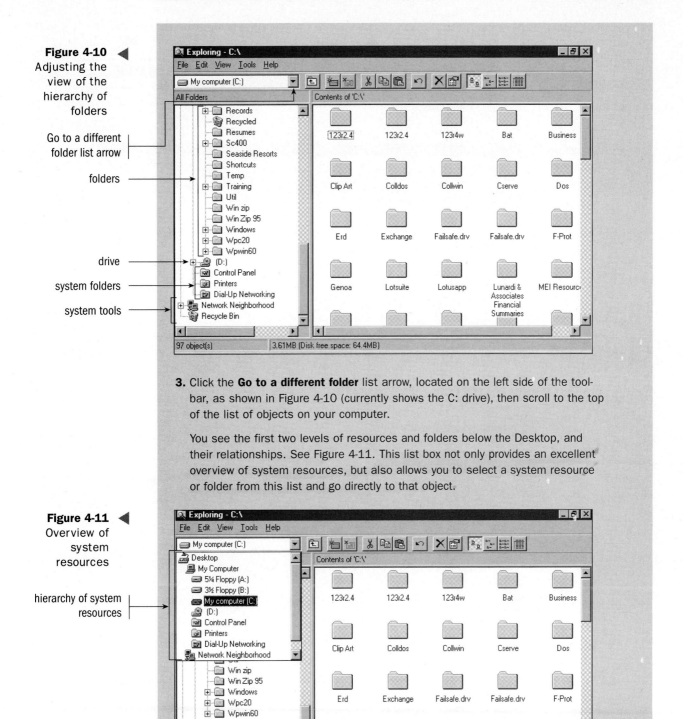

3. Click the **Go to a different folder** list arrow, located on the left side of the tool-bar, as shown in Figure 4-10 (currently shows the C: drive), then scroll to the top of the list of objects on your computer.

You see the first two levels of resources and folders below the Desktop, and their relationships. See Figure 4-11. This list box not only provides an excellent overview of system resources, but also allows you to select a system resource or folder from this list and go directly to that object.

Figure 4-11 ◀
Overview of
system
resources

hierarchy of system
resources

4. Click the **Desktop** icon. You quickly scroll back to the top of the All Folders window, and the Contents window changes to show you not the contents of the drive C: but the icons of the objects on the desktop. See Figure 4-12. Your view might differ from that shown in the figure. The second vertical dotted line from the left side of the All Folders windows shows what objects are subordinate to My Computer, your computer's drives.

Figure 4-12 ◄
Contents of the
desktop

current folder ──▶

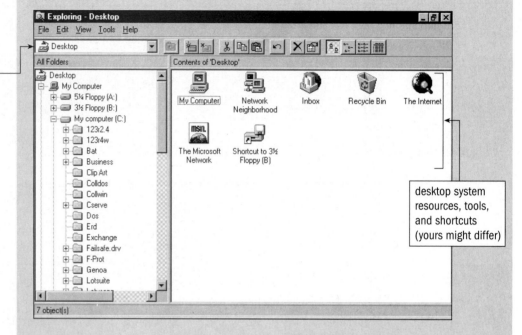

desktop system
resources, tools,
and shortcuts
(yours might differ)

5. Scroll to the bottom of the list of objects in the All Folders window.

In the All Folders window, you should see a folder for the Control Panel and one for Printers below My Computer. If you have a CD-ROM drive, you will see that it also is subordinate to My Computer. The objects below My Computer are the ones that you see when you open My Computer. However, here those resources are shown within the overall hierarchy of all your system resources.

6. Insert your Student Disk into a floppy disk drive. Make sure you are using the correct Student Disk for this tutorial, identified in the "Read This Before You Begin" section at the beginning of this book.

7. Click the **Go to a different folder** list arrow, locate and click the name of the disk drive that contains your Student Disk. You see the contents of the highest level folder on this drive in the Contents window. See Figure 4-13. Notice that in the All Folders window there is a plus sign next to the icon for the floppy disk drive that contains your Student Disk. You can click this plus sign to expand the folder listing in the All Folders window. Don't worry if your screen looks slightly different.

Figure 4-13 ◀
Contents of
floppy disk
drive folder

current folder ──→

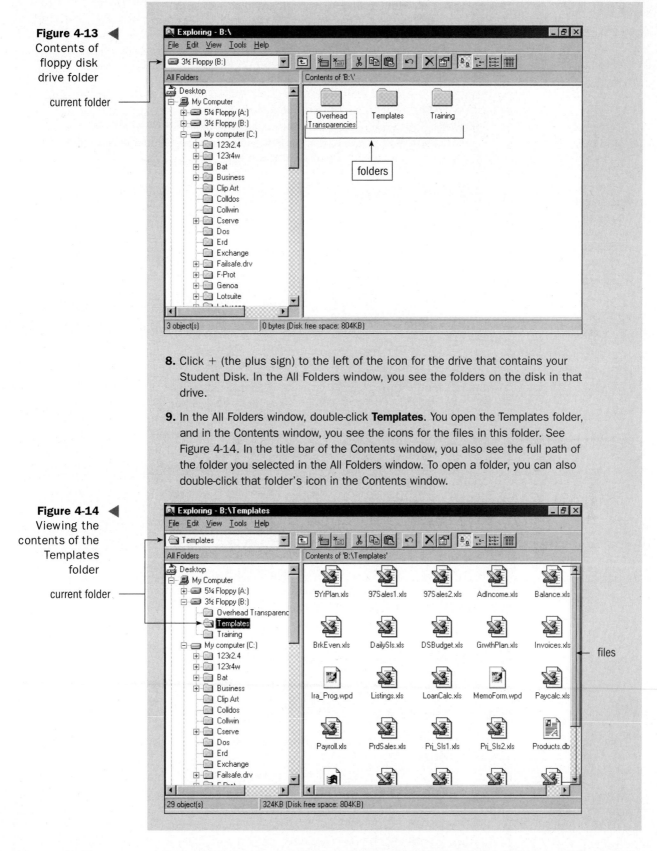

8. Click + (the plus sign) to the left of the icon for the drive that contains your Student Disk. In the All Folders window, you see the folders on the disk in that drive.

9. In the All Folders window, double-click **Templates**. You open the Templates folder, and in the Contents window, you see the icons for the files in this folder. See Figure 4-14. In the title bar of the Contents window, you also see the full path of the folder you selected in the All Folders window. To open a folder, you can also double-click that folder's icon in the Contents window.

Figure 4-14 ◀
Viewing the
contents of the
Templates
folder

current folder ──→

Jason wants to examine the shortcut menu for his floppy disk drive to see what options are available to him on his new computer system. He asks you to open the shortcut menu.

To display the shortcut menu for your floppy disk drive:

1. Right-click the **disk drive icon** for your floppy disk drive. Windows Explorer displays a shortcut menu that shows options available on your computer. See Figure 4-15. Your options might differ from those shown in the figure. For example, if you are connected to a network, you will see options for changing network settings. If you aren't running virus software, you won't have a Scan for Viruses option. No matter what other options you might have, you can explore the contents of that disk drive, open the disk drive folder, use the Find feature, copy the disk in that drive, format the disk in that drive, create a shortcut to that drive (if you don't already have one), and explore the drive's properties.

Figure 4-15
The shortcut menu for the current floppy disk drive

selected drive

menu options for selected drive

2. Click the **drive** icon again to close the shortcut menu.

Keep Windows Explorer open for the next section.

Whether Jason opens up My Computer or Windows Explorer, he can select a specific drive and view its contents, and he can display a shortcut menu with the same set of options for using and managing the resources within his computer.

Using Find to Locate Files

Jason's hard disk, like that of his co-workers, has hundreds of folders and subfolders and within each folder or subfolder many different files for both applications and documents. Jason uses different strategies when he needs to find a specific file among the thousands of files on his computer.

Today, applications consume an increasing amount of storage space on hard disks. For example, if you perform a complete installation of Windows 95, you might have 44 folders and subfolders that contain over 1,400 files and occupy close to 83MB of storage space on your hard disk. If you perform a complete installation of the Microsoft Office Professional, you might have 34 folders and subfolders that contain over 600 files and occupy over 77MB of storage space.

As you are working on your computer system, you might need to work with a certain file whose location you can't recall. Or, you might be troubleshooting a problem and need to locate a program file or a set of configuration files. You might even set aside time on a slow day to examine the contents of your hard disk so that you can remove duplicate copies of files (and maybe even folders), move misplaced files to the correct folder, and archive folders and files that you no longer need.

To simplify these operations, you can use the Find tool available from Windows Explorer, the Start menu, and other convenient locations to find a folder, file, or set of files by employing a variety of techniques that uniquely identify an object or set of objects. You can search for a folder or file based on all or part of the name of that folder or file. You can search for files created or modified between two dates or during a recent period of time, such as the last month or the last week. If you cannot remember a file's name, you can even search for text within a file or look for a file based on its size. You can limit searches to specific types of documents produced by applications and to certain locations on your computer. Furthermore, you can combine two or more of these features to customize the search so that you use all the information you remember about a folder or file to quickly locate it.

HELP DESK

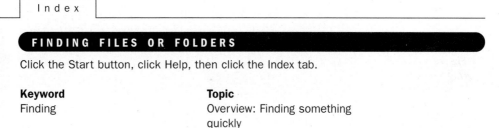

Index

FINDING FILES OR FOLDERS

Click the Start button, click Help, then click the Index tab.

Keyword	**Topic**
Finding	Overview: Finding something quickly

Finding a File with an Entire Filename

Jason's supervisor, Nadine, asks him to prepare several loan analyses for an upcoming meeting later that afternoon. She needs some ball park figures about the costs of financing a loan to purchase additional equipment. Jason recalls that he created a loan analysis spreadsheet about a year ago. Although he has just restored all his original folders and files to his new computer, he cannot recall whether that file is stored in a folder on his hard disk or on the diskette that holds documents that he needs when he carries work home. He asks you to use the Find feature in Windows Explorer to locate a file named LoanCalc.xls, and he suggests that you start the search from My Computer.

To find a file:

1. Click **Tools** on the Windows Explorer menu bar, point to **Find**, then click **Files or Folders**. The Find: All Files window opens. See Figure 4-16. Your Look in list box might show a different folder.

Figure 4-16 ◀
Find: All Files
window

what to search for ——

where to search ——

search all subfolders ——

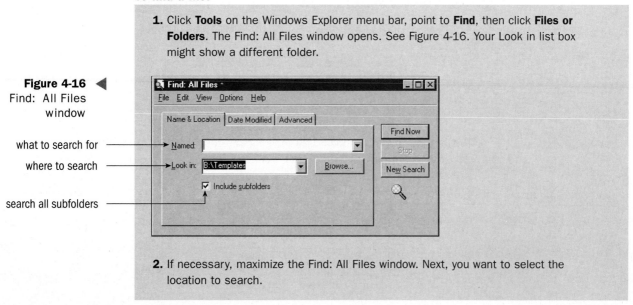

2. If necessary, maximize the Find: All Files window. Next, you want to select the location to search.

3. Click the **Look in** list arrow, then click **My Computer**. Your selection appears in the Look in list box. By selecting My Computer, you are instructing Windows 95 to check all components within your computer system, including all floppy and CD-ROM drives. To specify the file's name, you enter it in the Named list box.

4. Click the **Named** list box, then type **LoanCalc.xls** in the list box.

You can use mixed case, uppercase, or lowercase when specifying a folder or file name.

5. If it is not already selected, click the **Include subfolders** check box to select it. In most cases, you want Windows 95 to search all subfolders.

6. Click the **Find Now** button. Windows expands the Find: All Files window, and in the Files Found area, Windows 95 lists one file that has the name you specified. See Figure 4-17. The LoanCalc.xls file is in the Templates folder on Jason's disk. In the status bar at the bottom of this window, Windows 95 reports the number of files found. The latter information is useful when you search for and find a large number of files that meet the conditions you specify.

Figure 4-17 ◀
Searching for
a file

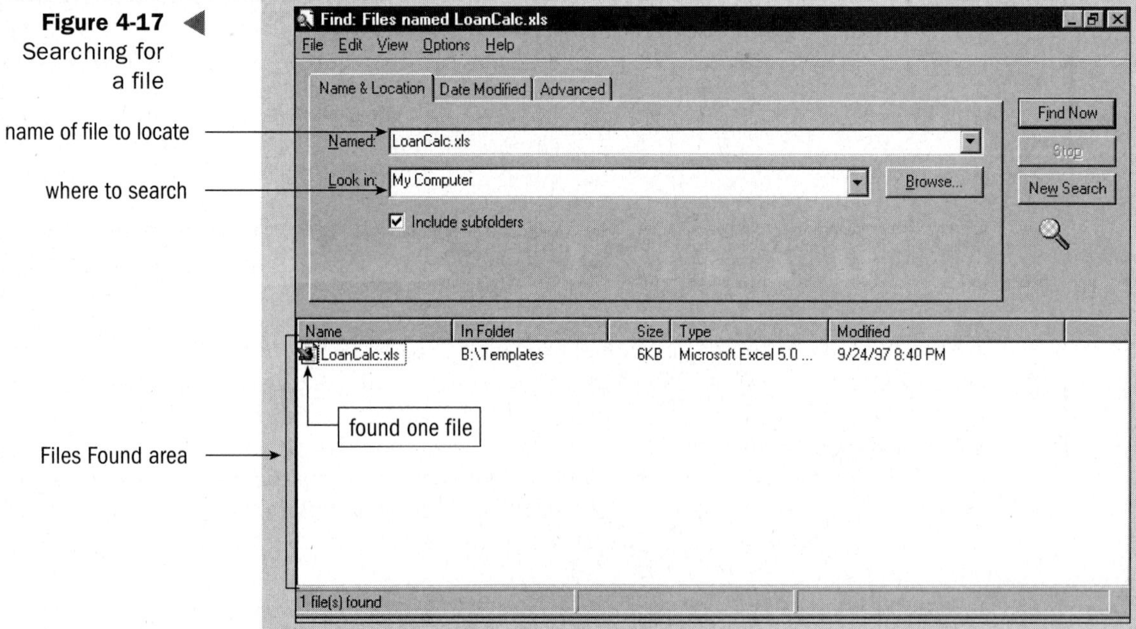

name of file to locate ──────

where to search ──────

Files Found area ──────▶

TROUBLE? If Windows 95 does not find the file, check the Named and Look in list boxes, and verify that you have entered the filename correctly and started the search from My Computer.

TROUBLE? On a network or large hard disk drive, the search might take a few minutes. If the search seems to be taking too long, and if Windows 95 has already found the file you specified, click the Stop button to stop the search.

7. In the Files Found area, right-click the **LoanCalc.xls** icon, click **Quick View**, then, if necessary, maximize the Quick View window. Jason has found the loan analysis model that he needs to start this next project.

TROUBLE? If you have not yet installed Quick View on your computer, you will not see the Quick View option on the File menu. Quick View is included with the Accessories component, and you can install it with the Add/Remove Programs application in the Control Panel. If you do not see Quick View on the shortcut menu, go to the next step.

8. Click the **Close** button ⊠ to close the Quick View window, click the **Close** button ⊠ to close the Find: All Files named LoanCalc.xls window, then click the **Close** button ⊠ to close Windows Explorer.

REFERENCE window

SEARCHING FOR A FOLDER OR FILE USING WINDOWS EXPLORER

- Click Tools, point to Find, then click Files or Folders.
- After the Find: All Files window opens, indicate where the search should start by selecting a drive or location from the Look in list box.
- Specify the name of a folder or file in the Named list box.
- Click the Find Now button.

Although the loan analysis model that Jason found calculates a monthly mortgage payment on a home purchase, Jason can quickly adapt it to an equipment purchase loan and come up with the figures Nadine needs for her afternoon meeting.

Finding a File Using Part of a Filename

So that its management staff can plan an expansion of MultiGrain Cereals' product line, the CEO asked Nadine to prepare a sales projection that forecasts the most likely growth of the company over the next several years. Nadine asks Jason to locate copies of the sales projection templates that he used last year to forecast this year's growth.

If you work with many different files or only use certain files one or twice a year, you might not remember all of a file's name, yet the part of the name that you remember might be enough to locate the file. In other instances, you might create a set of files that contain the same type of information, but you provide each of them with a slightly different filename to distinguish them from each other. Later, you can locate all of them, then decide which one meets your needs.

Windows 95 can find files using whatever information you enter in the Named list box, whether it is a complete filename with a file extension, part of a filename (even just a few characters), or just a file extension.

You can start a Find from different locations on your computer. For example, if you are working on your desktop, you can start a Find by using the Start Menu. You do not need to open Windows Explorer first. You can also access Find from shortcut menus for drives.

When Jason named those files, he included the phrase "Sls" (for Sales) as part of their filenames so that he could easily locate them again. He asks you to search for those files on his disk.

To locate files using part of a filename:

1. Click the **Start** button, point to **Find**, then click **Files or Folders**. The Find: All Files window opens.

2. Maximize the Find: All Files window.

3. In the Named list box, type **Sls**.

4. Click the **Look in** list arrow, then click the name of your floppy disk drive.

5. Click the **Find Now** button. In the Files Found area, Windows 95 lists six files in the Overhead Transparencies and Templates folders that have "Sls" somewhere in the filename. See Figure 4-18. The two files Jason wants to find are Prj_Sls1.xls and Prj_Sls2.xls, and they are located in the Templates folder.

Figure 4-18
Searching for sales projections

file specification

where to search

found six sales projections

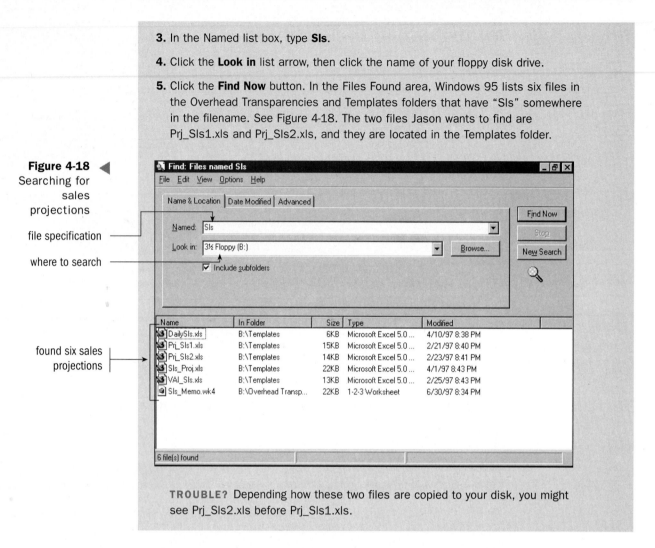

TROUBLE? Depending how these two files are copied to your disk, you might see Prj_Sls2.xls before Prj_Sls1.xls.

Right after you locate the two templates that Nadine requested, Nadine and Jason discuss which template to use to create the sales projection. Nadine also tells him that she will prepare a short presentation for senior management based on that projection and asks him to locate copies of the overhead transparencies that he produced with PowerPoint. She can then take the results shown in his projection and summarize them by adapting one of the overhead transparencies.

Jason realizes that finding these files will be easy because all these files have ppt as their file extension. He asks you to use the same approach to locate these files.

To locate files with a specific file extension:

1. In the Named list box, click **Sls** to select it.

2. Type **ppt**

3. Click the **Find Now** button. In the Files Found area, Windows 95 lists four files in the Training folder that have "ppt" somewhere in the filename. Nadine can adapt any of these transparencies as she prepares her presentation. Keep the Find: All Files named ppt window open for the next section.

FINDING FILES WITH PARTIAL FILENAMES

- Open Find from Windows Explorer or from the Start menu.
- Select a drive or location in the Look in list box.
- In the Named list box, type all or a portion of the folder or file-name that you want to find.
- Click the Find Now button.

Nadine thanks Jason for preparing the sales projection so quickly and for locating the PowerPoint files so that she can assemble her presentation.

Using Wildcards to Find a File

While Jason was on vacation for a week, a temporary employee prepared a report on out-standing invoices for the director of accounting. Now, Jason needs to update that report. However, he does not know the name of the file that contains the report. Since his tem-porary replacement would have used dBASE for Windows to prepare the report, he deduces that the file is likely to have the file extension rpt. He can use that information as a lead in locating the file.

Sometimes, you might want to more precisely define a selection of files. For example, suppose you have produced a variety of reports using dBASE for Windows. When you pro-duce and save reports with the Crystal Reports application included in dBASE, it uses rpt as the file extension. If you use "rpt" as the criteria for locating these files, you might also locate other files that contain "rpt" somewhere in the filename, such as Bdgt_rpt.doc, and these other files might have been produced with an application other than Crystal Reports.

To perform a more selective search, you can use one or more wildcards. A **wildcard** is a symbol that substitutes for all or part of a filename. One wildcard, the asterisk (*), substitutes for any number of characters in the main part of the filename or in the file extension. The other wildcard, the question mark (?), substitutes for a single character at a specific position in the filename. For example, if you want to locate all files that have rpt as their file extension, you would use *.rpt as your condition. The asterisk tells Windows 95 to search for files with any filename, and the "rpt" limits the search to those files with this file extension.

As another example, you might want to locate a series of budget documents for dif-ferent years. You could use 9?Budget.Doc to locate those files that have any character at the second position in the filename. Using that file specification, you might locate files by the names of 96Budget.Doc, 97Budget.Doc, and 98Budget.Doc.

Jason asks you to use the asterisk wildcard as part of a file specification to locate the report file that he needs.

To locate a file with the asterisk wildcard:

1. In the Named list box, click **ppt** to select it.

2. Type ***.rpt**

3. Click the **Find Now** button. In the Files Found area, Windows 95 lists Invoices.rpt and indicates that it is in the Overhead Transparencies folder.

Jason is glad he searched for the file. He would not have expected the file to be in the Overhead Transparencies folder. If he had looked in the folders where he would have thought someone would have saved it, he would not have found it. After Jason updates this report, prints a new copy, and then moves it to the right folder, it is lunch time.

While Jason is at lunch, Nadine needs to locate a copy of a product sales report that Jason prepared earlier in the week for her. She asks you to find the report for her. She does not know the name of the report, but suggests that you might look for a report that starts with "P" for "Product."

To locate files that start with the letter "P":

1. In the Named list box, click ***rpt** to select this file specification, then type **P**

2. Click the **Find Now** button. In the Files Found area, Windows 95 lists 23 files that have the letter "P" or "p" somewhere in the filename. See Figure 4-19. Note that it also found two folders with this character in its folder name. Since this selection is not what you want, you decide to use the asterisk wildcard.

Figure 4-19 ◀
Searching for a
character in a
filename

search for this
character

folders found

files found

number of files found

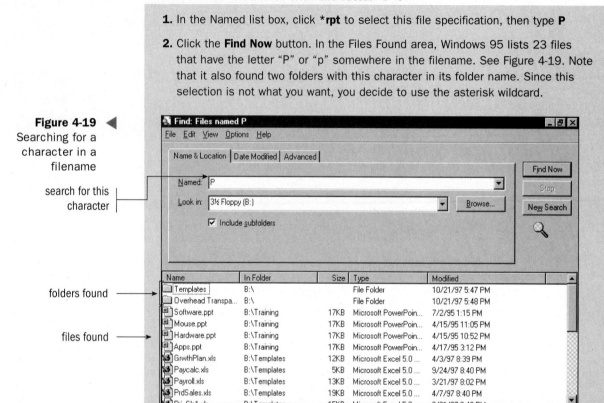

3. In the Named list box, click **P** to select it, type **P*** as your new search condition, then click the **Find Now** button. Now, you have narrowed your selection down to 8 filenames that start with the letter "P" and that have any file extension. The file labeled Prdsales.xls is probably the one that Nadine is looking for.

You tell Nadine you think you have found the file she needs. You view the file, and she verifies that it is the right file. She makes a change, saves the file, then prints a copy of the report.

After Jason returns from lunch, he decides to look for two other sales projection reports that he prepared a few months ago for a subsidiary of MultiGrain Cereals, so that he can update those reports. He asks you to search for two files named 97Sales1.xls and 97Sales2.xls. You decide to use the question mark wildcard to locate both files at the same time.

To select files using the question mark wildcard:

1. In the Named list box, click **P*** to select it, type **97Sales?.xls** as your search condition, then click the **Find Now** button. In the Files Found area, Windows 95 lists two files that meet this condition: 95Sales2.xls and 95Sales1.xls. Next, you want to view the contents of these two files before you print copies of them.

2. Right-click the **97Sales2.xls** icon then click **Quick View**. The Quick View window shows part of the contents of 97Sales2.xls. See Figure 4-20. This file shows sales for four different regions in the United States. You used this information to produce a pie chart that shows sales by region, but because the chart is on a separate page you do not see the chart. Before you print a copy of this file, you want to make sure it contains the chart.

Figure 4-20 ◄
Using Quick
View to
examine a
found file

view of sales
summary

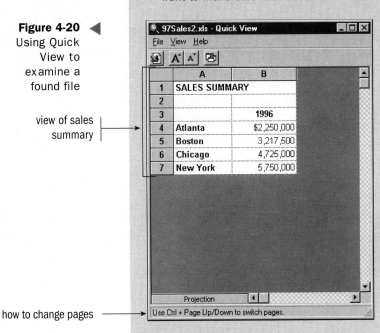

how to change pages

3. Click **View** on the Quick View menu bar and, if Page View is not already selected, click **Page View**. The Quick View feature displays a full page view of the first page of the file. See Figure 4-21. To turn to the next page, you can click the left arrow in the upper-right corner of the previewed page.

Figure 4-21 ◄
Switching to
full page view

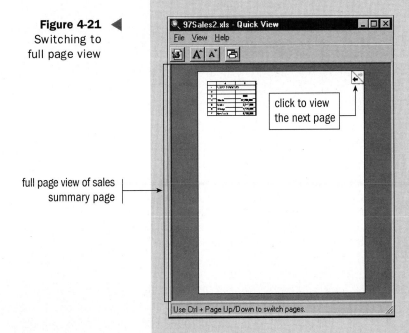

click to view
the next page

full page view of sales
summary page

4. Click the left arrow in the upper-right corner of the page preview window. Windows 95 flips pages and displays a color view of the pie chart included with this spreadsheet. See Figure 4-22.

Figure 4-22
Viewing the
next page in
the file

pie chart summarizing
sales

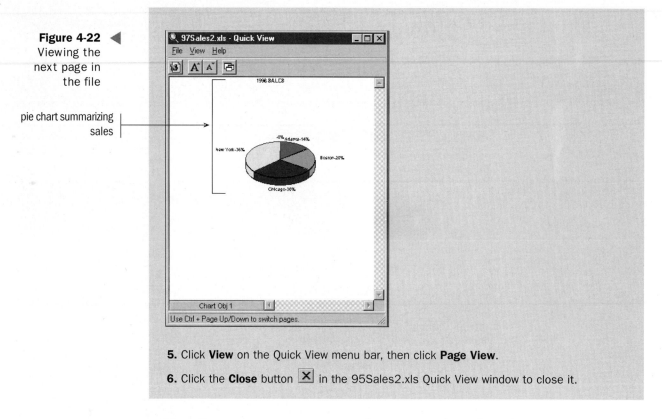

5. Click **View** on the Quick View menu bar, then click **Page View**.

6. Click the **Close** button ☒ in the 95Sales2.xls Quick View window to close it.

Next, Jason wants you to examine the contents of 97Sales1.xls to make sure it is the other file that he needs.

To view the contents of 97Sales1.xls:

1. Right-click the **97Sales1.xls** icon then click **Quick View**. Now you see a Quick View window for 97Sales1.xls. This file shows sales for four different locations within a region.

2. Click **View**, then click **Page View** to switch to a full page view.

3. Click the **left** arrow in the upper-right corner of the page preview window. Windows 95 flips pages and displays a bar chart included with this spreadsheet.

4. Click the **Close** button ☒ in the 97Sales1.xls Quick View window to close this window.

5. Click the **Close** button ☒ for the Find: All Files named 97Sales?.xls window to close it.

Before he leaves for the evening, Jason realizes that the use of wildcards will save him valuable time as he looks for, and verifies with the Quick View feature, the files he needs for a specific project. Even if he knows the filename and where it is located, the Find feature allows him to go directly to a file without opening folders.

If you want to take a break and resume the tutorial at a later time, you can do so now. If you are on a network, close any open applications and dialog boxes, and leave Windows 95 running. If you are using your own computer, click the Start button on the taskbar, click Shut Down, click Shut down the computer, and then click the Yes button. When you resume the tutorial, launch Windows 95 again, place the Student Disk for this tutorial in the appropriate drive, and then continue with the tutorial.

● ● ●

Searching for a File by Date

After Jason arrives at work the following morning, Nadine asks him to locate a file that the two of them put together within the last year. Nadine shows him the printed copy of that file. Although he does not remember the filename, he can tell from the date on the printed document that he worked on the file last April. He can use this information to find the file.

If you are looking for folders or files created at a certain point in time, you can specify a date search condition. On the Date Modified tab, you can instruct Windows 95 to locate files that were created or modified between two dates. You can also locate files created or modified during a recent period of time. So, for example, you could locate all files created or modified during the previous month or the last two weeks.

Jason tells you that the file Nadine wants is on your floppy disk drive, and suggests that you use the shortcut to your floppy disk drive then use the Find option on the shortcut menu.

To search for files using a date condition:

1. On the desktop, right-click the **shortcut** to your floppy disk drive, then click **Find** on the shortcut menu. The Find: All Files window opens.

2. Click the **Date Modified** tab. On the Date Modified tab, you can choose to search for all files, specify a date range to locate files created or modified between two dates, or locate files created or modified during a specified number of previous months or days. See Figure 4-23. You want to enter a date range that starts with April 1st and extends through April 30th.

Figure 4-23
Viewing options on the Date Modified tab

specify a time frame

choose a recent period of time

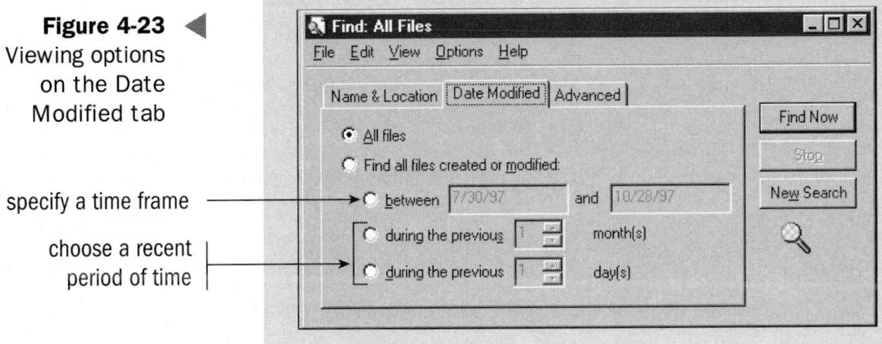

3. Click the **Find all files created or modified** radio button, then click the **between** radio button.

4. Press **Tab** then, in the starting date text box, type **4/1/97**

5. Press **Tab** then, in the ending date text box, type **4/30/97**

6. Click the **Find Now** button, then, as Windows 95 searches for files that fall within this date range, maximize the Find: All Files window. Windows 95 locates 12 files in different folders with dates of creation or modification that fall between 4/1/97 and 4/30/97.

If you enter a search condition that selects a large group of files, as occurred in this case, you might want to change the way in which Windows 95 displays the information you see in the Files Found area. By clicking the button at the top of each column of information, you can arrange information in a column in either ascending or descending order, and you can also adjust the size of each column of information.

To arrange the found files in alphabetical order by name:

1. Click the **Name** column button. Windows 95 arranges the filenames in ascending order by filename. Before he examines these files, Jason wants to view the full name of the application that produced each of these files.

2. Point to the border between the In Folder and Size columns, and when the pointer changes to ⊞, double-click the **border**. The In Folder column widens to show long folder names.

3. Point to the border between the Type and Modified columns, and when the pointer changes to ⊞, double-click the **border**. The Type column widens to show long application names.

4. Scroll through the list of files. Jason notices that the files in the Files Found area are from the Overhead Transparencies and Templates folders. See Figure 4-24. He also notices that most of the files were produced with Microsoft Excel.

Figure 4-24 ◀
Finding files created during April

time period

files created or modified during April

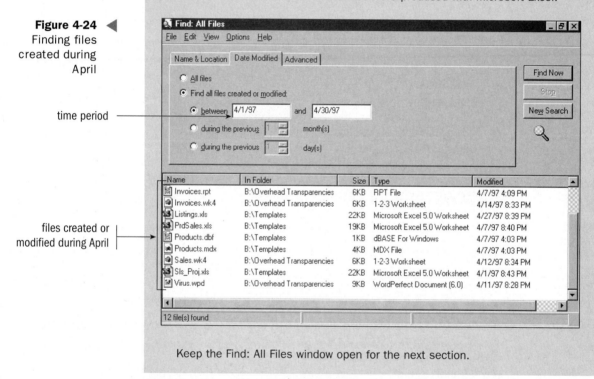

Keep the Find: All Files window open for the next section.

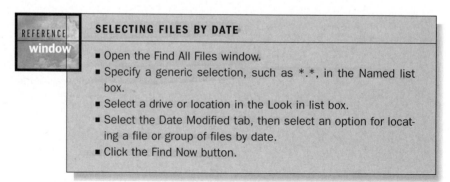

REFERENCE
window

SELECTING FILES BY DATE

- Open the Find All Files window.
- Specify a generic selection, such as *.*, in the Named list box.
- Select a drive or location in the Look in list box.
- Select the Date Modified tab, then select an option for locating a file or group of files by date.
- Click the Find Now button.

Jason spots the file Sls_Proj.xls in the Templates folder, the one Nadine needs. He lets her know that he found the file so that she can begin working on the changes she needs to make to that file.

Finding Files Using Multiple Criteria

Nadine asks Jason to prepare a list of all the files that contain financial projections that he has developed over the last year. As part of Jason's upcoming yearly performance appraisal, Nadine wants to highlight the fact that he has developed invaluable financial models that the company depends on for analyzing data and for preparing financial projections and forecasts.

On the Advanced tab of the Find: All Files window, you can search for files using three options. First, you can search for files produced by specific applications. This is especially valuable if you do not remember a file's name, but do remember the name of the application used to produce the file. Second, if you want to find a single file or a group of files that contains a specific word or phrase within the document(s), you can search for them by specifying the text stored in the file. Finally, you can even search for files that have a minimum or maximum file size. You can combine these options to limit the file selection to a smaller group of files.

To prepare the list that Nadine wants, Jason must locate files that have three features in common. First, each file was produced with Microsoft Excel 5.0. Second, each file has an XLS file extension, indicating a worksheet file produced by Microsoft Excel. And third, each file contains the word "Projection" somewhere within the document. Jason asks you to specify this information on the Advanced tab and locate the files he needs to prepare the list for Nadine.

To locate files using a combination of advanced criteria:

1. On the Date Modified tab in the Find: All Files window, click the **All Files** radio button. If you inadvertently keep the date selection that you last used for your last find operation, then that option will also apply to your next search.

   TROUBLE? If you do *not* have Microsoft Excel 5.0 on your computer or if you do *not* know if this application is installed on your computer, click the **Name & Location** tab, then type ***.xls** in the Named list box. Then you can search for spreadsheets produced with different versions of Microsoft Excel.

2. Click the **Advanced** tab, and make sure Windows 95 is set to search All Files and Folders.

3. If you *do* have Microsoft Excel 5.0 on your computer, then click the **Of type** list arrow, scroll through the list of applications and document types, and locate and click **Microsoft Excel 5.0 Worksheet**.

   TROUBLE? If you see Microsoft Excel Worksheet, or a reference to another version of Microsoft Excel on your computer, then do not select this option. Refer to the previous **TROUBLE.**

4. Click the **Containing text** box, then type **Projection**.

   Since the search is not case-sensitive, Windows will look for all combinations of uppercase, mixed case, and lowercase letters.

5. Click the **Find Now** button and *be patient*. Windows 95 finds 9 files that either have the XLS file extension *or* that are Microsoft Excel 5.0 worksheets *and* that have the word "Projection" in the file. See Figure 4-25. The order of your files might differ from that shown in the figure. Since searching for text within a file might turn into a time-consuming process on a large hard disk drive or a network drive, you might want to use it only in emergencies. Also, if Find locates and displays the file you need in the Files Found area, you can click the Stop button to stop the search at that point so that you do not waste time searching for uneeded files.

Figure 4-25 ◄
Searching for
spreadsheets
that contain
the word
"Projection"

search this
application's files

look for this word in
the file

found nine
spreadsheets with the
word "Projection"

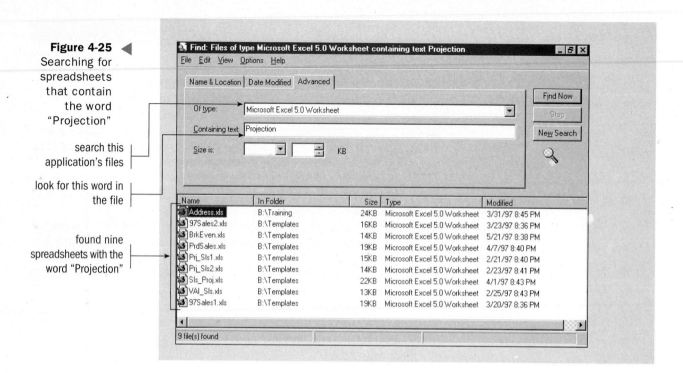

Leave the Find dialog box with these search results open so that you can use them in the next section.

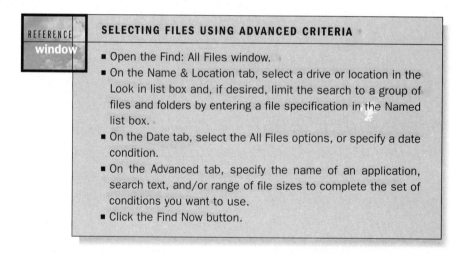

REFERENCE
window

SELECTING FILES USING ADVANCED CRITERIA

- Open the Find: All Files window.
- On the Name & Location tab, select a drive or location in the Look in list box and, if desired, limit the search to a group of files and folders by entering a file specification in the Named list box.
- On the Date tab, select the All Files options, or specify a date condition.
- On the Advanced tab, specify the name of an application, search text, and/or range of file sizes to complete the set of conditions you want to use.
- Click the Find Now button.

Jason provides Nadine with the list of files that she needs for his performance appraisal. Along with this information and the other contributions that Jason has made to the department, Nadine wants to request a generous 11% merit increase for Jason.

Saving Search Criteria

After locating the list of files that Nadine needs, it occurs to Jason that it would be useful to save these search criteria, because he can use them again to compile updated lists of these spreadsheet models that Nadine and he regularly use. Plus, he can repeat this search again before his next performance appraisal a year from now.

If you create a complex set of search criteria, you can save the conditions that you specified so that you can use them later. When you save the conditions for a search, Windows 95 creates an icon on the desktop for that search condition. You can leave the saved search icon on the desktop, or you can move it to a folder that you frequently use so that it and other saved searches do not clutter your desktop.

HELP DESK

Index

SAVING SEARCH CRITERIA

Click the Start button, click Help, then click the Index tab.

Keyword	**Topics**
Saving	Saving the results of a search for files or folders

Jason asks you to save the results of this last search, so that he can use it every several months to update his list of financial models.

To save a search result:

1. Click **File** then click **Save Search**. Although nothing appears to happen, Windows 95 has placed an icon for this saved search on the desktop.

2. Click the **Close** button ☒ to close the Find dialog box, then close any other open windows. Now you can see the icon for the last search that you performed. See Figure 4-26. The text you see is the name of the file; it contains the search conditions and FND is the file extension for that file. The label for your saved search icon might differ from that shown in the figure. Next, Jason asks you to move this object to your Student Disk.

Figure 4-26 ◄
Saving search
criteria

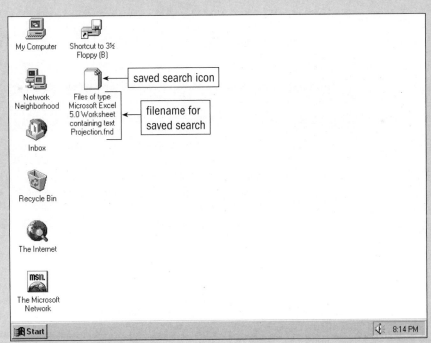

3. Right-click the **saved search** icon, then click **Cut** on the shortcut menu.

4. Double-click the **shortcut** to your floppy disk drive, then maximize the window.

5. If you do not see a toolbar, click **View** then click **Toolbar**.

6. If you do not see large icons, click the **Large Icons** button on the toolbar.

7. Click the **Paste** button on the toolbar. Windows 95 displays a Moving dialog box, then you see the saved search icon in the highest level folder on your Student Disk. See Figure 4-27. Now, Jason asks you to test this saved search and verify that it still works.

Figure 4-27 ◀
Moving a saved
search to a
floppy disk

current drive

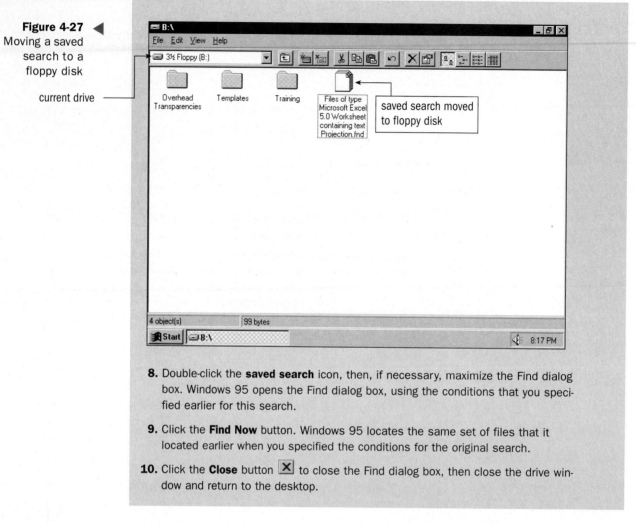

saved search moved
to floppy disk

8. Double-click the **saved search** icon, then, if necessary, maximize the Find dialog box. Windows 95 opens the Find dialog box, using the conditions that you specified earlier for this search.

9. Click the **Find Now** button. Windows 95 locates the same set of files that it located earlier when you specified the conditions for the original search.

10. Click the **Close** button ☒ to close the Find dialog box, then close the drive window and return to the desktop.

The ability to recall a complex set of search conditions by using a saved search will benefit both Jason and Nadine. Periodically, they are faced with important projects and short deadlines, so they must be able to locate files quickly. Even though they might know the name and location of a file, using a saved search with Find will save even more time.

Creating a Folder Using Windows Explorer

Jason and Nadine discuss the possibility of creating a set of saved searches so that they can quickly locate, preview, open, and print financial models. They also decide to store these saved searches in a separate folder, so that they both know where to go to find a saved search.

You can use Windows Explorer to create folders, rename folders, cut and paste folders, cut and copy folders, and delete folders. The techniques for performing these operations are the same as the ones that you learned in the previous tutorial.

Jason asks you to create a folder named Searches so that Nadine and he can save each new saved search in the same folder.

To create a folder:

1. Click the **Start** button, point to **Programs**, then click **Windows Explorer**.

2. After Windows Explorer opens, locate and click the **disk drive** icon in the All Folders window for the floppy disk drive that contains your Student Disk.

3. If you see a plus sign to the left of your floppy disk drive icon in the All Folders window, then click the **plus sign** to expand the folder structure.

4. If you do not see large icons in the Contents window, click the **Large Icons** button on the toolbar.

5. Click **File**, point to **New**, then click **Folder**. A new folder appears in the Contents window and *also* in the All Folders window. Now, you can name the folder.

6. Type **Searches** then press the **Enter** key. Windows 95 renames the folder in both windows. See Figure 4-28.

Figure 4-28 ◄
Creating a
folder for saved
searches

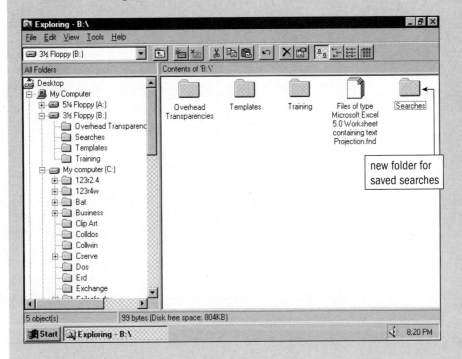

7. Drag the icon for your saved search to the top of the new Searches folder. Windows Explorer moves the saved search to the Searches folder.

8. Double-click the **Searches** folder. The saved search is now stored in the Searches folder.

9. Click the **Up One Level** button on the toolbar, and keep Windows Explorer open for the next section.

REFERENCE window

CREATING A FOLDER WITH WINDOWS EXPLORER

- Open Windows Explorer.
- Select the disk drive or folder that will contain the new folder.
- Click File, point to New, then click Folder.
- Enter a name for the new folder then press the Enter key.

Nadine and Jason decide to create a searches folder on each of their disks for saved searches so they can find templates quickly and easily.

Copying a Folder

Nadine calls a meeting of her department to discuss their schedules and workloads for the next six months. Now that the management at MultiGrain Cereals has decided to expand its product line, their department will be busy preparing a variety of financial analyses, models, and projections. Nadine emphasizes the importance of organizing folders and files logically, and of using new Windows 95 features, such as saved searches, to stream-line their work. She also reminds everyone of the importance of having duplicates of their working files stored in different locations. These features will not only benefit them during this upcoming busy period, but will also make life easier when their co-workers cover for them while they are away on vacation.

In Windows Explorer, you can easily copy folders and files from one location to another on the same disk or a different disk. If you want to copy a folder from one disk to another, you select the folder on the source disk and drag the folder to the location on the destination disk where you want to store that folder.

Jason asks you to first rename the Templates folder to Company Templates to empha-size the importance of the files in this folder to the entire company. Then, he wants you to copy the Company Templates folder to your hard disk so that you have copies of the important files in this folder.

If you are working in a computer lab, make sure you have permission to copy a folder to a hard disk or network drive before you perform this operation.

To rename then copy the Templates folder:

1. In the Contents window, right-click the **Templates** folder, then click **Rename** on the shortcut menu.

2. Click before **Templates** to place the insertion point before the folder name, type **Company** and press the **Spacebar**, then press the **Enter** key. Windows 95 now displays the new name of this folder, Company Templates. Next, check to make sure the hard disk or network drive does not already have a folder named Company Templates.

3. If necessary, adjust your view of the All Folders window so that you see the fold-ers on your hard disk drive that start with the letter "C."

   TROUBLE? If there is already a folder named Company Templates and you work in a computer lab, check with your instructor or technical support person before you continue. Another student might have left a copy of this folder on that hard disk, and the technical support person or you might be able to remove it or over-write it and continue with the tutorial. If you are working on your own computer and there is already a folder named Company Templates, rename that folder so that you can complete this section of the tutorial.

4. Drag the Company Templates folder to the hard disk drive in the All Folders win-dow, as shown in Figure 4-29, until Windows 95 highlights the name of the hard disk drive. The plus sign in the lower-right corner of the icon you are moving indi-cates you are making a copy.

Figure 4-29 ◀
Dragging a
copy of a folder
to another drive

selected destination ──────

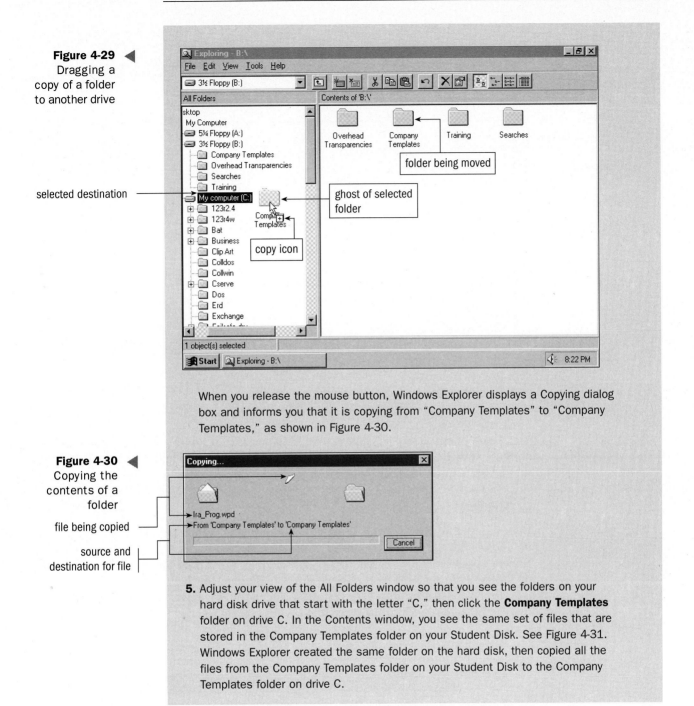

When you release the mouse button, Windows Explorer displays a Copying dialog box and informs you that it is copying from "Company Templates" to "Company Templates," as shown in Figure 4-30.

Figure 4-30 ◀
Copying the
contents of a
folder

file being copied ───

source and
destination for file

5. Adjust your view of the All Folders window so that you see the folders on your hard disk drive that start with the letter "C," then click the **Company Templates** folder on drive C. In the Contents window, you see the same set of files that are stored in the Company Templates folder on your Student Disk. See Figure 4-31. Windows Explorer created the same folder on the hard disk, then copied all the files from the Company Templates folder on your Student Disk to the Company Templates folder on drive C.

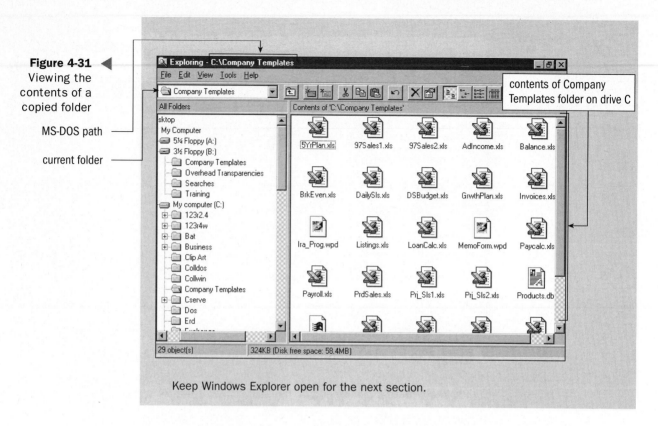

Figure 4-31 ◀
Viewing the
contents of a
copied folder

MS-DOS path ——

current folder ——

contents of Company
Templates folder on drive C

Keep Windows Explorer open for the next section.

If Jason needs to make a quick copy of important files on his hard disk for Nadine, another co-worker, or even himself, he can reverse this process and copy a folder and its files from his hard disk to a floppy disk.

Deleting a Duplicate Folder

In her departmental meeting, Nadine also emphasized the importance of removing unneeded folders and files to conserve hard disk space.

If you need to remove a folder from your hard disk or from a floppy disk, you can use the Delete button on the Windows Explorer toolbar. If you have enabled the use of the Recycle Bin on your computer, then the contents of the deleted folder are sent to the Recycle Bin and remain in the Recycle Bin until you empty it.

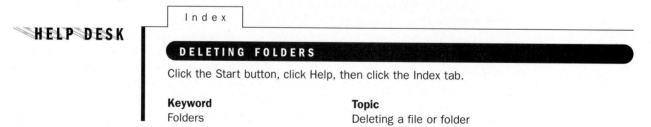

HELP DESK

Index

DELETING FOLDERS

Click the Start button, click Help, then click the Index tab.

Keyword
Folders

Topic
Deleting a file or folder

Jason asks you to show a new co-worker how to copy a folder from a hard disk to a floppy disk. Rather than add more folders to your hard disk, you decide to remove the folder that you just copied to your hard disk so that you can show her how to copy that same folder back to the disk again.

To remove a folder:

1. Adjust your view of the All Folders window until you locate the folder named Company Templates on drive C.

2. Click the **Company Templates** folder on your hard disk.

3. Click the **Delete** button ☒ on Windows Explorer toolbar. Windows Explorer displays a Confirm Folder Delete dialog box. See Figure 4-32. You are asked to confirm that you want to remove this folder and send its contents to the Recycle Bin.

Figure 4-32 ◀
Confirming a
folder deletion

prompt for verification

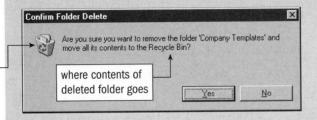

where contents of
deleted folder goes

4. If you have selected the correct folder, click the **Yes** button; otherwise, click the **No** button and repeat Steps 1 through 4 again. Windows Explorer displays a Deleting dialog box and removes the folder from your hard disk.

REFERENCE
window

DELETING A FOLDER WITH WINDOWS EXPLORER

- Open Windows Explorer.
- In the All Folders window, locate the folder you want to delete, then click the folder to select it.
- Click the Delete button on the Windows Explorer toolbar.
- Verify that you have selected the correct folder, then click the Yes button in the Confirm Folder Delete dialog box; otherwise, click the No button.

After restoring this folder on his hard disk, Jason decides to set aside the last hour of the day to check his hard disk drive and remove any unnecessary folders and files, and to make copies of important folders and files.

Moving a File

Jason's next project calls for him to move one of the spreadsheet templates stored in the Company Templates folder to another folder, and then prepare an overhead transparency for the next meeting of the company's financial staff.

With Windows Explorer, you can move files from folder to folder on the same drive or to another drive. You select the folder and then the file or files you want to move. Next, you use drag-and-drop or cut-and-paste to move the files to another folder. Which method you use depends on where you are moving the file to. If you want to move a file to a folder *on the same disk drive*, you can use drag-and-drop to drag it from its current location to the new folder. Windows 95 will then move the file. However, if you drag a file *to another drive*, Windows 95 will copy the file, not move it. If you use cut-and-paste instead of drag-and-drop, Windows 95 will move the file, even if you select another drive. Cut-and-paste removes the file from its current location, then Windows 95 pastes the file in the folder and drive that you select.

HELP DESK

Index

COPYING FILES AND FOLDERS

Click the Start button, click Help, then click the Index tab.

Keyword
Files

Topic
Overview; Using drag and drop

Jason asks you to move the file named Products.xls from the Company Templates folder to the Overhead Transparencies folder.

To move a file to another folder on the same drive:

1. In the All Folders window, click the **disk drive** icon for your Student Disk.

2. In the All Folders window, click the **Company Templates** folder. In the Contents window, you see the files in this folder.

3. Adjust your view so that you can see the file named Products.xls, then click the **Products.xls** icon.

4. Drag the Products.xls icon from the Contents window to the Overhead Transparencies folder in the All Folders window, as shown in Figure 4-33. Windows Explorer displays a Moving dialog box, and moves the file to the Overhead Transparencies folder.

Figure 4-33 ◄
Moving a file
from one folder
to another

ghost of a selected file

source folder

destination folder

file being moved

```
Exploring - B:\Company Templates                           _ |□| X
File  Edit  View  Tools  Help

[Company Templates      ▼]  [toolbar icons]

All Folders                    Contents of 'B:\Company Templates'

op                             5TrPlan.xls  Sr Sales1.xls  Sr Sales2.xls  Admcome.xls  Balance.xls
Computer
5¼ Floppy (A:)
3½ Floppy (B:)
  Company Templates            BrkEven.xls  DailySls.xls  DSBudget.xls  GrwthPlan.xls  Invoices.xls
  Overhead Transparencies
  Searches           Products.xls
  Training                     Ira_Prog.wpd  Listings.xls  LoanCalc.xls  MemoForm.wpd  Paycalc.xls
My computer (C:)
  123r2.4
  123r4w
  Bat                          Payroll.xls  PrdSales.xls  Pri_Sls1.xls  Pri_Sls2.xls  Products.db
  Business
  Clip Art
  Colldos
  Collwin
  Cserve
  Dos                          Products.mdx  Products.xls  Quotes.xls  Raises.xls  Salary.xls
  Erd
  Exchange

1 object(s) selected        15.0KB
```

5. In the All Folders window, click the **Overhead Transparencies** folder. The file named Products.xls is now in the Overhead Transparencies folder.

   TROUBLE? If you do not find the file in this folder, you accidentally placed it in another folder. Open adjacent folders, locate and select the file, then drag it to Overhead Transparencies.

6. Click the **Up One Level** button 🔼 on the toolbar to return to the first folder on your disk.

MOVING A FILE IN WINDOWS EXPLORER

- Open Windows Explorer.
- Select the drive then the folder that contains the file you want to move.
- Select the file by clicking it.
- If you want to move the file to a folder on the same drive, drag the file from the Contents window to the folder in the All Folders window.

or

- If you want to move the file to a folder on another drive, click the Cut button, double-click the folder in the All Folders window that you want to move the file to, then click the Paste button.

Now that Jason has moved Products.xls to the Overhead Transparencies folder, he can open the file and adapt it for use as a transparency.

Printing Folder Contents

Jason asks you to document the contents of the Company Templates folder by printing a list of the files contained in that folder. He suggests that you open this folder, then switch to the Small Icons view so that you can copy the screen's contents and print it with the Paint accessory.

To document the contents of the Company Templates folder:

1. In the Contents window, double-click the **Company Templates** folder.

2. Click the **Small Icons** button on the toolbar.

3. Press **Alt + Print Screen**. A copy of the active window is placed on the Clipboard.

4. Click the **Close** button to close Windows Explorer.

5. Click the **Start** button, point to **Programs**, point to **Accessories**, then click **Paint**.

   TROUBLE? If you can't find the Paint accessory on the Accessories menu, it's possible that your site didn't install Paint. Check the Accessories menu again. If the WordPad accessory is installed, you can use it instead of the Paint accessory. If you cannot find either accessory, ask your instructor or technical support person for a suggestion on which application to use. If you are using your own computer, you can use the Windows 95 Setup disk to find and install the Paint and WordPad accessories.

6. Click **Edit** on the Paint menu bar, then click **Paste**.

   TROUBLE? If a message box appears asking to enlarge the bitmap, click the Yes button. The contents of the Clipboard appear in the Paint window.

7. Make sure your printer is on and operational.

8. Click **File**, click **Print**, and then click the **OK** button in the Print dialog box after you check the Print settings. You now have a hard copy of the contents of the Company Templates folder on your Student Disk.

9. Click **File** then click **Exit**.

10. If a Paint dialog box appears asking if you want to save your file, click the **No** button. Windows 95 again returns you to the desktop, and the Paint button disappears from the taskbar.

Jason thanks you for the copy of the contents of the Company Templates folder, and files this record with his other documentation.

Creating a Windows Explorer Shortcut

Since Windows Explorer is an important part of Windows 95 and since it provides a visual overview of the organization of drives and folders within a computer, Nadine asks Jason and her other employees to create a shortcut to Windows Explorer on their desktop so that they can quickly open it as they work.

To speed up access to Windows Explorer and further customize your desktop, you can create a shortcut to Windows Explorer by using the desktop's shortcut menu. When you use this feature, you must specify the location and filename of the application that you want to create a shortcut to. Unlike creating a shortcut to a specific drive from My Computer window, you must browse the folder structure of a disk until you locate and select the application.

HELP DESK

Index

CREATING SHORTCUTS TO PROGRAMS AND FILES

Click the Start button, click Help, then click the Index tab.

Keyword	**Topic**
Shortcuts	Overview: Creating shortcuts to programs and files

Jason asks you to add a shortcut to Windows Explorer on his desktop.

To create a shortcut to Windows Explorer:

1. Right-click the **desktop**, point to **New**, then click **Shortcut** on the New menu. A Create Shortcut dialog box opens. See Figure 4-34. Windows 95 prompts you to type in the Command line text box the location and name of the item for which you want to create a shortcut. If you do not know the exact location and name of the item, you can use the Browse button to find it.

Figure 4-34 ◄
Creating a desktop shortcut

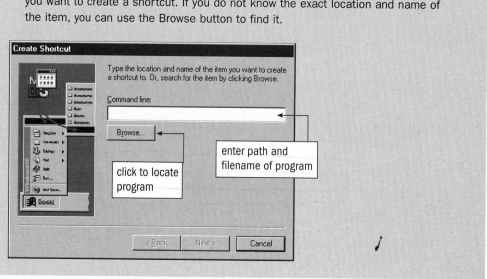

2. Click the **Browse** button. In the Browse dialog box, you can specify where to look, which folder to use, and what types of files to locate. See Figure 4-35. Since Windows Explorer is a Windows tool, you assume the program file will be in the Windows folder.

Figure 4-35 ◀
Browsing for a
program

browse this folder ——

subfolders on
drive C

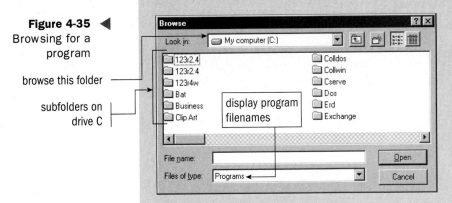

display program
filenames

3. Scroll until you locate the Windows folder, click the **Windows** folder, then click the **Open** button. The Look in list box shows you that you are currently looking in the Windows folder. Now you can locate the name of the program file that starts Windows Explorer.

4. Scroll until you locate the file named Explorer.exe or Explorer, click **Explorer.exe** or **Explorer**, then click the **Open** button.

If you do not see file extensions on your filenames, then the option for viewing MS-DOS file extensions is not enabled.

5. You return to the original Shortcut dialog box, and Windows inserts the full path for Windows Explorer. See Figure 4-36.

Figure 4-36 ◀
Creating a
shortcut for
Windows
Explorer

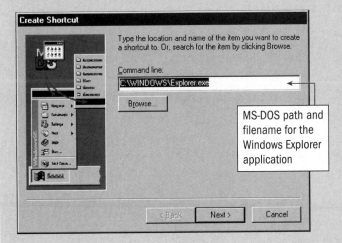

MS-DOS path and
filename for the
Windows Explorer
application

6. Click the **Next** button. In the Select a name for the shortcut text box, you can type a name for the shortcut icon.

7. Type **Explorer** in the Select a name for the shortcut text box.

8. Click the **Finish** button. Windows 95 places a shortcut to Windows Explorer on your desktop. See Figure 4-37.

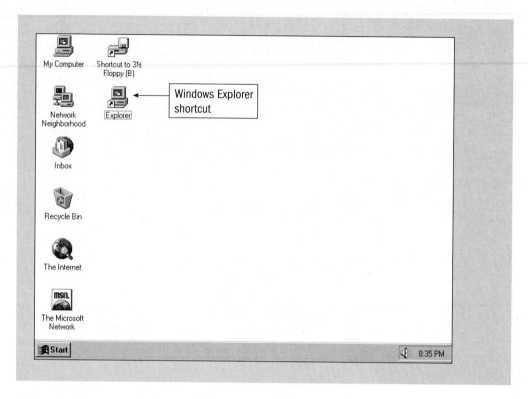

Figure 4-37
Windows
Explorer
shortcut on the
desktop

Jason asks you to test this shortcut and make sure it is operating properly.

To test the Explorer shortcut:

1. Double-click the shortcut for Windows Explorer. The Windows Explorer window opens, and you see the contents of your hard disk.

2. Click the **Close** button ❎ to close the window and return to the desktop.

You can use this same approach to create other types of shortcuts for system resources, applications, and folders that you want to place on your desktop.

REFERENCE
window

CREATING A SHORTCUT FROM THE DESKTOP

- Right-click the desktop to display the desktop's shortcut menu.
- Point to New on the shortcut menu, then click Shortcut on the New menu.
- In the Create Shortcut dialog box, enter the full path of the application or program you want to create a shortcut for, or use Browse to locate the filename of the system resource, application, folder, or file for which you want to create a shortcut.
- Click the Next button, then, if necessary, type a label for the shortcut.
- Click the Finish button.

Tutorial Assignment

Nadine has asked Jason to present a workshop for other members of the finance department on how to design effective spreadsheet models. To prepare for this upcoming workshop, Jason needs to pull together a set of files that illustrate the points that he wants to make during his presentation. To start, he wants to make a copy of his current floppy disk, then search for the files that he will use to illustrate how to develop spreadsheet models. In this tutorial assignment, you will make a copy of the Student Disk that you used in this tutorial, and use that new copy for the remainder of the tutorial assignment as well as the case problems.

1. Insert your Student Disk into a floppy disk drive.
2. Open Windows Explorer.
3. In the All Folders window, select the floppy disk drive that contains your Student Disk.
4. Right-click the disk drive icon, select Copy Disk on the shortcut menu, then copy the contents of your Student Disk to a newly formatted, blank disk.
5. Open the Find: All Files window, then maximize the window.
6. On the Name & Location tab, select and delete any entry in the Named list box, then, if necessary, select your floppy disk drive as the drive to search.
7. Check the Date Modified tab and, if necessary, select the option for searching for all files.
8. On the Advanced tab, choose Microsoft Excel 5.0 Worksheet as the type of application file to search for. If you do not have Microsoft Excel on your computer, select the Name & Location tab, then specify *.XLS in the Named list box.
9. On the Advanced tab, enter "Analysis" as the text to search for, then start the search.
10. After Windows 95 locates the files that contain this text, double-click the border between the In Folder and Size columns to widen the In Folder column. The files Jason wants are Adincome.xls and BrkEven.xls, and they are stored in the Company Templates folder.
11. If Quick View is installed on your computer, use it to view the contents of Adincome.xls. Change to full page view, examine the graph, then close the Quick View window.
12. *Optional*: If you have Microsoft Excel 5.0 or 7.0 on your computer, double-click Adincome.xls and examine the actual contents of the file. Notice the differences between Quick View and the actual file's contents, then close Microsoft Excel.
13. Close the Find: All Files window.
14. Select the floppy disk drive that contains your Student Disk, then create a folder named Presentations on your floppy disk.
15. Open the Company Templates folder, then select and drag Adincome.xls and BrkEven.xls to the Presentations folder in the All Folders window. If you prefer, you can select and drag one file at a time to the Presentations folder.
16. Select the Presentations folder in the All Folders window, and verify that Adincome.xls and BrkEven.xls are now in this folder.
17. Click the Up One Level button on the Windows Explorer toolbar to close the Presentations folder.
18. Select View, point to Arrange Icons, then select by Name.
19. Press Alt + Print Screen to copy the folder structure of your floppy disk to the Clipboard.
20. Open the Paint accessory from the Start menu. Use Paste on the Edit menu to paste the contents of the Clipboard into the drawing area, then print a copy of the pasted image. Exit Paint without saving the file.
21. Close Windows Explorer.

Case Problems

1. Updating Financial Records at Grassilli Vineyards Grassilli Vineyards is a small but flourishing company that produces high-quality Cabernet wines. Marie Retherford, one of the partners in this company, prepares financial analyses for herself and the other two owners. After a busy summer and fall, Marie now has some time to update her records. So that she can keep track of her financial analyses, Marie asks you to search for all the documents that she has created from last May through last August.

1. Insert your Student Disk into a floppy disk drive.
2. Open the Find: All Files window from the Start Menu, then maximize the window.
3. On the Name & Location tab, enter "*.*" (which selects all files) in the Named box, then select your floppy disk drive as the drive to search.
4. Check the Advanced tab and, if necessary, select All Files and Folders in the Of type box, then select and delete any entry in the Containing text box.
5. On the Date Modified tab, select the between option, enter "5/1/97" as the starting date, enter "8/31/97" as the ending date for the search, then start Find.
6. Arrange the results in order by filename, and adjust the width of the In Folder and Type columns to show the full folder and application names.
7. Press Alt + Print Screen.
8. Open the Paint accessory, paste the contents of the Clipboard into the drawing area, print the pasted image, then exit Paint without saving.
9. Close the Find: All Files window.

2. Creating Folders for Business Records at Garrison's Auto & Truck Repair During the summer months, Adam Garrison works at his father's business, Garrison's Auto & Truck Repair to earn additional money for college. This summer his father wants him to organize the business records on his computer, and create copies of folders that contain important files. Adam asks you to copy the contents of the Company Templates and Searches folder to a new folder on drive C named Garrison's Business Records.

If you work in a computer lab, make sure you have permission to copy files to a hard disk or network drive.

1. Insert your Student Disk into a floppy disk drive.
2. Open Windows Explorer and, in the All Folders window, select the floppy disk drive that contains your Student Disk.
3. If necessary, select drive C in the All Folders window.
4. Create a new folder named Garrison's Business Records.
5. Select your floppy disk drive in the All Folders window.
6. Select then drag a copy of the Company Templates and the Searches folders to the Garrison's Business Records folder on drive C. *Note:* If you prefer, you can select and drag one folder at a time.
7. Open the Garrison's Business Records folder on drive C, and verify that you copied the Company Templates and Searches folders to this folder.
8. Press Alt + Print Screen.
9. Open the Paint accessory, paste the contents of the Clipboard into the drawing area, then print the pasted image, and exit Paint without saving.
10. Select the Garrison's Business Records folder on drive C, then delete the folder.
11. Close Windows Explorer.

3. Evaluating Disk Usage at Computer Resources, Inc. Computer Resources, Inc. offers its clients a spectrum of services ranging from consulting and training to on-site installation, setup, and configuration of computers. Like other types of businesses that focus on computer training, Computer Resources must install a wide variety of applications on their computer systems. Julie Shannon and her assistant are responsible for tracking all the client documents and business records of Computer Resources. At the end of every quarter, Julie evaluates the usage of storage space on the company's computers to determine how efficiently that space is used. She and her assistant periodically archive files that have not been accessed for more than six months, or large files that require a large amount of storage space. Julie asks you to examine your computer and locate files that you have not used since May 1st. She also asks you to locate large files and determine whether you still need them.

1. Insert your Student Disk into a floppy disk drive.
2. Open the Find: All Files window from the floppy disk shortcut's shortcut menu, then maximize the window.
3. On the Name & Location tab, enter "*.*" (which selects all files) in the Named list box, then if necessary, select your floppy disk drive as the drive to search.
4. Check the Advanced tab and, if necessary, select All Files and Folders in the Of type box, then select and delete any entry in the Containing text box.
5. On the Date Modified tab, select the between option, enter "3/20/96" as the starting date, enter "3/20/97" as the ending date for a search, then start Find.
6. Arrange the results in order by filename, and then adjust the width of the In Folder and Type columns to show the full folder and application names.
7. Press Alt + Print Screen.
8. Open the Paint accessory, paste the contents of the Clipboard into the drawing area, print the pasted image, and exit Paint without saving.
9. On the Date Modified tab, select the option for locating all files.
10. On the Advanced tab, specify that you want to locate all files that are at least 20KB in size, then start the Find. *Note:* The first Size list box allows you to select "at least," "at most," or no qualifier. In the second Size list box, you can use the spin box arrows to increase or decrease the number of KB (Kilobytes).
11. Arrange the results in order by filename, then adjust the width of the In Folder and Type columns to show the full folder and application names.
12. Press Alt + Print Screen.
13. Open Paint, then paste the contents of the Clipboard into the drawing area, print the pasted image, then exit Paint without saving the file.
14. Close the Find: All Files window.

4. Compiling Document Lists at Doran & Traversi Word Processing Services Doran & Traversi Word Processing Services prepare a variety of legal and medical documents for their clients. Some of the documents are directly transcribed from tape, while other documents are prepared from draft versions of documents provided by their client. Since their clients work with Microsoft Word and WordPerfect for Windows, the owner of Doran & Traversi have installed both applications on their computers. Chad Malloy keeps track of client documents, and organizes those documents in folders so that the staff at Doran & Traversi can easily locate these client documents. One of Chad's co-workers recently worked on some client documents at home, and has given Chad his diskette so that Chad can copy those files to his computer. Since the diskette has other files, Chad must search for the Microsoft Word and WordPerfect files. He asks you to search for both sets of files using wildcards.

1. Insert your Student Disk into a floppy disk drive.
2. Open Windows Explorer and, in the All Folders window, select the floppy disk drive that contains your Student Disk.
3. Open the Find: All Files window, then maximize the window.
4. Check the Date Modified tab and, if necessary, choose the option for searching for all files.

5. Check the Advanced tab and, if necessary, select All Files and Folders in the Of type box, then select and delete any entry in the Containing text box.

6. On the Name & Location tab, enter *.doc *.wpd in the Named list box, and select your floppy disk drive as the drive to search. *Note:* If you specify two criteria in the Named box, separated by a space, Find locates files (and folders) that meet both conditions.

7. Arrange the results in order by filename, then adjust the width of the In Folder and Type columns to show the full folder and application names.

8. Press Alt + Print Screen.

9. Open the Paint accessory, paste the contents of the Clipboard into the drawing area, print the pasted image, then exit Paint without saving the file.

10. Close the Find: All Files window, then close Windows Explorer.

Using Troubleshooting Tools

Developing Troubleshooting Tools

Yellow Brick Road Child Care Services

CASE Yellow Brick Road Child Care Services provides child care for parents with limited incomes so that those parents can continue to work and further their job skills and education. Yellow Brick Road relies on income from tuition fees and grants, as well as funding from both private and public programs. Three months ago, as the result of the generosity of its corporate sponsors, it received donations of six new Pentium computers with Windows 95, a laser printer, and software. The administrative staff now uses these computers to produce a wide variety of documents, including financial and program reports, grant applications, and its annual report.

Yellow Brick Road also relies on a committed core of volunteers who are skilled professionals in the community. Some of these volunteers work full time at other jobs, some are self-employed, and some are retirees. Wei Chiu works with five other full-time and part-time staff in the administrative offices. One of her important responsibilities as office manager is to provide computer support to other staff members. She often consults with Stephanie Arnold, a computer troubleshooting specialist who donates four hours of time per month to the center on both software and hardware problems. Stephanie has assisted Wei and the other staff members in installing software, configuring and customizing their computers, and troubleshooting printer problems.

Developing a Troubleshooting Strategy

Now that the staff has become more comfortable with their new computers, Stephanie presents a one-hour workshop for the administrative staff on how to troubleshoot problems with a computer. Stephanie emphasizes that when faced with a problem on your computer system, you can combine your experience and knowledge with the resources available within Windows 95. As you troubleshoot a problem, you can use the following guidelines and techniques to assist you in the task:

■ **Define the problem**. First, you want to make sure you know the exact nature of the problem. If, for example, a co-worker's printer is not working properly, ask questions that will provide you with the information you need to troubleshoot the problem. Was she able to print at all? Were there problems with the quality of the printed document? Is this the first time she has encountered that problem? When was she last able to print a document without any problems? Did she or anyone else make changes to the configuration of her computer? Were any error messages displayed?

■ **Analyze the problem**. Using the information that you have acquired about the problem, you then analyze the problem. For example, if a co-worker changes the configuration on his computer and then is unable to print, could the problem be caused by the change in configuration? Or is there a possibility of some other type of error, such as a hardware problem or a change in a software setting?

■ **Identify the source of the problem**. To provide you with more information about the nature of a problem, you can devise other tests that help you identify the cause of the problem. For example, if a co-worker is unable to print a document with a specific application, you could open another application and print a document produced with that application. If you are able to print with this other application, then you check the print settings for the first application. If you cannot print with any of the applications installed on a computer, then check the operating system's configuration settings for the printer.

■ **Check hardware and software settings**. Check both hardware and software settings and, if the settings have been changed, restore the settings to their original values.

■ **Draw on all the resources you have to resolve the problem**. Check the online Help provided with your operating system and applications. It might provide you with some ideas and direction, or it might even have special troubleshooting tools. Check readme files provided with software that you install on your computer. A **readme** file is a text file (often named Readme.txt) that contains troubleshooting information or more up-to-date information on newly installed hardware and software. For example, in the Windows folder, there is a readme file named Printers.txt that contains information about installing and using printers with Windows 95. Check any reference manuals provided with your hardware or software. If the manufacturer of the product you purchased has a technical support line, call and talk to a technical support person about the problem. He or she might know the answer immediately, or might be able to replicate the problem and then determine how to resolve it. Some companies operate bulletin board services that you can dial into, post a question about a problem you are having, and check back later to find out if a technical support person or another user has possible solutions to the problem. Also, talk to coworkers or friends who might be familiar with specific types of hardware and software.

- **Consider other alternatives**. If you attempt to troubleshoot a problem and cannot resolve it, consider other possible causes for a problem. For example, if you cannot print a document that you printed a few days ago, you might consider the possibility of an infection by a computer virus. A **computer virus** is a program that gains access to a computer, usually via an infected diskette, and adversely affects the performance of a computer system. For example, the Dark Avenger computer virus randomly deletes sectors on a hard disk. If a printer driver is stored in the sector that the Dark Avenger virus deletes, then you will not be able to print.

During her presentation of troubleshooting strategies, Stephanie also emphasizes that staff members can simplify the process of troubleshooting problems on a computer by following certain common-sense guidelines, precautions, and preventive measures:

- **Develop an understanding of how your computer functions.** If you understand how the basic processes within a computer function, such as how a computer boots, then you are in a better position to analyze and resolve problems that might arise. You should understand what happens when your computer boots, how Windows 95 configures and manages the resources within your computer, and also what happens when you shut down your computer.

- **Acquaint yourself with the troubleshooting tools on your computer.** Operating systems include a variety of features or utilities for troubleshooting problems and for optimizing the performance of a computer system. Learn about these utilities and how they function. Periodically optimize your computer, and eliminate small problems before they become major problems.

- **Document hardware and software settings.** Prior to the occurrence of a problem, you should have a copy of the correct settings for different hardware devices and software applications on your computer so that, if the need arises, you can check the current settings on your computer against settings that have previously worked.

- **Back up your computer.** Periodically back up the installed software, with its configuration settings, and the document files on your computer. If you lose an important document file, you can restore it from the backup copy. If program files are accidentally deleted, you can restore a copy of your software from a backup disk.

- **Use anti-viral software.** As of August, 1995, close to 6,300 computer viruses have been identified, and two or three new computer viruses are discovered daily. Purchase and install anti-viral software on your computer. Use that software to periodically check your computer and diskettes that you insert into your computer's disk drives. If the anti-viral software includes a virus interceptor, load the virus interceptor. A **virus interceptor** is a program that monitors your computer for computer viruses while you work with other software, and that automatically checks diskettes inserted into disk drives. Since new viruses are discovered daily, you must update the software every two or three months.

After Stephanie completes her presentation on troubleshooting strategies, she and Wei meet to go over in more detail the troubleshooting tools available in Windows 95.

The Booting Process

Stephanie emphasizes first that Wei should know what happens during booting so that she can be a more effective troubleshooter.

When you turn on a computer system, the microprocessor locates and executes start-up **routines**, or programs, to identify and enable devices, perform a Power-On Self-Test, and then locate and load the operating system. The software contained in the BIOS (Basic Input/Output System) contains instructions for communicating with hardware devices. The software is stored on a ROM (Read-Only Memory) BIOS chip. If your computer has a Plug and Play BIOS, then the first routine identifies, enables, and configures Plug and Play devices. If your computer has a legacy BIOS, then all the devices are enabled. The term **legacy** refers to devices that do not support the Plug and Play standards defined by Microsoft Corporation in conjunction with hardware manufacturers.

The **Power-On Self-Test** (or **POST**) is another routine that checks for hardware errors, including memory errors. After the POST, another routine checks drive A for the operating system software. If drive A contains the operating system files, then the computer boots from that drive and disk then loads the operating system software into memory. If drive A does not contain a floppy disk, then the routine examines drive C. Once it locates the operating system files on that drive, it loads the operating system into memory so that it can then manage the operation of the computer system. If drive A contains a floppy disk that does not have the operating system on it, then you will see the familiar "Non-system disk or disk error" message appear every time you boot your computer with a disk left in drive A by mistake. If this occurs, you remove that disk from the drive and press any key to continue the booting process from drive C. Some computers are configured to check drive C first, then drive A, for the operating system. Also, for those computers that check drive A first, one common means for infecting a computer with a computer virus is to leave an infected floppy disk in drive A and then boot.

This type of boot is called a **cold boot** because you start by powering on the computer. To perform a **warm boot**, your computer is already on, and you either press the Reset button on your desktop or tower unit or press the Ctrl, Alt, and Delete keys simultaneously. During the warm boot, or **system reset**, you reboot the computer, but it does not perform the POST. Instead, it locates and loads a copy of the operating system into memory. The warm boot is useful if your system locks up and does not respond. No matter what type of boot you perform, the important thing to remember is that you boot a computer from drive A or from drive C.

The name of the real mode Windows 95 operating system file that loads first is Io.sys. Recall that real mode refers to the MS-DOS operating mode in which the microprocessor can only access 1MB of memory. Io.sys contains the information for continuing the booting process. This operating system file combines the functions of the MS-DOS files named Io.Sys, which handled input and output operations; Msdos.Sys, which managed disks, drives, folders, and files; and the MS-DOS configuration file named Config.Sys, which loaded device drivers. Io.sys loads Himem.sys, the device driver for managing extended memory; Ifshlp.sys (Installable File System Helper), the device driver for accessing the Windows 95 filing system; Setver.exe, the device driver that provides DOS applications with the DOS version number; and either Dblspace.bin or Drvspace.bin, the device drivers that provide access to disk drives compressed with either the DoubleSpace or the DriveSpace disk compression utilities available in MS-DOS 6.0, 6.1, 6.2, 6.21, and 6.22, as well as Windows 95.

The Windows 95 Msdos.sys file performs a completely different function than the MS-DOS operating system file by the same name. It now contains special startup values, such as the paths for locating important Windows 95 files as well as booting options that Windows 95 needs to start your computer.

After loading Io.sys, the Windows 95 operating system loads and processes real mode (or MS-DOS mode) components. It examines the contents of Config.sys and Autoexec.bat, and loads any real mode device drivers needed for DOS applications. Config.sys is an MS-DOS system startup file that contains **directives**, or commands, for further configuring the operating system. Autoexec.bat is an MS-DOS system startup file for customizing a computer. Using these two files, Windows 95 loads device drivers and Terminate-and-Stay-Resident utilities to maintain backward compatibility with DOS and Windows 3.1 applications. A **Terminate-and-Stay-Resident** program, or **TSR**, is one that remains in memory and performs some function in the background as you work with other programs. The memory used by a TSR is not available for use by other programs. In contrast, when an operating system loads an application, it allocates memory to the application. Once you exit the application, the operating system reclaims the memory used by that application so that you can use it for another application or a utility. An example of a TSR is a virus interceptor. On many systems, the operating system loads the virus interceptor when the computer boots, and the virus interceptor remains in memory and monitors your computer while you work with other applications.

During this real mode phase of the booting process, Win.com loads the core components of Windows 95. Then, Windows 95 switches to protected mode, and loads the remainder of the operating system files as well as the virtual device drivers. Recall that protected mode is an operating mode in which the microprocessor can address more than 1MB of memory, provide memory protection features, and use 32-bit (rather than 16-bit) processing. These operating system files include Kernel32.dll, which contains the main Windows 95 components; Krnl386.exe, which loads the Windows 95 device drivers; Gdi.exe and Gdi32.exe, which contain the code for the graphic device interface; and User.exe and User32.exe, which contain the code for the user interface.

As Wei can tell from Stephanie's description of how a system boots under Windows 95, the booting process is a complex and involved process that proceeds in phases. The process involves many different program files that provide compatibility with DOS and Windows 3.1 applications, and provides access to the new Windows 95 operating system and its features.

Making a Startup Disk

Stephanie notes that, because of the complexity of the Windows 95 booting process, each computer should have its own Startup Disk for troubleshooting problems with a hard drive or Windows 95.

When you first install Windows 95 on a computer system, it asks if you want to make a Startup Disk. If you choose to make a Startup Disk, Windows 95 copies the operating system files and utilities that allow it to boot your system from drive A to the Startup Disk.

You cannot make a Startup Disk using drive B because the BIOS routine that looks for the operating system files only checks a floppy disk in drive A and the hard disk in drive C. If you are experiencing trouble with Windows 95 or with your hard disk drive C, you can boot your computer with the Windows 95 Startup Disk in drive A. Then, you can attempt to troubleshoot the problems.

HELP DESK

Index

CREATING A STARTUP DISK

Click the Start button, click Help, then click the Index tab.

Keyword
Startup disk, creating

Topic
To create a startup disk

Following Stephanie's advice, Wei asks you to prepare a Startup Disk for her computer and one for your computer.

If you did not make a Windows 95 Startup Disk when you first installed Windows 95 on your computer system, if someone else installed Windows 95 but did not provide you with a Startup Disk, or if you want a second copy of the Startup Disk, you can make one by using the Add/Remove Programs Wizard in the Control Panel folder.

To complete the following tutorial steps, you will need a floppy disk for drive A. You will also need a copy of the Windows 95 CD-ROM installation disc or the Windows 95 installation disks. If you do not have access to these disks, then you cannot complete the following section and should continue with the next section.

To make a Windows 95 Startup Disk:

1. Click the **Start** button, point to **Settings**, then click **Control Panel** on the Settings menu. The Control Panel opens. See Figure 5-1.

Figure 5-1
Control Panel
window

choose to create a
Startup Disk

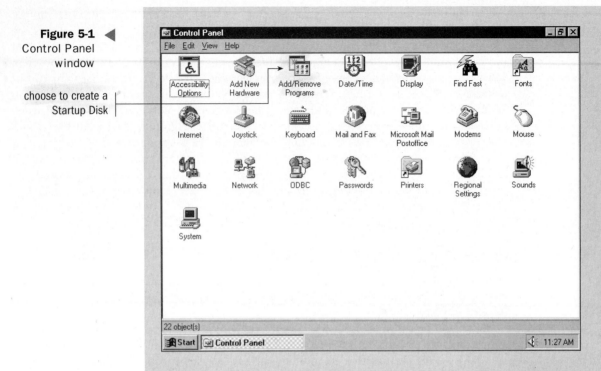

2. Double-click the **Add/Remove Programs** icon. The Add/Remove Programs
Properties dialog box opens.

3. Click the **Startup Disk** tab. On the Startup Disk property sheet, Windows 95
explains the value of having a Startup Disk. See Figure 5-2.

Figure 5-2
Add/Remove
Programs
Properties
dialog box

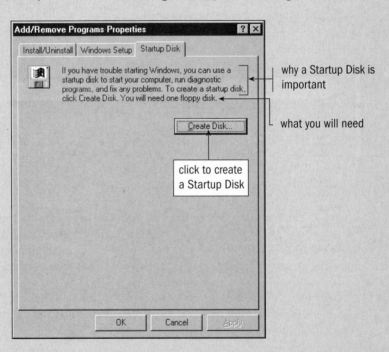

why a Startup Disk is
important

what you will need

click to create
a Startup Disk

4. Click the **Create Disk** button. The first Insert Disk dialog box prompts for either
your Windows 95 CD-ROM disc or one of your installation disks.

TROUBLE? If you are on a network, you might not need to insert an installation
disk. Instead, you will probably see the prompt described in Step 5 that requests
that you insert a floppy disk into drive A. Do so, then continue with Step 6.

5. Insert your Windows 95 CD-ROM disc into the CD-ROM drive, or the appropriate installation disk into a floppy disk drive, then click the **OK** button. The next Insert Disk dialog box prompts you to label a disk "Windows 95 Startup Disk" and to insert that disk into drive A. You will need a new disk for drive A. *Do not use any of your Student Disks; if you do, you will erase them.*

6. Insert the newly labeled "Windows 95 Startup Disk" into drive A, then click the **OK** button. Windows 95 then copies operating system files and utilities to the new Startup Disk.

   TROUBLE? If Windows 95 does not recognize the disk that you insert into drive A, remove that disk and try another disk. If you still have problems with Windows 95 recognizing a disk, format the disk under Windows 95.

7. After Windows 95 completes the process of making a Startup Disk, click the **OK** button to close this dialog box, then close the Control Panel.

REFERENCE window

MAKING A STARTUP DISK

- Click the Start button, point to Settings, then click Control Panel on the Settings menu.
- Double-click the Add/Remove Programs icon.
- n the Add/Remove Programs dialog box, click the Startup Disk tab.
- Click the Create Disk button and follow the steps as Windows 95 prompts you.

Wei has all staff members create a Startup Disk to guarantee them access to their computers if they experience problems with Windows 95, the booting process, or the hard disk drive itself.

Viewing the Files on a Startup Disk

To reinforce what Stephanie told her about the importance of the Startup Disk and the booting process, Wei wants to examine the files on her copy of the Startup Disk.

Since the Startup Disk contains operating system files for booting your computer system, as well as specific utilities for troubleshooting problems, it is important to be familiar with the contents of the Startup Disk. Also, you might want to add other system files and utilities to that disk to assist you in troubleshooting problems.

Wei suggests that you also examine your copy of the Startup Disk, so that you can decide whether you want to add any other utilities to the disk.

To view the contents of the Startup Disk:

1. Double-click the **My Computer** icon.

2. In the My Computer window, double-click the **disk drive icon** for drive A, then maximize the drive A window.

3. If you do not see a toolbar, click **View** then click **Toolbar**.

4. Click **View**, click **Options**, then click the **View** tab. On the View property sheet, you have an option for displaying the MS-DOS path.

5. If it is not already selected, click the **Display the full MS-DOS path in the title bar** check box.

6. If it is selected, click the **Hide MS-DOS file extensions for file types that are registered** check box to remove the check mark.

7. If necessary, in the Hidden files section, click the **Show all files**, then click the **OK** button.

8. If necessary, click the **Large Icons** button ⬚ on the toolbar. Figure 5-3 shows the files on the Startup Disk.

Figure 5-3 ◄
Viewing the
contents of a
Startup Disk

system startup files ——————

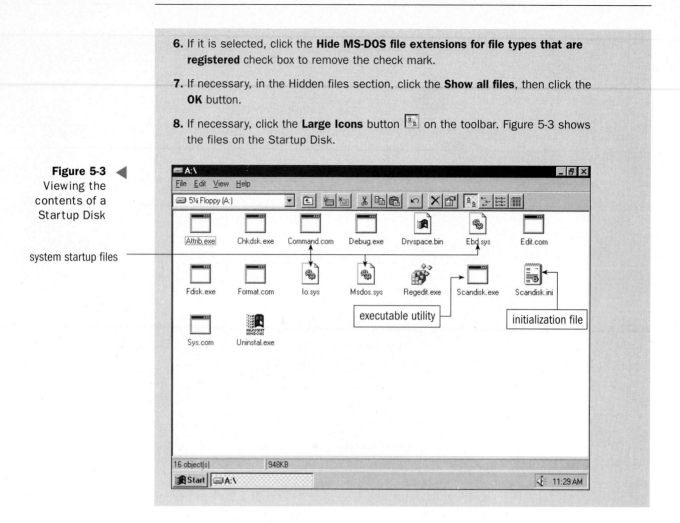

You see the Windows 95 real mode operating system files Io.sys, Msdos.sys, Ebd.sys, Command.com, and either Drvspace.bin or Dblspace.bin. Ebd.sys contains a setting that identifies this diskette as an emergency Startup Disk. Command.com displays a MS-DOS like command prompt on the screen, interprets commands entered at the command prompt, and locates and loads programs. A **command prompt** is a user interface that allows you to issue commands to the operating system. The command prompt shows the current drive and the current directory (or folder). For example, the command prompt for drive A might appear as A:\> and the one for drive C might appear as C:\>. The backslash symbol (\ ) after the drive name refers to the root directory, or the first folder, created on the disk when it was formatted. If you ever need to start your computer with the Startup Disk, you will not see the Windows 95 graphical user interface. Instead, you will see a command prompt for drive A. To work with your computer, you must enter commands at the command prompt and, therefore, be familiar with how to use MS-DOS commands and utilities.

The other files are utilities provided with Windows 95. Figure 5-4 identifies each of these utilities, and lists the filenames of the executable and supporting files for each utility as well as the use or uses of each utility. All of these utilities, except Regedit.exe and Uninstal.exe, are available in different versions of MS-DOS and IBM-DOS (or PC-DOS). Windows 3.1 has its own version of Regedit.exe.

Figure 5-4 ◀
Startup Disk
Files

Utility	Filename(s)	Use(s)
Attribute	Attrib.exe	A file and folder utility that (1) displays information on the attributes of files and folders, and (2) changes the attributes of files and folders
Check Disk	Chkdsk.exe	A disk analysis utility that (1) checks the status of the filing system and reports errors in the logical structure of a disk, (2) corrects certain types of errors in the logical structure of a disk, and (3) reports on the utilization of disk storage space and memory
Debug	Debug.exe	A debugging utility for testing and debugging executable DOS programs
Editor	Edit.com	A text editor for creating and modifying configuration files
FDisk	Fdisk.exe	A disk utility for creating partitions on a hard disk
Format	Format.com	A disk utility for formatting a hard disk or floppy disk
Registry Editor	Regedit.exe	Opens the Registry Editor so that you can view or change Registry information [Important Note: **Do not change the Registry; instead, use the Control Panel.**]
ScanDisk	Scandisk.exe Scandisk.ini	A disk analysis and disk repair utility that (1) checks the status of the filing system and reports errors in the logical structure of a disk, (2) corrects certain types of errors in the logical structure of a disk, and (3) checks and repairs defective sectors on a disk. Note: The INI file is an **initialization file** that contains configuration settings used by the ScanDisk utility.
System	Sys.com	A system utility that copies the operating system files from one disk to another disk
Uninstall	Uninstal.exe	A utility that uninstalls Windows 95 and restores the previous MS-DOS and Windows versions to your computer

To start any of these utilities, you type the first part of the filename as a command at the command prompt and specify the correct **syntax**, or wording, for the command. For example, to format a disk with the Format utility on the Startup Disk, you type FORMAT followed by a space and the name of the disk drive that you want to format. To obtain Help information on how to use any of these utilities, you type the name of the utility at the command prompt followed by a space and the Help switch (/?). For example, to obtain Help on how to use the format utility, you would type FORMAT /? then press the Enter key. Later, when you explore how to start an MS-DOS session under Windows 95, you will learn more about working at the command prompt.

You should be cautious with three of these utilities—Fdisk.exe, Regedit.exe, and Uninstal.exe. The Fdisk utility will remove all the partitions from your hard disk and in the process delete everything stored on the hard disk, and you cannot reverse this process. When you **partition** a hard disk, you divide it into one or more logical drives. For example, you might partition a hard disk into one disk drive called drive C, or you might partition it into two drives, one called drive C and the other called drive D. The Regedit utility allows you to access the Windows 95 Registry—the set of databases where Windows 95 stores all its system and user configurations. If you open the Registry and make a change to a setting, Windows 95 might not function. The Uninstal.exe allows you to remove Windows 95 from your computer, and reinstall the previous version of MS-DOS and Windows 3.1. However, if the Windows 95 Setup install program does not create a file named W95undo.dat on drive C when you first installed Windows 95, then you cannot uninstall Windows 95 with the Uninstall utility. Also, do not use Uninstal.exe if you compressed your hard disk after installing Windows 95 on your computer system.

In addition to the booting files and utilities on your Startup Disk, you might want to copy other important files, such as Config.sys, Autoexec.bat, Win.ini, and System.ini, as well as device drivers for hardware components, into a special folder on your Startup Disk so that you can restore these files on your hard disk. Win.ini and System.ini are Windows 3.1 initialization files that contain configuration settings for Windows 3.1. During booting, Windows 95 examines the contents of the MS-DOS and Windows 3.1 configuration and initialization files so that it has all the settings that it needs to maintain backward compatibility with MS-DOS and Windows 3.1 applications.

If you need to modify the MS-DOS or Windows 3.1 configuration and initialization files on either drive C or on the Startup Disk in drive A, you can use the Edit utility on the Startup Disk or your hard disk drive. Edit.com is a Windows 95 utility that starts the MS-DOS Editor, a simple text editor, for viewing and editing configuration and initialization files. This utility is included on your Startup Disk in case you cannot access the same utility on your hard disk drive.

Testing a Startup Disk

When Stephanie first discussed the importance of a Startup Disk with Wei, she urged Wei to test the Startup Disk after she made it. Stephanie told her that she should not wait until an emergency arises and then hope that the Startup Disk works properly. Wei asks you to test your new Startup Disk too.

If you are working in a computer lab, do not perform the following steps without the permission of your instructor or the technical support person, because these steps require that you restart the computer.

To test the Startup Disk:

1. Close the drive A window, then, if necessary, close the My Computer window.

2. Make sure the Startup Disk is in drive A.

3. Click the **Start** button then click **Shut Down**.

4. When the Shut Down Windows dialog box appears, click the **Restart the computer** radio button, then click the **Yes** button.

TROUBLE? If a message box appears telling you that a user is connected to your machine and asking if you want to continue, click the No button and skip the remaining three steps. You are on a network, and rebooting might cause other users to lose their work if you continue.

After your computer boots from the Startup Disk in drive A, you see a command prompt for drive A. See Figure 5-5. The Startup Disk works, and you can use it anytime you need to troubleshoot a problem with Windows 95 or your hard disk. Now you want to use the DOS Version (VER) command to report the current version of the operating system.

Figure 5-5 ◄
Viewing the
Windows 95
command
prompt
interface

```
                    Award Software, Inc.
                    System Configurations

  CPU Type        : 80486DX2-S      Base Memory      :   640K
  Co-Processor    : Installed       Extended Memory  : 15360K
  CPU Clock       : 66MHz           Cache Memory     :   256K

  Diskette Drive  A : 1.2M , 5.25 in.   Display Type     : EGA/VGA
  Diskette Drive  B : 1.44M, 3.5 in.    Serial Port(s)   : 3F8 2F8
  Hard Disk Drive C : User Type ,  504MB Parallel Port(s) : 378
  Hard Disk Drive D : None


Starting Windows 95...



Microsoft(R) Windows 95
    (C)Copyright Microsoft Corp 1981-1995.

command prompt ──────►A:\>
```

5. At the command prompt, A:\>, type **VER** then press the **Enter** key. The Version command reports that you are using Windows 95, and that its version number is 4.00.950. Your version number might be different.

6. Remove the Startup Disk from drive A.

7. Press the **Reset** button, or press **Ctrl** + **Alt** + **Delete** simultaneously to reboot your computer and start Windows 95.

You might want to seriously consider the possibility of having two, or perhaps three, Startup Disks. If you rely on only one Startup Disk, you might be surprised to find that when you most need it, the disk has developed a bad sector and you cannot boot your computer with it. Why, though, would you need three Startup Disks? If you boot with your first Startup Disk and discover that it does not work, your immediate response is to insert your second Startup Disk and try again. If you then lose your second Startup Disk, it will most likely occur to you that the drive itself might be malfunctioning. Before you use your third and only remaining copy of a Startup Disk, you service drive A.

REFERENCE window	**USING A STARTUP DISK**
	▪ Close all open applications, documents, or windows.
	▪ Insert the Startup Disk into drive A.
	▪ Click the Start button, then click Shut Down.
	▪ Click Restart the computer, then click the Yes button.
	▪ After booting is complete, you will see a command prompt for drive A.
	▪ Troubleshoot any system problems.
	▪ After you resolve any problems, remove the Startup Disk from drive A.
	▪ Press the Reset button, or press Ctrl + Alt + Delete.

Your Startup Disk, as well as Wei's, works without any problems. She makes two other copies of the Startup Disk, and stores them in a safe, easily accessible place that she can find if she ever needs them. She suggests that you do the same.

Performing an Interactive Boot

The following week, Stephanie and Wei meet for lunch to talk about potential problems that might arise when starting Windows 95. Stephanie explains to Wei that if, for any reason, Windows 95 fails to start properly, it will display a Startup menu with a list of booting options. If Windows 95 detects problems on your computer, it will recommend that you restart your computer in Safe mode, so that it can rebuild damaged files. Then, if you reboot again, it will reexamine your computer and its components and attempt to reconfigure itself so that it can start properly. You can also open the Startup menu yourself during the booting process by pressing the F8 key when the "Starting Windows 95" message appears on your screen. Then, Windows 95 will display a Startup menu with different options for starting your computer.

HELP DESK

Index

PERFORMING AN INTERACTIVE BOOT

Click the Start button, click Help, then click the Index tab.

Keyword	Topic
Interactive start	Starting your computer without starting Windows

What you see on the Windows 95 Startup menu depends on the configuration of your computer. Your Startup Menu might include some, or all, of the following options, all of which disable certain components of your operating system so that you can determine what is working and what isn't:

- Normal

- Logged (\BOOTLOG.TXT)

- Safe mode

- Safe mode without compression

- Safe mode with network support

- Safe mode command prompt only

- Step-by-step confirmation

- Command prompt only

- Previous version of MS-DOS

After you choose one of these options, Windows 95 uses settings in Msdos.sys to determine what device drivers to load and what paths it needs for system files.

The Normal option is the default option and, if you choose this option, Windows 95 attempts to go through the complete booting process. The Logged option starts up the system by creating a special startup log called Bootlog.txt. In Bootlog.txt, Windows 95 records what processes were performed and the status of those processes. You can open this file with WordPad, Editor, Notepad, or Write, then examine the sequence of operations that occur during booting, and find out which processes failed and which succeeded. This information might help you and a technical support person, or consultant, to determine how best to proceed in repairing your system.

The Safe mode option starts Windows 95, but only loads device drivers for the mouse, keyboard, and video display unit. Safe mode bypasses Windows 95, Windows 3.1, and MS-DOS startup files, Config.sys, Autoexec.bat, Win.ini, and System.ini, so that you can examine and correct problems with these configuration files. As noted earlier, you can open these files with the Edit utility on the Startup Disk. However, before you make changes to these files, make a copy of the file, print a copy of the file, and make sure you know the effects of the changes you make. To understand the commands and settings included in these configuration and initialization files, you should have a strong background in the use of MS-DOS and Windows 3.1.

HELP DESK

Index

STARTING WINDOWS IN SAFE MODE

Click the Start button, click Help, then click the Index tab.

Keyword	Topic
Safe mode	To start Windows in safe mode

If Windows 95 does not boot properly, if it locks up while you are using it, if it stalls for an extended period of time, if hardware components such as the video display unit and printer do not work properly, or if Windows 95 does not perform reliably and predictably, boot your computer using the Safe mode option, then attempt to troubleshoot the problem. The first thing you should do after rebooting in Safe mode is restart Windows 95, and see if it can rebuild damaged files and reconfigure itself. If rebooting does not work, you can compare the contents of Msdos.sys, Config.sys, Autoexec.bat, Win.ini, and System.ini with your printed copies of these files to verify that the current settings are correct. Even if you are unfamiliar with the contents of the MS-DOS startup files and the Windows 3.1 initialization files, you do have two other important options. You can restore Windows 95 operating system files from a recent backup, or you can reinstall Windows 95 from your original set of disks or CD-ROM disk. If you choose to reinstall Windows 95, it asks if you want to perform a complete installation of all files or if you want to replace only damaged or missing files.

The Safe mode with network support option, if available on the Startup menu, is similar to the Safe mode option, except Command.com and network drivers are loaded so that you can troubleshoot problems that occur in a networking environment and that require a network connection to resolve the problems. As noted earlier, Command.com is important because it displays the command prompt, interprets commands that you enter at the command prompt, and locates and loads program files from the command prompt.

The Safe mode command prompt only option loads Command.com and either Dblspace.bin or Drvspace.bin, but does not load Windows 95. Instead, you work from a command prompt. This option is useful when the Safe mode option does not work, or if you need to work from a command prompt to troubleshoot system problems.

The Step-by-step confirmation option displays each line in Config.sys and Autoexec.bat, and prompts you as to whether or not you want to execute the directives in Config.sys and the commands in Autoexec.bat. To understand what options to choose, and what happens if you decide to load or not load a device driver or TSR, you should have a strong background in the use of MS-DOS. During the Step-by-Step Confirmation, you are also prompted as to whether you want to load the DoubleSpace or DriveSpace drivers so that you can access compressed disk drives, process the Registry, create a start-up log file called Bootlog.txt, start Windows 95, and load Windows drivers. If Windows 95 fails to load properly, the Registry database files might not contain all the necessary configuration information for Windows 95, or it might be damaged.

The Command prompt only option starts Windows 95 by using the Windows 95, Windows 3.1, and MS-DOS system startup files, and processes the contents of the Registry, then displays the command prompt. Instead of troubleshooting problems within Windows 95, which might not be functioning properly, you or a technical support person can troubleshoot them from the command prompt.

The Previous version of MS-DOS, if available, starts the version of MS-DOS that was previously installed on a computer. This option provides you with a wider range of DOS utilities for troubleshooting system problems; however, again, you must have a strong background in the use of MS-DOS and these utilities.

If your hard disk is compressed, then you might also see a Safe mode without the compression only option on the Startup menu. Using this option, Windows 95 loads Command.com, but does not load a disk compression driver to manage access to compressed drives. This option might be useful if you are experiencing problems with a compressed drive or cannot access that compressed drive.

Wei suggests that you display the Startup menu, and select the Safe mode option so that you are familiar with the process for using the Windows 95 Startup menu.

When you reboot your computer, you need to watch the screen closely so that you can press the F8 key when you see the message "Starting Windows 95." You only have two seconds to select this option before the booting process continues. Also, when you switch from one operating mode to another, Windows 95 boots more slowly, so you must be patient.

 If you are working in a computer lab, do not perform the following steps without the permission of your instructor or the technical support person, because these steps require that you restart the computer.

To boot in Safe mode:

1. Click the **Start** button then click **Shut Down**.

2. Click the **Restart the computer** option, then click the **Yes** button.

3. When you see the message "Starting Windows 95" displayed on the monitor, press the **F8** key. After you press the F8 key, the Windows 95 Startup menu appears. See Figure 5-6. Your Startup menu options might differ from those shown in this figure.

TROUBLE? If you miss the "Starting Windows 95" message, you must wait until Windows 95 completely boots, then repeat Steps 1 through 3.

Figure 5-6
Displaying the
Windows 95
Startup menu

Startup menu

shortcut key for Safe
mode

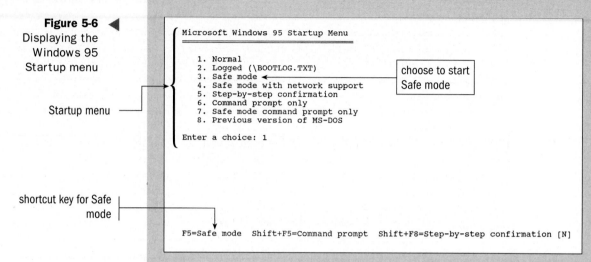

```
Microsoft Windows 95 Startup Menu

   1. Normal
   2. Logged (\BOOTLOG.TXT)
   3. Safe mode          ◄───────   choose to start
   4. Safe mode with network support          Safe mode
   5. Step-by-step confirmation
   6. Command prompt only
   7. Safe mode command prompt only
   8. Previous version of MS-DOS

Enter a choice: 1




F5=Safe mode  Shift+F5=Command prompt  Shift+F8=Step-by-step confirmation [N]
```

4. Press [↓] until you highlight the Safe mode option, press the **Enter** key, then wait until Windows 95 boots using Safe mode.

TROUBLE? If you are working on a network, highlight the Safe Mode with Network Support option.

As noted earlier, your computer will boot more slowly when you select another option for starting Windows 95. Even though you might think that something is wrong, be patient. Before Windows 95 displays the contents of the desktop, it displays a Desktop dialog box in which it explains that you are using a special diagnostic mode for troubleshooting Windows 95 problems. It notes that problems might be caused by your network connection or by your hardware. It suggests that you open the Control Panel, check and, if necessary, change settings, then restart Windows 95. It also warns you that not all devices will be available while you are using Safe mode. You can also select Safe mode by pressing the F5 key on your keyboard (the Safe mode shortcut key) when you see the Startup menu, or by typing the number of the Startup menu option for Safe mode.

5. In the Desktop dialog box, click the **OK** button. You now see the desktop, and in the four corners of the screen, you see the message "Safe mode." See Figure 5-7. If your computer is connected to a network, Windows 95 does not display the Network Neighborhood icon because it is not available while working in Safe mode.

Figure 5-7 ◀
How the
desktop
appears in Safe
mode

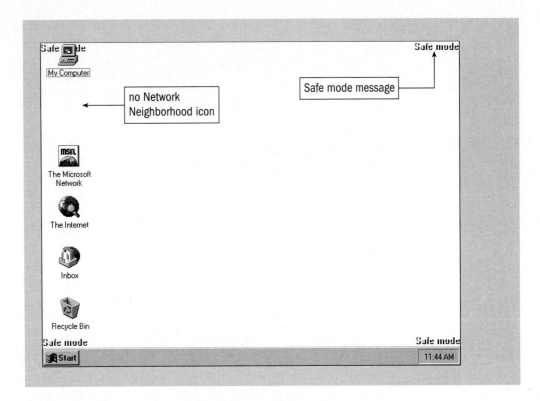

After checking the Control Panel settings, Wei asks you to restart Windows 95 and let it reboot by itself without any intervention on your part.

To restart Windows:

1. Click the **Start** button, then click **Shut Down**.

2. Click the **Restart the computer** radio button, then click the **Yes** button. Again, your computer will boot more slowly when you switch back to the Normal process for starting Windows 95. Even though you might think that something is wrong, be patient. Eventually, you will see your desktop.

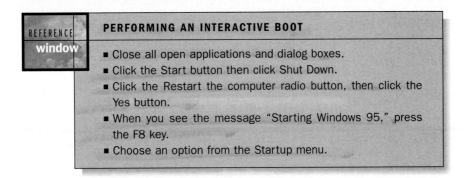

REFERENCE
window

PERFORMING AN INTERACTIVE BOOT

- Close all open applications and dialog boxes.
- Click the Start button then click Shut Down.
- Click the Restart the computer radio button, then click the Yes button.
- When you see the message "Starting Windows 95," press the F8 key.
- Choose an option from the Startup menu.

Wei now knows what to expect if Windows 95 fails to start properly and how to work with the Startup menu. Furthermore, if she has to troubleshoot a problem on the telephone with Stephanie or another technical support person, she will have a better idea of how they might want her to start her computer.

If you want to take a break and resume the tutorial at a later time, you can do so now. If you are on a network, close any open applications and dialog boxes, and leave Windows 95 running. If you are using your own computer, click the Start button on the Taskbar, click Shut Down, click Shut down the computer, and then click the Yes button. When you resume the tutorial, launch Windows 95 again, and then continue with the tutorial.

● ● ●

Using the Print Troubleshooter

During Stephanie's workshop on troubleshooting computer problems, she told the staff that they can use Windows 95 Troubleshooters to solve problems with both hardware and software components.

Once you have defined a problem, you can open a **Troubleshooter** from online Help that guides you step-by-step through the process of analyzing and identifying the source of a hardware or software problem. At each step, the Troubleshooter asks you a question and, depending on your response, the Troubleshooter might ask you another question in an attempt to more precisely define the problem. It might ask you to check and change settings, or it might ask you to perform some type of test. One of the primary advantages of using the online Help Troubleshooters is that they provide you with a starting point for solving a problem. Although the Troubleshooters might not be able to resolve all the different types of problems that you might encounter on a computer, they do help you look for common types of problems. The Troubleshooters use many of the features described earlier on developing a troubleshooting strategy to pinpoint and solve problems.

For example, if you are having a problem with your printer, you can use the Print Troubleshooter. Printer problems are quite common, because applications have a wide variety of printing options that you can combine in different ways. Plus, these applications must work on computer systems that use different types of printers.

While working with her computer, Wei has a printing problem. She asks you to use the Print Troubleshooter to help solve it. She describes the problem to you: she opened Windows Explorer and selected two readme files, Tips.txt and Printers.txt, in the Windows folder so that she could print them. Tips.txt contains additional time-saving tips for working with Windows 95. Printers.txt contains information on the use of different types of printers, the use of TrueType fonts, and network printing. When she attempted to print the files, Notepad displayed the error message shown in Figure 5-8. The error message informed Wei that Notepad could not print the Printers.txt file, and suggested that Wei check the printer connection and verify that the printer is configured properly. Before she makes changes to the configuration of her computer, Wei wants you to open the Print Troubleshooter from online Help and, if possible, identify the source of the problem.

Figure 5-8 ◀
Notepad print
error warning

To use the Print Troubleshooter.

1. Click the **Start** button then click **Help**. The Help Topics Windows Help window opens.

2. If necessary, click the **Index tab**.

3. In the Step 1 box, type **trouble**. In the index entries list box, Windows 95 selects and highlights the "troubleshooting" index entry. See Figure 5-9. Now you need to locate the Help topic for troubleshooting printing problems.

Figure 5-9
Searching for
troubleshooting
Help

search text

index entry

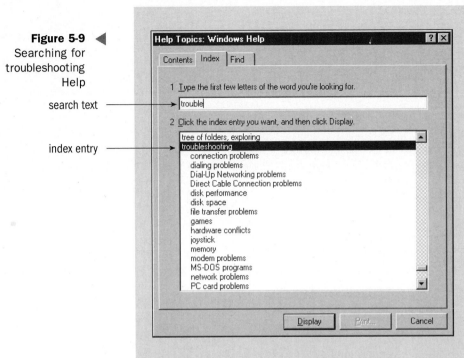

4. Scroll down the index entries list box until you locate the index entry "printing problems," click **printing problems** in the index entries list box, then click the **Display** button. Windows Help locates and displays the Print Troubleshooter in a Windows Help window. See Figure 5-10. The introductory paragraph informs you that this troubleshooter helps identify and solve printer problems, and tells you to select an option under "What's wrong?" to follow the suggested steps to fix the problem. Since Wei was unable to print one of the two documents she selected, you decide to try the first option.

Figure 5-10
Opening the
Print
Troubleshooter

what the Print
Troubleshooter does

click to start
troubleshooting your
printer

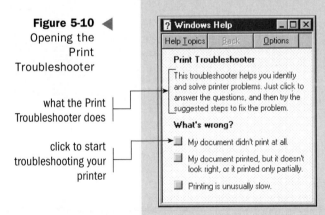

5. Under "What's wrong?," click the **button** to the left of "My document didn't print at all." The next Windows Help window, labeled "Try printing a test page," suggests printing a test page. See Figure 5-11.

Figure 5-11
Option for
printing a test
page

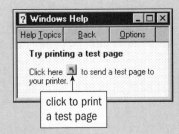

6. If necessary, check the status of your printer, and make sure your printer is on and operational.

7. In the Windows Help window, click the **arrow** button to print a test page. A Printer Test Page dialog box appears. See Figure 5-12. If you have more than one printer, you can select the printer you want to test.

TROUBLE? If no dialog box appears and you are running other applications, the dialog box might be hidden on the desktop behind the other open windows (no icon appears on the taskbar for this dialog box). Right-click the taskbar then click Minimize All Windows. The Printer Test Page dialog box should now appear. If you still can't find the Printer Test Page dialog box, your network might not be set to display one. In that case, skip to Step 9.

Figure 5-12 ◀
Option for selecting a printer

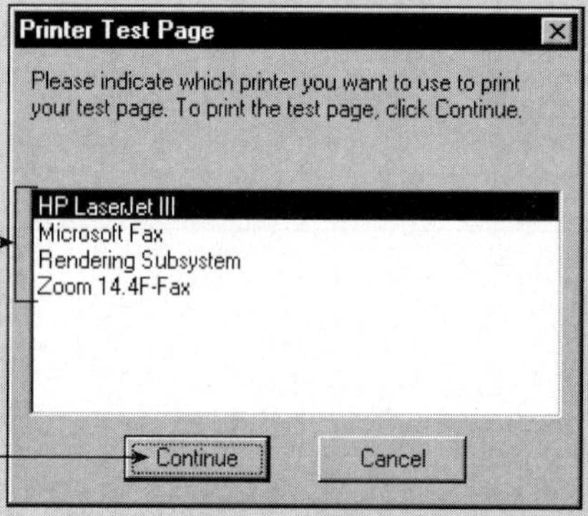

select a printer name ⟶

click to continue ⟶

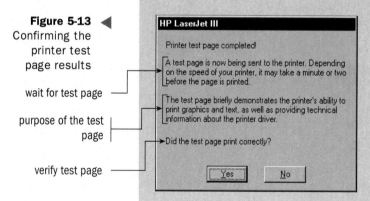

8. In the Printer Test Page dialog box, click a **printer name** then click the **Continue** button. A Printer dialog box explains that this test determines your printer's ability to print text and graphics. See Figure 5-13. It also notes that the test provides technical information on your printer. Then, it asks if your printer is working properly. Before you answer this question, you want to examine the test page.

Figure 5-13 ◀
Confirming the printer test page results

wait for test page ⟶

purpose of the test page ⟶

verify test page ⟶

9. Retrieve the printed copy of the test page from your printer. Figure 5-14 shows a sample of a Windows 95 Printer Test Page for a Hewlett Packard LaserJet III. Your test page might differ. The test page informs you that, if you can read this information, you have correctly installed your printer.

Figure 5-14 ◀
A Windows 95
Printer Test
Page

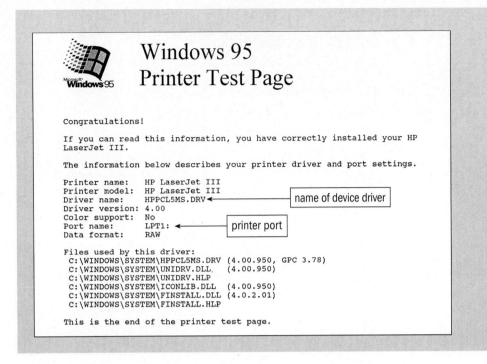

The printer test page provides useful information on your printer, including a list of the files used by the printer driver. For example, the printer driver for the Hewlett Packard LaserJet III used in this figure is stored in a file named Hppcl5ms.drv. In the list of the full path names of files used by this device driver, you can tell that this device driver is stored in the System subfolder below the Windows folder on drive C on the computer used for this figure. This device driver is a Windows 95 device driver for Windows version 4.00.950. The supporting files are Unidrv.dll, Unidrv.hlp, Iconlib.dll, Finstall.dll, and Finstall.hlp. The filenames with the dll file extension are dynamic link libraries. A **dynamic link library**, or **dll**, is a file with executable program code that provides support to one or more software applications. The filenames with the file extension hlp are Windows Help Files. From the information on this Printer Test Page, you also know that this printer is connected to LPT1:.

Even though the printer printed a test page correctly, Wei suggests that you continue to trace the potential source of the problem she encountered with her printer.

To continue the troubleshooting process:

1. Click the **Yes** button. The next Windows Help window tells you that the printer is set up correctly, and asks if the problem is fixed. See Figure 5-15. If this last step had solved Wei's problem, she would click the Yes button and close the Print Troubleshooter. Wei tries to print the help files again, and encounters the same problem. She must now search for other possible causes.

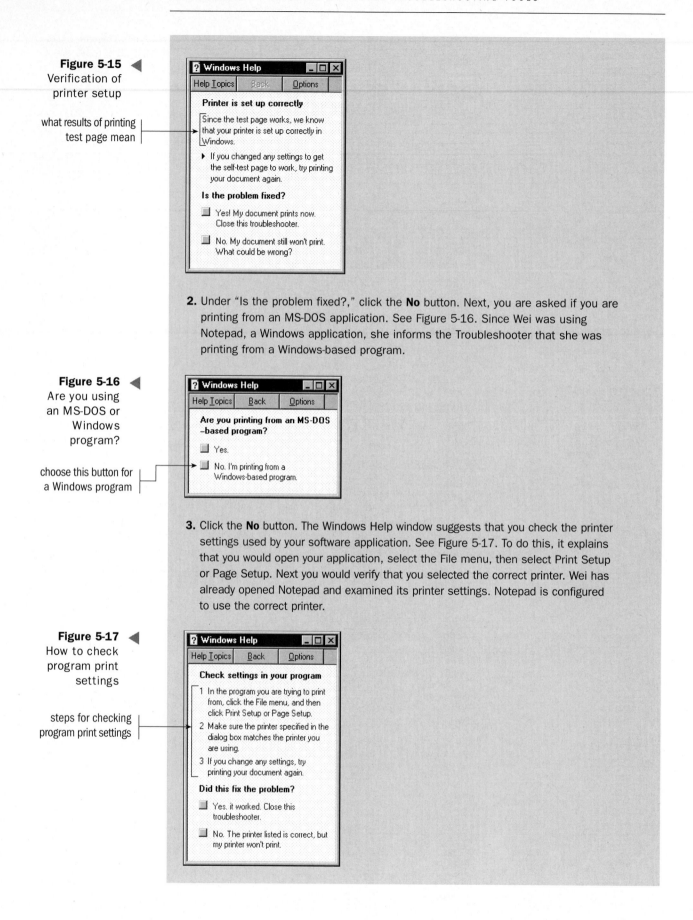

Figure 5-15 ◀
Verification of
printer setup

what results of printing
test page mean

Figure 5-16 ◀
Are you using
an MS-DOS or
Windows
program?

choose this button for
a Windows program

Figure 5-17 ◀
How to check
program print
settings

steps for checking
program print settings

2. Under "Is the problem fixed?," click the **No** button. Next, you are asked if you are printing from an MS-DOS application. See Figure 5-16. Since Wei was using Notepad, a Windows application, she informs the Troubleshooter that she was printing from a Windows-based program.

3. Click the **No** button. The Windows Help window suggests that you check the printer settings used by your software application. See Figure 5-17. To do this, it explains that you would open your application, select the File menu, then select Print Setup or Page Setup. Next you would verify that you selected the correct printer. Wei has already opened Notepad and examined its printer settings. Notepad is configured to use the correct printer.

4. Under "Did this fix the problem?," click the **No** button, then maximize the Windows Help window. The next Windows Help window suggests that you capture the printer port. See Figure 5-18. Wei explains that this option is one you would try if you were connected to a network. Since her computer is not connected to a network, you want to know what other options you can try.

Figure 5-18 ◀
Option for capturing printer port

steps for testing network printing

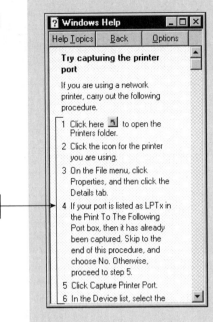

5. If necessary, scroll down to view the remainder of the information in the Windows Help window, then under "Did this fix the problem?," click the **No** button.

In the next Windows Help window, Windows 95 recommends that you change the timeout setting for your printer. See Figure 5-19. If your documents contain complex graphics or numerous fonts, you might need to increase the timeout value for that printer. For individuals who use Windows applications and include graphics and fonts in their documents, a timeout setting that is too low will quite likely cause a problem at some point in time. If you are printing more than one document at a time, you might also need to increase the timeout setting. Wei suggests that changing the timeout might solve the problem, and suggests that you keep these Help instructions on the screen as you try them.

Figure 5-19 ◀
Suggestions for changing timeout settings

why you might want to change timeout settings

steps for locating timeout settings

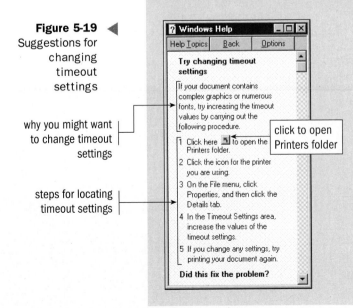

6. Click the **Options** button, point to **Keep Help on Top**, then click **On Top**.

7. Restore the Windows Help window to its original size.

Now, you are ready to follow the instructions for changing the timeout settings.

To check the timeout setting:

1. In Step 1 of the Windows Help window, click the **arrow** button. Windows 95 opens the Printers folder. See Figure 5-20.

Figure 5-20 ◀
Opening the
Printers folder
window and
keeping Help
open

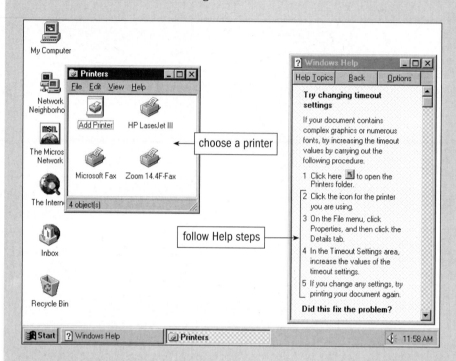

2. Click the **icon** for the printer you are using.

3. Click **File** then click **Properties**. A printer Properties dialog box opens.

4. If necessary, drag the printer Properties dialog box to the left so that you can view the contents of this dialog box and the Windows Help window at the same time.

5. In the printer Properties dialog box, click the **Details** tab. In the Timeout settings section, there are two timeout settings. See Figure 5-21. The Not selected setting instructs Windows 95 to wait a specific number of seconds for the printer to become on line before it reports an error. The Transmission retry setting instructs Windows 95 to wait for a specific number of seconds for the printer to print before it reports an error. If you print large documents, multiple copies of documents, documents with graphics, and documents with multiple fonts, then you might need to increase the Transmission retry setting. Wei and you notice that the Transmission retry setting is set to 0 (zero).

Figure 5-21 ◀
Selecting the
property sheet
with timeout
settings

printer port

printer driver

timeout settings

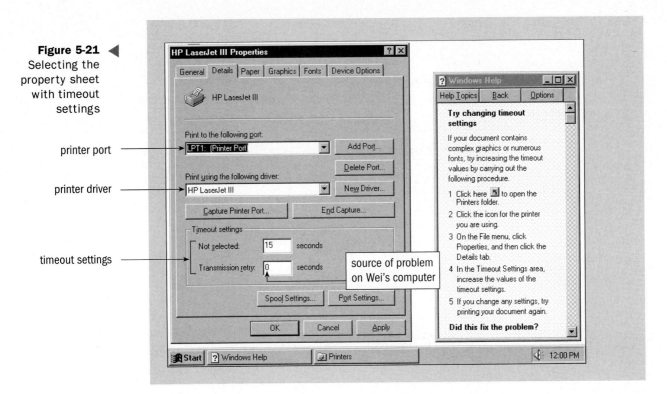

Wei thinks that you have located the source of the problem. She suggests that you increase the setting to 90, then close the dialog box so that she can try to print the same two documents again. Wei repeats the same steps that she tried previously, and Notepad prints copies of both files without displaying an error message. Now that you have located the source of the problem, Wei suggests that you close the Print Troubleshooter.

To close the Print Troubleshooter:

1. In the Windows Help window, scroll down until you can see the see options under "Did this fix the problem?," then click the **Yes** button. The Windows Help window closes.

2. Close the printer property sheet and the Printers folder window.

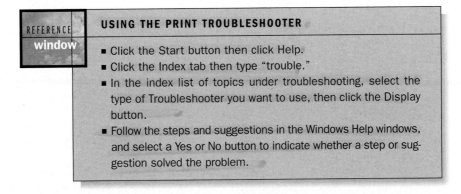

REFERENCE
window

USING THE PRINT TROUBLESHOOTER

- Click the Start button then click Help.
- Click the Index tab then type "trouble."
- In the index list of topics under troubleshooting, select the type of Troubleshooter you want to use, then click the Display button.
- Follow the steps and suggestions in the Windows Help windows, and select a Yes or No button to indicate whether a step or suggestion solved the problem.

The other Troubleshooters available in Windows 95 are:

- Disk Space Troubleshooter
- Memory Troubleshooter
- Joystick Troubleshooter
- Disk Defragmenter Troubleshooter
- Dial-Up Networking Troubleshooter
- Direct Cable Connection Troubleshooter

- Hardware Conflicts Troubleshooter
- Modem Troubleshooter
- MS-DOS Troubleshooter
- Network Troubleshooter
- PC Card (PCMCIA) Troubleshooter
- Windows Setup Troubleshooter

Wei notes that you can access all these Troubleshooters in the same way that you accessed the Print Troubleshooter, by selecting Help from the Start menu, then by entering "trouble" as the search entry on the Index tab.

If you use any of the Troubleshooters to help you solve a problem, your responses to each step in the troubleshooting process determine what type of information that Troubleshooter displays next and what suggestions it offers. In some cases, you might find that you do not find a solution to your problem. If this occurs, start over, follow another set of options and find out where they lead.

If you exhaust all the possible troubleshooting options available with a Troubleshooter, it informs you that you have run into a problem that it cannot help you solve. If this occurs, you have to look elsewhere for the solution to the problem. You might have to refer to your hardware or application software manuals, your Windows 95 manuals, and any special help files provided with Windows 95. You might have to contact the vendor who sold you the hardware or software, the manufacturer of the hardware or software, or Microsoft Corporation. You might even have to call in a consultant or technical support person. The Windows Troubleshooters, however, are your first best step.

Plug and Play

Since Yellow Brick Road Child Care receives a major part of its funding from the state, the director must prepare frequent program status reports and other types of documents for the state. These reports are time-consuming because staff must not only compile all the data but also present it in the proper format required by the state funding agency. To complicate matters, the turnaround times for these reports are usually very short. Wei recommends to the director that they purchase a modem for one of the computers so that they can transmit the documents electronically to the proper state funding agency.

After the director approves the purchase, Wei asks Stephanie for a recommendation on the type of modem that they should buy. Stephanie strongly urges that Wei purchase a modem that supports the Plug and Play standards in Windows 95. Then, when Wei connects the modem, Windows 95 will automatically configure it so that it works properly. If Wei purchases a legacy device that does not support Plug and Play, then Wei might have to hire someone to install and configure the modem with the computer. Stephanie mentions that the use of Plug and Play components reduces the amount of time you must spend troubleshooting problems on your computer system, and it reduces the cost of expensive hardware and software support. Furthermore, businesses who rely on computers to produce income experience less down time and less loss of income.

One of the major problems faced by users in the past was the overly complex process for installing and configuring new hardware devices, such as modems, so that they would work properly. To reduce the support costs and the personal frustration associated with installing new hardware components, hardware manufacturers now follow a set of specifications or standards, called Plug and Play, to produce hardware components that Windows 95 configures automatically without any involvement on your part, other than connecting the device to the computer. The goal of Plug and Play is simple: You plug in the device, turn on your computer, and the device works.

During the booting process, Windows 95 examines your computer and its components, and then configures the computer. If Windows 95 detects a new hardware component that supports the Plug and Play standards, it automatically loads the device drivers for that hardware component and then configures the device so that it works. For Plug and Play to work properly, your computer must include the following features:

- **Plug and Play BIOS.** During the booting process, routines, or programs, in the Plug and Play BIOS identify, enable, and configure Plug and Play devices automatically. For legacy devices, the BIOS enables devices, but does not identify or configure them for the operating system.

- **Plug and Play devices.** For a hardware device to be automatically detected and configured with the proper device drivers, it must be a Plug and Play device. If you purchase a legacy device (that is, it does not support Plug and Play standards) for your computer, you will have to install MS-DOS device drivers for their operation and configure the devices. Also, legacy devices might not function as reliably as Plug and Play devices.

- **Plug and Play operating system.** One of the important new features in Windows 95 is that it supports the use of Plug and Play devices. Windows 95 stores configuration information on Plug and Play devices in its Registry. When you install a new Plug and Play device, it checks the resources currently used by Plug and Play devices in the Registry so that it can properly configure the new device without introducing conflicts between hardware devices. Although Windows 95 does attempt to automatically detect and configure legacy devices that do not support Plug and Play standards, this process more than likely will require assistance from you.

Stephanie recommends that Wei and any other staff members who might shop for new hardware components, or even new computer systems, carefully question the sales people and verify that the devices or computer that they are purchasing fully implements Plug and Play specifications adopted by Microsoft and many hardware manufacturers. The time she invests in determining whether a hardware device is Plug and Play will more than make up for the time required to install and configure that component. Furthermore, a Plug and Play device will result in less performance and troubleshooting problems.

Using Device Manager

During Stephanie's workshop, she recommended that all staff members open Device Manager and print a copy of the configuration settings for their hardware. If someone inadvertently changes a configuration setting, then Wei can use their documentation to restore the correct setting. Likewise, if a conflict develops when they install a new hardware component, then Wei or another technical support person can use this information to resolve the hardware conflicts.

Device Manager not only provides an important overview of the components of your computer, but also shows the configuration settings that Windows 95 uses for both Plug and Play and legacy devices. Device Manager is therefore an important tool for viewing information on the configuration of hardware components within your computer system and for changing configuration settings as you try to install new hardware and troubleshoot hardware conflicts.

Before you make changes to the configuration settings in Device Manager, make sure you understand the effect that might have on your computer. Furthermore, make sure you have a record of your computer's current configuration settings before you change any settings. If you change a configuration setting in Device Manager, you might create a conflict with another hardware device and that device might not work, or your computer might become unstable or not function at all.

Wei asks you to open Device Manager, and start the process of documenting the setup and configuration of your computer by printing a view of the category of devices contained in your computer. As you examine specific device settings, you can then print a summary report that shows more detail on the configuration of that device.

To open Device Manager:

1. Right-click the **My Computer** Icon, then click **Properties** on the shortcut menu.

2. Click the **Device Manager** tab. On the Device Manager tab, you can view information on devices by type or by connection.

3. If necessary, click the **View devices by type** radio button. In the View devices by type box, you see a list of the hardware device types on your computer. See Figure 5-22. Although your computer will have some of the types of devices shown in this figure, you might have others as well. The plus sign next to each device type category indicates that there are one or more devices within that category. If you see a red **X** through an icon for a device, then that hardware device has been disabled for some reason. If you see an exclamation mark with a circle around it **!** through an icon for a device, then there is a problem with the configuration for that hardware device. If you see a question mark next to a hardware icon, then Windows 95 does not know what to do with that hardware device. If you examine the property sheets for a hardware device with any of these notations, Windows 95 will display information on the problem. Before you print your system summary, Wei asks you to print a copy of this view of devices, so that you have a visual record of your computer's components.

Figure 5-22 ◄
Opening Device
Manager

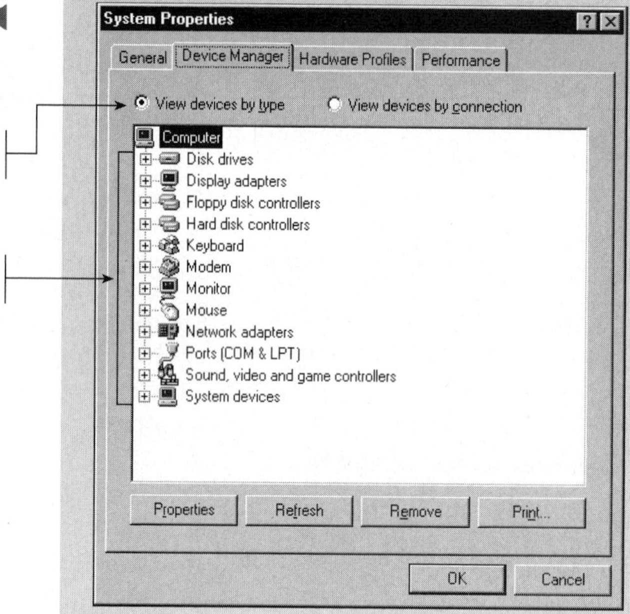

choose to list devices
by type

types of devices
within computer

4. Press **Alt + Print Screen**. Although nothing appears to happen, a copy of the active window has been placed on the Clipboard.

5. Click the **Start** button, point to **Programs**, point to **Accessories**, then click **Paint**.

6. Click **Edit**, then click **Paste**. The contents of the Clipboard appear in the Paint window.

   TROUBLE? If a message box appears asking you whether you want to enlarge the bitmap, click the Yes button.

7. Make sure your printer is on and operational.

8. Click **File**, click **Print**, then click the **OK** button in the Print dialog box after you check the Print settings.

9. Click **File**, click **Exit**, then if Paint displays a Paint dialog box and asks if you want to save your file, click the **No** button.

Wei points out to other staff members that, if a problem arises on their computer, it is easier to define the nature of the problem, analyze it, and locate the source of the problem if each person knows what devices are available in their computer, how those devices function, and how those devices are configured.

In the View devices by type box, Windows 95 provides an overview of the organization of the types of hardware devices within your computer. Every computer system has categories for Disk drives, Display adapters, Floppy disk controllers, Hard disk controllers, Keyboard, Monitor, Mouse, Ports (COM & LPT), and System devices. In the Disk drives category, Windows 95 lists information on each of the hard disk drives and floppy disk drives in your computer. In the Display adapters, Floppy disk controllers, and Hard disk controllers categories, Windows 95 lists information on the types of adapters or controllers in your computer. An **adapter** is a circuit board or card that connects one system component with another and that enables those components to work together. A **controller** is a circuit board or card that controls a peripheral device, such as a hard disk or floppy disk. Adapter and controller cards are connected to the **motherboard**, or main system board, within the system unit of the computer. The **system unit** is the unit that houses the main system board with the microprocessor, coprocessors, and electronic circuitry as well as any circuit boards attached to the motherboard, the power supply, and the drives. The Keyboard, Monitor, and Mouse categories identify the brand of each of these components. The System devices category contains information about the system board and components on the system board. The Ports (COM & LPT) identify the types of ports in your computer. A **port** is a connection for attaching a cable from a peripheral device, such as a monitor, printer, or modem, to circuit boards that are connected to the system board. The ports are located on the back of the system unit, and provide an electronic pathway for transferring data to and from peripheral devices.

You might see categories for other types of optional devices, such as a modem and sound, video, and game controllers. If your computer is connected to a network, then you will see a Network adapters category.

Understanding Parallel and Serial Ports

Recently, Wei had to troubleshoot a configuration problem with one of the serial ports on her computer. Fortunately, after setting up her new computer, she had printed a report on the configuration settings of the parallel and serial ports in her computer, and was able to use this information to resolve the problem.

Recall that ports provide a means for connecting a variety of peripheral, or external devices, such as a printer or modem, to your computer. Computers have two types of ports, parallel and serial, that differ in how data is transmitted to and from a device. Figure 5-23 illustrates the differences in how data is transmitted over a parallel and serial cable. Assume, for example, you have a laser printer connected to a parallel port on your computer. When you issue the command to print a document, a code for each character is transmitted to the printer. The code consists of eight binary digits, or eight bits, that distinguish that character from all other characters. For example, the ASCII code for the letter U is 01010101. **ASCII** (an acronym for American Standard Code for Information Interchange) is a coding scheme used and recognized by many different types of computers and programs. The parallel cable that connects your computer and printer via a parallel port has eight different lines for transmitting data to the printer. Each of the eight bits for a character, such as the letter U, is transmitted to the printer down a different line in the printer cable. Not only are the eight bits transmitted at the same time from the computer, but they arrive at the printer at the same time. Once the printer has the eight binary digits that identify a specific character, it can print that character.

Figure 5-23 ◀
Parallel vs.
serial
transmission

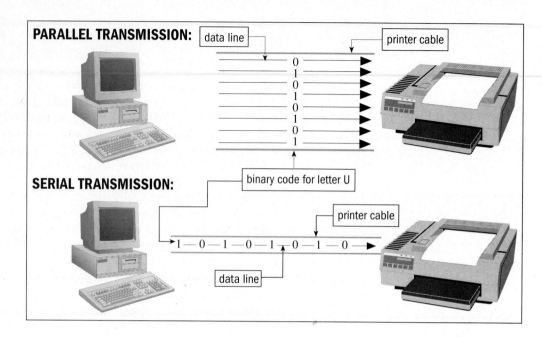

If you have a laser printer connected to a serial port, the serial port connecting the computer to the printer has only one data line for transmitting bits to the printer. When the eight binary digits that represent the letter U are transmitted to the printer, each bit travels down the same data line, one after another. Once the last binary digit for a character arrives at the printer, the printer can print the character.

Parallel transmission is faster than serial transmission; however, parallel transmission requires a special type of cable. The cable must not be longer than 6–15 feet in length; otherwise, interference in the transmission of data occurs. Although serial transmission is slower than parallel transmission, the cable can be up to 500 feet in length. In an office situation, where several people often share the same expensive laser printer, those individuals who are located in different offices at different distances from the printer are connected to the printer using a serial connection. If one or two individuals have their desks in close proximity to the printer, those individuals can be connected to the same printer using a parallel connection.

During the booting process, Windows 95 assigns names to each of the devices in a computer, including the ports. Each device is assigned a **device name**. For example, the device name A: is assigned to the first floppy disk drive, B: to the second floppy disk drive (if available), and C: to the first hard disk drive. Figure 5-24 summarizes common device name assignments.

Figure 5-24 ◀
Device name
assignments

Device Name	Meaning	Assigned To
LPT1	Line printer 1	First parallel port
LPT2	Line printer 2	Second parallel port
LPT3	Line printer 3	Third parallel port
PRN	Printer	First printer port (same as LPT1)
COM1	Communications port 1	First serial port
COM2	Communications port 2	Second serial port
COM3	Communications port 3	Third serial port
COM4	Communications port 4	Fourth serial port
AUX	Auxiliary device	First serial port (COM1)
CON	Console unit	Keyboard and monitor
CLOCK$	System clock	System clock
A:	Drive A	First floppy disk drive
B:	Drive B	Second floppy disk drive, or first floppy disk drive (if there is no second floppy disk drive)
C:	Drive C	First hard disk drive
NUL	Null device	"Bit Bucket"

The first parallel port is assigned the device name LPT1: (which stands for Line Printer 1). Although device names typically end with a colon, you can use all of the device names, except for drive names, without the colon. PRN (which stands for Printer) is assigned as an alternative device name for LPT1. LPT2 and LPT3 are assigned to the second and third parallel ports. LPT1, LPT2, and LPT3 are commonly referred to as parallel printer ports because, in the past, printers were commonly connected to these ports. However, today, you can connect other types of devices, such as modems, to parallel ports.

COM1 (which stands for Communications Port 1) is assigned to the first serial port. COM2, COM3, and COM4 are assigned to the second, third, and fourth serial ports. Peripheral devices, such as a mouse and modem, are connected to a computer via a serial port.

Wei suggests that you display the ports on your computer so that you know what ports Windows 95 recognizes and what ports are available for connecting peripheral devices.

To view the types of ports in a computer:

1. Click the **plus sign** to the left of Ports (COM & LPT).

On the Device Manager property sheet, you now see the names of the ports in your computer. See Figure 5-25. Your ports might differ from those shown in the figure. On the computer used for this figure, there are two serial ports, COM1 and COM2, and one parallel port, LPT1.

Figure 5-25 ◀
Viewing the
types of devices
in the Ports
(COM & LPT)
category

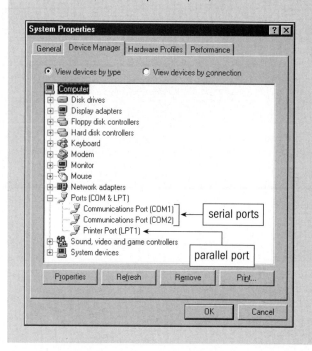

From the Device Manager property sheet, you can use the Print button to print three types of reports that summarize information on the configuration of devices.

- **Resource Summary Report**. You can print a short summary report that identifies features of your computer, such as the processor type (i.e., an 80486DX), and that includes a more technical summary of resource usage.

- **Selected Resource Report**. You can print a short report on a class of devices or on a specific device. This report shows the types of resources used by a device, and provides information on the device drivers that Windows 95 uses to interact with that device.

- **System Resource Report**. This report is a multi-page report that includes a system summary, plus information on every device in your computer. For example, one section of the report summarizes information on the disk drives in your computer.

Wei asks you to print a Selected Resource Report for the Ports (COM & LPT1) device category for your computer, so that you have a record of the current settings used by Windows 95 for those ports. Later, after you have verified that your computer is working properly and that all the configuration settings are correct, you can print a full System Resource Report.

To print a Selected Resource Report on your ports:

1. In the View devices by type, click **Ports (COM & LPT)**.

2. Click the **Print** button.

In the Type of report section on the Print dialog box, you can select a type of report. See Figure 5-26.

Figure 5-26
Printing a
Selected
Resource
Report

choose to print a
report on this device

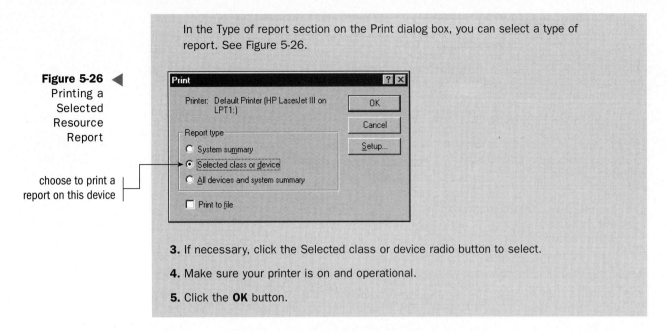

3. If necessary, click the Selected class or device radio button to select.

4. Make sure your printer is on and operational.

5. Click the **OK** button.

Wei points out that the report lists information on one or two types of system resources used by ports. Although this information is technical, it is important to be familiar with the concept and use of IRQ and I/O address settings. If your computer contains legacy devices, and if a conflict develops between two hardware devices, then you will have to change the IRQ setting, the I/O address setting, or both settings. If your computer has Plug and Play devices, Windows 95 will automatically resolve hardware conflicts and change the IRQ and I/O address settings.

IRQ is an acronym for Interrupt ReQuest, and refers to a hardware interrupt request line. A **hardware interrupt** is a signal transmitted from a hardware device to the micro-processor when the device is ready to send or accept data. Each device has its own interrupt request line. When two devices attempt to use the same interrupt request line, a hardware conflict develops, and one or both devices do not work. The operating system uses the I/O address assigned to a device to send signals to a specific peripheral device, such as a parallel or serial port. Each device must have its own address assignment so that the operating system can communicate with that device; otherwise, hardware conflicts develop.

Windows 95 automatically configures both Plug and Play devices, as well as legacy devices, so that IRQ and I/O address conflicts do not occur. However, if you change a device's configuration in Device Manager, it is possible to "accidentally" create a hardware conflict.

Jose Sanchez, assistant director of the center, tells Wei that he is unable to print any documents on his computer. Wei opens the Print Troubleshooter and attempts to print a test page; however, the Print Troubleshooter displays the error message shown in Figure 5-27. The Print Troubleshooter informs Wei that she should verify that the printer is connected to a valid port. The phrase "valid port" immediately leads Wei to suspect that the printer port might not be properly configured. She checks Device Manager on Jose's computer.

Figure 5-27
Verifying Jose's
printer problem

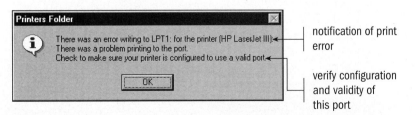

notification of print
error

verify configuration
and validity of
this port

After she opens Device Manager, she notices that Windows 95 is displaying a red "X" **X** mark on the connection icon next to LPT1, as shown in Figure 5-28. Wei asks you to look at each property sheet to verify and, if necessary, correct the configuration settings.

Figure 5-28
Checking
Device
Manager on
Jose's
computer

disabled device

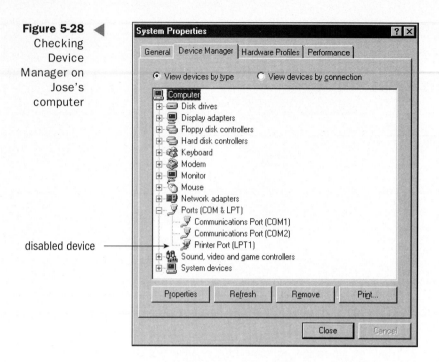

To check the property sheets for LPT1:

1. Click **Printer Port (LPT1)** then click the **Properties** button. Device Manager displays the General tab for the Printer Port (LPT1) Properties dialog box. See Figure 5-29. Some of the information on your General tab will differ from the one shown in this figure. On the computer used in this figure, Windows 95 reports in the Device status section that this device is disabled. The Code 22 identifies a specific type of problem. When you call a technical support number, such as for Microsoft Corporation, a technician can use this code to identify the source of the problem. In the Device usage section, Windows 95 shows what configuration this device uses. You can use online Help to get more information on this configuration.

Figure 5-29
Checking the
status of Jose's
printer port

device status section
shows device is
disabled

troubleshooting code

no configuration
selected for this
device

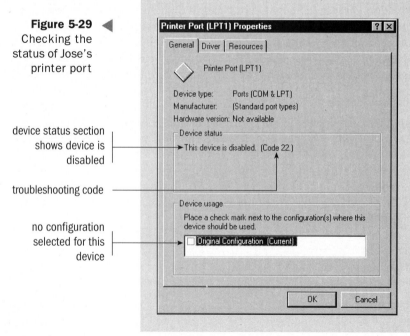

2. Click the ? button, then click the **configuration** listed in the Device usage box. In the pop-up Help window, Windows 95 explains that if there is a check mark in a configuration box, then Windows 95 enables that configuration for that device and loads the appropriate device driver(s). See Figure 5-30. If you remove the check mark from a configuration check box, then you disable that configuration for the device and its driver(s). If you disable a device and then enable it later, you might need to restart your computer so that Windows 95 can load the appropriate device drivers for communicating with that device.

Figure 5-30 ◀
Obtaining Help on the device's configuration is disabled

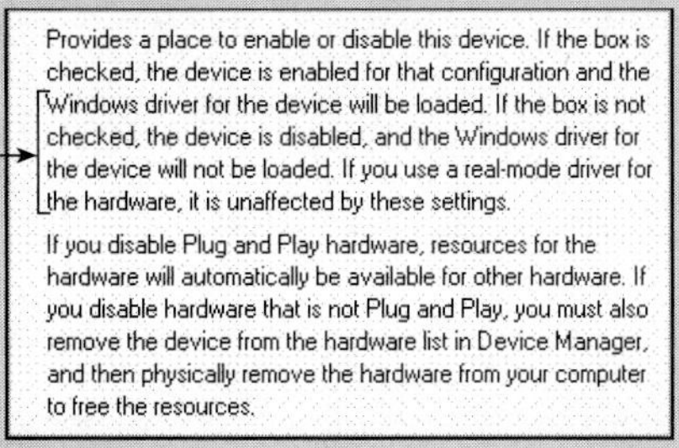

what happens if device configuration is disabled

> Provides a place to enable or disable this device. If the box is checked, the device is enabled for that configuration and the Windows driver for the device will be loaded. If the box is not checked, the device is disabled, and the Windows driver for the device will not be loaded. If you use a real-mode driver for the hardware, it is unaffected by these settings.
>
> If you disable Plug and Play hardware, resources for the hardware will automatically be available for other hardware. If you disable hardware that is not Plug and Play, you must also remove the device from the hardware list in Device Manager, and then physically remove the hardware from your computer to free the resources.

3. Click the **pop-up window** to close it. Wei thinks you have found the source of the problem, but asks you to quickly check the other settings before she makes any changes to the configuration of Jose's computer.

4. Click the **Driver** tab. The device driver shown for LPT1 on the computer used for Figure 5-31 is a virtual device driver (VxD). Recall that a virtual device driver is a driver that enables more than one application to work with the same device. In the File details section, Windows 95 displays information (if available) on the vendor that produced the driver, the driver version, and copyright information. In this figure, the device driver Lpt.vxd is provided by Microsoft Corporation with Windows 95.

TROUBLE? If your property sheet doesn't have a Driver tab, skip to Step 5.

Figure 5-31 ◀
Viewing information on the printer port's device driver

virtual device printer for parallel port

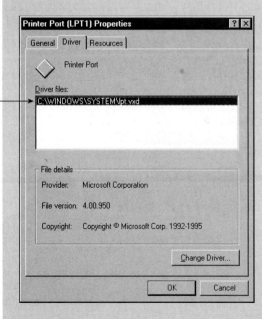

5. Click the **Resources** tab. The Resources tab displays the I/O address used to identify and communicate with the LPT1 port. See Figure 5-32. In the Conflicting device list section, Windows 95 notes any resource conflicts for this device.

Figure 5-32
Viewing
resources used
by a parallel
port

I/O address setting

no conflicts with I/O
address

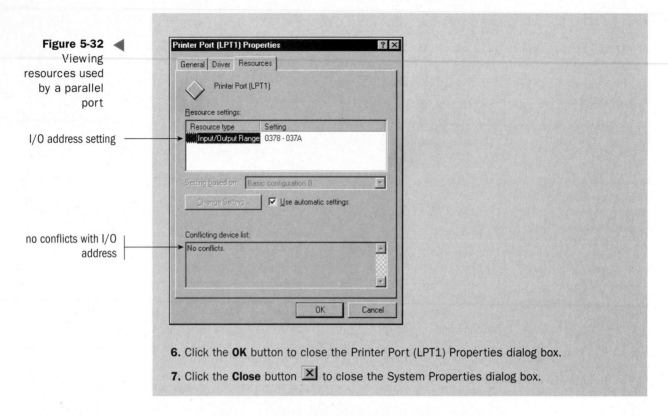

6. Click the **OK** button to close the Printer Port (LPT1) Properties dialog box.

7. Click the **Close** button [X] to close the System Properties dialog box.

Wei thinks that someone might have opened Device Manager and accidentally disabled LPT1 on Jose's computer by removing the configuration for this device. Wei enables the configuration for the LPT1 port on Jose's computer, then closes the Printer Port (LPT1) Properties dialog box. On the Device Manager property sheet, Windows 95 now shows that the device is no longer disabled. Now, Jose is able to print a report on the financial status of the programs at the center for the Board of Directors' meeting tonight.

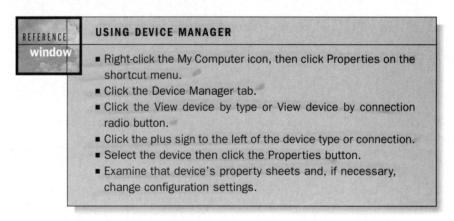

REFERENCE
window

USING DEVICE MANAGER

- Right-click the My Computer icon, then click Properties on the shortcut menu.
- Click the Device Manager tab.
- Click the View device by type or View device by connection radio button.
- Click the plus sign to the left of the device type or connection.
- Select the device then click the Properties button.
- Examine that device's property sheets and, if necessary, change configuration settings.

● ● ●

At their next weekly staff meeting, Wei reminds everyone that the Windows 95 Troubleshooters and Device Manager are two of the most important tools that they have for troubleshooting configuration problems and for verifying configuration settings. In many instances, as you use Windows 95 Troubleshooters, they will recommend that you open Device Manager and check settings. Furthermore, from Device Manager, you can print reports that document your system's settings.

Tutorial Assignment

Jessica Thompson, one of Wei's coworkers, has tried several times to print the same document, but she runs into the same problem each time—only part of the page prints. She tells Wei that she has successfully printed other documents with the same application, and the page layout settings in the application that she is using are correct. Wei asks you to use the Print Troubleshooter to locate the source of the problem, correct the problem, and, as a precaution, print a Selected Resource Report for the printer's port.

1. Click the Start button then click Help.
2. On the Index tab, type "trouble."
3. When the index entry "troubleshooting" appears in the index entries list box, click the Display button.
4. In the Topics Found dialog box, locate and select the topic "Troubleshooting Printer Problems," then select the Display button.
5. Click the Options button, then point to Keep Help on Top, then, if necessary, click On Top so that this Help window always stays on top.
6. Read the information on the Print Troubleshooter in the Windows Help window, then, under "What's wrong?," select the button "My document printed, but it doesn't look right, or it printed only partially."
7. Read the information on "My document doesn't look right" in the next Windows Help window, then select the button "Only a partial page printed."
8. Read the information on checking the paper orientation in the next Windows Help window. You might need to adjust your view of this window with the scroll bars. After checking with Wei, you find out that the paper orientation is properly set in the application. In Step 3, select the Help button that opens the Printers folder.
9. Following the instructions in Step 4 of the Windows Help window, click the printer icon in the Printers folder window, click File, then click Properties.
10. Following the instructions in Step 5, click the Paper tab and check the settings for paper orientation on your computer.
11. Assume that the paper orientation on Jessica's computer was incorrect, that Jessica changed this setting, and that she can now print her document. Under "Did this fix the problem?" in the Windows Help window, click the button labeled "Yes! My document prints now. Close this troubleshooter."
12. Click the Details tab, and in the Print to the following port list box, note the name of the printer port.
13. Close the printer Properties dialog box, then close the Printer folders window.
14. Right-click the My Computer icon, click Properties, then click Device Manager.
15. If necessary, click the View devices by type radio to select this option.
16. Click the plus sign next to the Ports (COM & LPT1) device category, then click the name of the printer port on your computer.
17. Make sure your printer is on and operational.
18. Click the Print button, then in the Type of report section, select the Selected class or device option. Click the OK button to print the report.
19. Close the System Properties dialog box.

Case Problems

1. Adding System Files to a Startup Disk at Muelrath & Harbaugh Dental Group Muelrath & Harbaugh services include family dentistry, oral surgery, cosmetic dentistry, periodontics, dental hygiene, restorative dentistry, dentures, and implants. Maria Sanchez, the office manager, has prepared Startup Disks for all the computers used in the firm. Now, she wants to add important system files to those disks. So that she can complete this project before the end of the day, she asks you to assist her.

For this case problem, use the Startup Disk that you prepared in this tutorial.

1. Insert the Startup Disk into drive A.
2. Open Windows Explorer, then select drive A in the All Folders window.
3. Select File on the menu bar, point to New, select Folder, and name the new folder System Files.
4. Select the plus sign next to drive A in the All Folders window to show the new folder.
5. In the Look in list box, select drive C.
6. Select Tools on the menu bar, point to Find, then select Files or Folders.
7. In the Named list box on the Name & Location tab of the Find: All Files dialog box, type "System.ini," then select the Find Now button.
8. In the Files Found area, select the copy of System.ini that you found in the Windows folder, and drag this copy of System.ini from the Find: All Files dialog box to the System Files folder on the Startup Disk.
9. Repeat the same process for Win.ini, and drag a copy of this file to the System Files folder on the Startup Disk.
10. Close the Find: All Files dialog box.
11. Check the main folder on drive C (C:\) and, if you see the MS-DOS configuration files, Config.sys and Autoexec.bat, drag copies of these files to the System Files folder on the Startup Disk in drive A.
12. Open the System Files folder on the Startup Disk.
13. Press Alt + Print Screen, open Paint, paste the contents of the Clipboard into the drawing area, then print the pasted image, and exit Paint without saving the file.
14. Close Windows Explorer.

2. Documenting COM1 & COM2 at A & E Construction Company A & E Construction Company is a medium-sized firm that provides general construction services to commercial businesses and residential properties. Zhou Qiao, one of the administrative employees, recently installed a new printer on COM1 and a Plug and Play modem on COM2. He wants you to document the settings for his serial ports.

1. Right-click the My Computer icon, then select Properties from the shortcut menu.
2. When the System Properties dialog box opens, select Device Manager.
3. If necessary, select the View devices by type option.
4. Select the plus sign to the left of Ports (COM & LPT).
5. Select Communications Port (COM1).
6. Make sure your printer is on and operational.
7. Select the Print button, then in the Type of report section, select the Selected class or device option. Select the OK button to print the report.
8. On your printed copy of the settings for COM1, identify the type of device that is connected to COM1.

9. If you have a device connected to COM2, print a Selected Resource Report for COM2, then, on the printed report, identify the type of device that is connected to COM2.
10. Close the System Properties dialog box.

3. Developing a Strategy for Troubleshooting Hardware Conflicts at Monterey Training Associates Monterey Training Associates contracts with businesses to provide custom training for employees whose jobs now require them to use a computer. After two weeks of on-site training, a company's employees are ready to apply their new skills to their jobs. Mary Woznicki, a computer specialist, and her assistant, Nathan Russell, prepare the computers for each contract training session and troubleshoot hardware and software conflicts. Mary wants you to test the hardware conflict troubleshooter in Windows 95 and prepare a short summary of how best to use this troubleshooter.

1. Select the Start button then select Help.
2. On the Index tab, enter "trouble."
3. When the index entry "troubleshooting" appears in the index entries list box, select the Display button.
4. In the Topics Found dialog box, locate and select the topic "Troubleshooting hardware conflicts" then select the Display button.
5. Select the Options button, then point to Keep Help on Top on the shortcut menu, then, if necessary, click On Top.
6. Read the information on the Hardware Conflicts Troubleshooter in the Windows Help window, then select the Display an overview of the process option.
7. Maximize the window, then read the information on "Overview of resolving conflicts."
8. Prepare a one-page report that (a) describes how a hardware conflict occurs, (b) lists two approaches that you can use to resolve hardware conflicts, and (c) outlines the strategies you can use to resolve a hardware conflict with the Device Manager.
9. Close the Hardware Conflicts Troubleshooter.

4. Using the Disk Space Troubleshooter at Morrisey & Dubois Law Offices Morrisey & Dubois Law Offices specializes in the preparation of bond documents for major state reconstruction projects. Since each bond document and its associated files require a large amount of storage space, one of the problems they constantly face is finding extra disk storage space on their computer's hard disks. Holly Lorenz works as their librarian and computer support specialist. She asks you to prepare a list of the ways in which the other support staff can free up storage space on their hard disks. You decide to open the Disk Space Troubleshooter and use it to help you prepare the information Holly needs.

After you open the Disk Space Troubleshooter, do not select or implement the option for using DriveSpace disk compression.

1. Select the Start button then select Help.
2. Select the Contents tab, then open the Troubleshooting book.
3. From the list of troubleshooting topics, click the topic "If you need more disk space," then click the Display button.
4. When the Disk Space Troubleshooter opens, prepare a list of five ways in which you can free up more space on your hard disk.
5. Select the Options button, point to Keep Help on Top, then, if necessary, click On Top.
6. Select the option for Emptying the Recycle Bin, restore the Windows Help window to its original size, and try the steps suggested by the Disk Space Troubleshooter.

7. Click the Back button to return to the window that contains suggestions for freeing up disk space.

8. Select the Remove Windows components that you don't use option.

9. In the next Windows Help window, click the arrow button to open the Add/Remove Programs dialog box.

10. Which tab in the Add/Remove Programs dialog box does the Disk Space Troubleshooter display?

11. Why would the Disk Space Troubleshooter recommend that you might want to consider removing Windows components?

12. Close the Add/Remove Programs dialog box, then close the Windows Help window.

Opening DOS Sessions

Working with DOS Applications at The Travis Foundation

OBJECTIVES

In this tutorial you will:

- Learn about the importance of compatibility with DOS applications
- Examine the characteristics of a Virtual DOS Machine
- Create a desktop shortcut for a DOS application
- Open a DOS application from the desktop
- Copy data from a DOS application to a Windows 95 application
- Use MS-DOS mode
- Configure memory for a DOS application
- Print copies of the DOS system startup files
- Add a DOS application to the Start menu

The Travis Foundation

CASE

The Travis Foundation is a philanthropic foundation that derives its income primarily from corporate giving programs and its own business investments. Each year graduating high school students compete for hundreds of scholarships offered by The Travis Foundation. These scholarships support students for four years while they pursue interdisciplinary programs at colleges or universities overseas.

Marie Arias manages the foundation's corporate giving programs, and oversees a staff of 11 employees. Over the last 10 years, Marie and her staff have produced spreadsheets that track corporate donations using Lotus 1-2-3 Release 2.4 for DOS. They use WordPerfect 5.1 for DOS to produce their annual report on corporate giving, as well as reports, correspondence, and forms. Although her staff now works on computers that use Windows 95 as their operating system, Marie and her staff still depend heavily on the DOS applications that they have used for years and the documents that they produced with those DOS applications. Marie wants each staff member to create shortcuts to their DOS applications, learn how to start and use their DOS applications from the Windows 95 desktop, and configure the applications so that they perform optimally.

The Importance of DOS and DOS Applications

Prior to upgrading to Windows 95, Marie learned that Windows 95 not only offered many new features for enhancing and optimizing the performance of computers, but also provided support for the DOS applications that businesses and companies have used over the years.

In the 14-year period prior to the introduction of Windows 95, DOS was the primary operating system used on microcomputers by both businesses and millions of individuals around the world. During that time, DOS applications and games proliferated. Even with the introduction of the Windows 95 operating system, many businesses and users still rely on DOS applications.

During the development of Windows 95, Microsoft Corporation decided that it was important to provide compatibility with the DOS operating system as well as DOS and Windows 3.1 applications and games. Some DOS applications did not function properly under Windows 3.1 because they needed direct access to system resources, including memory, and therefore had to be started directly from the DOS prompt rather than from Windows 3.1. DOS games, in particular, did not function well under Windows 3.1 because the software for these games assumed that they were the only program running on the system. Furthermore, they placed heavy demands on the resources within the computer. Although Windows 3.1 handled access to hardware within the computer, the software for DOS games attempted to bypass Windows 3.1 and interact directly with the computer's hardware, thus creating conflicts with Windows 3.1.

Because many users still rely on DOS applications, Windows 95 provides support for their use. With Windows 95 you can open DOS applications and games from the desktop, or you can start DOS applications and games from a DOS window. However, even with this increased support for DOS applications and games, you might find that certain applications and games will not function properly unless you open them from a DOS window or until you boot your computer in MS-DOS mode and load the program from the DOS prompt, as you'll see later in this tutorial.

There are other compelling reasons for advanced users to learn DOS in the Windows 95 environment. DOS is important in configuring legacy devices for use under Windows 95. Recall that a legacy device is a hardware component that does not support the new Plug and Play standards adopted for Windows 95. Although Windows 95 provides support for Plug and Play technologies, many computers still have legacy devices, including CD-ROM drives, modems, and sound cards that don't meet the new specifications of Windows 95. To ensure that these devices work properly, users need to know how to modify the DOS system startup files.

DOS is also important for troubleshooting Windows 95 problems. If Windows 95 does not start, you can boot your computer from a Startup Disk. Then, from a DOS-like command prompt, you can attempt to troubleshoot problems, make backups, and restore important Windows 95 system files. For all these reasons, Windows 95 users still find it useful to learn DOS fundamentals. This book is not intended to teach the DOS operating system but only to introduce you to situations in which you might encounter DOS in the Windows 95 environment. To learn DOS sufficiently to be able to use it effectively in troubleshooting situations, you need to take a comprehensive course on DOS or turn to a text that focuses on basic and advanced concepts and features of the DOS operating system.

The Virtual DOS Machine

In order to run a DOS application, Windows 95 must simulate the type of environment that a DOS application expects to find when it operates solely under DOS. For example, Windows 95 accesses and uses memory differently than DOS and DOS applications. For a DOS application to function properly under Windows 95, Windows 95 must manage memory in the same way that DOS manages memory for itself and DOS applications.

When you boot a computer that uses Windows 95 as its operating system, Windows 95 executes the commands in the DOS system startup files, Config.sys and Autoexec.bat. Not only does it load real-mode components such as DOS device drivers and TSRs (Terminate-and-Stay-Resident utilities), but it also stores specific settings in the DOS environment. As you learned earlier, real mode is a microprocessor operating mode in which the computer functions as an 8086 or 8088 microprocessor, and the microprocessor can only access the first megabyte of memory. The **DOS environment** is an area of memory that contains system and application settings. DOS and software applications check the contents of the DOS environment to locate settings that they need to operate properly.

When you open a DOS application under Windows 95, Windows 95 creates a Virtual DOS Machine for that application. A **Virtual DOS Machine** (or **VDM**) is a complete operating environment for a DOS application. The VDM contains a copy of real-mode device drivers and TSRs as well as DOS environment settings. Windows 95 allocates part of the system's resources, such as memory, to that application and also provides access to all the other system resources that the DOS application needs to operate properly. Plus, Windows 95 provides protection for the memory space allocated to that application. If you open another DOS application, Windows 95 creates another Virtual DOS Machine for that application. Each Virtual DOS Machine operates independently of all other VDMs. Within a VDM, the DOS application operates as if it has access to all the computer's resources, and the application is not supposed to be aware of Windows 95 or any other applications running under Windows 95. However, you might find that certain DOS games detect the presence of Windows 95, and they will either not operate properly, or they might freeze up your computer.

By using Virtual DOS Machines, Windows 95 attempts to isolate each DOS application from every other DOS application to prevent conflicts and system crashes resulting from one DOS application trying to use the memory space of another DOS application.

Using MS-DOS 7.0

When you install Windows 95 on your computer system, it renames the DOS operating system files and places its own versions of those same operating system files in the root directory of drive C. Recall that Windows 95 uses the terms "folder" and "subfolder" to refer to groups of logically related files on a hard disk, while MS-DOS uses the terms "directory" and "subdirectory."

Windows 95 changes the names of the DOS operating system files Io.sys, Msdos.sys, and Command.com, used by your computer's previous version of DOS, to Io.dos, Msdos.dos, and Command.dos. After renaming the DOS operating system files, Windows 95 installs new versions of Io.sys, Msdos.sys, and Command.com that are part of the operating system files that Windows 95 uses to boot your computer and load itself. By keeping important files from the previous version of DOS that you used on your computer, you have the ability to boot with your previous version of DOS.

Depending on the DOS version that you use on your computer system, Windows 95 also deletes approximately 35 of the DOS utilities stored in the DOS subdirectory on drive C when you first install Windows 95. Below the Windows directory on drive C, Windows 95 creates a subdirectory called Command that contains new versions of the DOS utilities that it deleted from the DOS subdirectory.

MS-DOS 7.0, the new version of DOS included with Windows 95, is an integral part of the Windows 95 operating system. Windows 95 includes program code that handles certain basic and important DOS functions, such as obtaining the date and time and accessing drives. The fact that MS-DOS is integrated into Windows 95 makes sense from a logical standpoint because to be a successful product in the marketplace Windows 95 must provide compatibility with DOS and DOS applications.

Searching for a Program File

So that she can quickly start her DOS applications from the Windows 95 desktop, Marie wants to create shortcuts for Lotus 1-2-3 Release 2.4 for DOS and her other DOS applications. Before she can create a Lotus 1-2-3 shortcut, she must locate the executable program file for that DOS application. Marie asks you to use the Find feature on the Start menu to locate the folder for the program that starts Lotus 1-2-3.

HELP DESK

Index

FINDING A PROGRAM OR FILE QUICKLY

Click the Start button, click Help, then click the Index tab.

Keyword   **Topics**
Finding   Overview: Finding something quickly

Marie suggests that you start by searching for all files that begin with the name "123" on drive C.

This tutorial demonstrates how to set up the DOS application Lotus 1-2-3 under Windows 95. If you don't have Lotus 1-2-3 loaded, you can still go through the tutorial using another application. You will, however, have to know the location of the executable program file for the application you choose to use in order to perform the steps in this tutorial. Ask your instructor or technical support person to suggest a specific application located on your school's network. Or you can try to search for a DOS application program file on your own. For example, if WordPerfect 5.1 is installed on your computer, search for program files that begin with "Wp." If you do not have any DOS applications installed on your computer, you can search for the MS-DOS 7.0 application called the MS-DOS Editor, which is provided with Windows 95, by looking for files that begin with "Edit." The MS-DOS Editor, like the Windows 3.1 Notepad application, is a simple text editor for creating and modifying text files, such as the Windows 95 and DOS configuration files.

The figures used for this tutorial will illustrate how to work with a DOS application by using Lotus 1-2-3 Release 2.4 for DOS. Although your screen views might differ from those shown in the tutorial, you will find that the property sheets and other options that you use are very similar. The most important thing to remember is that the logic for working with a DOS application under Windows 95 is the same no matter what application you use.

If you are working in a computer lab and your instructor or technical support person provides the name of the DOS application that you should search for, make sure you have the location, including the name of the network drive (if applicable) for which you should search.

Before you start the search, you must set viewing options so that you can see file extensions, and are able to identify program files from other types of files that might have similar names.

To set viewing options:

1. Double-click the **My Computer** icon. The My Computer window opens.

2. Click **View** on the menu bar, then click **Options**.

3. Click the **View** tab.

4. If selected, click the **Hide MS-DOS file extensions for file types that are registered** check box to remove the check mark.

5. Click the **OK** button to close the Options dialog box.

6. Click the **Close** button ☒ to close the My Computer window.

Now you are ready to start the search for the program file for a DOS application on your computer.

To search for a program's executable file:

1. Make sure you are at the Windows desktop.

2. Click the **Start** button, point to **Find**, then click **Files or Folders**. The Find: All Files window opens.

3. If necessary, click the **Name & Location** tab, then in the Named list box, type the filename of the executable program file that you want to search for, *but do not type the file extension*. For example, if you are searching for MS-DOS Editor, you would type Edit; for a DOS release of Lotus 1-2-3, you would type 123; and for a DOS release of WordPerfect, you would type WP (without a period).

4. If the name of your hard disk drive does not appear in the Look in list box, click the **Look in** list arrow, then locate and click the **name** of your hard disk drive or the network drive that contains the DOS application.

5. Make sure that the Include subfolders check box is selected. Figure 6-1 shows the entries you would use to search for all folders and files named 123 on drive C. If you are searching for another DOS application, the entry you type in the Named list box will differ, and the name of the drive in the Look in list box might also differ.

Figure 6-1 ◀
Searching for
an executable
program file

what to look for ────
where to look ────

search all
subdirectories

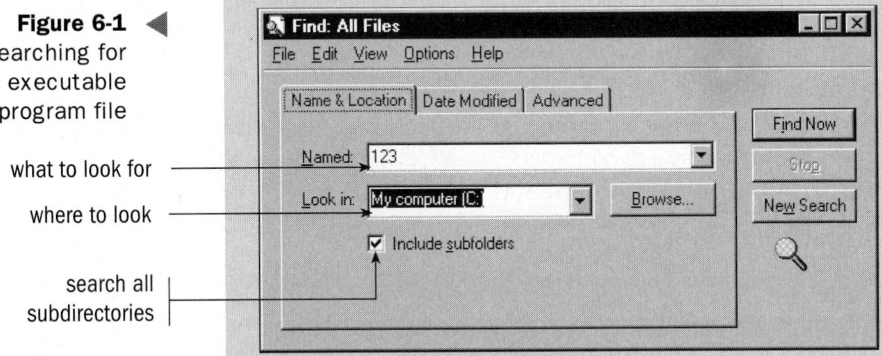

6. Click the **Date Modified** tab, then, if necessary, click the **All files** radio button.

7. Click the **Advanced** tab, then, if necessary, click the **Of type** list arrow, then click **All Files and Folders**.

8. If the Containing text box and the Size is list box contain entries from a previous use of the Find feature, select those entries and press the **Delete** key.

9. Click the **Name & Location** tab, click the **Find Now** button, then, as Windows 95 searches for matching folders and files, click the **Maximize** button ☐. Windows 95 locates all folders and files that match the file specification you entered in the Named list box. See Figure 6-2. Your list of found folders and files will differ from that shown in the figure, even if you search for the same application (Lotus 1-2-3) used for this figure.

Figure 6-2 ◀
Selecting the
executable
program
filename

executable program
file

number of files found

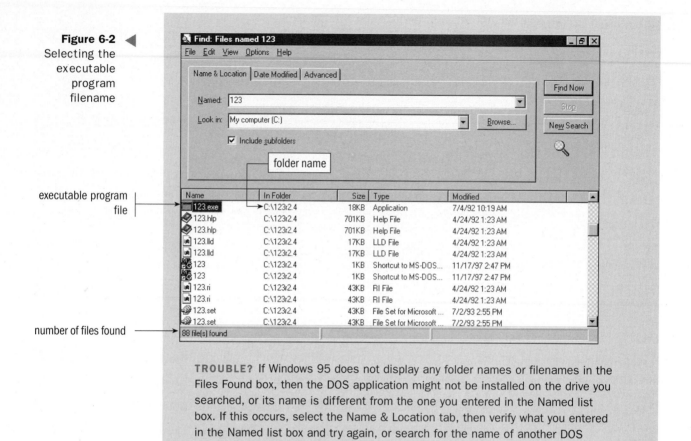

TROUBLE? If Windows 95 does not display any folder names or filenames in the Files Found box, then the DOS application might not be installed on the drive you searched, or its name is different from the one you entered in the Named list box. If this occurs, select the Name & Location tab, then verify what you entered in the Named list box and try again, or search for the name of another DOS application.

Creating a Shortcut for a DOS Application

Next, you need to locate the name of the executable program file in the Files Found box. Executable program files for DOS applications will have exe (for "executable") or com (for "command") as their file extension. For example, the executable program file for Lotus 1-2-3 is "123.exe"; for WordPerfect, "Wp.exe"; and for the MS-DOS Editor, "Edit.com." To make the process of locating the program filename easier, you can first alphabetize the folder names and filenames. Then, you can create the shortcut.

To locate the executable program file:

1. Click the **Name** column button in the Files Found box.

   TROUBLE? If the folder and filenames appear in reverse alphabetical order, click the Name button a second time.

2. Scroll through the list of folders and filenames until you locate the name of the executable file for your DOS application, then click the **executable program filename**. In Figure 6-2, the executable program filename 123.exe is selected. If you are searching for the MS-DOS Editor, your executable filename will be Edit.com. If you are searching for WordPerfect, your executable filename will be Wp.exe. You can use the information in the Type column to identify executable files from other types of files that might have similar names. By default, Windows 95 identifies files with the file extension com as MS-DOS applications, and those with the file extension exe as just applications.

3. Write down the folder and full filename of the executable program file that contains your DOS application (widen the In Folder column to see the entire path, if necessary). You will need to know this information later.

4. Right-click the **executable program filename** for your DOS application, then click **Create Shortcut** on the shortcut menu. Windows 95 displays a Shortcut dialog box that informs you it cannot create a shortcut here, but it can create it on the desktop.

5. In the Shortcut dialog box, click the **Yes** button.

6. After the Shortcut dialog box closes, click the Find:All Files window's **Close** button ⊠. The Find: All Files window closes, and you return to the desktop where Windows 95 placed the shortcut for the DOS application. See Figure 6-3. If you searched for the MS-DOS Editor or another DOS application, your shortcut icon might be different.

Figure 6-3 ◀
Placing a
shortcut to
a DOS
application on
the desktop

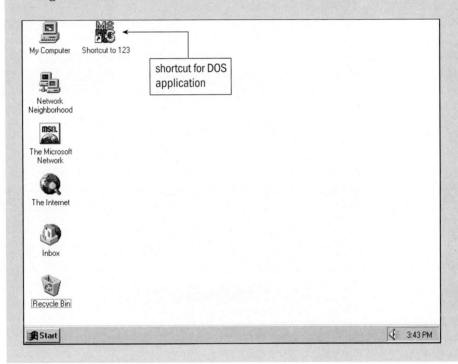

Now, Marie has a shortcut to one of her DOS applications on the desktop.

Changing a Desktop Shortcut Icon

You show Marie her new shortcut, and she asks if it is possible to change the icon, currently the standard MS-DOS icon, so that it more closely represents her DOS application.

Figure 6-3 shows the icon that Windows 95 uses for MS-DOS. You can change the icon by opening the shortcut property sheet and selecting an icon that reminds you of your DOS application.

To select another icon for the DOS application shortcut:

1. Right-click the **DOS application shortcut**, then click **Properties** on the shortcut menu. Windows 95 displays the Shortcut Properties dialog box for your DOS application. In Figure 6-4, the name of the dialog box is "Shortcut to 123 Properties."

Figure 6-4 ◀
Shortcut
Properties
dialog box for a
DOS
application

General property
sheet

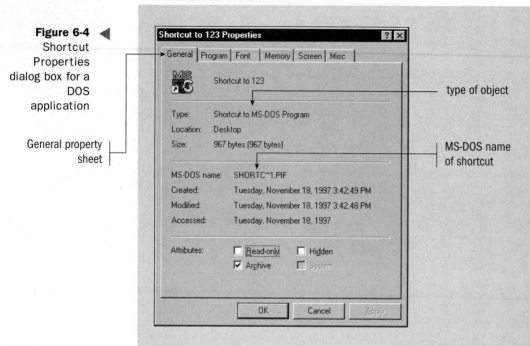

type of object

MS-DOS name
of shortcut

Your dialog box name might be different. On the General property sheet, Windows 95 displays information on the type of shortcut along with the MS-DOS name of the shortcut. In this figure, the type of object is a Shortcut to MS-DOS Program, and the MS-DOS name of the shortcut file is SHORTC~1.PIF. The file extension pif stands for "Program Information File." The PIF Editor in Windows 3.1 allowed you to specify settings for Program Information Files so that you can run DOS applications. Now, you do the same thing with property sheets.

2. Click the **Program** tab. On the Program property sheet, the first box shows the name assigned to the shortcut on the desktop. See Figure 6-5. Your shortcut name might be different.

Figure 6-5 ◀
Program
property sheet
for a DOS
application

drive, path, and
filename of DOS
application

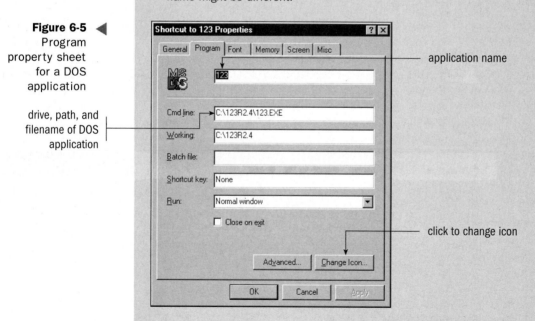

application name

click to change icon

If you want to change the label that Windows 95 uses to identify the DOS application on the desktop, you enter a new label in the name text box. The Cmd line (for "command line") text box contains the path and filename of the program file that Windows 95 executes. The Working text box lists the name of the folder from which this application will automatically load files and where it will automatically save files. You might want to specify another folder as the default folder in the Working text box. Then, when you double-click the icon for your DOS application, you will access files in that folder. The Run list box allows you to specify how the application will appear when first started. If you click the list arrow, you can change from a "Normal window" option to "Minimized" or "Maximized." If you choose "Minimized," a button will appear on the taskbar when you open the DOS application. You can then switch to that window by clicking the taskbar button. The "Normal window " and "Maximized" options produce the same result for DOS applications.

3. Click the **Change Icon** button. The Change Icon dialog box opens. See Figure 6-6.

Figure 6-6 ◀
Selecting a
new icon for a
desktop
shortcut

name of file with
icons

choose an icon

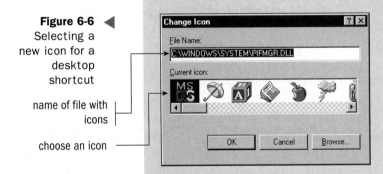

In the File Name text box, you see the path and filename of the file that contains the icons shown in the Current icon list box. You can scroll through the Current icon box and select one of the available icons.

4. Use the scroll arrows to scroll right and left until you locate an icon that you want to use for your DOS application, click the **icon** you want to use then click the **OK** button in the Change Icon dialog box. After the Change Icon dialog box closes, you see the icon that you chose in the upper-left corner of the Program property sheet.

5. Click the **OK** button to close the Shortcut Properties dialog box for your DOS application. The new icon for the shortcut now appears on the desktop. See Figure 6-7.

Figure 6-7 ◀
New DOS
application icon

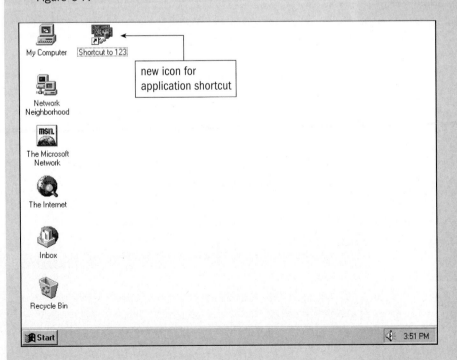

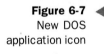

In this figure, the icon for money is used because Lotus 1-2-3, like other spreadsheet applications, is commonly used for financial analyses and projections.

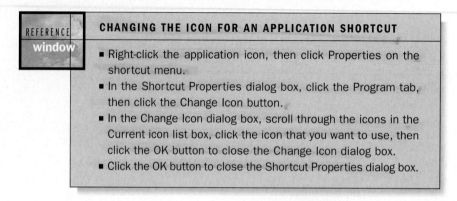

REFERENCE window

CHANGING THE ICON FOR AN APPLICATION SHORTCUT

■ Right-click the application icon, then click Properties on the shortcut menu.
■ In the Shortcut Properties dialog box, click the Program tab, then click the Change Icon button.
■ In the Change Icon dialog box, scroll through the icons in the Current icon list box, click the icon that you want to use, then click the OK button to close the Change Icon dialog box.
■ Click the OK button to close the Shortcut Properties dialog box.

Marie thinks the icon that you chose fits the DOS application better than the default one provided by Windows 95.

Opening a DOS Application from the Desktop

Now that you have created a shortcut to a DOS application and added it to your desktop, Marie wants you to open the application, then open one of your documents, and verify that you can work with the DOS application without any problem.

To open a DOS application using a shortcut:

1. Double-click the **DOS application shortcut**. Windows 95 opens the DOS application. In Figure 6-8, you see the application interface for Lotus 1-2-3 Release 2.4 for DOS. The view for your DOS application will differ if you chose another DOS application.

Figure 6-8 ◀
Opening a DOS application from the desktop

application interface for DOS application

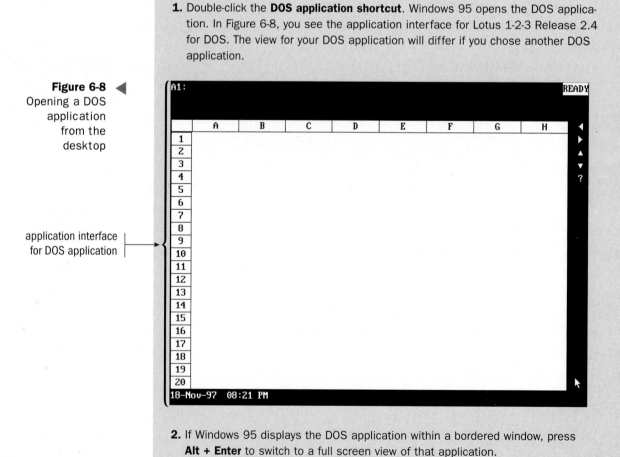

2. If Windows 95 displays the DOS application within a bordered window, press **Alt + Enter** to switch to a full screen view of that application.

3. Open a document that you produced with your DOS application. Figure 6-9 shows a spreadsheet with a three-dimensional bar graph, both of which were produced by Marie with Lotus 1-2-3 Release 2.4 for DOS.

Figure 6-9 ◀
Opening a
document for a
DOS
application

spreadsheet

three-dimensional bar
graph placed as a
graphic object

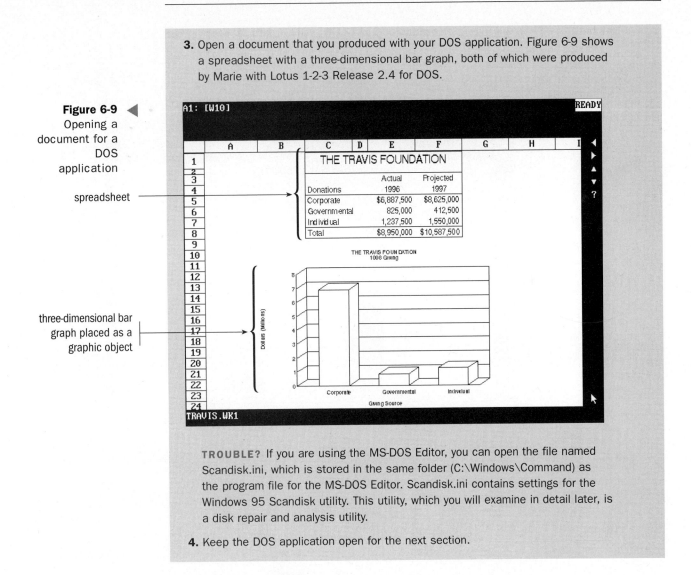

TROUBLE? If you are using the MS-DOS Editor, you can open the file named Scandisk.ini, which is stored in the same folder (C:\Windows\Command) as the program file for the MS-DOS Editor. Scandisk.ini contains settings for the Windows 95 Scandisk utility. This utility, which you will examine in detail later, is a disk repair and analysis utility.

4. Keep the DOS application open for the next section.

You have verified that you can open your DOS application from the shortcut that you placed on the desktop.

Using a DOS Application in a Window

Marie and her staff need to produce an annual report that draws on the information stored in documents that they produced this last year. To save time and effort, Marie decides to extract this information from documents her staff produced with DOS applications, and then place that information in documents that she is now producing with Windows 95 applications.

When you open a DOS application, you can switch from a full screen view to a windowed view, or vice versa, and you can display a toolbar that enables you to make changes to window and property settings directly from the MS-DOS application window. You can open other applications, and copy information from one application to another. When you switch from a full screen view to a windowed view, you might not be able to see all the elements of the DOS application's interface.

Marie asks you to switch to a windowed view, display the MS-DOS toolbar, and copy part of the document to Paint or WordPad.

To change to a windowed view of the DOS application:

1. Press **Alt + Enter** then, if necessary, click the **Maximize** button 🗖. Windows 95 now displays the DOS application within an MS-DOS window. See Figure 6-10.

Figure 6-10 ◄
Displaying
a DOS
application in
an MS-DOS
window

application menu
icon

application button

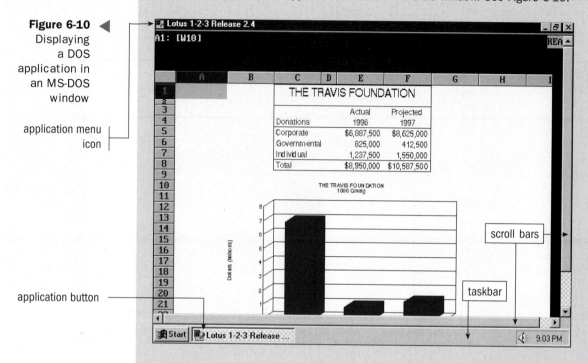

The window has its own title bar, with the name of the DOS application, plus Minimize, Restore, and Close buttons. Vertical and horizontal scroll bars allow you to adjust your view of the window. You can see the taskbar at the bottom of the window with the Start button. You can open one or more other applications with the Start button, and then switch between those applications. The applications can include Windows 95, Windows 3.1, and DOS applications.

2. Click the **application icon** located to the left of the DOS application name on the title bar. Windows 95 displays an application menu. See Figure 6-11.

Figure 6-11 ◄
Displaying an
application
menu in an MS-
DOS window

application menu

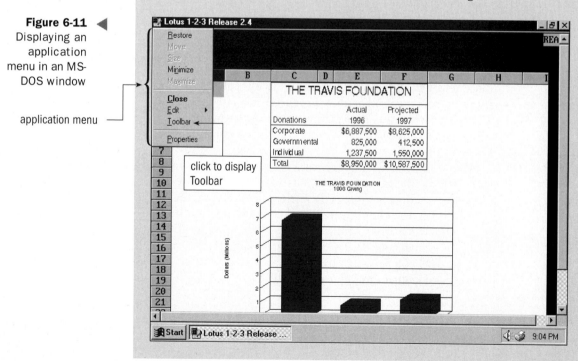

From this menu, you can resize or close the window, hide or display a toolbar, and change properties of the DOS application.

3. If you do not see a check mark next to Toolbar, then click **Toolbar**; otherwise click outside the menu to close the menu. Windows 95 displays an MS-DOS toolbar for the DOS application window. See Figure 6-12.

Figure 6-12
Displaying the
MS-DOS
Toolbar

Mark button   Copy button   Paste button   Full screen button   Properties button

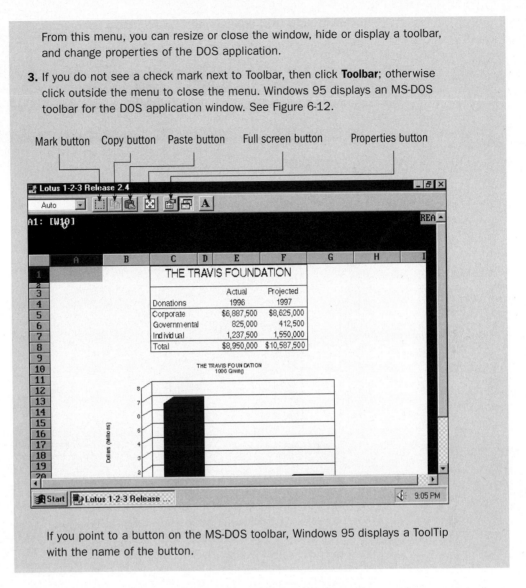

If you point to a button on the MS-DOS toolbar, Windows 95 displays a ToolTip with the name of the button.

The buttons on the MS-DOS toolbar allow you to change the font (provided the DOS application does not directly control the screen), change to full screen view, and display the Properties dialog box for the application. You can also mark, or select, part of the contents of a document for copy and paste operations.

Marie suggests that you select and copy part of the document, and paste it into Paint.

To copy from a DOS application to a Windows application:

1. Click the **Mark** button 🔲 on the MS-DOS toolbar.

2. Point to the upper-left corner of the area that you want to select, then drag through the text, spreadsheet, or graphic in the document to the lower-right corner of the area that you want to select, similar to the area selected in Figure 6-13.

Figure 6-13 ◀
Selecting an area to copy

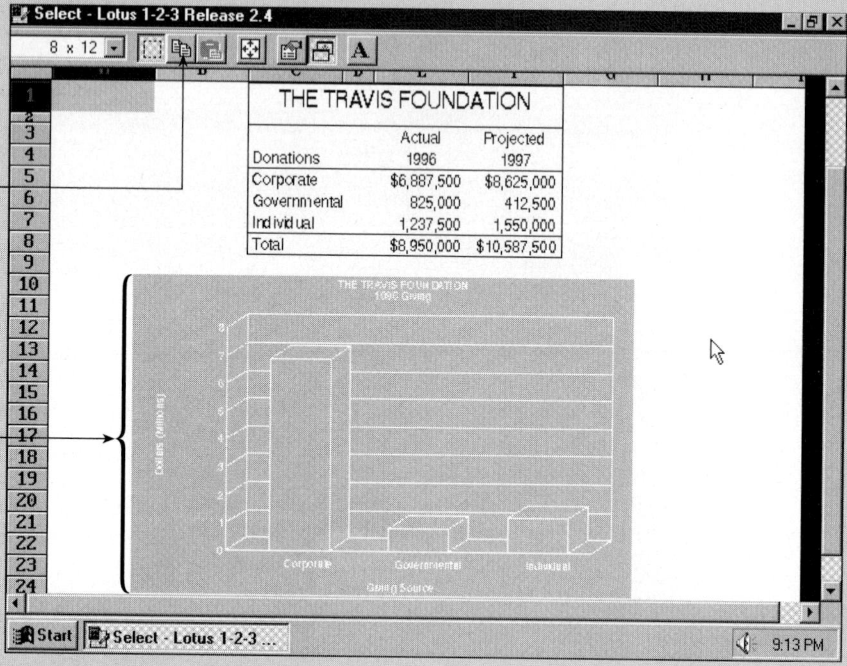

Copy button ───

area marked for copying │

As you select an area within a document, the area appears highlighted.

TROUBLE? If you are unable to select a button, an area with the mouse, or a menu name on the menu bar, press the Alt key to access the menu bar, press the Enter key to select the File menu, then type X for Exit. Right-click the desktop shortcut for your DOS application, then click Properties. Click the Misc tab, remove the check marks from the boxes in the Mouse section labeled Quick Edit and Exclusive mode, then click the OK button. Then, repeat Steps 1 and 2.

3. Click the **Copy** button 🔳 on the MS-DOS toolbar. The highlighting disappears from the selected area.

4. Click the **Start** button, point to **Programs**, then point to **Accessories**.

5. If you are copying text, click **WordPad**; if you are copying graphics, click **Paint** on the Accessories menu.

6. After WordPad or Paint opens, click **Edit** on the menu bar, then click **Paste**. Windows 95 pastes the copied image from the DOS application into the WordPad or Paint application window. In Figure 6-14, a graph from a Lotus 1-2-3 spreadsheet is pasted in the drawing area of the Paint application window.

Figure 6-14
Pasting an
object from
a DOS
application into
a Windows
application

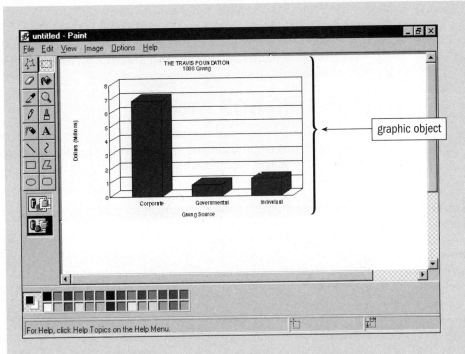

graphic object

7. Make sure the printer is on and operational, then click **File** on the menu bar, click **Print**, then when the Print dialog box opens, click the **OK** button.

8. Click **File**, click **Exit**, then when the WordPad or Paint dialog box opens, click the **No** button to exit without saving. You return to the DOS application window.

9. Close the DOS application window using the program's quit or exit command, and return to the desktop.

TROUBLE? If you attempt to exit a DOS application window with the Close button, Windows 95 might display a warning that it cannot shut down the program automatically. It will also recommend that you exit the program with that program's quit or exit command. Then, it will ask if you want to terminate the program and run the risk of losing any unsaved information. If this occurs, click the No button in the program warning dialog box, then issue the appropriate command for exiting that application. For example, to exit the MS-DOS Editor, you select Exit on the File menu. To exit Lotus 1-2-3, you type a slash (/), click Quit, then click Yes. To exit WordPerfect 5.1, you press the F7 key, then verify whether you want to save the document, and indicate that you want to exit.

REFERENCE
window

COPYING DATA FROM A DOS APPLICATION TO A WINDOWS APPLICATION

- If necessary, press Alt + Enter to switch to a windowed view, then display the MS-DOS toolbar.
- Click the Mark button on the MS-DOS toolbar, then drag to select the area that you want to copy.
- Click the Copy button on the MS-DOS toolbar.
- Click the Start button, then locate and open the Windows application from the Programs menu.
- Click Edit on the menu bar, then click Paste.

You report to Marie that it is easy to copy and paste images and text from a DOS application to a Window application, especially when you work in an MS-DOS window where you can display a toolbar and select buttons on the Windows 95 taskbar. Before you start a new project, Marie asks you to copy the remainder of the information that she will need to start on the annual report.

Using MS-DOS Mode

After returning from a staff meeting, Marie opens Lotus 1-2-3 so she can compile some additional information she needs to produce the foundation's annual report. Immediately, she notices problems with her view of the worksheet area in Lotus 1-2-3, similar to the one shown in Figure 6-15.

Figure 6-15 ◄
Problems with the display of a spreadsheet on Marie's computer

random white patches in the worksheet area

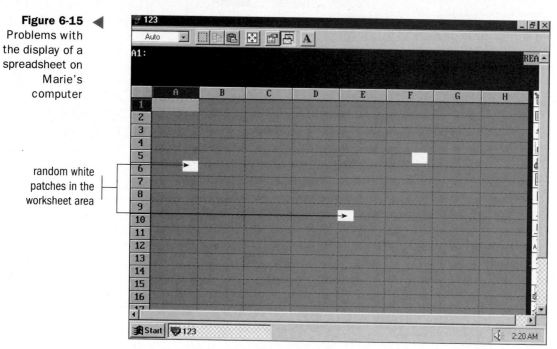

She also notices that Lotus 1-2-3 is responding very slowly.

HELP DESK

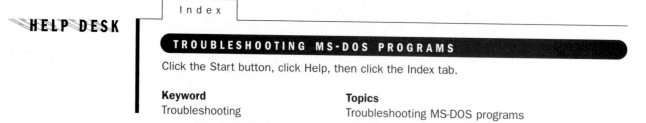

Index

TROUBLESHOOTING MS-DOS PROGRAMS

Click the Start button, click Help, then click the Index tab.

Keyword
Troubleshooting

Topics
Troubleshooting MS-DOS programs

If you encounter problems opening and using a DOS application directly from the desktop, such as a distortion of the application's interface, restart your computer using MS-DOS mode. Then, locate and start the DOS application from the MS-DOS prompt, and determine whether this approach to using your DOS application resolves the problems you encountered. Your application will then run in what is called exclusive MS-DOS mode. In **exclusive MS-DOS mode**, Windows 95 cannot run any other applications or processes.

After closing Lotus 1-2-3, Marie asks you to restart your computer in MS-DOS mode, then start Lotus 1-2-3 and evaluate whether this approach to using Lotus 1-2-3 eliminates the problems that she noticed.

Before you continue with the tutorial, you must know the full path name of the subdirectory that contains your DOS application. Earlier, you wrote down this information. If you no longer have this information or do not remember it, you must use the Find feature on the Start menu to locate the executable program filename and path for the DOS application. After you locate this information, close the Find window, and continue with these steps.

 If you are working in a computer lab or on a network, do not perform the following steps without the permission of your instructor or the technical support person, because these steps require that you restart the computer.

To start your computer in MS-DOS mode:

1. Close all open applications and dialog boxes.

2. Click the **Start** button, click **Shut Down**, click **Restart the computer in MS-DOS mode?**, then click the **Yes** button.

   TROUBLE? If Windows 95 displays a blank screen with only the mouse pointer and does not restart your computer, then your computer has locked up. Press the Reset button to restart Windows 95, then try this step again.

   After Windows 95 restarts your computer, it might place you in the Windows subdirectory on drive C. See Figure 6-16.

Figure 6-16 ◀
Restarting
Windows 95 in
MS-DOS mode

command prompt

drive name

subdirectory name

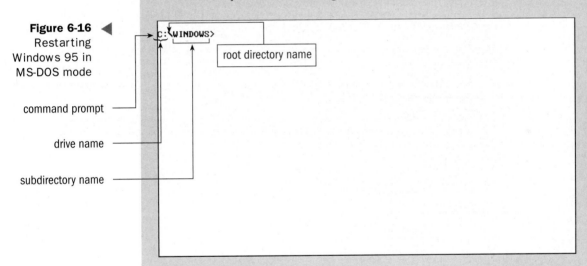

root directory name

You can determine the current directory by examining the command prompt. The first part of the command prompt shows the current drive by displaying the device name for the drive. Immediately after the drive name, you see a backslash symbol that is the DOS notation for the root directory. After the reference to the root directory, DOS displays the path to the current directory. For example, if your command prompt shows C:\WINDOWS, then you are in a subdirectory named Windows located below the root directory of drive C.

Unlike Windows 95, which operates in **graphics mode** so that it can display graphic images, icons, fonts, and colors, and also control the screen resolution and other characteristics of the video display unit, DOS operates in text mode. **Text mode** is a simple and fast display mode that uses one font to display text, numbers, symbols, and special characters. As you can see from Figure 6-16, in text mode, all that appears is text; there are no icons, colors, or any graphical figures.

To start a DOS application from the command prompt, you type the name of the executable program file. For example, to start Lotus 1-2-3 from the command prompt, you would type "123" and press the Enter key, since the name of the Lotus 1-2-3 executable program file is "123.exe." You could also type the MS-DOS file extension, but it is unnecessary. MS-DOS and Windows 95 treat files that have either a com or exe file extension as executable programs.

If Windows 95 or DOS does not know the path to the subdirectory where the executable program file is stored, then it displays the message "Bad command or file name." If this occurs, you can change to the subdirectory that contains the executable program file first by using the Change Directory (CD) command, then you can type the name of the DOS application. However, to change to the subdirectory, you must know the path.

Next, you want to change to the subdirectory where your DOS application is stored before you load it.

In the next set of steps, you will use the path of your DOS application that you jotted down earlier.

To change to the subdirectory with your DOS application:

1. If the command prompt displays the name of a disk drive that is different than the drive where your DOS application is stored, type the drive name where your DOS application is stored, then press the **Enter** key. For example, if your DOS application is stored on drive C, type C: then press the Enter key. You must type a colon immediately after the letter of the alphabet that identifies the drive. The command prompt will change to show the new drive.

2. At the command prompt, type **CD** then press the **Spacebar**, type the **path name** that identifies where your DOS application is stored, then press the **Enter** key. For example, if you are using Lotus 1-2-3 and if its path is C:\123R2.4W, then you would type CD C:\123R2.4. If its path is C:\LOTUS, you would type CD C:\LOTUS then press the Enter key. After you enter this command, the command prompt changes to show the name of the subdirectory that contains your DOS application. See Figure 6-17.

Figure 6-17 ◀
Changing
directories at
the command
prompt

Change Directory
command

updated command
prompt shows current
directory

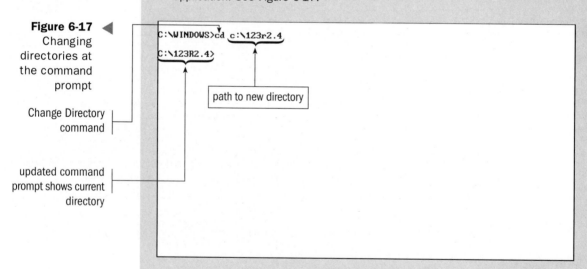

path to new directory

TROUBLE? If you see the error message "Invalid directory," you do not have the proper path name. First, make sure you typed the path name correctly and that you included a backslash symbol (\) immediately before the path name, as described in the examples for this step. If you still see an error message, restart your computer and load Windows 95, then use the Find feature to locate the executable program filename and path for your DOS application. After you locate this information, close the Find window, then try these steps again.

3. To start your DOS application, type the **executable program filename**, then press the **Enter** key. For example, if you want to start Lotus 1-2-3, type 123 then press the Enter key. If you want to start WordPerfect, type WP then press the Enter key. If you want to start the MS-DOS Editor, type EDIT then press the Enter key.

Windows 95 loads your DOS application. See Figure 6-18.

Figure 6-18
Loading a DOS application in MS-DOS mode

application interface →

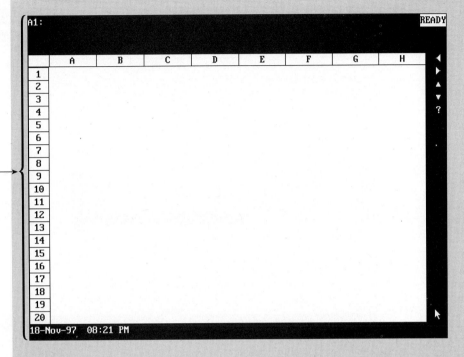

4. Open a document produced with the DOS application that you are using.

5. Press **Alt + Enter** and note that nothing happens. Windows does not allow you to switch to a windowed view while you are using MS-DOS mode. Also, you cannot start other applications while in MS-DOS mode. You can only work with one application or utility at a time. When you finish using the application or utility, you must exit it before you can use another application or utility.

6. Exit the DOS application.

7. When you see the command prompt, type **EXIT** then press the **Enter** key. After a short pause, Windows 95 loads itself and you see the Windows 95 desktop.

TROUBLE? If Windows 95 does not load, then press the Reset button on your computer.

Although using MS-DOS mode resolved Marie's problem, she wants to explore other possibilities for eliminating the video display problems and the slow response times. One of her staff members suggests that they examine how her DOS application uses memory, since memory problems are common to DOS applications.

If you want to take a break and resume the tutorial at a later time, you can do so now. If you are on a network, close any open applications and dialog boxes, and leave Windows 95 running. If you are using your own computer, click the Start button, click Shut Down, click Shut down the computer, and then click the Yes button. When you resume the tutorial, launch Windows 95 again, and then continue with the tutorial.

● ● ●

Understanding DOS Memory Usage

In a recent 1-2-3 session Marie opened one of her Lotus 1-2-3 spreadsheets and expanded the size of the spreadsheet by adding other ranges that summarized corporate, governmental, and individual giving to The Travis Foundation. A few minutes later, Lotus 1-2-3 displayed an Error dialog box, shown in Figure 6-19, indicating that memory was full.

Figure 6-19 ◀
Out of memory
error in a DOS
application

Out of memory error ⟶

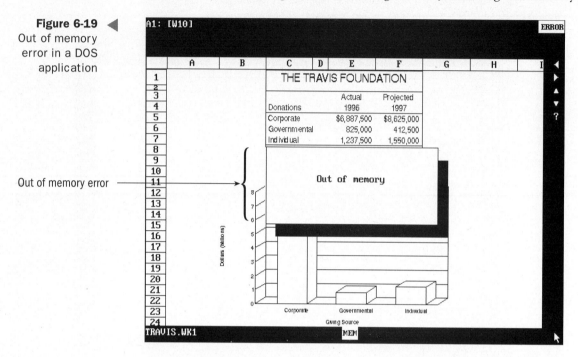

Marie used the Worksheet Status command to display information on memory, as shown in Figure 6-20.

Figure 6-20 ◀
Viewing the
status of
available
memory

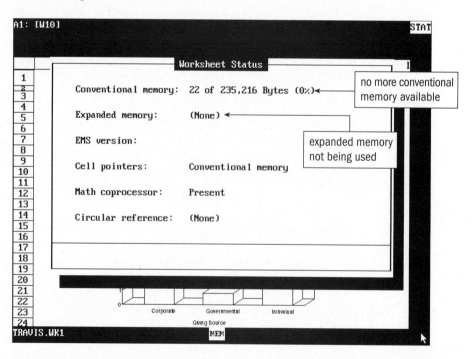

The Worksheet Status dialog box showed that she had almost 0% of conventional memory left. She also noticed that Lotus 1-2-3 was not using any expanded memory. Since Marie could not continue her work, she had to exit the spreadsheet application without saving her most recent changes.

HELP DESK

Index

TROUBLESHOOTING MEMORY PROBLEMS

Click the Start button, click Help, then click the Index tab.

Keyword
Troubleshooting

Topics
Memory troubleshooter

On computers that rely on DOS as the operating system, the availability of conventional memory has become the primary limiting factor in the performance of those computers. Because DOS operates in real mode, the microprocessor is limited to accessing only one megabyte of memory. As a result, DOS itself, DOS device drivers, DOS TSRs, DOS applications, and DOS utilities must all operate within the first megabyte of memory. Even if a computer has additional memory, DOS and DOS applications have limited or no access to that memory.

Under DOS, memory is organized differently than it is under Windows 95. The Windows 95 operating system treats all of a computer's available memory as one sequential address space. In contrast, on a computer that uses DOS as its operating system, memory is organized into regions, each of which has different properties. Figure 6-21 illustrates the organization of memory on systems that use DOS as the operating system.

Figure 6-21 ◀
The organization
of memory

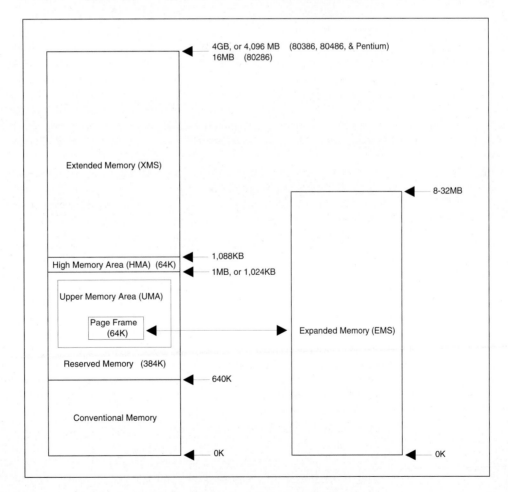

The first 640KB of memory from 0KB to 640KB is **conventional memory**. DOS manages conventional memory. DOS, device drivers, TSRs, and DOS applications are loaded into conventional memory.

The next 384KB of memory from 640KB to 1024KB (or 1MB) is **reserved memory**. This memory is reserved as address space for video display adapters, network adapters, and the ROM-BIOS (ROM Basic Input/Output System). What is important about reserved memory for those who want to optimize memory on their computer is that only part of reserved memory is actually used as address space for these system components. You can use memory managers to claim the additional unused space for DOS. A **memory manager** is a device driver that manages the use of a specific region of memory. Memory managers are important not only because they claim unused and available memory, but also because they prevent one program from attempting to access the memory space used by another program. If one program attempts to use part of the memory used by another program and if there is no memory manager that decides which program uses which part of memory, then your computer system "locks up" and does not respond to your commands.

If you use memory managers to claim unused regions of reserved memory, that extra memory is then referred to as the **Upper Memory Area (UMA)**. Upper memory adds to the total amount of conventional memory available to DOS, and DOS can load device drivers and TSRs into the Upper Memory Area. By loading as many device drivers and TSRs as will fit into the Upper Memory Area, more conventional memory becomes available for your DOS applications, and you can create larger documents with those applications.

Extended memory is the memory above 1MB. If you purchase a computer system today, that computer more than likely will automatically include 4, 8, or 16MB of extended memory. You also have the option of adding more extended memory at the time of purchase or later. Although Windows 95 is designed to operate on computer systems with 4MB of extended memory, it functions optimally if your computer has 16MB or more of extended memory.

The first 64KB of extended memory from 1024KB to 1088KB is called the **High Memory Area (HMA)**. If your computer uses DOS 5.0 or later, then you can use a memory manager to move all or most of DOS and its data structures to the High Memory Area and, again, free up more conventional memory for your DOS applications, even under Windows 95.

Expanded memory is an additional type of memory that is separate from both conventional and extended memory. Prior to the availability of extended memory in computer systems, expanded memory was commonly used to increase the total amount of memory available to DOS applications. Expanded memory provided a means for applications to circumvent the fact that the first microprocessors, the 8088 and 8086, could not address more than 1MB of memory and therefore could not use extended memory. Expanded memory was added to those computer systems by inserting an adapter or card with expanded memory chips on the system board within the computer's system unit. An expanded memory manager program was also included with the board to access the memory on the expanded memory board. Today, for commonly used DOS applications such as Lotus 1-2-3, WordPerfect, and dBASE that can work with expanded memory, you can use a memory manager to convert part of the extended memory available in a computer system to expanded memory. In essence, you are simulating expanded memory without having to buy and add an expanded memory board to your computer.

To use expanded memory, the expanded memory manager creates a page frame in the Upper Memory Area or in conventional memory for swapping small banks of data to and from expanded memory. A **page frame** is a 64KB region of memory that is divided into four pages of equal size. Each **page** is 16KB of memory within the page frame. Expanded memory is slower than extended memory, because the expanded memory manager must swap small blocks of program code or data to and from expanded memory. However, since DOS applications can use expanded memory, but not extended memory, you still improve the performance of those applications by converting extended memory to expanded memory. Plus, you can create larger documents because DOS applications like Lotus 1-2-3, WordPerfect, and dBASE can store data in expanded memory.

The two memory managers used by DOS, Windows 3.1, and Windows 95 are Himem.sys and Emm386.exe. Himem.sys manages extended memory, the High Memory Area (HMA), and the Upper Memory Area (UMA). Himem.sys allocates extended memory to applications that can use that type of memory. It also allocates memory in the High Memory Area to DOS, so that DOS can load itself into the High Memory Area.

Once Himem.sys claims unused space in reserved memory, Emm386.exe divides what is now called Upper Memory Area into upper memory blocks (or UMBs) so that DOS can load device drivers and TSRs into the Upper Memory Area. Emm386.exe is also the memory manager that can convert all or part of extended memory to expanded memory for those DOS applications that use expanded memory but not extended memory.

Himem.sys and Emm386.exe work cooperatively with Windows 95, Windows 3.1, and DOS to manage all the memory within your computer system.

When you use a DOS application under Windows 95, it creates a Virtual DOS Machine (or VDM) that simulates the memory organization that DOS applications and DOS games require in order to function properly. Plus, it uses the memory managers Himem.sys and Emm386.exe to provide DOS, DOS applications, and DOS games with access to different types of memory within the Virtual DOS Machine. When you boot your computer, Windows 95 reads and executes the contents of Config.sys and Autoexec.bat, the MS-DOS system startup files, so that it knows how to configure memory for DOS applications. This feature provides compatibility with existing DOS applications and DOS games.

When you use a Windows application under Windows 95, Windows 95 still uses the MS-DOS memory manager Himem.sys to manage the extended memory within your computer. However, it does not require Emm386.exe for Windows applications. With Himem.sys, Windows 95 manages all the available memory within your computer as one single address space, and it allocates address space to each application that you start under Windows 95. Once you close a Windows application, Windows 95 reclaims the memory used by that application so that it becomes available for other applications.

When you attempt to optimize memory for DOS applications and games, remember that the two types of memory that you might need to configure properly are conventional memory and expanded memory.

Configuring Memory for a DOS Application

Marie asks you to examine the property sheet for the DOS application that she is using, determine why she encountered memory problems, and, if possible, figure out how to correct the problem so that she can complete her project. She reminds you that her DOS application is using conventional memory, but not expanded memory.

To examine memory usage for a DOS application:

1. Right-click the **DOS application shortcut** on the desktop, then click **Properties** on the shortcut menu.

2. After the Properties dialog box for your DOS application opens, click the **Memory** tab. The Memory tab on your computer might show results different from those in the figure. See Figure 6-22.

Figure 6-22 ◄
Viewing
memory
settings

not configured for
expanded memory

click to view details
on expanded memory

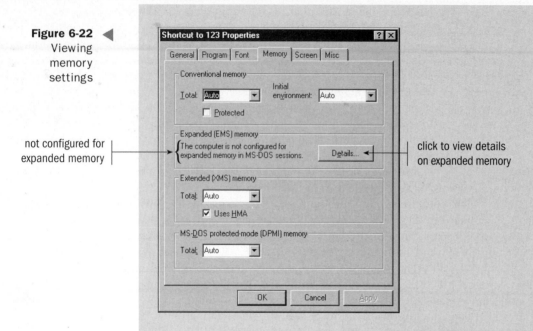

In the Conventional memory section, Windows 95 is automatically set to make available whatever conventional memory the DOS application needs. So, conventional memory is not likely to be the source of the memory problems on Marie's computer. You then notice in the Expanded (EMS) memory section that Windows 95 reports that Marie's computer is not configured to use expanded memory in MS-DOS sessions. You want to find out the reason why. Your property sheet might show that the use of expanded memory is enabled.

3. If you see a Details button in the Expanded (EMS) memory section, click the **Details** button; otherwise skip to Step 5. The dialog box labeled with the MS-DOS name for the file that contains the information on using the shortcut explains that the "device=EMM386" line in Marie's Config.sys file contains the "noems" keyword. See Figure 6-23. "Noems" is an abbreviation for "no expanded memory specification." Windows 95 suggests that you use Notepad to remove that keyword and then restart your computer. Do not attempt to change memory settings on this property sheet unless you know what you are doing, because Windows 95 might not function properly.

Figure 6-23 ◄
How to enable
expanded
memory

where the problem
lies

how to resolve
problem

SHORTC~1.PIF

The 'device=EMM386' line in your CONFIG.SYS contains the 'noems'
keyword. To enable expanded memory, use Notepad to remove that
keyword and restart the system.

OK

4. If you used the Details button in the last step, click **OK** button to close the dialog box.

5. Click the **OK** button to close the properties dialog box for the shortcut to your DOS application.

EXAMINING MEMORY USAGE FOR AN APPLICATION

- Right-click the application shortcut on the desktop, then click Properties on the shortcut menu.
- When the Shortcut Properties dialog box opens, click the Memory tab.
- Examine and, if necessary, change memory settings.
- Click the OK button to close the Shortcut Properties dialog box.

You immediately inform Marie that expanded memory is not enabled on her computer. Once you enable that memory, she should not have any further problems.

Using Notepad to Examine Config.sys

Now that you have identified the likely source of the memory problems on Marie's computer, you can open and examine Config.sys and determine whether you need to change the setting that enables Windows 95 and DOS applications to convert part of extended memory to expanded memory.

Like other types of configuration files in Windows 95, Windows 3.1, and DOS, Config.sys and Autoexec.bat are simple text files that contain a set of commands which are executed during the booting of a computer. The commands in Config.sys are called directives, and they configure DOS by changing default settings built into DOS and by enabling DOS to work with software and hardware devices. For example, device drivers, such as a mouse driver, CD-ROM driver, or a memory manager, load from Config.sys. The commands in Autoexec.bat customize your working environment for your benefit. For example, you might load TSRs that configure sound cards and CD-ROM drives.

Before you make any changes to these files, you should make sure you have duplicate copies of the contents of these files, or you should print a copy of each file. Then, you can restore the files to their original condition if you inadvertently make a change that you don't want. Also note that it is beyond the scope of this book to discuss handling of DOS system files. See an appropriate DOS text for information on working with Config.sys and Autoexec.bat.

You can view, print, and make changes to these files using the MS-DOS Editor Notepad, Sysedit, or WordPad. The MS-DOS Editor and Notepad are text editors. Sysedit is a utility introduced in Windows 3.1 for opening, changing, and printing MS-DOS and Windows 3.1 configuration files. WordPad can open and save text files.

Next, you want to open Notepad, and then open and print Config.sys. Marie suggests that you also print a copy of Autoexec.bat so that you have records of the settings in these two DOS system startup files.

If you are working in a computer lab or network, you can view and print but not make changes to these files.

To print then view the contents of the DOS system startup files:

1. Click the **Start** button, point to **Programs**, point to **Accessories**, click **Notepad**, then click the **Maximize** button in the Notepad application window. Figure 6-24 shows the Notepad application window.

Figure 6-24 ◀
Opening the
Notepad
application

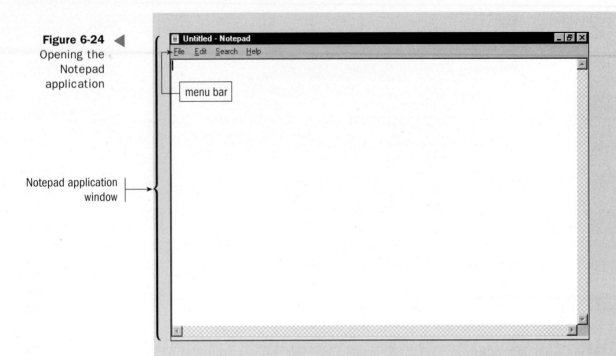

Notepad application
window

menu bar

2. Click **File** then click **Open**. In the Open dialog box, you select the drive, folder, and file that you want to open. See Figure 6-25.

Figure 6-25 ◀
Opening a file

where to look for file

select a folder

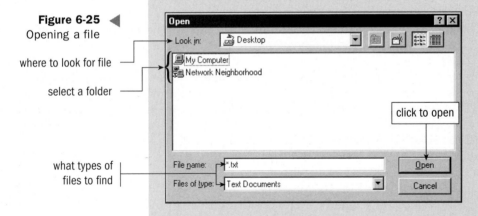

what types of
files to find

click to open

3. Click the **Look in** list arrow, then click the listing for drive C. In the Look in box, you see a list of the folders on drive C.

4. Click the **Files of type** list arrow, then click **All Files (*.*)**.

5. Scroll through the folders and files in the Look in box, and locate and click **Config.sys**, as shown in Figure 6-26, then click the **Open** button.

Figure 6-26 ◀
Opening
Config.sys

current folder

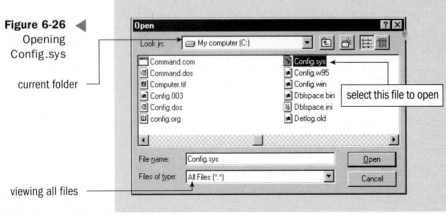

select this file to open

viewing all files

In the Notepad application window, you will see all or part of the contents of your Config.sys file. See Figure 6-27.

Figure 6-27 ◄
Viewing the contents of a Config.sys file

commands for loading memory managers →

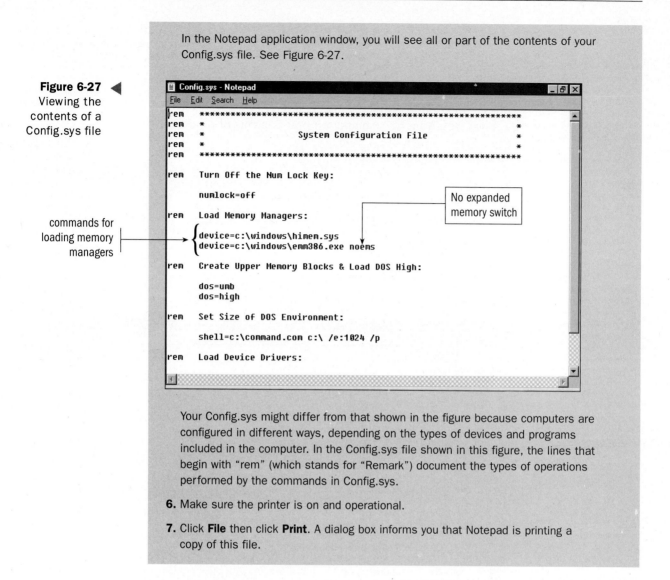

Your Config.sys might differ from that shown in the figure because computers are configured in different ways, depending on the types of devices and programs included in the computer. In the Config.sys file shown in this figure, the lines that begin with "rem" (which stands for "Remark") document the types of operations performed by the commands in Config.sys.

6. Make sure the printer is on and operational.

7. Click **File** then click **Print**. A dialog box informs you that Notepad is printing a copy of this file.

In Figure 6-27, the section labeled "Load Memory Mangers" lists two device commands that load the Windows 95, Windows 3.1, and DOS memory managers. The first device command loads Himem.sys, which manages extended memory, the High Memory Area (HMA), and the Upper Memory Area (UMA). The second device command loads Emm386.exe, which divides the Upper Memory Area into Upper Memory Blocks (UMBs). The noems switch at the end of this command line indicates to Emm386.exe that there is no expanded memory. A **switch** is an optional parameter, or piece of information, that changes the way in which a program operates. The noems switch means that any extended memory in the computer is used only as extended memory. Remember that Emm386.exe can convert extended memory to expanded memory for applications that use expanded memory. If you replace the switch "noems" with the switch "ram," then Emm386.exe will convert part of extended memory to expanded memory. Your command line would then read:

device=c:\windows\emm386.exe ram

If you are using DOS applications like Lotus 1-2-3, WordPerfect, and dBASE, all of which benefit from the availability of expanded memory, change the switch from "noems" to "ram," restart your computer so that MS-DOS and Windows are configured with the new switch, then open your DOS application. You will find that you eliminate memory problems that you previously had, and that you can build larger documents.

If you are working on your own computer and have encountered this exact same problem with one or more of your DOS applications, you might want to make this change now and use the Save command on the File menu to update your Config.sys file. Then, reboot your computer, and work your DOS applications.

If you are working in a computer lab or on a network, do not change any of the settings in the Config.sys file.

Next, you want to open and print the contents of Autoexec.bat.

To print a copy of Autoexec.bat:

1. Click **File**, then click **Open**. Notepad remembers that you opened the folder for drive C, and that you chose to view all files.

2. Scroll through the folders and files in the Look in box, and locate and click **Autoexec.bat**, then click the **Open** button.

3. If Notepad displays a Notepad dialog box and asks you if you want to save your changes to Config.sys, click the **No** button. In the Notepad application window, you will see all or part of the contents of your Autoexec.bat file. See Figure 6-28.

Figure 6-28 ◄
Viewing the contents of an Autoexec.bat file

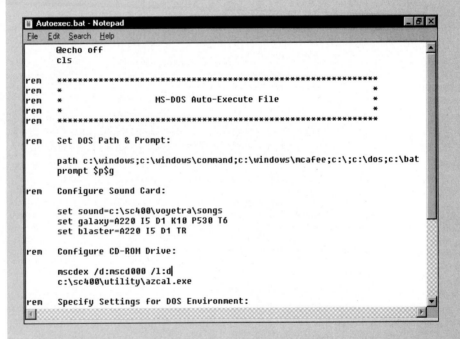

Your Autoexec.bat might differ from that shown in the figure because computers are customized in different ways. Like the Config.sys file, the lines that begin with "rem" document the types of operations performed by the commands in Autoexec.bat.

6. Make sure the printer is on and operational.

7. Click **File** then click **Print**. A dialog box informs you that Notepad is printing a copy of this file.

8. Click **File** then click **Exit**. If Notepad displays Notepad dialog box and asks you if you want to save your changes, click the **No** button.

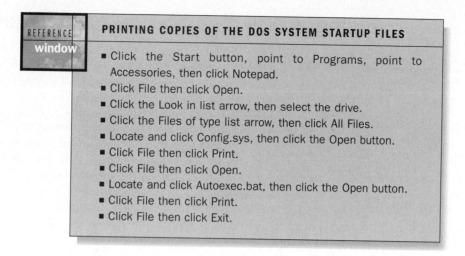

REFERENCE
window

PRINTING COPIES OF THE DOS SYSTEM STARTUP FILES

- Click the Start button, point to Programs, point to Accessories, then click Notepad.
- Click File then click Open.
- Click the Look in list arrow, then select the drive.
- Click the Files of type list arrow, then click All Files.
- Locate and click Config.sys, then click the Open button.
- Click File then click Print.
- Click File then click Open.
- Locate and click Autoexec.bat, then click the Open button.
- Click File then click Print.
- Click File then click Exit.

After opening Config.sys on Marie's computer, you show her that her computer is not configured to use expanded memory. She changes the noems switch to the ram switch, saves the change to Config.sys, exits Notepad, and restarts her computer. Marie next examines the Memory property sheet for the shortcut to her DOS application, and discovers that Windows 95 is configured to provide her DOS application with whatever expanded memory it needs. Then, she opens Lotus 1-2-3, and uses the Status command on the Worksheet menu to display the current status of her computer. Lotus 1-2-3 can now access all of extended memory and use it as expanded memory, as shown in Figure 6-29.

Figure 6-29
Optimizing
memory usage
on Marie's
computer

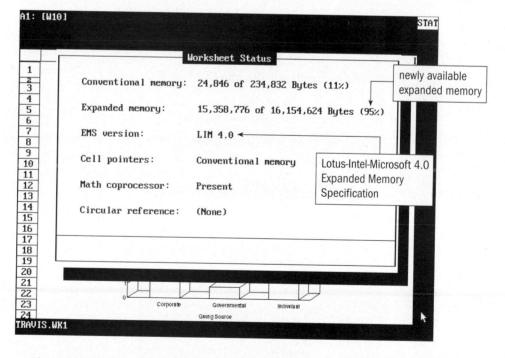

She opens her spreadsheet file, and reconstructs the changes that she lost when she encountered the memory errors. Thanks to your efforts, her DOS application is now working properly.

Marie recommends that the two of you discuss the importance of properly configuring DOS applications under Windows 95 at the next staff meeting, and demonstrate how to check and change memory settings.

Adding a DOS Application to the Start Menu

Marie realizes that her desktop is becoming cluttered with too many shortcuts. After she starts Windows 95, she has to spend what seems like an inordinate amount of time looking for the shortcut she needs. She decides to add her DOS application to the Start menu, and remove it from the desktop.

Windows 95 automatically adds applications designed for Windows to the Start menu when you first install those applications. However, it does not automatically add DOS applications. If you want to place a DOS application on your Start menu, or perhaps even create a folder for DOS applications, then you must open the Taskbar Properties dialog box, select the Start Menu Programs tab, then complete a series of steps to locate and add the application to the Start menu. If you periodically use a DOS application, it makes more sense to add it to the Start menu than to add yet another shortcut on your desktop.

Since her desktop also has a variety of shortcuts, Marie asks you to add the DOS application to her Start menu.

HELP DESK

Index

CUSTOMIZING THE START MENU

Click the Start button, click Help, then click the Index tab.

Keyword
Start menu

Topics
Overview: Customizing your Start menu

Marie asks you to add Lotus 1-2-3 to her Programs menu.

If you are working in a computer lab or on a network, you might not be able to make changes to the Programs menu.

To add an application to the Start menu:

1. Point to an empty area of the taskbar, right-click the **taskbar**, then click **Properties**. The Taskbar Properties dialog box opens.

2. Click the **Start Menu Programs** tab. The Customize Start Menu section allows you to add or remove programs from the Start menu. See Figure 6-30.

Figure 6-30 ◀
Customizing
the Start menu

click to add a
program to the
Start menu

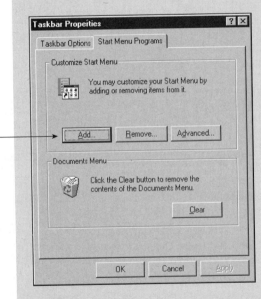

3. In the Customize Start Menu section, click the **Add** button. Windows 95 displays a Create Shortcut dialog box, and asks you to enter the path and name of the program you want to add to the Start menu. See Figure 6-31.

Figure 6-31 ◀
Prompt to enter
the location
and name of
the program

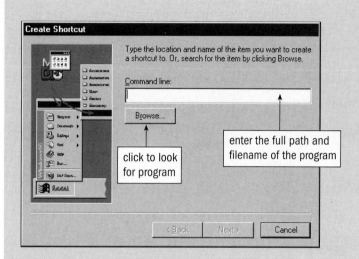

click to look
for program

enter the full path and
filename of the program

If you do not know the path and name of the program, you can use the Browse
button to locate and select it.

4. In the Create Shortcut dialog box, click the **Browse** button. A Browse dialog box
opens. See Figure 6-32.

Figure 6-32 ◀
Browsing for a
program file

look in drive C

select a folder

display program
filenames

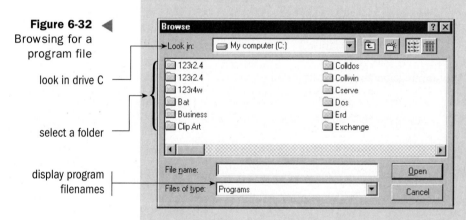

5. If the Look in list box does not display a reference to drive C, click the **Look in**
list arrow, then locate and click the **listing** for drive C.

6. Scroll through the Look in list, locate and click the **folder** that contains the executable program file for your DOS application, then click the **Open** button. The
application folder opens. See Figure 6-33.

Figure 6-33 ◀
Locating the
program folder
and file

look in this
application folder

select a program file

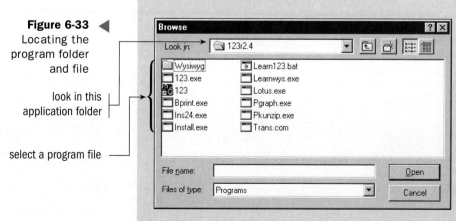

Your application folder might have a different name, and contain different files.

7. Locate and click the **executable program filename**, then click the **Open** button. Windows 95 displays the path and name of the DOS application in the Create Shortcut dialog box. See Figure 6-34.

Figure 6-34 ◀
The full path
and filename of
a DOS
application

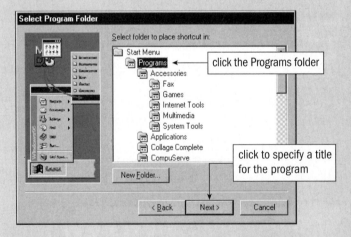

Your path and filename might differ from that shown in the figure.

Next you specify where you want the application name to appear on the Start menu, and select a title for the application.

To add the application to the Start menu:

1. In the Create Shortcut dialog box, click the **Next** button. Windows 95 opens the Select Program Folder dialog box. See Figure 6-35.

Figure 6-35 ◀
Selecting a
folder on the
Start menu for
the program
shortcut

You can select an existing folder, or even create a new folder on the Start or Programs menus.

2. If the Programs folder is not highlighted, click the **Programs** folder, then click the **Next** button. Windows 95 displays the Select a Title for the Program dialog box. See Figure 6-36.

Figure 6-36 ◀
Prompt for a
title to appear
on the
Programs menu

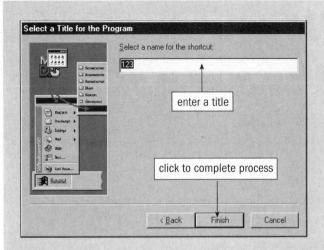

3. In the Select a name for the shortcut text box, type a name for the DOS application you are using, then click the **Finish** button. For example, if you are adding Lotus 1-2-3 to the Start menu, you might type Lotus 1-2-3 for DOS in the text box.

4. In the Taskbar Properties dialog box, click the **OK** button to close this dialog box and complete the process of adding an application to the Start menu.

Now, you want to start the DOS application by using the Start menu, so that you know it is working properly.

To start your DOS application from the Start menu:

1. Click the **Start** button then point to **Programs**. Your DOS application is listed on the Programs menu. Figure 6-37 shows the name of the Lotus 1-2-3 for DOS application on the Programs menu.

Figure 6-37 ◀
Viewing a new
addition to the
Programs menu

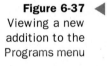

2. Click the **name** of your DOS application on the Programs menu. Windows 95 opens your DOS application from the Start menu.

3. Close your DOS application and return to the desktop.

ADDING A DOS APPLICATION TO THE START MENU

- Right-click the taskbar then click Properties on the shortcut menu.
- Click the Start Menu Programs tab.
- In the Customize Start Menu section, click the Add button.
- In the Create Shortcut dialog box, click the Browse button.
- In the Look in list box, locate and click the drive you want to search.
- In the Look in box, locate and click the folder that contains the executable program file, then click the Open button.
- Locate and click the executable program filename, then click the Open button.
- In the Create Shortcut dialog box, click the Next button.
- In the Select Program Folder dialog box, click the name of the folder where you want to add the application, then click the Next button.
- In the Select a Title for the Program dialog box, type a name for the DOS application, then click the Finish button.
- In the Taskbar Properties dialog box, click the OK button.

Marie notices that it is easy to select her DOS application from the Start menu because Windows 95 places it in alphabetical order with the rest of the applications.

Removing a Shortcut from the Desktop

You might not want the DOS application shortcut you just created to remain on your desktop, so delete the shortcut from your desktop.

To remove a shortcut from the desktop:

1. Right-click the **shortcut** to your DOS application, then click **Delete** on the shortcut menu. Windows 95 displays a Confirm File Delete dialog box, and asks if you want to send the shortcut to the Recycle Bin.

2. Click the **Yes** button. Windows 95 removes the shortcut from the desktop.

3. If you change your mind and want to keep this shortcut on your computer's desktop, you can right-click the **Recycle Bin**, click **Open** on the shortcut menu, right-click the **name** of the shortcut in the Recycle bin, then click **Restore** on the shortcut menu. Windows 95 will then move the shortcut from the Recycle Bin and restore it to the desktop.

Removing an unneeded shortcut is a good way to keep your desktop uncluttered.

Removing an Application from the Start Menu

Rather than list the name of each DOS application that she uses on the Programs menu, Marie decides to create a folder for those DOS applications. After creating this folder on the Start menu, and after adding each of her DOS applications to this folder, she asks you to remove the original DOS application that you added to her Start menu.

To remove an application from the Start menu:

1. Point to an empty area of the taskbar, right-click the **taskbar**, then click **Properties**. The Taskbar Properties dialog box opens.

2. Click the **Start Menu Programs** tab.

3. In the Customize Start Menu section, click the **Remove** button. Windows 95 displays a Remove Shortcuts/Folder dialog box. See Figure 6-38.

Figure 6-38 ◀
Removing an application from the Programs menu

select the application name

click to remove

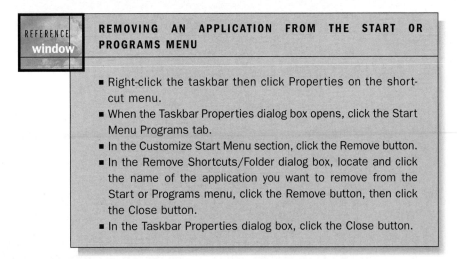

4. In the Remove Shortcuts/Folder dialog box, locate and then click the **name** of the application that you added to the Programs menu, click the **Remove** button, then click the **Close** button.

5. In the Taskbar Properties dialog box, click the **OK** button.

6. Click the **Start** button then point to **Programs**. Windows 95 has removed the DOS application from the Start menu.

7. Click the **Start** button again to close the Programs and Start menus.

REFERENCE
window

REMOVING AN APPLICATION FROM THE START OR PROGRAMS MENU

- Right-click the taskbar then click Properties on the short-cut menu.
- When the Taskbar Properties dialog box opens, click the Start Menu Programs tab.
- In the Customize Start Menu section, click the Remove button.
- In the Remove Shortcuts/Folder dialog box, locate and click the name of the application you want to remove from the Start or Programs menu, click the Remove button, then click the Close button.
- In the Taskbar Properties dialog box, click the Close button.

● ● ●

At her next weekly staff meeting, Marie discusses the process for configuring and customizing the DOS applications that she and her staff rely on to update and produce the documents that track corporate giving at The Travis Foundation.

Tutorial Assignment

Another important DOS application used by staff at The Travis Foundation is WordPerfect 5.1. Marie and the members of her department prepare memos, correspondence, reports, tables, and an annual report with this DOS application. Also, once a year staff prepare a special newsletter that profiles recent recipients of their scholarships. Marie wants you to prepare a desktop shortcut for WordPerfect 5.1, open WordPerfect 5.1, and open a document. She also wants you to check memory settings to verify that it is functioning optimally on your computer.

As you complete this tutorial assignment, choose a DOS application different than the one that you used for this chapter's tutorial. If you need assistance in selecting a DOS application and a document to open, ask your instructor or technical support person for suggestions. If you can't perform a copy and paste operation, close the DOS application, open the Properties dialog box for the DOS application, select the Misc tab, and, in the Mouse section, deactivate the QuickEdit and Exclusive mode options.

1. Click the Start button, point to Find, then click Files or Folders.
2. In the Named list box on the Name & Location tab of the Find window, enter all or part of the name of the DOS application you want to search for, select the drive you want to search, and verify that the search will include all subfolders.
3. On the Date Modified tab, select all files, then on the Advanced tab, verify that the search will include All Files and Folders. As you check these tabs, remove settings that might affect your search.
4. Start the find and, as the find progresses, maximize the window.
5. Right-click the filename of the DOS application that you intend to use, choose the option to create a shortcut on the desktop, then close the Find window.
6. Right-click the desktop shortcut for your DOS application, click Properties on the shortcut menu, click the Program tab, click the Change Icon button, locate and select a new icon for your desktop shortcut, then close the Change Icon and Shortcut Properties dialog boxes.
7. Double-click the new desktop shortcut for your DOS application.
8. Use the Alt + Enter key combination to switch to a windowed view, then open the application menu, and choose the option to display the MS-DOS toolbar.
9. Open a document created with this DOS application, or create and save a document.
10. Click the Mark button, use the mouse to select text or graphics within the document, then click the Copy button.
11. Open the WordPad or Paint application from the Start menu, click Paste on the Edit menu to paste a copy of the text or graphics into WordPad or Paint, print a copy of the pasted image, then close WordPad or Paint without saving.
12. Close your DOS application and return to the desktop.
13. Right-click the desktop shortcut for your DOS application, then select Properties from the shortcut menu.
14. Select the Memory tab in the Shortcut Properties dialog box.
15. If expanded memory is not enabled, click the Details button to view how to configure expanded memory, then close the informational dialog box.
16. Press Alt + Print Screen, open Paint, paste the contents of the Clipboard into the drawing area, then print the pasted image, and exit Paint without saving the file.
17. Close the Shortcut Properties dialog box.
18. If you are working in a computer lab, or if you want to remove the desktop shortcut for this DOS application, right-click the shortcut, click Delete on the shortcut menu, then confirm the file deletion.

Case Problems

1. Creating a Shortcut to the MS-DOS Prompt at Bytes, Bits & Nibbles Bytes, Bits & Nibbles is a small computer dealership that sells PCs, peripherals, software, and books. Bytes, Bits & Nibbles also has a small service department for repairing PCs. One of BBN's employees, Antonio Hernandez, sells computers and assists customers in customizing their new systems. For a self-employed client that relies on her DOS applications for both business and personal use, Antonio asks you to create a desktop shortcut for the MS-DOS Prompt application. This desktop shortcut will open an MS-DOS window from which his client can start any DOS application she wants.

1. Click the Start button, point to Find, then click Files or Folders.
2. In the Named list box on the Name & Location tab of the Find window, type COMMAND.COM then select drive C.
3. On the Date Modified tab, select all files, then on the Advanced tab, verify that the search will include All Files and Folders. As you check these tabs, remove settings that might affect your search.
4. Start the find and, as the find progresses, maximize the window.
5. Since Windows 95 might find several copies of Command.com, locate the Command.com stored in C:\, the root directory of drive C.
6. Right-click the Command.com icon, choose the option to create a shortcut on the desktop, then close the Find window.
7. Double-click the MS-DOS Prompt desktop shortcut.
8. If the MS-DOS Prompt application opens in full screen view, use the Alt + Enter key combination to switch to a windowed view.
9. Use the CD command to change from the current directory (shown in the command prompt) to the directory that you used in the chapter tutorial.
10. Type the command to load the DOS application that you worked with in this tutorial, open a document, then close the DOS application.
11. At the command prompt, type EXIT to exit the MS-DOS Prompt application and return to the desktop.
12. Right-click the MS-DOS Prompt shortcut, select Properties from the shortcut menu, then select the Memory tab in the Shortcut Properties dialog box.
13. Press Alt + Print Screen, open Paint, paste the contents of the Clipboard into the drawing area, then print the pasted image, and exit Paint without saving the file.
14. Close the MS-DOS Prompt Properties dialog box.
15. Right-click the MS-DOS Prompt shortcut, then select Cut from the shortcut menu. Insert your Student Disk into a drive, open the My Computer window, open a window for the drive that contains the floppy disk, select Paste from the Edit menu, then close the drive and My Computer windows.

2. Creating a Shortcut to the System Configuration Editor at Amalgamated Insurance
Amalgamated Insurance is a large firm that offers it customers health and dental insurance, life and disability insurance, and retirement plans. Nancy Zheng, a microcomputer specialist, tests various system configurations on her computer before she implements them on her coworkers' computers. So that she can quickly document different configurations that she tests, she wants to create a shortcut to the System Configuration Editor, a utility provided with Windows 3.1. This utility automatically opens all the Windows system configuration files in a separate Notepad window. She asks you to locate the program, create a desktop shortcut for the program, and open and test the program.

The System Configuration Editor will open specific configuration files used by Windows 95 on your computer. Do not make any changes to these configuration files because the changes might affect the performance of your computer.

1. Click the Start button, point to Find, then select Files or Folders.
2. In the Named list box on the Name & Location tab of the Find window, type SYSEDIT then select drive C.

3. On the Date Modified tab, select all files, then on the Advanced tab, verify that the search will include all files and folders. As you check these tabs, remove settings that might affect your search.

4. Start the find and, as the find progresses, maximize the window.

5. After Windows 95 locates Sysedit.exe in C:\Windows\System, right-click the Sysedit.exe icon, choose the option to create a shortcut on the desktop, then close the Find window.

6. Right-click the shortcut to Sysedit.exe, click Rename on the shortcut menu, then type System Configuration Editor and press the Enter key to change the name for this shortcut.

7. Double-click the shortcut to the System Configuration Editor.

8. After Sysedit opens all the Windows configuration files, maximize the System Configuration Editor application window.

9. Select Cascade from the Window menu to display overlapping views of all the windows opened by the System Configuration Editor.

10. Press Alt + Print Screen, open Paint, paste the contents of the Clipboard into the drawing area, then print the pasted image, and exit Paint without saving the file.

11. Close the System Configuration Editor application window and return to the desktop. *If you are prompted to save any changes to a configuration file, click the No button.*

12. Right-click the System Configuration Editor shortcut, then select Cut from the shortcut menu. Insert your Student Disk into a drive, open the My Computer window, open a window for the drive that contains the floppy disk, select Paste from the Edit menu, then close the drive and My Computer windows.

3. Creating Shortcuts to Config.sys and Autoexec.bat at Telano Bonding Corp Telano Bonding Corp provides a professional bonding service for counties, municipalities, developers, and individuals. Cory Childers, an employee who prepares the contracts for these bonding services, is updating the configuration of his computer system. As he reconfigures the CD-ROM drive, a legacy device on his computer, he wants to simplify the process of opening Config.sys and Autoexec.bat so that he can test different configurations quickly. He asks you to create shortcuts to these two configuration files using the MS-DOS Editor.

As you complete this case problem, do not make any changes to Config.sys and Autoexec.bat because the changes might affect the performance of your computer.

1. Click the Start button, point to Find, then select Files or Folders.

2. In the Named list box on the Name & Location tab of the Find window, type EDIT then select drive C.

3. On the Date Modified tab, select all files, then on the Advanced tab, verify that the search will include the All Files and Folders option. As you check these tabs, remove settings that might affect your search.

4. Start the find and, as the find progresses, maximize the window.

5. After Windows 95 locates Edit.com in C:\Windows\Command, right-click the Edit.com icon, choose the option to create a shortcut on the desktop, then close the Find window.

6. Right-click the shortcut to MS-DOS Editor, click Rename on the shortcut menu, then type OPEN CONFIG.SYS and press the Enter key to change the name for this shortcut.

7. Right-click the Open Config.sys shortcut, select Properties from the shortcut menu, then select the Program tab.

8. Click at the end of the Cmd line box, press the Spacebar, then type C:\CONFIG.SYS so that the command line reads:
   C:\WINDOWS\COMMAND\EDIT.COM C:\CONFIG.SYS

9. Click the OK button to close the Open Config.sys Properties dialog box.

10. Double-click the Open Config.sys shortcut. Windows 95 opens the MS-DOS Editor then opens Config.sys.

11. Close the MS-DOS Editor. If the MS-DOS Editor asks you if you want to save your changes, click the No button.

12. Right-click the Open Config.sys shortcut, then select Copy from the shortcut menu.

13. Right-click the desktop, then select Paste from the shortcut menu to paste another copy of the shortcut on the desktop. The duplicate of this shortcut is named Copy of Open Config.sys.

14. Right-click the Copy of Open Config.sys shortcut, click Rename on the shortcut menu, then type OPEN AUTOEXEC.BAT and press the Enter key to change the name of this shortcut.

15. Right-click the Open Autoexec.bat shortcut, select Properties from the shortcut menu, then select the Program tab.

16. In the Cmd line text box, click before the "C" in CONFIG.SYS, drag to highlight and select CONFIG.SYS, then type AUTOEXEC.BAT so that the command line now reads:

    C:\WINDOWS\COMMAND\EDIT.COM C:\AUTOEXEC.BAT

17. Click the OK button to close the Open Autoexec.bat Properties dialog box.

18. Double-click the Open Autoexec.bat shortcut. Windows 95 opens the MS-DOS Editor, then opens Autoexec.bat.

19. Close the MS-DOS Editor. If the MS-DOS Editor asks you if you want to save your changes, click the No button.

20. Right-click the Open Config.sys shortcut, select Properties from the shortcut menu, then select the Program tab in the Open Config.sys Properties dialog box.

21. Press Alt + Print Screen, open Paint, paste the contents of the Clipboard into the drawing area, then print the pasted image, and exit Paint without saving the file.

22. Close the Open Config.sys Properties dialog box and return to the desktop.

23. Right-click the Open Config.sys shortcut, then select Cut from the shortcut menu. Insert your Student Disk into a drive, open the My Computer window, open a window for the drive that contains the floppy disk, select Paste from the Edit menu.

24. Right-click the Open Autoexec.bat shortcut, then select Cut from the shortcut menu. Select the drive window, then select Paste from the Edit menu.

25. Close the drive and My Computer windows.

4. Automating the Formatting of Disks at Rottiers Enterprises Rottiers Enterprises uses AutoCAD to prepare engineering blueprints, topographic maps and surveys for contractors, builders, landscape services, and county agencies. Mirielle Rottiers and her staff need to frequently format and reformat floppy disks so that they can provide clients with copies of files that they produce with AutoCAD. She asks you to prepare a desktop shortcut that starts the formatting utility provided with Windows 95. She also wants this program to automatically place the label "Rottiers" on each disk.

To complete this case problem, you will need a disk that you can format. Also, the disk's storage capacity must match that of the disk drive you are using. For example, you need to use a high-density disk for a high-density drive and a double-density disk for a double-density drive. If you are working in a computer lab and do not know the storage capacity of the computers disk drive or drives, ask your instructor or technical support person.

1. Click the Start button, point to Find, then select Files or Folders.

2. In the Named list box on the Name & Location tab of the Find window, type FORMAT then select drive C.

3. On the Date Modified tab, select all files, then on the Advanced tab, verify that the search will include the All Files and Folders option. As you check these tabs, remove settings that might affect your search.

4. Start the find and, as the find progresses, maximize the window.

5. After Windows 95 locates Format.com in C:\Windows\Command, right-click the Format.com icon, choose the option to create a shortcut on the desktop, then close the Find window.

6. Right-click the shortcut to Format.com, select Rename from the shortcut menu, then type FORMAT DISK and press the Enter key to change the name for this shortcut.

7. Right-click the Format Disk shortcut, select Properties from the shortcut menu, then select the Program tab.

8. Click at the end of the Cmd line text box, press the Spacebar, then type A: /V:ROTTIERS. If you are using drive B instead of drive A, substitute B: for A:. The command line should read:

     C:\WINDOWS\COMMAND\FORMAT.COM A: /V:ROTTIERS

   Note: The /V switch labels the disk.

9. Click the OK button to close the Format Disk Properties dialog box.

10. Double-click the Format Disk shortcut.

11. When the format utility in the Format window prompts for a disk, insert a blank disk into the disk drive, then press the Enter key.

12. After the formatting is complete, you will see a summary of the storage capacity of the disk and then a prompt asking you if you want to format another disk. Type N for No.

13. When the title bar displays "Finished - FORMAT," click the Close button to close the Format window.

14. Open the My Computer window, right-click the drive that contains the newly formatted disk, then select Properties from the shortcut menu.

15. When the Properties dialog box for the disk drive opens, press Alt + Print Screen, open Paint, paste the contents of the Clipboard into the drawing area, then print the pasted image, and exit Paint without saving the file.

16. Close the drive Properties dialog box, then close the My Computer window.

17. Right-click the Format Disk shortcut, then select Cut from the shortcut menu. Insert your Student Disk into a drive, open the My Computer window, open a window for the drive that contains the disk, select Paste from the Edit menu, then close the drive and My Computer windows.

Backing Up Files

Implementing a Backup Strategy at Multimedia
Enterprises International

OBJECTIVES

In this tutorial you will:

- Learn why backups are important

- Examine two types of backup storage media

- Examine backup strategies

- Learn about Microsoft Backup and its capabilities

- Back up a folder

- Restore a folder

- Perform a tape backup

CASE

Multimedia Enterprises International, Inc.

Multimedia Enterprises International, Inc. (MEI) is a large Boston corporation that produces Plug and Play multimedia kits that include the latest CD-ROM technology, high-quality sound cards and speakers, and multimedia games and educational software. Jonathan Bauman works as a contracts specialist for Multimedia Enterprises International, Inc. and develops new contracts for joint ventures with other companies.

Jonathan and his co-workers rely on his records for contract negotiations with current and new clients. To ensure that he always has a copy of all the documents that he produces for each contract negotiation, Jonathan periodically creates two backups of his contract files, one that he stores in his office for easy access, and one that he stores off-site in a special fireproof facility. A **backup** is a copy of data usually stored in a separate location from your computer, often on an efficient storage medium like a tape, that ensures you won't lose your work in case of an emergency or computer failure. A backup usually includes all of the document files that an individual creates on his or her computer.

The Importance of Backing Up Files

Like many others who depend on their computers in their job, Jonathan understands the importance of regular backups. Several years ago, Jonathan's hard disk drive was accidentally infected with the Dark Avenger computer virus. Dark Avenger is a **polymorphic virus** that changes itself every time it makes a new copy of itself, thereby making it difficult for anti-viral software to detect the presence of this type of virus infection. Before it was finally detected and identified, the Dark Avenger virus caused substantial damage to the software and document files on Jonathan's computer. Fortunately, after he removed the virus, Jonathan was able to restore his document files from backups that were free of the virus.

If Jonathan had not made backups of his installed software and files, he would have had to reinstall the operating system and all the other applications that he uses on his hard disk. Then, he would have had to customize his operating system as well as each of the software applications. Finally, he would have had to reconstruct all his contract documents from scratch, using printed copies of those files.

In 1994, when hard disk storage capacities commonly ranged from 340-540MB, Microsoft Corporation estimated it would take an average of 2,000 hours to replace lost files on a typical hard disk. Furthermore, it is also estimated that more than 90% of computer users do not back up the data on their hard disks. With the dramatic increase in storage capacities of hard disk drives in subsequent years, restoring the contents of a hard disk drive from scratch would be a formidable task.

Even though hard disk drives have improved so that they are more reliable than ever, they do periodically fail and are still susceptible to damage from power surges, shock, and computer viruses. If you operate your own business, or if you are employed by a business, you cannot afford to lose important files, nor can you afford the time and cost required to reconstruct them. A regular backup of your hard disk is like an insurance policy. It protects your investment in your business.

Types of Backup Media

The two most common types of media used for backups are floppy disks and tapes. Floppy disks are inexpensive, but if you want to back up a major portion of your hard disk, or the entire hard disk, disks become a less viable backup medium. Not only would you need many disks, you would also have to constantly swap disks in and out of the disk drive that you use for the backup.

If you need to back up a large amount of data, you should consider purchasing a tape drive and using tapes as your backup media. A **tape drive** is a drive unit in which you can insert tapes that are similar in appearance to cassette tapes. Although you must invest several hundred dollars in a tape drive, and although tapes are more expensive than disks, one of the primary advantages of a tape drive is its high storage capacity. Depending on the size of your hard disk and the storage capacity of the tapes you use in your tape drive, you might be able to store the entire contents of a hard disk on one tape. If you also use data compression, you can store even more data on a tape. **Data compression** refers to the use of one or more techniques by a backup utility to store data so that it takes up less space on tapes or disks than the data would require on a hard disk. In the case of the Microsoft Backup utility, it combines all the files that you back up into one larger file so that disk space is used more efficiently. On a hard disk or floppy disk, each file is allocated a certain number of clusters of storage space; however, the file may not use all the storage space within the last cluster. Recall that a cluster consists of one or more sectors of storage space. When a backup utility combines all the backed up files into one larger file, one file immediately follows another file, so no space is wasted. Because of the large storage capacity of tapes, the actual cost for backups drops to a few cents or less per megabyte of backed up data when you use data compression.

No matter what type of backup medium you choose, you will discover that backing up data, especially the entire contents of a hard disk, takes time. However, it is one of the most important tasks that you perform on a computer system.

Developing a Backup Strategy

When Jonathan was first hired at Multimedia Enterprises International, Inc., he discussed various backup strategies with the staff in the company's data system department so that he could develop a procedure for making reliable backups.

To protect your time and investment in the files that you produce on your computer, you should develop a backup strategy that will enable you to restore files to your computer if you encounter some type of problem and lose important files. The backup strategy that you choose depends on several factors: (1) the backup utility and its capabilities; (2) the type of media that you use for your backups; (3) the number of files that you need to back up; and (4) the size of the files.

Your backup strategy should always include a full backup at regular intervals, such as every month or quarter; this interval is called the **backup cycle**, which generally begins by backing up your whole system, then continues with backups of important files at shorter intervals, and ends with the next full backup. A **full backup** represents the start of a backup cycle and might include the entire contents of your hard disk. Or, to save time and effort, you might limit your full backups to folders that contain just your document files. The files contained in these folders are quite important because you are constantly changing and updating them.

You do not need to back up folders that contain software as frequently as you back up those that contain document files, because the software and its settings usually do not change as dramatically or as frequently as the contents of document files. After you install and configure a software application on your computer system, you might want to back it up once so that you can install a new copy later if the need arises. It is easier to restore an installed version of a software application than it is to install the software from the original set of disks and then modify the default document layout and print settings for that software application.

If you perform a full backup each month, you can perform either an incremental or a differential backup on a weekly or daily basis. An **incremental backup** is a backup that includes only those files that you created or changed since your last full *or* last incremental backup. By performing a full backup followed by periodic, incremental backups, you can restore all the files you have worked on during a backup cycle.

For example, after you perform a full backup, you can perform your first incremental backup at the end of the first week. This backup includes all files that you created or modified during the first week. At the end of the second week, you perform your second incremental backup. This backup includes all files that you created or modified during the second week. At the end of the third week, you perform your third and last incremental backup. This backup includes all files you created or modified during the third week. At the end of the month, you perform a new full backup that includes all files, and starts a new backup cycle. Figure 7-1 illustrates the use of incremental backups.

Figure 7-1 ◀
Using a full
backup with
incremental
backups

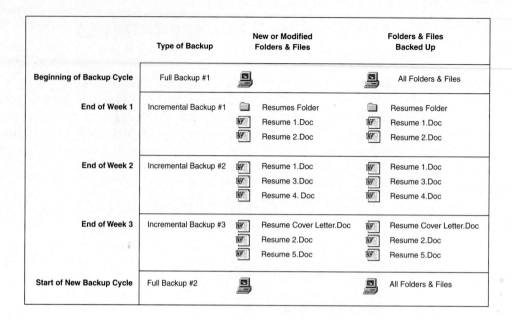

It is a good habit to keep two or three of the most recent backup sets and alternate them. When you start the next backup cycle, you should use a new set of tapes or disks. If you attempt to restore files from your most recent backup, and find that that backup set is defective, then you can turn to the backup set from the previous month. The next month, you can use the backup tapes or disks that you used two months ago for the next backup cycle. By using this approach, you will always have backup sets for the two most recent backup cycles. If you need to restore all the files from a backup set, you restore your last full backup and then each of the incremental backups in the order in which you produced them.

One advantage of incremental backups is that you have different versions of the same file stored in different backup sets, and you therefore can locate and restore a specific version of a file.

A **differential backup** is a backup that includes all new and modified files since your last full backup. Unlike an incremental backup, which only backs up files since your last full or incremental backup, a differential backup includes everything you've worked on after the full backup at the beginning of the backup cycle. Each new differential backup includes the files backed up during the previous differential backup. For example, after you perform a full backup, you might perform your first differential backup at the end of the first week. This backup includes all files that you created or modified during the first week, since the full backup. At the end of the second week, you perform your second differential backup. This backup includes all files that you created or modified during the first *and* second weeks, again since the full backup. At the end of the third week, you perform your third and last differential backup. This backup will include all files that you created and modified during the first, second, *and* third weeks, since the full backup. At the end of the month, you perform a new full backup that includes all files, and then you start a new backup cycle with a new set of tapes or disks. Figure 7-2 illustrates the use of differential backups. If you need to restore files to a hard disk, you use your last full backup and your last differential backup in that backup cycle.

Figure 7-2 ◀
Using a full
backup with
differential
backups

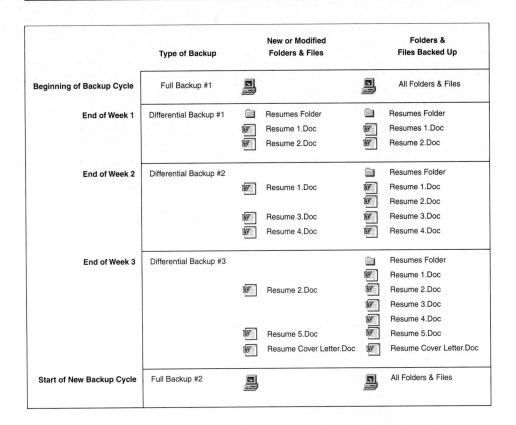

	Type of Backup	New or Modified Folders & Files		Folders & Files Backed Up
Beginning of Backup Cycle	Full Backup #1			All Folders & Files
End of Week 1	Differential Backup #1	Resumes Folder		Resumes Folder
		Resume 1.Doc		Resumes 1.Doc
		Resume 2.Doc		Resume 2.Doc
End of Week 2	Differential Backup #2			Resumes Folder
		Resume 1.Doc		Resume 1.Doc
				Resume 2.Doc
		Resume 3.Doc		Resume 3.Doc
		Resume 4.Doc		Resume 4.Doc
End of Week 3	Differential Backup #3			Resumes Folder
				Resume 1.Doc
		Resume 2.Doc		Resume 2.Doc
				Resume 3.Doc
				Resume 4.Doc
		Resume 5.Doc		Resume 5.Doc
		Resume Cover Letter.Doc		Resume Cover Letter.Doc
Start of New Backup Cycle	Full Backup #2			All Folders & Files

After the first differential backup, subsequent differential backups take longer than the corresponding incremental backup because you are backing up all files that you created or modified since the full backup. Unlike the incremental backup, differential backups keep only the most recent versions of files. However, if you keep each of your differential backup sets, you might be able to find previous versions of some files on a differential backup set. Although differential backups take longer than incremental backups, it is easier to restore files from differential backups because you only have to restore the last backup set. In contrast, if you use incremental backups and need to restore all the files, you restore your full backup and then restore each of your incremental backup sets.

No matter what type of backup strategy you choose to implement, you should have at least two and maybe three backup sets of each backup cycle. It is also a good idea to store one set of backups off-site. In fact, some insurance companies require you to store backups off-site before they will insure your data.

Like insurance policies, backups are invaluable when you need them. For example, you might find yourself in a situation where you need to reconstruct all of your company's business records after a major disaster, like an earthquake or fire, or some other incident, like a theft.

Using Microsoft Backup

Ever since Jonathan installed Windows 95 on his computer a year ago, he has used the Microsoft Backup utility included in Windows 95 to make backups. Jonathan's backup cycle lasts one month: he combines a full backup at the beginning of the month with incremental backups once a week. He chose incremental backups over differential backups because an incremental backup makes it easier to restore a previous version of a document from one of his backup sets.

Microsoft Backup allows you to perform three types of operations: Backup, Restore, and Compare. The Backup component backs up all or part of a hard disk onto some type of permanent storage medium, such as a tape or diskette. The Restore component restores folders and files from a backup set. The Compare component either compares backed up files with the original copies of those files, or restored files with the original copies of those files, to verify that a backup or restore operation functioned properly.

You can use Microsoft Backup to perform full and incremental backups. When you perform a full backup, you usually select the entire contents of a drive, or a group of folders and the files within those folders. If you intend to back up your entire computer system, though, you can't simply select drive C. When you perform a full backup of drive C, Microsoft Backup does not automatically include important parts of the Windows 95 operating system, such as the Registry files. If you want to back up the entire computer system, you select the file set called Full System Backup. Microsoft Backup automatically creates this file for you, so that you do not inadvertently exclude an important part of your computer system when you attempt a full system backup. In contrast to a full backup, which includes only selected folders and files, a full system backup includes not only the contents of a drive that you select, but also the Windows 95 operating system files.

Performing a Partial Backup

Jonathan stores original copies of all his contract files on drive C in a folder named MEI. He is ready to start a new backup cycle, and wants to back up all the files contained in this folder. He wants you to use Microsoft Backup to perform a full backup of this folder and its subfolders and files. If he ever needs to restore the entire folder, a subfolder, groups of files, or even a single file, he can use this full backup. When Jonathan backs up this folder, he is performing a **partial backup** of his computer system rather than a full system backup. The partial backup allows him to focus on his most important files, and complete the backup in the shortest possible time.

Before you can back up this folder, you must copy the folder from your Student Disk for this tutorial to the hard disk on the computer you are using. The "Read This Before You Begin" page at the beginning of this book tells you which Student Disk you should use for Tutorial 7.

If you are working in a computer lab on computers that do not have a hard drive, follow the instructions provided by your instructor or technical support person on how to complete this section.

To copy the MEI folder onto a hard drive:

1. Make sure you see the Windows desktop, then insert your Student Disk labeled MEI Inc. into a floppy disk drive.

2. Start Windows Explorer, using the Windows Explorer shortcut if you have one or by clicking the **Start** button, pointing at **Programs** on the Start menu, then clicking **Windows Explorer** on the Programs menu.

3. If necessary, click the **Large Icons** button [⊞] on the toolbar to display large icons in the Contents window.

4. After the Windows Explorer opens, click the **Go to a different folder** list arrow, then click the **disk drive** icon for the drive that contains your Student Disk. On your Student Disk, you will have one folder, named MEI_Inc. See Figure 7-3.

Figure 7-3 ◀
The Multimedia
Enterprises,
Inc. folder

current drive ────────▶

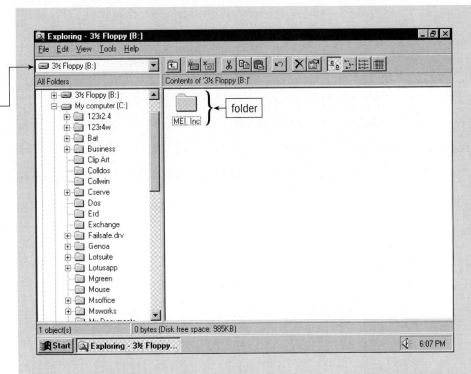

5. Drag the **MEI_Inc** folder to the folder for drive C, as shown in Figure 7-4, then release the mouse button. Windows Explorer displays a Copying dialog box as it copies the MEI_Inc folder to drive C.

Figure 7-4 ◀
Dragging a
copy of the
Multimedia
Enterprises,
Inc. folder to a
hard disk drive

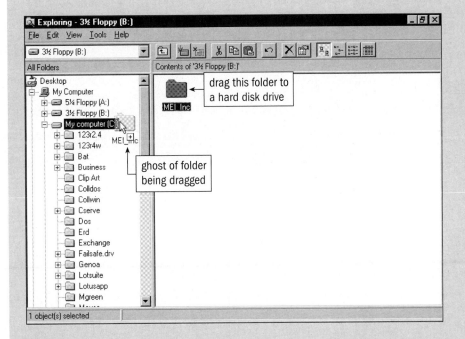

TROUBLE? If Windows Explorers displays a Confirm Folder Replace dialog box, then a folder by that name already exists on your hard disk drive. Click the No button to cancel the operation. If you are working in a computer lab, another student might have left the folder on the hard disk. Ask your instructor or technical support person if it can be removed or renamed. Remove or rename the folder by using its shortcut menu, then repeat this step.

6. In the All Folders list box, click the **disk drive** icon for drive C.

7. Remove your Student Disk from the floppy disk drive.

Before you perform the full backup, Jonathan wants you want to examine the MEI_Inc folder so that you are familiar with the folder's contents.

To view the contents of the MEI_Inc folder:

1. In the All Folders list box, use the vertical scroll bar to locate the folder named MEI_Inc on your drive C, then click the **MEI_Inc** folder name.

2. Click the **plus sign** to the left of the MEI_Inc folder name. Jonathan has organized his work files into eight folders within the MEI_Inc folder. See Figure 7-5.

Figure 7-5 ◄
Viewing the contents of the Multimedia Enterprises, Inc. folder

expanded folder structure

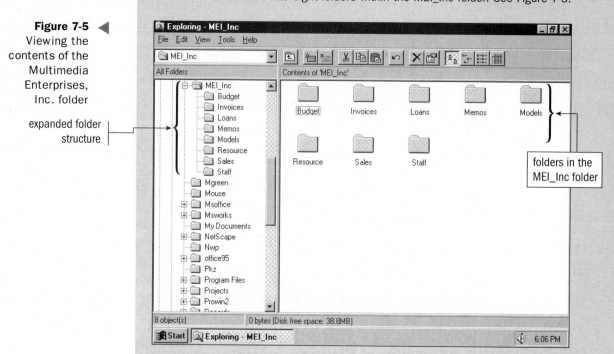

3. In the All Folders list box, click the **Sales** folder. Jonathan has placed all the files he uses to project and track sales for different contracts into one folder. See Figure 7-6.

Figure 7-6 ◄
Viewing the contents of the Sales folder

click to open folder

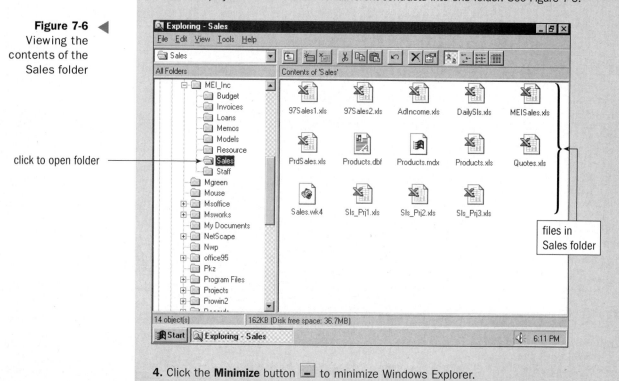

4. Click the **Minimize** button ▬ to minimize Windows Explorer.

Now that you are familiar with the contents of the MEI_Inc folder, you can start the process for performing a full backup.

Starting Microsoft Backup

The backup process includes three basic steps: (a) selecting each folder and file you want to back up, (b) selecting the destination drive to back up to, and (c) starting the backup. Before you start a backup, you can also define the settings you need for that backup and then store them in a file that Microsoft Backup refers to as a **file set**. The filename for the file set has the file extension of set. Windows 95 stores this file in the Accessories folder. Whenever you need to perform the same type of backup again, this file set contains all the settings you need.

To perform these steps you will need a blank, formatted disk. Make sure you do not use one of the Student Disks that contains the tutorial files.

To start Microsoft Backup:

1. Insert a blank, formatted diskette in a floppy disk drive. *Do not use one of your Student Disks because Microsoft Backup will erase its contents.*

2. Click the **Start** button, point to **Programs** on the Start menu, point to **Accessories** on the Programs menu, point to **System Tools** on the Accessories menu, then click **Backup** on the System Tools menu. The Welcome to Microsoft Backup dialog box opens. See Figure 7-7. This Welcome dialog box explains that you can use Microsoft Backup to back up files from a hard disk to a floppy disk or tape, then it outlines the steps for performing a backup.

Figure 7-7 ◀
Welcome to Microsoft Backup dialog box

what you use Backup for

steps for backing up a folder or file

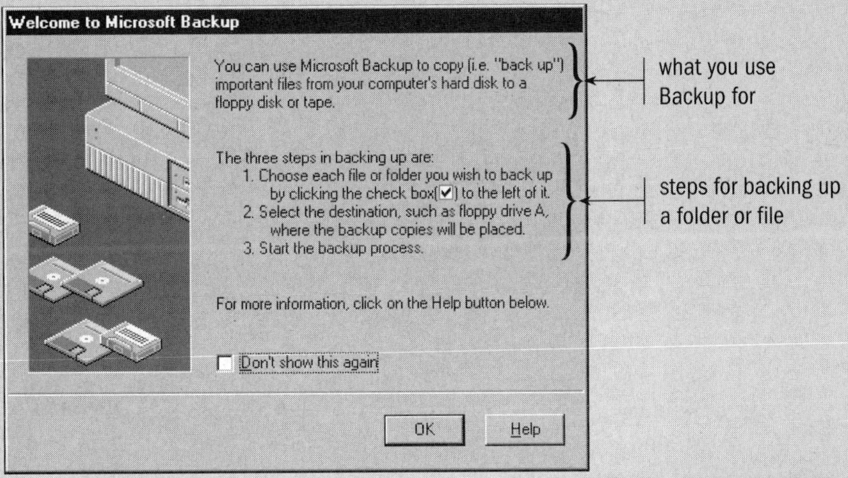

TROUBLE? Before you can start Microsoft Backup, it must be installed on your computer system. If you are working on your own computer and have not already installed Microsoft Backup, open the Control Panel, start the Add/Remove Programs Wizard, and select the Disk Tools option from the Windows Setup tab to install Backup.

TROUBLE? If the Welcome dialog box does not appear, it's possible that a previous user disabled it. If the dialog box does appear, you can disable it yourself if you do not want to see it in the future: simply click the Don't show this again check box. Until you are more familiar with Microsoft Backup, you might want to continue to display this Welcome dialog box as a reminder of what to do.

3. If necessary, click the **OK** button to close the Welcome dialog box. Microsoft Backup opens, then displays a Microsoft Backup dialog box that tells you it automatically created a full backup set named Full System Backup. See Figure 7-8.

Figure 7-8
The Microsoft
Backup
dialog box

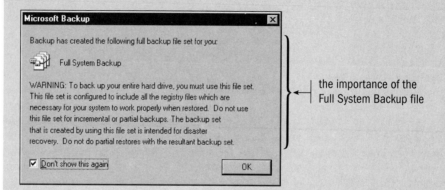

the importance of the
Full System Backup file

This dialog box informs you that you should use this file set to perform a full system backup of your hard disk drive, because this file set also backs up the Registry files that are needed to properly restore your computer system. It also warns you that you should not use this file set for incremental or partial backups. The full system backup is designed to restore your entire computer system, which includes the Windows 95 operating system files, in the event of a disaster, such as a hard disk failure or damage caused by a computer virus infection.

TROUBLE? If you do not want to see this Microsoft Backup dialog box in the future, click the Don't show this again check box. Since this warning is important, you might want to continue to display the Microsoft Backup window until you are more familiar with Microsoft Backup.

4. If necessary, click the **OK** button to close the introductory Microsoft Backup dialog box explaining the Full System Backup set.

The Untitled - Microsoft Backup window now appears as shown in Figure 7-9; it contains tabs for performing a Backup, Restore, and Compare. You use the Backup tab to back up folders and files on your hard disk, the Restore tab to restore folders and files on your hard disk, and the Compare tab to verify that the backed up files are identical to the original files. In the Select files to back up list box, Microsoft Backup displays the basic components in your computer system that you can choose to back up. Your window might look different, depending on your computer.

Figure 7-9
Microsoft
Backup window

Backup menu bar

Backup tab

click to view folders
and files on drive C

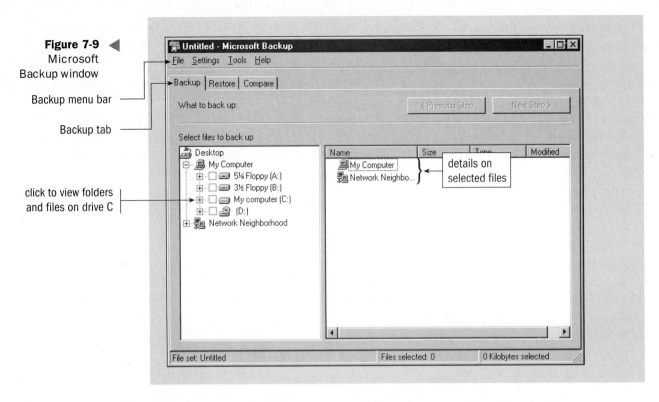

Now that you have started Microsoft Backup, you next select the files you want to back up, in this case, the MEI_Inc folder.

Selecting the Files to Back Up

After opening Microsoft Backup, you select the files to back up. If, for example, you want to back up all the files on drive C, you click the empty selection box to the left of drive C in the Select files to back up list box. Microsoft Backup then displays a File Selection dialog box and selects all the folders and all the files in each folder on drive C.

To back up one or more folders, you first expand the folder listing for drive C, then you select the individual folders you want to back up. Once you select a folder, Microsoft Backup selects all the files in that folder. You then have the option of deselecting files so that they are not included in the backup.

HELP DESK

| Index |

SELECTING FILES FOR A BACKUP

Open Microsoft Backup, click Help on the menu bar, click Help Topics, then click the Index tab.

Keyword
Defining file sets

Topic
To define a set of files to be backed up

Since Jonathan asked you to just back up the MEI_Inc folder, you need to select that folder and its contents.

To select the MEI_Inc folder:

1. In the Select files to back up list box, click the **plus sign** to the left of the symbol for your hard disk drive where the MEI_Inc folder is located.

   Do not click the empty selection box to the left of the hard disk drive. Microsoft Backup now shows the folders on that drive. See Figure 7-10.

Figure 7-10 ◀
Selecting a
hard disk drive
for a backup

expanded folder
structure

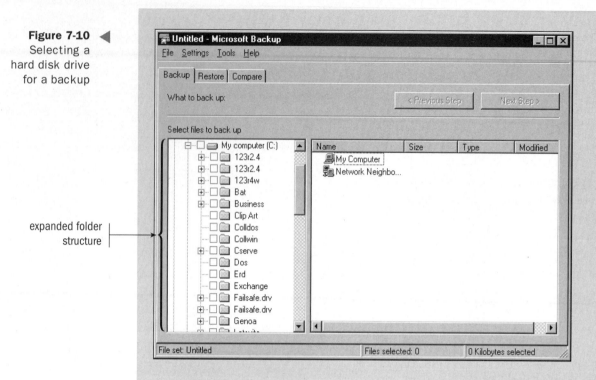

The status bar at the bottom of the Microsoft Backup window shows that you have not selected any files yet.

2. Use the horizontal scroll bar to locate the MEI_Inc folder.

3. Click the **empty selection box** to the left of the MEI_Inc folder, then click the **plus sign** to the left of the MEI_Inc folder. The status bar shows that you have now selected 40 files which use a total of 439 kilobytes of storage space. See Figure 7-11. By selecting the MEI_Inc folder, you have specified that all its sub-folders and their files be included in the backup.

Figure 7-11 ◀
Selecting the
Multimedia
Enterprises,
Inc. folder

folders selected
for the backup

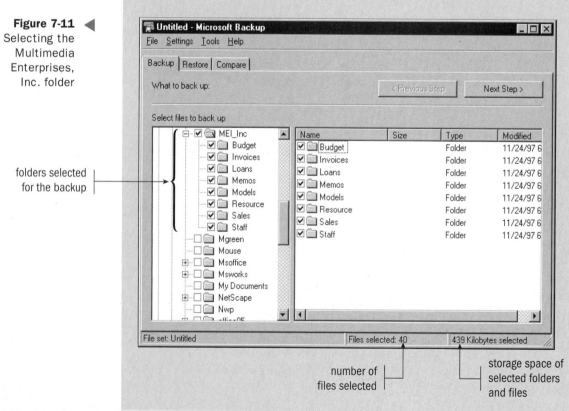

number of
files selected

storage space of
selected folders
and files

4. In the Select files to back up section, click the **Sales** folder. Microsoft Backup displays the contents of the Sales folder in the window to the right of the one that shows the folder structure of the hard disk drive or network drive. See Figure 7-12. Note that each file in the Sales folder has a check mark in the selection box to the left of the filename. If you click one of these selection boxes, you remove that file from the backup selection.

Figure 7-12
Viewing files in the Sales folder selected for the backup

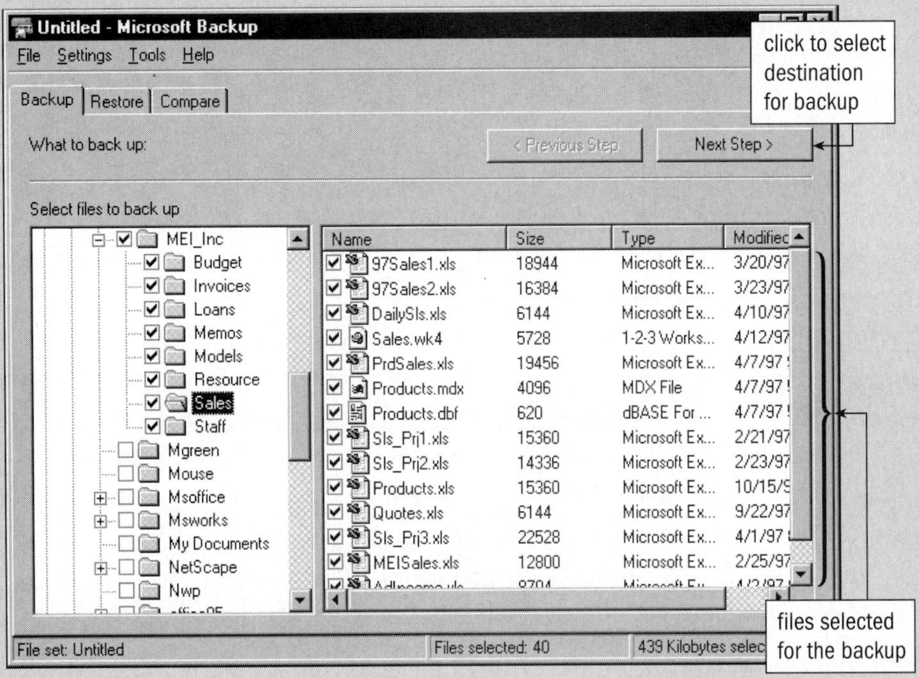

Specifying the Destination Drive

Next, you specify the destination drive that Microsoft Backup will use to store the backup copies. Since you want to store your backup on a floppy disk, you need to specify a floppy disk drive as your destination drive.

To select the destination drive:

1. Click the **Next Step** button. Microsoft Backup modifies the Backup tab so that you can now indicate where to back up to. See Figure 7-13. In the Select a destination for the backup section, Microsoft Backup lists the names of locations on your computer system as well as the names of your drives. If you have a tape drive, an icon appears for that tape drive. If you do not have a tape in the tape drive, Microsoft Backup indicates that it is "Waiting for tape."

Figure 7-13 ◄
Selecting a
destination for
the backup

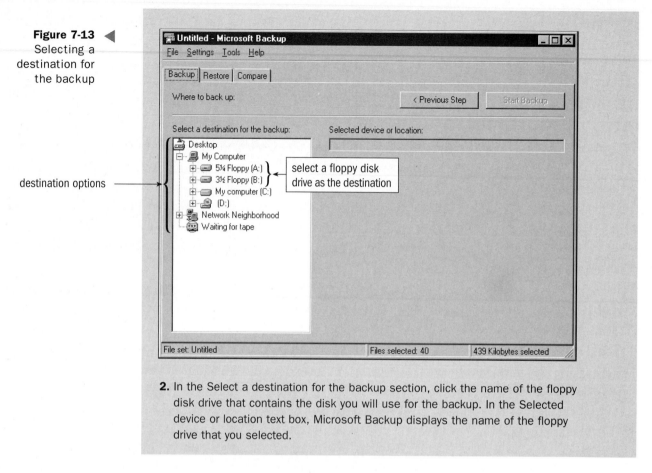

destination options →

2. In the Select a destination for the backup section, click the name of the floppy disk drive that contains the disk you will use for the backup. In the Selected device or location text box, Microsoft Backup displays the name of the floppy drive that you selected.

You have selected the folder and files for the backup, and you have selected the destination drive that contains the disk that will store the backup.

Saving a Backup Selection in a File Set

Next, you want to define a backup selection, then save it in a file set. The file set contains any folder or file selections you specify for a backup. By saving your specifications to a file set, you can simply open that file to run the same backup.

To save your folder and file selection in a file set:

1. Click **File** on the menu bar, then click **Save As**. In the Save As dialog box, you can specify which folder to use for your file sets as well as the file name for the file set. See Figure 7-14. By default, Microsoft Backup saves your file sets with the set file extension in the Accessories folder.

Figure 7-14 ◄
Saving backup
settings

save file set
in this folder

file set for a full
system backup

enter a name
for the file set

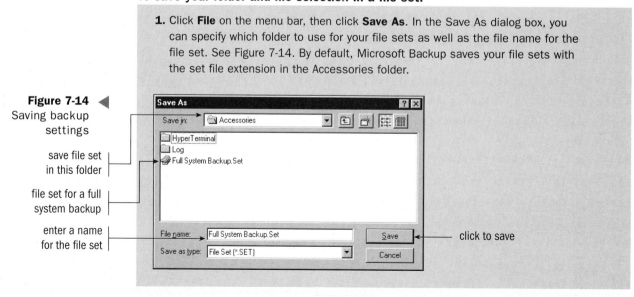

click to save

2. In the File name text box, type **MEI** immediately followed by the last four digits of your social security number, then type **A**.

For example, if the last four digits of your social security number are "7642," then your file set name would be "MEI7642A." The letter "A" indicates the first backup that you will perform today. If you perform more than one backup on the same day and name your file sets with eight-character filenames, you might want to use some naming scheme that distinguishes one backup from another.

3. Click the **Save** button. The Save As dialog box closes.

Now that you have stored the settings for this backup, you can open the file set at any time using the Open File Set command on the File menu, and repeat the same type of backup again. The backup will include the same folders and files, and the destination drive will be the same.

Specifying Backup Options

Since you are starting the beginning of a backup cycle, you want to make sure Microsoft Backup performs a full backup instead of an incremental backup. Also, Jonathan asked you to use the options for verifying the backup and compressing data on the backup disk.

To view optional backup settings:

1. Click **Settings** on the menu bar, then click **Options**. Microsoft Backup displays a Settings - Options dialog box with tabs for specifying four types of settings.

2. Click the **Backup** tab, then make sure your backup settings match those shown in Figure 7-15. The options you are enabling include ones for a full backup, verification of the backup process, and the use of data compression.

Figure 7-15 ◄
Selecting
optional
backup
settings

select the full
backup option

select to verify
backup data

select to
compress data

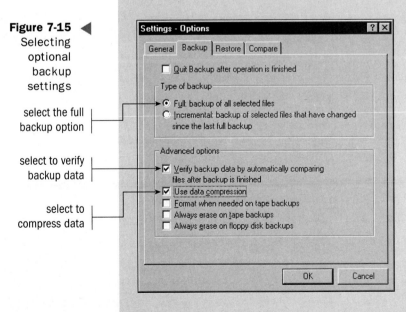

3. Click the **OK** button. Now you are ready to start the backup.

4. Click the **Start Backup** button.

The Backup Set Label dialog box opens. In this dialog box you specify the name for your backup set. The **backup set** is the file that contains all your compressed data that you are storing on your floppy disk drive. You can give your backup set the same name as the file set; you can easily tell them apart because the file set has the set file extension whereas the backup set has the qic file extension, as you'll see in a moment.

5. In the Backup set text box, type **MEI** followed immediately by the last four digits of your social security number, then type **A**. If you perform more than one backup with the same backup file set, then you assign a label to distinguish one backup set from another. See Figure 7-16.

Figure 7-16 ◀
Naming the
backup set

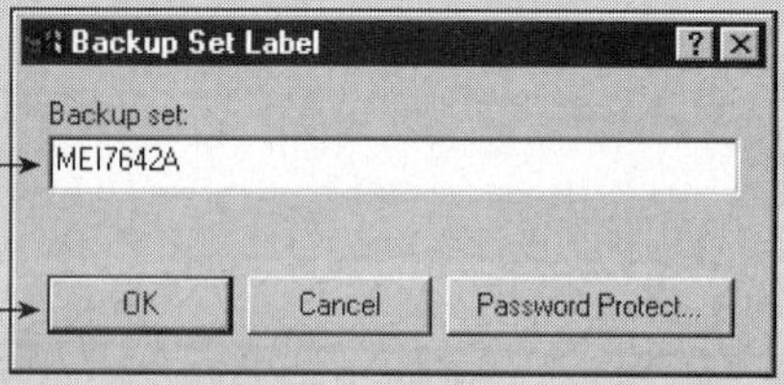

enter a name for
the backup set

click to start backup

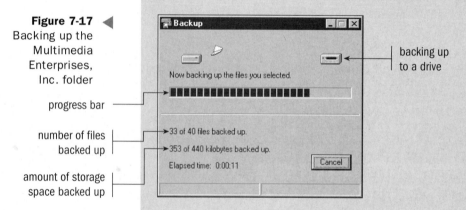

6. Click the **OK** button. Microsoft Backup starts the backup, and the Backup dialog box shows the progress of the backup. See Figure 7-17.

Figure 7-17 ◀
Backing up the
Multimedia
Enterprises,
Inc. folder

progress bar

number of files
backed up

amount of storage
space backed up

backing up
to a drive

The progress bar shows how much of the backup is completed, and the dialog box tracks the number of files backed up, out of the total number of files, and the amount of storage space backed up, out of the total storage space occupied by these files. It also shows you the elapsed time. After it completes the backup, Microsoft Backup displays a Compare dialog box and performs a compare operation. This step compares the backed up files with the original files. If Backup encounters any errors, it reports them on the status bar of this dialog box. Then, a Microsoft Backup window informs you the operation is complete.

7. Click the **OK** button to close the Microsoft Backup dialog box, then click the **OK** button to close the Compare dialog box. If you wanted to make a second or third backup set, you would start another backup using the same settings and a new set of disks or a new tape.

8. Click the **Close** button ⊠ to close the Microsoft Backup window and return to the desktop.

PERFORMING A PARTIAL BACKUP OF A DRIVE

- Click the Start button, point to Programs on the Start menu, point to Accessories on the Programs menu, point to System Tools on the Accessories menu, then click Backup on the System Tools menu.
- If necessary, click the OK button to close the Welcome dialog box, then click the OK button to close the Microsoft Backup window.
- In the Select files to back up list box, locate the folder on your hard disk drive that you want to back up, then click the empty selection box to the left of the folder name.
- Click the Next Step button.
- In the Select a destination for the backup list box, click the name of the floppy disk drive (or tape drive) that contains the disk (or tape) you will use for the backup.
- Click File on the menu bar, click Save As, type a file set name in the File name text box, then click the Save button.
- Click Settings on the menu bar, then click Options.
- In the Settings - Options dialog box, click the Backup tab, activate those settings you want to use, deactivate any settings you do not want to use, then close the Settings - Options dialog box.
- Click the Startup Backup button, enter a backup set label name, then click the OK button to start the backup.
- After the backup and compare, click the OK button to close the Microsoft Backup dialog box, then click OK to close the Compare dialog box.
- Close Microsoft Backup.

You have completed the backup process. The file set contains the settings for the backup, while the backup set contains the backed up and compressed data. If you store your document files in more than one folder, as many people do, you will need to select more than one folder for your backup. After you select the first folder, you would follow the same approach to select each of the other folders.

Examining the Backup Disk

Jonathan asks you to examine the contents of the backup disk to verify that the backup worked without any problems.

To view the contents of the backup disk:

1. Click the **Windows Explorer** button on the taskbar.

2. In the All Folders list box, locate and click the name of the floppy disk drive that contains your backup disk. On the backup disk is one file with a qic file extension. The qic file extension added to the backup file on the backup disk refers to a standard that conforms to specifications developed by the Quarter Inch Cartridge (QIC) Standards Committee for backing up data on a desktop computer system.

3. Click the **Details** button 🏛 on the toolbar. In the Type column, Windows 95 identifies this file as a Backup Set for Microsoft Backup. See Figure 7-18. All the folders and files that you backed up are stored in this one file. Note that this backup file, which contains a backup of 439KB of data, is 233KB in size. If you had not selected data compression on the Backup tab, your backup file would have been larger than the combined sizes of all the files you backed up because Microsoft Backup stores additional information about the location of the folders and files you backed up.

Figure 7-18 ◀
Viewing the
backup set file

current drive

backup set filename

size of
compressed file

type of file

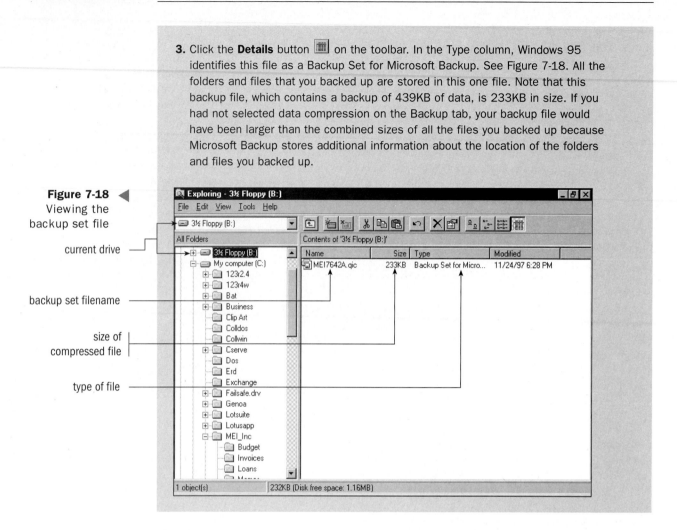

You have successfully backed up Jonathan's contract files, and verified that the backup process worked properly.

If you want to take a break and resume the tutorial at a later time, you can do so now. If you are on a network, close Windows Explorer and any other open applications and dialog boxes, and leave Windows 95 running. If you are using your own computer, you can click the Start button on the taskbar, click Shut Down, click Shut down the computer, and then click the Yes button. When you resume the tutorial, launch Windows 95 again, open and minimize Windows Explorer, then continue with the tutorial.

● ● ●

Restoring a Folder

Some of the contract files in Jonathan's folder have become corrupted, and he is unable to use these files. A **corrupted file** is a program or document file whose contents have been altered as the result of a hardware, software, or power failure. If you encounter a problem similar to Jonathan's, if you accidentally delete a folder or files within a folder, or if your hard disk drive fails, then you can restore files from you backup sets. If a folder no longer exists on the hard disk drive, then Microsoft Backup will rebuild the folder and any sub-folders below that folder.

Before you restore the contents of a backup set, you must specify the name of the file set that contains the settings you used when you backed up the folders and files. Then, the folders and files are restored to their original locations.

Index

RESTORING FOLDERS AND FILES

Open Microsoft Backup, click Help on the menu bar, click Help Topics, then click the Index tab.

Keyword
Restoring files

Topic
Restoring backed up folders and files

Jonathan asks you to rename the folder that contains the corrupted files, then attempt to restore the contents of the MEI_Inc folder from his backup set. Once he can verify the integrity of the files restored to his hard disk drive, then he can remove the folder with the corrupted files.

To rename a folder:

1. Click the **Windows Explorer** button on the taskbar, or if you closed Windows Explorer, open it from the Start menu or a desktop shortcut.

2. In the All Folders list box, locate and right-click the **MEI_Inc** folder on your hard disk drive, then click **Rename** on the shortcut menu.

3. Type **MEI_Old** then press the **Enter** key to rename the folder.

4. Click the **Minimize** button ▬ to minimize Windows Explorer.

Now, you can restore the MEI_Inc folder from your backup set for Jonathan.

To restore a folder:

1. Click the **Start** button, point to **Programs** on the Start menu, point to **Accessories** on the Programs menu, point to **System Tools** on the Accessories menu, then click **Backup** on the System Tools menu.

2. If you see a Welcome to Microsoft Backup dialog box, click the **OK** button and, if you see a Microsoft Backup dialog box explaining the use of the Full System Backup file set, click the **OK** button.

3. Click the **Restore** tab.

4. In the Restore from section, click the name of the floppy disk drive that contains your backup disk.

5. In the Backup Set list box, click the backup set filename, **MEI####A** (the #### corresponds to the last four numbers of your social security number), then click the **Next Step** button.

6. In the Select files from the backup set list box, click the **empty selection box** to the left of the MEI_Inc folder name. Your Restore tab should be similar to that shown in Figure 7-19.

Figure 7-19 ◀
Selecting
folders and files
to restore

backup set filename ⎯⎯⎯⎯⎯⎯⎯⎯→

backed up drive ⎯⎯⎯⎯⎯⎯⎯→

folder to restore ⎯⎯⎯⎯⎯⎯⎯→

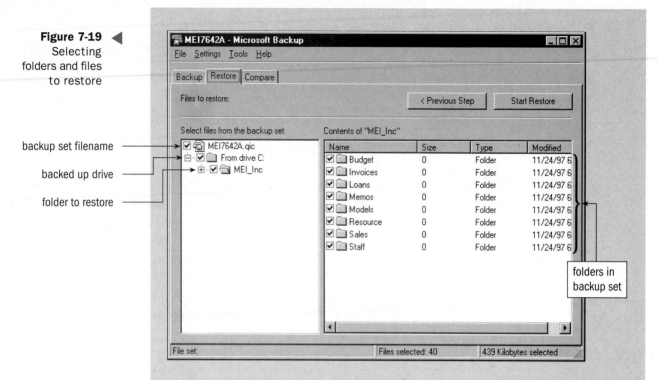

folders in
backup set

7. Click **Settings** on the menu bar, then click **Options**, click the **Restore** tab, set
   your restore options to match those shown in Figure 7-20, then click the **OK** button. The options you are enabling include ones for restoring files to their original
   locations, verifying the restored files with the original files stored on disk, and
   overwriting any existing files.

Figure 7-20 ◀
Selecting
optional restore
settings

select to restore
to original locations

select to verify
restored data

click to overwrite
existing files

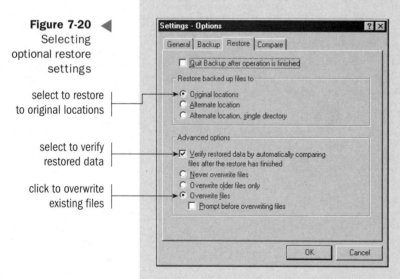

In the Restore backed up files to section, you can restore files to their original
locations or to an alternate location. If you select the Overwrite files option,
Microsoft Backup automatically overwrites any files on the destination disk that
have the same names as the files in the backup set. If you select this option,
you can have Backup prompt you before it overwrites any files.

8. Click the **Start Restore** button. The Restore dialog box shows the progress of
   the restore operation and then the compare operation. See Figure 7-21. After the
   restore and compare are complete, Microsoft Backup displays the Microsoft
   Backup window.

Figure 7-21 ◀
Restoring the
Multimedia
Enterprises,
Inc. folder
and files

progress bar ⎯

number of files
restored

amount of storage
space restored

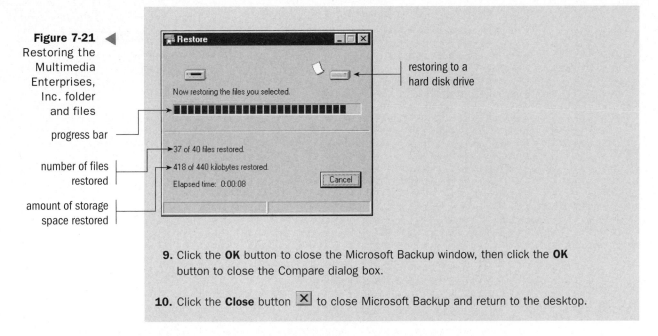

restoring to a
hard disk drive

9. Click the **OK** button to close the Microsoft Backup window, then click the **OK** button to close the Compare dialog box.

10. Click the **Close** button ⊠ to close Microsoft Backup and return to the desktop.

The Restore operation worked without any problems, and you have restored Jonathan's MEI_Inc folder and its contents.

Before you tell Jonathan that you have restored his folder to his hard disk drive, you want to verify that the folder was rebuilt by Microsoft Backup and that it contains Jonathan's files.

To check the folder structure:

1. Click the **Windows Explorer** button on the taskbar, then, if necessary, click the **Maximize** button ▢. Next, you need to update the Windows Explorer window by having it examine your hard disk again.

2. Click the **Go to a different folder** list arrow, then click the **disk drive** icon for your hard disk.

3. Click **View** on the menu bar, then click **Refresh**.

4. In the All Folders list box, locate and click the **MEI_Inc** folder, then click the **plus sign** to the left of the MEI_Inc folder. Windows Explorer shows the folders in the newly restored MEI_Inc folder. See Figure 7-22.

Figure 7-22 ◀
Verifying a
restore

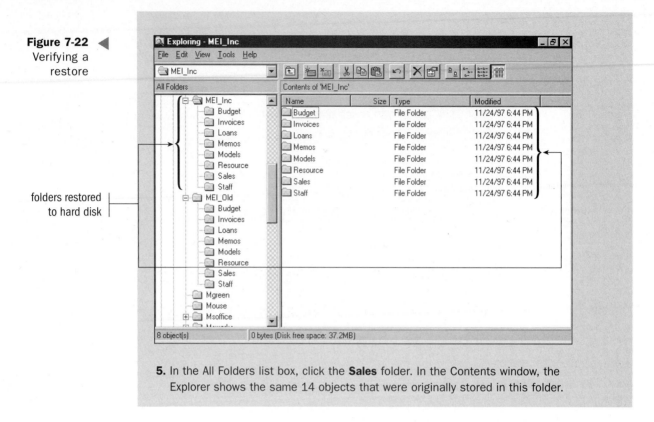

folders restored
to hard disk

5. In the All Folders list box, click the **Sales** folder. In the Contents window, the
Explorer shows the same 14 objects that were originally stored in this folder.

In the previous restore operation, you restored the entire MEI_Inc folder and all its
subfolders and files. If you inadvertently delete a subfolder within a folder, you can
restore that subfolder and its files using a similar approach. If you accidentally delete an
important file or set of files, then you can restore the file or files from the same backup
set, again using the same process.

If you are working in a computer lab, you must remove the MEI_Inc and MEI_Old folders from the hard disk drive of the computer you are using so that other students can practice the skills in this tutorial. If you are working on your own computer, you might want
to remove these folders so that you can use this storage space for other folders and files.

To remove the MEI_Inc and MEI_Old folders:

1. In the All Folders list box, locate and right-click the **MEI_Inc** folder on drive C,
then click **Delete** on the shortcut menu.

2. When Windows Explorer displays a Confirm Folder Delete dialog box and asks if
you want to move the folder's contents to the Recycle Bin, click the **Yes** button.

   If Windows Explorer displays a Confirm File Delete dialog box, click the **Yes to all**
   button. Windows Explorer removes the MEI_Inc folder.

3. In the All Folders list box for Windows Explorer, locate and right-click the **MEI_Old**
folder on drive C, then click **Delete** on the shortcut menu.

4. When Windows Explorer displays a Confirm Folder Delete dialog box and asks if
you want to move the folder's contents to the Recycle Bin, click the **Yes** button.

5. If Windows Explorer displays a Confirm File Delete dialog box, click the **Yes to all**
button. Windows Explorer removes the MEI_Old folder.

6. Click the **Close** button ⊠ to close Windows Explorer.

Performing a Full-System Tape Backup

Jonathan recently installed a tape backup drive into his computer. Now he can periodically perform full backups of the entire contents of his hard drive onto tape. The backup tapes that he produces will be very important, because he will be able to restore his entire system, including the Windows 95 operating system and its configuration files, from his backup tapes.

To perform a full system backup of your hard disk drive, you must use a backup utility designed for Windows 95. You cannot use the backup utilities included with Windows 3.1 or 3.11 or the ones included with DOS. These utilities do not support the use of long filenames.

Microsoft Backup works only with certain types of tape drives produced by certain manufacturers since 1992. If Microsoft Backup does not recognize your tape drive, then you might need to contact your tape drive manufacturer to find out what backup software you can use under Windows 95.

HELP DESK

Index

RESTORING FOLDERS AND FILES

Open Microsoft Backup, click Help on the menu bar, click Help Topics, then click the Index tab.

Keyword	**Topics**
Tape drives	Tape drives that are compatible with Backup
	Verifying that your tape drive will work with Backup

To complete this section, your computer system must have a tape backup drive, and you must have one or more formatted tapes for that tape drive. If you do not have a tape drive, skip this section. Also, since the tape backup might take an hour or more, perform the backup at a convenient time.

If you are working on a network, you will not be able to complete this section. Instead, skip this section.

To perform a full system backup:

1. Insert a formatted tape into your tape drive.

2. Click the **Start** button, point to **Programs** on the Start menu, point to **Accessories** on the Programs menu, point to **System Tools** on the Accessories menu, then click **Backup** on the System Tools menu.

3. If you see a Welcome to Microsoft Backup window, click the **OK** button, and if you see a Microsoft Backup window explaining the use of the Full System Backup file set, click the **OK** button.

4. Click **File** on the menu bar, then click **Open File Set**. Windows 95 displays the Open dialog box. See Figure 7-23. In the Look in list box, you can see the name of the previous backup you performed for MEI.

Figure 7-23 ◄
Selecting the
Full System
Backup
file set

click to select
this file set

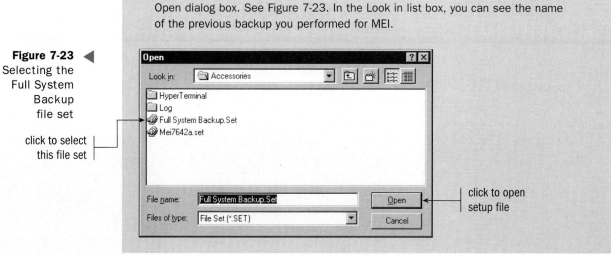

click to open
setup file

5. In the Look in list box, click the **Full System Backup.Set** icon, then click the **Open** button. A Microsoft Backup dialog box informs you that it is copying the settings in the system registry. See Figure 7-24. Recall that the Registry is a set of database files that store all the user and system configurations. These settings are important to back up.

Figure 7-24
Copying settings in the registry for a full system backup

copying registry settings

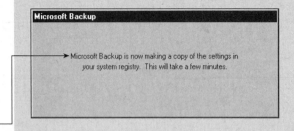

Then Microsoft Backup displays a File Selection dialog box that shows you the number of files that it is selecting for the backup, and the storage space required for those files. See Figure 7-25.

Figure 7-25
Selecting folders and files for a full system backup

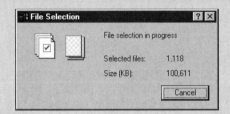

Then you return to the Full System Backup - Microsoft Backup window. See Figure 7-26. On the computer used for this figure, Microsoft Backup selected 11,041 files that occupy 429,892KB of storage space.

Figure 7-26
Files selected for a full system backup

contents of drive C selected

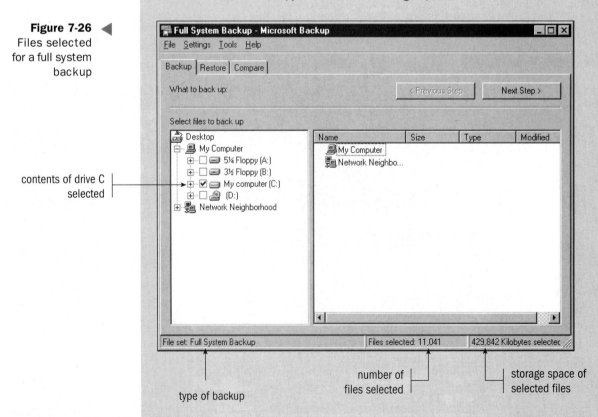

type of backup

number of files selected

storage space of selected files

After Microsoft Backup selects all the files on your hard disk, you can verify the backup options and then start the backup process. As noted earlier, the backup process may take an hour or more to complete. If you select a compare, the amount of time increases substantially.

To continue the full system backup:

1. Click **Settings** on the menu bar, click **Options**, click the **Backup** tab, and verify that the Full backup and use data compression options are enabled, then click the **OK** button. You might also want to select the verify backup data option to guarantee that the backup is reliable; however, if you do, the backup will take even longer.

2. Click the **Next Step** button. If your tape drive is compatible with Microsoft Backup, you will see a tape drive icon in the Select a destination for the backup section.

   TROUBLE? If you do not see a tape drive icon in the Select a destination for the backup list box, click **Tools** on the menu bar, then click **Redetect Tape Drive**. If Microsoft Backup does not detect the tape drive, then the tape might be damaged, or the tape drive might not be compatible with Microsoft Backup, and you might not be able to use this utility to back up to your tape drive. Or you might need to clean the tape drive head. If Microsoft Backup does not recognize your tape drive, then you cannot complete this section.

3. In the Select a destination for the backup list box, click the **tape drive** icon, as shown in Figure 7-27, then click the **Start Backup** button.

Figure 7-27 ◀
Selecting a destination for the full system backup

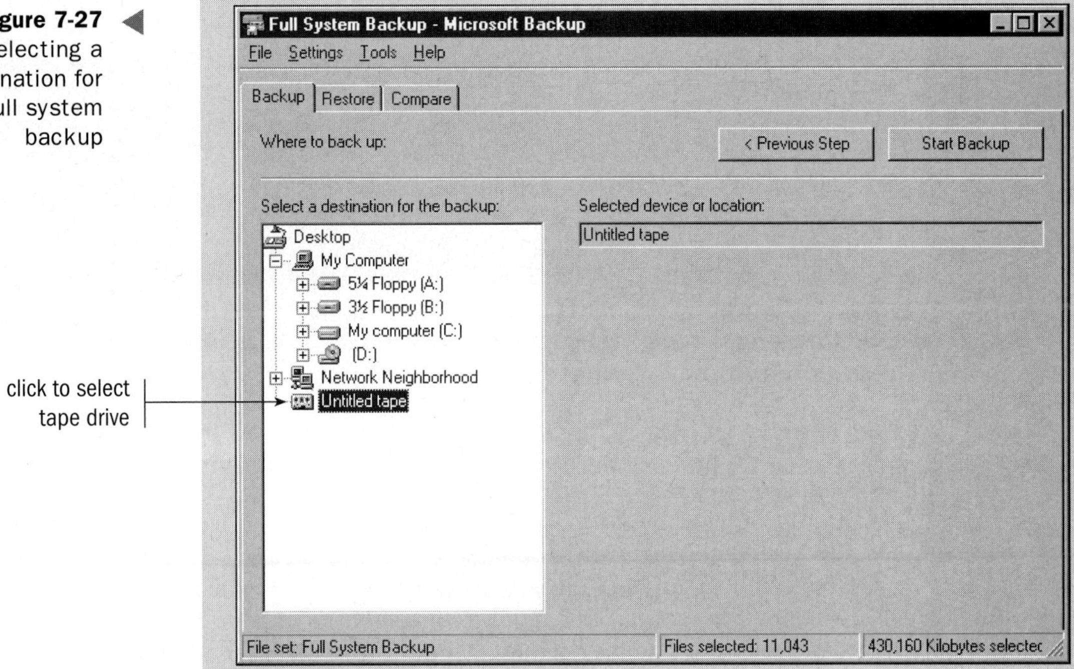

click to select tape drive

4. In the Backup Set Label dialog box, type **Full System Backup #1** then click the **OK** button. Microsoft Backup then starts backing up your hard disk drive. The Backup dialog box will report the progress of the backup. In Figure 7-28, over an hour and a half have elapsed since the start of the backup.

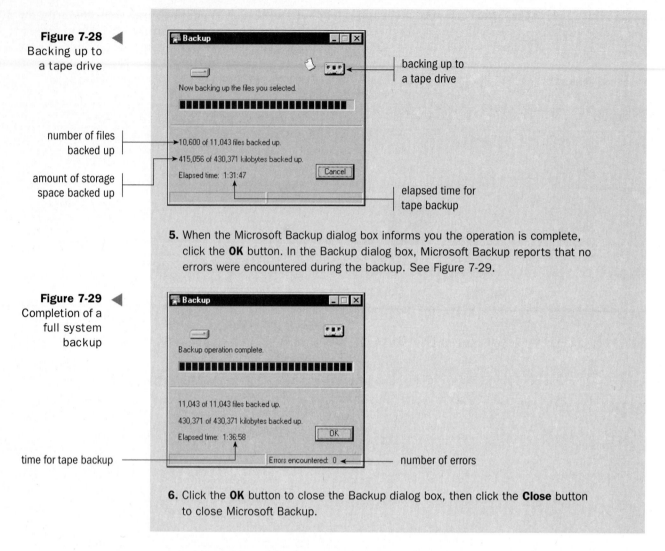

Figure 7-28
Backing up to
a tape drive

backing up to
a tape drive

number of files
backed up

amount of storage
space backed up

elapsed time for
tape backup

5. When the Microsoft Backup dialog box informs you the operation is complete, click the **OK** button. In the Backup dialog box, Microsoft Backup reports that no errors were encountered during the backup. See Figure 7-29.

Figure 7-29
Completion of a
full system
backup

time for tape backup

number of errors

6. Click the **OK** button to close the Backup dialog box, then click the **Close** button to close Microsoft Backup.

You have successfully completed a full backup of Jonathan's computer without any problems or errors. To restore files from the tape, you follow the same type of process that you performed earlier when you restored from a disk; however, you select the tape drive as the object from which to restore files.

Restoring DOS & Windows 3.1 Backups

If your computer originally contained Windows 3.1 and MS-DOS before you installed Windows 95, then you might have made backups using the Microsoft Windows Backup utility, the Microsoft Backup utility for MS-DOS 6.0, 6.2, and 6.22, or the Backup utility for different versions of DOS through MS-DOS 5.0 and IBM-DOS 5.0. If you want to restore backups that you made with one of these utilities, then you must use the same utility that you used to create the backups. If you used the DOS Backup utility in a version of MS-DOS or IBM-DOS, then you should use the Restore utility for that same version of MS-DOS or IBM-DOS to restore files onto your hard disk.

No matter what type of backup utility you use, you should label your backup disks or tapes with the name of the utility that you used to produce the backup. You should also include that utility's software version number so that you can properly restore files from any of the different types of backup sets that you have made.

●   ●   ●

Jonathan takes his tape from the tape backup to MEI's safety deposit box, reassured that if disaster strikes, he'll be able to recover with ease at least his data.

Tutorial Assignment

Jonathan wants you to make a backup of the Sales and Models folders within the MEI_Inc folder. Furthermore, he wants you to validate your backup by renaming the Sales folder and then restoring a new copy of the Sales folder from your backup set.

   To complete this tutorial assignment, you will need your Student Disk with the MEI_Inc folder and the disk that you used for backups.

1. Insert your Student Disk into a floppy disk drive.
2. Open Windows Explorer, select the floppy disk drive that contains your Student Disk, drag a copy of the MEI_Inc folder from your Student Disk to your hard disk drive, then minimize Windows Explorer.
3. Remove your Student Disk from the floppy disk drive, and insert your backup disk. *Note*: As long as there is room on your backup disk, you can add additional backups to the same disk.
4. Open My Computer and format your backup disk so that you can use it for a new backup.
5. Open Microsoft Backup.
6. In the Select files to back up list box, expand the folder structure for your hard disk drive, then locate and expand the structure of the MEI_Inc folder.
7. In the Select files to back up list box, select the empty selection boxes for the Sales and Models folders.
8. Click the Next Step button.
9. In the Select a destination for the backup list box, select the floppy disk drive that contains your backup disk.
10. Click File on the menu bar, click Save As, enter a name for the backup file set in the File name text box, then click the Save button. You might want to enter a name similar to the one you used in the chapter's tutorial, except use "B" to indicate that it is the next backup you performed on the MEI_Inc folder.
11. Click Settings on the menu bar, click Options, then click the Backup tab.
12. On the Backup tab, select the options for performing a full backup, for verifying the backup data, and for using data compression, then close the Settings - Options dialog box.
13. Click the Start Backup button and, when the Backup Set Label dialog box opens, enter a name for the backup set that is identical to the name of the file set, then click the OK button.
14. After the backup and compare operations are complete, close the Microsoft Backup window, then close the Compare dialog box.
15. Open Windows Explorer, rename the Sales folder to Misc, then minimize Windows Explorer.
16. Click the Restore tab, select the name of your floppy disk drive that contains your backup disk, select the backup set filename, then click the Next Step button.
17. In the Select files from the backup set list box, display the backed up folders below MEI_Inc, then click the empty selection box for the Sales folder.
18. Press Alt + Print Screen, open Paint, paste the contents of the Clipboard into the drawing area, then print the pasted image, and exit Paint without saving.
19. Click the Start Restore button, and after the restore and compare are complete, close the Microsoft Backup window, then close the Compare dialog box.
20. Close Microsoft Backup, then click the Windows Explorer button on the taskbar.
21. Click View on the menu bar, then click Refresh.
22. Click the Sales folder, then verify that Microsoft Backup restored the original Sales folder and its files.
23. Remove the MEI_Inc folder from your hard disk drive, then close Windows Explorer.

Case Problems

1. Backing Up Files at First Mortgage Corporation First Mortgage Corporation offers FHA, VA, and conventional loans to prospective home owners. Juan Mercado works as a finance officer for one of First Mortgage Corporation's branches. At the end of each week, Juan backs up important files that he has worked on during the previous week. He wants you to perform his next weekly backup.

1. Insert your Student Disk into a floppy disk drive.
2. Open Windows Explorer, select the floppy disk drive that contains your Student Disk, then rename the MEI_Inc folder to FMCorp.
3. Drag a copy of the FMCorp folder from your Student Disk to your hard disk drive, then minimize Windows Explorer.
4. Rename the FMCorp folder on your Student Disk to MEI_Inc.
5. Remove your Student Disk from the floppy disk drive, then insert your backup disk.
6. Open Microsoft Backup.
7. In the Select files to back up list box, expand the folder structure for drive C, then locate and expand the structure of the FMCorp folder.
8. Click the Budget folder to display the files in this folder, then click the selection boxes for the files named Qtr4.xls and Final.xls.
9. Click the Loans folder, then click the selection box for the file named Invest.xls.
10. Click the Models folder, then click the selection boxes for the files named GrwPlan.xls and 5YrPlan.xls.
11. Click the Next Step button
12. In the Select a destination for the backup list box, select the floppy disk drive that contains your backup disk
13. Click File on the menu bar, click Save As, and in the Save As dialog box, enter a name for the backup file set in the File name box, then click the Save button.
14. Click Settings on the menu bar, click Options, then click the Backup tab.
15. On the Backup tab, select the options for performing a Full backup, for verifying the backup data, and for using data compression, then close the Settings - Options dialog box.
16. Click the Start Backup button and, when the Backup Set Label dialog box opens, enter a name for the backup set that is identical to the name of the file set, then click the OK button.
17. After the backup and compare operations are complete, close the Microsoft Backup window, then close the Compare dialog box.
18. Click Options on the menu bar, click Settings, then click the Restore tab. Enable the setting that prompts you before overwriting existing files, then close the Options - Settings dialog box.
19. Click the Restore tab, select the name of your floppy disk drive that contains your backup disk, select the backup set filename, then click the Next Step button.
20. In the Select files from the backup set list box, select the empty selection box for the FMCorp folder, click the plus sign to expand the folder structure, then select the Models folder.
21. Press Alt + Print Screen, open Paint, paste the contents of the Clipboard into the drawing area, then print the pasted image, and exit Paint without saving.
22. Click the Start Restore button and, as Microsoft Backup prompts you whether you want to overwrite each of the five files, click the Yes button.
23. After the restore and compare are complete, close the Microsoft Backup window, then close the Compare dialog box.

2. Backing Up the Start Menu Folder at Voice Mail Communications, Inc. Voice Mail Communications, Inc. sells voice messaging systems to businesses and corporations in New England. Isabel Hernandez, a consultant at Voice Mail Communications, has customized her Start menu so that she can quickly access records on various clients and projects. Since she has invested a great deal of time and effort in customizing her Start menu, she wants you to back up her Start Menu folder, then examine the backup set and verify that it contains the contents of the Start menu.

1. Open Microsoft Backup.
2. In the Select files to back up list box, expand the folder structure for drive C, then locate and expand the Windows folder.
3. Locate and select the selection box for the Start Menu folder, then expand the Start Menu folder structure.
4. Select the Programs folder below the Start Menu folder.
5. Click the Next Step button.
6. In the Select a destination for the backup list box, select the floppy disk drive that contains your backup disk.
7. Click File on the menu bar, click Save As, and, in the Save As dialog box, enter a name for the backup file set in the File name box, then click the Save button.
8. Click Settings on the menu bar, click Options, then click the Backup tab. On the Backup tab, select the options for performing a full backup, for verifying the backup data, and for using data compression, then close the Settings - Options dialog box.
9. Click the Start Backup button and, when the Backup Set Label dialog box opens, enter a name for the backup set that is identical to the name of the file set, then click the OK button.
10. After the backup and compare operations are complete, close the Microsoft Backup window, then close the Compare dialog box.
11. Click the Restore tab, select the name of your floppy disk drive that contains your backup disk, select the backup set filename, then click the Next Step button.
12. In the Select files from the backup set list box, select the selection box for the Windows folder, the selection box for the Start Menu folder, then the selection box for the Programs folder.
13. In the Contents section, double-click the Start Menu folder, then double-click the Programs folder to display the selected folders from this backup set.
14. Press Alt + Print Screen, open Paint, paste the contents of the Clipboard into the drawing area, then print the pasted image, and exit Paint without saving.
15. Close Microsoft Backup without restoring the contents of the backup set.

3. Developing a Backup Strategy for Ross and Bauer Ross and Bauer is a consulting firm that assists city and regional managers in long-range planning. Carmen Ortega works as a staff biologist who consults with city and regional planners on the impact that growth and development will have on the natural resources of a region. Carmen wants to develop a backup strategy that will enable her to reconstruct her records should she experience problems with her computer. She asks you to analyze the following concerns, and develop a comprehensive backup strategy.

- Carmen wants to restore the entire system in the event drive C fails.
- On her drive C, she has folders organized by project, resource, and client.
- Since each project usually requires in-depth analysis and development of long-range proposals, she works on the same projects for one to two years. During this time, she works with the same set of files each day.
- During each backup cycle, she wants to keep backup copies of the most recent versions of her files. Since each draft of a file is thoroughly reviewed before it is updated, Carmen does not need to restore earlier versions of her files.

Using the factors listed above, answer the following questions.
1. What type of backup strategy should Carmen use?
2. What types of backups should Carmen perform to ensure that she can restore her entire system and her working folders?
3. What types of option settings should she specify for these backups? Are there any options that might simplify the backup process?
4. Using the factors listed above, outline the backup process in a table using the following table format. See Figure 7-30.

Figure 7-30 ◄

Backup schedule	Type of backup	What to include in the backup
First of the month		
End of first week		
End of second week		
End of third week		
Beginning of next month		

4. Developing a Backup Strategy for Redwood County Water Agency The Redwood County Water Agency recently hired Anthony Fenwick to use AutoCAD to prepare maps from aerial photos of the different habitats within the county. Since each map represents a major investment of time and resources for the water agency, Anthony must develop a backup strategy that will enable him to restore any of the maps that he produces. Anthony wants you to use the following factors to assist him in identifying the best backup strategy.

- Anthony stores all of his drawing files in a folder named Maps on his hard disk drive.
- He wants to be able to restore previous versions of each map from his backup set, in the event a map becomes corrupted. Then, he can reconstruct the remainder of that map.
- Anthony might also need to retrieve an earlier version of map from a backup set so that he can produce a new variation of the same map.

    Using the factors listed above, answer the following questions.
    1. What type of backup strategy should Anthony use?
    2. What types of backups should Anthony perform to ensure that he can restore the folder that contains his maps, or individual drawings?
    3. What types of option settings should he specify for these backups? Are there any options that might simplify the backup process?
    4. How many copies of each backup set should Anthony keep, and where should those backups be stored?
    5. Using the factors listed above, outline your backup process in a table using the following table format. See Figure 7-31.

Figure 7-31 ◄

Backup schedule	Type of backup	What to include in the backup
First of the month		
End of first week		
End of second week		
End of third week		
Beginning of next month		

TUTORIAL 8

Optimizing Disks

Optimizing the Storage of Files on Disks

OBJECTIVES

In this tutorial you will:

- Learn about the importance of the ScanDisk utility

- Check a disk for errors

- Undelete files from the Recycle Bin

- Learn what causes file fragmentation

- Use the Disk Defragmenter to optimize a disk

- Check the status of a disk's fragmentation

CASE

Harris & Banche

Harris & Banche is a large advertising agency that handles product advertising, public relations, sales promotions, and direct marketing services for its corporate clients. Teri Caldwell, an employee in their Atlanta branch, works as a telecommunications specialist. As part of her management responsibilities, Teri oversees two employees who work as microcomputer specialists and who provide support to other employees. Teri and her staff have decided to promote a new program that will encourage other staff members to optimize and maintain the performance of their computers. **Disk optimization** refers to the steps you can take to reorganize the use of storage space on a disk so that the operating system can efficiently and quickly locate folders and files.

Teri and her staff have discussed implementing a regular disk optimization routine at Harris & Banche. Teri, in particular, wants her staff to train the other employees to use two of the important Windows 95 disk maintenance utilities: **ScanDisk**, which checks a disk for errors, and the **Disk Defragmenter**, which ensures that data are stored most efficiently on a disk. Another important part of disk maintenance is deleting old files, and Teri wants to encourage the employees to save hard disk space by regularly deleting files, but she also wants to be sure they understand how to recover deleted files from the Windows 95 Recycle Bin. She asks her staff to focus their training sessions on developing a regular disk maintenance schedule that includes a disk check using ScanDisk, then a close examination of a disk's contents to delete unneeded files, and then a defragmentation to reorganize the disk for optimal efficiency.

The Importance of the ScanDisk Utility

Teri's first priority is to implement a regular disk check routine at Harris & Banche. The ScanDisk utility in Windows 95 examines disks for errors and, where possible, repairs errors. When you first install Windows 95 on your computer, it automatically uses ScanDisk to check the hard disk for errors before it installs itself on the hard disk. This utility checks and fixes the following parts of a hard disk drive or floppy disk drive:

- File Allocation Table (FAT)
- folder or directory structure
- filing system
- long filenames
- physical surface of the disk
- compressed volume files

Recall that the File Allocation Table contains information on whether each allocation unit or cluster on a disk is available, is in use, marks the end of a file, or is defective (i.e., contains a bad cluster). This information is so important to the operating system that it keeps and updates two copies of the File Allocation Table. If the operating system cannot read the disk clusters that contain the first copy of the File Allocation Table (FAT1) for the information it needs, then it reads the disk clusters that contain the second copy of the File Allocation Table (FAT2). As noted earlier, Windows 95 uses the MS-DOS File Allocation Table as its foundation, but also adds the capability for tracking long filenames.

The folder or directory structure is also quite important because Windows 95 uses it to locate and store files on a disk. Each folder or directory is a file that contains the name, extension, size, date, time, and attributes of each file in a folder, as well as the starting cluster of each file in that folder or directory. Windows 95 uses this starting cluster to find all the other parts of a file, because the starting cluster points to the next cluster, and each subsequent cluster points to the next cluster until Windows 95 reaches the last cluster, which has an end-of-file mark. The ScanDisk utility examines the entire folder or directory structure of a disk to ensure that it is functional and intact.

When ScanDisk checks the integrity of the filing system, it looks for the presence of lost clusters and cross-linked files. A **lost cluster** is a cluster on a disk that contains data that once belonged to a program or a document file. In the File Allocation Table, there is no record to indicate which file the lost cluster belongs to. Lost clusters might develop when a power failure occurs, when you reboot a computer system after it locks up, or when a brownout (a diminished supply of power) or a power surge occurs. In these cases, the operating system might not be able to record any remaining information it has on the location of all clusters of a file in the File Allocation Table or the starting cluster in the folder or directory file. Over time, lost clusters might increase in number, waste valuable disk space, and lead to further disk errors. Lost cluster errors are the most common type of problem encountered on hard disks.

When ScanDisk repairs lost clusters, it assigns a new filename to each **chain**, or sequence of lost clusters that once belonged to a file, and stores the new filename in the top-level folder or the root directory. The first file is named File0000, the second File0001, the third File0002, and so on. After ScanDisk converts each chain of lost clusters to a new file, you can attempt to open the file with WordPad or Notepad and examine its contents. In some cases, you might recognize text that belongs to a word processing file, and you might be able to combine the contents of this file with the original file. Usually, you will see only extraneous characters or symbols, and will not be able to identify whether the file is a program file or a data file. In most cases, you just delete the files that contain the lost clusters. If a program fails to operate properly or at all, you reinstall that program on your hard disk or restore it from a backup set. If you are missing part of a data file, you can restore it from a backup set.

A **cross-linked file** is a file that contains at least one cluster which belongs to, or is shared by, two (or perhaps more) files. In most cases, you will find that one file is cross-linked with only one other file through just one cluster. In the File Allocation Table, the operating system has recorded the cross-linked cluster as the next available cluster for two different files. When you retrieve and change one of these files, the other file is automatically updated. ScanDisk repairs cross-linked files by copying each file to a new location and removing the original files so that the files are no longer cross-linked. When you open one of the two files, you might find that it is intact. When you open and examine the other file, you might find that part of the document is missing and that extraneous characters have replaced the original contents of that section of the document.

The primary purpose of the ScanDisk utility is to check for problems in the logical structure of a disk and for physical defects on the surface of a disk. The **logical structure** of a disk is its File Allocation Tables, its filing system, the folder or directory structure, and filenames. ScanDisk checks the validity of filenames and verifies that the names do not contain characters, such as a question mark or asterisk, that are not allowed. If ScanDisk finds defects on the disk's surface, it attempts to move any data stored in those defective clusters to new locations on the disk before it marks those defective clusters as unusable.

If your computer system has a compressed hard drive, or if you compress floppy disks, the ScanDisk utility can check the integrity of the compressed volume files on those disks. A **compressed volume file** is a file that contains all the folders and files that were originally stored on an uncompressed disk. By combining all the folders and files into one larger file, disk space is more efficiently used.

HELP DESK

Index

USING SCANDISK

Click the Start button, click Help, then click the Index tab.

Keyword	**Topic**
ScanDisk, using	Checking your disk's surface, files, and folders for errors

Before you run the ScanDisk utility, you should close all other programs that you are using, including applications and other utilities. If the ScanDisk utility finds a defective cluster, it attempts to move the data in that bad cluster to another location on the disk. An open program might be using that same cluster, so you should close the program first. While it is checking a hard disk, ScanDisk might detect a change made to the status of the disk by a program, even if you have closed all open applications. If this occurs, ScanDisk will automatically restart. If ScanDisk keeps restarting, stop and then close ScanDisk. Open the Start menu, select Shut Down, select the option for restarting Windows 95, then run ScanDisk again.

Using ScanDisk

As she works with the employees, Teri emphasizes the importance of using the ScanDisk utility on a regular basis to check and maintain the integrity of hard disks and floppy disks that contain important company documents. She points out that it is easier to repair problems while they are relatively minor, rather than wait until the problems become more serious and perhaps impossible to repair. For example, if too many lost clusters build up on a hard disk, the operating system might not recognize the disk as one that was originally formatted with that operating system, and the disk might fail.

Recently, Multimedia Enterprises International, Inc., one of Harris & Banche's many corporate clients, sent their advertising rep a floppy disk with copies of files that they use to prepare financial projections and analyses. Teri asks you to use the ScanDisk utility to verify the integrity of the disk before her staff distributes copies of it to employees who will work with Multimedia Enterprises' files.

To start ScanDisk:

1. If necessary, close all open applications and utilities, and return to the desktop.

2. Insert your original copy of the Multimedia Enterprises International, Inc. disk into a floppy disk drive. Make sure you are using the correct Student Disk for this tutorial, identified in the "Read This Before You Begin" page at the beginning of this book.

3. Click the **Start** button, point to **Programs**, point to **Accessories**, point to **System Tools**, then click **ScanDisk** on the System Tools menu. The ScanDisk dialog box for the default drive opens. See Figure 8-1. At the top of this dialog box, you can select the drive or drives you want to scan.

Figure 8-1 ◀
Choosing a
drive to scan

click to select a drive
to scan

click for a Thorough
scan

click to repair disk
errors during the scan

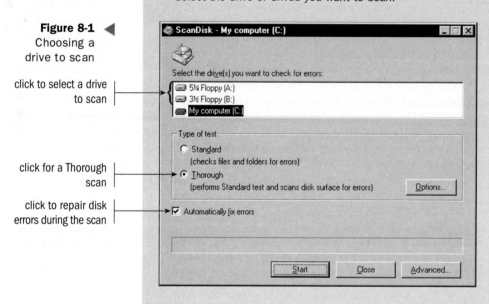

4. In the Select the drive(s) you want to check for errors list box, click the **name** of the floppy disk drive that contains your Student Disk.

Next, you choose the type of scan that you want ScanDisk to perform. You have two options. In the Type of test section, you can choose either Standard or Thorough. The Standard test only checks folders and files for errors. It does not check the surface of the disk for defects. The Thorough test includes the Standard test, so this option not only checks folders and files for errors, but it also checks the surface of the disk for errors.

Since you have not scanned the MEI disk before, you decide to do a Thorough test.

To select the type of test:

1. Click the **Thorough** radio button. You can also specify options for a Thorough test, but not for the Standard test.

2. Click the **Options** button. The Surface Scan Options dialog box opens. See Figure 8-2.

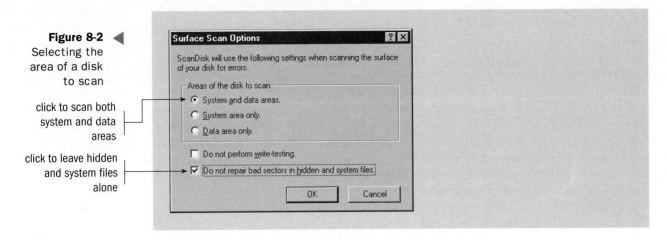

Figure 8-2
Selecting the
area of a disk
to scan

click to scan both
system and data
areas

click to leave hidden
and system files
alone

In the Areas of the disk to scan section, you can choose to scan the system and data areas, the system area only, or the data area only. The system area of a disk contains the boot sector or boot record, the File Allocation Tables, and the top-level folder or directory file. The data area of a disk contains the operating system software, application software, utility software, and document files that you regularly use. If ScanDisk finds errors in the system area of a disk, it more than likely will not be able to fix them, and the disk might then become unusable. If ScanDisk finds errors in the data area of a disk, it attempts to move the data to another part of the disk, and then mark the defective cluster as unusable. If ScanDisk cannot move the data to another location, you more than likely have lost that data. You should use the option for checking both the system and data areas, so that you know as soon as possible if a problem is developing on your hard disk.

You also have the option of limiting the ScanDisk operation by selecting one or both of the two check boxes in the Surface Scan Options dialog box. If you select the Do not perform write-testing option, ScanDisk reads the contents of each cluster to determine whether the cluster is defective. If you do not enable this option, ScanDisk not only reads the contents of each cluster, but it also writes the contents back to the same cluster to determine whether the cluster is defective. Reading the contents of a cluster, and then writing the contents back to the same cluster, means that ScanDisk takes longer to check the integrity of a disk, but the test is more thorough.

If you select the Do not repair bad clusters in hidden and system files option, ScanDisk will not move any data stored in a cluster that is part of a hidden or system file. This feature is important because operating systems create hidden and system files at specific locations on a disk and expect to find those files at those locations later. Also, some software applications check a hidden file stored in a specific location on a disk to verify that the application is a properly registered, and not a pirated, version of the software product. If you do not select this option, ScanDisk attempts to move any data stored in a bad cluster that is part of a hidden or system file. When you think about it, the latter option actually might be more useful than the first one. If an important hidden or system file is stored in a bad cluster, an operating system, application, or utility can't access the information it needs from the bad cluster. If ScanDisk is able to move the data, then the operating system, application, or utility might still be able to function properly. When ScanDisk moves a cluster, it updates the File Allocation Tables so that the operating system and software applications can locate specific files. If you are concerned that ScanDisk might move a sector that should not be moved, then enable the Do not repair bad clusters in hidden and system files option.

After examining these options, you decide that you want to check both system and data areas, perform write-testing, and, if necessary, repair bad clusters where part of a hidden or system file might be stored.

To specify surface scanning options:

1. Choose the surface scan options shown in Figure 8-2.

2. Click the **OK** button to return to the ScanDisk dialog box.

In the ScanDisk dialog box, you can also choose whether you want ScanDisk to automatically repair errors using its default settings. To change the default settings that ScanDisk uses, you use the Advanced button. If you disable the Automatically fix errors option, ScanDisk asks each time it encounters an error how you want to correct it.

Before you decide whether to use this option, you want to check the settings that ScanDisk uses for correcting errors.

To view the settings for correcting errors:

1. Click the **Advanced** button. In the ScanDisk Advanced Options dialog box, you can control six different types of settings for automatically correcting errors. See Figure 8-3.

Figure 8-3
Selecting advanced scanning options

click to display a summary

click to add scan results to log file

click to repair cross-linked files

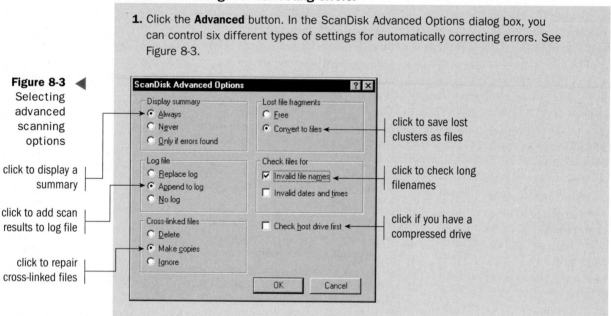

click to save lost clusters as files

click to check long filenames

click if you have a compressed drive

The six Advanced options are:

- **Display summary**. Specify whether you want to see a summary of the results that ScanDisk finds when it checks a disk. The summary tells you whether ScanDisk found and repaired any errors. In most cases, you will want to see a summary so that you know what types of errors occurred. The summary might provide you with important information that allows you to pinpoint the source of problems and troubleshoot your system before those same types of problems occur again, or even to anticipate future problems.

- **Log file**. Specify how you want to keep a record of each ScanDisk session. If you select the Replace log or Append to log options, ScanDisk saves detailed information about the results of its findings and any changes that it made to the disk in a special file called a **log file**. The log file, named Scandisk.log, is stored in the top-level folder or root directory of drive C. The Replace log option replaces the previous version of the Scandisk.log with a new one the next time you run ScanDisk. The Append to log option adds the results of the next ScanDisk operation to the results of the previous one. If you choose the No log option, ScanDisk does not create this log file, and it does not save its results. The log file is useful, because you might need to go back and check the log file if you experience problems with your computer system after you perform a ScanDisk operation. The Append to log is the most useful option because it allows you to keep a running history of ScanDisk's findings and changes to a disk. In the case of a hard disk, this information might be invaluable, although obviously the file will grow in size with time. Since the ScanDisk log is a simple text file, you can open it with the Notepad accessory, make any changes you need to the file, and, if necessary, print a copy of the log.

- **Cross-linked files**. Specify how ScanDisk should handle cross-linked files. If you choose the Delete option, ScanDisk deletes the cross-linked files. You might not want this option because one of the two files might be intact. Plus, you might want to know which two files are cross-linked and what those files contain. For example, are the two cross-linked files ones that contain information on your company's latest cash flow status and your company's quarterly tax return? If so, you might want to attempt to save the files or at least print their contents before you try to correct the problem. If you choose this option to automatically delete cross-linked files, consider performing frequent backups. If you choose the Make copies option, ScanDisk makes a copy of the cross-linked cluster for each of the two cross-linked files. The information in the cluster where the cross link occurred is more than likely data that belongs to one of the two files, but not to both. However, this option improves your chances of recovering one file intact and most of the other file. If you choose the Ignore option, ScanDisk does not change the cross-linked files in any way, and leaves the cross-linked files on the disk. Later, if you try to use one of these cross-linked files, the software application that you use to open the file might fail, or the damage to the cross-linked files might become more extensive. But you might want to do a backup of your files before you attempt to correct the problem with ScanDisk.

- **Lost file fragments**. Specify how ScanDisk should handle lost clusters. If you choose the Free option, ScanDisk deletes the lost clusters and frees up the disk space. This is important because lost clusters waste valuable disk space that could be used more productively by other files or as "elbow room" for your operating system. If you choose the Convert to files option, ScanDisk assigns names, such as File0000, File0001, and File0002, to each chain of lost clusters, and stores the recovered files in the top-level folder or root directory of the disk. One advantage of converting lost clusters to files is that you can then examine the files and determine whether they contain any important information. More often than not, these files are not useful, because you see only extraneous characters when you view the contents of the files. In most cases, lost clusters were produced from temporary files created by the operating system, applications or utilities. A **temporary file** is a file that contains data that a program is processing. Once the processing is done, the temporary file is deleted. However, if the power fails, or if your computer locks up and you reboot, then the temporary files might remain on disk as lost clusters. If you do choose the option to convert lost clusters to files, then examine the files immediately after the ScanDisk operation and delete any of these files you do not need.

- **Check files for**. Specify whether you want ScanDisk to check files for both invalid filenames and invalid dates and times. If a file has an invalid name, such as a filename with two extensions, the application that produced that file might not be able to open it. An invalid date or time for a file affects how the file is listed in Windows Explorer and in directory listings from the command prompt when you open a DOS session. Also, an invalid date or time might affect the operation of an application or other type of program, such as a backup utility. It is important to note that lost clusters, cross-linked files, an invalid filename, or an invalid date and time for a file might also indicate the presence of a computer virus. You should purchase, and use, an anti-viral software program that checks for and removes computer viruses, that monitors your computer as you work, and that checks disks inserted into the floppy drives.

- **Check host drive first**. Click if you use a disk compression utility to compress your hard disk or a floppy disk. The **host drive** is the drive that contains the compressed volume file. If you have a compressed hard disk, you should always use this option because problems on the compressed drive probably result from problems on the host drive.

From your examination of these options, you decide to always display a summary, append ScanDisk's results to the existing log file, make copies of cross-linked files, convert lost clusters to files, and check files for invalid filenames.

To specify advanced settings:

1. Choose the options in the ScanDisk Advanced Options dialog box shown in Figure 8-3.

2. If you are working on a compressed drive, click the **Check host drive first** check box if it is not already selected.

3. Click the **OK** button to return to the ScanDisk dialog box.

4. If the Automatically fix errors check box is not already selected, click this check box.

5. Click the **Start** button. The progress bar shows the status of the ScanDisk operation. See Figure 8-4.

Figure 8-4
Scanning a
floppy disk

drive being checked

scanning the
data area

progress of scan

cluster being
examined

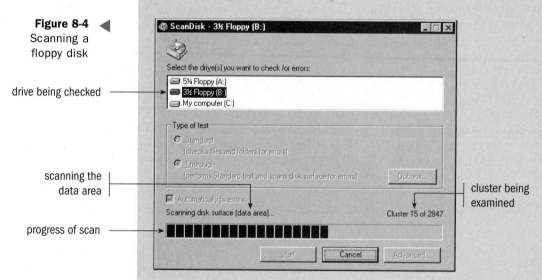

ScanDisk checks the File Allocation Tables, the folders and files, the system area, and finally the data area of the disk. Not only does ScanDisk report on the task it is currently performing, but it also shows which cluster number it is currently examining when it checks the data area of a disk. Notice that ScanDisk grays or dims all the option buttons, check boxes, and command buttons, except for the Cancel button. You cannot change any of the settings once ScanDisk starts, although you can cancel the ScanDisk operation. It might take four or five minutes, or more, to scan the disk. When ScanDisk finishes, it displays a ScanDisk Results dialog box with its findings. See Figure 8-5.

Figure 8-5
Viewing the
results of a
scan

no errors found during
the scan

summary of disk
space usage

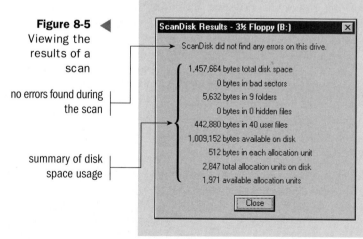

Your summary might differ from that shown in the figure. If your disk contained errors that ScanDisk recognizes, then you will see the message "ScanDisk found errors on this drive and fixed them all" at the top of the ScanDisk Results dialog box. Plus, it will report on any bad clusters it found.

6. In the ScanDisk Results dialog box, click the **Close** button. You return to the ScanDisk dialog box.

7. Click the **Close** button ☒ to close the ScanDisk dialog box.

REFERENCE window

USING THE SCANDISK UTILITY

- Click the Start button, point to Programs, point to Accessories, point to System Tools, then click ScanDisk on the System Tools menu.
- In the ScanDisk dialog box, click the disk drive you want to scan.
- In the Type of test section, click the type of scan you want to perform.
- Click the Options button and, in the Surface Scan Options dialog box, click the settings you want to use, then close the dialog box.
- Decide whether you want ScanDisk to automatically fix errors.
- Click the Advanced button and, in the ScanDisk Advanced Options dialog box, click any advanced settings you want to use, then close the dialog box.
- Click the Start button and, when ScanDisk completes its check of the disk, click the Close button to close the ScanDisk Results dialog box, then click the Close button to close the ScanDisk dialog box.

As Teri and her assistants work with other employees, they emphasize that the ScanDisk utility is the most important utility that one can use on a regular basis to check a hard disk drive and floppy disks for errors and to repair those errors before they become more serious and unrepairable. Microsoft Corporation recommends that you use the ScanDisk utility as frequently as you can. If you are faced with a busy schedule and time constraints and cannot use the ScanDisk utility on a daily or weekly basis, use the ScanDisk utility at least once a month.

Undeleting Files

As part of a regular disk maintenance program, a natural step after performing a disk scan is the **purging**, or deleting, of unneeded folders and files, including files created from lost clusters, to recover and increase disk space. At Harris & Banche, regular file deletion is a particularly important task, because clients regularly send disks containing important (and often large) business files, such as product sales, analyses, and projections to Harris & Banche employees, so that the firm can analyze their client's current business activity and develop more effective advertising campaigns. Harris & Banche employees copy these files into client folders on their hard drives, use them to help develop advertising strategies, and then archive them to conserve space when they are no longer needed. However, sometimes an employee might need to restore a folder or file that they accidentally deleted, so Teri wants to make sure that employees at Harris & Banche know how to recover deleted folders and files.

When you delete a file from a hard disk, Windows 95 either moves the file to the Recycle Bin or it deletes the file completely, depending on what you've specified in the Recycle Bin property sheet. If you choose to use the Recycle Bin, Windows 95 moves deleted files to a folder on drive C called Recycled, in which case you can recover, or undelete, files and restore them to your hard disk. You can periodically empty the Recycle Bin so that deleted files do not take up valuable storage space on your disk. However, after you empty the Recycle Bin, you cannot recover deleted files. Also, the Recycle Bin only stores files deleted on a hard disk. If you delete a file from a floppy disk, the file is not moved to the Recycle Bin. You have to use some other utility to recover the file.

Multimedia Enterprises International, Inc. recently sent you a disk, and Teri asks you to copy one of the folders on it to drive C, delete the folder, then recover the folder and its files from the Recycle Bin so that you'll have the skills to recover files when you really need them.

If you are working on a computer that does not have a hard disk drive, then you cannot complete this section of the tutorial. Instead, you might want to read, but not complete, the steps so that you are familiar with how the Recycle Bin works.

To copy one of the MEI_Inc folders to drive C:

1. If necessary, close any open applications or utilities and return to the desktop.

2. Insert your original copy of the Multimedia Enterprises International, Inc. disk into a floppy disk drive. Make sure you are using the correct Student Disk for this tutorial, identified in the "Read This Before You Begin" page at the beginning of this book.

3. Double-click the **My Computer** icon, the click the **Maximize** button 🗖.

4. If you do not see a toolbar, click **View** on the menu bar, click **Toolbar**, then, if necessary, click the **Large Icons** button ⧉ on the toolbar.

5. Click **View** on the menu bar, point to **Arrange Icons**, then click **by Drive Letter**.

6. Double-click the **disk drive** icon for drive A (or drive B), and when the drive folder opens, click the **MEI_Inc** folder, then click the **Copy** button ⧉ on the toolbar.

7. Click the **Up One Level** button ⧉ on the toolbar.

8. Double-click the **disk drive** icon for drive C, then click the **Paste** button ⧉ on the toolbar. Windows 95 displays a Copying dialog box as it copies the MEI_Inc folder to drive C. See Figure 8-6.

Figure 8-6 ◄
Copying a folder to a hard disk

file being copied ——

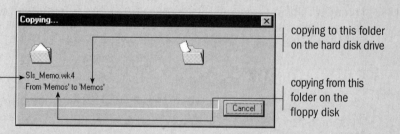

copying to this folder on the hard disk drive

copying from this folder on the floppy disk

TROUBLE? If there is already a copy of the MEI_Inc folder on drive C, Windows 95 displays a Confirm Folder Replace dialog box. If this occurs, click the Yes to All button to replace the contents of that folder with the contents of the MEI_Inc folder from the floppy disk.

9. Click **View** on the menu bar, point to **Arrange Icons**, then click **by Type**. You should now see a folder named MEI_Inc. See Figure 8-7.

Figure 8-7 ◀
The MEI_Inc
folder

current drive

folder copied to the
hard disk

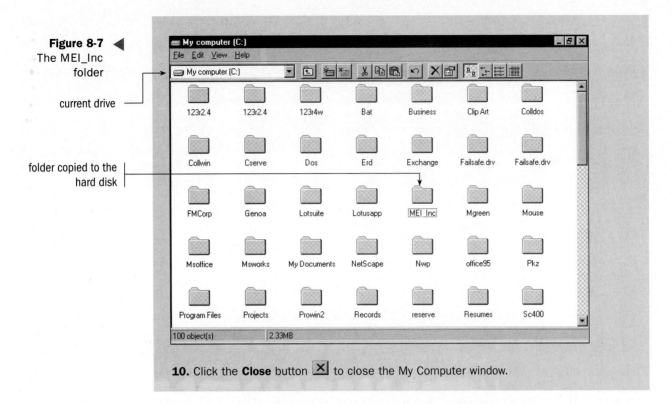

10. Click the **Close** button ⊠ to close the My Computer window.

Teri notes that this is the fastest way to copy a client folder, with all its subfolders and files, from a client disk to your hard disk drive so that you can then work with a client's files.

Verifying the Properties of the Recycle Bin

Before you delete any files in this folder, you want to verify that the Recycle Bin is enabled and that Windows 95 is using the proper settings for recovering deleted files from drive C.

To check the property settings for the Recycle Bin:

1. Right-click the **Recycle Bin** icon, then click **Properties** on the shortcut menu. On the Global tab in the Recycle Bin Properties dialog box, the Do not move files to the Recycle Bin. Remove files immediately on delete option indicates whether Windows 95 will move deleted folders and files to the Recycle Bin or whether it will permanently delete folders and files. See Figure 8-8.

Figure 8-8
Verifying
properties of
the Recycle Bin

click to use the same
settings for all drives

do not enable if you
want to recover
deleted files

click to confirm the
deletion of folders
and files

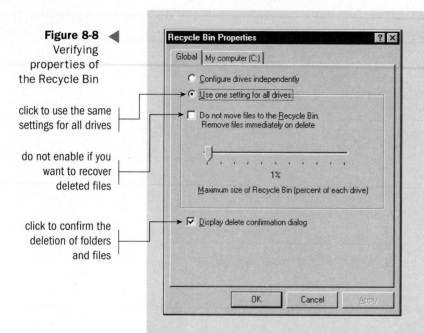

2. If necessary, click the **Use one setting for all drives** radio button to enable this feature.

3. If necessary, click the **Do not move files to the Recycle Bin. Remove files immediately on delete** check box to deselect this option. Now Windows 95 will move deleted files to the Recycle Bin.

4. If necessary, click the **Display delete confirmation dialog** check box to enable this option. By enabling confirmation, you reduce the chances of inadvertently deleting the wrong folder or file.

5. Click the **OK** button to close the Recycle Bin Properties dialog box.

When you work on a different computer from the one you typically use, you should check the settings for the Recycle Bin before you start deleting folders and files from that computer's hard disk.

Restoring a Folder with its Files

Teri emphasizes that, after you enable the Recycle Bin, you can safely delete folders and files from a hard disk drive. If you need to recover a deleted folder or deleted files, you open the Recycle Bin, select the files you want to restore, then select the Restore option on the File menu. The files are restored to their original folder(s). If a folder no longer exists, Windows 95 recreates the folder before restoring files to that folder.

Teri asks you to delete the entire folder, then restore all its files.

To examine the process for recovering a deleted folder and its files:

1. Double-click the **My Computer** icon, then double-click the **disk drive** icon for your hard disk drive.

2. Click the **MEI_Inc** folder, then click the **Delete** button ☒ on the toolbar. Windows 95 displays a Confirm Folder Delete dialog box, asking you if you want to remove the MEI_Inc folder and its contents and move them to the Recycle Bin. See Figure 8-9.

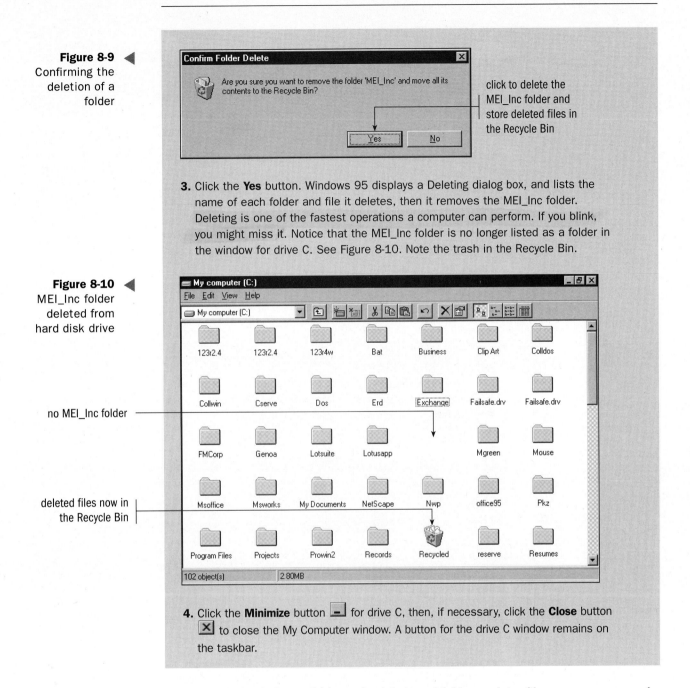

Figure 8-9
Confirming the
deletion of a
folder

click to delete the
MEI_Inc folder and
store deleted files in
the Recycle Bin

3. Click the **Yes** button. Windows 95 displays a Deleting dialog box, and lists the name of each folder and file it deletes, then it removes the MEI_Inc folder. Deleting is one of the fastest operations a computer can perform. If you blink, you might miss it. Notice that the MEI_Inc folder is no longer listed as a folder in the window for drive C. See Figure 8-10. Note the trash in the Recycle Bin.

Figure 8-10
MEI_Inc folder
deleted from
hard disk drive

no MEI_Inc folder

deleted files now in
the Recycle Bin

4. Click the **Minimize** button ⬛ for drive C, then, if necessary, click the **Close** button ⬛ to close the My Computer window. A button for the drive C window remains on the taskbar.

After accidentally or deliberately deleting a folder and its files, you can open the Recycle Bin and restore the folder and its files. Since the Recycle Bin is usually set to a certain size, you should restore deleted files as soon as you realize you need them.

You want to recover the MEI_Inc folder that you just deleted.

To recover a deleted folder:

1. Right-click the **Recycle Bin** icon, then **Open** on the shortcut menu, then maximize the Recycle Bin window. In the Recycle Bin window, you see a list of the files that you deleted and moved to the Recycle Bin. See Figure 8-11. If the Recycle Bin already contained deleted files before you deleted the MEI_Inc folder, then you will also see those files in the Recycle Bin. On the status bar, Windows 95 shows the number of objects in the Recycle bin. You might have more objects in your Recycle Bin. Now, you want to restore all these files.

Figure 8-11 ◀
Viewing the
contents of the
Recycle Bin

deleted files

number of objects in
the Recycle Bin

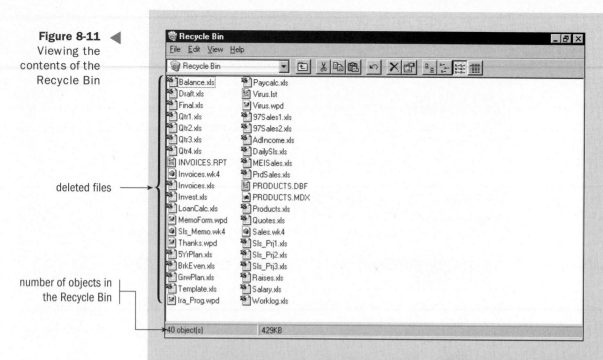

The Explore option on the shortcut menu opens an Exploring - Recycle Bin window similar to the Windows Explorer's window. You can perform the same types of operations if you choose Explore instead of Open.

2. If necessary, click **View** on the menu bar, then click **Toolbar.**

3. If necessary, click the **Details** button 🗐 on the toolbar. The Recycle Bin contains columns for the filename, its original location, the date it was deleted, the type of file, and the size of the file. See Figure 8-12.

Figure 8-12 ◀
Displaying
details on
deleted files

Original Location
column button

original locations of
deleted files

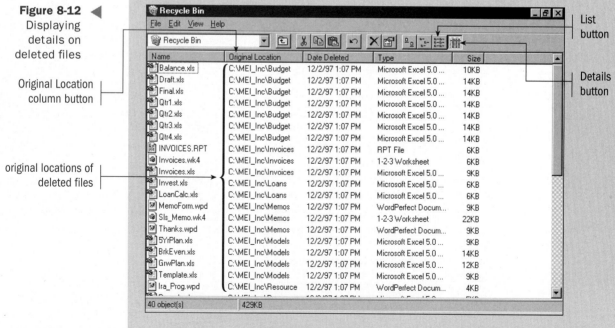

List
button

Details
button

4. If necessary, click the **Original Location** column button. Windows 95 displays the deleted files in alphabetical order by folder name.

By organizing deleted files in the Recycle Bin in order by the file's original location, you can easily select and restore all the files in a folder.

TROUBLE? If the deleted files are listed in reverse alphabetical order by folder name, click the Original Location column button again.

5. Click the List button [icon] on the toolbar. Now, you can see more files within the same window.

6. Locate and click the **Balance.xls** icon, press and hold the **Shift** key, click the **Worklog.xls** icon, then release the Shift key. Windows 95 selects all the deleted files that fall between Balance.xls and Worklog.xls. If you had wanted to restore only one file, you select just that file. If you had wanted to restore nonadjacent files, you press the Ctrl key while you click each file.

7. Click **File** on the menu bar, then click **Restore**. Windows 95 displays a Moving dialog box as it moves the deleted files back to their original folders. It also must recreate the original folder structure. Then, the Recycle Bin no longer displays those deleted files. You can also use the Undo Delete option on the Edit menu to restore deleted files.

8. Click the **Close** button [icon] to close the Recycle Bin.

9. Click the taskbar button for the drive C window.

10. Click **View** on the menu bar, point to **Arrange Icons**, then click **by Type**. Windows 95 displays the restored folder named MEI_Inc. See Figure 8-13.

Figure 8-13 ◀
Restored folder

folder restored from
the Recycle Bin

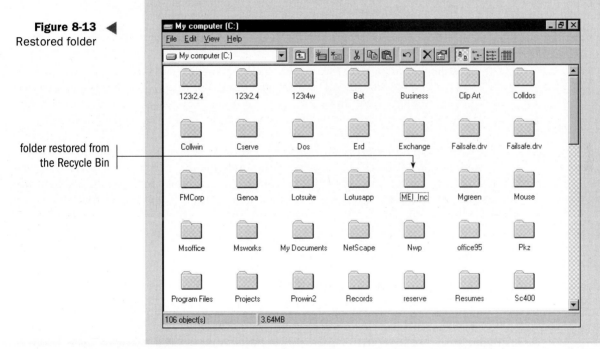

So that you do not waste valuable space that Windows 95 and application software packages might need, it is important to periodically review the contents of the Recycle Bin and decide whether you want to restore any files or whether you want to empty the Recycle Bin.

Since you no longer need the MEI_Inc folder that you used to test the process of deleting and undeleting files, you can remove the folder from drive C.

To remove the MEI_Inc folder:

1. Click the **MEI_Inc** folder, then click the **Delete** button ☒ on the toolbar.

2. In the Confirm Folder Delete dialog box, click the **Yes** button.

3. Click the **Close** button ☒ to close the window for the drive C folder. Notice that the Recycle Bin now contains the files that you just deleted.

REFERENCE
window

RESTORING FILES FROM THE RECYCLE BIN

- Right-click the Recycle Bin icon, then click Open on the shortcut menu.
- Click the Original Location column button to organize deleted files by their original folder names in alphabetical order.
- Select the file or files you want to restore by clicking an individual filename, by pressing the Ctrl key while you click the name of each of the files you want to restore, or by clicking the name of the first file while you hold the Shift key and click the name of the last file in the group of filenames.
- Click File on the menu bar, then click Restore to restore all the selected files.
- Close the Recycle Bin.

If you store your important files, as well as those of any clients you might have, on your hard disk drive, then you can take advantage not only of the greater storage capacity and faster operation of the hard disk drive, but you can also enable the Recycle Bin and, at a later date, recover any files that you might have accidentally or deliberately deleted.

If you want to take a break and resume the tutorial at a later time, you can do so now. If you are on a network, close any open applications and dialog boxes, and leave Windows 95 running. If you are using your own computer, click the Start button on the taskbar, click Shut Down, click Shut down the computer, and then click the Yes button. When you resume the tutorial, launch Windows 95 again, and then continue with the tutorial.

● ● ●

Defragmenting Disks

During her weekly staff meeting, Teri tells her staff that, in addition to using ScanDisk to check for and repair errors on a disk, another important way to optimize the performance of your hard disk drive is to use a defragmenting utility. A **defragmenting utility** is a program that rearranges the files on a hard disk or a floppy disk so that all parts of each file are stored in consecutive clusters.

As you create, modify, and save files to a hard disk or a floppy disk, Windows 95 attempts to store the different parts of each file in contiguous, or adjacent, clusters. However, over time, as you add, delete, and modify files, Windows 95 might have to store different parts of a file in noncontiguous, or nonadjacent, clusters that are scattered across the surface of a disk. The file is then called a **fragmented file**.

Each time you issue a command to retrieve a file from a hard disk or a floppy disk, the read/write heads (the device within a disk drive that retrieves and records data from and on the disk) must locate each of the file clusters and reassemble those clusters so that the software application that you are using can work with the entire file or with a large portion of a file. Likewise, when you issue a command to save a new or modified file to a hard disk or a floppy disk, Windows 95 must locate available clusters for that file. If a file is stored in noncontiguous clusters, it takes the read/write heads longer to write the file to the hard disk or floppy disk. The problem is compounded if all or a majority of the files on a hard disk or a floppy disk are fragmented.

So that you have a better understanding of how file fragmentation occurs, let's examine a simple example of how file fragmentation might occur. Assume you have used a disk heavily over the last six months. You have added files to the disk, and you have deleted and modified files on the disk. As a result of these changes, Windows 95 has used all of the clusters on the disk at one time or another to store parts of files. Let's also assume that part of this disk contains three files (Figure 8-14).

Figure 8-14 ◄
An example of files arranged in contiguous clusters on a disk

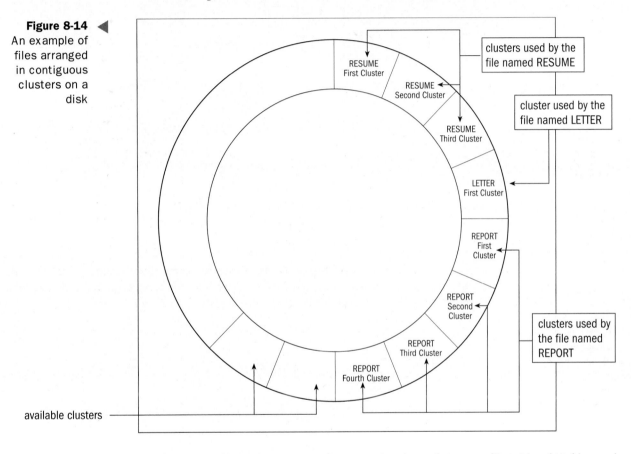

clusters used by the file named RESUME

cluster used by the file named LETTER

clusters used by the file named REPORT

available clusters

You have a file with a resume that occupies three clusters, a file with a brief letter that occupies the next available cluster, a file with a report that occupies the next four clusters, and two other clusters that are now available for use again. You decide you no longer need the letter, so you delete it. By removing this file, you have created an available cluster (Figure 8-15).

Figure 8-15 ◀
Windows 95
frees a cluster
after a file
deletion

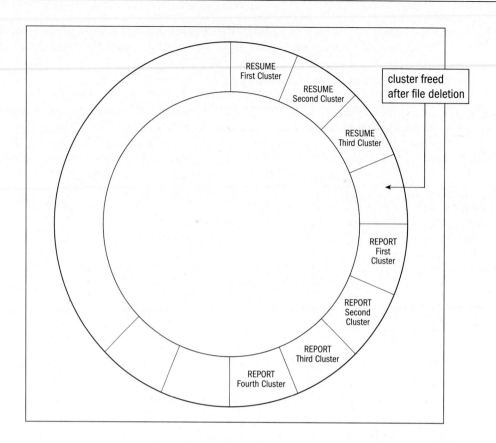

Now you prepare a bid proposal and save it to the same disk. Windows 95 uses the cluster that was previously occupied by the letter and the next two available clusters, located after the clusters containing the report (Figure 8-16).

Figure 8-16 ◀
Windows 95
produces a
fragmented file
by storing it in
noncontiguous
clusters

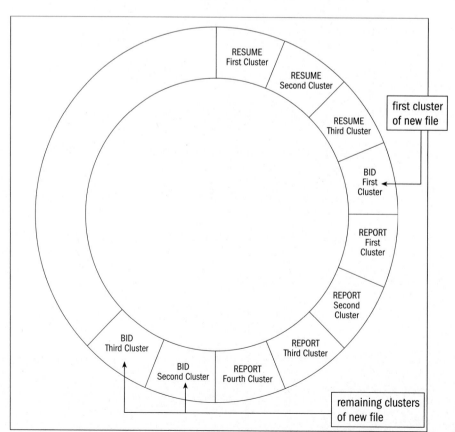

The file with the bid proposal becomes a fragmented file because it is stored in non-contiguous clusters. From this example, you can see that if you reduce the size of files or delete files from a disk, you free up clusters that Windows 95 might use later for part of yet another file. If you increase the size of files or add new files to a disk, Windows 95 stores the files in noncontiguous clusters if the disk does not contain enough consecutive clusters to hold the entire file.

By using a defragmenter, you can eliminate or reduce file fragmentation on a disk. If all of the clusters of a file are stored in adjacent clusters, the read/write heads can then quickly retrieve the contents of that file, and this improves the performance of your computer. If a file is fragmented, the read/write heads must keep moving to different sites on a disk in order to locate all the parts of a file, and this slows down the performance of your computer. Defragmenting utilities therefore eliminate file fragmentation and improve a computer's response time.

HELP DESK

Index

USING THE DISK DEFRAGMENTER

Click the Start button, click Help, then click the Index tab.

Keyword
Defragmenting your hard disk

Topic
To speed up your hard disk by using Disk Defragmenter

Before you run the Disk Defragmenter, you should close all other programs that you are using, including applications and other utilities. Since the primary function of the Disk Defragmenter is to rearrange data stored on disk, you do not want to have any open programs that are currently accessing data that might be moved to another location. Also, you should not use a defragmenting utility designed to operate under your previous version of MS-DOS and that might still be installed on your hard disk. While it is checking a hard disk for errors prior to defragmentation, the Disk Defragmenter might detect a change made to the status of a disk by a program, even if you have closed all open applications. If this occurs, the Disk Defragmenter will automatically restart. If the Disk Defragmenter keeps restarting, stop and then close the Disk Defragmenter. Open the Start menu, select Shut Down, select the option for restarting Windows 95, then run the Disk Defragmenter again.

Using the Disk Defragmenter

Over the last few weeks, Teri has noticed that it takes longer and longer for Windows 95 to retrieve and record information on the Multimedia Enterprises disk. She decides that it is time to use the Windows 95 Disk Defragmenter to optimize the organization of files on this disk. She asks you to optimize her disk with the Disk Defragmenter while she attends an important management meeting.

To start the Disk Defragmenter:

1. Close all open applications and utilities, and return to the desktop.

2. Insert your original copy of the Multimedia Enterprises disk into a floppy disk drive. Make sure you are using the correct Student Disk for this tutorial, identified in the "Read This Before You Begin" page at the beginning of this book.

3. Click the **Start** button, point to **Programs**, point to **Accessories**, point to **System Tools**, then click **Disk Defragmenter** on the System Tools menu. In the Select Drive dialog box, you choose the disk drive you want to defragment. See Figure 8-17.

Figure 8-17 ◀
Selecting a
drive to
defragment

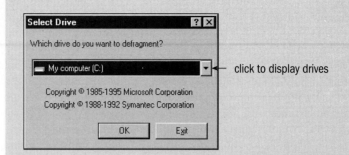

click to display drives

4. Click the **Drive** list arrow, click the **name** of the drive that contains your Student Disk, then click the **OK** button. In the Disk Defragmenter dialog box, the defragmenter informs you what percentage of your disk is fragmented. See Figure 8-18. If the percentage is low or zero, the defragmenter will tell you that you do not need to defragment the disk now. No matter what the defragmenter recommends, you can still defragment the disk if you want. However, before you start the defragmentation process, you can choose the Advanced button and specify how the Disk Defragmenter will perform the defragmentation.

Figure 8-18 ◀
Summary of
fragmentation
analysis

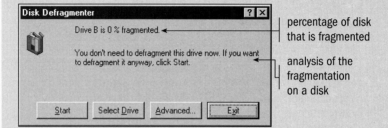

percentage of disk
that is fragmented

analysis of the
fragmentation
on a disk

5. Click the **Advanced** button. In the Advanced Options dialog box, you can specify the defragmentation method, enable or disable error checking, and specify whether you want to use these settings in the future. See Figure 8-19.

Figure 8-19 ◀
Selecting
advanced
options for
defragmenting
a disk

click for a full
defragmentation

click to check for
errors on drive

click to use settings
just this time only

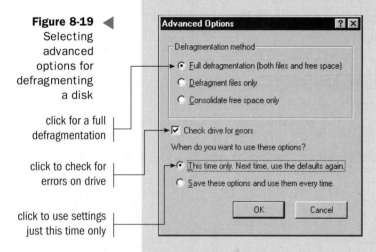

The Disk Defragmenter includes three options for defragmenting a disk:

■ **Full defragmentation (both files and free space).** Rearranges the storage space on a disk by storing parts of each file in consecutive clusters and by removing free space, or empty space, between files. By removing the free space between files, Windows 95 can no longer use that space to store parts of a file, and you reduce the amount of file fragmentation that will occur in the future. Because this defragmentation option performs more functions, it takes longer.

- **Defragment files only.** Eliminates file fragmentation by storing the parts of a file in consecutive clusters but leaving free space between files. If you do not remove the unused space between files, Windows 95 stores parts of new or modified files in that empty space, and fragmented files accumulate at a faster rate on your disk. The advantage of this option is that it does reduce file fragmentation, and it is faster than the Full defragmentation option.

- **Consolidate free space only.** Removes the empty space between files, but does not eliminate file fragmentation. By removing the empty space between files, new files are stored in consecutive clusters following the files already stored on disk. However, if you modify an existing file, and increase its size, that file might become fragmented. Again, this option is faster than the Full defragmentation option.

Prior to the actual defragmentation, you can choose to have the Disk Defragmenter check the disk for errors. If a disk has errors, then the defragmenter cannot properly defragment all the files on a disk. Even though you might use ScanDisk on a weekly or monthly basis, it is a good idea to always enable the option for error checking prior to a defragmentation. You also have the option of using the settings you choose just for this session or for all future sessions.

You decide to use error checking and to perform a full defragmentation of the Multimedia Enterprises disk.

To specify defragmentation settings:

1. Make sure your settings are identical to those shown in Figure 8-19, then click the **OK** button. You return to the Disk Defragmenter dialog box. Now, you can start the defragmentation.

2. Click the **Start** button. Since the process will take a few minutes, continue to read through and perform the steps, which ask you to do things during the defragmentation process. The Disk Defragmenter displays a Defragmenting dialog box that shows you the progress of the defragmentation. See Figure 8-20. You can view more details on the defragmentation as the disk defragments.

Figure 8-20 ◀
Defragmenting
a floppy disk

rearranging the
floppy disk

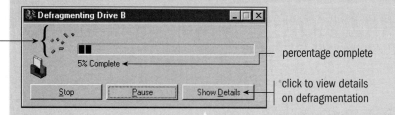

percentage complete

click to view details
on defragmentation

3. Click the **Show Details** button. The Disk Defragmenter displays a map of the disk. See Figure 8-21. The map of your disk might vary from that shown in the figure. If your disk has bad clusters, then you will see boxes with red lines through them. Although Windows 95 can still store files on a disk with bad clusters, you should not use a disk with a large number of bad clusters, because it might fail and you would lose all the files on it.

Figure 8-21 ◄
Viewing a map
of the
defragment-
ation process

optimized areas

unoptimized areas

free space

process of
defragmentation

click to view a legend

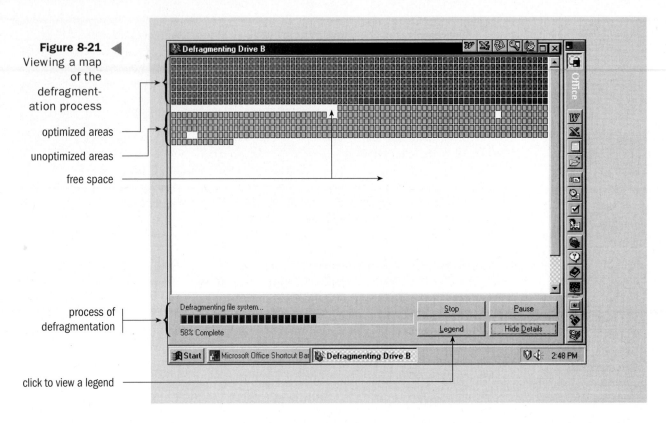

In this map, each block, or rectangle, represents one disk cluster. As the Disk Defragmenter defragments a disk, it moves disk clusters from one location to another so that the contents of each file are stored in consecutive clusters. During this process, the blocks that represent disk clusters move around the screen as the Disk Defragmenter rearranges storage space on the disk.

The Disk Defragmenter displays different colors and patterns for different blocks. If you want to display information on the meaning of these different colors and patterns, you can display a map legend.

To display the map legend:

1. Click the **Legend** button. In the Defrag Legend dialog box, the Disk Defragmenter explains the meaning of the different colors and patterns used for blocks. See Figure 8-22.

Figure 8-22 ◄
Displaying a
legend for the
map

what boxes on
map mean

one box represents
one cluster

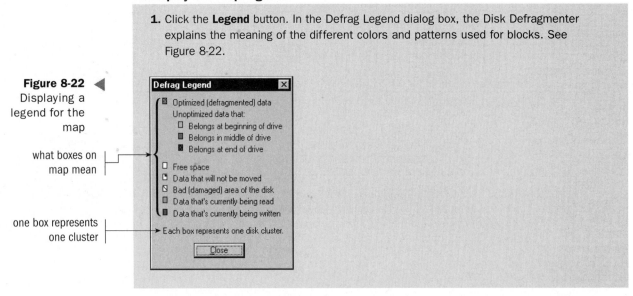

A blue block on the map represents an optimized, or defragmented, disk cluster. Some disk clusters must remain unoptimized because the operating system uses these disk clusters for specific system files. Some of these unoptimized areas are at the beginning of the drive, some are in the middle of the drive, and some are at the end of the drive. The Disk Defragmenter identifies these three types of unoptimized areas by using blocks with different colors.

White areas denote free, or unused, storage space on the disk. In fact, you might see blocks of white that appear as if they are background areas. The Disk Defragmenter also identifies disk clusters that contain operating system data that cannot be moved, as well as bad, or damaged, clusters of the disk.

As the Disk Defragmenter rearranges storage space on the disk, it reads one or more blocks, or disk clusters, either to move data stored in one or more disk clusters to another location, or to free up space after a block of disk clusters so that it can record data in that storage space. After it reads one or more blocks of disk clusters, it either writes or records the data in those disk clusters to another temporary storage location on disk or, if the data in those disk clusters are part of the same file, it records those blocks of disk clusters in the empty space that follows previous disk clusters of that same file. You can think of this process as being similar to the process of rearranging building blocks to create a pattern or object that has some meaning. The Disk Defragmenter keeps shuffling disk clusters around until all the disk clusters used by each file are stored in consecutive sectors on the disk.

When the Disk Defragmenter reads blocks of disk clusters, these blocks are shown in green. When it writes blocks of disk clusters to a new location, then these blocks are shown in red.

Now that you understand the map legend, you want to close it so you can view the defragmentation process.

To view the defragmentation:

1. In the Defrag Legend dialog box, click the **Close** button.

2. View the remainder of the disk defragmentation or optimization.

   Be patient. Depending on the size of the disk, the amount of fragmentation, and the type of microprocessor, the defragmentation process might take five minutes or more. When the Disk Defragmenter has defragmented the entire disk, it displays a Disk Defragmenter dialog box, asking you if you want to quit the Disk Defragmenter.

3. Click the **Yes** button. You return to the desktop.

REFERENCE
window

DEFRAGMENTING A FLOPPY DISK

- Close all open applications and utilities.
- Click the Start button, point to Programs, point to Accessories, point to System Tools, then click Disk Defragmenter on the System Tools menu.
- Click the Drive list arrow in the Select Drive dialog box, then click the name of the drive that you want to defragment.
- Click the Advanced button, select options for defragmenting a disk, then close the Advanced Options dialog box.
- Click the Start button in the Disk Defragmenter dialog box to start the defragmentation.
- After defragmentation is complete, click the Yes button in the next Disk Defragmenter dialog box.

You should optimize disks, especially your hard disk, on a regular basis. On a hard disk, file fragmentation can build up quickly and slow down the performance of your computer. The first time you optimize a hard disk with the Disk Defragmenter, it will take time. However, after that, the defragmentation proceeds more quickly because part of the hard disk is already optimized.

Checking the Status of a Disk's Fragmentation

During the meeting, Teri notes that if you create and modify a large number of files each day, then you will have to defragment your hard disk drive and floppy disks more frequently than if you work on your computer system only occasionally and create and modify a small number of files. Like the ScanDisk utility, you should defragment a hard disk at least once a month if you are a moderate to heavy user, or when you start to notice that your computer is responding more slowly.

Using My Computer, you can periodically check information that Windows 95 keeps on the amount of fragmentation of each disk drive so that you can determine when to defragment a disk.

Teri asks you to check the amount of file fragmentation on the hard disk drive of one of your coworkers who is currently on vacation. When she worked on that computer earlier in the day, she noticed that its response time was quite slow.

If you are working on a computer that does not have a hard disk drive, then you will not be able to complete this section. Instead, you can continue with the Tutorial Assignment which follows this section.

To check information on a disk's fragmentation:

1. Double-click the **My Computer** icon.

2. In the My Computer window, right-click the **disk drive** icon for your hard disk drive, then click **Properties** on the shortcut menu.

3. In the Properties dialog box for your hard disk drive, click the **Tools** tab. The Tools property sheet reports on when you last checked your computer system's hard disk drive for errors, performed a backup of that disk drive, and optimized that disk by eliminating file fragmentation. See Figure 8-23.

Figure 8-23
Viewing the status of error-checking, backups, and defragment-ation on a hard disk drive

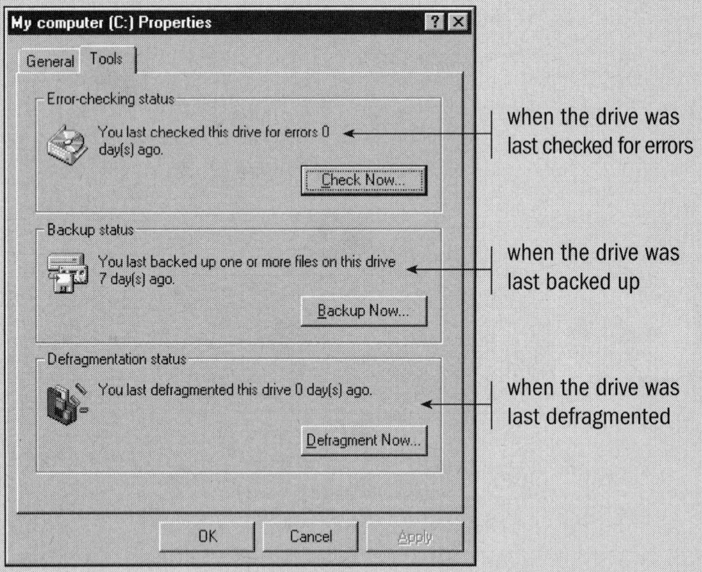

when the drive was last checked for errors

when the drive was last backed up

when the drive was last defragmented

If you click the Check Now, Backup Now, or Defragment Now button, you can start any of these three utilities from this dialog box.

4. After you examine the information on file fragmentation, you can either choose to defragment your hard disk now, or you can click the **OK** button to close the dialog box.

5. After you close the Properties dialog box or complete the defragmentation of your hard disk, click the **Close** button ☒ to close the My Computer window.

Tutorial Assignment

Teri just hired a new staff member, Michael Everett, to assist her with her duties as a telecommunications specialist. In order to bring Mike up to speed as fast as possible, she makes a copy of a client disk, then asks Mike to scan it for errors and defragment it. So that Mike knows how to recover deleted files, she also wants him to copy the client folder from the disk to drive C, open the client folder and delete the Sales sub-folder, then restore that subfolder from the Recycle Bin.

1. Insert your Student Disk into a floppy disk drive.
2. Open ScanDisk, then choose the name of your floppy disk drive from the ScanDisk dialog box.
3. If necessary, choose the Standard type of scan.
4. Open the Advanced Options dialog box and, if necessary, choose the options to always produce a summary, append the scan results to the current log, make copies of cross-linked files, convert lost clusters to files, and check files for invalid filenames. If you are working on a compressed disk drive, choose the option to check the host drive first. Then close the Advanced Options dialog box.

5. Start the scan and, when ScanDisk displays a summary of its results, press Alt + Print Screen, open Paint, paste the contents of the Clipboard, print the pasted image, then close Paint without saving the image.
6. Close any dialog boxes and return to the desktop.
7. Open the Recycle Bin Properties dialog box and, on the Global tab, verify that one setting is used for all drives, that deleted files are moved to the Recycle Bin, and that Windows 95 displays a delete confirmation dialog box prior to deleting files, then close this dialog box.
8. Open the My Computer window, open your floppy drive folder, then copy the MEI_Inc folder from your Student Disk to a hard disk drive.
9. Open the MEI_Inc folder on the hard disk drive, "accidentally" delete the Sales folder, and then verify the deletion.
10. Minimize the MEI_Inc folder, close the drive C window, then close the My Computer window.
11. Open the Recycle Bin, display the toolbar, and display the deleted files so that you know the original locations of the files.
12. Choose only the files you deleted, restore them to their original locations, and then close the Recycle Bin.
13. Open the MEI_Inc folder, verify that you have restored the contents of the Sales folder, then close the MEI_Inc folder and return to the desktop.
14. Open the Disk Defragmenter, then choose the drive that contains your Student Disk.
15. Open the Advanced Options dialog box and, if necessary, choose the options for a full defragmentation, checking the drive for errors, and using these set-tings just this time only, then close the dialog box.
16. Start the defragmentation, then choose the option for displaying details of the defragmentation process.
17. After the defragmentation is complete, close the Disk Defragmenter and return to the desktop.

Case Problems

1. Scanning a Hard Disk at Sheshmani's Carpet Care Center Sheshmani's Carpet Care Center is a small business that repairs and cleans carpets, rugs, draperies, and office partitions. Patrick Sydow, a partner in the company, uses a computer to handle all cus-tomer transactions, schedule work crews, track cash flow, and prepare tax statements. Since he maintains all the business records on this one computer, he periodically scans the hard disk drive and repairs any errors. While he is away on a short business trip, he asks you to scan his hard disk drive.

To complete this case problem, the computer you use must have a hard disk drive.

1. Open ScanDisk and select a hard disk drive on your computer.
2. Select the option for performing a Thorough test.
3. Open the Surface Scan Options dialog box, and if necessary, choose the option for scanning both the system and data areas. Also, choose the option for not repairing areas that contain hidden and system files, then close the dialog box.
4. Open the ScanDisk Advanced Options dialog box and, if necessary, choose the options to always display a summary, append the scan results to the current log, make copies of cross-linked files, convert lost clusters to files, and check files for invalid filenames. If you are working on a compressed disk drive, choose the option to check the host drive first. Then close the ScanDisk Advanced Options dialog box.
5. Start the scan of your hard disk drive.
6. When ScanDisk displays the ScanDisk Results dialog box, press Alt + Print Screen, open Paint, paste the contents of the Clipboard into Paint, print the pasted image, then close Paint without saving the image.
7. Close the ScanDisk Results dialog box, then close the ScanDisk dialog box and return to the desktop.
8. Open the My Computer window, then open the hard disk drive folder.
9. Check the hard disk drive for the presence of files that contain lost clusters. If present, the files will have names similar to File0000, File0001, File0002, and so on. Use the Notepad or WordPad application to open each of these files and examine their contents. If the files do not contain any important information, or if the files contain unreadable characters, then delete the files from the hard disk.

2. Defragmenting a Hard Disk at the Westside Radiology Medical Lab The Westside Radiology Medical Lab conducts specific tests, such as Computerized Tomography, Nuclear Medicine, Ultrasound Imaging, Magnetic Resonance Imaging (MRI), and general diagnostic X-rays, for physicians and hospitals who refer patients under their care. Marna Tennyson, a medical technician, uses one of the lab's computers to keep patient information and test results. Since the information on this computer is constantly being updated and changed, Marna uses the Disk Defragmenter once a month to eliminate file fragmentation and optimize the performance of the hard disk drive. Since she is going to be busy this week running a series of tests on patients, she asks you to defragment her hard disk drive.

To complete this case problem, the computer you use must have a hard disk drive.

1. Open the Properties dialog box for your hard disk drive, then select the Tools tab.
2. Press Alt + Print Screen, open Paint, paste the contents of the Clipboard into Paint, print the pasted image, then close Paint without saving the image.
3. On the Tools tab, click the Defragment Now button and, when the Disk Defragmenter dialog box opens, click the Select Drive button, choose the name of your hard disk drive from the Select Drive dialog box, then close the Select Drive dialog box.
4. Open the Advanced Options dialog box and, if necessary, choose the options for a full defragmentation, checking the drive for errors, and using these settings just this time only, then close the dialog box.
5. Start the defragmentation.
6. Choose the option for displaying details of the defragmentation process.
7. After the defragmentation is complete, close the Disk Defragmenter dialog box, close the Properties dialog box for your hard disk drive, close the My Computer window, and return to the desktop.

3. Recovering Folders at Data Recovery Services Data Recovery Services (DRS) is a small business that specializes in the recovery of data from damaged hard disks. Many of its customers are small business and home users who inadvertently delete data from their hard disk drives, and do not know how to recover that data. Abigail Noakes, a data recovery specialist, needs to recover a folder that a local small business owner accidentally deleted. She asks you to open the Recycle Bin and recover the folders while she attempts to recover data from another customer's hard disk drive that failed.

To complete this case problem, the computer you use must have a hard disk drive.

1. Open the Recycle Bin Properties dialog box, verify that deleted files will be moved to the Recycle Bin, then close this dialog box.
2. Insert your Student Disk into a floppy disk drive.
3. If the Recycle Bin does not contain any files that you think you might want to recover later, empty the Recycle Bin.
4. Open the My Computer window, then open the drive window for your floppy drive.
5. Copy the MEI_Inc folder from the disk to the hard disk on your computer.
6. Change the name of the MEI_Inc folder on the hard disk drive to DRS_Inc (do not include a period after "Inc").
7. Open the DRS_Inc folder, then delete the Budget, Loans, and Resource folders.
8. Minimize the DRS_Inc folder, then, if necessary, close the drive window and close the My Computer window.
9. Open the Recycle Bin, display the toolbar, then switch to Details view.
10. Double-click the border between the Original Location and Date Deleted columns to widen the Original Location column to accommodate the widest entry.
11. Adjust your view so that you can see the deleted files originally stored in the Budget, Loans, and Resource subfolders below the DRS_Inc folder.
12. Press Alt + Print Screen, open Paint, paste the contents of the Clipboard into Paint, print the pasted image, then close Paint without saving the image.
13. Choose the deleted files from the Budget and Loans folders, restore them to their original locations, then close the Recycle Bin.
14. Open the DRS_Inc folder from the taskbar, and verify that the Budget and Loans folder and their files were successfully restored to their original locations.
15. Since you no longer need the DRS_Inc folder on your hard disk, delete the folder and all its contents, then return to the desktop.

4. Recovering a Deleted File at Peninsula Business Forms Peninsula Business Forms designs a variety of forms, such as computer checks, invoices, labels, tags, mailers, letterhead, and envelopes, for its customers. Kyle Lebakos, one of Peninsula Business Forms' designers, deleted a folder that contained invoice formats which he thought the company no longer used. However, after deleting this folder, he discovered that it contained a file with an invoice format popular among customers. While he completes the other forms he needs to design today, he asks you to recover this deleted file.

To complete this case problem, the computer you use must have a hard disk drive.

1. Open the Recycle Bin Properties dialog box, verify that deleted files will be moved to the Recycle Bin, then close this dialog box.
2. Insert your Student Disk into a floppy disk drive.
3. If the Recycle Bin does not contain any files that you think you might want to recover later, empty the Recycle Bin.
4. Open the My Computer window, then open the drive window for your floppy disk drive.
5. Copy the MEI_Inc folder from the floppy disk to the hard disk on your computer.
6. Change the name of the MEI_Inc folder to PBF_Inc (do not include a period after "Inc").
7. Open the PBF_Inc folder, then delete the Invoices folder.
8. Minimize the PBF_Inc folder, then, if necessary, close the drive window and close the My Computer window.
9. Open the Recycle Bin, display the toolbar, then switch to Details view.

10. Double-click the border between the Original Location and Date Deleted columns to widen the Original Location column to accommodate the widest entry.

11. Adjust your view so that you can see the deleted files originally stored in the Invoices subfolder below the PBF_Inc folder.

12. Press Alt + Print Screen, open Paint, paste the contents of the Clipboard into Paint, print the pasted image, then close Paint without saving the image.

13. Choose the deleted file named Invoices.wk4, restore it to its original location, then close the Recycle Bin.

14. Open the PBF_Inc folder and verify that the file named Invoices.wk4 is stored in the recreated Invoices folder.

15. Since you no longer need the PBF_Inc folder on your hard disk, delete the folder and all its contents, then return to the desktop.

Working with Applications

Preparing a Company Logo

CASE

Visual Arts, Inc.

Visual Arts, Inc. is one of the largest graphics design agencies on the East Coast. Over the last five years, the company has experienced a phenomenal rate of growth. Brandon Tolbert is a graphics artist who has worked at Visual Arts since its inception, and now oversees the work of all the designers at the firm. Many of their projects call for them to build documents that include objects from different applications, like a brochure created in a desktop publishing package that includes document files created in a word processor and graphics files created in graphics packages. Brandon and his staff have found that Windows 95 makes it easy to move objects among documents, no matter what application created them.

Now that Brandon is in management he no longer works actively in the design department, so he no longer keeps the complex, memory-intensive and space-demanding graphics design packages on his computer. He does, however, use the quicker and smaller Windows 95 applets like Paint and WordPad when he wants to draft quick suggestions for his design department to implement.

Naomi Morita, the president of Visual Arts, has asked Brandon and his staff to design a new company logo. She wants him to develop a couple of designs and then circulate them among the other employees at Visual Arts.

Like Windows 3.1, Windows 95 includes a set of accessories, called **applets**, that provide access to features commonly found in major types of applications, but applets take less space and make far fewer demands on a computer system than full-featured applications. Depending on your installation of Windows 95, you might or might not have access to the following applets:

■ **WordPad** is a word processing application similar to Microsoft Word 6.0 and the Write application included in Windows 3.1.

■ **Paint** is a graphics application similar to Paintbrush in Windows 3.1. With Paint, you can create freeform drawings, and you can insert graphics images from the Clipboard or from other files.

■ **Clipboard Viewer**, which allows you to view the contents of the Clipboard in different file formats and, if you prefer, save the contents of the Clipboard to a file on disk, and **Clipbook**, a network utility, which allows you to cut and paste images locally or across a network.

- **Character Map** allows you to select symbols from different font sets, place the symbols on the Clipboard, and then insert them into documents that you are preparing.

- **Quick View,** a tool that you have already used, allows you to view the contents of files without opening the files.

- **Calculator** is an application that simulates a hand-held calculator and allows you to perform simple and complex calculations.

- **Phone Dialer** allows you to dial telephone numbers using a telephone line connected to your computer. You can store commonly used telephone numbers so you can speed dial those numbers, and you can keep a log of telephone calls.

- **HyperTerminal** is a communications program that allows you to connect to another computer system, such as an online service, that is not using Windows 95.

- **Dial-up Networking** allows you to use your computer at work, home, or on the road to connect to a computer network that is running Windows 95 so that you can access files and network resources, such as printers.

- **Direct Cable Connection** allows you to establish a parallel or serial connection between two computers. You specify whether the computer you are using is the **host**–the computer with the resources you want to access–or the **guest**–the computer you will use to access resources from a host computer. Then, the application makes the connection for you.

- **Winpopup** and **Chat** allow you to send and receive messages over a network.

- **Net Watcher** allows you to monitor the network server and network connections.

- **System Monitor** allows you to visually monitor the performance of your computer system with color charts. For example, you can view the number of concurrent processes managed by the operating system.

- **Resource Meter** allows you to view system resource levels. When activated, it places an icon on the taskbar. When you double-click the icon, you see a status report on the percentage of system resources currently in use.

- **ScanDisk,** a utility for analyzing and repairing disk errors.

- **Backup,** a utility for backing up all or part of a hard disk to tape or floppy disks.

- **Defragmenter,** a utility for optimizing the performance of a disk by eliminating file fragmentation and empty space between files.

- **DriveSpace,** a utility that increases the storage space on a hard disk from 60–100% by creating a compressed drive.

If you are running the Microsoft Plus! pack, you will find:

- An enhanced **DriveSpace** disk compression utility that supports compressed drives up to 2GB in size and higher compression rates.

- **Compression Agent** that compresses files and disks when your computer is idle, rather than when you are working on a file.

- **System Agent,** a scheduling program that runs programs, such as ScanDisk and Compression Agent, at scheduled times.

All these tools provide you with a wide variety of resources, and enrich your working environment.

Installing and Uninstalling Applications

Brandon and his staff meet and discuss possible designs for the new company logo. After agreeing on two ideas, Brandon decides to use Paint to draft the logos. After, he will use WordPad to prepare a memo to all staff, and insert copies of his logo designs into the memo. He asks you to get started for him while he hurries to a meeting. Before you can create the memo, you must install WordPad on your computer.

In a standard installation of Windows 95, the most common applets are already included, but if you or your network administrator were short on space when installing Windows 95, you might have opted to leave them out. Windows 95 makes it easy to install software applications and utilities on your computer and, if disk space is a premium, to remove applications and utilities. You can use the Add/Remove Programs Wizard to install software from floppy disk drives and CD-ROM drives. For programs designed for Windows 95, the installation process for a Windows application involves few or no steps other than inserting the disks or CD-ROM disc required for the installation.

HELP DESK

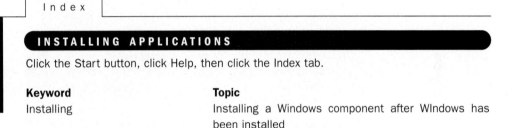

Index

INSTALLING APPLICATIONS

Click the Start button, click Help, then click the Index tab.

Keyword	Topic
Installing	Installing a Windows component after WIndows has been installed

If you know that WordPad is already installed on the computer you are using, skip the remainder of this section and continue with the section entitled "Multitasking, Task-Switching, and Multithreading."

Since WordPad is included with the Accessories component of Windows 95, you can check the Accessories menu to determine if this application is already installed.

To determine if WordPad is already installed on your computer:

1. Click the **Start** button, point to **Programs**, then point to **Accessories** on the Program menu. Windows 95 displays the Accessories menu. See Figure 9-1.

Figure 9-1 ◄
Accessories
menu

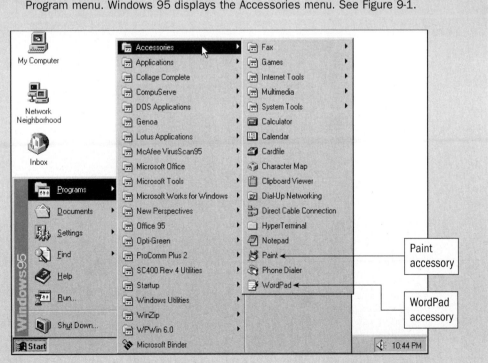

2. Check the Accessories menu for WordPad.

3. Click the **Start** button again to close the Start menu.

If WordPad is listed on the Accessories menu, skip to the next section entitled "Multitasking, Task-switching, and Multithreading." If it is not listed on the Accessories menu, then you need to install this application. *To install this application, you must have access to the Windows 95 CD-ROM installation disc, or the Windows 95 installation disks. If you do not have the Windows 95 installation CD-ROM disc or the disks, then you will not be able to complete the majority of this tutorial.*

If you are working in a computer lab, skip the following steps, because Windows 95 suggests that you restart your computer after you install an accessory. Instead, ask your system administrator to install it if it is not already installed.

To install WordPad on your computer:

1. Double-click **My Computer**, double-click the **Control Panel** folder, then click the **Maximize** button ▢ .

2. Double-click the **Add/Remove Programs** icon. The Add/Remove Programs Properties dialog box opens. You can install and uninstall applications on the Install/Uninstall tab, shown in Figure 9-2. The Uninstall box lists the names of applications that Windows 95 can automatically remove from your computer.

Figure 9-2 ◀
The property
sheet for
installing and
uninstalling
applications

applications that
Windows 95
can uninstall
(yours will differ)

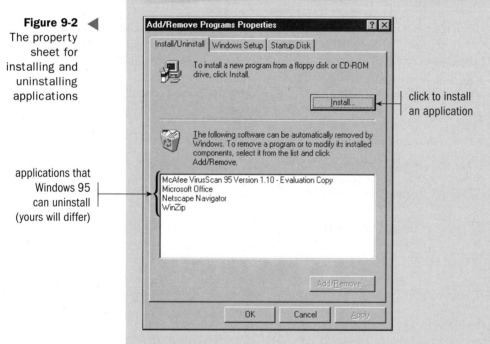

click to install
an application

If you do not see the name of an application that you want to remove in this box, check the documentation that came with that application so you know how to remove it properly from your computer.

3. Click the **Windows Setup** tab. The Components list box displays the Windows 95 components that you can install on your computer system. See Figure 9-3.

Figure 9-3 ◀
The property
sheet for
installing and
uninstalling
Windows
components

components that
you can install

description of
selected component

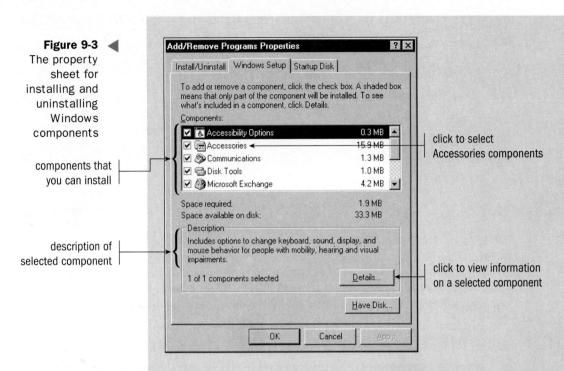

click to select
Accessories components

click to view information
on a selected component

If there is a check mark on a white background in the selection box to the left
of a component name, all of the applications included with that component are
already installed. If the selection box is partially shaded, then some of the
applications for that component are installed, but others are not installed. If the
selection box is empty, then none of the applications for that component are
installed.

4. In the Components list box, click **Accessories**, then click the **Details** button. The
Accessories dialog box lists the accessories included with Windows 95. See
Figure 9-4.

Figure 9-4 ◀
Selecting
accessories
to install

accessories (your list
might not have all
accessories selected)

description of
selected accessory

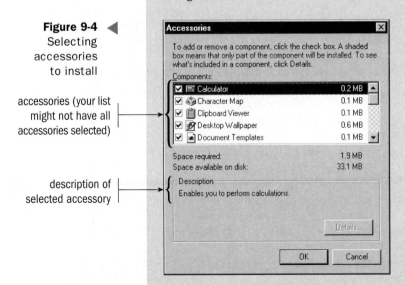

5. In the Components list box, locate the WordPad component, click the **selection
box** to the left of the WordPad component, then click the **OK** button in the
Accessories dialog box.

6. Insert the original Windows 95 installation disk if prompted, then click the **OK** button. After Windows 95 installs WordPad, the System Settings Change dialog box informs you that you must restart the computer before the settings take effect.

7. Click the **Yes** button to verify that you want to restart your computer.

8. When you see the desktop, click the **Control Panel** taskbar button, then click the **Close** button ⊠ to close the Control Panel.

You can also use the Add/Remove Programs Wizard to remove Windows 95 applications, but not DOS or Windows 3.1 applications. If a software application comes with an uninstall utility, you should use that utility to remove the software application from your computer, rather than merely deleting the folder or folders that contain the software application. During the installation of a Windows application, supporting files are copied to different folders on your hard disk drive, not just to the folder that contains the software application. An uninstall utility will locate and remove all files that were originally installed with that application, no matter where they are stored.

HELP DESK

Index

UNINSTALLING APPLICATIONS

Click the Start button, click Help, then click the Index tab.

Keyword
Removing

Topic
To remove a program from your computer

REFERENCE
window

INSTALLING AND UNINSTALLING APPLICATIONS

- Click the Start button, point to Settings, then click the Control Panel folder.
- After the Control Panel window opens, double-click the Add/Remove Programs icon.
- If you want to install an application from a floppy disk or CD-ROM disc, click the Install button on the Install/Uninstall property sheet of the Add/Remove Programs Properties dialog box and follow the directions provided by Windows 95.
- If you want to remove a Windows 95 application, or change its installation, select the application in the Add/Remove list box, then click the Add/Remove button and follow the directions provided by Windows 95.
- If you want to install a Windows 95 component and are not working on a network, click the Windows Setup tab, click the selection box for the group that contains the Windows 95 component you want to install, click the Details button, click the selection box for the Windows 95 component, then click the OK button and follow the directions provided by Windows 95. Note: If you are working in a networked environment, the network administrator handles the installation of software.
- Click the OK button to close the Add/Remove Properties dialog box.

After returning from his meeting, Brandon thanks you for installing WordPad on his computer.

Multitasking, Task-switching, and Multithreading

In today's workplaces individuals increasingly look for more ways to improve their productivity and meet important deadlines critical to the success of their businesses. Brandon, for example, works with graphics, text, and data in several different applications at a time to produce documents. He needs to be able to switch rapidly from one application to the next and to move from document to document within an application to extract information. Furthermore, because many different demands are made on his time, he must initiate a task in one application and, while that application performs the task, switch to another application and continue working. For example, he might put the finishing touches on a long document, then print that document in the background while he begins the next document with yet another application.

The Windows 95 operating system supports three features that meet Brandon's needs: multitasking, task-switching, and multithreading. **Multitasking** is an operating system feature that permits you to open and use more than one application at the same time. Windows 95 therefore supports multiple tasks, or what Microsoft calls multiple **processes**, by allocating a share of the system resources to each application that you open. Although each application or task does not run at exactly the same time, the operating system handles each process so that each application or task thinks it is the only process that is running. Depending on the type of system you use, this sharing of the microprocessor and other system resources might happen so fast that you have the impression that the tasks are running simultaneously. Another advantage of multitasking is that you can also **task-switch**, or change, from one application to another so that you can work with different applications and documents at the same time.

Windows 3.1 supports cooperative multitasking, while Windows 95 supports both cooperative and preemptive multitasking. In the Windows 3.1 **cooperative multitasking environment**, the currently running application periodically relinquishes control of system resources so that the operating environment can permit another application access to those same system resources. Once the currently running application yields control to the operating system, you can then switch to, and use, another running application. This approach has its disadvantages. You must wait until a running application completes a task and yields control to the operating system so that another application's task can start. For example, you might have to wait for a spreadsheet application to calculate values for a complex loan analysis table before you can use your communications software to connect to an on-line service. As one process operates, you wait for the hourglass to change to a pointer so that you can then perform some other function. Another disadvantage of working in a cooperative multitasking environment is that the entire system might crash if the currently running application crashes.

In the Windows 95 **preemptive multitasking environment**, the Windows 95 operating system assigns priorities to the processes that it manages and decides at any given point in time whether to take control away from, or give control to, an application. This approach provides a more stable and reliable operating environment. However, this type of multitasking works only with Win32-based applications. Continuing with the earlier example, while your spreadsheet application calculates values for a complex loan analysis table, you can switch to your communications software, connect to an on-line service, and download files. To provide backwards compatibility with applications designed for earlier versions of Windows, Windows 95 cooperatively multitasks those applications.

Another important feature of preemptive multitasking for newer Win32-based applications is **multithreading**, the ability of an operating system to execute more than one sequence of program code for a single application at the same time. When you run an application that supports multithreading, the operating system manages a single task or process. Within that process, the operating system supports the execution of one or more **threads**, or units of program code, for that application. The net effect is that multi-threading improves the speed of the applications that you run. For example, in a spread-sheet application, one thread might be recalculating a complex table of values while another thread updates a three-dimensional chart produced from those calculations. Although Windows 95 supports the use of multithreading, the application you use must also support multithreading.

In the future, computer systems will allow **symmetric multiprocessing.** In a computer system with more than one microprocessor, each thread can execute simultaneously in a different processor, thereby further improving the performance and speed of your system. Today's microcomputers rely on one microprocessor that might receive assistance for complex graphics or numerical calculations from a co-processor. Future microprocessors will shift between multiple tasks so quickly that the user thinks each application's task is occurring simultaneously. For operating systems like Windows NT (but not Windows 95) that currently support symmetric multiprocessing and that operate on computers with more than one microprocessor, each microprocessor can be assigned a separate task and be performing those tasks simultaneously.

Multitasking and Task-switching

In a few days, Brandon will join other company representatives for contract negotiations with a new client. He needs to prepare a schedule of that day's events. While he attends a preparatory meeting for the new contract negotiations, Brandon asks you to prepare a schedule for him for the day of the contract negotiations. He also wants you to locate and print the preliminary design of a new company logo to which he can make the agreed-upon changes.

First, you will open WordPad, then open Find. While you are using WordPad to produce the schedule, the Find feature can look for the copy of the design for the company logo.

To open WordPad and Find:

1. If necessary, close all open applications and dialog boxes, and return to the desktop. Be sure you are using the correct Student Disk for this tutorial, identified in the "Read This Before You Begin" page at the beginning of this book.

2. Insert your Student Disk in a floppy disk drive.

3. Click the **Start** button, point to **Programs**, point to **Accessories**, then click **WordPad** on the Accessories menu. The WordPad application window opens. See Figure 9-5.

Figure 9-5 ◀
WordPad
application
window

menu bar ——

toolbar ——

format bar ——

ruler bar ——

status bar ——

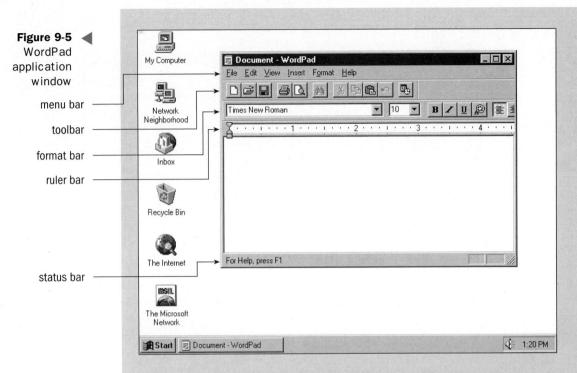

4. Click the **Start** button, point to **Find**, then click **Files or Folders** on the Find menu. The Find: All Files window opens. See Figure 9-6.

Figure 9-6 ◀
Opening the
Find: All Files
window

enter name of file
or folder to locate

click to start
search

click to select
floppy disk drive

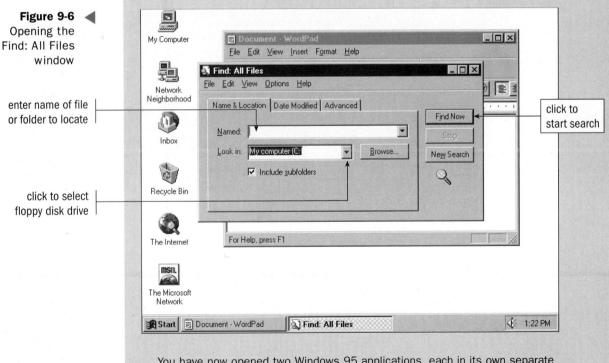

You have now opened two Windows 95 applications, each in its own separate window. Next, you want to adjust your view so that you can see both windows.

5. Right-click an empty area of the taskbar. Windows 95 displays a shortcut menu that contains three options for arranging open windows. See Figure 9-7.

Figure 9-7 ◀
Tiling windows

Find: All Files window ———

Find: All Files
taskbar button

WordPad
taskbar button

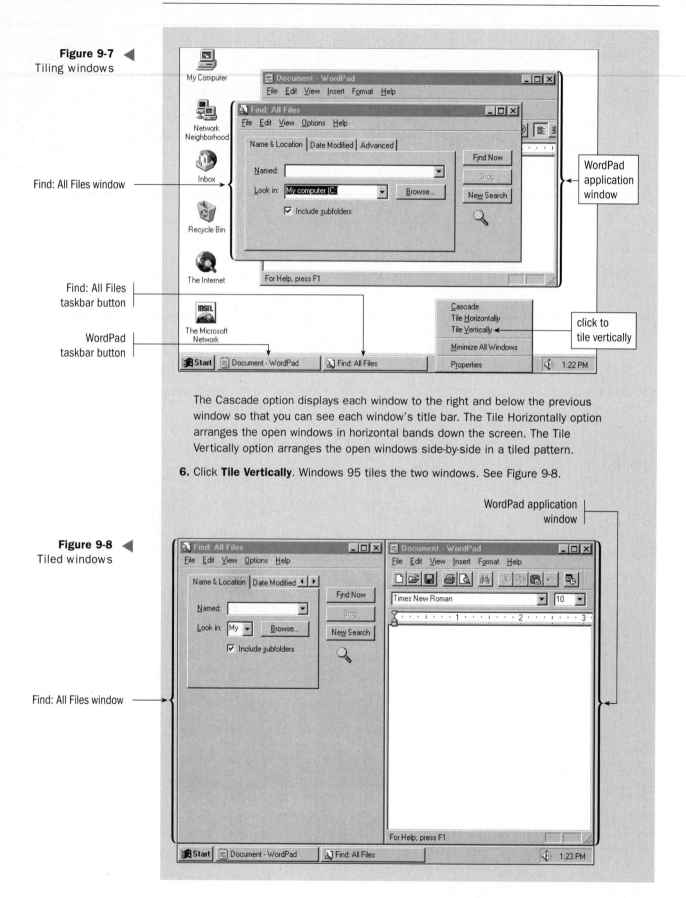

WordPad
application
window

click to
tile vertically

The Cascade option displays each window to the right and below the previous window so that you can see each window's title bar. The Tile Horizontally option arranges the open windows in horizontal bands down the screen. The Tile Vertically option arranges the open windows side-by-side in a tiled pattern.

6. Click **Tile Vertically**. Windows 95 tiles the two windows. See Figure 9-8.

WordPad application
window

Figure 9-8 ◀
Tiled windows

Find: All Files window

Now you can start the Find operation and, while Windows 95 is looking for the file you want to print, you can create a short schedule in WordPad.

To multitask:

1. Click the **title bar** of the Find: All Files window to select this application, then click the **Maximize** button ⬜ of the Find: All Files window.

2. Click the **Look in** list arrow, click the **icon** for drive A (or drive B), then click the **OK** button to continue.

3. Click the **Restore** button 🗗 to restore the Find: All Files window to its original size.

4. In the Named text box, type **Logo**, click the **Find Now** button, then click the **title bar** for the WordPad application window. Notice that Windows 95 continues its search for the file with the company logo in the Find: Files named Logo window even though WordPad is now the active window.

5. Type **SCHEDULE** then press the **Enter** key three times.

6. Press the **Spacebar** twice, type **7:00 AM**, press the **Tab** key, type **Design Meeting**, then press the **Enter** key.

7. Press the **Spacebar** twice, type **9:00 AM**, press the **Tab** key, type **Client Meeting**, then press the **Enter** key.

8. Type **12:00 PM**, press the **Tab** key, type **Client Lunch**, then press the **Enter** key.

9. Press the **Spacebar** twice, type **3:00 PM**, press the **Tab** key, then type **Conference Call**. Your final schedule should look like the one in Figure 9-9.

Figure 9-9 ◄
Your final
document

Brandon's schedule —

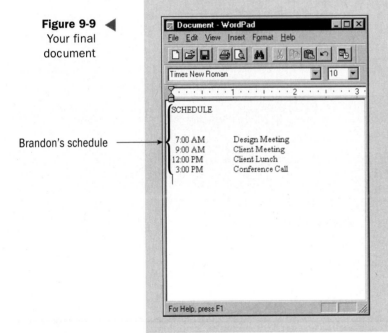

By this time, Find should have already located the file named VAI_Logo.Bmp on your Student Disk and stopped searching. As you work with these two applications, Windows 95 is multitasking. While one application searches for a file in the background, you are creating a new document in another application. Now that you have completed the schedule, you can save it.

Using Long Filenames

If you use applications designed for Windows 95, then you can use long filenames to more clearly identify the contents and use of a file. A long filename can be up to 255 characters in length and can include special symbols or characters, such as the ampersand (&), pound sign (#), dollar sign ($), percentage symbol (%), apostrophes (' and '), as well as opening and closing parentheses and spaces.

If you assign a long filename to a file, Windows 95 automatically creates an alias that provides backward compatibility with DOS and Windows 3.1, or Win16, applications. An **alias** is an MS-DOS filename that follows the rules and conventions for 8.3 filenames (that is, names that allow 8 characters and then a 3-character extension). An alias consists of the first six characters of the long filename, followed by a tilde (~) and then a number and the first three characters after the last period in a long filename. Any spaces in a long filename are not used in the alias. For example, if you had a folder named Visual Arts, Inc., Windows 95 would assign it an alias of VISUAL~1. A file named Company Logo (2).Bmp becomes COMPAN~1.BMP. Note that mixed case and lowercase are converted to uppercase. If the alias name already exists, then an **algorithm**, or formula, increments the number until a unique filename is found. For example, if you have three Microsoft Word files named "Memo to CEO on Quarterly Report," "Memo to CEO on Monthly Planning Meeting," and "Memo to CEO on Staff Benefits," Windows 95 would assign them respective aliases of MEMOTO~1.DOC, MEMOTO~2.DOC, and MEMOTO~3.DOC. You and the applications that you use cannot determine the alias that Windows 95 assigns for long filenames. If you use a filename that follows the 8.3 filenaming convention for DOS and Win16 applications, then the long filename and alias are the same.

The use of aliases is a necessary feature because many applications do not yet support long filenames. The folder and filenames on the Student Disks in this book all conform to the old 8.3 rule for this very reason: networks at some colleges and universities might not yet accommodate long filenames.

Microsoft recommends that you limit your use of long filenames in the root directory or top-level folder of a disk, because the initial formatting of a disk limits the number of files that the root directory or folder can track. The file that contains the information on files that you see in the root directory or top-level folder is a fixed size. If you use long filenames, you use up more of the storage space allocated for filenames and therefore cannot store as many files in the root directory.

To save the schedule:

1. If you do not see a toolbar below the WordPad menu bar, click **View** on the menu bar, then click **Toolbar**.

2. In the WordPad application window, click the **Save** button 🖫 on the toolbar.

3. When the Save As dialog box opens, click the **Save in** list arrow, then click the **disk drive** icon of the drive that contains your Student Disk.

4. In the Save in list box, double-click the **Vai** folder. Windows 95 opens the Vai folder and shows you the names of the subfolders.

5. In the Save in list box, locate and double-click the **Staff** folder.

6. In the File name text box, double-click **Document.doc**.

   TROUBLE? Your system might not be configured to display file extensions. Don't worry if they don't appear throughout this tutorial.

7. If the computer you are using supports the use of long filenames, type **Brandon's Schedule.wri** as your filename; otherwise, type **Schedule.wri**. *Do not type the period after Schedule.wri.*

8. Click the **Save** button.

9. Click the **Close** button ⊠ to close WordPad and your document.

Now you can switch to the Find: All Files named Logo window, and open the file that contains the design of the company logo.

To select and open the file with the logo:

1. Click the **title bar** for the Find: All Files named Logo window, then click the **Maximize** button ◻. Windows 95 found one file, VAI_Logo.Bmp in the Designs folder. See Figure 9-10.

Figure 9-10 ◀
Opening a
found file

double-click to
open Paint file

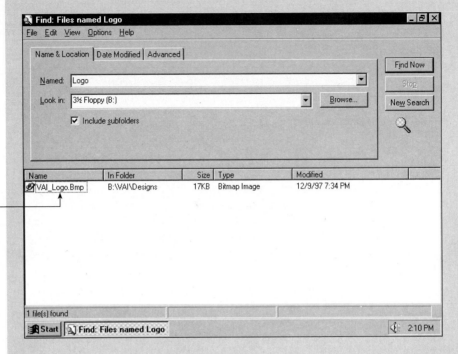

2. Double-click **VAI_Logo.Bmp**. Windows 95 opens the Paint application, and then opens VAI_Logo.Bmp. See Figure 9-11. Windows 95 associates the file extension Bmp with the Paint application. Now, you can print a copy of this logo design.

Visual Arts, Inc. logo

Figure 9-11 ◀
Viewing
a design
for the new
company logo

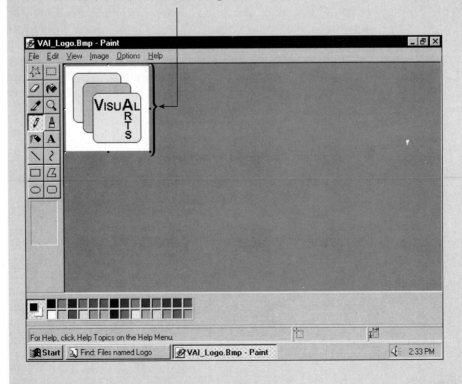

3. Make sure your printer is on and operational.

4. Click **File** on the menu bar, click **Print**, and when the Print dialog box opens, click the **OK** button.

5. Click the **Close** button to close the Paint window. You return to the Find: All Files named Logo window.

6. Click the **Close** button ☒ to close the window.

REFERENCE
window

TO MULTITASK AND TASK-SWITCH:

- Open the first application that you want to use, then open one or more documents that you created with this application.
- Open each of the next applications that you want to use, then open one or more documents that you created with each of these applications.
- To switch to another application, click the taskbar button for that application.
- To switch to another document within the same application, use the application's Window menu.

If you open and then print a multi-page document or a document with graphics, you can print the document in the background and open another application and file and continue to work. With the multitasking feature in Windows 95, you do not have to wait until a document prints before you can perform another task on your computer system.

Placing Documents on the Desktop

If you want immediate access to a document, you can drag a copy of that document onto the desktop. Then you can open the document by double-clicking it. After you double-click, Windows 95 locates and opens the application, then the file that contains the document. This feature is useful if you work with the same document each day or if you have important documents that you might need to access in a hurry. Also, you can use this feature to place reminders on the desktop. For example, if you keep a list of scheduled appointments in a file, you can drag a copy of the file onto the desktop. Then, when you need to check an appointment or add another appointment to your schedule, you can double-click the desktop icon and open the file with this information.

So that Brandon can easily locate his schedule, you decide to place a reminder on his desktop.

To copy the WordPad file with Brandon's schedule to the desktop:

1. Double-click the **shortcut** to your floppy disk drive or, if you removed the short-cut, double-click **My Computer**, then double-click the **disk drive** icon for your floppy disk drive. You now see the Vai folder in the floppy drive window.

2. Double-click the **Vai** folder. Next, you see the folders within this folder.

3. Double-click the **Staff** folder. Now you see the files contained with this folder. See Figure 9-12.

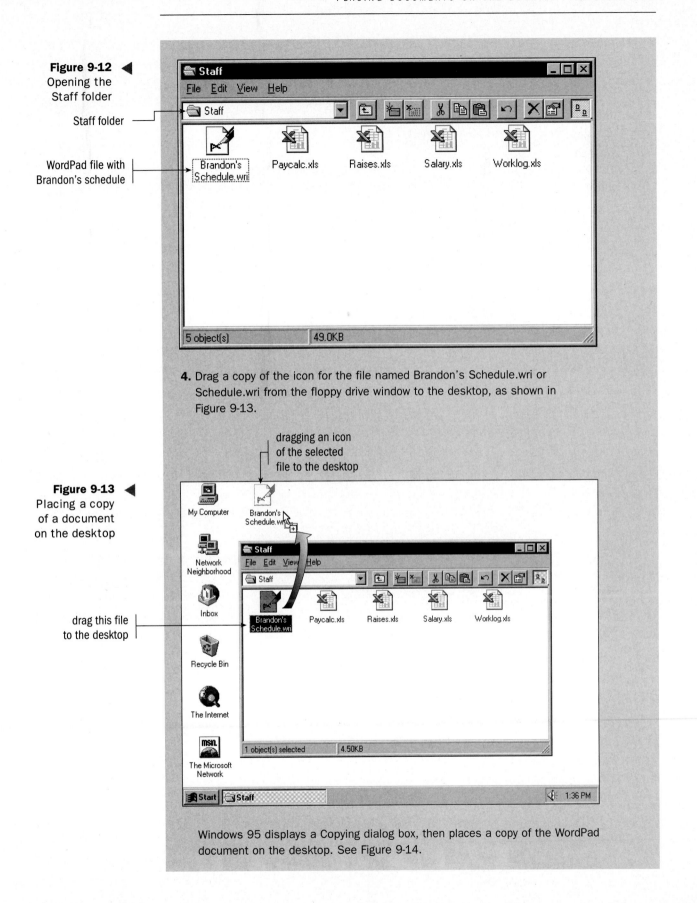

Figure 9-12 ◀
Opening the
Staff folder

Staff folder —

WordPad file with
Brandon's schedule

4. Drag a copy of the icon for the file named Brandon's Schedule.wri or
Schedule.wri from the floppy drive window to the desktop, as shown in
Figure 9-13.

dragging an icon
of the selected
file to the desktop

Figure 9-13 ◀
Placing a copy
of a document
on the desktop

drag this file
to the desktop

Windows 95 displays a Copying dialog box, then places a copy of the WordPad
document on the desktop. See Figure 9-14.

Figure 9-14
Copy of
schedule file
placed on
desktop

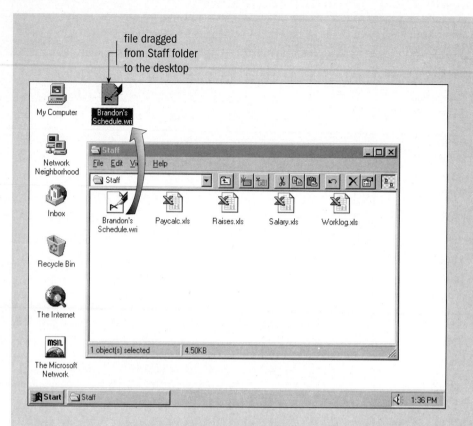

5. Close the floppy drive window, then, if necessary, close the My Computer window.

6. Double-click the **desktop** icon for the file named Brandon's Schedule.wri or Schedule.wri. Windows 95 opens WordPad, and displays the contents of the file in the WordPad application window. See Figure 9-15. Brandon now has a way to quickly view his schedule for that day.

Figure 9-15
Opening the file
with Brandon's
schedule

copy of Brandon's
schedule in WordPad
application window

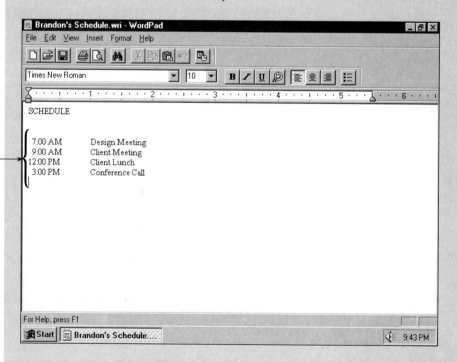

7. Click the **Close** button to close the WordPad application window and return to the desktop.

The object-oriented approach of Windows 95 simplifies operations like the one that you just performed. You can also drag copies of folders to the desktop, so that you can double-click the folder to open it and view its contents. If you open and work with the same folder on a daily basis, you can save yourself time and effort. You do not need to first open My Computer, then open a drive window. You do, however, have to decide how many shortcuts you want on your desktop, because your desktop might become cluttered. Figure 9-16 shows the contents of Brandon's desktop. He organizes his desktop icons and shortcuts into groups that include system tools, Windows applications, utilities, DOS applications, folders and files, and drives. By organizing his tools into logical groups, he can more easily find what he needs.

Figure 9-16
How Brandon organizes his desktop

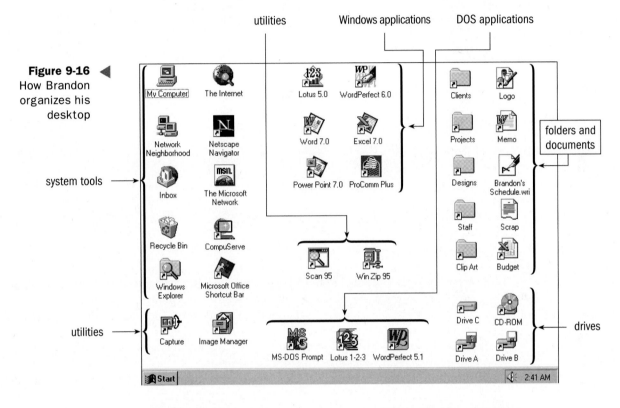

Creating a Company Logo with Paint

Using the preliminary design for the new company logo as a guideline, Brandon wants you to use the Paint application to draft a new logo and then to circulate a memo containing the logo to all staff, asking them for their opinions.

To open Paint:

1. Click the **Start** button, point to **Programs**, point to **Accessories**, then click **Paint** on the Accessories menu. The Paint application window opens. See Figure 9-17.

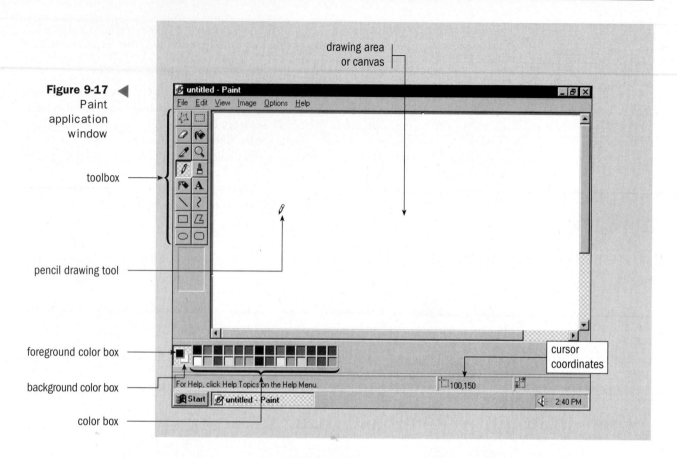

Figure 9-17 ◀
Paint
application
window

The majority of the application window consists of the drawing area, or canvas, where you create or modify a drawing. On the left side of the application window, below the title and menu bars, is a tool box that contains various tools for creating drawings. If you point to one of the buttons in the tool box, a ToolTip appears, identifying the name and purpose of the tool. Near the bottom of the window is a color box from which you can choose foreground and background colors.

You want to start by choosing black as the foreground color and a shade of red as the background color. Then, you want to draw the first of the three shapes for the logo, the red square with a black border.

To draw a red square with a black border:

1. Click the **black color box** in the first row of the left corner of the color box, then right-click the pink or **lighter shade of red color box** in the second row in the right corner of the color box. To the left of the color box, you see the foreground and background colors you selected. See Figure 9-18.

Figure 9-18
Selecting
foreground and
background
colors

click to use as
foreground color

foreground color

background color

right-click to use as
background color

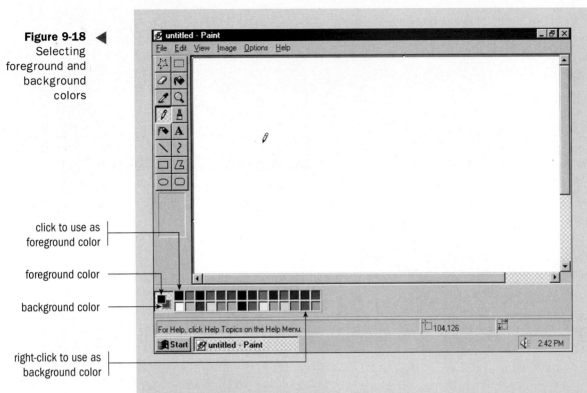

2. Click the **Rectangle tool** button near the bottom of the first column of the tool box. Below the tool box, Paint displays three types of shapes that you can produce with this tool: a hollow rectangle, a filled rectangle with a border, and a filled rectangle without a border. See Figure 9-19.

Figure 9-19
Choosing the
Rectangle tool

click to use
Rectangle tool

click to select a
filled rectangle
with a border

cursor

current cursor
coordinates

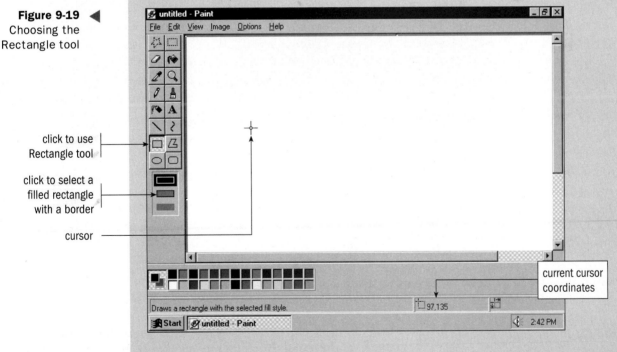

3. Click the **filled rectangle with a border** in the box below the tool box. To assist you in positioning and defining the area for an object, Paint displays cursor coordinate boxes on the status bar. The first of the two boxes shows your starting position, the second the area you are defining as you drag the mouse.

If you hold the Shift key while you draw a shape, then Paint constrains that shape. For example, when you draw with the Ellipse tool and the Shift key, you produce a perfect circle.

4. Position the mouse pointer + near the coordinates 50,50 in the drawing area, press and hold the **Shift** key, drag the mouse to the right and down until you extend the square to 75x75 then release the mouse button and the Shift key. The square you draw should be similar to the one shown in Figure 9-20.

Figure 9-20
Drawing a square with a black border and filled with red color

square pasted onto canvas

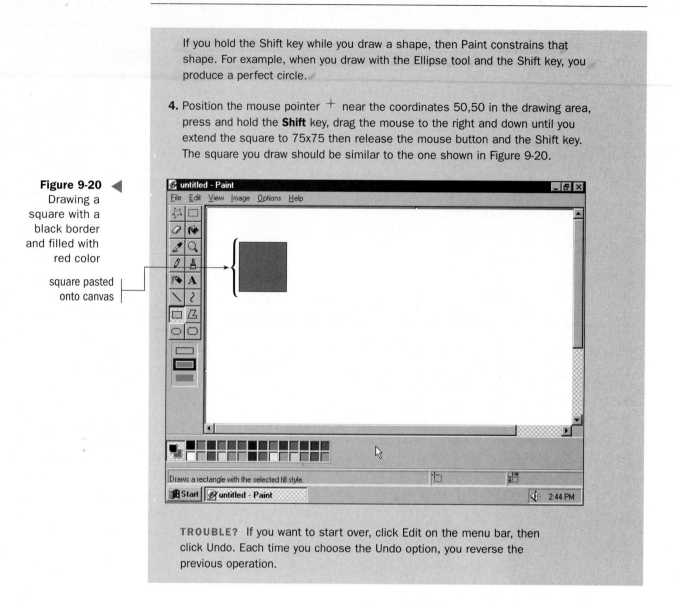

TROUBLE? If you want to start over, click Edit on the menu bar, then click Undo. Each time you choose the Undo option, you reverse the previous operation.

The coordinates are measured in pels or pixels, both abbreviations for picture elements. A **pel** or **pixel** is the smallest element on a video display screen for displaying a color. On a color display, a combination of red, green, and blue phosphors constitutes a pel. When electrons strike the red, green, and blue phosphors, a solid color or shade appears on the video display.

Next, you want to draw a bright blue rounded square with a black border to the right and below the red square. As you draw this object, you want it to overlap and cover part of the red square. Then, you want to draw a light yellow circle with a black border in the center of the two squares.

To draw the blue rounded square:

1. Right-click the **bright blue color box** in the second row of the color box.

2. Click the **Rounded Rectangle tool** button in the second column of the tool box, then click the **filled rectangle with a border** in the box below the tool box.

3. Position the mouse pointer + near the coordinates 85,85 in the drawing area, press and hold the **Shift** key, drag the mouse to the right and down until you extend the square to 75x75, then release the mouse button and the Shift key. The square you draw should be similar to the one shown in Figure 9-21.

Figure 9-21
Drawing a
rounded square
with a black
border and
filled with
blue color

rounded square
pasted onto canvas

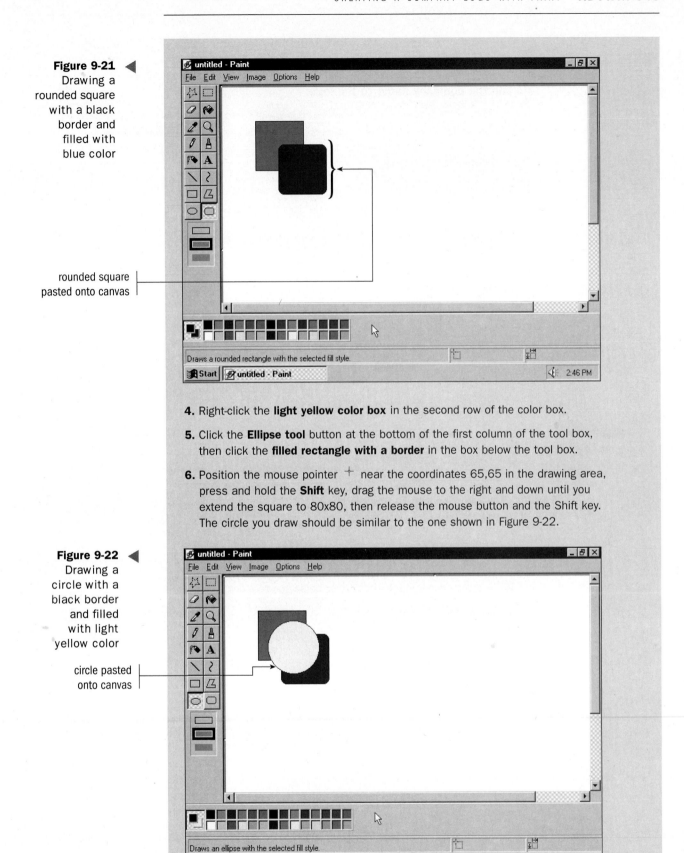

4. Right-click the **light yellow color box** in the second row of the color box.

5. Click the **Ellipse tool** button at the bottom of the first column of the tool box, then click the **filled rectangle with a border** in the box below the tool box.

6. Position the mouse pointer ✛ near the coordinates 65,65 in the drawing area, press and hold the **Shift** key, drag the mouse to the right and down until you extend the square to 80x80, then release the mouse button and the Shift key. The circle you draw should be similar to the one shown in Figure 9-22.

Figure 9-22
Drawing a
circle with a
black border
and filled
with light
yellow color

circle pasted
onto canvas

To complete the design, you want to add the company name, Visual Arts, in the center of the circle.

To add the company name to the logo:

1. Click the **Text tool** button. In the box below the tool box, Paint displays two options for adding text. See Figure 9-23. The first option displays the text on the background color; the second displays the text against the background color already on the canvas.

click to use Text tool

Figure 9-23
Selecting the
Text tool

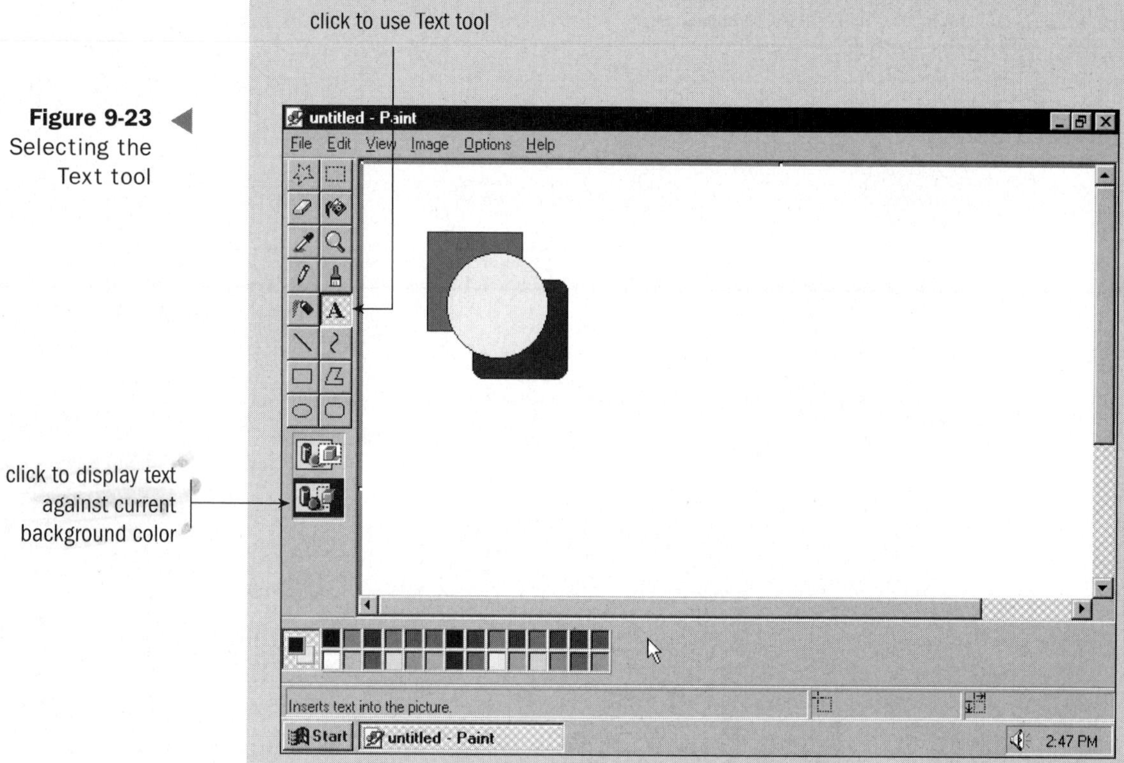

click to display text
against current
background color

2. Click the second option in the box below the tool box.

3. Click in the upper-left corner of the light yellow circle, as shown in Figure 9-24. Paint displays a selection rectangle and the Text toolbar.

Figure 9-24 ◀
Entering text

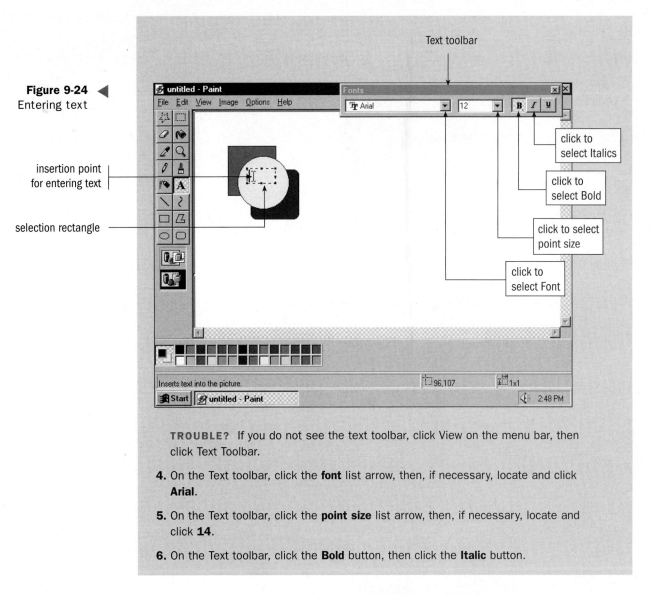

Text toolbar

insertion point
for entering text

selection rectangle

click to
select Italics

click to
select Bold

click to select
point size

click to
select Font

TROUBLE? If you do not see the text toolbar, click View on the menu bar, then click Text Toolbar.

4. On the Text toolbar, click the **font** list arrow, then, if necessary, locate and click **Arial**.

5. On the Text toolbar, click the **point size** list arrow, then, if necessary, locate and click **14**.

6. On the Text toolbar, click the **Bold** button, then click the **Italic** button.

When you place text in a drawing, Paint displays a **selection rectangle**, a dashed border that defines where the text will appear. As long as you see the selection rectangle, you can change the height or width of the selection rectangle, and you can move the selection rectangle and the text. Once you click a blank area of the canvas or select another tool, you paste, or anchor, the text onto the canvas. If you look closely at a selection rectangle, you will see small black squares, called **handles**, located at the corners and midsections of the selection rectangle. You use the handles to change the size of the selection rectangle.

Now you are ready to add the first part of the company name, and position it within the light yellow circle.

To enter and position the first part of the company name:

1. Click inside the selection rectangle, then type **Visual**.

   TROUBLE? The last two or three characters of the word Visual will more than likely appear on a separate line. That's all right. You will adjust the width of the selection rectangle so the word fits on one line in Step 2.

2. Point to the handle located in the middle of the right side of the selection rectangle and when the mouse pointer changes to a ↔, drag the handle to the right until the word Visual fits on one line, as shown in Figure 9-25.

Figure 9-25 ◄
Widening the
selection
rectangle to fit
text on one line

drag handle to widen
selection rectangle

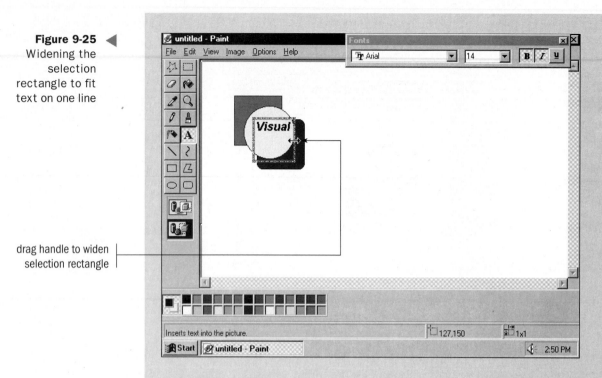

3. Point to the dashed border between handles and, when the mouse pointer changes to ![cursor], drag the selection rectangle and text to center the text within the top of the light yellow circle, as shown in Figure 9-26. As you drag, you will see a thick gray border that shows the new position where the text will appear once you release the mouse button.

outline of new
location for selection
rectangle and text

Figure 9-26 ◄
Moving the
selection
rectangle and
the text

drag border to
move selection
rectangle and text

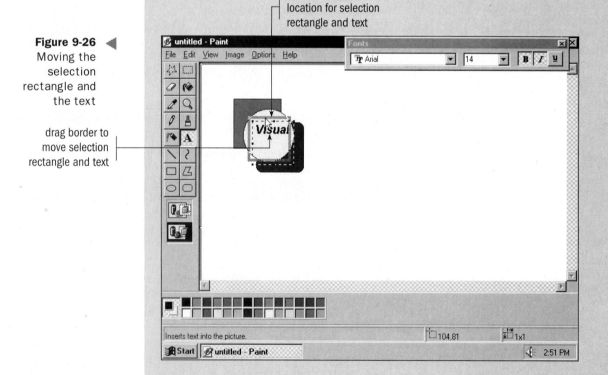

TROUBLE? If your first attempt to center the text does not work, repeat the same process and reposition the text again.

TROUBLE? If the selection rectangle disappears, click Edit on the menu bar, then click Undo, click inside the light yellow circle, and repeat Steps 1 through 3.

4. Click a blank area of the canvas to paste the text onto the drawing.

5. With the Text tool still selected, click below the word Visual in the light yellow circle, then type **Arts**.

6. Point to the dashed border between the handles and, when the mouse pointer changes ⌖, drag the selection rectangle and text to center the text below the word Visual, then click a blank area of the canvas to paste the text onto the drawing. Although your final drawing does not need to be exactly like the one shown in Figure 9-27, it should be similar in appearance.

Figure 9-27 ◀
Final design for
company logo

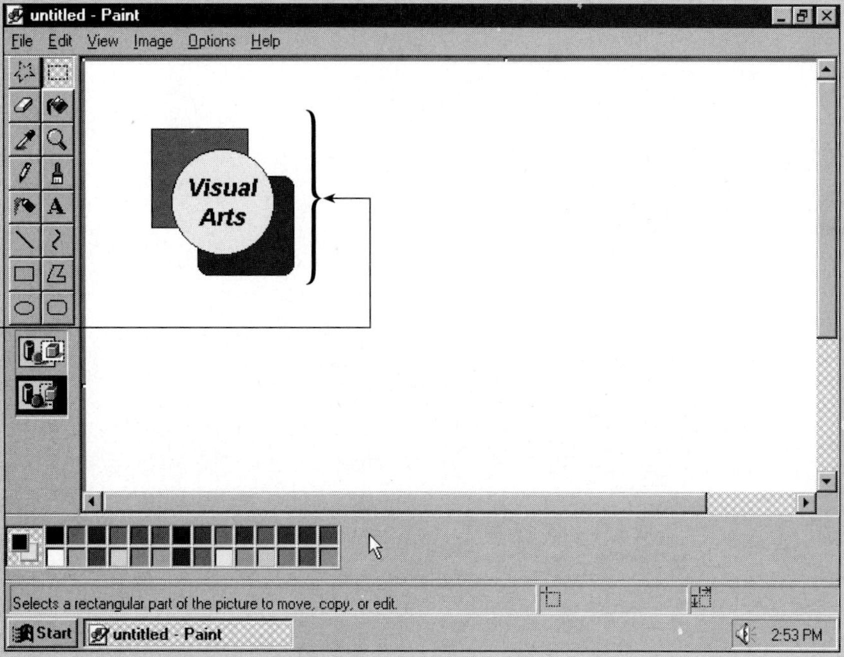

completed design ────

Saving a Drawing

You can use two different approaches to saving a drawing. If you choose the Save As command on the File menu, you can save the drawing in a file on disk. This approach not only saves the actual drawing, but also *all* the white space around the drawing and, as a result, the file on disk might be close to 300K in size.

An alternate approach is to save only the drawing and a small amount of white space around the drawing. This approach can reduce the file size by as much as 95% so that the file is only about 20K in size, and thereby saves space on a disk. To use this approach, you first have to select the part of the drawing that you want to save, then choose Copy To on the Edit menu.

To conserve disk space, you decide to select the part of the drawing that contains the logo and save it to disk.

To copy a drawing to disk:

1. Click the **Select tool** button located at the top of the second column of the toolbox.

2. Position the mouse pointer above and to the left of the upper-left corner of the drawing, leaving a small white space at the top and to the left of the drawing, drag to draw a selection rectangle around the drawing, as shown in Figure 9-28, then release the mouse button.

Figure 9-28 ◄
Selecting the
drawing to save

selection rectangle
around drawing
to save

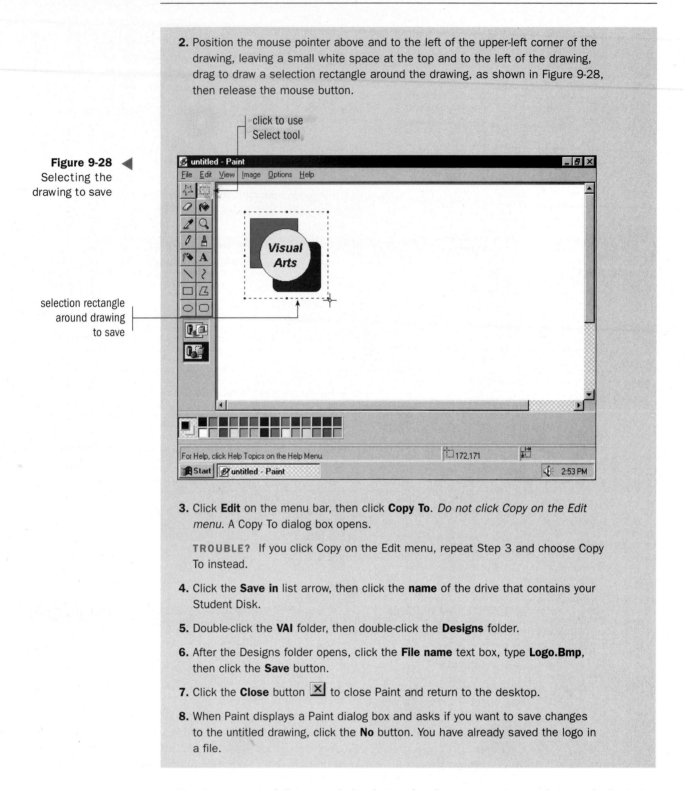

3. Click **Edit** on the menu bar, then click **Copy To**. *Do not click Copy on the Edit menu.* A Copy To dialog box opens.

   TROUBLE? If you click Copy on the Edit menu, repeat Step 3 and choose Copy To instead.

4. Click the **Save in** list arrow, then click the **name** of the drive that contains your Student Disk.

5. Double-click the **VAI** folder, then double-click the **Designs** folder.

6. After the Designs folder opens, click the **File name** text box, type **Logo.Bmp**, then click the **Save** button.

7. Click the **Close** button ☒ to close Paint and return to the desktop.

8. When Paint displays a Paint dialog box and asks if you want to save changes to the untitled drawing, click the **No** button. You have already saved the logo in a file.

You have successfully created the design for the company's new logo with the Paint application.

If you want to take a break and resume this tutorial at a later time, close all open applications and remove your Student Disk from the floppy disk drive. When you resume the tutorial, start Windows and insert your Student Disk into a floppy disk drive.

Object Linking and Embedding

Now that Brandon has decided on the design of the company's logo, and created a drawing of that design with Paint, he wants you to create a memo to all staff and include in the memo a copy of the logo, along with another variation of that design, so that he can solicit any additional suggestions or feedback from the staff before presenting the draft for approval to the president of the company. After you create the memo with WordPad, he wants you to insert a copy of the designs into the document that contains the memo.

Object Linking and Embedding, often referred to as **OLE** (pronounced "oh-lay"), is a technology that enables you to use information from a document produced by one application in a document produced by another application. Microsoft introduced Object Linking and Embedding in Microsoft Windows 3.1, and referred to it as OLE 1.0. In Windows 95, Microsoft has improved on this technology, and the new standard is referred to as OLE 2.0.

One of the more common uses of Object Linking and Embedding is to insert a table or a chart from a spreadsheet into a document that you produce with a word processing application. For example, Deborah Woods, a financial analyst at Visual Arts, Inc., prepares a yearly report that summarizes the financial performance of the company. After she uses a word processing application to prepare the main body of that report, she inserts a table of financial data and a three-dimensional bar chart that illustrates the company's performance. The spreadsheet and bar chart come from a separate document created with a spreadsheet application.

When you insert an object from another document into the current document, you can either create a link or embed the object. If you create a **link**, the current document stores the name of the file that contains the original object. Each time you open the document that contains the link, the current application examines the file, referred to as the **source document**, that contains the original object and updates the view of that object that you see in the current document. If you need to create documents that depend on data stored in a source document, then you can create links from each new document to the source document. Whenever you update the data in the source document, all documents with links to the source document are automatically updated when you next open those documents. However, the embedded object has information that identifies the application that produced the original object.

HELP DESK

> Index
>
> **EMBEDDING OBJECTS**
>
> Click the Start button, click Help, then click the Index tab.
>
> | Keyword | Topic |
> | --- | --- |
> | OLE | Linking information between documents |

When you **embed** an object, a copy of the object is pasted into the current document, and there is no link with the original file. If you make a change to the object in the source document, the embedded object does not change.

HELP DESK

> Index
>
> **EMBEDDING OBJECTS**
>
> Click the Start button, click Help, then click the Index tab.
>
> | Keyword | Topic |
> | --- | --- |
> | OLE | Embedding information in another document |

You can edit both linked and embedded objects. If you double-click a linked object, you open the application that produced the original object. After you edit the object, you exit the application and return to the document with the link, and the link is automatically updated to reflect changes in the original object. If you double-click an embedded object using OLE 2.0, the current application's application window changes and displays menus and tools appropriate to the application that produced the original object. You can then edit the embedded object in place. This feature is called **visual editing**. In OLE 1.0, if you double-clicked an embedded object inserted into a document from another file, Windows 3.1 opened the original application and displayed the object in another window so that you could modify it.

The applications that you use must support Object Linking and Embedding; otherwise, you cannot use this technology. For those applications that do support this technology, you will discover that there are differences in the type of support provided by these applications. For example, some applications might support the newer OLE 2.0 standards, while others support OLE 1.0. Furthermore, some applications can only act as a source for objects to other applications, some applications can only store objects from other applications, and other applications can perform both functions.

Brandon asks you to prepare the memo for him, and to insert copies of the new logo designs into the memo.

To open the WordPad application and enter the text of the memo:

1. Click the **Start** button, point to **Programs**, point to **Accessories**, then click **WordPad** on the Accessories menu. Windows 95 opens the WordPad application.

2. Click **File** on the menu bar, then click **Page Setup**. In the Page Setup dialog box, you can specify the paper size, paper source, orientation, and margins for a document. See Figure 9-29.

Figure 9-29 ◀
Specifying page
layout settings

preview of document

paper size

paper orientation

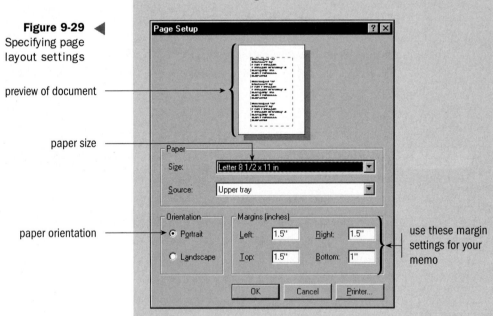

use these margin
settings for your
memo

3. In the Margins (inches) section, if necessary, double-click each of the margin settings, change them to the settings shown in Figure 9-30, then click the **OK** button.

4. Click the **Font** list arrow, then locate and click the **Arial** font.

TROUBLE? If your computer does not contain the Arial font, select another font, such as Times New Roman.

5. Click the **Font Size** list arrow, then locate and click **14**.

TROUBLE? If your computer does not contain a 14-point option for the font you selected, choose another point size close to 14 points.

6. Type the text shown in Figure 9-30. Leave five blank lines between the first and second paragraphs of the memo so that you can insert copies of the company logo.

Figure 9-30 ◀
Creating a
memo on
prospective
company logos

enter this text
into WordPad

MEMO

TO: Staff

FROM: Brandon Tolbert

RE: Company Logo

DATE: December 7,1997

Our design artists have just developed two designs for the new company logo.

leave five blank
lines between here

If you have any suggestions for changes to these designs, please discuss them with me as soon as possible. We hope to make a final decision on the new logo within the next few months.

7. Click the **Save** button 🖫 on the toolbar, and when the Save As dialog box opens, click the **Save in** list arrow, then click the **name** of the drive that contains your Student Disk.

8. Double-click the **VAI** folder, then double-click the **Designs** folder.

9. After the Designs folder opens, double-click **Document.doc** in the File name text box, type **Proposal.doc**, then click the **Save** button.

Inserting a Linked Object

Brandon wants you to insert a copy of the new logo design into the memo as a linked object. If he uses Paint to make any last minute changes to the original design, then the copy of the logo design in the WordPad memo will be automatically updated when he opens the file.

To insert a linked object:

1. If necessary, use the scroll bars to adjust your view so that you can see the blank space between the first and second paragraphs.

2. Click the blank line below the first paragraph, then use the arrow keys to position the insertion point on the third line below the first paragraph.

3. Press the **Tab** key twice to move the insertion point two tabs to the right.

4. Click **Insert** on the menu bar, then click **Object**. WordPad displays an Insert Object dialog box. See Figure 9-31. Your Object Type list box will vary depending on what applications you have installed.

Figure 9-31 ◀
Choosing an object to insert into the WordPad memo

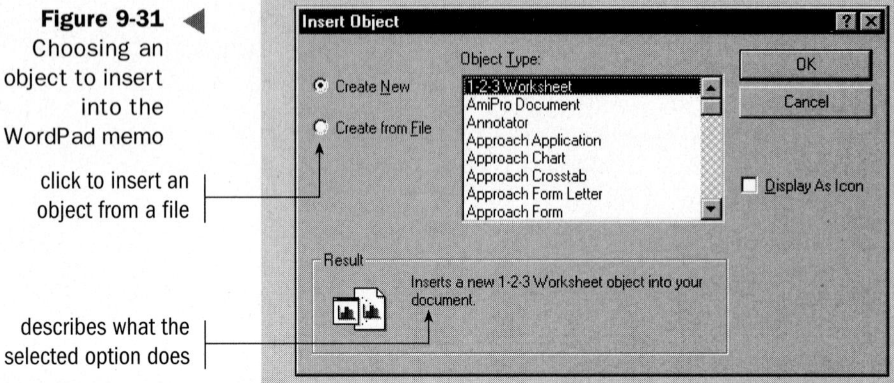

click to insert an object from a file

describes what the selected option does

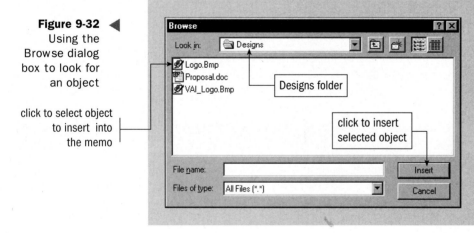

From this dialog box, you can insert a new object, or you can insert an object from an existing file. In the Object Type list box, Windows 95 lists the types of files that you can insert as objects. You also have the option of inserting an object into a document as an icon.

5. Click the **Create from File** radio button, then click the **Link** check box. In the Result section, Windows 95 explains what this selected option does. Next, you need to locate the file to which you want to establish a link.

6. Click the **Browse** button. WordPad opens the Browse dialog box. See Figure 9-32.

TROUBLE? If the Look in list box does not display an open Designs folder, click the Look in list arrow, click the name of the floppy drive that contains your Student Disk, double-click the VAI folder, double-click the Designs folder, click Logo.Bmp, then click the Insert button.

Figure 9-32 ◀
Using the Browse dialog box to look for an object

click to select object to insert into the memo

Designs folder

click to insert selected object

7. Click **Logo.Bmp**, then click the **Insert** or **Open** button. You return to the Insert Object dialog box. See Figure 9-33. In the File text box, you see the path to the file that contains the object you want to insert into your WordPad document. The file type is identified by Windows 95 as a Bitmap Image.

Figure 9-33 ◄
The path to the source document

type of file

creates a link

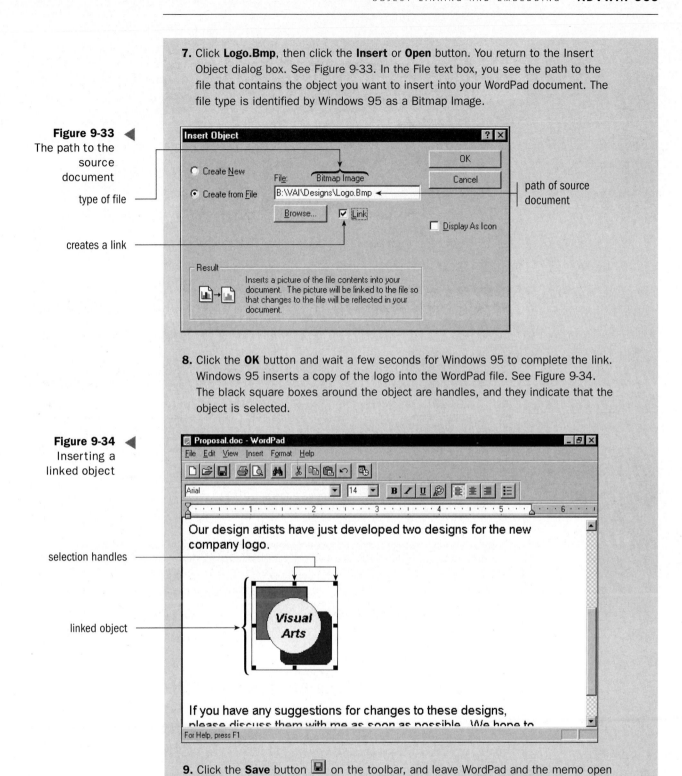

path of source document

8. Click the **OK** button and wait a few seconds for Windows 95 to complete the link. Windows 95 inserts a copy of the logo into the WordPad file. See Figure 9-34. The black square boxes around the object are handles, and they indicate that the object is selected.

Figure 9-34 ◄
Inserting a linked object

selection handles

linked object

9. Click the **Save** button 🖫 on the toolbar, and leave WordPad and the memo open for the next section.

INSERTING A LINKED OBJECT IN WORDPAD

- Open the WordPad application.
- Click Insert on the menu bar, then click Object.
- In the Insert Object dialog box, click the Create from File radio button.
- Click the Link check box.
- Click the Browse button, locate the file that contains the object you want to insert into the current file, click the Insert button, then click the OK button in the Insert Object dialog box.

You have successfully inserted an object into a document and created a link to the original object.

Editing a Linked Object

Brandon wants to make one small change to the original design. He wants to change the pink or light red color to a darker red.

Once you insert a linked object into a document, you can double-click that object to open the application that created the object and the file that contains the original object. After you make whatever changes you want to make to the original object, you exit the application and return to the file that contains the linked object. Windows 95 then updates the linked object so that it reflects any changes you made to the original object.

To follow this process more closely and ensure that the changes you are making to the original object are also reflected in the linked copy of that object, you can tile the application windows so that you can see the original and the linked objects.

HELP DESK

Index

UPDATING LINKED OBJECTS

In WordPad, click Help on the menu bar, click Help Topics, then click the Index tab.

Keyword	Topic
Updating	Editing linked objects

To edit the linked object:

1. Double-click the **linked object**. Windows 95 opens the Paint application, then opens the document with the original design of the logo. See Figure 9-35.

Figure 9-35 ◄
Opening the
link to the
original object

Paint application
window

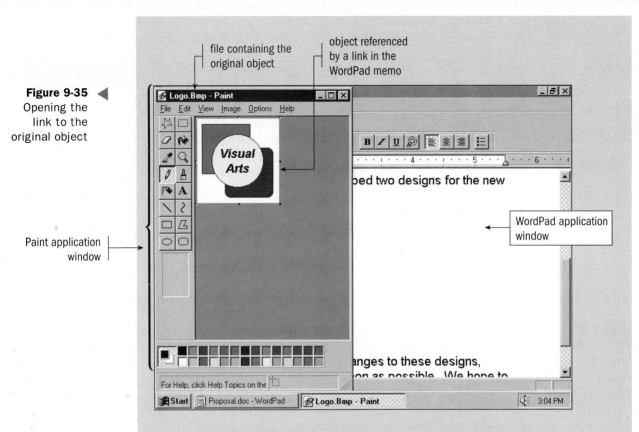

2. Right-click the **taskbar**, then click **Tile Vertically** on the shortcut menu.

3. Use the scroll bars to adjust your view of the Paint and WordPad applications windows so that you can see the original logo and the linked object at the same time.

   Now, you can make a change to the original logo design in the Paint window.

4. If necessary, click the Paint application window to select it.

5. Click the **bright red box** in the second row of the color box.

6. Click the **Fill with Color tool** button in the second row of the second column of the tool box.

7. Click inside the border of the pink or light red square. Paint fills the area within the square with a bright red color. Notice that the color of the pink or light red square in the linked object in the WordPad window also changes to bright red.

8. In the Paint window, click **File** on the menu bar, then click **Save**.

9. In the Paint window, click the **Close** button ⊠ to close the application.

10. In the WordPad window, click the **Maximize** button ☐.

REFERENCE
window

EDITING A LINKED OBJECT

- Double-click the linked object.
- Once Windows 95 opens the original application that produced the object and the file with the original object, modify the contents of the original object.
- Save the changes to the file that contains the original object.
- Exit the application that produced the object.

Creating links to objects in other files is one important way in which you can build compound documents that draw on resources stored in other files.

Embedding an Object

After talking to another staff member, Brandon decides to include another design for the company logo in the memo. Since the second logo design is going to be a variation of his original design, he wants you to embed, rather than link, a copy of the original logo design, then make some modifications to that design. If you embed a copy of the original logo, any changes you make to this copy will not affect the original logo design in the Paint file. Also, you can still edit the design with Paint even though it is now stored in a WordPad document. The process for embedding an object is very similar to that for inserting a linked object, except you do not create a link to the object you insert.

Brandon asks you to make this additional change to the memo before you print and distribute it.

To insert an embedded object:

1. If necessary, use the scroll bars to adjust your view so that you can see the blank space between the first and second paragraphs and the linked object.

2. Press the **End** key to move the insertion point to the right of the object, then press the **Tab** key three times to move the insertion point three more tabs to the right.

3. Click **Insert** on the menu bar, then click **Object**.

4. In the Insert Object dialog box, click the **Create from File** radio button. *Do not click the Link check box.*

5. Click the **Browse** button.

6. In the Browse dialog box, locate and click **Logo.Bmp**, then click the **Insert** or **Open** button.

7. After you return to the Insert Object dialog box, click the **OK** button and wait a few seconds for Windows 95 to complete the embedding. Again, Windows 95 inserts a copy of the logo into the WordPad memo; however, this time there is no link. See Figure 9-36.

Figure 9-36 ◀
Embedding
an object

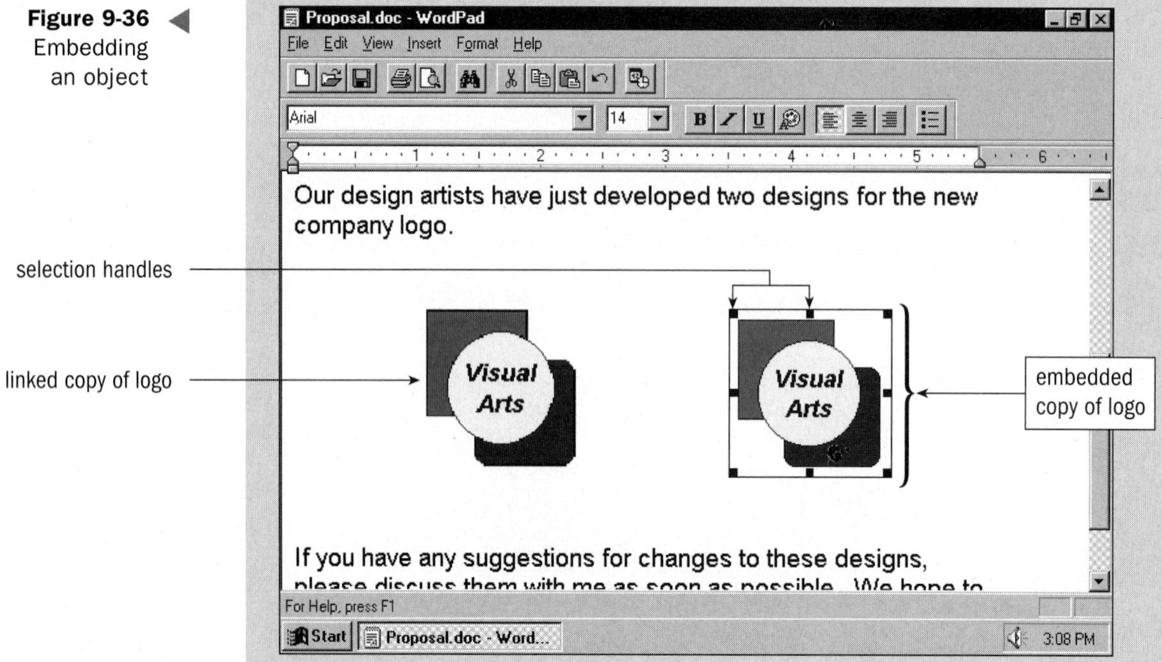

selection handles

linked copy of logo

embedded
copy of logo

8. Click the **Save** button on the toolbar.

REFERENCE
window

INSERTING AN EMBEDDED OBJECT IN WORDPAD

- Open the WordPad application.
- Click Insert on the menu bar, then click Object.
- In the Insert Object dialog box, click the Create from file radio button.
- Click the Browse button, locate the file that contains the object you want to insert into the current file, click the Insert or Open button, then click the OK button in the Insert Object dialog box.

You have successfully embedded a copy of the same object into your document.

Editing an Embedded Object

Since there is no link to the original object, you can modify this object without affecting the original object. If you double-click the embedded object, Windows 95 displays the object in a special window within the WordPad application window. Windows 95 replaces WordPad's menu bar, toolbar, and format bar with the menu bar, tool box, and color box in Paint. You are still working with the selected object in its actual location within WordPad, but the interface now contains the tools available in Paint for editing this object. As mentioned earlier, Microsoft calls this OLE 2.0 feature visual editing.

HELP DESK

Index

EMBEDDING OBJECTS

Click the Start button, click Help, then click the Index tab.

Keyword	Topic
OLE	Embedding information in another document

Brandon wants you to edit the second copy of the logo so that it includes two small light green circles with black borders in the upper-right and lower-left corners of the logo.

To edit the selected object:

1. Double-click the **embedded object** on the right. The object appears in a special window with scroll bars so that you can adjust your view of the object. See Figure 9-37. The gray border around the object and the handles indicate that the object is selected. Although you are still in the WordPad application window, as shown by the information on the title bar, you now see the Paint interface. You can still see the text of the memo in the window.

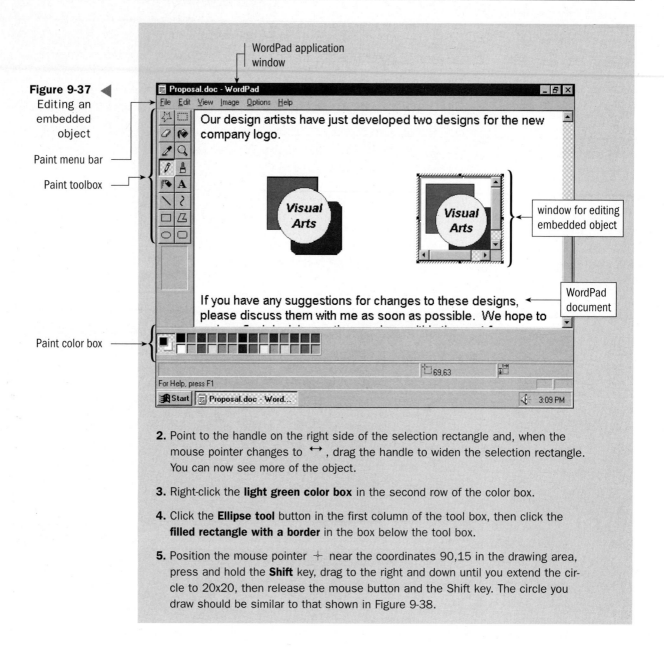

Figure 9-37
Editing an embedded object

Paint menu bar

Paint toolbox

Paint color box

2. Point to the handle on the right side of the selection rectangle and, when the mouse pointer changes to ↔ , drag the handle to widen the selection rectangle. You can now see more of the object.

3. Right-click the **light green color box** in the second row of the color box.

4. Click the **Ellipse tool** button in the first column of the tool box, then click the **filled rectangle with a border** in the box below the tool box.

5. Position the mouse pointer ＋ near the coordinates 90,15 in the drawing area, press and hold the **Shift** key, drag to the right and down until you extend the circle to 20x20, then release the mouse button and the Shift key. The circle you draw should be similar to that shown in Figure 9-38.

Figure 9-38 ◀
Adding a circle
to an
embedded
object

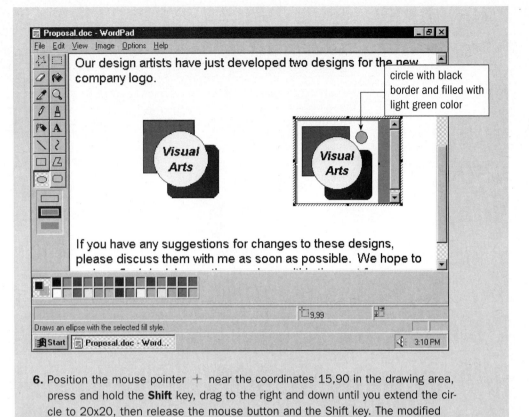

6. Position the mouse pointer ✛ near the coordinates 15,90 in the drawing area, press and hold the **Shift** key, drag to the right and down until you extend the circle to 20x20, then release the mouse button and the Shift key. The modified drawing should now be similar to that shown in Figure 9-39.

Figure 9-39 ◀
Adding another
circle to the
embedded
object

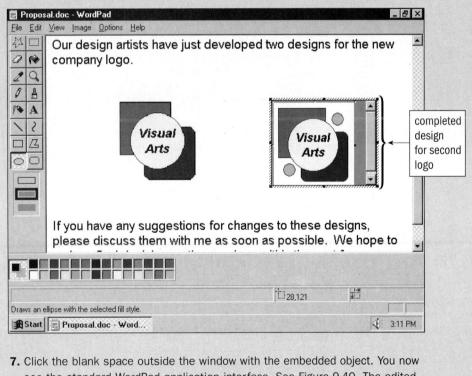

7. Click the blank space outside the window with the embedded object. You now see the standard WordPad application interface. See Figure 9-40. The edited object is now displayed within the WordPad memo.

Figure 9-40
View of linked
and embedded
objects in
WordPad memo

WordPad
components restored

linked object

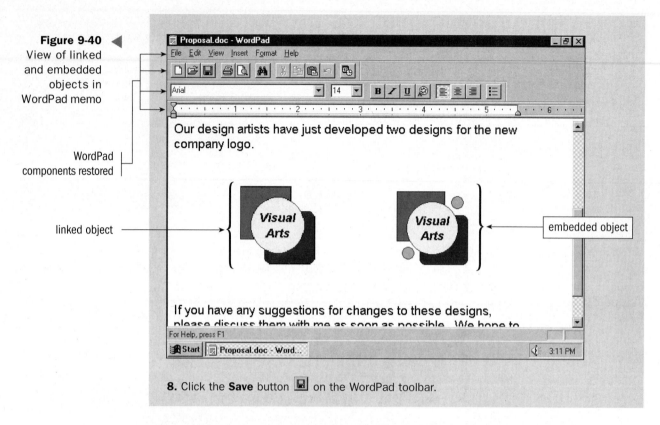

embedded object

8. Click the **Save** button 🖫 on the WordPad toolbar.

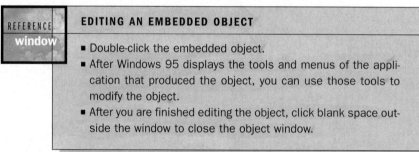

REFERENCE
window

EDITING AN EMBEDDED OBJECT

■ Double-click the embedded object.
■ After Windows 95 displays the tools and menus of the application that produced the object, you can use those tools to
  modify the object.
■ After you are finished editing the object, click blank space outside the window to close the object window.

Printing the Memo with Linked and Embedded Objects

Now you are ready to print a copy of the staff memo that includes proposed designs for
the new company logo.

To print the memo:

1. Make sure your printer is on and operational.

2. Click the **Print** button 🖨 on the toolbar.

Using the new Object Linking and Embedding technology in Windows 95 applications,
you have created a compound document with both linked and embedded objects.

Using Scrap

Several weeks later, Naomi Morita, the president of Visual Arts, Inc., chooses the second
of the two designs for the new company logo, based on the overwhelming preference for
this design by the entire staff. She asks Brandon to send another memo to all the employees, informing them of the new company logo.

Another way to assemble documents from parts of other documents is to create one or more "scraps" and place them on the desktop. A **scrap** is a file that Windows 95 automatically creates when you drag all or part of a file onto the desktop. The scrap might consist of text or any other type of object stored in a file. If you double-click the scrap, you open the application that produced the original document, even though there is no link to the file where the original object is currently stored.

When you need to include the scrap in a document, you open the document and then drag the scrap from the desktop into the document.

HELP DESK

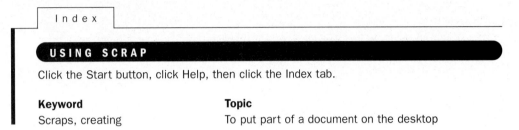

Index

USING SCRAP

Click the Start button, click Help, then click the Index tab.

Keyword	**Topic**
Scraps, creating	To put part of a document on the desktop

Brandon asks you to prepare another memo to the staff, with the new company logo. He suggests that you drag a copy of this logo onto your desktop, then drag a copy of the scrap into the new memo you prepare.

To create scrap from the memo:

1. Click the **Restore** button 🗗 to return the WordPad application window to its original size, then, if necessary, move or adjust the size of the window so that you can see an open area of your desktop.

2. If necessary, use the scroll bars to adjust your view so that you can see the second of the two logos. See Figure 9-41. The second logo is the embedded object that contains two light green circles as part of the logo's design.

Figure 9-41 ◄
Preparing to
create scrap

drag embedded
object to desktop

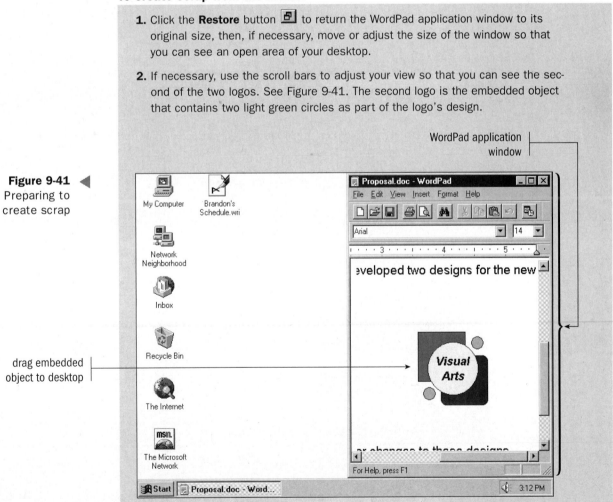

3. Click the **embedded object** and drag it to an empty area of the desktop, then release the mouse button. Windows 95 creates a scrap, or file, that contains a copy of the embedded object. See Figure 9-42.

Figure 9-42 ◄
Scrap on
the desktop

embedded object ———

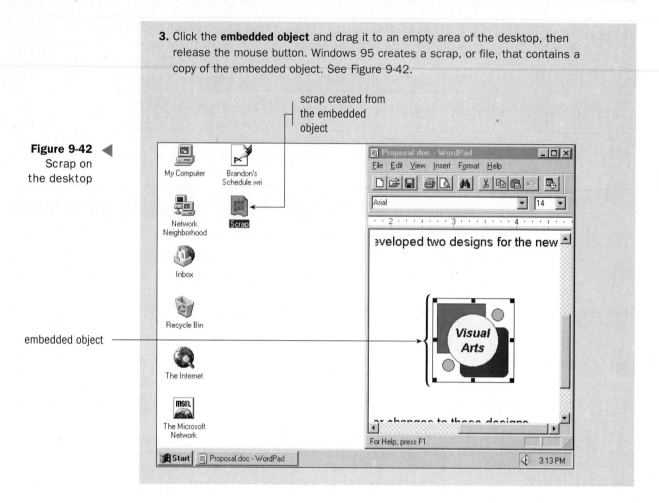

Now, you need to create a new file that contains the memo announcing the official company logo. To complete the memo, you will drag a copy of the scrap from the desktop into the new file.

To create a new file:

1. Click the **Maximize** button 🔲 to maximize the WordPad application window.

2. Click the **New** button 🔲 on the toolbar. WordPad displays a New dialog box. In the New document type list, you can choose from one of three file types—Word 6 Document, Rich Text Document, and Text Document. A Word 6 Document can be opened and edited in Microsoft Word 6.0 for Windows. A Rich Text Document includes character formatting and tabs that many types of word processing applications recognize. A Text Document has unformatted text.

3. Click the **OK** button.

4. If WordPad displays a WordPad dialog box asking if you want to save changes to Proposal.doc, click the **Yes** button. WordPad saves and closes Proposal.doc, then opens a new file.

5. Click **File** on the menu bar, click **Page Setup**, and, if necessary, in the Margins (inches) section, change the Top, Left, and Right margins to 1.5 inches and the Bottom margin to 1 inch, then click the **OK** button.

6. Click the **Font** list arrow, then locate and click the **Arial** font.

TROUBLE? If your computer does not contain the Arial font, select another font, such as Times New Roman.

7. Click the **Font size** list arrow, then locate and click **14**.

   TROUBLE? If your computer does not contain a 14-point option for the font you selected, choose another point size close to 14 points.

8. Type the text shown in Figure 9-43. Leave five blank lines between the first and second paragraphs of the memo so that you can insert a copy of the new company logo.

Figure 9-43 ◄
Creating
a memo
on the new
company logo

enter this text
into WordPad

```
MEMO

TO:            Staff

FROM:          Brandon Tolbert

RE:            Company Logo

DATE:          January 1,1998

Based on the overwhelming preference expressed by the staff, Naomi
Morita, the President of Visual Arts, Inc., has chosen the following
design for the new company logo:




I would like to thank all of you for your support, suggestions, and
recommendations as we explored designs for a new company logo
over the last few months.
```

leave five blank
lines between here

9. Click the **Save** button 🖫 on the toolbar, and when the Save As dialog box opens, type **Logo.doc** in the File name text box, then click the **Save** button.

10. Click the **Restore** button and, if necessary, move or adjust the size of the WordPad application window so that you can see the scrap on the desktop.

Now you are ready to include a copy of the new company logo into the file.

To drag scrap into a file:

1. If necessary, use the scroll bars in the WordPad application window to adjust your view so that you can see the blank lines between the first and second paragraphs of the memo.

2. Drag a copy of the scrap from the desktop into the new file and, when the insertion point appears on the third line following the first paragraph, release the mouse pointer. Windows 95 inserts the new company logo into the new file at the position of the insertion point. See Figure 9-44.

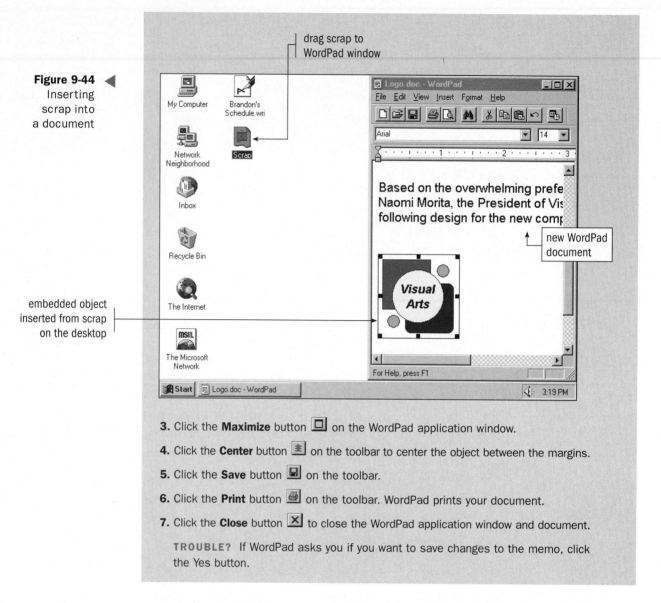

Figure 9-44
Inserting
scrap into
a document

drag scrap to
WordPad window

new WordPad
document

embedded object
inserted from scrap
on the desktop

3. Click the **Maximize** button on the WordPad application window.

4. Click the **Center** button on the toolbar to center the object between the margins.

5. Click the **Save** button on the toolbar.

6. Click the **Print** button on the toolbar. WordPad prints your document.

7. Click the **Close** button to close the WordPad application window and document.

   TROUBLE? If WordPad asks you if you want to save changes to the memo, click the Yes button.

The operations that you just performed are possible because of the Object Linking and Embedding technology included in Windows 95 and in the applications that support this technology.

Since you no longer need the scrap and the schedule, you decide to delete them.

To delete the scrap and schedule:

1. Right-click the **scrap**, then click **Delete** on the shortcut menu.

2. When prompted as to whether you want to send the scrap to the Recycle Bin, click the **Yes** button.

3. Right-click **Brandon's schedule** document, then click **Delete** on the shortcut menu.

4. When prompted as to whether you want to send this icon to the Recycle Bin, click the **Yes** button.

By using the new Object Linking and Embedding technology in Windows 95, Brandon and his staff can quickly and easily produce compound documents that contain embedded and linked objects derived from documents produced by other applications.

Tutorial Assignment

Brandon's next project is to design a letterhead. He asks you to create a design similar to the one shown in Figure 9-45 using Paint and WordPad.

Figure 9-45 ◀
Design for
Visual Arts,
Inc.'s new
company
letterhead

Visual Arts, Inc.
250 Montgomery Street
San Francisco, CA 94014

1. Insert your Student Disk into a floppy disk drive.
2. Open Paint then maximize the Paint application window.
3. Click the Text tool, choose a font (such as Arial) from the Text toolbar, and then set the point size to 18.
4. Type the company name, "Visual Arts, Inc.", widen the selection rectangle so that the company name fits on one line, then click on the canvas to paste the text into the drawing area.
5. Change the point size to 14, click below the company name, type "250 Montgomery Street", press the Enter key, type "San Francisco, CA 94014", widen the selection rectangle so that the street address and city, state, and zip each fit on a single line, then click on the canvas to paste the text into the drawing area.
6. Click the Line tool, click the option for a medium-sized line in the box below the toolbox, press and hold the Shift key, drag to draw a line below the city, state, and zip code, then release the mouse button and the Shift key.
7. Click the Select tool, draw a selection rectangle around the company name, address, and graphics line. Leave enough space below the graphics line so that you can add a second one later.
8. Click Edit on the menu bar, click Copy To, and, when the Copy To dialog box opens, select the drive that contains your Student Disk, select the VAI folder, select the Designs folder, double-click the File name text box, type "Ltrhead.Bmp", then click the Save button.
9. Close Paint.
10. Open WordPad.
11. Click File on the menu bar, click Page Setup, set the Top margin to 1.5 inches, set the Left, Right, and Bottom margins to 1 inch, then click the OK button.

12. Click Insert on the menu bar, click Object, and in the Insert Object dialog box, click the Create from File radio button, click the Link check box, then click the Browse button.

13. In the Browse dialog box, click the Look in list arrow, select the drive that contains your Student Disk, double-click the VAI folder, double-click the Designs folder, click Ltrhead.Bmp, click the Insert button, then click the OK button in the Insert dialog box.

14. After Windows 95 inserts the contents of Ltrhead.Bmp as a linked object into your WordPad document, press the End key, then press the Tab key three times to move the insertion point three tab stops to the right.

15. Click the Start button, point to Programs, point to Accessories, then click WordPad on the Accessories menu to open a second copy of this application.

16. Click the Open button on the toolbar, and in the Open dialog box, click the Look in list arrow, select the drive that contains your Student Disk, double-click the VAI folder, double-click the Designs folder, click Logo.doc, then click the Open button.

17. Use the scroll bars to locate the company logo, click the embedded object, click the Copy button on the toolbar.

18. Click the taskbar button for your other WordPad document, which contains the linked object, then click the Paste button on the toolbar to paste a copy of the embedded object from your other WordPad document.

19. Double-click the linked object that has the company name and address and, when Paint opens the file that contains the original object, click the Line tool in the first column of the toolbox, and press the Shift key while you draw a second graphics line below the first one. Indent the second line, and extend it a short distance to the right of the first line.

20. Click File on the menu bar, click Save, click File again, then click Exit.

21. After you return to your WordPad document that contains the letterhead, click File on the menu bar, then click Save As. When the Save As dialog box opens, click the Look in list arrow, select the drive that contains your Student Disk, double-click the VAI folder, double-click the Designs folder, click the File name text box, type "Ltrhead.Doc", then click the Save button.

22. Print a copy of the letterhead that you designed, then close the WordPad application window.

23. Click the taskbar button for the WordPad document that contains the company logo, click File on the menu bar, then click Exit.

Case Problems

1. **Creating a Brochure Design for Greene's Remodeling Company** Greene's Remodeling Company provides affordable remodeling services to its residential and commercial clients. Greene's has contracted with Cyndi Chiara, a local design artist, to create a design for a new brochure that will advertise their remodeling services. Cyndi asks you to prepare the design from a sketch that she has prepared. Use Figure 9-46 as a guideline for preparing your own design.

Figure 9-46 ◀
Design for Greene's Remodeling Services' business brochure

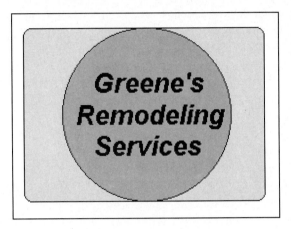

1. Insert your Student Disk into a floppy disk drive.
2. Open Paint.
3. Click the Rounded Rectangle tool in the second column of the tool box, click the option for creating an object with a border in the box below the tool box, select the black color box as the foreground color, and the light blue color box as the background color in the color box, click near the coordinates 50,50 then drag to near the coordinates 250x175.
4. Click the Ellipse tool in the first column of the toolbox, click the option for creating an object with a border in the box below the toolbox, click the black color box as the foreground color, and click the light green color box as the background color in the color box, press and hold the Shift key, click near the coordinates 90,50 then drag to the right and down until the circle touches the other side of the rounded rectangle, then release the Shift key and the mouse button.
5. Click the Text tool in the second column of the toolbox, choose a font (such as Arial) from the Text toolbar, set the point size to 22, then click the Bold and Italics buttons.
6. Type "Greene's", widen the selection rectangle so that the first part of the company name fits on one line, move the selection rectangle so that the text is centered just above the midpoint of the circle, then click on the canvas to paste the text into the drawing area.
7. Type "Remodeling", widen the selection rectangle so that the next part of the company name fits on one line, move the selection rectangle so that the text is centered below the text "Greene's", then click on the canvas to paste the text into the drawing area.
8. Type "Services", widen the selection rectangle so that the last part of the company name fits on one line, move the selection rectangle so that the text is centered below the text "Remodeling," then click on the canvas to paste the text into the drawing area.
9. Enhance the design in any other ways that you prefer.

10. Click the Select tool in the first column of the toolbox, draw a selection rectangle around the design, click Edit on the menu bar, click Copy To and, when the Copy To dialog box opens, select the drive that contains your Student Disk, select the VAI folder, select the Designs folder, double-click the File name text box, type "Greenes.Bmp", then click the Save button.

11. Click File on the menu bar, click Print, then click the OK button.

12. Click File on the menu bar, click Exit and, when prompted to save changes to "untitled," click the No button.

2. Creating a Mailer for Country Gazebos, Inc. Country Gazebos, Inc. designs and builds gazebos for clients who live in country homes. The owner, Michael Rupe, wants to create a design for an upcoming mailer to prospective customers. He asks you to prepare a draft of the design using WordPad and one of the Paint files included with Windows 95. Once you complete this design, he will hire a desktop publisher to prepare the mailer.

1. Insert your Student Disk into a floppy disk drive.

2. Open WordPad.

3. Click File on the menu bar, click Page Setup, set the Top margin to 1.5 inches, set the Left, Right, and Bottom margins to 1 inch, then click the OK button.

4. Click the Font box list arrow, then select a font of your own choosing.

5. Click the Font Size box list arrow, then click 36 (or a point size close to 36).

6. Click the Center button on the toolbar, type "Country Gazebos, Inc.", then press the Enter key two times.

7. Click the Font Size box list arrow, then click 24 (or a point size close to 24).

8. Type "CUSTOM-DESIGNED" (in caps), press the Enter key twice, type "GAZEBOS", press the Enter key twice, type "FOR COUNTRY-STYLE SETTINGS", then press the Enter key four times.

9. Click Insert on the menu bar, click Object, and in the Insert Object dialog box, click the Create from File radio button, *do not click the Link check box*, then click the Browse button.

10. In the Browse dialog box, click the Look in list arrow, select the drive that contains your Student Disk, double-click the VAI folder, double-click the Designs folder, click Ltrhead.Bmp, click the Insert button, then click the OK button in the Insert dialog box.

11. Click Insert on the menu bar, click Object, and in the Insert Object dialog box, click the Create from File radio button, *do not click the Link check box*, then click the Browse button.

12. In the Look in list box, select drive C, locate and double-click the Windows folder, locate and select Forest.Bmp, click the Insert button in the Browse dialog box, then click the OK button in the Insert Object dialog box. *Note*: If you do not have a file named Forest.Bmp, select another Paint file to embed into your WordPad document.

13. Click the Print Preview button on the toolbar, verify that the text and embedded object fit on one page, then click the Close button to close the Paint window. *Note*: If the text and embedded object do not fit on one page, adjust your margin settings and, if necessary, delete blank lines between the lines of text and the text and the embedded object.

14. Click File on the menu bar, click Save As, and when the Save As dialog box opens, click the Look in list arrow, click the name of the drive that contains your Student Disk, double-click the VAI folder, double-click the Designs folder, click the File name box, type "Gazebos.Doc", then click the Save button.

15. Click File on the menu bar, then click Print, then click the OK button.

16. Click File on the menu bar, then click Exit to close WordPad.

3. Creating Desktop Icons for Paint Files at Reichman's Nursery Reichman's Nursery specializes in the collection and propagation of plants for landscaping newly-built developments. Johanna Alvarez, the nursery manager, wants to design new business cards, letterhead, brochures, and flyers for the upcoming business season. She asks you to create icons for Paint files included with Windows 95 and place them on the desktop. Later, she will print copies of these files so that she can assemble various designs by cutting-and-pasting images together.

1. Open Windows Explorer, restore the Windows Explorer window to its original size, then, if necessary, adjust the size of the window so that you can see blank space on your desktop.
2. In the All Folders window, locate and click the Windows folder.
3. If necessary, click the Details button.
4. In the Contents of Windows window, click the Type column button to arrange files in alphabetical order by their file type. If necessary, use the scroll bars to adjust your view of this window.
5. In the Contents of Windows window, use the scroll bars to locate Bitmap Image Files (Paint files).
6. Drag the Forest.Bmp file to the desktop. *Note*: If you don't have this Paint file, right-click another Paint file, click Quick View to view the contents of the file, click the Close button to close Quick View, then select and drag the file to the desktop. If you accidentally open a file in Paint, close Paint, then try again.
7. Locate and drag Leaves.Bmp, or another Bitmap Image file, to the desktop.
8. Locate and drag another Bitmap Image file of your own choosing to the desktop.
9. Close Windows Explorer.
10. Double-click one of the Bitmap Image file icons on the desktop to open Paint and the file with the bitmap image.
11. Click File on the menu bar, click Print, then click the OK button.
12. Close the Paint window.
13. Right-click one of the Bitmap Image file icons on the desktop, click Cut on the shortcut menu, open Windows Explorer, locate and click the Windows folder in the All Folders section, then click the Paste button to restore this file to where it was originally stored.
14. Repeat the same process to restore the other two Bitmap Image files on your desktop back to the Windows folder.

4. Preparing Training Materials at PC Trainers PC Trainers specializes in workshops that focus on advanced Windows 95 topics. Instructors, lab directors, technical support staff, and other contract trainers sign up for their courses so that they can improve their own job skills. May-Ling Chung, one of the staff trainers, asks you to prepare an overview of Object Linking and Embedding for her, so that she can develop a handout for an upcoming workshop on OLE 2.0 in Windows 95 using the form shown in Figure 9-47.

Figure 9-47 ◄

CHARACTERISTICS OF OBJECT LINKING AND EMBEDDING		
	OBJECT LINKING	**OBJECT EMBEDDING**
Does Windows 95 maintain a link to the original document? (List Yes or No for each of these OLE processes.)		
Does a change to the original document affect the document with a linked or embedded object? (List Yes or No for each of these OLE processes.)		
Does a change to an object affect the original document? (List Yes or No for each of these OLE processes.)		
How do you insert a linked or embedded object? (Concisely list the steps you would use in WordPad for each OLE process.)		
How do you update a linked or embedded object? (Concisely list the steps you would use in WordPad for each OLE process.)		
How do you move a linked or embedded object? (Concisely list the steps you would use in WordPad for each OLE process.)		
Note whether each of these OLE features supports visual editing. (List Yes or No for each of these OLE processes.)		

Connecting to Networks and the Internet

Searching the Internet for Resorts

In this tutorial you will:

- Learn about networks

- Log onto a network and use Winchat, an online communication utility

- Learn about online services, the Internet, and the World Wide Web

- Explore the organization of The Microsoft Network

- Search for information on The Microsoft Network

- Open the Internet Center folder

- Access the Internet

- Browse the World Wide Web

- Use the Internet Explorer to search the Internet

CASE

Seaside Resorts, Inc.

Each year, thousands of people swarm to the sunny beaches of southern California and Mexico as well as to the beautiful seashores and beaches of Hawaii. Seaside Resorts, Inc. provides diverse vacation packages for locations along the west coast of the United States, Mexico, and Hawaii. One of Seaside Resorts' goals is to expand its vacation packages to include the Fiji Islands and other islands in the South Pacific.

Michela Roberts recently began working at the San Francisco headquarters of Seaside Resorts. Her supervisor, Maria Herrera, wants Michela to evaluate the feasibility of advertising the company's vacation packages on the Internet and to design a new brochure highlighting the magnificence of the Fiji Islands.

The Importance of Networks

During her first week at Seaside Resorts, Maria orients Michela to her new job and to the resources available to her. Michela will work jointly with co-workers in the same department on specific projects. Like other employees, Michela will be working on a network where she can share files with her co-workers and access a high-performance laser printer for producing near-typeset quality documents.

A **network** is a group of computers and other hardware devices, such as printers, that are connected together so that the computers can share hardware resources, software resources, and files. Each computer has a **network adapter card** that controls the transmission of data between the computer and the network cabling that connects that computer to all the other computers and devices within the network. A network operating system allocates resources and manages all the operations within the network. Any computer on a network can access the same printer or any other available hardware device, such as a modem. A user at any computer can access the same software applications and utilities, and can share document and data files with other computers and individuals on the network. Networks are important to **workgroups**, or individuals who work together as a group, and require access to shared resources. By sharing resources, businesses receive a faster return on their investments, and employee productivity increases.

There are two common types of network arrangements: client/server networks and peer-to-peer networks. In a **client/server network**, a central computer provides file, printer, and communication support to other computers on the network. See Figure 10-1.

Figure 10-1 ◀
Client/server
network

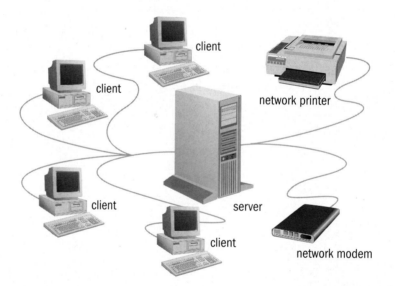

The central computer is called the **server**, and the computers that request and use the services available on the server are called **clients**. The server contains the network operating system, the installed software applications, and user document and data files. Larger and more complex client/server networks might include one or more file servers dedicated to the management of files and one or more print servers that manage printing on the network.

The **file server** is a specialized server that contains the files produced by applications, and may allow more than one user to access the same shared file at the same time. This later feature is important in business environments, where many users might need to access and update the same customer database. The **print server** is a specialized server that accepts print jobs from different computers on the network, **spools** or stores print jobs on disk, recognizes user priorities, and reports the status of print jobs. One important advantage of a client/server network is that, by acting as a central repository of all resources, it provides for more efficient management and control of data, and therefore offers greater security. Plus, it provides a standardized and predictable working environment for all users on the network. However, the client/server network is more complex to set up and manage, requires more expensive hardware and software, and requires a greater investment in resources and training.

In a **peer-to-peer network**, the simplest type of network arrangement, each computer can access and share the printers, hard disk drives, and CD-ROM disc drives on other computers within the network. See Figure 10-2.

Figure 10-2 ◄
Peer-to-peer
network

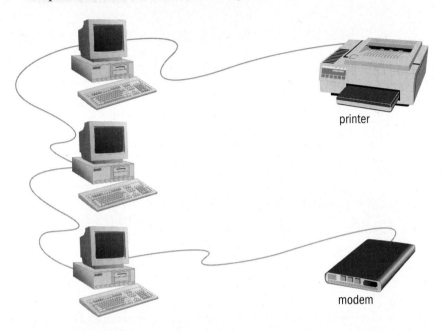

printer

modem

Each computer acts as both a client and a server. A peer-to-peer network is ideal for a small group of users and their computers. A peer-to-peer network is easy-to-install and is far less expensive than a client/server network, but it does not have the powerful management and auditing features found in client/server networks.

If you see a Network Neighborhood icon on your desktop, then Windows 95 has detected the presence of a network. The Windows 95 installation program not only detects a network connection, but also automatically installs and configures the network client, adapter, protocol, and service. The **client** refers to the type of client software used on the network you want to connect your computer to. This software allows you to use files and printers on other computers on the same network. For example, your client might be a Novell network that uses the NetWare operating system. As noted earlier, the **adapter** is the network card that physically connects your computer system to a network. Windows 95 installs the appropriate software driver or drivers for the network adapter.

The **protocol** is the language that computers use to communicate with each other over a network. All the computers on a network must use the same protocol. Two common types of protocols are the TCP/IP (Transmission Control Protocol/Internet Protocol) protocol and the IPX/SPX (Novell's Internetwork Packet Exchange/Sequential Packet Exchange) protocol. The **service** refers to the installation of peer file and printer sharing services, as well as other types of network services. For example, you might select a service that allows your computer to share files and printers with other computers on the same network.

Index

HELP DESK

THE MICROSOFT NETWORK

Click the Start button, click Help, then click the Index tab.

Keyword	**Topic**
Networks	Overview: What is a network?

If you need to install network support on your computer after you have already installed Windows 95, you can open the Control Panel, then the Network folder, and install the necessary network components. In the Network dialog box, you use a Configuration property sheet similar to the one shown in Figure 10-3 to select a client, install an adapter, and select a protocol and service.

Figure 10-3 ◄
Configuration
tab in Network
dialog box

installed network
components

type of client
network

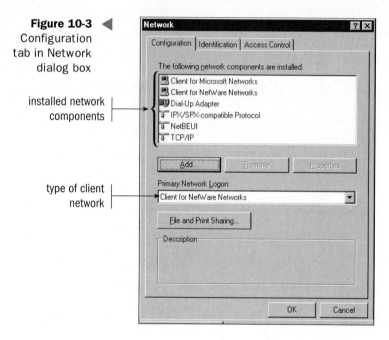

You use an Identification property sheet similar to the one shown in Figure 10-4 to provide a name for your computer, a workgroup name, and a description of your computer that identifies it on the network.

Figure 10-4 ◄
Identification
tab in Network
dialog box

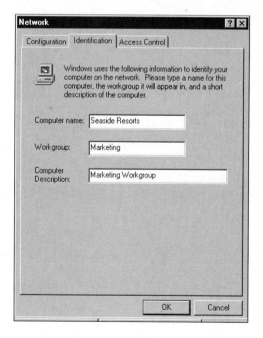

You use an Access Control property sheet similar to the one shown in Figure 10-5 to specify how shared resources will be used. For example, you can specify a password for each resource, or allow specific users and groups access to a resource.

Figure 10-5 ◀
Access Control
tab in Network
dialog box

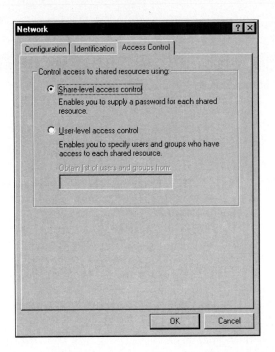

When you open My Computer, you explore and access the resources and features of your computer system. Likewise, when you open Network Neighborhood, you can explore and access the resources of other computer systems that form part of a network, as well as other networks.

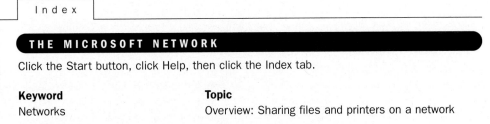

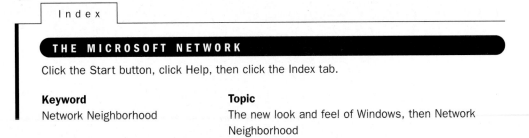

Connecting to a Network

After her first few days at her new job, Michela's supervisor provides her with her network login and password so that she can sign onto the company's Novell network. Michela has a few moments before she must leave for a meeting, so she decides to verify that her login and password work properly.

HELP DESK

Index

THE MICROSOFT NETWORK

Click the Start button, click Help, then click the Index tab.

Keyword	Topic
Networks	Overview: Connecting to a network

Before you can complete the rest of this section and the next one on network utilities, not only must your computer be connected to a network, but Windows 95 must also be configured to support that network. If your computer system is not connected to a network, then skip this section and continue with the section entitled "Using The Microsoft Network."

As you complete this tutorial, your view of your specific network and its resources will differ from those shown on the Novell network in the figures.

To connect to your network:

1. Make sure you see the Windows 95 desktop.

2. Double-click **Network Neighborhood**. Windows 95 opens the Network Neighborhood dialog box. See Figure 10-6. In the Network Neighborhood window, you might see an Entire Network icon as well as icons for one or more specific networks that you can connect to through your computer. The names of your workgroup network or networks will differ from those shown in the figure.

   TROUBLE? If your computer displays an Enter Network Password dialog box after you power on your computer, you can log in directly to the network after you specify your user name, password, and login server name. If you choose not to log in immediately into the network, you can always connect to the network later with Network Neighborhood.

Figure 10-6 ◀
Network
Neighborhood
window

3. If the Network Neighborhood contains an Entire Network icon, double-click the **Entire Network** icon. In the Entire Network window, Windows 95 displays all the networks that are available from the computer system you are using. See Figure 10-7. You will see the name of your network or networks. By opening this window, you have an overview of all the networks that are connected together to the network that you are most likely to use.

Figure 10-7 ◀
Entire network
window

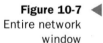
click to open
Michela's network

Seaside Resorts has access only to its own network, but in a large university setting, you might have access to many workgroups and networks.

4. Click the **Close** button ☒ to close the Entire Network window.

5. In the Network Neighborhood window, double-click **your network server name**. Windows 95 displays an Enter Network Password dialog box, and prompts you to enter your password. See Figure 10-8. You will see your user name in the User name text box. If you enable the "Connect as guest" option, Windows 95 will connect you to the network even if you do not have a login and password; however, you might have limited privileges on that network.

Figure 10-8 ◄
Entering a network user name and password

enter user name

enter password

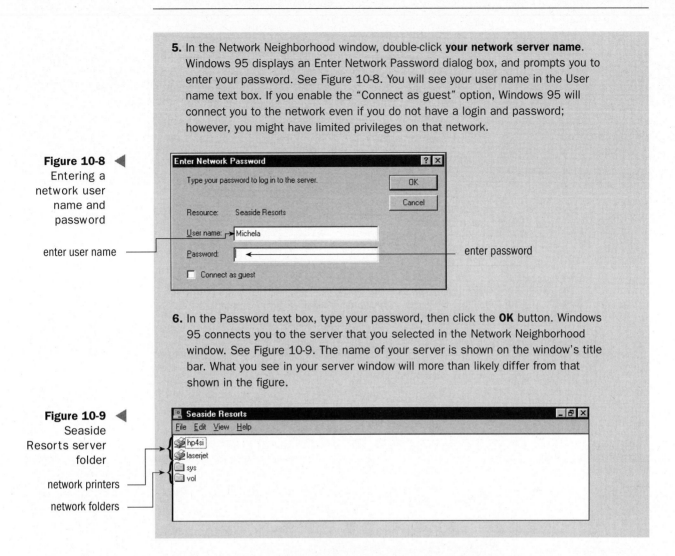

6. In the Password text box, type your password, then click the **OK** button. Windows 95 connects you to the server that you selected in the Network Neighborhood window. See Figure 10-9. The name of your server is shown on the window's title bar. What you see in your server window will more than likely differ from that shown in the figure.

Figure 10-9 ◄
Seaside Resorts server folder

network printers

network folders

After you connect to a network, you use the same techniques and skills that you have used in earlier tutorials to select and open folders and files, and to run applications. However, now that you are connected to a network, you will more than likely have access to most of the hardware and software resources on the network, as well as access to files that are shared by one or more users on the network.

Network Utilities

Michela quickly learns that Windows 95 includes a useful utility, Winchat, for users who work on a network. With Winchat, you can have an online conversation with another user on a network without having to leave your office. If you are working on a network with different network software, like Novell, you might have a different utility for online conversations. Read through this section to see how online conversing works.

Before she logs off the network, Michela wants to send a message to her supervisor, Maria, to remind her that she will be leaving shortly for a client meeting.

The Winchat utility must be installed on your network before you can complete the following tutorial. If your network is running Windows 95 network software, you can install it from your CD-ROM installation disc by using the Add/Remove Programs folder and the Windows Setup tab. To locate the program file, click the Have Disk button, open the Other folder and then the Chat folder. If you don't have access to the CD-ROM installation disc, then skip this section and continue with the section entitled "Using The Microsoft Network."

To use Winchat to send a message to another user on a network:

1. Click the **Start** button, point to **Programs**, point to **Accessories**, then click **Chat** on the Accessories menu. The Chat window opens.

If your Winchat program displays the name "Winchat" on the Accessories menu, click it to open the Chat window.

2. Type the message shown in Figure 10-10.

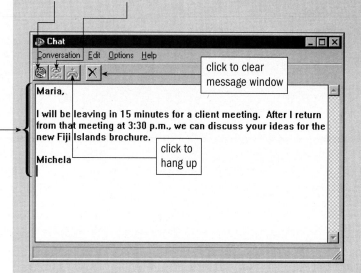

Chat window

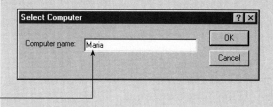

3. Click the **Dial** button ⊕ on the toolbar. In the Select Computer dialog box, type the name of one of the computers attached to your network, then click the **OK** button. Michela types "Maria," the name of Maria's computer, as shown in Figure 10-11. Windows 95 sends your message to the computer you specified.

Figure 10-11 ◀
Select
Computer
dialog box

enter name of
computer

TROUBLE? If a message appears in the status bar indicating that the other computer did not respond, click the Dial button again, and enter the correct name of the computer in the Select Computer dialog box, then click the OK button and try again. If the computer doesn't respond, you can't use Chat to send the message. Make sure you entered the correct name of the remote computer. You must know its name before you can connect.

Chat only works when the other user is working at the remote computer. The remote user hears a ringing sound and sees the Chat icon blinking in the taskbar. The remote user then clicks the Chat icon to see your message. As soon as the remote user activates the Chat window, your window changes to show two sections: one for your messages and one for the remote user. Maria sends a response to Michela that looks like Figure 10-12.

Figure 10-12
Maria's response

message sent by Michela

response sent by Maria

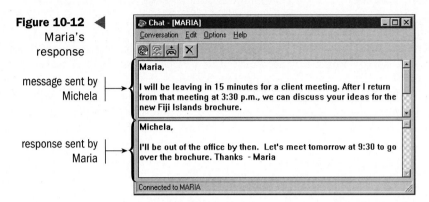

You can continue sending messages back and forth as long as you want the conversation to continue. When you are ready to end the conversation, either you or the remote user can hang up the phone.

To hang up:

1. Click the **Hang Up** button on the Chat window toolbar.

2. Click the **Close** button to close the Chat window.

This messaging utility allows you to communicate quickly with other users on a network without having to play telephone tag and without having to hunt someone down, but of course it only works when the remote user is available to answer the chat ring.

Michela is now ready to log off the network so that she can leave for her client meeting. How you log off the network depends on the network operating system you are using, whether you want to return to the desktop or leave the Windows 95 operating environment entirely, and whether your network requires user access validation. Many sites ask users to log off the network so an unauthorized user can't sit down at a computer and gain access to private network files.

To log off a network:

1. Click the **Start** button, then click **Shut Down**.

2. In the Shut Down Windows dialog box, click **Close All Programs And Log On As A Different User**, then click the **Yes** button.

The Enter Network Password dialog box appears. At some sites, network administrators prefer you to leave your computer with this dialog box open, so that the next user can sit down at the computer and enter his or her password. Other sites with different network operating systems might have configured the network so that you bypass the Windows 95 password system entirely.

Michela leaves her computer with this dialog box open.

Seaside Resorts' network enables all its employees to share the hardware and software resources on the network, communicate directly with other network users, and to share important files as they complete workgroup projects.

Online Services, the Internet, and the World Wide Web

If you are using a university computer, you probably have Internet access through your school, in which case you might not need an online service. However, if you own your computer or are thinking of purchasing one, you will find this section useful. In either case, you should read this section to familiarize yourself with the resources Microsoft makes available through Windows 95 to users who want to take advantage of the "Information superhighway." Michela, like many others, is already familiar with the use of online services. A year ago, she and her husband purchased communications software and a modem, and became members of a online service popular among home computer users. Whenever they have any spare time from their busy jobs, they explore the features of their online service.

An **online service** is a business that provides dial-up access to information stored on its computer system. You can access databases or libraries with a wealth of information on many different topics or subject areas, use e-mail services that permit you to transmit and receive messages and documents to others on the same online service or on another online service, use bulletin boards where you can post messages, and download documents, graphic images, shareware, and freeware. When you **download** files from an online service, you are copying the file from the online service to your computer. **Shareware** is software that is made available to you for a test period. If you decide to use the software after that test period, then you send the author of the shareware a fee that permits you to license and use that person's product. **Freeware** is software that is made available to you at no cost.

In addition to providing access to business, financial, and technical information, online services also provide other types of useful information on current events, weather, and sports. You can access newspapers and magazines, and even make travel reservations. Many also provide shopping services from which you can purchase products.

Online services also provide Internet access. The **Internet** consists of thousands of inter-connected networks located in countries all around the world. Each **network** consists of one or more computers that provide access to a rich diversity of resources. The **World Wide Web** is an Internet service that simplifies the process for locating and using information stored on the Internet.

Popular online services include companies such as America Online, CompuServe, Delphi, Genie, The Microsoft Network, and Prodigy, to name a few. You might have automatic Internet access at your university, and your university might not offer access to The Microsoft Network. If it doesn't, you won't be able to complete the rest of this tutorial, although you can reach the Microsoft Network directly from the Internet by using an Internet Web browser like Netscape or Mosaic. Your system administrator can tell you how. Your instructor can tell you how much of this tutorial you will be able to complete based on the access you have.

To use an online service, your computer must have communications software and a modem. **Communications software** manages the transmission of data between your computer and another computer that you access over a telephone line or perhaps even a direct connection. A **modem** is the hardware device that mediates the physical transfer of the data between computers. When you are transmitting data, the modem converts the electronic signals inside your computer into audio signals so that it can transmit that data over a telephone line to another computer. When you are receiving data, the modem converts audio signals on a telephone line into electronic signals on your computer. Using a modem and communications software, you can dial up an online service and connect to its network. Then, you can access the services available on that network.

You also have to become a member of the online service that you intend to use. The membership entitles you to access the online service and, like any other business, you are charged fees for using the online service.

All these online services place a wealth of information at your fingertips. No matter what type of information you need, you can access an online service or connect to the Internet, and in seconds, find that information and download it to your computer. Today, businesses are advertising their products and services on online services and the Internet, where they can easily reach millions of people.

Using The Microsoft Network

Seaside Resorts, like many other businesses, has purchased computers with Windows 95 so that they can use The Microsoft Network as their primary online service. Not only can they draw on the resources available on The Microsoft Network, but they can also access the Internet and World Wide Web.

The Microsoft Network (MSN) offers access to MSN and Internet e-mail, bulletin boards, MSN and Internet newsgroups, and chat rooms where you can conduct online discussions with other members on topics of your own choosing. Like other online services, MSN provides information on current events, news, weather, sports, and other topics of interest.

HELP DESK

Index

THE MICROSOFT NETWORK

Click the Start button, click Help, then click the Index tab.

Keyword
Microsoft Network (MSN)

Topic
Overview: Taking a test drive on the information highway

The Microsoft Network is an integral part of the Windows 95 operating system, and one of the significant new features of Windows 95 that distinguishes Windows 95 from other operating systems. The Microsoft Network user interface is similar to the Windows 95 user interface. You can navigate The Microsoft Network in the same ways that you use My Computer and Windows Explorer on your own computer system. You can use the same types of features available in Windows 95. For example, you can display and use toolbars, create shortcuts, use shortcut menus, and use drag and drop to move or copy folders and files. You can switch between The Microsoft Network and applications and documents on your computer system.

Before you can become a member, you must install the software that enables you to access The Microsoft Network from Windows 95. If you didn't install this software when you installed Windows 95, you can use the Add/Remove Programs application in the Control Panel to select The Microsoft Network component from the Windows Setup tab. After you install The Microsoft Network, you can then open it to apply for an account on it.

Microsoft Corporation has automated the process for connecting to The Microsoft Network and becoming a member. When you first access The Microsoft Network, Microsoft Corporation transmits membership application forms to you so that you can complete the necessary information required to become a member, and then disconnects you from The Microsoft Network. Next, you complete the application forms. You provide information about yourself, read and accept an agreement for using The Microsoft Network, select a payment plan, and provide a credit card number for your billing charges. Once you complete this information, Windows 95 automatically transmits the information to Microsoft Corporation via The Microsoft Network. Microsoft Corporation then provides Windows 95 with a local telephone number that permits you to connect to The Microsoft Network. As part of this process, you also provide a member ID of your own choosing and a password. If you prefer, you can use a fictitious name or handle to protect your identity when you are on line.

Michela has just completed the process for becoming a member of The Microsoft Network. Next, she wants you to connect to The Microsoft Network, and look for information on vacation packages offered by other businesses. By examining what other businesses offer, she can develop new ideas of her own for advertising strategies that Seaside Resorts might use on The Microsoft Network.

Before you can complete this tutorial, you must have an account on The Microsoft Network and, of course, a connection to The Microsoft Network. If you want to become a member of The Microsoft Network, install The Microsoft Network component, then double-click The Microsoft Network icon and complete the membership application process before you start the tutorial. If you do not have an account of your own, or access to an account at your college, you might want to read, but not keystroke, the tutorial steps so that you are familiar with the use of The Microsoft Network and the rich diversity of resources that it offers.

When you connect to The Microsoft Network, you are not automatically connected to the Internet. That is a separate process that you perform either from The Microsoft Network, or from your desktop, as you will see later in the tutorial.

The features and resources on The Microsoft Network, as well as other networks, change daily. As you step through the tutorial, your screens might be different from those shown in the figures. The important thing to remember is that the procedures described in this tutorial for using The Microsoft Network are the same even if the figures don't match.

To connect to The Microsoft Network:

   1. On your desktop, double-click **The Microsoft Network** icon. Windows 95 displays a Sign In dialog box. See Figure 10-13. In the Sign In box, you see your Member ID. If this is the first time you have used The Microsoft Network, you will need to enter your password. If you enable the Remember my password option, you will not need to enter your password again.

Figure 10-13 ◀
Logging onto
The Microsoft
Network

enter password

enable option to
remember password

click to change
settings

click to connect to
The Microsoft
Network

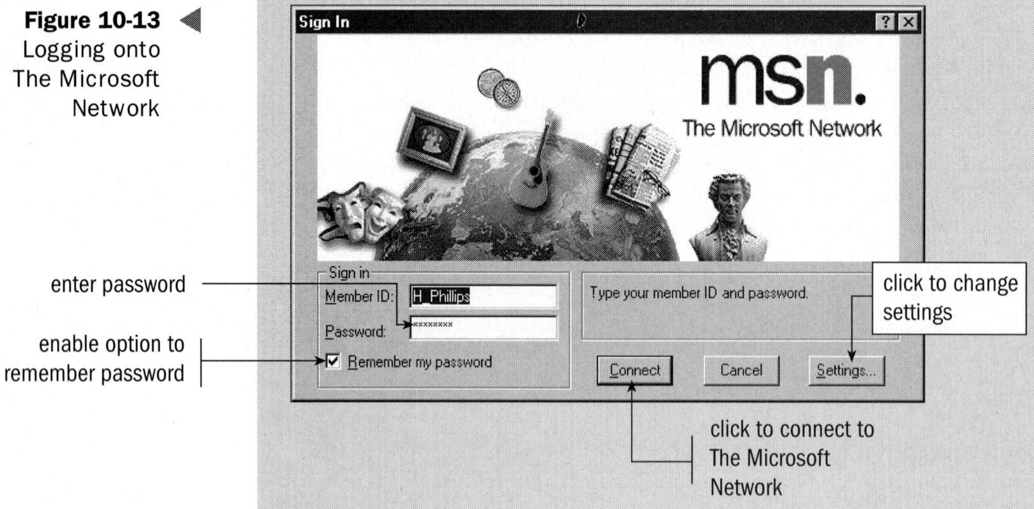

TROUBLE? If you do not have The Microsoft Network icon on your desktop, then you have not installed that Windows component. Install the Microsoft Network component now from the Control Panel's Add/Remove Programs utility (click the Windows Setup tab), then repeat Step 1.

2. If necessary, enter your password in the Password text box, then click the **Connect** button. Your modem dials your primary access number. Once your modem establishes a connection to The Microsoft Network, your account is verified, then you will briefly see MSN Central before an Online Viewer prepares a view of MSN Today. See Figure 10-14. MSN Today provides you with tools for accessing information on current events, activities, presentations, and services. On the left side of the screen, you see a list of options that might include the following categories: MSN Life, MSN Spectrum, Home and Family, MSN Computing, MSN Sports, Kids & Co., Business & Finance, MSN News, Events Calendar, and MSN Central. The remainder of the window contains icons for special events and options. You can click any of the categories on the left side of the screen or any of the icons to access information.

Figure 10-14
Viewing current
events and
options in MSN
Today

click to open a
guidebook

click an option
to go to

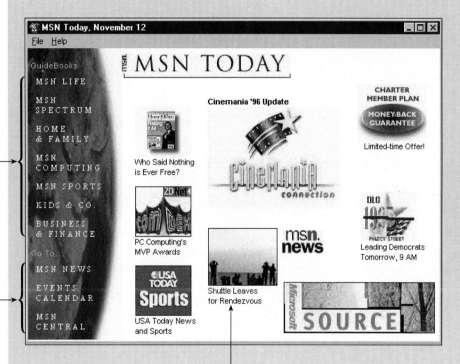

click to view news

TROUBLE? If this is the first time you have connected to The Microsoft Network, a Welcome to The Microsoft Network window opens with a welcoming message from the owner of Microsoft Corporation, Bill Gates. From this window you can meet other Microsoft employees and explore other Network opportunities. Click the Welcome window Close button and then continue with the steps. You might also see MSN Today very briefly, then see MSN Central. The next time you connect to The Microsoft Network, you will see MSN Today.

TROUBLE? If you see The Microsoft Network dialog box, informing you that you have received new mail on The Microsoft Network and asking if you want to open your inbox now, click the No button.

3. Click the **Close** button [X] to close MSN Today. You now see MSN Central. See Figure 10-15. MSN Central is actually your starting point for accessing all the services and features available on The Microsoft Network. On the MSN Central screen, there are five buttons for MSN Today, E-mail, Favorite Places, Member Assistance, and Categories. Notice that MSN Central has a menu bar and toolbar similar to the ones you use in Windows 95. Also, the Help menu provides help information about The Microsoft Network and its resources and features.

Figure 10-15 ◀
Viewing
services in
MSN Central

MSN toolbar ——

services ——

click to open
Categories folder

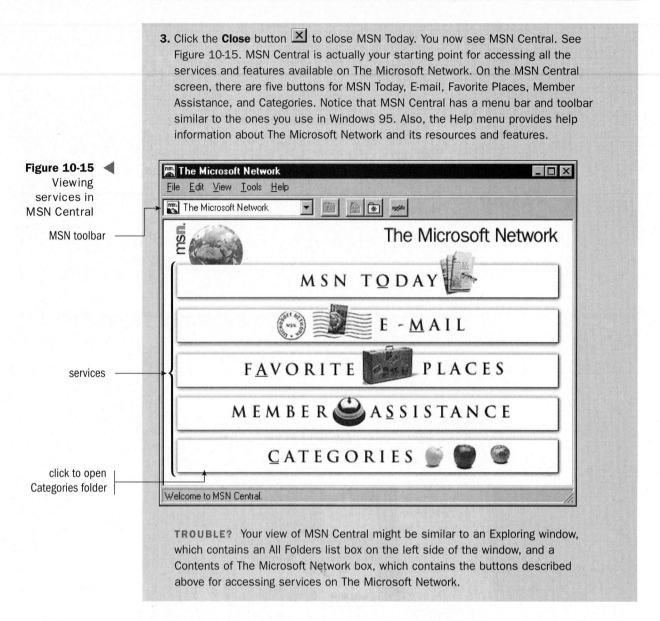

TROUBLE? Your view of MSN Central might be similar to an Exploring window, which contains an All Folders list box on the left side of the window, and a Contents of The Microsoft Network box, which contains the buttons described above for accessing services on The Microsoft Network.

When you access The Microsoft Network, MSN Today is automatically opened so that you can immediately find out about new events, World news, and new developments. You can then return to MSN Central to access other services.

The E-Mail button accesses The Microsoft Network service that allows members to send mail to, and receive mail from, other members as well as from individuals who use the Internet.

Favorite Places is a folder where you can store shortcuts to your favorite folders, bulletin boards, and chat rooms. By opening Favorite Places and clicking a shortcut, you can go directly to a folder, bulletin board, or chat room that you visited previously.

Member Assistance is a folder where Microsoft provides assistance to members. You can obtain information about your account, billing, and statements of charges.

The Categories button opens a folder that contains icons for all the different forums offered on The Microsoft Network. A **forum** is a collection of services on a specific topic, such as Computers & Software. Within each forum, you will find folders for each of the services in the forum. Each forum has a **kiosk**, or online information booth, that explains the purpose of the forum and identifies the individual who acts as the forum manager. You might also find folders with libraries of files that you can download (or copy down) to your computer system, **bulletin boards** where you can read other members' messages and post messages of your own for members to read, and **chat rooms** where you can carry on conversations with other members while all of you are online at the same time.

Michela asks you to open the Categories folder and find out if there is a folder devoted to travel.

To open the Categories folder:

1. Click the **Categories** button. You now see forums for a variety of member interests, such as Arts & Entertainment, Business & Finance, Computers & Software, and The Internet Center. See Figure 10-16. Michela suggests you set viewing options as you do when you navigate Windows folders, then open the Interest, Leisure & Hobbies folder.

Figure 10-16
Viewing the contents of the Categories folder

forums →

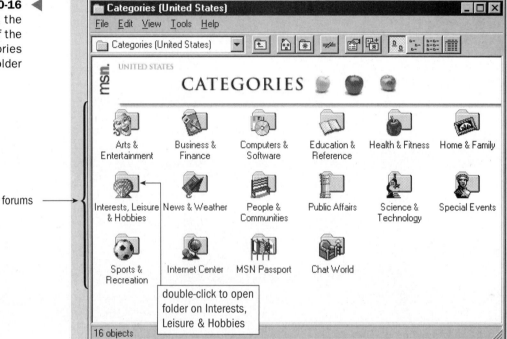

TROUBLE? It is important to note that over time, online services grow and change. You might see forums and other options that were not available when these figures were created.

2. If you do not see a Toolbar in the Categories folder, click **View** on the menu bar, then click **Toolbar**.

3. Click **View** on the menu bar, click **Options**, click the **Folder** tab, then, if necessary, click the **Browse MSN folders by using a single window that changes as you open each folder** radio option and click the **OK** button.

4. Double-click the **Interests, Leisure & Hobbies** folder. After opening this folder, you immediately notice that there is a Travel folder. See Figure 10-17.

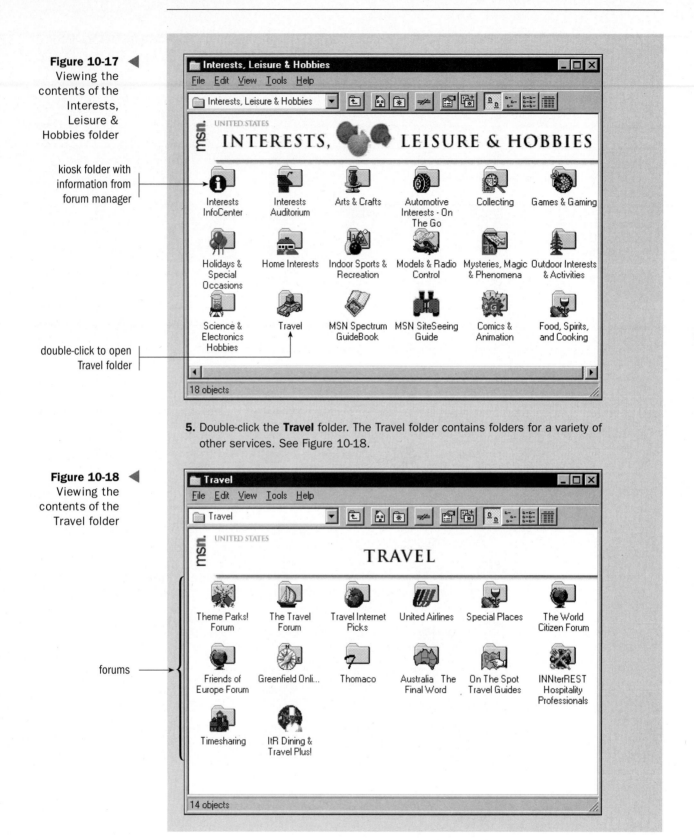

Figure 10-17 ◀
Viewing the
contents of the
Interests,
Leisure &
Hobbies folder

kiosk folder with
information from
forum manager

double-click to open
Travel folder

5. Double-click the **Travel** folder. The Travel folder contains folders for a variety of other services. See Figure 10-18.

Figure 10-18 ◀
Viewing the
contents of the
Travel folder

forums

Searching The Microsoft Network

So that you can more quickly locate the types of information that Michela needs to develop new advertising strategies for Seaside Resorts, you decide to search for information on resorts. Since Hawaii is one of the most popular vacation packages for Seaside Resorts' customers, you decide to focus on resorts in Hawaii.

To search for information on The Microsoft Network:

1. Click **Tools** on the menu bar, point to **Find**, then click **On The Microsoft Network** on the Find menu. The Find: All MSN services window opens.

2. In the Containing text box, type **Hawaii** then set the remainder of your settings to match those in Figure 10-19.

Figure 10-19
Searching for information on Hawaii

enter search topic

search in these places

search all services

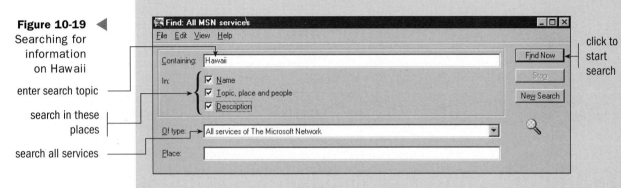

click to start search

The Find: All MSN services window is similar to the Find: All Files window you use with Windows 95. In the Containing text box, you can enter a word or phrase that identifies the type of information you want to locate. If you select the Name check box, the search will include the names of services on The Microsoft Network. If you select the Topic, place and people check box, the search will include each service's keywords for topic, place, and people. If you select the Description check box, the search will include the description for each service. The Of type list box includes options for searching all services of The Microsoft Network, folders and forums, bulletin boards and file libraries, chat rooms, multimedia titles, kiosks and other files, Internet newsgroups, and all services (MSN and Internet). In the Place text box you can enter the name of a specific geographic area.

3. Click the **Find Now** button. The Find window displays the results of its search.

4. Click the **Type** column button once to arrange the items in the Found box in alphabetical order of Type. See Figure 10-20.

Figure 10-20 ◄
Results of
searching The
Microsoft
Network for
information on
Hawaii

click to arrange
results in order by
type of item

bulletin board folders

chat room

download-and-run
files

folders

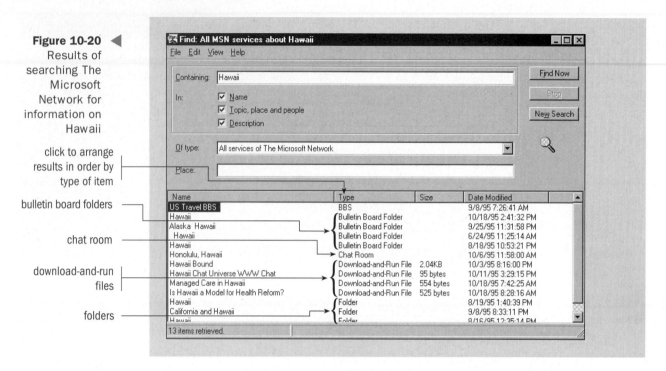

You tell Michela that you have located bulletin board folders, a chat room, download-and-run files, and folders all of which contain information about Hawaii. A download-and-run file is one that The Microsoft Network downloads and then immediately opens within the application that created it.

Opening a Bulletin Board Folder

Michela suggests that you examine a bulletin board folder on Hawaii, and find out whether Seaside Resorts might benefit from using one of these vehicles as an advertising tool.

Businesses and individuals post messages in bulletin board folders so that you can examine those messages at your convenience. You can also post responses to messages.

To open a bulletin board folder:

1. In the Name column, right-click **Alaska Hawaii**, then click **Open** on the shortcut menu and *be patient*. The Alaska Hawaii (Read Only) window opens with a list of locations for Alaska and Hawaii. See Figure 10-21. The paper clip to the right of an item in the subject column indicates that there is a file that you can download to your computer and then open after you select that item.

Figure 10-21 ◄
Viewing the
contents of the
Alaska Hawaii
Bulletin Board
folder

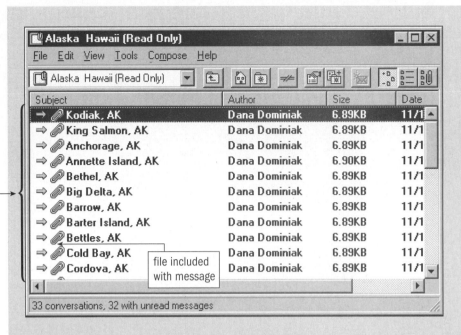

messages with
information on places
in Alaska

file included
with message

33 conversations, 32 with unread messages

TROUBLE? If you do not see a bulletin board folder named Alaska Hawaii, right-click the name of another bulletin board folder, then click Open on the shortcut menu.

TROUBLE? If you do not see any messages listed in your window, click Tools on the menu bar, then click Show All Messages.

2. Adjust your view so that you see the listing for Honolulu, HI.

3. Right-click **Honolulu, HI**, then click **Open** on the shortcut menu.

In the (Read-Only) Honolulu, HI window, a message tells you to double-click on the icon and then choose Download and Open to view the contents of the message. See Figure 10-22.

Figure 10-22 ◄
Viewing the
contents of the
Honolulu, HI
message

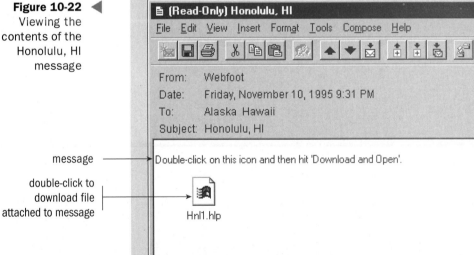

message

double-click to
download file
attached to message

From: Webfoot
Date: Friday, November 10, 1995 9:31 PM
To: Alaska Hawaii
Subject: Honolulu, HI

Double-click on this icon and then hit 'Download and Open'.

Hnl1.hlp

4. Double-click the icon. An Attached File Properties dialog box opens. See Figure 10-23. The Status option on the General property sheet informs you that this file has been approved by the forum manager for downloading.

Figure 10-23 ◀
Attached File
Properties
dialog box

how long it will take
to download file

file approved by
forum manager

no cost

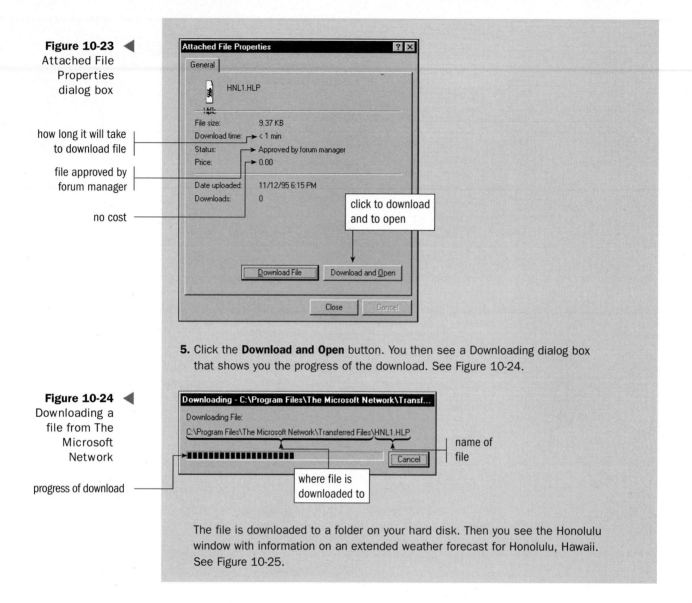

5. Click the **Download and Open** button. You then see a Downloading dialog box that shows you the progress of the download. See Figure 10-24.

Figure 10-24 ◀
Downloading a
file from The
Microsoft
Network

progress of download

The file is downloaded to a folder on your hard disk. Then you see the Honolulu window with information on an extended weather forecast for Honolulu, Hawaii. See Figure 10-25.

Figure 10-25 ◀
Viewing the
contents of the
downloaded file

weather forecast for
Honolulu, Hawaii

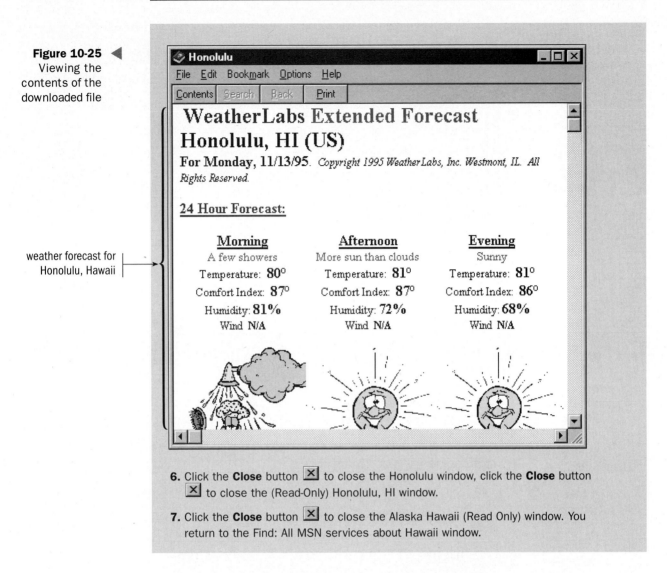

6. Click the **Close** button ☒ to close the Honolulu window, click the **Close** button
☒ to close the (Read-Only) Honolulu, HI window.

7. Click the **Close** button ☒ to close the Alaska Hawaii (Read Only) window. You
return to the Find: All MSN services about Hawaii window.

Although the window with the weather forecast for Honolulu, Hawaii, was not what
Michela expected to find, she realizes that this find will be useful, because many clients
ask about weather conditions just prior to a flight. Now, she knows how to find this
information when she needs it.

Opening a Folder

Michela asks you to next try one of the Hawaii folders, and find out if businesses advertise in these folders.

*To complete this next section, you must have Microsoft Word or WordPad installed on
your computer. The Microsoft Network will download a file, open Microsoft Word or
WordPad, and then open the document. Also, you might be prompted to pay a nominal
charge.*

To open a folder:

1. In the Name column, right-click a recent listing for a Hawaii Folder then click
Open on the shortcut menu. The Hawaii window opens. See Figure 10-26. The
Hawaii window contains icons for documents that contain information about pop-
ular areas in Hawaii visited by vacationers.

Figure 10-26 ◀
Viewing the
contents of the
Hawaii folder

documents that you
can download

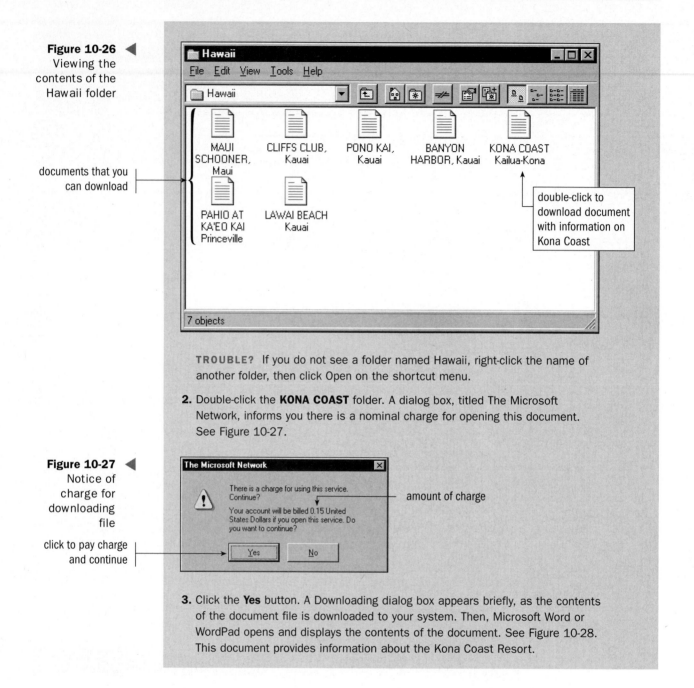

double-click to
download document
with information on
Kona Coast

TROUBLE? If you do not see a folder named Hawaii, right-click the name of
another folder, then click Open on the shortcut menu.

2. Double-click the **KONA COAST** folder. A dialog box, titled The Microsoft
Network, informs you there is a nominal charge for opening this document.
See Figure 10-27.

Figure 10-27 ◀
Notice of
charge for
downloading
file

click to pay charge
and continue

amount of charge

3. Click the **Yes** button. A Downloading dialog box appears briefly, as the contents
of the document file is downloaded to your system. Then, Microsoft Word or
WordPad opens and displays the contents of the document. See Figure 10-28.
This document provides information about the Kona Coast Resort.

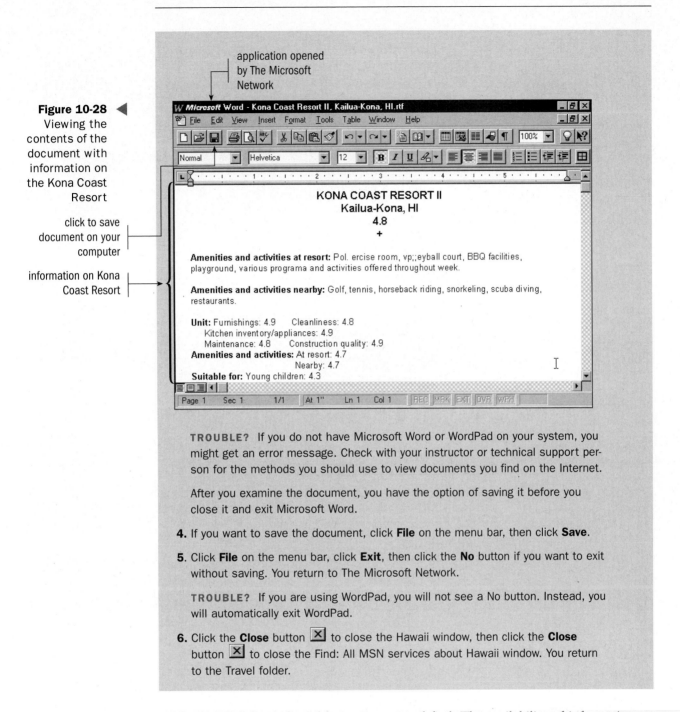

Figure 10-28 ◄
Viewing the
contents of the
document with
information on
the Kona Coast
Resort

click to save
document on your
computer

information on Kona
Coast Resort

TROUBLE? If you do not have Microsoft Word or WordPad on your system, you might get an error message. Check with your instructor or technical support person for the methods you should use to view documents you find on the Internet.

After you examine the document, you have the option of saving it before you close it and exit Microsoft Word.

4. If you want to save the document, click **File** on the menu bar, then click **Save**.

5. Click **File** on the menu bar, click **Exit**, then click the **No** button if you want to exit without saving. You return to The Microsoft Network.

TROUBLE? If you are using WordPad, you will not see a No button. Instead, you will automatically exit WordPad.

6. Click the **Close** button ☒ to close the Hawaii window, then click the **Close** button ☒ to close the Find: All MSN services about Hawaii window. You return to the Travel folder.

Again, Michela is pleased by an unexpected find. The availability of information on different resort sites will prove useful in helping customers choose tailor-made vacation packages.

Opening a Forum

As Michela has discovered, The Microsoft Network provides access to unexpected and useful types of information as you use its services. Michela, however, would still like to locate some examples of advertising by other companies. She suggests that you open one of the forums in the Travel folder.

To open a forum:

1. Double-click the **INNterREST Consumer Dining & Travel** icon and, when the INNterREST Hospitality Forums window opens, click the **Maximize** button ▢. You have finally located another business that advertises on The Microsoft Network and, at the same time, accessed its global network that provides information on dining, travel, and marketplace. See Figure 10-29.

Figure 10-29 ◄
Viewing options
available in a
forum

a global dining and
travel online network

click to open Travel
folder for this forum

TROUBLE? If you do not see the INNterREST Consumer Dining & Travel icon, you can double-click another icon that you think might lead you to an advertiser and work on your own, or you can read, but not complete, the remainder of the steps in this section.

2. In the INNterREST Hospitality Forums window, point to **TRAVEL** and, when the mouse pointer changes to 🖑, click **TRAVEL**. You open the ItR Travel PLUS! folder. See Figure 10-30. This folder provides individuals interested in a vacation package with additional information as they plan a vacation.

Figure 10-30 ◀
Viewing the
contents of an
advertiser's
folder

option provided by
advertiser for making
accommodations
and reservations

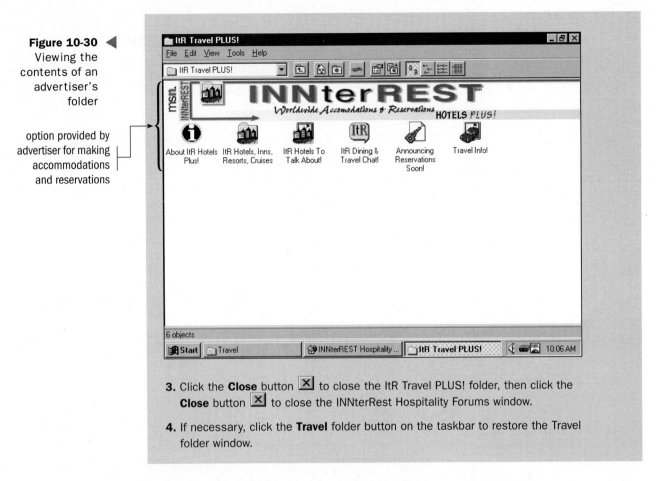

3. Click the **Close** button ☒ to close the ItR Travel PLUS! folder, then click the
Close button ☒ to close the INNterRest Hospitality Forums window.

4. If necessary, click the **Travel** folder button on the taskbar to restore the Travel
folder window.

After finding the information on the INNterRest Hospitality Forums and the ItR
Travel PLUS! folder, Michela decides to further research the possibility of developing a
comparable service on The Microsoft Network for Seaside Resorts.

She asks you to search using the more general topic "resorts," and find out what other
information might be helpful to her.

To search for information on resorts:

1. Click **Tools** on the menu bar, point to **Find**, then click **On The Microsoft Network**
on the Find menu.

2. After the Find: All MSN services window opens, type **resorts** in the Containing
text box, then click the **Description** check box.

3. Click the **Find Now** button and, when the search is complete, click the **Type** column button once to arrange the items in the Found box in alphabetical order of
Type. See Figure 10-31.

Figure 10-31 ◀
Searching The
Microsoft
Network for
information on
resorts

click to arrange
results in order by
type of item

right-click to display
shortcut menu

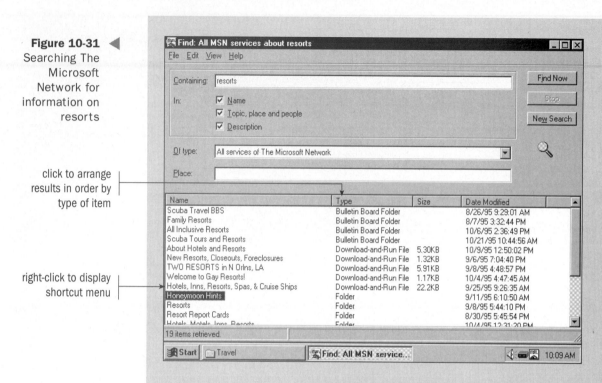

4. Right-click **Hotels, Inns, Resorts, Spas, & Cruise Ships** in the Name column,
then click **Open** on the shortcut menu. In the Hotels, Inns, Resorts, Spas, Cruise
Lines window, you discover a business that helps other businesses design advertising for The Microsoft Network. See Figure 10-32.

Figure 10-32 ◀
Accessing a
service
provided by a
business

options for features
you might use for your
online advertising

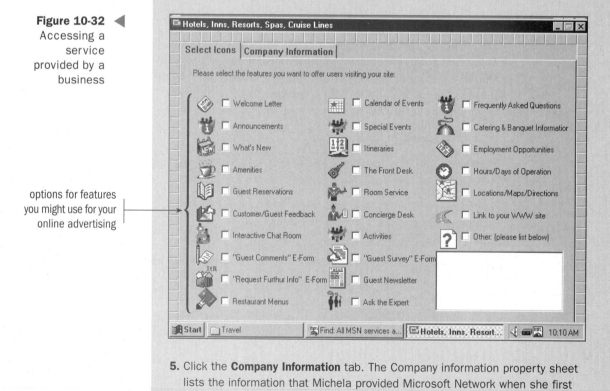

5. Click the **Company Information** tab. The Company information property sheet
lists the information that Michela provided Microsoft Network when she first
registered. See Figure 10-33.

Figure 10-33 ◀

Viewing
company
information on
Michela
Roberts and
Seaside
Resorts

registration
information provided
by Michela; yours will
contain information
you provided
Microsoft when you
registered for an
account, or it might
be blank

how to order service

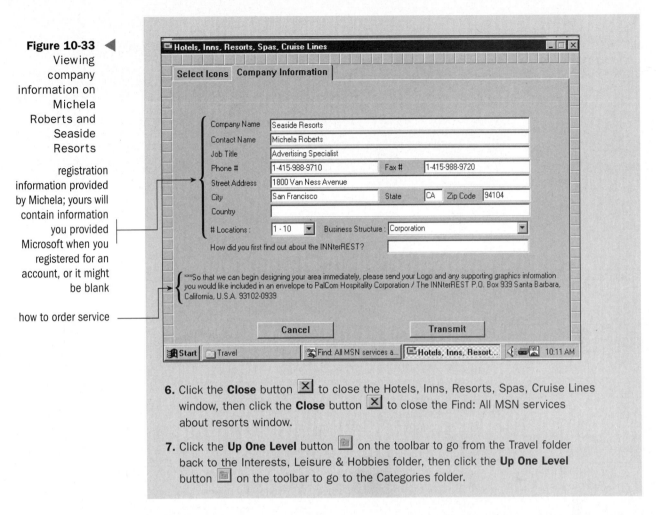

6. Click the **Close** button ☒ to close the Hotels, Inns, Resorts, Spas, Cruise Lines window, then click the **Close** button ☒ to close the Find: All MSN services about resorts window.

7. Click the **Up One Level** button 🖿 on the toolbar to go from the Travel folder back to the Interests, Leisure & Hobbies folder, then click the **Up One Level** button 🖿 on the toolbar to go to the Categories folder.

You have found some valuable information for Michela. She is going to recommend that Seaside Resorts contract with this company to design custom advertising for The Microsoft Network.

Opening The Internet Center Folder

Michela wants you to open The Internet Center folder, find out what resources are available, and figure out how to install the software she needs to access the Internet and the World Wide Web.

To open The Internet Center folder:

1. Double-click **The Internet Center** icon. In the Internet Center folder, Microsoft provides information on how to get on the Internet and World Wide Web, rules for using the Internet, Internet software, and even an Internet Cafe! See Figure 10-34.

Figure 10-34 ◀
Viewing the
contents of The
Internet Center
folder

double-click to
display information
on how to get on the
Internet

Internet
etiquette

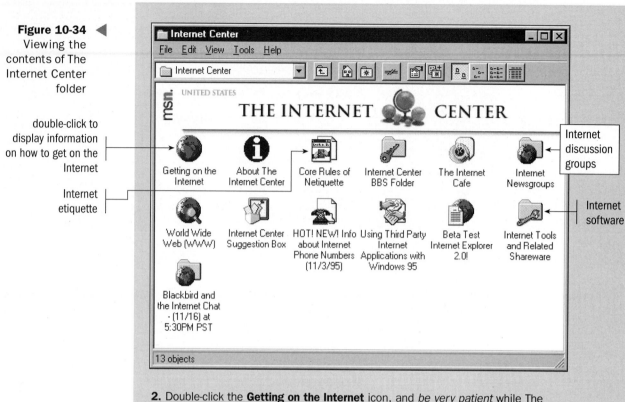

Internet
discussion
groups

Internet
software

2. Double-click the **Getting on the Internet** icon, and *be very patient* while The
Microsoft Network downloads the necessary information into a window on your
computer system. In the Getting on the Internet window, Microsoft explains that
you can use MSN to exchange electronic mail with anyone who has an Internet
address, to read and post messages in Internet newsgroups, to browse the World
Wide Web. See Figure 10-35. If you have not downloaded the necessary software
for accessing the Internet through The Microsoft Network, you can use the Upgrade
Instructions button on this screen to set up your computer system. The buttons at
the top of the screen provide more information on Getting on the Internet.

Figure 10-35 ◀
Getting on the
Internet
window

click to view
information on how
to browse the World
Wide Web

what you can do on
the Internet

click to download
software for
accessing the Internet

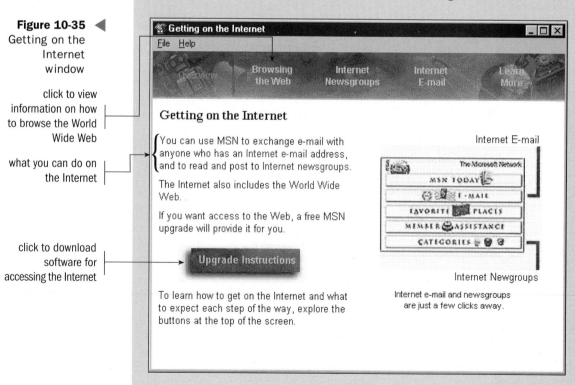

3. Point to the **Browsing the Web** button and, when the pointer changes to 🖑, click the **Browsing the Web** button. In the Getting on the Internet window, Microsoft notes that the Web consists of millions of pages of information on a wide variety of subjects. See Figure 10-36. If you click the check mark to the left of one of the paragraphs of information, you can learn more about the Web.

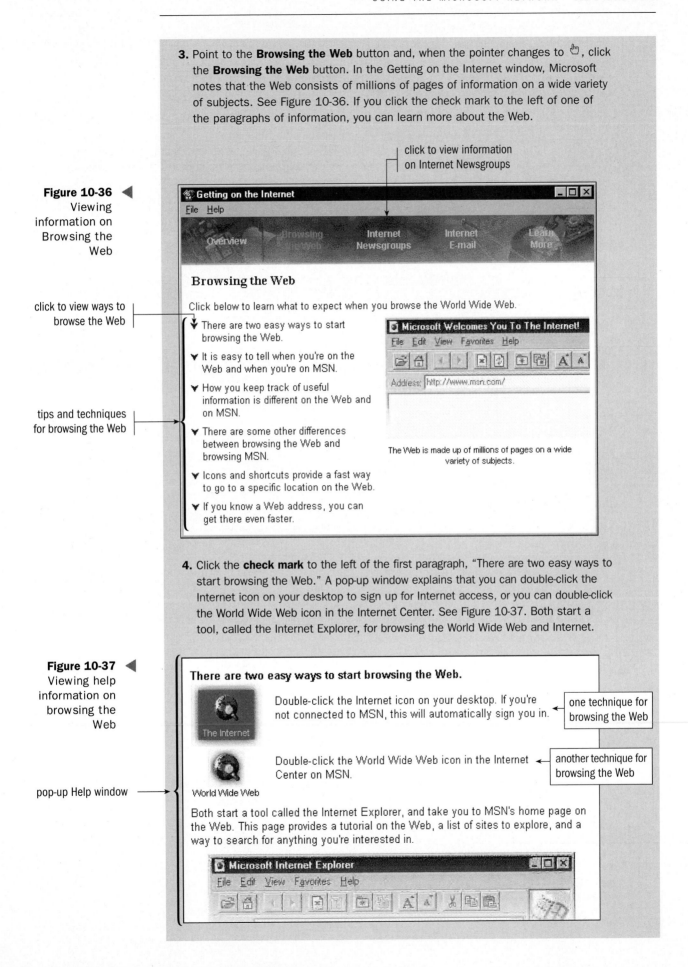

Figure 10-36
Viewing information on Browsing the Web

click to view information on Internet Newsgroups

click to view ways to browse the Web

tips and techniques for browsing the Web

4. Click the **check mark** to the left of the first paragraph, "There are two easy ways to start browsing the Web." A pop-up window explains that you can double-click the Internet icon on your desktop to sign up for Internet access, or you can double-click the World Wide Web icon in the Internet Center. See Figure 10-37. Both start a tool, called the Internet Explorer, for browsing the World Wide Web and Internet.

Figure 10-37
Viewing help information on browsing the Web

pop-up Help window

one technique for browsing the Web

another technique for browsing the Web

5. Click the **pop-up window** to close it.

6. Once you have explored the other topics on Browsing the Web, click the last **pop-up window** to close it.

7. Click the **Internet Newsgroups** button. Microsoft explains that there are Internet newsgroups on every conceivable subject. See Figure 10-38. You can access those newsgroups in the Internet Center. You can also learn more about newsgroups by selecting a check mark next to one of the three topics in this window.

click to view information on Internet E-mail

Figure 10-38 ◀
Viewing help information on using Internet newsgroups

tips on newsgroups

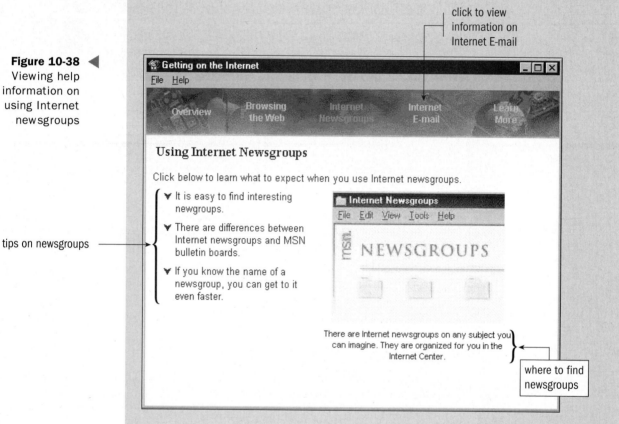

where to find newsgroups

8. Once you have explored the topics on Using Internet Newsgroups, click the last **pop-up window** to close it.

9. Click the **Internet E-mail** button. Microsoft explains that your Inbox (on your desktop) stores mail you receive from other MSN members, as well as individuals on the Internet. See Figure 10-39.

Figure 10-39 ◄
Viewing help
information on
using Internet
E-mail

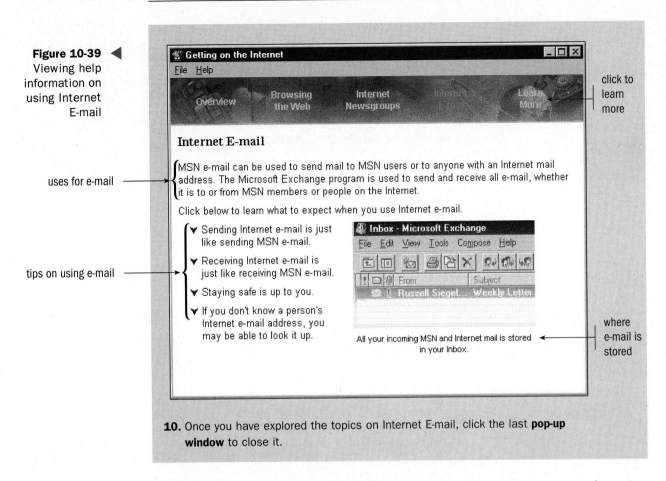

click to
learn
more

uses for e-mail

tips on using e-mail

where
e-mail is
stored

10. Once you have explored the topics on Internet E-mail, click the last **pop-up window** to close it.

The last button in the Getting on the Internet provides you with more information about using The Microsoft Network, the Internet, and the World Wide Web. Michela notes that it's important to examine this information, so that you understand the terminology and features common to the Internet and World Wide Web.

To learn more:

1. Click the **Learn More** button. Microsoft explains that the World Wide Web is a system for locating and using resources on the Internet. See Figure 10-40. You can click any of the commonly used terms to learn more about their meaning. Furthermore, you can click the four icons at the bottom of the window for more information on the Internet and the World Wide Web. For example, you can step through a tutorial on how to use the Internet.

Figure 10-40
Options for
learning more
about MSN and
the Internet

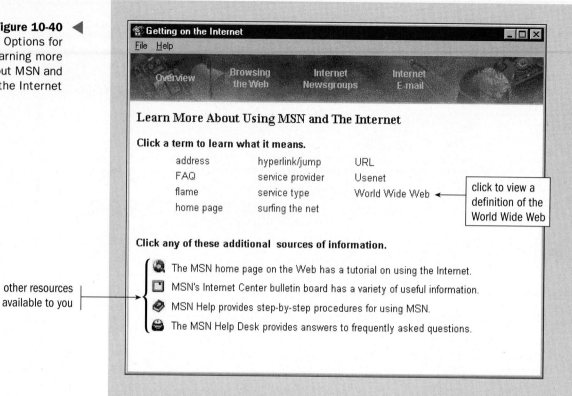

other resources
available to you

2. Click the **World Wide Web** term. In a pop-up window, Microsoft explains that the Internet Explorer is the Web browser tool you use to explore the World Wide Web.

3. Click the **pop-up window** to close it.

4. Click the **URL** term. Microsoft explains that URL, an abbreviation for Uniform Resource Locator, is an address for a specific location on the Internet.

5. Click the **pop-up window** to close it.

6. Click the **home page** term. Microsoft explains that both companies and individuals have their own page, or screen, on the World Wide Web. If you click a highlighted term or icon, you jump to another Web page with related information.

7. Click the **pop-up window** to close it.

8. Click the **surfing the net** term. Microsoft explains that this term means the same as browsing or exploring the Internet.

9. After you explore these additional sources of information, close any open pop-up window, then click the **Close** button ☒ to close the Getting on the Internet Window and return to The Internet Center.

Since you have finished your search of information on The Microsoft Network, you are ready to sign out.

To disconnect from The Microsoft Network:

1. Click the **Sign Out** button 🖅 on the toolbar.

   TROUBLE? If you do not see a toolbar, click View on the menu bar, then click Toolbar.

2. When The Microsoft Network dialog box displays a prompt asking you to verify that you want to disconnect from The Microsoft Network, click the **Yes** button.

Michela has to leave for a meeting where she and others will discuss new advertising strategies. The information that you have collected for her will help her in planning new advertising campaigns.

If you want to take a break and resume this tutorial at a later time, close all open applications and remove your Student Disk from the floppy disk drive. When you resume the tutorial, start Windows and insert your Student Disk into a floppy disk drive.

• • •

Accessing the Internet

Seaside Resorts wants to expand its current vacation packages to include the Fiji Islands and other islands of the South Pacific. Michela offers to search the Internet for information on the Fiji Islands, and then use that information to prepare brochures for clients.

The easiest way to connect to the Internet is through a service provider, such as The Microsoft Network, because the service provider has all the tools you need to browse the net. The use of a **Web browser**, such as the Internet Explorer available on The Microsoft Network, provides an easy-to-use graphical user interface with tools for locating the information you need on the World Wide Web and the Internet.

When you first access the Internet with a Web browser, you are placed at a Web site's home page. A **Web site** is a computer or network for a corporation, business, or online service, such as The Microsoft Network, that provides access to the World Wide Web. At each Web site, you might access one or more Web pages. A **Web page** is a document that displays text and images, but it might also include options for displaying video, sound, and animation. The first Web page you see at a Web site is that site's **home page**. The home page provides you with information about the site and also about what's available at that site.

Each Web page includes links to other Web pages at the same site or at other Web sites. These links, called **hypertext links**, consist of underlined text, sometimes displayed in a color, such as blue, as well as images surrounded by a blue or black border. If you point to a hypertext link and click, you access another Web page somewhere on the World Wide Web. You can always identify a hypertext link, because the mouse pointer changes to 🖑 when you place the mouse pointer over the hypertext link. The use of hypertext links on the World Wide Web allows you to focus on finding the information you need, rather than attempting to figure out which Web site contains what you need.

HELP DESK

Index

THE INTERNET

Click the Start button, click Help, then click the Index tab.

Keyword	**Topic**
Internet	Overview: Introduction to the Internet

Depending on where you live, the number you use to connect to The Microsoft Network might also be the same number you use to connect to the Internet. In some locations, you have to dial a long-distance number so that you can connect to the Internet through The Microsoft Network. If you have to use a different number, then you need to sign out of The Microsoft Network and select the Internet icon on your desktop so that you can connect to The Microsoft Network through a long-distance line.

Michela asks you to find a home page that contains information on the Fiji Islands.

As you navigate the Internet, you must be patient. It takes time to access other computers on the Internet and even more time to display Web pages that contain graphics images.

The version of Internet Explorer that you use might differ from that shown in the figures, because Microsoft Corporation periodically upgrades this Web browser. However, the screens and options will more than likely be similar to those shown in the figures so that you can continue with the tutorial. If you attempt to connect to the Internet and if there is a new version of the Internet Explorer, you might be prompted to download the upgrade before you can proceed.

To connect to the Internet:

1. Double-click the **Internet** icon on your desktop. The Connect To dialog box opens. See Figure 10-41. The Connect To dialog box shows the name of the provider you use to connect to the Internet, your member ID or name, and the access number.

TROUBLE? If your access number for the Internet is the same as the one for The Microsoft Network, you will see a dialog box similar to the one for signing on to The Microsoft Network.

Figure 10-41 ◀
Connecting to the Internet through The Microsoft Network

click to connect to the Internet

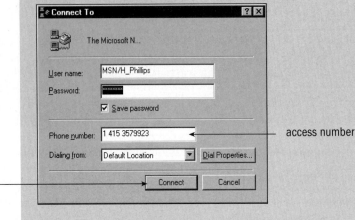

access number

2. Click the **Connect** button. You then see a Connecting to The Microsoft Network dialog box. Wait for the MSN Welcomes You to The Internet!-Microsoft Internet Explorer Web page window to open. From this window, you can start your exploration of the Internet. See Figure 10-42. Below the toolbar is an address box that lists the URL (Uniform Resource Locator) or address on the Internet that you are currently accessing.

Figure 10-42 ◀
MSN Welcomes You To the Internet! - Microsoft Internet Explorer home page

URL address

MSN's Internet home page

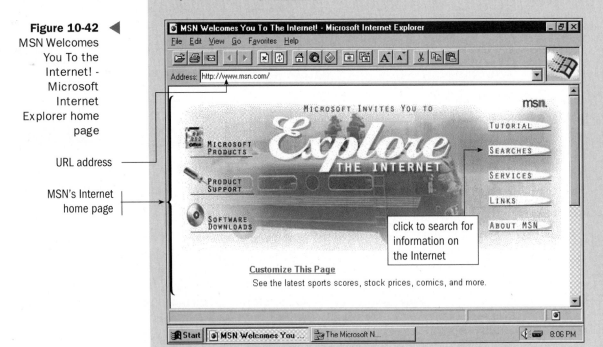

3. Click the **Searches** button. The Internet Searches Web page opens. See Figure 10-43. In this window, four search services allow you to search for information on the Internet.

Figure 10-43 ◀
All Internet
Searches -
Microsoft
Internet
Explorer
web page

search services

click to enter a
search condition

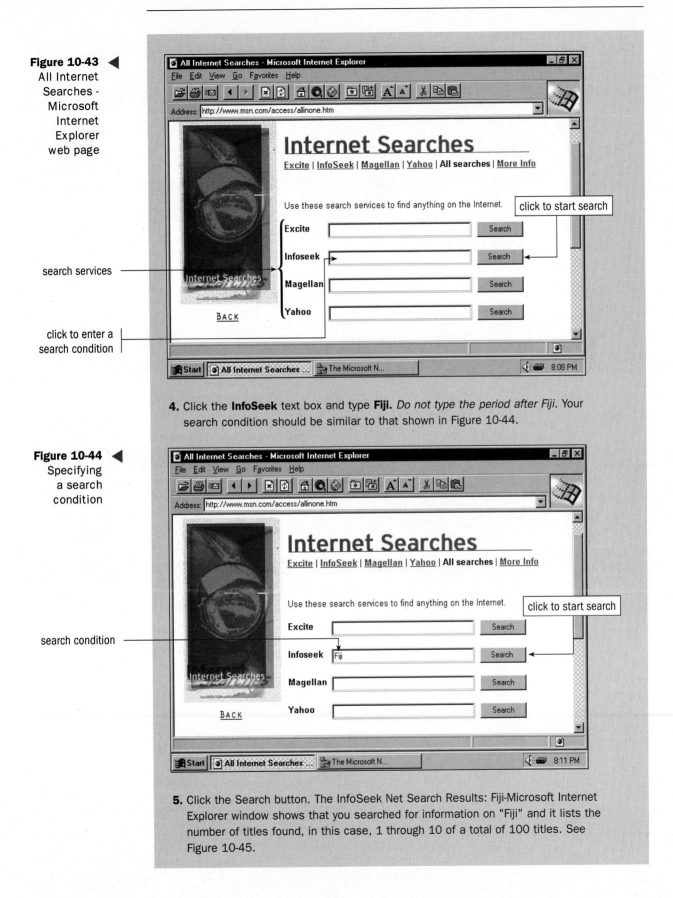

4. Click the **InfoSeek** text box and type **Fiji.** *Do not type the period after Fiji.* Your search condition should be similar to that shown in Figure 10-44.

Figure 10-44 ◀
Specifying
a search
condition

search condition

5. Click the Search button. The InfoSeek Net Search Results: Fiji-Microsoft Internet Explorer window shows that you searched for information on "Fiji" and it lists the number of titles found, in this case, 1 through 10 of a total of 100 titles. See Figure 10-45.

Figure 10-45
Results
of searching
the Internet

what you
searched on

titles listed

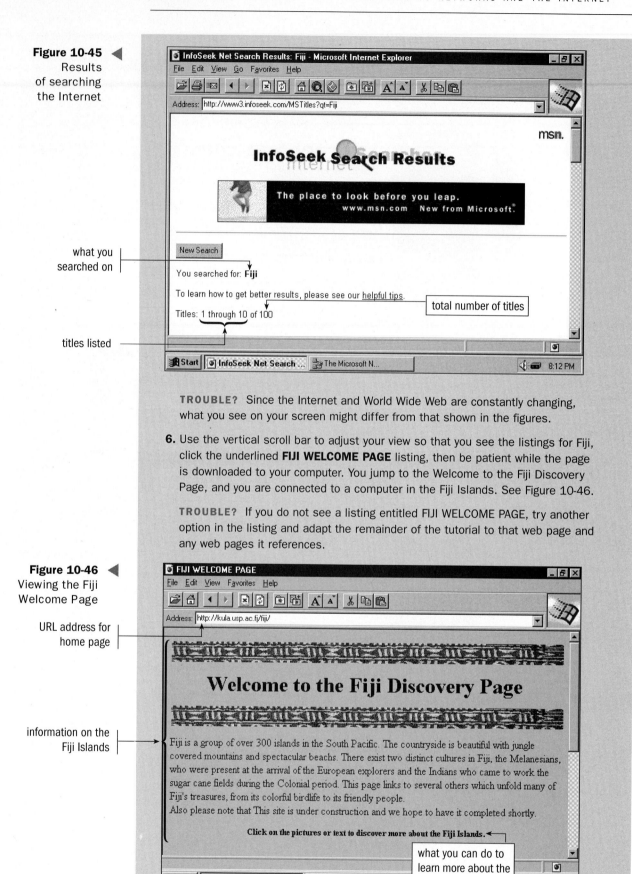

TROUBLE? Since the Internet and World Wide Web are constantly changing, what you see on your screen might differ from that shown in the figures.

6. Use the vertical scroll bar to adjust your view so that you see the listings for Fiji, click the underlined **FIJI WELCOME PAGE** listing, then be patient while the page is downloaded to your computer. You jump to the Welcome to the Fiji Discovery Page, and you are connected to a computer in the Fiji Islands. See Figure 10-46.

TROUBLE? If you do not see a listing entitled FIJI WELCOME PAGE, try another option in the listing and adapt the remainder of the tutorial to that web page and any web pages it references.

Figure 10-46
Viewing the Fiji
Welcome Page

URL address for
home page

information on the
Fiji Islands

what you can do to
learn more about the
Fiji Islands

If you see underlined text on a Web page, you can click the underlined text to jump to a Web page with information on the underlined topic. If you see a border around a graphics image on a Web page, you can click the image and display the image in a larger size. If you see a border around an icon for a sound, and if your computer has a sound card and speakers, you can click the icon to hear spoken words or music.

The Address box lists the URL for the Web page that you just accessed. At the bottom of this home page, you are prompted to click on the pictures or text to discover more about the Fiji Islands.

To view and select a picture:

1. Use the vertical scroll bar to adjust your view so that you see the pictures on this home page, as shown in Figure 10-47. By clicking one of these four pictures, you can view information and more pictures on Birdlife, People, Sea Life, and the Landscape.

Figure 10-47 ◀
Viewing links
you can access
from the
Fiji Welcome
home page

where you are
on the Internet

hypertext links

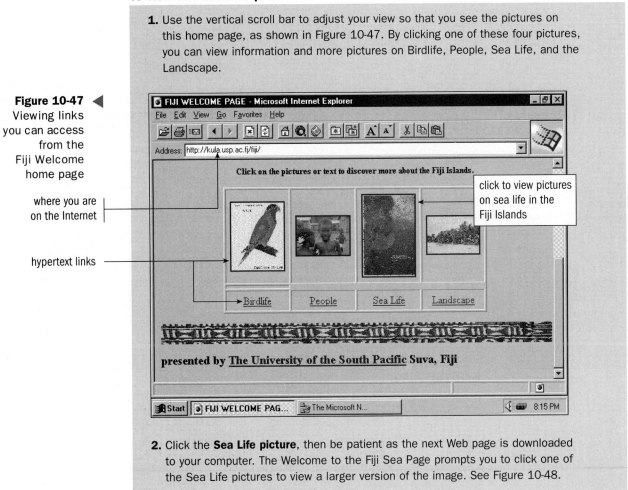

2. Click the **Sea Life picture**, then be patient as the next Web page is downloaded to your computer. The Welcome to the Fiji Sea Page prompts you to click one of the Sea Life pictures to view a larger version of the image. See Figure 10-48.

Figure 10-48 ◀
Welcome to the
Fiji Sea Page

3. Click the **Corals picture**, then be patient as the image is downloaded to your computer. The coral.jpg at kula.usp.ac.fj window displays a larger version of the Corals picture you viewed on the previous Web page. See Figure 10-49. You decide to save a copy of the picture to show Michela.

Figure 10-49 ◀
Viewing a
larger version
of the picture
on corals

click to go to MSN's
home page

right-click image to
view shortcut menu
for copying image to
your disk

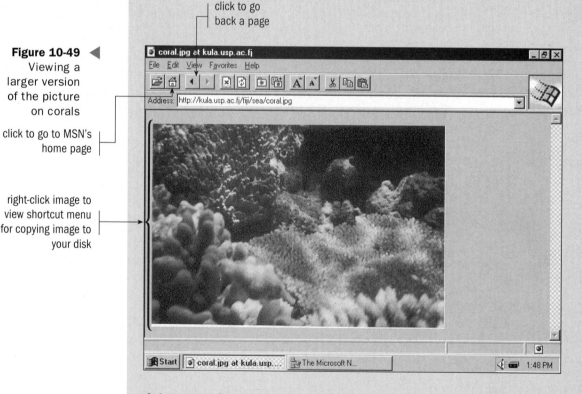

4. Insert your Student Disk into a floppy disk drive.

5. Right-click the **picture**, then click **Save Picture As** on the shortcut menu.

6. When the Save As dialog box opens, double-click the **disk drive** icon in the Save in list box for the drive that contains your Student Disk, then, if necessary, change to the top-level folder of your Student Disk. Select the default filename in the File name text box, type **coral** then click the **Save** button.

7. Click the **Back** button ◄ on the toolbar to go back to the Welcome to the Fiji Sea Page.

8. Click the **Back** button ◄ to return to the Welcome to the Fiji Discovery Page.

Printing a Web Page

Before you exit the Internet, you want to print a copy of the Welcome to the Fiji Discovery Page. Michela can use this Web page to compile a new brochure on the Fiji Islands.

To print your search results:

1. Make sure your printer is on and operational.

2. Click **File** on the menu bar, click **Print**, then click the **OK** button.

3. Click the **Open Start Page** button 🏠 on the toolbar to return to the MSN Welcomes You To The Internet window.

   TROUBLE? If you do not see a toolbar, click View on the menu bar, then click Toolbar.

4. Click **File** on the menu bar, click **Exit**, and when asked if you want to disconnect from The Microsoft Network, click the **Yes** button.

Michela is delighted with the progress that she has made in developing new advertising strategies for Seaside Resorts. Not only is The Microsoft Network easy to use, but the Internet Explorer simplifies the use of the Internet. The Microsoft Network and the Internet will prove invaluable in expanding and advertising Seaside Resorts vacation packages.

Tutorial Assignment

Each season Seaside Resorts prepares and prints a magazine that includes articles of interest to its customers. Maria has asked Michela to write a short article on some aspect of safety that would be useful for its customers. Michela asks you to sign onto The Microsoft Network, search for information on safety, then download and print that information so that she can prepare her article.

To complete this tutorial assignment, you must have a modem, access to an account on The Microsoft Network, and Microsoft Word or WordPad on your computer.

1. Double-click The Microsoft Network icon on the desktop.
2. In the Sign In dialog box, click the Connect button.
3. After you connect to The Microsoft Network, close MSN Today and return to MSN Central.
4. Click Tools on the menu bar, point to Find, then click On The Microsoft Network on the Find menu.
5. When the Find: All MSN services window opens, type "safety" (without the quotation marks) in the Containing text box.
6. If necessary, enable the In options for searching by Name, Topic, place and people, and Description.
7. If necessary, in the Of Type list box, choose All services of The Microsoft Network.
8. Click the Find Now button.

9. After the search is complete, you might see as many as eight Download-and-Run files on safety. If possible, in the next step select a safety folder appropriate to the area of the country where you live.

10. Right-click one of the Download-and-Run Files on safety, then click Open on the shortcut menu.

11. After the Download-and-Run file opens in Microsoft Word on your computer, click File on the menu bar, then click Print to print a copy of the safety information.

12. If you want to save this information in a file on your Student Disk, click File on the menu bar, then click Save As. In the Save As dialog box, select the drive that contains your Student Disk, then click the Save button.

13. Click File on the menu bar, then click Exit to close Microsoft Word and the download-and-run file.

14. Close the Find: All MSN services about safety window.

15. Click the Sign Out button, then click the Yes button to verify that you want to disconnect from The Microsoft Network.

Case Problems

1. Preparing a Multimedia Presentation at JME Technologies, Inc. JME Technologies, Inc. is a firm that develops new multimedia products for the home computer market. Julio Tempone, an employee at JME Technologies, is developing a multimedia presentation for a group of potential investors. He asks you to check The Microsoft Network for tools that might prove useful for his upcoming presentation.

To complete this tutorial assignment, you must have a modem, access to an account on The Microsoft Network, and Microsoft Word or WordPad on your computer.

1. Connect your computer to The Microsoft Network.
2. If necessary, close MSN Today and return to MSN Central.
3. Open the Categories folder.
4. Open the Computers & Software folder.
5. Open the Multimedia & CD-ROM folder.
6. Press Alt + PrintScreen to copy the Multimedia & CD-ROM folder to the Clipboard, open Paint, paste a copy of the image from the Clipboard into Paint's drawing area, print a copy of the image, then exit Paint without saving the image.
7. If the Multimedia & CD-ROM folder contains the Quick Multimedia Tester! icon, double-click the Quick Multimedia Tester! icon, and wait for The Microsoft Network to download a file with information on multimedia features into Microsoft Word, click the File Types button, click the Options button, click Print Topic, then click the OK button to print information on multimedia file types. *Note*: The Quick Multimedia Tester! allows you to test your computer and determine its multimedia capabilities so that you can enjoy this new emerging technology. If you want to save this downloaded file, click File on the menu bar, click Save As and, in the Save As dialog box, select the drive that contains your Student Disk, then click the Save button. Finally, click File on the menu bar, then click Exit to close Microsoft Word and the file you downloaded.
8. If the Quick Multimedia Tester! icon is not available, then choose another option within this folder, such as a newspaper, magazine, folder, bulletin board, or library and examine the available options. Use WordPad to prepare a one-page article on your findings, then print a copy of that article.
9. Sign out of The Microsoft Network.

2. Preparing a Brochure on Artificial Intelligence at Gifford Associates Gifford Associates prepares training aids for use by businesses, schools, and governmental agencies. Trisha Reyes, a designer at Gifford Associates, asks you to search The Microsoft Network for information on basic AI (Artificial Intelligence) concepts and definitions of commonly-used AI terms.

To complete this tutorial assignment, you must have a modem, access to an account on The Microsoft Network, and Microsoft Word or WordPad on your computer.

1. Connect your computer to The Microsoft Network.
2. Open the Categories folder.
3. Open the Computers & Software folder
4. Open the Emerging Computer Technologies folder
5. Open the Artificial Intelligence Forum.
6. Open the Introducing...AI! folder.
7. If the AI Definitions Help File icon is available, open this Help file. After The Microsoft Network downloads this file onto your computer and opens Microsoft Word, click the Options button, click Print Topic, then click the OK button to print. If you want to save this downloaded file, click File on the menu bar, click Save As and, in the Save As dialog box, select the drive that contains your Student Disk, then click the Save button. Finally, click File on the menu bar, then click Exit to close Microsoft Word and the file you downloaded.
8. If the AI Definitions Help File icon is not available, then choose another option within this folder, such as a newspaper, magazine, folder, bulletin board, or library and examine the available options. Use WordPad to prepare a one-page article on your findings, then print a copy of that article.
9. Sign out of The Microsoft Network.

3. Preparing a News Article at Tri-City News Tri-City News is a business that publishes a weekly newspaper with articles of interest to the professional and business community that it serves. Marc Langer was recently hired to prepare a weekly article on the Information Superhighway. Marc asks you to search The Microsoft Network for recent news on the future of the Information Superhighway.

To complete this tutorial assignment, you must have a modem, access to an account on The Microsoft Network, and Microsoft Word or WordPad on your computer.

1. Connect your computer to The Microsoft Network.
2. Open the Categories folder.
3. Open the Computers & Software folder.
4. Open the Networking & Telephone folder.
5. Open the SuperHighway News folder.
6. Open the SuperHighway News: Free Daily News bulletin board, then double-click a subject, such as The state of the Superhighway, that is of interest to you. Click File on the menu bar, then click Print to print a copy of the message.
7. If the SuperHighway News: Free Daily News bulletin board is not available, then choose another option within this folder, such as a newspaper, magazine, folder, bulletin board, or library and examine the available options. Use WordPad to prepare a one-page article on your findings, then print a copy of that article.
8. Close the message window, then sign out of The Microsoft Network.

4. Downloading NASA Images at Danville Observatory Danville Observatory presents multimedia planetary slide shows on Friday and Saturday nights prior to public viewings of the planets using its telescope. Angela Washington, the presenter at the observatory, asks you to download an image of the great red spot on the planet Jupiter from The Microsoft Network for inclusion in an upcoming slide show.

To complete this tutorial assignment, you must have a modem, access to an account on The Microsoft Network and Internet access on your computer.

1. Connect your computer to the Internet.
2. Click the option to Explore the Internet.
3. Click the option for Internet Searches.
4. Use InfoSeek or another search tool to locate information on Jupiter.
5. Locate a home page that contains an image of the great red spot on Jupiter, then open that home page.
6. After you display the image, click File on the menu bar, click Print, then click the OK button.
7. Right-click the image and, on the shortcut menu, click Save Picture As. When the Save As dialog box opens, double-click the disk drive icon in the Save in list box for the drive that contains your Student Disk, select the default filename in the File name text box, type Great Red Spot, then click the Save button.
8. Click the Open Start Page button.
9. Click File on the menu bar, then Exit.
10. Sign out of The Microsoft Network.

Designing Custom Desktops and Stationery

Vista Travel Agency

CASE

The travel agents at Vista Travel Agency assist their clients in planning vacation packages for tourist spots along the west coast. Many of their customers have toured well-known places, such as Yosemite National Park. To provide a more interesting working environment for employees at Vista Travel Agency, Peke Akua and her staff have decided to display a background image of an outdoors scene, such as a view of Yosemite, on their desktop. They also want to develop some new stationery, envelopes, and office note pads that contain a small part of this same outdoors image. To increase their chances of finding an interesting and attractive background image, they decide to search the Internet. Once they decide on a final image to use, they will prepare a design for new stationery and then adapt that design to the envelopes and office note pads.

Peke asks you to examine the Internet and the bit mapped image files on your computer, select an image, and use it as wallpaper for your desktop. When you design the new letterhead for Vista's stationery, she wants you to embed two objects: a logo design with the company name and a selected portion of the desktop wallpaper.

If you do not have access to the Internet, skip Steps 1 through 6 and start with Step 7.

1. Connect your computer to the Internet, either through direct university access, through The Microsoft Network as described in Tutorial 10, or through your own service provider.

2. Open the Search tool available to your Internet browser. Search for bit mapped image files by using options such as "images," "wallpaper," and "backgrounds." Make sure the search includes the option that might include these words as part of a description of the object.

3. After the search is complete, select and open folders, bulletin board folders, and download-and-run files, and examine the types of images that are available. Select one that contains a scenic view of interest to you. (Note: If your service provider informs you that there is a fee for downloading a file, you have the option of canceling the download if you do not want to pay the fee. Then, you can examine other options that might be available. Also, make sure you download bit mapped images, so that you can open and use those images in Paint. Ask your instructor or technical support person for a particular file and location if necessary.)

4. Open each of the files that contain downloaded images, and display each of them as wallpaper on the desktop one at a time so that you can view the full impact that the image makes. (Note: You can copy the file with the image to the Windows directory so that you can select it as wallpaper, or while you have the file with the image open in Paint, you can select the File menu, select Set Wallpaper (Tiled), then minimize Paint to view the scene on your desktop.)

5. Use the Find feature on the Start menu to locate files with the file extension bmp on your computer's hard disk drive or drives. If you find one or more files with images of interest to you, open each of the files in Paint, choose the option to display the image as wallpaper, then minimize Paint so you can see the desktop.

6. Select one of the images you obtained from the Internet or your computer to use for the remainder of this case problem. Open the one you want to use as wallpaper, and set the option in Paint for displaying it as wallpaper.

7. Select the Pick tool in the Paint toolbox, select a small area of the image, then select the Copy To option from the Edit menu, and save the selected area in a file on disk. Close the Paint file with the complete image without saving.

8. Open a new Paint file, and create a logo to use as letterhead. For the logo, use the company's name, Vista Travel Agency, and draw lines or include other graphics elements available in Paint to accent and enhance the logo.

9. Select the Pick tool in the Paint toolbox, select the area that contains the text and any graphic elements you have added to the drawing, then select the Copy To option from the Edit menu, and save the selected area in a file on disk. Close Paint, but do not save the image with all the surrounding white space. (*Note:* By using the Copy To option, you do not save all the background white space around the image.)

10. To design the stationery, open WordPad, and embed a copy of the logo in the upper left-corner of the page. Then, if necessary, tab to position the insertion point closer to the right margin, and embed a copy of the object that contains a partial view of the desktop background wallpaper.

11. After you save a copy of the new stationery design, print a copy of the WordPad document. Then, close WordPad and any other open applications, and return to your desktop.

12. Press Alt + Print Screen to copy an image of the desktop wallpaper to the Clipboard, open Paint, paste the contents of the Clipboard into the Paint drawing area, change the print orientation to landscape, then print a copy of the desktop image. Exit Paint without saving the image pasted into the Paint drawing area.

Customizing Windows 95

CASE

Novak, Giorgi, Jirresis & Echeverria

The attorneys at Novak, Giorgi, Jirresis & Echeverria specialize in the preparation of state, county, and municipal bond documents. Not only are bond documents typically several hundred pages long, but the attorneys must prepare and submit these documents within relatively tight time frames. Jeffrey Shimmel works as a microcomputer systems specialist at the company's headquarters in Boston, Massachusetts. Jeffrey has launched a program to customize the desktops of the computers at each attorney's desk as well as those used by the support staff to streamline each person's access to important features on his or her computer. As part of one phase of his project, he wants to add folders for commonly used options, such as Communications programs, to the Programs menu and then group those communications programs together for ease of selection.

Jeffrey asks you to assist him in customizing your desktop. He wants you to add Optimize System, Communications, and Protect System folders to the Programs folder on the Start menu.

If you work in a computer lab, ask your instructor or the technical support staff in the laboratory whether you can make changes to the Start menu.

As you look for program files on your computer, you might also need to check folders other than the C:\Windows folder. For example, you might find some programs in the C:\Program Files or the C:\Program Files\Accessories folders.

1. Open the Taskbar Properties dialog box, and select the Start Menu Programs tab.

2. Use the Advanced button to open the Exploring C:\Windows\Start Menu window.

3. In the All Folders list box, select the Programs folder, then select the option for creating a new folder below the Programs folder. Name the new folder Optimize System, then close the Exploring window.

4. In the Taskbar Properties dialog box, use the Add button to open the Create Shortcut dialog box.

5. In the Create Shortcut dialog box, use the Browse button to open a Browse dialog box.

6. In the Browse dialog box, locate and open the Windows folder, then locate and open Defrag.exe.

7. After Windows 95 adds the MS-DOS path for Defrag.exe to the Create Shortcut dialog box, use the Next button to open the Select Program Folder dialog box.

8. In the Select Program Folder dialog box, locate and select the Optimize System folder, then use the Next button to open the Select a Title for the Program dialog box.

9. Enter the title "Defragment Disk" (without the quotation marks) as the title for this program option, then use the Finish button to add this option to the Start menu.

10. Close the Taskbar Properties dialog box, open the Start menu, point to Programs, then point to Optimize System menu, and verify that the Defragment Disk option is included as an option on the Optimize System menu.

11. Close the Start menu.

12. Repeat the same process to add the following menu options to the Optimize System menu:

Program	Check	Menu Option
Drvspace.exe	C:\Windows	Compress Disk
Scandskw.exe	C:\Windows	Scan Disk

Tip: If you already have shortcuts to these programs in another folder, you can copy them from that folder to the Optimize System folder while you are working in the Exploring C:\Windows\Start Menu folder.

13. Add a Communications folder to the Programs menu.

14. Add the following menu options to the Communications menu. (Note: You might not have all of these programs or installed components on your computer. Use the ones that you do have on your computer.)

Program	Check	Menu Option
Dialer.exe	C:\Windows	Phone Dialer
Faxcover.exe	C:\Windows	Create Fax Cover
Faxview.exe	C:\Windows	View Fax
Ftp.exe	C:\Windows	File Transfer Protocol
Telnet.exe	C:\Windows	Use Telnet

If you have fax software like Delrina WinFax PRO, add it to your menu as well.

15. Add your communications program, online service, and Web browser to the Communications folder on the Programs menu. For example, if you have ProComm Plus for Windows (a communications program), The Microsoft Network, CompuServe or America Online (online services), or Internet Explorer or Netscape Navigator (a Web browser), add shortcuts to these programs in the Communications folder. If you have Internet utilities like Eudora Mail, add them as well.

16. Add a Protect System folder to the Programs menu, and add the following menu option to this folder:

Program	Check	Menu Option
Backup.exe Backup	C:\Program Files\Accessories	Windows 95

17. Add your anti-viral scanner and virus interceptor to the Protect System folder on the Programs menu. For example, if you have VirusScan95 for Windows or McAfee's anti-viral scanners and Vshield (a virus interceptor), add shortcuts to these programs in the Protect System folder.

18. *Optional:* If you have the Windows 95 CD-ROM installation disc, search for the Emergency Recovery Disaster utility, copy it to a folder on your hard disk, and then add an option for starting this program to the Protect System folder on the Programs menu. Tip: This utility backs up to diskette important Windows 95 system files.

19. *Optional:* Create a Network Utilities folder on the Programs menu, and add the following utilities as menu options to the Network Utilities folder:

Program	Check	Menu Option
Directcc.exe	C:\Windows	Cable Computers
Netwatch.exe	C:\Windows	Monitor Network Activity
Winchat.exe	C:\Windows	Chat
Winpopup.exe	C:\Windows	Display Messages

20. Display the Start menu, the Programs menu, then the Optimize System menu.

21. Press Alt + Print Screen, open Paint, paste the image of the desktop into the drawing area, print the image, then exit Paint without saving the image.

22. Repeat the same process to print copies of the Communications, Protect System, and, if available, the Network Utilities menu that you created.

Providing Client Support

CASE

Safeguards Unlimited

Over the last 11 years while she worked as a microcomputer support specialist for a company in Silicon Valley, Karin Moresco noticed how few precautions employees and businesses take to safeguard their data. She discovered that employees with heavy workloads and frequent deadlines do not have the time to optimize their computers or develop and implement an effective backup strategy. After hearing on the news that close to 90% of businesses do not back up their data or do not perform effective backups, she decided to start her own business and provide these basic types of support services.

As part of the process of defining the types of services she wants to offer to local businesses, Karin decided to include the following services as part of a comprehensive protection plan:

- Create an Emergency Recovery disk with important Windows 95, Windows 3.1, and MS-DOS system files for each computer station.

- Use ScanDisk to check for and repair hard disk errors.

- Use Disk Defragmenter to fully optimize a hard disk.

- Use Backup to perform a full system backup of a client's computer systems.

- Perform selective backups once a week.

- Create a Startup Disk for each computer station.

Karin has already interested several clients in her new package of services. Before starting with her first client, she asks you to step through as many of these features as possible.

To complete the first part of the case problem (Steps 1 through 11), you need a 3.5-inch, high density diskette.

1. Open My Computer and format two diskettes. If you have completed all of the tutorials in this text, you can use the same diskettes rather than start with a new set of diskettes. Label one diskette Emergency Recovery Disk.

2. Open a window for one of the diskettes you just formatted, and create the following folders on that diskette: Windows 95 System Files, Windows 3.1 System Files, and MS-DOS System Files.

3. Use the Find feature on the Start menu to locate all files in the C:\Windows folder with the file extension ini. Maximize the Find window, then click the Name column button to arrange the files in order by filename.

4. Right-click the taskbar then tile the Find and My Computer windows vertically.

5. From the Files Found section in the Find window, select and copy System.ini to the Clipboard.

6. Click the floppy disk drive window, double-click the Windows 3.1 System Files folder, and then paste System.ini into this folder.

7. Repeat this process to select and copy Win.ini to the Windows 3.1 System Files folder on your floppy disk drive.

8. Use the Go to a different folder list box to return to the main folder on your floppy disk drive.

9. Open the Windows 95 System Files folder, then copy Protocol.ini from the Find window to the Windows 95 System Files folder.

10. In the Find window, change the file specification and search for all files with the dat file extension in the C:\Windows folder.

11. Select and copy User.dat and System.dat to the Windows 95 System Files Folder on your floppy disk.

12. Use the Go to a different folder list box to return to the main folder on your floppy disk drive, then open the MS-DOS System Files folder.

13. In the Find window, change the file specification to search for all files in the main folder of drive (C:\), and remove the option to search all subfolders. Start the Find, and after the Find is complete, arrange the folders and filenames in C:\ in alphabetical order.

14. Select and copy Config.sys and Autoexec.bat to the MS-DOS System Files Folder on your floppy disk.

15. Close the floppy disk drive window, then maximize the Find window.

16. In the Find window, change the search condition to *.* (for all files) and activate the option to search all subfolders. When the Find is complete, arrange the folder and filenames in alphabetical order, and widen the Name and In Folder columns to show the full filename and folder name.

17. Press Alt + Print Screen, open Paint, paste the image on the Clipboard to the drawing area, print the image, then close Paint without saving the image.

18. Close the Find and floppy disk drive windows.

19. Start the ScanDisk utility and check drive C for errors using the following settings:

Type of test:	Thorough
	Automatically fix errors
Display summary:	Always
Log file:	Replace log
Cross-linked files:	Make copies
Lost file fragments:	Convert to files
Check files for:	Invalid file names
Areas of the disk to scan:	System and data areas
	Do not repair bad sectors in hidden and
	system files

20. After you complete the scan of drive C, close ScanDisk, open WordPad, then open ScanDisk.log in C:\, and print a copy of this file.

21. Start the Disk Defragmenter and optimize drive C by performing a full defragmentation of both files and free space.

22. Open the Backup utility, and in the Select files to backup section, click the name of your hard disk drive, but *do not* click the empty selection box and inadvertently select all folders and files in the main folder on drive C.

23. In the Contents section, click the Name column button to arrange folders and files in alphabetical order.

24. Locate and select the following files from the main folder on drive C to include in the backup: Autoexec.bat, Command.com, Config.sys, Io.sys, and Msdos.sys.

25. In the Select files to backup section, expand the folder structure for drive C.

26. Locate and click the Windows folder, but *do not* click the empty selection box and inadvertently select all folders and files in the folder.

27. In the Contents section, click the Name column button to arrange folders and files in alphabetical order.

28. Locate and select the following files from the Windows folder to include in the backup: Protocol.ini, System.ini, and Win.ini.

29. In the Select files to backup section, expand the folder structure for the Windows folder.

30. Locate and click the empty selection box for the Start Menu folder to include its folders in the backup selection.

31. After selecting the files, choose the Next button to proceed to the next step, then select the name of your floppy disk drive for the backup.

32. From the Settings menu, select Options, choose the option for a Full backup of all selected files in the Type of backup section, choose the option Use data compression in the Advanced options section, and then close the Options dialog box.

33. From the File menu, choose Save As, and in the Save As dialog box, save your settings under the filename "Selective System Backup" (without the quotation marks).

34. Start the backup, and when prompted for the Backup Set Label, enter "Selective System Backup."

35. After the backup is complete, close the Backup utility.

36. *Optional:* If you have not created a Startup Disk for your computer, open the Control Panel, select Add/Remove Programs, and from the Startup Disk tab, create a Startup Disk.

New Perspectives on

Advanced Windows 95

REFERENCES

Menu Bar Commands

My Computer

Opens a folder that contains icons used to organize your computer. This folder has four menus: **File, Edit, View,** and **Help.**

About Windows 95 (Help) Shows the program information on your version of Windows 95, as well as information on available memory and system resources.

Arrange Icons (View) Opens a cascading menu that contains options for arranging objects in a window.

    by Drive Letter Arranges drives alphabetically by name.

    by Type Arranges objects alphabetically by type.

    by Size Arranges objects by size in ascending order.

    by Free Space Arranges objects by their available free space.

    Auto Arrange Toggles between automatically arranging items and allowing free placement of items.

Capture Printer Port (File) Connects a specific printer to a network for use; available after selecting the Printers folder.

End Capture (File) Disconnects a specific printer from a network; available after selecting a printer icon.

Close (File) Closes the My Computer folder.

Copy (Edit) Creates a copy of the selected object and places the copy on the Clipboard. Ctrl + C is the keyboard shortcut for this command.

Copy Disk (File) Copies the contents of the selected disk to another hard disk or floppy disk; available after selecting a floppy drive.

Create Shortcut (File) Creates a rapid-access pathway for the selected item.

Cut (Edit) Removes the selected item and places it on the Clipboard. Ctrl + X is the keyboard shortcut for this command.

Delete (File) Deletes a shortcut, folder, or file.

Details (View) Shows pertinent information about each item in this folder.

End Capture (File) Disconnects a specific printer from a network; available after selecting a printer icon.

Explore (File) Opens an Exploring window or Windows Explorer for a drive or folder.

Find (File) Opens the Find All Files window to search the selected drive for folders or files; available after selecting a drive.

Format (File) Opens a dialog box that formats a floppy disk in the selected drive; available after selecting a drive.

Help Topics (Help) Opens Windows Help.

Invert Selection (Edit) Reverses which items are selected and which are not.

Large Icons (View) Displays items in the folder using large icons.

Line up Icons (View) Moves all of the icons in the window into a grid pattern; available in Large Icons and Small Icons views.

List (View) Presents the items in the folder as a list.

Open (File) Opens the highlighted drive or folder.

Options (View) Opens the Options window so that you can change display options.

Paste (Edit) Inserts the Clipboard contents at the selected location. Ctrl + V is the keyboard shortcut for this command.

Paste Shortcut (Edit) Creates a rapid-access pathway for the most recently copied or cut item.

Properties (File) Opens a Properties window that displays additional information about the item.

Refresh (View) Updates the active window's information.

Rename (File) Changes the name of the highlighted shortcut or folder.

Select All (Edit) Selects all items in a window. Ctrl + A is the keyboard shortcut.

Small Icons (View) Displays items in the selected folder using small icons.

Status Bar (View) Toggles the status bar on or off.

Toolbar (View) Toggles the icon toolbar on or off.

Undo (Edit) Reverses the last folder or file action. Ctrl + Z is the keyboard shortcut.

Explore Window and Windows Explorer

The Explore window is available from the File menu on most folders. It displays all of the folders and files contained within the selected folder. Windows Explorer is available from the Start menu.

About Windows 95 (Help) Shows the program information on your version of Windows 95, as well as information on available memory and system resources.

Arrange Icons (View) Opens a cascading menu that contains options for arranging items in a window; options depend on folder selected in All Folders section.

> **by Drive Letter** Arranges drives alphabetically by name.
>
> **by Comment** (Network Neighborhood) Arranges items alphabetically using the comment in their properties.
>
> **by Description** (Recycle Bin) Arranges items alphabetically using the comment in their properties.
>
> **by Type** Arranges items alphabetically by type.
>
> **by Size** Arranges items by size in ascending order.
>
> **by Date** Arranges items chronologically by date, from oldest to most recent.
>
> **by Free Space** Arranges items by their available free space.
>
> **by Name** Arranges icons alphabetically by name.
>
> **by Origin** (Recycle Bin) Arranges icons by the name of the folder of origin.
>
> **by Delete Date** (Recycle Bin) Arranges icons by the date they were deleted.
>
> **Auto Arrange** Toggles between automatically arranging items and allowing free placement of items.

Close (File) Closes an Exploring window.

Copy (Edit) Creates a copy of the selected item and places the copy on the Clipboard.

Create Shortcut (File) Creates a rapid-access pathway for the selected item.

Cut (Edit) Removes the selected item and places it on the Clipboard.

Delete (File) Deletes a shortcut, folder, or file.

Details (View) Shows pertinent information about each item in this folder.

Disconnect Network Drive (Tools) Disconnects the current network drive; available if Network Neighborhood is selected.

Empty Recycle Bin (File) Deletes all items from the Recycle Bin; available after selecting Recycle Bin.

Explore (File) Opens an Exploring window or Windows Explorer for a drive or folder.

Find (File) Opens the Find All Files window to search the selected drive for folders or files; available after selecting a drive.

Find (Tools) Opens the Find cascading menu that contains options on locating various items.

> **Files or Folders** Opens a Find All Files window that allows you to locate a specific file or folder.
>
> **Computer** Opens a Find All Files window that allows you to locate another computer in a network.

On The Microsoft Network Opens a Find: All Files window that allows you to locate folders and files on the Microsoft Network; available to account holders of The Microsoft Network.

Go to (Tools) Opens a Go To Folder dialog box that allows you to open another drive or folder.

Help Topics (Help) Opens Windows Help.

Invert Selection (Edit) Reverses which items are selected and which are not.

Large Icons (View) Displays items in the selected folder using large icons.

Line up Icons (View) Moves all icons in the window into a grid pattern; available in Large Icons and Small Icons views.

List (View) Presents the items in the selected folder as a list.

Map Network Drive (Tools) Assigns a drive letter to a network drive.

New (File) Opens a cascading menu with options for creating new folders, shortcuts, and files for registered applications.

    Folder Creates a new folder within the selected heading.

    Shortcut Creates a new shortcut to the selected item.

    Wave Sound Creates a new file for sound samples or compositions.

    Bitmap Image Creates a new file for bitmaps or other pictures.

    Text Document Creates a new file for a text document of any type.

    Briefcase Create a new briefcase file.

Open (File) Opens the selected folder or file.

Open with (File) Displays a dialog box for selecting the application to open the file with; available for file types that are not registered with Windows 95.

Options (View) Opens the Options window so that you can change display options.

Paste (Edit) Inserts the Clipboard contents at the selected location. Ctrl + V is the keyboard shortcut for this command.

Paste Shortcut (Edit) Creates a rapid-access pathway for the most recently copied or cut item.

Pause Printing (File) Temporarily stops selected printer from printing; available after selecting a printer.

Print Prints a file with its registered application.

Properties (File) Opens a Properties window that displays additional information about the item.

Purge Print Jobs (File) Removes all current print jobs from memory; available after selecting a printer.

Quick View (File) Opens a Quick View window so you can preview the contents of a file without opening the application that produced the file.

Refresh (View) Updates the active window's information.

Rename (File) Changes the name of the selected shortcut, folder, or file.

Restore (File) Puts the selected file back into its original folder.

Select All (Edit) Selects all items in a window. Ctrl + A is the keyboard shortcut.

Send To (File) Opens a cascading menu with options on places to copy the selected file.

    (Floppy Drive) Copies the file to the specified floppy disk drive.

    Fax Recipient Uses a copy of a file to create a fax.

    Mail Recipient Uses a copy of a file to create an e-mail message.

    My Briefcase Copies the file to a briefcase folder on another computer.

Set As Default (File) Identifies the selected printer as the default printer; available after selecting a printer.

Small Icons (View) Displays items in this folder using small icons.

Status Bar (View) Toggles the status bar on or off.

Toolbar (View) Toggles the icon toolbar on or off.

Undo (Edit) Reverses the last folder or file action. Ctrl + Z is the keyboard shortcut.

Recycle Bin

Windows 95 places items deleted from other folders into the Recycle Bin. When you empty the bin, all information in it is deleted. You can restore deleted files in the Recycle Bin to their original locations, as long as you have not emptied the Recycle Bin.

About Windows 95 (Help) Shows the program information on your version of Windows 95, as well as information on available memory and system resources.

Arrange Icons (View) Opens a cascading menu that contains options for arranging items in a window.

  by Name Arranges icons alphabetically by name.

  by Origin (Recycle Bin) Arranges icons by the name of the folder of origin.

  by Delete Date (Recycle Bin) Arranges icons by the date they were deleted.

  by Type Arranges items alphabetically by type.

  by Size Arranges items by size in ascending order.

  Auto Arrange Toggles between automatically arranging items and allowing free placement of items.

Close (File) Closes the Recycle Bin.

Copy (Edit) Creates a copy of the selected item and places the copy on the Clipboard. Ctrl + C is the keyboard shortcut for this command.

Create Shortcut (File) Creates a rapid-access pathway for the selected item.

Cut (Edit) Removes the selected item and places it on the Clipboard. Ctrl + X is the keyboard shortcut for this command.

Delete (File) Deletes a shortcut, folder, or file.

Details (View) Shows pertinent information about each item in the selected folder.

Empty Recycle Bin (File) Removes all deleted items from the Recycle Bin.

Help Topics (Help) Opens Windows Help.

Invert Selection (Edit) Reverses which items are selected and which are not.

Large Icons (View) Displays items in the selected folder using large icons.

Line up Icons (View) Moves all of the icons in the window into a grid pattern; available in Large Icons and Small Icons views.

List (View) Presents the items in this folder as a list.

Options (View) Opens the Options window so that you can change display options.

Paste (Edit) Inserts the Clipboard contents at the selected location. Ctrl + V is the keyboard shortcut for this command.

Paste Shortcut (Edit) Creates a rapid-access pathway for the most recently copied or cut item.

Properties (File) Opens a properties window that displays additional information about the item.

Refresh (View) Updates the active window's information.

Rename (File) Changes the name of the selected shortcut, folder, or file.

Restore (File) Puts the selected file back into its original folder.

Select All (Edit) Selects deleted files in the Recycle Bin. Ctrl + A is the keyboard shortcut.

Small Icons (View) Displays items in the selected folder using small icons.

Status Bar (View) Toggles the status bar on or off.

Toolbar (View) Toggles the icon toolbar on or off.

Undo (Edit) Puts the selected file back into its original folder. Ctrl + Z is the keyboard shortcut for this command.

Network Neighborhood

This window controls access to computers and other resources, such as printers, on a network.

About Windows 95 (Help) Shows the program information on your version of Windows 95, as well as information on available memory and system resources.

Arrange Icons (View) Opens a cascading menu that contains options for arranging items in a window.

by Name Arranges icons alphabetically by name.

by Comment Arranges items alphabetically using the comment on the property sheet.

Auto Arrange Toggles between automatically arranging items and allowing free dragging.

Close (File) Closes the Network Neighborhood window.

Copy (Edit) Creates a copy of the selected item and places the copy on the Clipboard.

Create Shortcut (File) Creates a rapid-access pathway for the selected item.

Cut (Edit) Removes the selected item and places it on the Clipboard.

Delete (File) Deletes a shortcut, folder, or file.

Details (View) Shows pertinent information about each item in the selected folder.

Explore (File) Opens an Exploring window or Windows Explorer for a drive or folder.

Help Topics (Help) Opens Windows Help.

Invert Selection (Edit) Reverses which items are selected and which are not.

Large Icons (View) Displays items in the selected folder using large icons.

Line up Icons (View) Moves all of the icons in the window into a grid pattern; available in Large Icons and Small Icons views.

List (View) Presents the items in the selected folder as a list.

Map Network Drive (File) Assigns a drive letter to a network drive.

Open (File) Opens the highlighted network or network resource.

Options (View) Opens the Options window so that you can change display options.

Paste (Edit) Inserts the Clipboard contents at the selected location. Ctrl + V is the keyboard shortcut for this command.

Paste Shortcut (Edit) Creates a rapid-access pathway for the most recently copied or cut item.

Properties (File) Opens a properties window that displays additional information about the item.

Refresh (View) Updates the active window's information.

Rename (File) Changes the name of the selected shortcut, folder, or file.

Select All (Edit) Selects all networks, network resources, or folders. Ctrl + A is the keyboard shortcut for this command.

Small Icons (View) Displays items in the selected folder using small icons.

Status Bar (View) Toggles the status bar on or off.

Toolbar (View) Toggles the icon toolbar on or off.

Undo (Edit) Reverses the last folder or file action. Ctrl + Z is the keyboard shortcut.

My Briefcase

This folder assists in moving files between two computers, and is used as a storehouse for work in progress.

About Windows 95 (Help) Shows the program information on your version of Windows 95, as well as information on available memory and system resources.

Arrange Icons (View) Opens a cascading menu that contains options for arranging the icons in this window.

Auto Arrange Toggles between automatically arranging items and allowing free dragging.

Close (File) Closes the My Briefcase folder.

Copy (Edit) Creates a copy of the selected item and places the copy on the Clipboard. Ctrl + C is the keyboard shortcut for this command.

Create Shortcut (File) Creates a rapid-access pathway for the selected item.

Cut (Edit) Removes the selected item and places it on the Clipboard. Ctrl + X is the keyboard shortcut for this command.

Delete (File) Deletes a shortcut, folder, or file.

Details (View) Shows pertinent information about each item in the selected folder.

Explore (File) Opens an Exploring window or Windows Explorer for a folder; available after selecting a folder.

Find (File) Opens the Find All Files window to search the selected drive for folders or files; available after selecting a folder.

Help Topics (Help) Opens Windows Help.

Invert Selection (Edit) Reverses which items are selected and which are not.

Large Icons (View) Displays items in the selected folder using large icons.

Line up Icons (View) Moves all of the icons in the window into a grid pattern.

List (View) Presents the items in the selected folder as a list.

Open (File) Opens the highlighted folder or file.

Options (View) Opens the Options window so that you can change display options.

Paste (Edit) Inserts the Clipboard contents at the selected location. Ctrl + V is the keyboard shortcut for this command.

Paste Shortcut (Edit) Creates a rapid-access pathway for the most recently copied or cut item.

Print (File) Prints the selected file.

Properties (File) Opens the Properties window to display additional information.

Refresh (View) Updates the active window's information.

Rename (File) Changes the name of the highlighted folder or file.

Select All (Edit) Selects every folder and file. Ctrl + A is the keyboard shortcut.

Send To (File) Opens a cascading menu with options on places to copy the selected file.

    (Floppy Drive) Copies the file to the specified floppy disk drive.

    Fax Recipient Uses a copy of a file to create a fax.

    Mail Recipient Uses a copy of a file to create an e-mail message.

    My Briefcase Copies the file to a briefcase folder on another computer.

Small Icons (View) Displays items in the selected folder using small icons.

Split from Original (Briefcase) Prevents the selected file from being overwritten by update commands.

Status Bar (View) Toggles the status bar on or off.

Toolbar (View) Toggles the icon toolbar on or off.

Undo (Edit) Reverses the last folder or file action. Ctrl + Z is the keyboard shortcut.

Update All (Briefcase) Replaces all unmodified files with files in the Briefcase.

Update Selection (Briefcase) Replaces unmodified files with files in the Briefcase.

Quick View Menus

The Quick View window allows you to preview the contents of files without opening the application that produced the files.

About Microsoft Quick View (Help) Shows the program information on your version of Microsoft Quick View, as well as information on available memory and system resources.

Exit (File) Closes the Quick View window.

Font (View) Opens a font dialog box to modify the font, point size, and script.

Landscape (View) Toggles the current page between portrait and landscape (side) views.

Help Topics (Help) Opens Windows Help.

Open File for Editing (File) Opens the appropriate program and selected file for editing.

Page View (View) Toggles between document and full page views.

Replace Window (View) Displays a new file in the current Quick View window.

Rotate (View) Rotates the current image ninety degrees.

Status Bar (View) Toggles the status bar on or off.

Toolbar (View) Toggles the icon toolbar on or off.

Shortcut Menus

Shortcut menus are accessed by clicking the right mouse button in a variety of situations. Here are some common menus.

Desktop

Arrange Icons Opens a cascading menu that contains options for arranging the icons in this window.

    by Name Arranges icons alphabetically by name.

    by Type Arranges items by type.

    by Size Arranges items in ascending order by size.

    by Date Arranges items in order by date and time.

    Auto Arrange Toggles between automatically arranging items and allowing free dragging.

Line up Icons Moves all icons in the window into a grid pattern.

New Opens a cascading menu with options for creating new folders, shortcuts, and files for registered applications.

    Folder Creates a new folder within the selected heading.

    Shortcut Creates a new shortcut to the selected item.

    Wave Sound Creates a new file for sound samples or compositions.

    Bitmap Image Creates a new file for bitmaps or other pictures.

    Text Document Creates a new file for a text document of any type.

    Briefcase Create a new briefcase file.

Paste (Ctrl + V) Inserts the Clipboard contents to the selected location.

Paste Shortcut Creates a rapid-access pathway for the most recently pasted item.

Properties Opens a properties window to display additional information about the item.

Undo Delete Undoes deletion of last desktop icon.

Undo (Ctrl + Z) Reverses the last folder or file action; available after performing certain desktop operations.

Undo Move Undoes move of last desktop icon.

Undo Rename Undoes rename of last desktop icon.

My Computer

Create Shortcut Creates a rapid-access pathway to My Computer.

Disconnect Network Drive Disconnects the current network drive.

Explore Opens an Exploring window for My Computer.

Find Opens the Find All Files window that allows you to locate a folder or file.

Map Network Drive Assigns a drive letter to a network drive.

Open Opens the My Computer window.

Rename Allows you to change the name of My Computer.

Properties Opens a properties window that displays additional information on My Computer.

Recycle Bin

Create Shortcut Creates a rapid-access pathway to the Recycle Bin.
Empty Recycle Bin Deletes all items from the Recycle Bin.
Explore Opens an Exploring window for the Recycle Bin.
Open Opens the Recycle Bin folder.
Properties Opens a properties window that displays additional information on the Recycle Bin.

Network Neighborhood

Create Shortcut Creates a rapid-access pathway to Network Neighborhood.
Disconnect Network Drive Disconnects the current network drive.
Explore Opens an Exploring window for Network Neighborhood.
Find Computer Searches for a computer on a network.
Map Network Drive Assigns a drive letter to a network drive.
Open Opens the Network Neighborhood folder.
Rename Allows you to change the name of Network Neighborhood.
Properties Opens a properties window that displays additional information on Network Neighborhood.
Who Am I Displays ID information about you for a particular network.

My Briefcase

Copy Creates a copy of the My Briefcase folder and places the copy on the Clipboard.
Create Shortcut Creates a rapid-access pathway to My Briefcase.
Cut Removes the My Briefcase folder and places it on the Clipboard.
Delete Deletes the My Briefcase folder.
Explore Opens an Exploring window for My Briefcase.
Open Opens the My Briefcase folder.
Paste Pastes a copied or cut file into the My Briefcase folder.
Properties Opens a Properties window that displays additional information on My Briefcase.
Rename Allows you to change the name of the My Briefcase folder.
Send To Opens a cascading menu with options on places to copy the selected file.
    (Floppy Drive) Copies the file to the specified floppy drive.
    Fax Recipient Uses a copy of a file to create a fax.
    Mail Recipient Uses a copy of a file to create an e-mail message.
    My Briefcase Copies the file to a briefcase folder on another computer.
Update All Update all files in the My Briefcase folder.

Toolbar Icons

My Computer Toolbar and the Explorer Toolbar

My Computer ▾   Takes you to a different folder.

Displays the next higher folder.

Assigns a drive letter to a network drive.

Disconnects the current network drive.

Removes the selected item and places it on the Clipboard.

Creates a copy of the selected item and places the copy on the Clipboard.

Pastes the Clipboard contents at the selected location.

Reverses the last folder or file action.

Deletes the selected item.

Opens a Properties dialog box.

Displays items in the selected folder using large icons.

Displays items in the selected folder using small icons.

Presents the items in the selected folder as a list.

Shows pertinent information about each item in the selected folder.

Quick View Toolbar

Opens the appropriate program to display the actual file for editing.

Increases the point size of the text in the current display.

Decreases the point size of the text in the current display.

Replaces the current contents of the Quick View window with a new file.

MS-DOS Toolbar

Auto ▾   Modifies the font and point size of text in an MS-DOS window.

Selects text in an MS-DOS window.

Places selected text in an MS-DOS window on the Clipboard.

Enters the text from the Clipboard into the MS-DOS window at the command prompt.

Toggles between an MS-DOS window and a full screen.

Opens the MS-DOS Properties dialog box.

Operates an MS-DOS program in the background of Windows 95.

Opens the MS-DOS Properties dialog box to view or change font options.

Help Button

Displays a pop-up Help window with context-sensitive help for the selected item.

Window Buttons

Reduces the open window to a button on the taskbar.

Increases the size of the open window to full screen.

Returns the window to its original size.

Closes the open window.

Commands Folder

These Window utilities, which you can run from a command prompt, are stored in the Commands folder below the Windows folder.

Attrib.exe Displays, assigns, or removes one or more file attributes.

Chkdsk.exe Examines the status of the hard disk drive, checks for errors and memory usage, and displays a status report for hard disk storage space and memory usage.

Choice.com A batch file command that displays one or more options for a user to choose from when the batch file is executed.

Debug.exe Program editor for executable files.

Deltree.exe Deletes a directory tree, all of its subordinate subdirectories, and all the files in the specified directories.

Diskcopy.com Copies the contents of one floppy disk to another floppy disk using the named drive or drives.

Doskey.com Provides more editing control on command lines via the keyboard.

Edit.com Loads the MS-DOS editor to edit or create text or ASCII files.

Extract.exe Uncompresses a compressed program file.

Fc.exe Compares files and provides descriptions of their differences.

Fdisk.exe Partitions and configures a hard disk into drives for use by MS-DOS.

Find.exe Locates text in a file.

Format.com Prepares floppy disks for a variety of purposes.

Keyb.com Configures a keyboard for a specific language.

Label.exe Displays, creates, changes, or deletes the label, or volume name, assigned to a disk.

Mem.exe Displays a memory usage report on total, conventional, upper, reserved, and extended memory.

Mode.com Configures system devices, including ports, the video display unit, and the keyboard.

More.com Allows you to advance one screen at a time through text files.

Move.exe Moves one or more files from one drive or directory to another drive or directory, or renames directories.

Mscdex.exe Allows access to CD-ROM drives by MS-DOS and Windows 95.

Nlsfunc.exe Adds natural language (foreign) support for MS-DOS.

Scandisk.exe Checks a drive for errors and repairs them.

Share.exe Enables file sharing and lockup capabilities for disk drives.

Sort.exe Sorts the output of DOS commands or text files.

Start.exe Starts a Windows 95 or MS-DOS program from the command prompt.

Subst.exe Assigns a drive name to a subdirectory.

Sys.com Creates a boot disk by copying the Windows 95 operating system files to the disk.

Xcopy.exe Copies subdirectories and files.

Xcopy32.exe A 32-bit version of the Xcopy.exe program, which copies subdirectories and files.

Glossary

? The question mark wildcard character used in a file specification to substitute for a single character in the filename or file extension

* The asterisk wildcard character used in a file specification to substitute for any and all characters in the filename or file extension, starting from the position of the asterisk

**** (1) The symbol for the root directory; (2) a delimiter that separates two folder or directory names in a path, or that separates a folder name and filename in a file specification

16-bit applications DOS applications that operate within the first 640KB of memory

16-bit chips Microprocessor chips, such as the 8088, 8086, and 80286, that internally process 16 bits of data at once

16-bit operating system An operating system, such as MS-DOS, that contains program code which enables it to function on earlier types of microprocessors (such as the 8088, 8086), which limits the operating system to addressing only 640KB of memory, and which operates on a computer with a microprocessor that processes 16 bits at a time

286 A computer system with an 80286 microprocessor

32-bit applications Windows 95 applications, such as Office 95, that utilize the full capabilities of Windows 95 and 80386 and later microprocessors

32-bit chips Microprocessor chips, such as the 80386 and 80486, that internally process 32 bits of data at once

32-bit operating system An operating system that contains program code which enables it to use the full capabilities of the 80386 and later microprocessors, including the ability to address more than 1MB of memory and provide memory protection features, and which operates on a computer with a microprocessor that processes 32 bits at a time

386 A computer system with an 80386 microprocessor

486 A computer system with an 80486 microprocessor

8086 The microprocessor chip used in XT compatibles introduced in 1983–84, capable of processing and transmitting 16 bits at a time, accessing 1MB of memory, and operating at a clock speed of 5 to 10MHz

8088 The microprocessor chip used in IBM PCs introduced in 1981 and PC/XTs introduced in 1983, capable of processing 16 bits at a time, transmitting only 8 bits at a time, accessing 1MB of memory, and operating at a clock speed of 5 to 8MHz

80286 A microprocessor chip introduced in 1984, used in ATs (IBM PC/ATs and 286s), capable of processing and transmitting 16 bits at a time, accessing 16MB of memory, and operating at a clock speed of 8 to 12MHz

80386DX A microprocessor chip introduced in 1985, used in 386DXs, capable of processing and transmitting 32 bits at a time, accessing 4GB of memory, and operating at a clock speed of 16 to 33MHz

80386SX A microprocessor chip introduced in 1988, used in 386SXs, capable of processing 32 bits at a time, transmitting only 16 bits at a time, accessing 16MB of memory, and operating at a clock speed of 16 to 20MHz

80486DX A microprocessor chip with a math coprocessor introduced in 1989, used in 486DXs, capable of processing and transmitting 32 bits at a time, accessing 4GB of memory, and operating at a clock speed of 25 to 50MHz

80486SX A microprocessor chip with a disabled math coprocessor introduced in 1991, used in 486SXs, capable of processing and transmitting 32 bits at a time, accessing 4GB of memory, and operating at a clock speed of 16 to 25MHz

80486DX2 A microprocessor chip with a math coprocessor introduced in 1992, used in 486DX2s, capable of processing and transmitting 32 bits at a time, accessing 4GB of memory, and operating at a clock speed of 50 to 66MHz

A: The drive name, or device name, assigned to the first floppy disk drive in a computer system

Accessibility Options A Windows 95 component that offers alternative ways for individuals with mobility, hearing, and visual disabilities to more efficiently interact with their computer, Windows 95, and applications

actions Operations you can do with or to an object

adapter, or **adapter card** A circuit board or card that connects one system component with another and enables those components to work together

adapter memory That portion of reserved memory in the region 640K to 1MB used for system-related operations, such as for video display adapters, network adapters, and the ROM-BIOS

add-in card A circuit board that is inserted in the system unit and connected to the main system board so that the computer system can work with a hardware component

address bus The combination of address lines that access memory

address lines The electronic circuitry used to access specific storage locations in memory

advanced user One who knows and understands the effects of different system settings, understands how a change in one setting might affect other settings on a computer, and knows how to restore settings on a system if a change in a setting adversely affects system performance

algorithm A formula or procedure for calculating or producing a result

alias An MS-DOS filename that follows the rules and conventions for 8.3 filenames—names that allow 8 characters and then a 3-character extension

allocation error An error in the allocation of space to a file on disk

allocation unit (1) One or more sectors used by an operating system as the minimum storage space when it allocates storage space on a disk to a file; (2) a cluster

analog Varying continuously over a range, such as the amplitude of a sound wave signal

anti-viral software A program that scans a disk for computer viruses and, where possible, removes computer viruses

applet A Windows 95 application that offers some of the features of a full-fledged software product devoted exclusively to a single use, such as word processing

application software Software that allows a user to accomplish a specific task on a computer system, such as word processing, spreadsheet, database, graphics, desktop publishing, or communications software

application-oriented interface An operating mode in which you open the software application you want to use, then you locate and open the document you want to use

archive To store less frequently used files on floppy disks

Archive attribute An attribute assigned to a file by the operating system to indicate that the file is a newly created file or a file that was modified since the last backup

ASCII The abbreviation for American Standard Code for Information Interchange, a coding scheme for representing characters and symbols

attribute A special characteristic, such as System, Hidden, Read-Only, or Archive, assigned to a folder or file by the operating system

Autoexec.bat A special, auto-executing MS-DOS startup file that is stored in the root directory of drive C and that contains commands executed by the operating system during booting to customize a computer

B: The drive name, or device name, assigned to the second floppy disk drive in a computer system

backup An additional copy of files kept on another type of storage medium, such as tapes or floppy disks, for an emergency

backup cycle A periodic cycle used to back up files on a hard disk and which starts with a full backup, includes additional backups of selected files, and then ends with the next full backup

backup set (1) a set of backup settings; (2) a set of tapes or floppy disks that contain duplicate copies of files stored on a hard disk

backward compatibility The ability to handle hardware and software designed for earlier types of computers and operating systems

bad sector A defective area on a hard disk or floppy disk that the operating system marks as unusable

baud rate The speed of transmitting data, in bits per second (commonly-used values are 9600, 14400, and 28800)

BBS The abbreviation for Bulletin Board Service

binary digit The digit 0 or 1 in the binary numbering system

BIOS The abbreviation for Basic Input/Output System

bit The abbreviation for a binary digit that consists of the number 0 or 1

boot To start a computer system

boot disk A floppy disk that contains operating system files needed to start a computer from drive A

boot record, or **boot sector** A hidden file or table that contains information about the version of the operating system used to format a disk and the physical characteristics of the disk, such as the number of bytes per sector, sectors per cluster, maximum number of files per disk, total number of sectors, and sectors per track

boot sector virus A type of virus that replaces the boot sector with its own program code to guarantee that it is automatically loaded into memory when the computer system boots

booting The process of powering on a computer system and loading the operating system into memory so that it can configure the computer system and manage the basic processes of the computer, including providing support for applications

Bulletin Board Service A service that provides information, and a mechanism for exchanging messages, for a particular interest group or for a specific topic

byte (1) The storage space required on disk or in memory for one character; (2) a combination of eight binary digits, or bits, used to encode a character, including letters of the alphabet, numbers, and symbols

C: The drive name, or device name, assigned to the first partition on the first hard disk drive in a computer system

cascade To arrange each open window in an overlapping pattern to the right and below the previous window

central processing unit The microprocessor chip that processes data under the direction of instructions in a program

chain A sequence of lost clusters that once belonged to a file

chat room An on-line feature that permits those logged onto the service to communicate with each other in what's called real time, i.e., at the moment

check box A box within a dialog box for activating or deactivating an option

click To quickly press and release a mouse button

client (1) A computer in a network that requests and uses services available on the server; (2) a network configuration option that informs Windows 95 of the type of client software used on the network you want to connect your computer to

client/server network A type of network in which a central computer provides file, printer, and communication support to other computers on the network

Clipboard An area of memory used to temporarily store data

clock speed A measurement of the timing of operations in a computer, measured in megahertz (MHz), which in turn reflects the speed at which a microprocessor executes program instructions.

cluster (1) One or more sectors used by an operating system as the minimum storage space when it allocates storage space on a disk to a file; (2) an allocation unit

cold boot Starting a computer system by turning on the power

COM1: The device name for the first communications, or serial, port in a computer system

COM2: The device name for the second communications, or serial, port in a computer system

COM3: The device name for the third communications, or serial, port in a computer system

COM4: The device name for the fourth communications, or serial, port in a computer system

Command.com The Windows 95, MS-DOS, PC-DOS, and IBM-DOS operating system file responsible for interpreting commands entered at the command prompt and for locating and loading an application, programming language, or utility

command line interface An operating system prompt at which you type commands in order to interact with the operating system and specify that it perform a task

communications software Software that enables you to use your computer system to communicate with other computer systems in the same office or in other offices around the country or world with the use of a modem and a telephone line connection or a direct connection

compressed drive A compressed volume file that functions as a real disk drive

compressed volume file A hidden file that contains all the folders and files that were originally stored on an uncompressed drive

compression The process by which DriveSpace, DoubleSpace, or another disk compression utility examines files for repetitive sequences that can be coded more compactly and then compresses the files

computer virus A program that adversely affects the performance of a computer system

connectivity support Features of an operating system that support the use of communications software and hardware, as well as networking, access to on-line services, the Internet, World Wide Web, and the use of portable computers

Config.sys A special, auto-executing MS-DOS startup file that is stored in the root directory of drive C and contains commands for configuring the operating system during booting

contiguous sectors Adjacent sectors of a file on a hard disk or floppy disk

control lines The electronic circuitry used to synchronize operations

Control Panel A group of options for customizing and configuring Windows 95 and a computer system

controller A circuit board or card that controls a peripheral device, such as a hard disk or floppy disk

conventional memory The base or standard memory that extends from 0K (zero K) to 640K

cooperative multitasking An operating mode in Windows 3.1 in which the currently running application periodically relinquishes control of system resources to Windows 3.1 so that Windows 3.1 can permit another application access to those same system resources

coprocessor An additional microprocessor that works in conjunction with the main microprocessor to dramatically increase the speed of mathematical calculations and processing of graphics

corrupted file A program or document file whose contents have been altered as the result of a hardware, software, or power failure

cross-linked file A file that contains at least one cluster which belongs to, or is shared by, two or more files

CPU The abbreviation for central processing unit, the microprocessor chip that processes data under the direction of instructions in a program

current directory The directory or subdirectory that is currently in use

current folder The folder that is currently open and in use

current window The currently selected window, identified by a highlighted title bar

customize To configure a computer system to meet a specific set of needs

CVF The abbreviation for compressed volume file

data bits The number of bits that constitute a character (usually 8)

data bus The electronic circuitry that connects the microprocessor with internal and external hardware components

data compression The use of one or more techniques by a backup utility to store data so that the data takes up less space on tape or a floppy disk than the data would require on a hard disk

data file A file that contains a document or data

data lines The electronic circuitry used to transmit and receive data from other hardware components

Dblspace.bin An operating system file that provides access to compressed drives

Dblspace.sys A device driver that loads Dblspace.bin into memory

default The setting or reference point a program uses until you specify another setting or reference point

defragmenting utility A program that rearranges files on a hard disk or a floppy disk so that all sectors of each file are stored in consecutive sectors, and that removes empty space between files

desktop (1) The background of the graphical user interface on which Windows 95 displays icons, the taskbar, menus, windows, and dialog boxes; (2) the Windows 95 folder that contains desktop shortcuts

destination disk The floppy disk that receives a duplicate copy of the contents of another floppy disk

device A component within a computer system, such as a keyboard, mouse, system unit, monitor (or video display unit), disk drive, or a printer

device driver A file with program code that enables the operating system to communicate with and control the operation of a hardware or software component

device name A name Windows 95 assigns to a device or hardware component

dialog box A box within which a program displays options for you to select, or useful information, including messages and warnings

differential backup A backup performed during a backup cycle and which includes all new or modified files since the last full backup

digital Consisting of data stored in discrete units, such as 0s and 1s

directive A command in the MS-DOS startup file Config.sys for configuring the operating system during the booting process

disk A device used to store program and data files

disk compression The process by which DriveSpace, DoubleSpace, or another disk compression utility examines files for repetitive sequences that can be coded more compactly and then compresses the files

disk drive A hardware component that records data onto or retrieves data from storage media, such as a hard disk or floppy disk

disk map A visual representation of the organization of clusters on a hard disk or floppy disk

disk optimization The steps one can take to reorganize the use of storage space on a disk so that the operating system can efficiently and quickly locate folders and files

display adapter A circuit board inside the system unit that controls the image displayed on the monitor

document-oriented interface An operating mode in which you locate and open the document you want to use, and then the operating system opens the application that originally produced the document

DOS The abbreviation for Disk Operating System, a generic name for three related operating systems: MS-DOS, PC-DOS, and IBM-DOS

DOS environment A small area of memory that contains system and application settings

double-click To quickly press twice and release a mouse button

double-density disk A 3½-inch floppy disk with a storage capacity of 720K, or a 5¼-inch floppy disk with a storage capacity of 360K

download The process of copying a file from another computer system to your computer system using communications software, a modem, and (usually) the telephone line

drag To hold down the left mouse button, move the mouse, and then release the mouse button, usually to select a group of filenames or to select and move an object or icon on the screen

drive A name assigned by the operating system to all or part of the storage space on a physical disk, like a hard disk, a floppy disk, or CD-ROM disc, or a virtual disk, like a RAM drive

drive folder (1) The first folder created on a disk or drive by a formatting program; (2) the root directory

drive name A device name that consists of a letter of the alphabet and a colon and that is assigned to a disk drive in a computer system

dynamic link library A file with executable program code (and the file extension dll) that provides support to one or more software applications

E-mail service An on-line service that supports the transfer of messages and mail

embedding The process of copying an object from a document in an application to another document produced by another application and retaining information on the application that originally produced the object

Emm386.exe A device driver that carves the upper memory area into upper memory blocks (UMBs) so that DOS can load device drivers and TSRs into the upper memory area, and that can convert all or part of extended memory into expanded memory for those DOS applications that use expanded memory but not extended memory

end-of-file marker The code in the File Allocation Table that identifies a cluster as the last cluster in use by a specific file

Energy Star computer A computer that contains software which will cycle down hardware components one at a time, decreasing or shutting off power, whenever the computer remains idle for a specific period of time

environment variable A name that Windows 95 or MS-DOS associates with a setting stored in the Windows or the DOS environment

exclusive MS-DOS mode A Windows 95 operating mode in which Windows 95 runs a DOS application, but cannot run any other applications or processes

executing Carrying out instructions in a program that is already loaded in memory

expansion slot A slot for inserting and attaching an adapter or add-in card to the motherboard

expanded memory Additional memory outside of conventional, upper, and extended memory that is added to a computer system for DOS applications by an expanded memory board or by converting extended memory into expanded memory

extended memory The memory above 1MB

external modem A modem that consists of a separate hardware unit that connects (usually) to one of the serial ports on a computer system

extra-high-density floppy disk A 3½-inch floppy disk with a storage capacity of 2.88M

FAT The abbreviation for File Allocation Table

file (1) A collection of data, such as a program or document, stored in a folder on disk; (2) a certain amount of storage space on a floppy disk or hard disk that is set aside for the contents of a program, document, or data file

File Allocation Table A file that contains a list of each allocation unit or cluster on a disk along with information on whether each allocation unit or cluster is available, in use, or defective (i.e., contains a bad sector)

file extension An additional one to three characters included after the main part of a filename, usually to identify the type of application that produced the file or the type of data in the file

file server A specialized server that contains the files produced by applications, and that may allow more than one user to access the same shared file at the same time

file specification The use of a drive name, path, filename, and wildcards to select one or more files

filename A name assigned to a program, document, or data file to identify the file's contents

filing system The use of specific techniques employed by an operating system to access data stored on disk

floppy disk A commonly-used storage medium that consists of a flat, circular plastic disk with a magnetic coating enclosed in a case for protection

folder An organized collection of objects such as files or other folders

format To prepare a floppy disk for use in a computer

forum A collection of services on a specific topic, such as Computers & Software, available on an on-line service

fragmented file A file stored in noncontiguous, or non-adjacent, sectors on a hard disk or floppy disk

freeware Software that is made available to you at no cost

full backup A backup that marks the start of a backup cycle and that includes all or part of the contents of a hard disk

Full format A type of format used on new or formatted disks to define the tracks and sectors on a disk, create a boot sector, new File Allocation Tables, and a new directory file, and perform a surface scan for defects

full path The notation that identifies the drive and sequence of folders that lead to a folder or a file on disk

G The abbreviation for gigabyte

GB The abbreviation for gigabyte

gigabyte 1,024 megabytes, or approximately one billion bytes, of storage space on disk

graphical user interface An interface that provides a more visual method for interacting with the operating system through the use of icons, multiple windows, menus with task-related lists, and dialog boxes

graphics adapter A video display card mounted in an expansion slot on the motherboard to control the display of text and graphics on the monitor

graphics mode A video display mode for displaying graphic images as well as text

guest An option for logging into another computer system, in some cases with restrictions on what you can do

GUI The abbreviation for graphical user interface, an interface that provides a more visual method for interacting with the operating system through the use of icons, multiple windows, menus with task-related lists, and dialog boxes

handles Small black squares that appear around an object to indicate that it is the currently selected object

hard disk An internal disk drive unit that consists of two or more unremovable metallic disks or platters with a magnetic coating on both surfaces of a disk, that stores substantially more data than a floppy disk, and that accesses data substantially faster than a drive unit for a floppy disk

hard disk partition table A file on a hard disk that contains information that identifies where each hard drive starts and which drive on the hard disk is the boot drive

hardware, or **hardware device** The physical components of a computer, such as the disk drives, a CD-ROM drive, a keyboard, monitor, printer, mouse, modem, and tape drive

hardware interrupt A signal transmitted from a hardware device to the microprocessor when the device is ready to send or accept data

help information Information provided by a program to assist you with a program task

Hidden attribute An attribute that indicates that the filename of a file should not be displayed in a list of files

High Color A feature of a 16-bit video display adapter that allows it to display 2^{16} or 65,536 colors

high-density disk A 3½-inch floppy disk with a storage capacity of 1.44M , or a 5¼-inch floppy disk with a storage capacity of 1.2M

high memory area The first 64K of extended memory from 1,024K (1MB) to 1,088K

Himem.sys A device driver that manages extended memory, the high memory area, and the upper memory area

HMA The abbreviation for high memory area

home page The first web page or document that you see at a web site

host computer A computer that contains resources you want to access

host drive The drive that contains the compressed volume file for a compressed drive

hypertext A technology for preparing documents in a way that you can create links to other documents within the body of the document you are creating and also include graphics, video, animation, and sound

hypertext link A link on a web page to another web page at the same site or at other web sites

icon An image or picture displayed on the screen to represent hardware and software resources (such as drives, disks, applications, and files) as well as tasks

incremental backup A backup performed during a backup cycle that includes only those files that you created or changed since your last full *or* last incremental backup

initialization file A file that contains initial settings used by a program

input The process of providing program instructions, commands, and data to a computer system so that it can accomplish a useful task with the data

Interactive Boot Selecting a booting option from the Windows 95 Startup menu

interface The means or ways in which you interact with a computer system

internal modem A modem that is mounted on a card and inserted into one of the expansion slots inside a computer

Internet A world-wide collection of thousands of interconnected networks that you can access with the use of communications software, a modem, and a telephone line

Interrupt Request Line, or **IRQ** A hardware interrupt request line used for transmitting signals from a hardware device to the microprocessor

I/O The abbreviation for input/output

Io.sys One of the Windows 95 and MS-DOS operating system files

K The abbreviation for kilobyte

KB The abbreviation for kilobyte

key combination Pressing two keys at the same time to issue a command to perform an operation

kilobyte 1,024 bytes—or approximately 1,000 bytes—of storage space on disk or in memory

kiosk An on-line service's information booth

LAN The abbreviation for local area network, a collection of computers and other peripherals joined by direct cable links and located relatively close to each other, usually in the same building, so that users can share hardware and software resources and files

laptop computer A small, lap-size microcomputer

laser printer A type of non-impact printer that uses a laser beam to form an electrostatic, or electrically charged, image on a rotating photosensitive drum, which in turn attracts toner and that uses heat to bond the toner to paper

launch To start an operating system or application

LCD The abbreviation for liquid crystal display, a type of display medium used with laptops and notebooks

legacy device A hardware device that does not support the Plug and Play standards defined by Microsoft Corporation in conjunction with hardware manufacturers

linking The process of copying an object from the document of an application to a document produced by another application and maintaining a link to the original object

list box A box within a dialog box that lists options from which to choose

loading Copying programs, documents, or data into a computer's memory

local area network A collection of computers and other peripherals joined by direct cable links and located relatively close to each other, usually in the same building, so that users can share hardware and software resources and files

log file A special file stored in the main folder on drive C in which ScanDisk saves detailed information about the results of its findings and any changes that it made to the disk

logical structure of a disk The combination of the File Allocation Tables, the filing system, the folder or directory structure, and filenames that Windows 95 uses to track allocation of space and files on a disk

lost cluster A cluster on a disk that contains data that once belonged to a program or a document file, but which is no longer associated with a file

LPT1: The device name for the first parallel port in a computer system

LPT2: The device name for the second parallel port in a computer system

LPT3: The device name for the third parallel port in a computer system

M The abbreviation for megabyte

map legend An explanation of the symbols used by the Defragmenter to identify cluster usage on a hard disk or floppy disk

Maximize button A button for enlarging a window to fill the entire screen

MB The abbreviation for megabyte

megabyte 1,024 kilobytes—or approximately one million bytes—of storage space on a disk or in memory

megahertz A unit of measurement representing millions of cycles per second

memory A set of storage locations where instructions and data are stored while you use a microcomputer

memory manager A device driver that manages the use of a specific region of memory

menu A list of command choices presented by a program

MHz The abbreviation for megahertz

microcomputer A single-user, personal computer system

microprocessor A special computer chip that constitutes the central processing unit of a microcomputer and that processes data using program instructions

Minimize button A button for reducing a window to a button on the taskbar

modem A hardware device that mediates the transmission of data between computers over telephone lines by converting digital signals to audio signals, or vice versa

modifier key A key, such as the Ctrl, Alt, or Shift key, that is pressed as part of a key combination

monitor A TV-like video screen that displays input and output

motherboard The main system board located within the system unit and that contains the microprocessor, coprocessor(s), supporting electronic circuitry, and expansion slots

mouse A hand-held device used to position a pointer on the screen so that you can select objects and options and perform specific operations

mouse pointer A type of cursor in the shape of an arrow or a rectangle that moves in the direction in which the mouse is moved over a desktop

MS-DOS Microsoft Disk Operating System; the brand of DOS used on IBM-compatibles

MS-DOS Editor A simple text editor for viewing and changing MS-DOS configuration files

MS-DOS path The notation that identifies the drive and sequence of folders that lead to a folder or a file on disk

Msdos.sys A Windows 95 and MS-DOS operating system file

multitasking An operating system feature that permits you to open and use more than one application at the same time

multithreading The ability of an operating system to execute more than one sequence of program code for a single application at the same time

network A group of computers and other hardware devices, such as printers, that are connected together so that the computers can share hardware resources, software resources, and files

network adapter card A circuit board inserted into a computer on a network to control the transmission of data between the computer and the network server that connects the computer to all the other computers and devices within the network

newsgroup An on-line group that shares information and commentary on defined topics

non-contiguous sectors Non-adjacent sectors of a file scattered across the surface of a hard disk or floppy disk

notebook computer A small microcomputer that can easily fit into a briefcase

object A component of your computer system. For example, each hardware device, software application, and document is an object, and each part of a document, such as a chart, is also an object

Object Linking and Embedding, or **OLE** A technology that enables you to use information from a document produced by one application in a document produced by another application, and retain either a link to the original document or a reference to the application that produced the original document

object-oriented operating system An operating system that treats each component of the computer as an object and that manages all the actions and properties associated with an object

On-line Help A Windows 95 feature that provides the user with assistance on the process for performing a task

on-line service A business or company that provides fee-based, dial-up access to information stored on its computer system(s)

operating environment   A program, like Windows 3.1, that displays a graphical user interface and performs many of the same functions as an operating system, except for booting a system and handling the storage and retrieval of data in files on disk

operating system   The software that manages the basic processes within a computer, coordinates the interaction of hardware and software, and provides support for the use of other software

option button   A small round button, also called a radio button, for selecting an option within a dialog box

output   The transmission of the results of computer processing to the user or to a storage site

output device   A hardware component used to display, print, or store information that results from processing data

overlay file   A file that contains a module of program code (such as a spelling checker) that is only loaded into memory when needed

page   16K of memory within a page frame

page frame   A 64K region of upper memory (or conventional memory) through which a memory manager swaps data for a DOS application from expanded memory into conventional memory, or vice versa

parallel transmission   The simultaneous transmission of eight bits down eight separate data lines in a cable

parallel port   A port or connection for transmitting data between the microprocessor and another component eight bits, or one byte, at a time

parameter   An optional or required item of information for a command

parent folder   The folder above the current folder in the folder structure of a drive

parity   An option for checking for data transmission errors using an extra bit

partial backup   A type of backup that includes only part of your hard disk drive's contents

partition   To divide a hard disk into one or more logical drives

path   The sequence of folder and folder names that identify the location of a folder or a file

PC-DOS   Personal Computer Disk Operating System, the brand of DOS originally used on IBM microcomputers

peer-to-peer network   A simple type of network in which each computer can access and share the printers, hard disk drives, and CD-ROM disk drives on other computers within the network

pel   The smallest element on a video monitor display that can be illuminated, also called a pixel

Pentium   A microprocessor chip with a math coprocessor introduced in 1993, used in Pentium PCs, capable of processing 32 bits at a time, transmitting 64 bits at a time, accessing an unlimited amount of memory, and operating at a clock speed of 60 to 120MHz or more

peripheral   An external hardware component, such as a printer or monitor, that is connected to the system unit

personal computer, or **PC**   A single-user, personal computer system

pixel   The abbreviation for a picture element, the smallest element on a video monitor display that can be illuminated

Plug and Play   A set of specifications for designing hardware so that the device is automatically configured when the computer boots

PNP   The abbreviation for Plug and Play

point   To move the mouse pointer to a specific area of the screen, usually to highlight a menu, command, drive name, filename, icon, or another object displayed on the screen

polymorphic virus   A computer virus that changes its program code each time it duplicates itself, so that each new copy is a variation of the original virus

pop-up window A small Help window that contains a brief explanation of a setting or option

port (1) An electronic pathway or connection for passing data between the computer's microprocessor and its peripherals; (2) a connection for attaching a cable from a peripheral device, such as a monitor, printer, or modem, to circuit boards connected to the main system board

POST The abbreviation for Power-On Self Test

Power-On Self Test A set of diagnostic programs executed during booting and used to test the system components—including memory—for errors

preemptive multitasking environment An operating mode in which the Windows 95 operating system assigns priorities to the processes that it manages and decides at any given point in time whether to take control away from, or give control to, a process

preformatted floppy disk A floppy disk formatted prior to sale

print queue A list of files waiting to be printed

print server A specialized server that accepts print jobs from different computers on a network, spools or stores print jobs on disk, recognizes user priorities, and reports the status of print jobs

printer A hardware component that produces a paper copy of text or graphics processed by the computer

PRN The device name for the first printer port in a computer system, usually LPT1:

process A task running on your computer

processing The ways in which a computer uses input to produce meaningful information, including arithmetic computations, logical comparisons, rearrangement of data, and the production of images or pictures, and sounds

program A detailed step-by-step set of instructions that tell the computer how to accomplish a task

program file A file that contains program instructions for an operating system, a software application, utility, or programming language

properties Characteristics of an object that you can view and sometimes change

property sheet A dialog box that displays information on the characteristics of an object

protected mode An operating mode that allows 80286, 80386, 80486, and subsequent microprocessors to address more than 1MB of memory and provide memory protection features

protocol (1) A set of rules governing the transmission of data with communications software; (2) a language that computers use to communicate with each other over a network

purge To remove or delete unneeded folders or files

Quick format A type of format in which the formatting program erases the contents of the File Allocation Tables and directory file, but skips the surface scan of a previously formatted disk

Quick View A Windows 95 feature that permits you to view the contents of a document without opening the application that produced the document

RAM The abbreviation for Random-Access Memory—your work space

Random-Access Memory (1) Temporary, or volatile, computer's memory used to store program instructions, input, processing, and output; (2) work space

read To retrieve instructions or data stored in memory or on disk

Read-Only attribute An attribute assigned to a file to indicate that you can read from, but not write to, the file

Read-Only file A file that you can read from, but not write to

Read-Only Memory Permanent memory which includes instructions for starting the computer system, for testing the system components at startup (the POST, or Power-On Self-Test), for locating drives A and C, and for transferring the operating system software from the disk in drive A or C to Random-Access Memory

real mode An operating mode used by 8088 and 8086 microcomputers in which the microprocessor can only address 1MB of memory

registered file A file associated with a specific application

Registry A set of databases that store system and user configuration information for Windows 95

reserved memory The upper memory area that extends from 640K to 1MB and that is reserved for system-related operations, such as for video display adapters, network adapters, and the ROM-BIOS (ROM Basic Input/Output System)

resident Remaining in memory

resolution The sharpness and distinctness of an image

Restore button A button for restoring a window to its original size

robustness The stability associated with an operating system and the system resources that it manages and protects

ROM The abbreviation for Read-Only Memory

ROM BIOS A computer chip that contains the program routines for the Power-On Self Test, for identifying and configuring Plug and Play devices, for communicating with peripheral devices, and for locating and loading the operating system

root directory The first directory created on a hard disk or floppy disk during formatting of the disk

routine A program executed during the booting process

Safe mode A booting option that bypasses the Windows 95, Windows 3.1, and MS-DOS startup files and only loads device drivers for the mouse, keyboard, and video display unit

scheme A combination of settings that include different colors, sizes, and formats

scrap A file that Windows 95 automatically creates when you drag all or part of a file onto the desktop

screen saver A program that either blanks a screen or displays moving images when you do not use the computer for a certain period of time

scroll arrows Up and down arrows on a scroll bar that indicate the direction in which you can move a window if you click with the mouse on the up or down arrow or scroll bar

scroll bar A bar with scroll arrows placed on the right hand side or bottom of a window so that you can adjust the view within the window with the mouse

scroll box A box in a scroll bar that is used to adjust the view onto a window in larger increments by dragging the scroll box with the mouse

scrolling A process by which you adjust the screen view with the scroll bars

sector (1) A division of a track that provides storage space for data; (2) the basic unit of storage space on a floppy disk or hard drive that holds 512 bytes of data

selection rectangle A dashed border defining a selected group of objects

serial transmission The transmission of each of the eight bits in a byte, one bit at a time down one data line in a cable

serial port A port or connection for sending information between the microprocessor and another component one bit at a time

server A central computer that contains the network operating system, the installed software applications, and user document and data files and that provides resources to other computers connected to the server

service A network configuration option that determines how resources, such as files and printers, are shared

setup file A file in which Backup stores settings for a specific type of backup

shareware Software that is made available to you for a trial period at little or no cost

shift-clicking The use of the Shift key and mouse to select a group of adjacent objects

shortcut (1) A feature that allows you to quickly access an object within your computer; (2) a file that points to an object, application, or document

shortcut keys Key combinations that allow you to quickly perform an operation or select a command

shortcut menu A menu that opens when you right-click an object and that displays menu options appropriate to that object

software A collection of computer programs that enable a computer to perform a useful task

source disk The floppy disk copied during a disk copy operation

source drive The disk drive that contains a floppy disk you want to copy

spool To store print jobs on disk until the printer is ready to process the print request

Startup Disk A disk that contains operating system files and auxiliary files and that is used for booting a computer from drive A

status bar A bar at the bottom of a window used to display help information, status information, cursor coordinates, and settings, such as the time

stop bits An additional bit or bits added to the data bits for a character to indicate that the transmission of a character is complete

subdirectory A directory that is subordinate to the root directory or to another subdirectory

surface scan (1) A part of the formatting process in which the formatting program records dummy data onto each sector of a disk and reads it back to determine the reliability of each sector; (2) the phase during which the ScanDisk utility examines the surface of a disk for defects

surfing the net Browsing the Internet or World Wide Web

SVGA The abbreviation for SuperVGA, a type of high-resolution video display adapter and monitor

switch An optional parameter, or piece of information, that modifies the way in which a program operates

syntax The correct wording for a command

Sysedit A program that opens the Windows 95, Windows 3.1, and MS-DOS configuration files

symmetric multiprocessing Executing threads of program code simultaneously in different microprocessors in the same computer

system architecture The internal design and coding of an operating system

system area The area of a disk that contains the boot sector, File Allocation Tables, and directory file

System attribute An attribute that identifies a file as an operating system file

system board The main board, or motherboard, with the microprocessor, supporting electronic circuitry, and expansion slots

system bus The network of electronic circuitry (data, address, and control lines) responsible for transmitting data and signals between the microprocessor and various components as well as storing information on the location of instructions and data in memory

system date The current date on a computer system

system disk A floppy disk that contains operating system files and that is used to start a computer from drive A

system files The program files that constitute the operating system software

system reset Rebooting a computer system by pressing the Reset button or by simultaneously pressing the Ctrl, Alt, and Del keys

system unit The unit that houses the main system board with the microprocessor, coprocessor(s), supporting electronic circuitry, expansion slots, and power supply as well as any circuit boards attached to the motherboard and disk drives

System.ini A Windows 3.1 configuration file that contains information on device drivers, network connections, and other system resources

system utility software Special programs provided with operating system software to enhance the performance of your computer system, such as optimizing the use of memory, maximizing the use of storage space on a hard disk, correcting errors on a hard disk, obtaining technical or diagnostic information about your computer system, or preparing floppy disks for use on a computer system

systems software The programs that manage the fundamental operations within a computer, such as starting the computer, loading or copying programs and data into memory, executing or carrying out the instructions in programs, saving data to a disk, displaying information on the monitor, and sending information through a port to a peripheral

tabbed dialog box A dialog box with tabs, each of which provides access to a different group of settings or options

tape drive A backup drive unit in which you can insert tapes that are similar in appearance to cassette tapes

task-switching The process of changing from one open task, or process, to another

taskbar A horizontal (or vertical bar) on the desktop that displays a Start button for starting programs or opening documents, as well as buttons for currently open software applications and documents

template A file that contains the structure, formatting, and data required for a specific type of document

temporary file A file used by a program to store a copy of the data that it is processing until it completes the operation

Terminate-and-Stay-Resident, or **TSR** program A program that remains in memory and performs some function in the background as you work with other programs

text box A box within a dialog box for entering a response

text editor A program for creating and editing simple text, or ASCII, files

text file A type of ASCII file

text mode A simple and fast video display mode for displaying text, including letters, numbers, symbols, and a small set of graphics characters using white characters on a black background

thread A unit of program code for an application that Windows 95 can execute at the same time as it is executing other threads

tile To arrange each open window side by side

title bar A bar at the top of a window for displaying the name of the open program and the currently open file

toggle key An on/off key that alternates between two uses each time you press the key

track A concentric recording band on a hard disk or floppy disk for storing data

Transmission retry A printer setting that instructs Windows 95 to wait for a specific number of seconds for the printer to print before it reports an error

Troubleshooter A Windows 95 Help feature that steps you through the process for locating and resolving a hardware or software problem

True Color A feature of a 24-bit video display adapter that allows it to display 2^{24} or 16,777,216 colors

TSR The abbreviation for Terminate-and-Stay-Resident, a program that remains in memory and is active while you use other programs

UMA The abbreviation for upper memory area

UMB The abbreviation for upper memory block

upper memory, or **upper memory area** Unused memory in the region that extends from 640K to 1MB and that can be claimed as address space by a memory manager

upper memory blocks The regions of unused memory in the Upper Memory Area claimed by a memory manager

URL The abbreviation for Uniform Resource Locator, the address of a specific site on the World Wide Web

user interface The combination of elements on the screen that lets you interact with the computer

VDM The abbreviation for Virtual DOS Machine

VESA Display Power Management Signaling (DPMS) A set of specifications that enable software to place the monitor in standby mode or turn it off when the monitor is inactive for a certain period of time

VFAT The Virtual File Allocation Table, an adaptation of the DOS File Allocation Table that permits Windows 95 faster disk access and that supports the use of long filenames

VGA The abbreviation for video graphics array, a type of video high-resolution display adapter and monitor

video accelerator adapter A video display card that assists the microprocessor with the task of drawing and displaying images

video card, or **video adapter** A video display card within the system unit that controls the display of the image on the monitor

Virtual 8086 mode An operating mode in which the 80386 and subsequent microprocessors can perform as multiple 8086 microprocessors

virtual device driver A device driver, or program, that manages a hardware or software resource so that more than one application can use that resource at the same time

Virtual DOS Machine A complete operating environment for a DOS application that contains a copy of real-mode device drivers and TSRs as well as DOS environment settings

virtual machine An operating environment in which the operating system simulates an 8086

virtual memory Space on a hard disk that an operating system uses as extra memory to supplement the memory available in RAM

virus interceptor A program that monitors your computer for computer viruses while you work with other software, and automatically checks floppy disks in disk drives

visual editing The process of editing an object within the current application's application window using the menus and tools appropriate to the application that produced the original object

volatile Dependent on the availability of power, and therefore temporary

VxD A virtual device driver for managing a hardware or software resource for more than one application

warm boot Starting a computer system by pressing the Reset button or by simultaneously pressing the Ctrl, Alt, and Del keys

web browser A software package, such as the Internet Explorer or Netscape, that enables you to browse, or surf, the World Wide Web

web page A document on the World Wide Web that displays text and images, but which might also include options for displaying video and animation and for producing sounds

web site A computer or network for a corporation, business, or on-line service, such as The Microsoft Network, that provides access to the World Wide Web

wildcard A symbol that substitutes for all or part of a filename in a file specification

Win.ini A Windows 3.1 configuration file that contains information on settings specified through options in the Control Panel

Win16-based applications DOS applications that operate within the first 640KB of memory

Win32-based applications Windows 95 applications, such as Office 95, that utilize the full capabilities of Windows 95 and 80386 and later microprocessors

window A defined rectangular area on the screen through which you use programs, view information, and display the contents of files

Windows environment A small area of memory that contains system and application settings

write protect To protect a floppy disk so that the operating system cannot record data onto the floppy disk

workgroups Individuals who work together as a group and require access to shared resources

World Wide Web An Internet service that uses a graphical user interface and web pages with hypertext links to other web pages to simplify the process for locating and using information on the Internet

write To record instructions or data in memory or on disk

Index

Task Reference

TASK	PAGE #	RECOMMENDED METHOD	NOTES
Accessibility options, choose	ADVWIN 80-81	Click Start button, point to Settings, click Control Panel, double-click Accessibility Options	
Accessory, start an	ADVWIN 13		See Reference Window "Starting an Accessory"
Active window, copy	ADVWIN 16	Press Alt + Print Screen	
Active window, paste	ADVWIN 16	Open application, click Edit, click Paste	
Application, install	ADVWIN 325		See Reference Window "Installing and Uninstalling Applications"
Application, uninstall	ADVWIN 325		See Reference Window "Installing and Uninstalling Applications"
Background, change	ADVWIN 54		See Reference Window "Changing the Desktop Background"
Backup, perform a partial	ADVWIN 281		See Reference Window "Performing a Partial Backup of a Drive"
Clock, show	ADVWIN 20	Right-click taskbar, click Properties, click Show clock check box	
Color schemes, change	ADVWIN 60		See Reference Window "Changing the Color Scheme"
Control Panel, opening	ADVWIN 191	Click Start button, point to Settings, click Control Panel	
Date, view or change	ADVWIN 21–22	Double-click clock on taskbar, click Date & Time tab	
Desktop Properties, view or change	ADVWIN 49–50	Right-click desktop, click Properties	
Device Manager, use	ADVWIN 220		See Reference Window "Using Device Manager"
Device Properties, view or change	ADVWIN 29		See Reference Window "Viewing Device Properties"
Directory, change	ADVWIN 242	Type CD, press Spacebar, type path name of directory, press Enter	
Disk, copy	ADVWIN 116		See Reference Window "Copying a Disk"
Disk, defragment	ADVWIN 313–317		See Reference Window "Defragmenting a Disk"
Disk, format	ADVWIN 104		See Reference Window "Formatting a Disk"
Disk, view contents of	ADVWIN 109	Double-click My Computer, double-click drive icon	
Disk Defragmenter, use	ADVWIN 313–317		See Reference Window "Defragmenting a Disk"

Task Reference

TASK	PAGE #	RECOMMENDED METHOD	NOTES
Display accessibility options, set	ADVWIN 91		See Reference Window "Setting Display Accessibility Options"
Document on desktop, place	ADVWIN 336	Open folder window, drag document icon onto desktop	
Drive properties, view	ADVWIN 118		See Reference Window "Viewing Drive Properties"
Drive shortcut, create a	ADVWIN 122		See Reference Window "Creating a Shortcut for a Floppy Disk Drive"
Embedded object, create a	ADVWIN 356–357		See Reference Window "Inserting an Embedded Object in WordPad"
Embedded object, edit a	ADVWIN 350		See Reference Window "Inserting a Linked Object in WordPad"
Energy saving, implement	ADVWIN 66		See Reference Window "Implementing Energy Saving Features"
File, copy	ADVWIN 140		See Reference Window "Copying a File from Folder to Folder"
File dates, searching for	ADVWIN 168		See Reference Window "Selecting Files by Date"
File, delete a	ADVWIN 125–126	Click file icon, press Delete key, confirm deletion	
File, drag a	ADVWIN 134, 179	Drag ghost of file icon to folder, then release mouse	See Reference Window "Moving a File in Windows Explorer"
File extensions, displaying	ADVWIN 108–109	Click View, click Options, click View tab, remove check mark from Hide MS-DOS file extensions for file types that are registered	
File, find a	ADVWIN 161		See Reference Window "Finding Files with Partial Filenames"
File, move a	ADVWIN 179		See Reference Window "Moving a File in Windows Explorer"
File, rename a	ADVWIN 124–125	Right-click file icon, click Rename, type new name, press Enter	
File, search for	ADVWIN 161		See Reference Window "Searching for a Folder or File Using Windows Explorer"
File using advanced criteria, search for a	ADVWIN 170		See Reference Window "Selecting Files Using Advanced Criteria"
Files, cut and paste	ADVWIN 137		See Reference Window "Moving a Group of Files to a Folder"
Files, display all	ADVWIN 150	Click View, click Options, click View tab, click Show all files	
Files, select a collection of	ADVWIN 137–138	Click first file icon, press Ctrl and click each other file	

Task Reference

Task Reference

TASK	PAGE #	RECOMMENDED METHOD	NOTES
Keyboard accessibility options, choose	ADVWIN 84		See Reference Window "Choosing Keyboard Accessibility Options"
Keyboard layout, select	ADVWIN 80		See Reference Window "Selecting a Keyboard Layout"
Link, creating a	ADVWIN 349		See Reference Window "Inserting a Linked Object in WordPad"
Link, editing a	ADVWIN 350		See Reference Window "Editing a Linked Object"
Message, send a	ADVWIN 378–379	Open Winchat, type message in Chat box, click Dial button 🖲, type name of a computer, click OK	
Microsoft Backup, start	ADVWIN 273	Click Start button, point to Programs, point to Accessories, point to System Tools, click Backup	
Mouse accessibility options, select	ADVWIN 89		See Reference Window "Selecting Mouse Accessibility Options"
Mouse properties, change	ADVWIN 87		See Reference Window "Changing Mouse Properties"
MS-DOS application, start	ADVWIN 242	Change to directory with DOS application, type command to load DOS application	
MS-DOS object, copy	ADVWIN 238	Click Mark button 🔲, drag to select object, click Copy button 🖺	
MS-DOS application memory usage, view	ADVWIN 249		See Reference Window "Examining Memory Usage for an Application"
MS-DOS mode, start in	ADVWIN 241	Click Start button, click Shut Down, click Restart the computer in MS-DOS mode?	
MS-DOS Path, display	ADVWIN 152		See Reference Window "Displaying the MS-DOS Path"
MS-DOS startup files, print	ADVWIN 253		See Reference Window "Printing Copies of the DOS System Startup Files"
MS-DOS toolbar, view	ADVWIN 236–237	Click application icon, click Toolbar	
Multitask, to	ADVWIN 329		See Reference Window "To Multitask and Task-Switch"
Network, connect to a	ADVWIN 376-377	Double-click Network Neighborhood, and log into a server	
Object, copy	ADVWIN 140	Click object, click Edit, click Copy	
Object, cut	ADVWIN 134–135	Click object, click Edit, click Cut	
Object, embed an	ADVWIN 350		See Reference Window "Inserting an Embedded Object in WordPad"
Object, paste	ADVWIN 136	Click Edit, click Paste	
Online Help, access	ADVWIN 35	Click Start button, click Help	

Task Reference

Task Reference

TASK	PAGE #	RECOMMENDED METHOD	NOTES
Start menu, remove an application from	ADVWIN 259		See Reference Window "Removing an Application from the Start or Programs Menu"
System Performance, view	ADVWIN 25–30	Right-click My Computer, click Properties, click Performance tab	
System Properties, view or change	ADVWIN 25	Right-click My Computer, click Properties	
Taskbar Properties, change	ADVWIN 14–15	Right-click taskbar, click Properties	
Task switch, to	ADVWIN 328		See Reference Window "To Multitask and Task-Switch"
The Microsoft Network, to connect to	ADVWIN 382	Double Microsoft Network icon, enter password, click Connect button	
The Microsoft Network, to disconnect from	ADVWIN 402	Click Sign Out button ⬜, verify disconnection	
The Microsoft Network, to search	ADVWIN 395–396	Click Tools, point to Find, click On The Microsoft Network, specify search conditions, click Find Now button	
Time, view or change	ADVWIN 21–22	Double-click clock on taskbar, click Date & Time tab	
Time zone, view or change	ADVWIN 21–23	Double-click clock, click Time Zone tab, drag time zone band to new location on map	
Toolbar, display	ADVWIN 110	Click View, click Toolbar	
Troubleshooter, start a	ADVWIN 202	Click Start button, click Help, click Index tab, type trouble, click index entry	
View options, set file	ADVWIN 114		See Reference Window "Changing Your View of Files"
Wallpaper, change	ADVWIN 56		See Reference Window "Changing the Wallpaper"
Window, browsing with a single	ADVWIN 108	Click View, click Options, click Folder tab, click Browse folders by using a single window that changes as you open each folder	
Window, close	ADVWIN 13	Click Close button ⬜	
Window, maximize	ADVWIN 12	Click Maximize button ⬜	
Window, minimize	ADVWIN 13	Click Minimize button ⬜	
Window, restore	ADVWIN 119	Click Restore button ⬜	
Windowed view, change to	ADVWIN 236	Press Alt + Enter	
Windows 95, restart	ADVWIN 201	Click Start button, click Shut Down, click Restart the computer	
Windows Explorer, open	ADVWIN 152–153	Click Start button, point to Programs, click Windows Explorer	